Why Rome Fell

Why Rome Fell

Decline and Fall, or Drift and Change?

Dr. Michael Arnheim

Barrister at Law
Sometime Fellow of St John's College
Cambridge, UK

FIRST EDITION

WILEY Blackwell

Registered Office
John Wiley & Sons, Inc., 111 River Street, Hoboken, NJ 07030, USA

Editorial Office
9600 Garsington Road, Oxford, OX4 2DQ, UK

For details of our global editorial offices, customer services, and more information about Wiley products visit us at www.wiley.com.

Wiley also publishes its books in a variety of electronic formats and by print-on-demand. Some content that appears in standard print versions of this book may not be available in other formats.

Library of Congress Cataloging-in-Publication Data
Names: Arnheim, M. T. W. (Michael T. W.), author.
Title: Why Rome fell : decline and fall, or drift and change? / Michael Arnheim.
Description: Hoboken, NJ : John Wiley & Sons, Inc., 2022. | Includes bibliographical references and index.
Identifiers: LCCN 2021038734 (print) | LCCN 2021038735 (ebook) | ISBN 9781119691372 (paperback) | ISBN 9781119691396 (pdf) | ISBN 9781119691389 (epub) | ISBN 9781119691341 (obook)
Subjects: LCSH: Rome--History. | Rome--Historiography. | Rome--Politics and government.
Classification: LCC DG209 .A76 2022 (print) | LCC DG209 (ebook) | DDC 945.6/32--dc23/eng/20211015
LC record available at https://lccn.loc.gov/2021038734
LC ebook record available at https://lccn.loc.gov/2021038735

Cover image: Jugate busts of Constantine (laureate) and Sol Invictus (radiate) on seven-solidus gold coin minted in 313 CE (Public domain)
Cover design by Wiley

Set in 11.5/14pt STIXTwoText by Integra Software Services, Pondicherry, India
Printed and bound by CPI Group (UK) Ltd, Croydon, CR0 4YY

C107000_280122

POSUI DEUM ADIUTOREM MEUM

To the Sacred Memory of My Beloved Parents

Dr Wilhelm Arnheim (1901–75)
A wise medical doctor and true polymath, with the driest sense of
humor
and

Mrs. Vicky Arnheim (1905–90)
A brilliant musician, gifted teacher,
dedicated social organizer,
Great cook, and loving mother
and

To the sacred memory of my beloved grandmother, "Oma"
Mrs. Martha Arnheim (1875–1965)
An eternally cheerful and optimistic, courageous spirit,
who taught me German, and whose wonderful
humorous tales
Of the old Germany will remain with me always.

Contents

About the Author

 Dr Michael Arnheim (commonly known as "Doctor Mike") is a practicing London Barrister, Sometime Fellow of St. John's College, Cambridge, and author of 23 published books to date, this being the twenty-third.

Born in Johannesburg, South Africa, to a German father and South African mother, he attended the prestigious King Edward VII School. As a 14-year-old schoolboy he was picked to join the "Quiz Kids" team of five capped and gowned teenagers appearing every Friday evening on South Africa's Springbok Radio, of which he became a stalwart member, "retiring" at the age of eighteen.

He entered Johannesburg's University of the Witwatersrand at the age of 16, taking a first-class B.A. in History and Classics at the age of 19, first-class Honours in Classics at 20 and an M.A. with distinction at the age of 21.

Michael Arnheim then went up to St. John's College, Cambridge, on a National Scholarship (later converted to a St. John's College scholarship, supplemented by a Strathcona Travel Exhibition). He was awarded a Cambridge Ph.D. in 1969 in record time, and in 1972, his doctoral dissertation was published by the Oxford University Press under the title of *The Senatorial Aristocracy in the Later Roman Empire.* In the meantime, he was elected into a Fellowship of St. John's College, Cambridge, where he combined research with a great deal of teaching for a number of colleges in Classics and Ancient History.

At the age of 31, Michael Arnheim was invited to take up the position of full Professor and Head of the Department of Classics back at his old university in South Africa. During his time in that position, he devised a new system of learning Latin, for which he wrote a series of Latin stories titled *The Adventures of Marcus*. He also taught his students Spanish under the title of "Modern Latin," using etymological links with English, along the lines later described in *Gateway English: How to Boost your English Word Power and Unlock New Languages* (2020.).

Despondent about the future of South Africa, Dr Arnheim returned to Britain, where he was called to the Bar by Lincoln's Inn in 1988, combining his practice of law with the writing of books (23 to date)—a combination that is still continuing.

Arnheim's books essentially belong to three main categories: history, religion, and law. His legal studies and practice soon made him aware of the injustice inherent in English law, resulting at least partly from what Lord Neuberger, the former President of the UK Supreme Court, had the courage in 2017 to describe as "a notable degree of disarray and a marked lack of reliable principle" in the whole vast field of the law of Tort. Arnheim's legal writings have tackled this serious but veiled problem with suggested practical solutions.

Arnheim also has an original take on religion—a classification of all religions, ancient and modern alike, as either "communal" or "creed" religions. Christianity and Islam, the two largest religions in the world today, are "creed" religions, based on a creed or set of beliefs. However, in the ancient world most religions, including the Roman "pagan" state religion, were "communal." Membership of a particular community, society or nation carried with it automatic membership of that community's religion. Everyone in a communal religion understood that every communty, society or nation has its own religion. So, communal religions are by definition tolerant—while creed religions are naturally intolerant. Every creed religion—and every denomination, grouping or sect of every creed religion—is based on a set of beliefs, which is taken to be "the truth." Anyone who does not accept this creed is a "heretic," a "pagan,," or an "unbeliever," and is punished accordingly. The dominance of Christianity in the later Roman Empire marked a sea-change in Roman and world history—the substitution of religious intolerance and persecution for toleration and freedom of worship.

This transformation is a major theme of the present book—together with a shift in the power structure, particularly in the West, an issue that has engaged Arnheim's interest since his undergraduate days, when he developed an original comparative analytical approach to history covering multiple societies spanning over three millennia, from early Greece to the present day. Focusing particularly on the power structure of these disparate societies, Arnheim developed the hypothesis that, regardless of outward appearances, all societies, past and present alike, belong to only one of two models of government: rule by an elite minority (oligarchy, morphing to aristocracy) on the one hand, or, on the other, rule by a single individual, or monarchy (whether the ruler is designated as king, president, dictator, or anything else.) This issue is pursued in the present book. The significance of power structure, a much neglected aspect of history, lies in its value as an analytical tool, and in its relationship to social mobility, liberty and equality.

For further information on Michael Arnheim, you may consult the Wikipedia article on him at en.wikipedia.org/wiki/Michael_Arnheim. You are also welcome to contact him by email at Counsel@arnheim-law.com.

Preface

This book has had a very long gestation period. Having developed an interest as an undergraduate in elite theory, I decided to test its applicability to the Later Roman Empire for my Cambridge Ph.D., on which I embarked in 1966. My doctoral supervisor, A.H.M. ("Hugo") Jones, the Cambridge Professor of Ancient History, had brought out his magisterial three-volume *Later Roman Empire* two years earlier. In my Ph.D. dissertation I emphasized Constantine's radical departure from his immediate predecessors' policy by reopening imperial appointments to members of the senatorial aristocracy in the West, from which they had been all but excluded. I concluded that this policy, perpetuated by Constantine's successors, effectively weakened the imperial government in the West—but not in the East—thus contributing to the fall of the western empire, and paving the way toward the medieval world.

My doctoral oral examination in 1969 turned out to be a surprisingly enjoyable occasion. My examiners, both Oxford men, were Peter Brown, then a Fellow of All Souls, and Professor W.H.C. ("Bill") Frend of Glasgow University. After a wide-ranging discussion, even including the Chinese mandarinate, both examiners suggested that my dissertation be published as a book, with specific mention of the Oxford University Press. Sure enough, in 1972, a revised version of my thesis duly appeared, under the Clarendon Press imprint, titled *The Senatorial Aristocracy in the Later Roman Empire*.

In 1971, while my book was in the press, Peter Brown, whose only previous book was a biography of Augustine of Hippo, brought out a slender, lavishly illustrated volume, with very few references, titled *The World of Late Antiquity*, spanning the period 150–750 CE, from the heyday of the "High Empire" until the end of the early Muslim conquests. Like myself, Brown emphasized continuity well beyond the "fall" of the western empire. But there the similarity ended.

To my surprise, Brown and his followers tend to view the period through rose-colored spectacles, labeling it all, and not least, Christianity—which became dominant in the fourth century—a "Good Thing." This overtly subjective and judgmental approach, from which most serious historians had been trying to free themselves for the past hundred years or more, inevitably led to special pleading and a distorted view of the period and of history generally.

After testing out my hypothesis about power structure and ethos in a number of different historical periods and societies in my *Aristocracy in Greek Society* (1977) and *Two Models of Government* (2016), interspersed with books on religion and law, I eventually decided to return to my original stamping ground.

The present work is a very different book from my 1972 publication, but the conclusions are not essentially different, though they are applied to a much wider canvas. The book's broad scope has also resulted in a certain amount of overlap between the chapters, giving the book something of a modular character. This feature is also designed to prevent misunderstanding, which is all too common in a subject as controversial as this.

The people whose help and assistance I have received over the years are too numerous to name. But I cannot omit to mention my former student and long-time friend Tom Malnati of Florida, to whom I owe a debt of gratitude for proofreading the whole book. All errors remaining are my own responsibility alone. The encouragement of my friend Jack Ward has probably brought the work to fruition sooner than would otherwise have been the case. And there have been many profitable discussions with colleagues and former students over the years.

I am privileged to have had the late Professor A.H.M. ("Hugo") Jones as my doctoral supervisor in Cambridge, behind whose slight frame and shy and retiring manner there lurked a powerhouse of erudition and intellectual brilliance. In the best tradition of academic history and scholarly research, his magisterial three-volume *Later Roman Empire* betrays no clue as to his political or religious beliefs. I also owe a great debt to my mentor, friend and colleague at St. John's, the late Professor John Crook, a gifted teacher and true polymath, combining an easy familiarity with Classical literature with a depth of knowledge of Ancient History and Roman Law, together with a linguistic facility in ancient and modern languages alike, not to mention skill as a classical clarinettist.

I am delighted to say that I have had a long and happy association with Wiley, starting with my *US Constitution for Dummies*, the first edition of which came out in 2009, and the second in 2018. I owe a debt of gratitude to the Wiley team with whom I have been working on this book: my managing editor, Andrew Minton, together with Todd Green, Skyler Van Valkenburgh, and latterly Will Croft as executive editor, and Ananth Ganesan. And thanks to the Oxford University Press for allowing me to quote from my *Senatorial Aristocracy in the Later Roman Empire*, published in 1972.

Any reader of this book is welcome to contact me with queries or comments at: Counsel@arnheim-law.com.

Dr. Michael Arnheim
Summer solstice, 2021

Introduction

Only a handful of Roman emperors are household names, and, of those, two, Augustus and Constantine, are pre-eminent but for very different reasons. Augustus established a form of government that would last for nigh on three centuries, and become a byword for stability, justice, and peace.

Constantine cast a long shadow by embracing Christianity and by establishing a new capital in Constantinople. Less well known, but long-lasting nevertheless, were his administrative and military reforms, including in particular his appointment to high civil (but not military) office in the West members of the senatorial aristocracy, who had been virtually excluded from any appointments under Diocletian.

A comparative thematic view will clarify the issues to be tackled in this study:

- **Monarchy:** From Augustus's victory over Antony in 31 BCE, Rome was a monarchy: First, the so-called Principate, which lasted until 284 then the "Dominate" under Diocletian and early Constantine until 312 in the empire as a whole and perpetuated in the East, or Byzantine Empire, until 1453, and, in the West, the new Constantinian model of monarchy, from around 312 until the fall of

Why Rome Fell: Decline and Fall, or Drift and Change?, First Edition. Michael Arnheim.
© 2022 John Wiley & Sons, Inc. Published 2022 by John Wiley & Sons, Inc.

the western empire, conventionally dated to 476, and beyond, in the "barbarian" successor states in the West.

- **Power structure:** There is a natural antipathy between monarchy and aristocracy or oligarchy. Strong monarchy ideally needs support from the lower classes against the aristocracy, which, however, should not be unduly antagonized.
  - This was well understood by Augustus, who cultivated the support of the Roman *plebs urbana*, which he had inherited from his adoptive father Julius Caesar, together with that of the army, and the *equites* (the second class in the state), while conciliating the senatorial aristocracy by allowing them to retain the bulk of provincial governorships.
  - The power of the emperor in the Dominate, as established by Diocletian, depended largely on the army and, also to some extent, on eunuch chamberlains. As perpetuated in Byzantium, the emperor came to be dependent on eunuch chamberlains and on the Church, with which he had a symbiotic relationship (sometimes inaccurately characterized as caesaropapism).
  - The model of government introduced by Constantine in the West had strict separation between civil and military officials. As far as the army was concerned, the emperor came to depend increasingly on "barbarian" military officials. On the civil side, members of the senatorial aristocracy exercised renewed influence through imperial appointments right up to the level of praetorian prefect—albeit mostly only for intermittent short periods—which, however, enabled them to combine office, landholding, and wealth in the same areas, and, to some extent, develop into a centrifugal force. The enhanced position of the aristocracy did not, however, rise to the level of power-sharing with the emperor (and later "barbarian" kings), let alone a hybrid power structure or oligarchy of any kind.
- **Social Mobility:** From the early Principate onward, the emperor elevated "new men," first from around Italy, and then from the provinces, to senatorial status. In the late third century this stopped, and emperors started appointing equestrians directly to governorships without bothering to make them senators first. This culminated under Diocletian, when the senatorial career became a cul-de-sac. This was reversed by Constantine, who not only appointed men of senatorial *birth* to office again, but also made a number of previously equestrian posts carry automatic senatorial status. But contrary to a common impression, this did *not* actually create "fusion," the creation of a "service aristocracy," or an "aristocracy of office" in the West, though it did have this effect in the

East. The difference was that the West already had a traditional hereditary senatorial aristocracy, which the East lacked. A high proportion of men appointed to senatorial posts in the West were of noble origin already, and in any case, they formed a proud caste, which in the fifth century added influential bishoprics (especially in Gaul) to their existing clutch of office, land, and wealth.

- **Aristocratic Ethos:** Stratified or hierarchical societies, which have always been the norm in most periods, have given rise to a general sense that people are unequal, and that birth and pedigrees matter. Four hundred and fifty years of aristocratic rule under the Roman Republic inculcated this aristocratic ethos into the very marrow of society, and it was not dispelled by the monarchical regime that followed it, down to the Middle Ages, and even into the West of today with its supposedly egalitarian ethos.

Why Did the West Fall?

At various points during the fifth century the western empire was gradually dismembered, and reconfigured as a shifting mosaic of "barbarian" kingdoms. How and why did this happen? In helping us to tackle this question we have two comparators: the Principate and the Byzantine Empire. Though under severe pressure, both internal and external, the Principate never succumbed. Secondly, though the western empire dissolved, the East survived for a thousand years, until 1453.

"Indissoluble Union and Easy Obedience"

How do these two comparisons help? In his inimitable rolling prose, and without undue exaggeration, Edward Gibbon (1737–94) pointed to "the indissoluble union and easy obedience that pervaded the government of Augustus and the Antonines." (Gibbon, Ch. 51.) Contrary to the special pleading of some modern writers, these two crucial cementing factors were absent in the later Roman Empire.

Tacitus (c.56–c.120) puts into the mouth of a Caledonian (Scottish) chieftain what has become a well-known indictment of Roman rule: "Robbery, slaughter, and plunder, they describe in lying words as empire, and where they make a desert, they call it peace" (Tac. *Agric.*, 29 f., tr. M. Arnheim). It is, of course, more than likely, that leaders of conquered peoples would not have thanked the Romans for depriving them of their liberty, and we know of several hard-fought conquests over the years. Yet, before long, the benefits of Roman rule came to be appreciated, especially when the Romans opened up their own senate and, indeed, the imperial purple itself, to provincials. Gibbon's point is brought home all the more forcefully when it is recognized that, whatever happened to the Roman Empire, it did not suffer the fate of the modern British, French, Portuguese, and Dutch colonial empires, which all came to an end as a result of local nationalist resistance. Roman citizenship was highly prized. *Civis Romanus sum* (I am a Roman citizen), famously proclaimed Paul of Tarsus in asserting his right to be tried before the emperor; and *peregrini* (free provincial subjects) would serve for twenty-five years in the Roman army in order to earn the coveted title of Roman citizen.

Lower down in the social scale, the Principate also epitomized social mobility. Unlike in the Greek city-states, for example, in Rome manumitted slaves or freedmen—*liberti* or *libertini* (for the distinction between them, see Mouritsen 2011, p. 65)—automatically became Roman citizens, with no bar on their owning property or amassing great wealth, or even holding responsible posts in government, as occurred particularly under Claudius. Successful freedmen were rewarded for their patriotism by being given a minor priesthood in the imperial cult as *seviri Augustales*, which even entitled them, like high magistrates, to be attended by a lictor. Trimalchio, the fictitious anti-hero freedman of Petronius's *Satyricon*, is inordinately proud of this honor, quite likely a true reflection of real life.

Caracalla's extension of citizenship to all free male inhabitants of the empire in 212 (though apparently done for tax reasons) is yet another illustration of Rome's policy of inclusiveness, which had already resulted in most emperors from Trajan (r. 98–117) onward being provincials.

Universal citizenship, however, had an adverse effect on military recruitment. Without an incentive for provincials to enlist, more "barbarians" were recruited than ever before, and conscription, introduced under Diocletian, continued as long as the western empire survived.

But Caracalla's policy of inclusiveness stopped short of inviting whole "barbarian" tribes to settle. In 213, for example, the highly Romanized Alemanni broke through the northern frontier of the Roman Empire with a view to settlement. Far from welcoming these would-be migrants, Caracalla pushed them back and strengthened the frontier against them. Why was the imperial government unable to hold back the "barbarians" who were similarly attracted to Roman civilization in the fourth and fifth centuries? And why did the West fall while the East survived?

The answer lies partly in the sheer strength of numbers involved in these later "barbarian" incursions, possibly driven by pressure on themselves by a westward push from the Huns. Deterred by Constantinople's strong strategic position and fortifications, the "barbarians" diverted their efforts to the West.

Divided Loyalties in a Fractured Society

However, the answer to our question must be sought largely in internal factors, and, in particular, in the divided loyalties of a fractured society, exactly the opposite of Gibbon's "indissoluble union and easy obedience" of the first two centuries of the Principate. The sentiment expressed in the famous line by Horace (65–8 BCE), *Dulce et decorum est pro patria mori* (It is sweet and fitting to die for your country), was probably widely shared during the *Pax Romana* (the Roman Peace) of the same period. (Horace *Od.* 3.2.)

When we come to the fourth century, we even hear of young men cutting off a thumb to beat the "draft." Judging by the number of laws against this practice, it may not have been as rare as modern writers tend to believe, and it so infuriated Valentinian I that, in 368, he ordered offenders to be burned alive. (CTh. 7.13.5.) There is no shortage of evidence of the unpopularity of conscription among the men themselves, and also among the large landowners whose duty it was to provide recruits.

The sack of Rome by the Goths in 410 and the Vandals in 455 elicited a great outpouring of grief among Christians and pagans alike, yet loyalty to the regime was generally so low among its subjects that the "barbarian" incursions generally met with very little resistance. This was the case even though the senatorial aristocracy undoubtedly benefited from having an overarching imperial structure in the West, enabling them to continue to combine office, land, and wealth in several provinces at the same time, which, however, effectively made them a centrifugal force. But, with their fortified estates, especially in Gaul, their disinclination to pay taxes, and their gradual control over the Church, many of them preferred to curry favor with their new masters rather than to attract their ire.

"The madness of the heretics must be curbed"
(CTh 16.5.65.)

Contrary to the frantic efforts of some modern writers, until Christianity became dominant with imperial favor under Constantine and his successors, the Roman Empire enjoyed not only religious toleration but indeed freedom of worship and religion. (See Chapter 10.)

The religious intolerance and persecutions instituted by the Christian Roman Empire, in East and West alike, fractured this unity. Even before 380, when Christianity became the exclusive official religion of the Empire, all those who were not adherents of that religion—and of its dominant denomination—found themselves the targets of incessant attacks, which sometimes spurred them into active disobedience. The usurper Firmus was able to hold out against the imperial government in Africa between 372 and 375, with the support of the Donatists, a "heresy" that was particularly popular in that area. The ousting of the Eastern Emperor Zeno by Basiliscus in 475 was achieved with the support of another group of "heretics," the Monophysites, who were very strong in Egypt and Syria, and who sided with the Muslims in their conquest of Egypt (639–646.) It is clear, from among other things, the long saga of the Altar of Victory, that there were a good many pagans in the aristocracy up to and beyond the end of the fourth century. It is significant that Eugenius, the puppet emperor chosen by Arbogast with the support of the Senate in 392, made a point of restoring the Altar of Victory to its place in the Senate house and appointed the influential pagan aristocrat Virius Nicomachus Flavianus as praetorian prefect of Italy. Significantly, Priscus Attalus, selected by the Visigoths as emperor in 409 and again in 414, was a pagan. Some modern writers, in their concern to kill off paganism as early as possible, have gone out of their way to disprove the existence of an active pagan resistance in the late fourth century. Yet pagans did not need to be activists in order to feel less than loyal toward an intolerant, persecuting government. And, though supposedly extinguished by 423, paganism clearly continued to have considerable numbers of adherents for a long time thereafter. As late as the reign of Justinian (527–565), John of Ephesus boasted of converting 70,000 pagans in Asia Minor, one of the most Christianized parts of the Empire, and, in addition, a large number of pagans, including some highly placed men, in Constantinople itself, which had been established as a Christian capital by Constantine in 330.

The poisonous religious atmosphere of the fragmented society that was the Christian Roman Empire helps to explain the divided loyalties that weakened the West in the face of the "barbarian" invasions and also the loss to the East of the bulk of its territory to the Muslims in the seventh century (some of which was, however, reconquered in the ninth and tenth centuries, only to be permanently lost in the aftermath of the Battle of Manzikert of 1071.)

So What?

How significant, then, was the "fall" of the western empire after all? In other words, what difference does it make whether the West fell, was pushed, or never came to an end at all? My own view is that the importance of this question has been grossly exaggerated. All the time and effort spent on the question of the fall of the Roman Empire could have been far better spent on the related, but quite separate, question of continuity and change. (See Chapter 5.)

East Is East, and West Is West

The significance of this question becomes all the more apparent by comparing continuity and change in the West with those same features in the East. Though what is now generally called the Byzantine Empire lasted over a thousand years (albeit for quite some time in a very shrunken state), its heritage is rather restricted. The only territory that can be considered a linear descendant of Byzantium in the modern world is that now occupied by Greece and the Greek-speaking part of Cyprus. In these two states alone is Greek the official language spoken as their first language by the population at large. This is a major negative feature. Though the Byzantines always thought of themselves as "Romans" (and Orthodox Christians are still referred to in Turkish as *Rûm*), their empire was essentially a Greek empire. From the time of Alexander the Great (356–323 BCE), Greek became the lingua franca of the Eastern Mediterranean even though Roman rule made Latin the official language of the whole Roman Empire until it was replaced in the East by Greek in 610.

In terms of religion, Byzantium has left a more robust heritage. The Eastern Orthodox Church, made up of a number of autonomous (or autocephalous) national churches, is today the second largest Christian denomination in the world, with 220 million adherents, largely concentrated in Eastern Europe. However, most of the autonomous churches have quite a tenuous connection with Byzantium. The liturgical language in most such churches is either Church Slavonic or a vernacular language, and though the Patriarch of Constantinople, known as the ecumenical patriarch, has priority over all other patriarchs, he is only *primus inter pares* (first among equals).

Another heritage of Byzantium which cannot be ignored is, ironically, the result of its demise, namely the rescue of thousands of Classical Greek texts, which were smuggled to the West after the fall of Constantinople in 1453 and are thought to have had some effect in developing the Italian Renaissance.

None of these features, however, really provides much continuity with the Byzantine Empire.

Gothia or Romania?

The position in regard to the western empire is very different. As the Visigoth King Athaulf (r. 411–415) recognized, no "barbarian" kingdom of Gothia would ever come into existence (Orosius 7.43.4–6). The only "barbarians" who gave their name to a country were the Franks and the Angles though the language of France is a Romance language, like those of most of the rest of the western empire, and that of England (an integral part of Britain, from the area's Roman name) has become suffused with Latin loanwords

The Roman Catholic Church, with its subdivision into dioceses and provinces, terms taken over directly from the Roman Empire, still has its headquarters in Rome, under a bishop who is called in Latin by the same title as the Roman emperor as head of the old pagan state religion: Pontifex Maximus (chief priest). Politically, too, the image of the western Roman Empire survives in the ideal of a united Europe. And a modern version of Roman Law still dominates the continent.

Three Revolutions

Constantine initiated the dominance of Christianity in the Roman world, though he was not actually baptized until on his deathbed in 337, and though Christianity did not become the sole official religion of the Empire until 380. The significance of this is that it replaced the tolerant communal Roman pagan state religion with an inherently intolerant creed religion, which has remained the dominant religion in Europe ever since. This represents both continuity and change, a major break with the past on the part of Constantine and his successors, and continuity from then on down to the present.

That revolution also had two major continuing spin-offs, namely the rise of Islam, a creed religion that became intolerant on the Christian model, and rabbinical Judaism, which, under the influence of Christianity, changed from a tolerant communal religion into an intolerant quasi-creed religion. (See Chapter 10.)

Constantine's second revolution was the establishment of Constantinople, which would come to be the permanent Christian capital of the Byzantine Empire until its fall to the Ottomans in 1453.

By bringing members of the senatorial aristocracy back into high office, Constantine effected a third revolution, which endorsed, boosted, bolstered, and reactivated the aristocratic ethos that had been the hallmark of Roman society from the early Republic. This revolution, too, proved long-lasting, surviving until the French Revolution, and still not entirely extinct. (See Chapter 5.)

Structural or Individual?

One important question that has not received sufficient attention is how much of the continuity of the western empire was structural, and how much was personal. We know, for example, that aristocracy and the aristocratic ethos survived the dissolution of the western empire. But who were the aristocrats who carried on this Roman tradition? Were they descendants of the old Roman senatorial aristocracy? Or were they "barbarian" aristocrats aping Roman manners and customs? The evidence is patchy, but the answer would appear to be a mixture of the two. (See Chapter 5.)

The Use of the Past

Tacitus claimed to have written *sine ira et studio*, (without anger or passion), or, in other words, without partiality either positive or negative. The great Greek historian Thucydides (c. 460–c. 400 BCE) wrote his *Peloponnesian War* in the belief that an accurate knowledge of the past would be useful for the future. (Thuc. 1.22.4.) The first prerequisite to this end must, therefore, be accuracy, and, as far as possible, objectivity. True objectivity is probably not an attainable goal, but that does not exempt historians from at least making the attempt.

The starting point must be choice of language. For example, the phrase, "the unnerving but mercifully brief reign of Julian" could not be anything other than overtly subjective, judgmental, hostile, and emotive (Brown 1997a, p. 638)—and even more so than "Williamanmary was a Good King," in *1066 And All That*, the witty parody of traditional British historical writing, written by W.C. Sellar and R.J. Yeatman and published in 1930.

Because Julian "the Apostate" (r. 361–363) is known chiefly for his anti-Christian religious policy, it can safely be concluded that the negative description of his reign is motivated by disagreement with that policy, which ties in with the same author's pro-Christian special pleading, and otherwise rose-tinted vision, inevitably plunging him headlong into a distorted view of the period. (See Chapter 12.)

Avoidance of overtly subjective, judgmental, and emotive language is important in itself, but also for another reason, namely, to use the study of the past as a tool for the future. But this can only be done on the basis of a tested empirical framework for the comparative study of different societies. There is nothing more disappointing than to see solid historical research run into a blind alley, for want of a properly analyzed framework, as happened to Sir Ronald Syme's potentially valuable work on Augustus. Having correctly characterized Augustus's rule as a monarchy, Syme opined that it was an oligarchy on the basis of a supposedly general "law" that "A monarchy rules through an oligarchy" (Syme, R., 1939, p. 8.)—a muddled conflation of two diametrically opposed forms of government. (See Chapter 1.) Chapter 6 illustrates how a correct formulation of power structure can be applied to different historical periods.

Part I

Transition from the Ancient to the Medieval World and Beyond

1

Rome
From Monarchy to Monarchy

This chapter is an analysis of the power structure of the Roman state from its foundation, traditionally dated 753 BCE, to the accession of the Emperor Diocletian in 284. The chapter is divided into two sections. Section A is an analytical narrative, while Section B is a discussion of some of the main discordant views propounded in modern writings.

My own view is that the early monarchy, on which there is very little reliable evidence, was replaced around 509 BCE by a "republic" dominated by an oligarchy or aristocracy. Thus far, the power structure of the Roman state conforms to a universal pattern that I identified in my Two Models of Government, *first published in 2016: monarchy succeeded by an oligarchy or aristocracy. By "oligarchy", I mean government by an elite minority, and "aristocracy" refers to a hereditary oligarchy.*

The accession of Julius Caesar's heir, known to history as Augustus, replaced the republican oligarchy with a thinly disguised monarchy that was able to satisfy, or at least placate, all sectors of society and to provide a stable form of government that lasted for some three hundred years.

Section A.   From Romulus to Diocletian

In the beginning, Rome was a monarchy. According to tradition, Rome, whose conventional founding date was 753 BCE, was first ruled by a succession of seven kings, starting with the eponymous Romulus, who,

Why Rome Fell: Decline and Fall, or Drift and Change?, First Edition. Michael Arnheim.
© 2022 John Wiley & Sons, Inc. Published 2022 by John Wiley & Sons, Inc.

if he existed at all, must have been named after the city rather than the other way round. The whole period of the monarchy is extremely shadowy. Our main authority for it is the Roman Historian Titus Livius, or Livy, whose great Roman History, titled *Ab Urbe Condita* ("From the Foundation of the City"), was written some 500 years after the fall of the monarchy, which is commonly dated to 509 BCE. Livy felt obliged to relate traditional tales and legends about the early history of Rome, but he also had access to earlier historical accounts, and he actually provides a list of no fewer than a dozen authors' names, the earliest being Quintus Fabius Pictor, whose history of Rome, written in Greek in around 200 BCE, survives only in fragmentary form.

The monarchy appears initially to have been not hereditary but elective, with the king being chosen by the Senate, an aristocratic council, and confirmed by the citizens meeting together in the Assembly known as the *Comitia Curiata*. The last three kings, Tarquinius Priscus, Servius Tullius, and Tarquinius Superbus ("Tarquin the Proud"), were reputedly Etruscans, and the monarchy seems to have become hereditary at that time, as the two Tarquins were either father and son or grandfather and grandson, and Servius Tullius was supposedly the younger Tarquin's father-in-law.

Livy's account of the last period of the monarchy paints a very confused picture, with Tarquinius Superbus initially cultivating the support of the Senate against Servius Tullius, his father-in-law, portrayed as a populist king, distributing conquered lands to the whole populace and enjoying widespread popular support. (Livy 1.46.1). Servius Tullius is even said to have been physically attacked by his son-in-law and murdered by Tarquin's entourage. (Livy 1.48). Once ensconced in power, we are told, Tarquin "...killed the leading senators who he believed had favored the cause of Servius." (Livy 1.49.2.1). This may indicate aristocratic opposition to his rule, which rather contradicts his earlier stance.

What, then, was the power-structure under the Roman monarchy? If the earlier kings really owed their position to election by the Senate, an aristocratic body, then that may point to an aristocratic regime from the start, with the king as essentially *primus inter pares* (first among equals). The last three kings, however, may possibly represent a period of Etruscan domination over Rome. So, the uprising that ended the monarchy may then be interpreted as the reclaiming by the indigenous Roman aristocracy of their previous pre-eminence against foreign domination. The only thing that appears to contradict this interpretation is the tradition that Lucius Junius Brutus and his co-conspirator Lucius Tarquinius Collatinus, who were chiefly instrumental in overthrowing Tarquin the Proud and would become the first two consuls of the new Republic, were both related to the king, and that Brutus had two of his sons put to death for siding with the ousted king. If there is any truth in this picture of a family feud, then it may be that Tarquin's overthrow was the result of internecine conflict within the Roman aristocracy.

Relics of Monarchy

Long after this time, there were some telltale signs that Rome had actually been a monarchy. These included the position of *interrex* and that of *rex sacrorum*. The *rex sacrorum* (literally, "king of the holy") was the patrician holder of the highest-ranking but largely ceremonial priesthood in the Roman state religion, who was in practice subordinate to the Pontifex Maximus (chief priest). The *rex sacrorum*, then, may be a relic of the religious functions originally carried out by the kings.

During the Republic, an *interrex* was elected by the Senate for five days only in order to hold elections when for some reason the consuls had been unable to do so. This office may possibly hark back to a time when there was a gap between two elective kings, causing an *interregnum*.

"Republic" and Democracy

The English word "republic" is a translation of the Latin *res publica*. The Latin adjective *publica* is a contraction of the non-existent **populicus*, from *populus*, "the people." So, *res publica* means, literally, "the people's thing, the people's business," hence "public or civil affairs, public or civil administration, public or civil power," and hence "the state, commonwealth, republic." (Lewis & Short.) It generally refers to the *Roman* state, as against foreign states, for which the word *civitas* was preferred, and from which (via the French) we have the English word "city."

It is important to note that, in referring to the Roman state, *res publica* did not identify any particular form of government and was still used to refer to the Roman state long after the Roman Republic had ceased to exist and when Rome was ruled by emperors. For example, in the dedication by Pliny the Elder (23–79) of his *Historia Naturalis* (Natural History) to the future Emperor Titus, he congratulates Titus on his service to *the state*, this term being expressed by *res publica*, written in 77, more than a century after the end of the Roman Republic. (Pliny, *Natural History*, 3.)

The term *res publica* clearly, therefore, carries no implication of democracy even though it is based on the word *populus*, meaning "the people," The acronym *SPQR*, for *Senatus Populusque Romanus* (The Roman Senate and People), a corporate designation of the Roman state, likewise carries no implication of democracy and is also not associated with a republican form of government. In fact, it is first encountered only in the late Republic and continued to be used well into Imperial times. Both the Arch of Titus, dating from 81 (CIL VI 945), and the Arch of Septimius Severus, constructed in 203 (CIL VI 1033), were dedicated to the memory of these emperors by The Roman Senate and People, the latter well over two centuries after the demise of the Roman Republic.

From One Brutus to Another

Whatever the precise explanation may be for the overthrow of the monarchy, there can be no doubt about the nature of the republic which replaced it. Far from being a democracy, it was controlled by a hereditary aristocracy that gradually morphed into an oligarchy. "Oligarchy," from the Greek, means literally "the rule of the few," whereas the literal meaning of "aristocracy," also of Greek origin, is "the rule of the best." Aristotle (384–322 BCE) used both terms to refer to minority rule, *aristokratia* being the "good" form and *oligarchia* the "bad" or "perverted" form. (Arist. Politics III.7.) My own usage of these terms is rather different. Aristocracy refers to rule by a hereditary elite and also to the membership of that elite, while "oligarchy" is used to refer to a non-hereditary ruling elite. And it is worth noting the Latin term *res publica* or *respublica* (republic) did not refer to the type of government or power structure but was a much more general term meaning essentially "the Roman state." (See sidebar).

According to our sources, the Latin word *rex* (king) and the whole idea of monarchy were taboo in the Roman Republic (and long afterward), which makes perfect sense because what an oligarchy dreads most is a strong ruler supported by the masses. But, as the history of the late Republic demonstrates, it would be a mistake to assume that this fear of monarchy was shared by the populace at large. Indeed, in times of crisis, the ordinary people would look to a strong leader to champion their cause against the oligarchy.

The Republican constitution, meaning the creation of the ruling oligarchy, was carefully constructed so as to prevent power from being concentrated in the hands of any one person. One of its main features was collegiality, or shared power, together with short terms of office, and rotation. The chief offices and institutions of state included the following:

Consuls: The king was replaced by two consuls with equal authority elected for a year at a time, each with the right to veto the other's actions. They alternated in holding supreme power *imperium* (supreme power) month by month. According to tradition, the consuls (possibly originally called praetors) had to be patricians until the *Lex Licinia Sextia* of 367 BCE threw the consulship open to plebeians as well, and the *Lex Genucia* of 342 BCE, which reserved one consulship for a plebeian every year but permitted both consuls to be plebeians (Livy 7.42.), The *Lex Genucia* also laid down the rule that a ten-year gap had to be left before an office-holder could be elected to the same office for a second term, but this was repealed in 217 BCE. (Livy 27.6.7.)

Other magistracies: All other regular executive magistracies, such as the praetorship, aedileship, and quaestorship, were similarly collegiate, being shared by several office-holders at the same time. They were elected for a year at a time and could be re-elected but only after a gap of ten years.

Tribunus plebis (Tribune of the plebs): An important office, traditionally said to have arisen out of the conflict between patricians and plebeians, known as the Conflict or Struggle of the Orders, which ended after about two centuries in 287 BCE. The tribunes, 10 in number after 457 BCE, were elected by the *Concilium Plebis*, an assembly of all Roman citizens except patricians. Tribunes could convene this body and preside over it. By the third century BCE, the tribunes also had the power to summon the Senate and put proposals to it. *Provocatio* (appeal against execution or flogging without trial) could be addressed to a tribune, but details are sketchy. A really important power held by tribunes was *intercessio*, the power to veto the action of any magistrate and even acts of the Senate, but no magistrate could veto the action of a tribune. Coupled with *sacrosanctitas*, or inviolability of their persons, a breach of which was punishable by death, these powers made tribunes extremely influential. According to persistent tradition, the tribunate was created to protect the original plebeians in the Conflict of the Orders.

These plebeians, or some of them, eventually fused with the patricians to form a composite patricio-plebeian aristocracy. The dating is much disputed, and it appears that it was only in 173 or 172 BCE that both consuls were plebeians for the first time (Cornell 1995, p. 337 f.)

However, there is really no need to dismiss Livy's detailed account. A simple explanation may be that, though it was constitutionally permissible from 342 BCE for both consuls to be plebeians, this law was not acted on until 173 BCE. The *Lex Genucia* was, after all, according to Livy, purely permissive and not mandatory. In other words, it *allowed* both consuls to be plebeians but did not require it. What is more significant is that, from 343 BCE onward, one consul was always a plebeian. These plebeians therefore formed an integral part of the senatorial aristocracy or oligarchy. So, who then made up the *plebs* whom we encounter in political activity in the late Republic, particularly from the time of the Gracchi, two hundred years after the *Lex Genucia*? Were they simply those plebeians from the early Republic who had been left behind when their more fortunate brethren joined the aristocracy? This seems unlikely as this later *plebs*, sometimes termed *plebs urbana* (urban plebs), is often portrayed as a mob, or what Cicero described as *faex Romuli* (the dregs of Romulus)." (Cicero *Ad Att.* 2.1.8.) Though created to protect the interests of a very different *plebs* in the early Republic, the tribunate was used to good effect by demagogues like the Gracchi in the late Republic on behalf of this more desperate *plebs*. In 48 BCE, *tribunicia potestas* (tribunician power) was granted to Julius Caesar, who, as a patrician was ineligible to hold the actual tribunate. In 23 BCE, this same power was bestowed by the Senate on Augustus for life, in addition to the *sacrosanctitas* of a tribune which he already had. Tribunician power was an important signal of the emperor's identification with the interests of the lower classes, and it was routinely bestowed on every emperor, usually upon his accession.

Censor: A very senior post in charge of taking the census of citizen numbers, open only to former consuls, again shared by two equal office-holders, elected originally for five years but later for eighteen months.

Senate: This was the most important deliberative body under the Republic, made up of former holders of the different executive magistracies. Until the passing of the Ovinian Law (*Lex Ovinia*) in 318 BCE, senators were appointed by the consuls and, after that date, by the censors. Under Sulla's reforms of 81 BCE, *quaestors* were granted automatic membership of the Senate. Consuls were invariably drawn from the ranks of the Senate.

Assemblies: Roman citizens were members of several Assemblies, arranged in slightly different ways: the *Comitia Curiata*, *Comitia Centuriata*, and *Comitia Tributa*. It was the *Centuriata* alone, in which the citizens were arranged along military lines, that had the power to declare war and to elect the highest-ranking magistrates, the consuls, praetors, and censors. Until 241 BCE, the *Centuriata* was effectively controlled by the aristocracy. It was then reorganised on more egalitarian lines, but subsequently reverted to the older arrangement. However, the Roman Republic never claimed to be a democracy, and the consuls, praetors, and censors were always chosen from the ranks of senators, regardless of the arrangement of the assembly. Besides these assemblies, there was the *Concilium Plebis*, which appears to have had the same arrangement and membership as the *Comitia Tributa*, with the exclusion of patricians.

Dictator: The only exception to the rule of shared power was the appointment of a *dictator* in an emergency, which was strictly limited to a tenure of six months. The Senate had to pass a decree (*senatus consultum*) instructing the consuls to nominate a dictator. The dictator would then appoint a *magister equitum* (master of the horse) to assist him and act as his deputy when necessary. Once appointed, the dictator had absolute power over the Roman state, superseding that of the consuls. The most admired type of Republican hero was someone like Cincinnatus, who, after resolving the immediate emergency in a fortnight, at once gave up his dictatorship and returned to his plough and to obscurity. The reason that Cincinnatus was fêted as an ideal Republican was that he had no interest in gaining personal power. After 202 BCE, the Senate would issue an emergency decree, labeled by modern historians *senatus consultum ultimum*, instead of appointing a dictator. The dictatorship was only revived much later on, in 82 BCE, first for L. Cornelius Sulla and then again for Julius Caesar in 46 BCE but, so far from preventing one-man rule, it was now used as a vehicle to achieve just that: bringing down the Republic.

"In the Consulship of Julius and Caesar"

A visceral fear of one-man rule is characteristic of oligarchies and aristocracies, not least in the case of the Roman Republic, where, as mentioned above, this fear was stemmed by collegiality and rotation of office. However, a less than persuasive argument is put forward against this view by Lintott, who opines that, "We would be wrong...to see collegiality in principle as a form of constitutional check: the multiplicity of magistrates was perhaps in origin intended rather as cover for a multiplicity of functions and insurance against the sudden death or disability of a magistrate." (Lintott, loc 1250.) The key word here is "perhaps." The only evidence for this view is that "...we find the praetors and quaestors generally each having separate functions, although the treasury came to be entrusted to a pair of quaestors, and the aediles, curule and plebeian, worked in pairs in the administration of the games"

(Ibid.). A key fact is that the consuls, who did *not* have "separate functions," had a veto power over each other. And, besides the power of the holder of a higher magistracy to forbid a lower magistrate from acting in a certain way, a magistrate could use the power of *intercessio*, as it was called, to cancel a *colleague's* action after it had occurred by acting in a contrary sense. But Lintott is anxious to wave this aside as well: "Where we find magistrates, other than tribunes, actually obstructing their colleagues in the late Republic, it is by exploiting their power of consulting the auspices in order to detect unfavourable religious omens" (Ibid.). This use of the auspices to block a colleague's actions was a well-known political ploy which only confirms its function as an attempt to prevent an individual from becoming too powerful. An extreme example of this (not mentioned by Lintott) was the attempt in 59 BCE by Julius Caesar's conservative co-consul, Marcus Calpurnius Bibulus, to block Caesar's populist legislation by closeting himself at home and issuing proclamations announcing bad omens, of which no proof was required. (Suetonius, Julius, 20.1.) As a result, Bibulus was sidelined, and some jokers signed mock-formal documents dated "Done in the consulship of Julius and Caesar" instead of "Bibulus and Caesar." (Ibid. 20.2.)

In sum, Bibulus's religiosity, whether genuine or feigned, is just an extreme example of a magistrate's armory to check and balance a colleague's actions—quite in keeping with the republican ethos of elite group power designed to prevent any one individual from becoming too powerful. Because of Caesar's popularity among the masses, Bibulus's attempts to block him backfired. When he opposed Caesar's land redistribution bill, he found himself attacked by an irate mob, which broke his *fasces* (the bundle of rods and an axe that symbolized his authority as a consul) and pelted him with feces. (Plutarch, *Cato the Younger*, 32.2.)

Violent conflicts like this foreshadowed the impending demise of the republic, with three civil wars in quick succession, first between Caesar and Pompey, then, after Caesar's murder, between the Caesarians and Caesar's assassins (the latter fighting for the continuance of the old oligarchical order), and, finally, between the two leading Ceasarians, Marcus Antonius and Caesar's heir, the future Augustus, who emerged as sole ruler of the Roman world after his victory over Antony at Actium in 31 BCE. But, before discussing the repercussions of this momentous event, let us take a step backward.

The Fall of the Republic

The last century of the Roman Republic was marked by confrontations between two groupings within the ruling oligarchy, one of which championed the cause, and depended on the support, of the lower classes, and the other, of a more "conservative" mindset, bent on the continued dominance of the senatorial elite. The terms "Populares" and "Optimates", used by Cicero in *Pro Sestio* in 56 BCE to describe these two groups, tend now to be rejected by historians. However, here I agree with Lintott that, "As for *optimates* and *populares*, even though they came from the same social class with its framework of individual and family connexions, this is no reason to deny the divergence of ideology highlighted by Cicero," with programs and leaders going back generations. Even if *popularis* politicians "...pursued their own interests more than those of the men they claimed to represent,....the mere possession of personal ambition does not disqualify a man from advancing the interests of others." (Lintott, A., p. 52 f.)

The long-smouldering antagonism between the *plebs urbana* (the urban masses, not to be confused with the original plebeians involved in the so-called Conflict of the Orders) and the dominant elements in the Roman oligarchy eventually burst into flames over the radical agrarian reforms proposed by Tiberius Gracchus with popular support.

The Gracchi Brothers

In 133 BCE, Tiberius Gracchus, a member of the patricio-plebeian aristocracy, plebeian on his father's side and patrician on his mother's, was elected tribune of the *plebs* and immediately introduced an ambitious program of land reform entailing redistribution of land from wealthy *nobiles* to the urban poor. Tiberius Gracchus's attempt to run for re-election was opposed by conservative senators, and violence erupted resulting in the clubbing to death of Gracchus and some 300 of his supporters.

Ten years later, in 123 BCE, Tiberius Gracchus's brother Gaius Gracchus was also elected tribune of the *plebs* and attempted to revive his late brother's program plus further measures to curb the power of the senatorial oligarchy. He had a broad base of support, made up not only of the urban poor but also of the agrarian poor and even some *equites* (equestrians, the wealthy class just below that of senator). However, his bid to extend Roman citizenship to non-Roman Italians cost him the support of a substantial number of the Roman urban poor, who were unwilling to share the privilege of Roman citizenship with outsiders. When Gaius Gracchus was defeated for re-election to the tribunate, there was a mass rally of his supporters on the Aventine Hill. The Senate declared a state of emergency by passing what is now termed a *senatus consultum ultimum*, and the pro-senatorial consul Lucius Opimius at the head of a force of armed supporters defeated Gaius Gracchus and his followers in a pitched battle. Gracchus committed suicide, and approximately 3,000 of his supporters were put to death in the proscriptions that followed.

Gaius Marius

The next popular leader was rather more successful. This was the great military reformer, a *novus homo* (new man) of equestrian origin, Gaius Marius, who was elected consul an unprecedented seven times between 107 and 86 BCE. Until the Marian reforms, only property owners were eligible to serve in the Roman army. What Marius did was to turn the Roman army into a professional standing army open to all citizens, no matter how poor. Soldiers were now recruited for an enlistment term of sixteen years. Marius's reforms offered the landless masses the opportunity to become paid professional soldiers, an offer that was enthusiastically taken up. Retired soldiers were given a pension and a plot of land in conquered territory. Marius also extended Roman citizenship to citizens of the allied Italian cities in return for service in the Roman army. While creating a much improved Roman standing army, Marius's reforms tended to transfer the troops' loyalty from the state to their general.

Sulla

Lucius Cornelius Sulla, nicknamed Felix (Lucky), from an impoverished patrician background, who as *quaestor* (deputy commander) to Marius in the Jugurthine War managed by a stratagem to capture King Jugurtha himself in 105 BCE. But Marius and Sulla soon crossed swords, leading eventually to Sulla's unprecedented march on Rome with his army in 88 BCE and again in 83 BCE. Sulla used his victory in 81 BCE to have himself appointed *dictator legibus faciundis et reipublicae constituendae causa* (dictator for the making of laws and for the settling of the constitution). This was the first time that Rome had a dictator since 202 BCE, but, unlike previous dictators, Sulla's appointment was for an indefinite period. He held it for just over a year, using his power to enact some far-reaching constitutional reforms intended to strengthen the Senate against popular institutions, notably the tribunate of the *plebs*. He then resigned and retired into private life to write his memoirs and, if Plutarch is to be believed, to devote himself to debauchery (Plutarch, Sulla, 37). But no tinkering with the constitution could save the Republic. Sulla's own career illustrated the fundamental truth that the future shape of the Roman government would be decided not by laws but by arms.

Pompey

The Roman Republic was now hurtling toward civil war, which was hastened by the fact that the Republic had become an unwieldy empire with trouble-spots needing urgent military attention. Sulla died in 78 BCE, and within less than ten years, most of his reforms would be rescinded by two of his former lieutenants on their return from successful military exploits: Gnaeus Pompeius, nicknamed Magnus and generally referred to in English as Pompey, and Marcus Licinius Crassus, one of the richest men in Rome, who were elected as joint consuls in 70 BCE.

Julius Caesar

The lineup for the final dénouement of the Republic took shape in 60 BCE, when the state was hijacked by an alliance between three strongmen in the so-called but unofficial First Triumvirate: Pompey, Crassus, and Caesar.

Gaius Julius Caesar was Marius's nephew, and he remained true to his uncle's populist politics. In Sulla's final purge of Marian partisans in 83 BCE, the seventeen-year-old Caesar was spared only through the intervention of his mother's family, which included supporters of Sulla and the Vestal Virgins because the young Caesar had been nominated as *flamen Dialis* (the high priest of Jupiter). In reluctantly sparing Caesar's life, Sulla is said to have predicted that Caesar would prove the ruin of the aristocracy, "...for in that Caesar there are many Mariuses.". (Suetonius, *Julius*, 1; Plutarch, *Caesar*, 1.)

Caesar early on showed his mettle. When captured by pirates, who demanded a ransom of twenty talents of silver, the young Caesar insisted that he was worth at least fifty. When released, he promised to return and crucify them all, which is exactly what he did. In 63 BCE, Caesar was elected against great odds to the prestigious position of Pontifex Maximus (chief priest) of the Roman state religion. After serving as praetor in 62 BCE, he was allotted the province of Hispania Ulterior (modern southeastern Spain), where he conquered two local tribes and, in 60 BCE, was hailed as *imperator* (commander) by his troops on the field of battle.

With the support of his partners, Pompey and Crassus, in the First Triumvirate, Caesar was elected consul in 59 BCE and successfully proposed a popular law redistributing public lands (*ager publicus*) to the poor. He also managed, in the face of "conservative" opposition, to be allotted as his proconsular command (the command that an ex-consul was given after his term of office) not one but three provinces: Illyricum (the Balkans), Cisalpine Gaul (northern Italy) and later also Transalpine Gaul (southern France). (Suetonius, *Julius*, 19.2.)

Caesar expanded Roman territory by his conquest of what was known as Gallia Comata (long-haired Gaul or northern France), which he publicized himself in his book *De Bello Gallico* (*The Gallic War*), inflicted on generations of schoolchildren right up to the present day.

Caesar's command had been extended to 50 BCE, by which time the Triumvirate had collapsed. Crassus had been killed in battle against the Parthians in 53 BCE; and Pompey had changed sides and become the champion of the Optimates, who now controlled the Senate and, unprecedentedly, made Pompey sole consul in 52 BCE. When Caesar's command ended in 50 BCE, he was ordered to disband his army and return to Rome as a private citizen, exposing him to possible prosecution. Instead, on January 10, 49 BCE, he chose to cross the Rubicon (the boundary between Cisalpine Gaul and Italy) with an armed legion, famously remarking (apparently in Greek) "the die is cast". (Plutarch, *Pompey*, 60.2; Plutarch, *Caesar*, 32.8.4; Suetonius, *Divus Julius*.)

Caesar was now at war with the Republic, which had entrusted its fortunes to Pompey. After Caesar's decisive victory over Pompey at Pharsalus in Greece in July 48 BCE, Caesar entered Rome as a conquering hero. He was named dictator, then won a second consulship in an election presided over by himself, and resigned his dictatorship after eleven days. In 48 BCE, he was named dictator again, this time for a year. Then in 46 BCE, after a few foreign interludes, he was named dictator for a year yet again and was designated as dictator for nine further years. As if this was not enough, Caesar was also elected to serve as consul (simultaneously with his dictatorship) three more times, for 46, 45, and 44 BCE. Julius Caesar was now king in all but name. To drive the point home, in early 44 BCE, he was named *dictator perpetuo* or *dictator in perpetuum* (dictator in perpetuity), the precise meaning of which is explained below. In accepting this title, Caesar effectively signed his own death warrant. Caesar was seen by the *Optimates* as threatening to bring to an end the 450-year-old Republic, and about sixty of them conspired to assassinate him, which occurred on the Ides of March (March 15) 44 BCE, one of the best-known dates in history.

It was Caesar's undoubted popularity with the masses coupled with his arrogance and habit of plain speaking that caused his downfall. He is said, for example, to have remarked "...that the Republic was nothing but a name, without substance or form; that Sulla had acted like an idiot by laying down the dictatorship; and that people ought to be more careful when speaking with him, and should take what he says as law.". (Suetonius, Ibid., 77.) Above all, not only was he unable to resist accepting most of the exceptional honours which were showered upon him, but he also did not seem to have recognized the likely backlash from the *Optimates*. According to Suetonius, among other honours accorded to him was the title *Pater Patriae* (Father of the Nation); several statues of himself, including one next to those of the seven kings of Rome; and a college of priests dedicated to himself. When, "...amidst the immoderate and unusual acclamations of the people...." (Ibid., 79), a man in the adulating throng placed on one of Caesar's statues a laurel crown encircled with a white fillet, a symbol of royalty, and two tribunes ordered the fillet to be removed and the man responsible for placing it there to be imprisoned, Caesar reprimanded the tribunes and dismissed them from office. This gave the impression, welcomed by the populace and feared by the *Optimates*, that he aspired to make himself king although when hailed by the people as *rex* (king), he responded jocularly, "I am Caesar, not Rex", Rex being a name as well as a title. And when his staunch supporter Mark Antony, as consul, on several occasions placed a laurel crown on Caesar's head, Caesar waved it aside and ordered it to be taken to the temple of Jupiter. (Ibid., 79.)

Caesar probably did not cry "*Et tu, Brute?*" ("You, too, Brutus?"), as suggested by Shakespeare, nor even, in Greek, "*Kai su, teknon?*" ("You, too, my child?"), as rather skeptically suggested by Suetonius and Cassius Dio, when he was stabbed by Marcus Junius Brutus, whom Caesar had taken under his wing. (Suetonius, Divus Julius, 84; Cassius Dio, 44.19.)

So out of touch with reality were Caesar's assassins that, according to Plutarch, they marched to the Capitol proudly brandishing their daggers full of confidence and fondly imagining that they would be fêted for saving the Republic and restoring "liberty." (Plutarch, *Caesar*, 67.3.)

In the immediate aftermath of the assassination, even Caesar's close friend, Mark Antony, was apparently unsure which way the wind was blowing. Plutarch, in his *Life of Antony*, says that Antony even gave the conspirators his son as a hostage, and entertained a leading conspirator, Cassius, to dinner while Lepidus, Caesar's master of the horse (lieutenant to Caesar as dictator), did the same for Brutus. (Plutarch, *Antony*, 13.) As consul, Antony convened the Senate, spoke in favour of an amnesty and of allotting provincial commands to both Brutus and Cassius and proposed a law abolishing the position of dictator forever. The Senate ratified these proposals, while voting to honour Caesar by giving him the posthumous title *divus* (the divine Julius), making him a minor deity, and confirming all Caesar's reforms (Plutarch, *Caesar*, 67.7; *Antony*, 14.)

Armed with his new command, Brutus issued coins with the motto LEIBERTAS, the old-fashioned spelling of *libertas* (liberty), and others with the legend EID MAR, an abbreviation for (the again intentionally archaic spelling of) *Idibus Martiis* meaning "on the Ides of March", together with a *pileus* (cap of liberty given to newly enfranchised slaves) and two daggers, celebrating Caesar's assassination. On the obverse was a portrait of Brutus described as *imp(erator)*, general. Mary Beard opines, "The portrayal of a living person on a Roman coin was taken as a sign of autocratic power." (Beard, p. 295.) Brutus certainly did not have "autocratic power," but was that what he was aiming at? Almost certainly not. The portrait of a living person on a coin *was* decidedly rare, but the name Brutus was closely identified in the Roman psyche with a fervent anti-monarchical tradition. Marcus Brutus himself claimed descent from the founder of the republic, Lucius Junius Brutus, who, according to persistent tradition, had been instrumental in ending the monarchy in 509 BCE, some 450 years earlier and whose portrait had appeared on coins minted by Marcus Brutus as moneyer at some time between 59 and 54 BCE. With the legends EID MAR, the date of Caesar's assassination, and LEIBERTAS, the watchword of the oligarchic republic, the message conveyed by Brutus's coins was *not* that he was aiming at autocratic power, but that he had emulated his iconic ancestor by liberating Rome from a tyrant who had enslaved it.

The populace, however, were incensed at the murder of their idol as the assassins soon learned when an unruly crowd descended on their houses intent on burning them down. As part of his lifelong devotion to the popular cause, in his will, Caesar bequeathed to the Roman people his gardens near the Tiber, and left every Roman man 300 sesterces.

Caesar's Heir

Probably the most significant provision of Caesar's will was his adoption of his nineteen-year-old great-nephew, Gaius Octavius who also inherited three quarters of his substantial estate. But before he could take power, he had to emerge victorious from a two-stage civil war, first against the conspirators and then against his erstwhile fellow triumvir Mark Antony.

Emerging victorious in 31 BCE from the Battle of Actium against Antony, the young Caesar established a new form of government, which, with modifications, was to last for three centuries, with repercussions down to the present day. But what sort of government was this to be? There is a great deal of confusion among modern writers about the nature and even the name of this new form of government. In common parlance, Augustus is generally referred to as the first Roman "emperor," and the system of government instituted by him as the "Roman Empire". But this is neither clear nor accurate. See the discussion below.

Avoiding Julius Caesar's Mistake

As an astute politician, Augustus took care not to make the same mistake that had cost Julius Caesar his life. Julius Caesar had ruled Rome as "dictator" for four years when he was appointed *dictator perpetuo* or *dictator in perpetuum* (literally, "dictator in perpetuity", commonly translated as "dictator for life" but more accurately dictator for an indefinite period). Acceptance of this title signaled the end of the Roman Republic, which had lasted for 450 years under an elite to whom one-man rule was carefully eschewed except for brief emergencies. Julius Caesar's position as *dictator perpetuo* posed a threat to this dominant minority, a number of whom, therefore, conspired to assassinate him on that fateful Ides of March, 44 BCE.

After his victory over Antony at Actium in 31 BCE, Augustus faced a serious dilemma. He was now master of the Roman world, but on what footing should his rule be placed? The title *rex* (king), which even Julius Caesar had refused, was anathema to the Republican aristocracy. But the title "dictator" was clearly also now off limits. The common people, who adulated Julius Caesar, had no objection to one-man rule, as was made clear in their outpouring of grief on Caesar's assassination. Indeed, they wanted a strong leader to champion their cause. So the young Caesar's game plan was to retain the support of the masses without offending the aristocracy, a daunting balancing act.

The Transmogrification of an Equestrian

The historic figure who is usually referred to as "Augustus" was born in 63 BCE into an equestrian family (i.e. the second rank, below that of senator). with the undistinguished name *Gaius Octavius*. In 44 BCE, on adoption in his great-uncle Julius Caesar's will, he immediately took his adoptive father's name: *Gaius Julius Caesar*. It was usual for an adoptive son to tack his own original *nomen* (name), in this case "Octavius," on to his new name as an additional *cognomen* (surname), often in adjectival form, so: "Octavianus." That is why he is generally referred to by modern historians during this period of his life as "Octavian", but he is not known ever to have used the name "Octavianus" himself. To his contemporaries, he was known simply as "Caesar," and this was his greatest asset with the masses as it enabled him to capitalize on his adoptive father's popularity. Moreover, besides having been a charismatic champion of the people, Julius Caesar was now a divinity, having been deified shortly after his death. So, in 42 BCE, the next step in Augustus's transmogrification was to add *Divi Filius* (son of a god or son of the divine (Julius)) to his name, which now became: *Gaius Julius Caesar Divi Filius*. In 38 BCE, in a masterstroke, both his forename "Gaius" and his clan name (*nomen gentilicium*) "Julius" were ditched and replaced by *Imperator* (commander), the victory title by which a successful general was hailed by his troops on the field of battle. This gave him a new identity: *Imperator Caesar Divi Filius*. But the culmination of his reinvention of himself came in 27 BCE when he was accorded by the Senate the title *Augustus* (the Sublime or the Revered), a sobriquet associated with Romulus, Rome's mythical founder. He then emerged in his full glory as *Imperator Caesar Divi Filius Augustus*.

Taking each component of this nomenclature separately:

Imperator: As Augustus tells us in his masterly autobiography, which came to be known as the *Res Gestae Divi Augusti*, he was hailed as *imperator* twenty-one times (RG §4). This was the traditional way in which a successful general was honoured by his troops on the field of battle. But, in a master stroke, he now adopted it as a forename. This designation, which came later to be used to mean emperor (and has given us the English word "emperor"), is the reason that the whole regime instituted by Augustus came to be known in English (and similarly in the Romance languages) as the Roman Empire. Because Roman emperors had never had the title of king, when Napoleon Bonaparte assumed monarchical powers he chose to call himself not king but emperor, which did not offend against his republican sensibilities as heir to the French Revolution.

Caesar: This is the only part of Augustus's final designation that was an actual name: Julius Caesar's *cognomen*. But it also became a title, later accorded to the emperor-designate and later still to a "junior" emperor, with the title *Augustus* reserved for "senior" emperors. It is the origin of the Russian imperial title *Tsar* or *Czar* and German *Kaiser*, and hence *Kaiserzeit* for the whole period ushered in by Augustus's accession to power.

Divi Filius: Being the son of a god was no mean feat, but Julius Caesar was reputedly already of divine stock before his deification as a descendant of the goddess Venus Genetrix, whose image accordingly appears on coins issued by earlier members of the Julian *gens* (clan). The Julii traced their descent from Venus through Iulus, the son of Aeneas, the mythical Trojan prince who was an ancestor of Romulus, the eponymous legendary founder of Rome. It was partly to celebrate this tradition that Vergil wrote his *Aeneid*.

Augustus: This designation meaning "the Sublime one" or "the Revered one," associated as it was with Romulus, gave the whole carefully crafted new self-image an aura of sanctity, and hinted at Augustus's claim to be the second founder of Rome. Augustus himself was to be deified on his death as were most of his successors. The jovial Emperor Vespasian (r. 69–79) famously quipped on his deathbed, "Oh dear, I think I'm becoming a god." (Suetonius, *Vespasian*, 23.4.) The deification of the emperor became the basis of the Imperial Cult, which was eventually extended to worship of the *genius* (attendant spirit) of the living emperor and, especially in the Eastern provinces, of the living emperor himself as well.

Augustus's Autobiography (*Res Gestae Divi Augusti*)

In his carefully crafted autobiography, Augustus managed to paint a composite picture of himself as a powerful populist leader and at the same time as the restorer of the republic in order to win the support of the *plebs urbana* (urban plebs) while conciliating the senatorial aristocracy at the same time. Here are a few choice extracts:

Victorious but merciful general: "I frequently waged civil and foreign wars by land and sea, and as victor I spared the lives of all citizens who sought pardon" (§3).

Recognition and modesty: "I twice celebrated a triumphal ovation and a curule triumph on three occasions, and was hailed as *imperator* twenty-one times, with the Senate decreeing more triumphs to me, all of which I refused" (§4.1).

Holder of Republican offices: "When I wrote this I had been consul thirteen times, and was holding tribunician power for the thirty-seventh time"(§4.4). "When offered the consulship [in 22 BCE] every year for the rest of my life, I did not accept it" (§5.3).

First Settlement: In 27 BCE, "having come to be in complete charge of everything by universal consent, I transferred the state (*res publica*) from my power (*potestas*) to the control (*arbitrium*) of the Roman Senate and People." In return for this, he was named "Augustus" by the Senate. "After this time I surpassed everyone in influence (*auctoritas*), but had no more power (*potestas*) than the others who were my colleagues in each magistracy" (§34).

Dictatorship refused: "The dictatorship was offered to me by both the people and the senate both when I was present and when I was absent from Rome in [22 BCE], but I did not accept it" (§5.1). In fact, in 22 BCE, there were food riots, with the urban masses calling on Augustus to become dictator to solve the problem. That was also the first year when Augustus for the first time declined the consulship, which so worried his loyal *plebs* that they refused to elect a second consul that year, ostensibly keeping the vacant seat open for Augustus. This concern erupted in riots in that year and also in 21 and 19 BCE. (Dio Cassius, 54.1, 54.6, 54.10.)

Benefactor of the poor: Augustus contrasts his refusal of the dictatorship in 22 BCE with his acceptance of the task of saving the corn supply during the corn shortage in that year, which he achieved "within a few days" and "at my own expense and effort" (§5.2). Augustus proudly records his bounty to the *plebs Romana*, or ordinary people of the capital: 500 sestertii to each member of the *plebs* under Julius Caesar's will in 44 BCE; 400 each from the spoils of war in 29 BCE; and another 400 sestertii, in 24 BCE, this time at his own expense; twelve rations of grain apiece at his own expense in 23 BCE; and 400 sestertii each for the third time in 11 BCE. The recipients of his bounty never numbered fewer than 250,000 people. But in 5 BCE, he gave 240 sestertii apiece to 520,000 members of the urban *plebs*. At the time of his triumph in 29 BCE, he gave 1,000 sestertii to 120,000 of his soldiers settled as *coloni* in Italy. And in 2 BCE, he gave 60 denarii (240 sestertii) apiece to the more than 200,000 members of the *plebs* then in receipt of public grain (§15).

Soldiers and veterans: Augustus paid out about 600 million sestertii for land in Italy to settle soldiers on as *coloni* in Italy and 260 million for provincial land. And he paid a further 400 million paid to soldiers on their retirement to their home towns (§16). Augustus founded colonies of soldiers in Africa, Sicily, Macedonia, and Spain plus 28 colonies in Italy (§28).

Tribunician power: In 23 BCE, Augustus was voted the tribunician power for life together with sacrosanctity of his person, which he had for some years and was a protection traditionally accorded tribunes of the *plebs* (§10.1). For more on tribunician power, see under the discussion of the Republican constitution, above.

Pontifex Maximus: Augustus was offered by the people the position of Pontifex Maximus (chief priest) of the Roman civic religion, which had been held by Julius Caesar, but he makes the point of stressing that he refused to accept it until the death of Lepidus (his former colleague in the Triumvirate), whom he studiously avoids naming but accuses of having taken the opportunity of civil war to "seize" the priesthood. Augustus's acceptance of the priesthood occurred in 12 BCE, "...with such a multitude pouring in to my election from the whole of Italy as has never been said to have occurred before" (§10.2).

Pax Augusta: "During my principate, the senate decreed three times that the Temple of Janus should be shut" to signify the attainment of peace by victory throughout the Roman Empire, which had only occurred twice before since the foundation of Rome over seven hundred years earlier (§13). Augustus's rule did indeed usher in about two centuries of peace, which is, therefore, sometimes labelled the *Pax Augusta*, or more usually *Pax Romana*.

Public works: Augustus provides us with an impressive list of his public works, including his rebuilding of the Senate-house and his restoration of 82 temples in one year (28 BCE) together with several new temples, including one to the Divine Julius (Caesar). We also read of the repair of aqueducts, including the doubling of the supply to the Marcian aqueduct (§19–20).

Games: Augustus paid for eight gladiatorial games, three athletics displays, 27 dramatic shows and 26 beast-hunts, and a massive mock sea battle involving 3,000 men in addition to the rowers of ships involved. Above all, there were the Secular Gamesof 17 BCE, a magnificent religious festival (§22). The Roman satirist Juvenal, writing about a century after Augustus, famously remarked that the Roman populace were keenly desirous of only two things: "bread and circuses" (*panem et circenses*). (Juv. 10.81.) Augustus's pandering to this desire is a mark of his populist side.

Pater Patriae: In 2 BCE "the senate, the equestrian order and the entire Roman people" gave Augustus the title *Pater Patriae* (Father of the Country)—the highest possible accolade that a Roman could be given.

Summary of bounty: Tacked on to his autobiography is an Appendix added after Augustus's death summarising his bounty: 600 million denarii to the treasury, the Roman *plebs*, and veterans; another impressive list of temples and other public works; an incalculable outlay (*impensa innumerabilis*) on games, dramatic shows, hunts and the mock sea battle; donations to towns destroyed by earthquake or fire; and grants to individual friends and senators to make up their property qualification.

Did Augustus Wield Sole Power?

Constitutional position—"first settlement": Augustus is at pains to stress the constitutional nature of his rule. He admits that he had complete power until 27 BCE but then claims to have handed back

the *res publica,* the government of the state, to the Roman Senate and
people—and, thereby, to have "restored the Republic", whose corporate designation was *Senatus Populusque Romanus* (The Roman
Senate and People), represented by the acronym SPQR. As mentioned above, there is no implication here of democracy. From 31 to
23 BCE, Augustus was consul, every year—the top Republican magistracy, which however it was unrepublican to hold so many times in
succession. Under the so-called "first settlement" (a modern label) of
27 BCE, in return for "restoring the Republic," Augustus was accorded
the title of "Augustus" borne as a name. Then comes the mock-mod-
est boast, the most memorable phrase in the whole autobiography:
"After this time I surpassed everyone in influence (*auctoritas*), but
had no more power (*potestas*) than the others who were my colleagues in each magistracy" (§34). This is not a very reliable picture
of the true position. For one thing, it omits Augustus's *imperium*
(command) over the provinces containing the greatest concentration
of legions: Syria, Cilicia, Cyprus, Gaul and Spain, together with
Egypt, which, since the defeat of Antony and Cleopatra, had effectively become part of Augustus's personal patrimony. He governed
all these provinces as consul, which was certainly not in keeping
with Republican traditions. Even less so was the sheer magnitude of
his vast *provincia*. As consul, he also had *imperium* in Rome and Italy
and could override the governors of all the provinces, which were
not directly under his control. It is also worth noting that, even before
his victory over Antony at Actium in 31 BCE, "the whole of Italy"
together with the Gallic and Spanish provinces, Africa, Sicily, and
Sardinia swore a personal oath of allegiance to him (§25.2). Augustus
does at least admit that he had more *auctoritas* ("influence") than
anyone else. *Auctoritas* was an intangible quality which could not be
made the subject of a formal grant but which enabled its holder to
exert his will more subtly by suggestion, without force or even command. (Cf. Some incorrect interpretations of *auctoritas*, like Michael
Grant's theory that it "devolved" from the emperor to the *consilium
principis*, the emperor's advisers). (Grant, M. 1971, pp. 130, 453.) I
agree with John Crook that *auctoritas* was not "...the kind of thing
that could 'devolve' or 'be transferred' at all." (Crook, J.A., 1955, p. 17
n.) Another implausible interpretation tries to limit Augustus's *auctoritas* to a single incident in 28 BCE on the ground that *auctoritas* is
not mentioned anywhere other than in Augustus's autobiography.
(Rowe 2013.) But why would we expect *auctoritas* to be mentioned in
the literary sources? It was not an official power but a nebulous quality, an aura of authority, which Augustus undoubtedly exuded in
large measure. The language is not complex and clearly relates to a

long period: "After this time..." The existence of Augustus's *auctoritas* over a long period is not in doubt. What is in doubt is Augustus's modest claim that it was *only* in respect of his *auctoritas* that he surpassed everyone else. The truth was that he surpassed everyone else not only in respect of his *auctoritas* but also in his formal *imperium*.

Constitutional position—"second settlement": In 23 BCE, after a life-threatening illness, Augustus's formal powers were placed on a slightly different footing from before. (Dio Cassius, 53.32.) In particular, he no longer continued to hold the consulship year after year, thus freeing up one of the two "ordinary" consulships for someone else to hold. But he retained control of his provinces, which was renewed at regular intervals for the rest of his life. He was now given *maius imperium*, "greater command", proconsular (instead of consular) power not only over his provinces but also in Rome itself, with the right to override all other provincial governors. In 22 BCE, Augustus handed back to the Senate the peaceful provinces of Gallia Narbonensis and Cyprus, but Illyricum was transferred to Augustus in 11 BCE and Sardinia in 6 CE; all new provinces were automatically entrusted to Augustus, and when the frontier was extended to the Danube, all troops in Macedonia were moved so as not to be under the control of the Senate. In the end, the only senatorial province with a garrison was Africa, with just one legion. Instead of the consulship, Augustus was now given *tribunicia potestas* (tribunician power) on an annual and indefinite basis, and this became the way Augustus and all subsequent emperors counted the years of their "reign". So, coins would normally show a number after the tribunician power, thus: "TRIB. POT. IV". In fact, Augustus may have been granted tribunician power long before 23 BCE, or at least some aspect of it, but it is in that year that the formal use of tribunician power as a reign tabulator begins. But why tribunician *power* and not simply the position of tribune, *tribunus plebis*? The formal reason is that, as a patrician by adoption, the emperor was ineligible to be elected a tribune. But, in fact, the emperors had more power than an actual *tribunus plebis* would have had during the Republic. One important power associated with tribunician power was the *ius auxilii*, or the right to come to the assistance of a citizen who complained of being oppressed by another magistrate). In Republican times, a tribune could exercise this power only in the city of Rome itself, but the imperial tribunician power extended throughout the Roman world. Augustus's tribunician power also gave him the right to submit legislative proposals to the *Concilium Plebis* the popular assembly, and to summon the Senate and submit motions to it as well. Another important power included in the tribunician power was the *ius intercessionis* the right to veto the acts of other magistrates, including the consuls, and the Senate itself. In addition, tribunician power gave the emperor *coercitio* (the right enjoyed by all magistrates to compel a reluctant citizen to obey his orders on pain of sanction). Above all, Augustus's *tribunicia potestas* carried with it *sacrosanctitas*, or inviolability of their persons, which meant that any assault on his person was prohibited by law. The position of tribune itself was low down on the traditional senatorial *cursus honorum*, or career structure, but, starting out as it did as a protection of the (original) plebeians against the patricians, the imperial tribunician power remained redolent of this ancient class struggle and enabled Augustus and his successors to stand as champions of the urban *plebs* against the senatorial aristocracy (see below).

Augustus and the urban*plebs*: Augustus established a bond with the urban *plebs* which his successors continued to maintain. In his important study titled *Plebs and Princeps*, Zvi Yavetz summed up the position in these words: "With the commencement of the Principate, the emperors became in a sense *patroni* of the entire urban *plebs*. The *tribunicia potestas* was an important advantage, while generous *largitiones* and proper conduct helped in no small measure to this end." (Yavetz 1988, p. 152.) However, a section of the *plebs* remained part of the *clientela* of major aristocratic houses. "Although the emperor was not officially referred to as *patronus* of all the *plebs*, there was a clear conflict between his influence and the patronage exercised by individual senators." (Ibid., p. 97.) Yavetz also plausibly suggests that "...the laws limiting the emancipation of slaves were likewise passed for no other reason but to restrict the private *clientela* of the senatorial aristocracy." (Ibid., p. 96f.) because a manumitted slave became a *libertus* or *libertinus* (in the later Roman Empire the two terms are used interchangeably, meaning freedman), who would automatically become a *cliens* to his former master as *patronus*. "As a general principle he (Augustus) prevented anyone (Agrippa being the exception that proves the rule) from bestowing *beneficia* (favors) on the masses." (Ibid., 97.) Later emperors followed the same pattern, and it is worth noting that the supposedly "bad" emperors got that reputation largely from their treatment of the upper echelons of society, while retaining the support of the *plebs*. (See Yavetz on Nero, Ibid., p. 153.)

Augustus and the Senate: In his autobiography Augustus makes a point of stressing that all his honors and titles were granted to him by the Senate and people in time-honored Republican fashion and that he refused the tainted title of dictator. The modest-sounding title *Princeps*, or "first citizen," which is mentioned three times in the autobiography in a very matter-of-fact way, was intended to suggest that Augustus was merely "first among equals", although the reality was very different. It is this title which has given the whole period from Augustus to the accession of Diocletian in 284 the designation of the Principate, as it is usually termed by historians, although it is commonly referred to by the general public simply as "the Roman Empire", from the title *imperator*, which, as we have seen, was adopted by Augustus as a forename. Augustus made much of restoring the Republican constitution. Elections to the traditional Republican magistracies were put on a firm footing, and provincial commands were reserved for those who had reached the praetorship and the consulship. But Augustus did not want the old *nobiles*, the top echelon of the Senate, to continue to monopolise these commands. So, he introduced into the Senate *novi homines*, "new men drawn from the length and breadth of Italy". (Jones 1955, p. 20.) As we are told in the Appendix to his autobiography, he even gave some personal "...grants to individual friends and senators to make up their property qualification", a way of introducing hand-picked friends to high office. Augustus also used as a counter-measure against the nobility the "ingenious electoral machinery of the *Lex Valeria Cornelia* of 5 CE, whereby, although the freedom of the *comitia* (popular assembly) was theoretically left untrammelled, a strong lead was given to it by ten centuries composed in the main of the very class whom Augustus wished to see elected to praetorships and consulates.... By the accession of Tiberius the monopoly of the *nobiles* had been broken, and a sufficient number of new men had been promoted to the higher ranks of the Senate to make it possible to entrust elections to the Senate itself." (*Ibid.*, p. 20 f.) It is important to realise, however, that being a member of the Senate was in itself no longer of great importance. Membership was only necessary in order to obtain appointment to provincial governorships, the overwhelming majority of which were in the gift of the emperor. Only the so-called senatorial provinces had governors allocated by the Senate. At the time of Augustus's death, in 14 CE, there were only ten of these.

Augustus and the *equites*: Augustus tried to bolster the *equites* ("equestrians", literally "knights"), the second rank in the state, as a counterweight to senators, relying on them as military commanders, tax collectors, and in many other capacities. He broadened the scope of the equestrian class, encouraging the Italian towns to nominate suitable entrants into this order. (Suetonius, Augustus, 46.)

Augustus and the army: Important though the army was to Augustus, I agree with Brunt and Moore that it would be "...a mistake to represent his power as depending mainly on the support of the army." (Brunt&/Moore (eds.), 1967: 15,) Augustus went out of his way to reward his troops and veterans and to settle them in *coloniae* ("settlements") all around Italy and the provinces. Augustus made sure that the army was largely under his control, and by the end of his reign, Africa was the only senatorial province with any troops at all (see above). And from the reign of the Emperor Gaius (Caligula) (37–41), the whole army was commanded by the emperor. The praetorian guard under a Praetorian Prefect came to play an increasingly important role in the Roman Empire, especially after the time of Augustus. And the setting up of the *cohortes urbanae*, (urban cohorts), a sort of police force for Rome, which, together with the *vigiles*, or (firemen), were seen as important factors contributing to Rome's generally peaceful existence for the better part of four centuries.

Consilium Principis: Augustus established the *Consilium Principis* or emperor's advisory council, a semi-informal body drawn from his much larger body of *amici* (friends), which he consulted from time to time. This arrangement continued right throughout the Principate and ultimately became more formalised as the *consistorium*, a department of state) under Diocletian. John Crook's learned study of the *Consilium* does, however, appear to overestimate the influence of the *Consilium* on imperial decision making. In the words of A.N. Sherwin-White, "It is by no means proved that the emperors regularly took the advice of a substantial body of *amici*, in any particular form, on most matters of high or low policy." (Sherwin-White 1957, p. 253.)

Augustus: "Optimi Status Auctor"?

Suetonius quotes an edict in which Augustus expresses the hope that he will be remembered by posterity as *optimi status auctor* (architect of the best state of affairs). (Suetonius, *Augustus*, 28.) In the *Aeneid*, similarly, Vergil predicts that Augustus will usher in *aurea saecula* (golden centuries) (Vergil, *Aeneid* VI. 791–807), a prediction that would prove prophetic.

But what was the nature of the regime that Augustus established? My own view is that Augustus was decidedly the sole ruler of the Roman world. To sum up my findings, Augustus's position depended on the following factors:

- Duly authorized *maius imperium*, initially as a consul and then later as a proconsul, enabling Augustus to override any other magistrate, including a consul;
- Duly authorized tribunician power, with the wide powers described above;

- The support of the urban *plebs* as their effective patron;
- The support of the *equites*;
- *Auctoritas* (influence) stemming from his connections and achievements;
- The support of the army, which, however, was *not* the mainstay of his power;
- *Amicitia*, a wide-ranging network of people linked to Augustus as their individual *patronus* or simply as *amici*, some of whom he would consult either formally, in the form of a *consilium* (council), or informally, *inter amicos* (among friends) but who had no decision-making powers. Contrary to Ronald Syme, this group did not constitute a party or an oligarchy of any kind (see below); and
- *Money*: Augustus inherited Julius Caesar's fortune to which he added the treasure of Egypt and other conquests. From this great fortune, which he had amassed, he was able to make lavish gifts to the people of Rome and others as is documented in the *Res Gestae Divi Augusti*. (See above.)

From Tiberius to Diocletian

For three centuries after the death of Augustus, the trend was toward greater autocracy on the part of the emperor together with a decline of the old aristocracy and recruitment to the Senate from an ever-widening circle both geographical and social. The ancient sources attribute the changes in the Senate to the deliberate policy of "bad" emperors like Tiberius, Domitian, Commodus and Septimius Severus. Modern writers tend to stress demographic factors. Thus, Mason Hammond: "The chief and continuing factor which necessitated the introduction of fresh blood into the Senate must have been a failure on the part of the old senatorial families adequately to perpetuate themselves." (Hammond 1957, p. 75.)

The low level of reproduction of the old senatorial families has probably been exaggerated because we know that it was imperial policy from the start to broaden the scope of recruitment. The Emperor Claudius (r. 41–54), for example, forced the resignation of a number of senators who no longer met the property qualification, and at the same time, he promoted the admission of senators from Gaul. In proposing the admission of Gallic senators in a famous speech to the Senate (preserved in the bronze Lyon Tablet), a different version of which was reported by Tacitus, Claudius made a point of mentioning that both Augustus and Tiberius had encouraged recruitment to the Senate of men of wealth and breeding from the provinces. Interestingly enough, Claudius's speech was interrupted with cries to the effect that

"Italy is not so weak as to be unable to provide its own capital city with a senate." Yet the Senate nevertheless passed a decree approving the emperor's policy. (Tacitus, Annals, 11.23; Sourcebooks.fordham. edu/ancient/48claudius.asp.) A number of detailed prosopographical researches were neatly summarised by Mason Hammond, showing that, of those senators whose origin is known, the proportion of provincials (i.e. non-Italians) increased steadily (with a couple of minor blips) as follows:

> Vespasian (r. 69–79)—16.8%
> Domitian (r. 81–96)—23.4%
> Trajan (r. 98–117)—34.2%
> Hadrian (r. 117–138)—43.6%
> Antoninus Pius (r. 138–161)—42.5%
> Marcus Aurelius (r. 161–180)—45.6%
> Commodus (r. 180–192)—44.7%
> Septimius Severus (r. 193–211) and Caracalla
> (r. 198–217)—57.4%
> Elagabalus (r. 218–222) and Severus Alexander
> (r. 222–235)—52.5%
> Third Century—56%
>
> (Hammond 1957, Ibid.)

Under Vespasian, therefore, provincials made up only one-sixth of senators of known origin. There is a major jump under Trajan, and from the end of the second century provincials made up more than half the senators of known origin.

According to Pierre Lambrechts, (as modified by Syme), in the period between 117 and 192, no fewer than 48 percent of *consulares* (ex-consuls) and presumably an even higher proportion of senators of lower grades were of non-senatorial and indeed provincial origin. (Pierrre Lambrechts 1936, l; Review by Syme 1937, p. 271 f.) It is important to note that Trajan was himself a provincial, from Spain, and practically all subsequent emperors were also provincials.

The ever-widening circle of senators, from whom most provincial governors were drawn, was an important reason for the stability and general tranquillity of the Roman Empire over a long period. In keeping with this trend, in the year 212, the Emperor Caracalla extended Roman citizenship to all inhabitants of the Roman world by means of the so-called *Constitutio Antoniniana*.

Augustus himself was already clearly the sole ruler of the Roman Empire, as we have seen, although he was anxious not to make this fact too obvious for fear of offending the element which had assassinated his adoptive father, Julius Caesar. Later emperors had no such qualms. The jurist Ulpian (170–228) famously declared, *Princeps legibus solutus est* (The emperor is exempt from the laws or The emperor is not bound by the laws) although this is sometimes interpreted to refer only to the marriage laws. That narrow interpretation is almost certainly wrong because the historian Cassius Dio (155–235) makes it clear that the phrase *legibus solutus* exempts the emperor from *all* laws, but he dates this back to 24 BCE in the reign of Augustus, which, if true, is certainly not mentioned by either Tacitus or Suetonius.

Another similar and equally famous formulation of imperial power, which is attributable to Ulpian, is, "*Quod principi placuit legis habet vigorem*" (What pleases the emperor has the force of law), which is said to derive from the *Lex de Imperio* (the law defining an emperor's power on his accession).

Can such sweeping powers be traced back to the *Lex de Imperio Vespasiani*, the law defining the powers of Vespasian, on his accession in the year 69? Unfortunately, only the latter part of the inscription promulgating this law has survived. This law provides that any candidate for a magistracy or other position of importance who is "commended" by the emperor shall be given "special consideration". There is also a blanket clause giving the emperor the "right and power" to execute anything that he considers to be "…in accordance with the public advantage and the dignity of divine and human and public and private interests" just as Augustus, Tiberius, and Claudius had done. The exact scope of this power is not clear, but it is significant that it is said to have belonged to Augustus as well, and it would presumably have been granted to all subsequent emperors. (*Ancient Roman Statutes*, 1961, p. 149 f.)

The well-known story about how Claudius became emperor is instructive. On the assassination of Claudius's nephew, the Emperor Gaius (Caligula) in the year 41, Claudius was cowering behind a curtain, when a common soldier, seeing Claudius's feet protruding below the curtain, pulled him out and recognized him. Claudius, fearing the worst, fell at his feet in supplication only to find himself hailed as emperor. This shows the deference and strong sense of loyalty of the ordinary people for their "betters" and for heredity, which was one of the reasons for the longevity of the Roman Empire. When the Julio-Claudian line ended with Nero, after a three-fold hiccup a new dynasty of the Flavians was briefly established by Vespasian and then from the accession of Nerva in 96 until the death of Marcus Aurelius in 180 a succession of "good emperors" was attainable thanks to adoption. None of these "good emperors" had sons of their own, but Marcus Aurelius was succeeded by his son Commodus, who unfortunately was not in his father's mould. Commodus's assassination in 192 was followed, after two more brief hiccups, by the Severan dynasty, which remained in power until 235. The next half century saw a large number of emperors taking power until the accession of Diocletian in 284, which introduced what modern historians call the "Dominate."

Here is a bird's-eye view of some major developments leading from the Principate to the Dominate (See Arnheim 1972, p. 21 ff.):

- Before long, consuls appear to have been directly appointed by the emperor. (Tacitus, Histories, 1.772, 2.71.3);
- Starting in the early Principate, the Senate's financial control was gradually eliminated. As an institution, the Senate was a mere cipher, happy to humor the emperor's every whim. But the same does not apply to senators as individuals. For, though some important posts were now held by equestrians or even by freedmen (especially under Claudius), the great majority of high imperial appointments continued to be reserved for senators until the second half of the third century. But senatorial status was in the emperor's gift, and emperors continually brought new blood into the Senate as we have seen. So the fact that most provincial governors were senators did not mean that these posts were reserved for the scions of old families;
- In the course of the third century, the old traditional framework was gradually abandoned, until by the end of the century, only very few posts of importance were open to senators. The tendency now was to bypass the Senate by appointing non-senators directly to a governorship without bothering to make them senators first;
- An ambiguous passage in *Aurelius Victor* has given rise to the belief that senators were deprived of military commands from the reign of Gallienus (260–68) onward (Aurelius Victor, 33 f., 37.5–6);
- Be that as it may, a number of non-military provinces also experienced a change from senatorial to equestrian governors;
- But while equestrians moved into the erstwhile preserves of senators, there was no movement the other way to produce Lambrechts's fabled "fusion" of the two orders (Lambrechts 1937, 107ff);
- This process culminated in the reign of Diocletian, who may justifiably lay claim to the title "Hammer of the Aristocracy", as I dubbed him in my book, *The Senatorial Aristocracy in the Later Roman Empire* (Arnheim 1972);
- The powers of the emperor are neatly summarised by Cassius Dio, who agrees with Ulpian that the emperor was above the law (Cassius Dio, 53.17.1, 18.1);
- Imperial trappings became increasingly grand. Nero was shown in his lifetime wearing the radiate crown of the sun, a symbol of divinity,

on some of his coins. In the late third century, this gave way to the jewelled diadem of the sun-god;

- By the third century, an oath by the emperor's *genius* was considered more binding than one by the gods;
- Everything connected with the emperor was given the epithet *sacrum* (sacred or holy); and
- Under Diocletian, the imperial court was well and truly decked out in Oriental trappings and an aura of cool aloofness on the one hand and abject self-abasement on the other pervaded everything.

Section B.   Two Disquieting Tendencies

There are two disquieting opposite tendencies current among writers on ancient history. One tendency is of undue negativity, what may be called the pooh-pooh mindset, dismissing out of hand ancient evidence, sometimes relating to whole periods. The danger here is that one may be throwing the baby out with the bathwater.

The opposite tendency is one of excessive uncritical acceptance of certain ancient evidence. The danger here is even greater, resulting as it may in a distorted or even completely false image of the period concerned. Though this tendency is the diametric opposite of the pooh-pooh tendency, the two tendencies sometimes coexist, surprisingly enough, even in the works of the same writer.

"The Fourth Century and the 'Conflict of the Orders' Belong in the Realm of Myth."

Much of the early history of Rome is based on tradition. But does that entitle us to dismiss it out of hand? T.J. Cornell's *The Beginnings of Rome* (1995), covering the period down to 264 BCE, has been criticized for adopting a "too trusting and overly optimistic" attitude to the ancient source material. (Forsythe 2005, p. 4.) At the opposite extreme from Cornell is Fergus Millar, who opines, "So far as 'real' history goes, we should forget the earlier Republic, and begin where contemporary evidence begins, in the time of Hannibal." (Millar 2002, p. 85 f.) Hannibal lived from 247 to about 182 BCE and fought Rome in the Second Punic War, which lasted from 218 to 203 BCE. Millar continues, "The fourth century and the 'conflict of the orders' belong in the realm of myth. Yet so apparently purist a decision will not really do either."—and so, he charitably stretches the period of "real" history two or three generations further back to allow for "collective memory."

Conflict of the Orders

Millar condemns as a "circular" definition this conclusion by Christian Meier as quoted by Karl-Joachim Hölkeskamp (2010) about the aristocratic monopoly of office in the Republic: "Whoever played a part in politics belonged to the aristocracy, and whoever belonged to the aristocracy played a part in politics." (Millar, Ibid., 94.) In fact, it is not circular at all. A parallel would be to say something like this: Any animal with a single horn on its head is a unicorn, and every unicorn has a single horn on its head. In other words, the class of animals with a single horn is closed. If you come across an animal with a single horn, you know that it must be a unicorn. And, if you come across a unicorn, you know it must have a single horn on its head. In other words, the two classes, that of unicorns and that of single-horned animals are coextensive.

This is not at all illogical. In fact, there are two aristocratic models that contrast with it. It is quite possible, for example, to have a society where political office is reserved to only certain aristocratic families or individuals while other aristocrats are left outside the magic circle. It is also possible for an aristocracy to be open, so that, while all or most of its members are engaged in politics, outsiders are not excluded. This latter model is actually a better fit for the Roman Republic than Meier's closed model because *novi homines*, or "new men," were able to gain admission to the dominant elite from an early date.

According to persistent tradition, at some time in the early Republic, a protracted Conflict of the Orders broke out between the *patricii* (patricians) and the *plebeii* (plebeians). Some modern writers have suggested an ethnic distinction between the two orders. Livy more plausibly identifies the patricians, the dominant elite in the early Republic, as descendants of the original senators appointed by Romulus. (Livy 1.8.) In the absence of evidence, it would be idle to speculate on the origins of the two groups.

But that should not prevent us from accepting the historicity of a conflict between the ruling elite and an element of the population excluded from power. It would be throwing the baby out with the bathwater to agree with Fergus Millar in consigning the fourth century (BCE) and the Conflict of the Orders to the realm of myth, as cited above. (Millar 2002, p. 85 f.) We have a very detailed account of the Conflict of the Orders from Livy writing in the time of Augustus, on the basis, as mentioned above, not only of tradition but also of earlier historical accounts.

There certainly are some problems with the details of the Conflict of the Orders as they have come down to us. One question that has exercised scholars is why several of the early consuls, including Lucius Junius Brutus himself, appear to have been plebeians at a time when only patricians were supposedly eligible. The answer may be that the clear distinction between the orders may only have developed later, but this is a puzzle-problem to which there is no definite solution.

Even if the details and dates of this protracted struggle as recounted by Livy, Dionysius of Halicarnassus, and other ancient sources are fictitious, there can be no doubt that from at least the third century BCE, the dominant elite in the Roman Republic was a combined patricio-plebeian aristocracy, which controlled not only the high magistracies of state, but also the senate, and the state religion. (See Stuart Stavely 2014.) It is significant that, from the fourth century BCE, every senatorial family was forever labeled as either patrician or plebeian, and the only way one could switch from one order to the other was by adoption, though entry to the plebeian part of the aristocracy was open to *novi homines* from outside.

"Monopoly of Office and Power"

But the fact that the Republic was dominated by a small elite is not in doubt. In rejecting this position, Millar was flying in the face of the evidence and opposing not only the Gelzer school of German scholars but also his own supervisor in Oxford, Sir Ronald Syme. (Syme 1939, p. 124.)

Gary Forsythe provides evidence of "...multiple offices shared by the same two individuals", one patrician and the other plebeian, between 366 and 264 BCE, the century before the First Punic War. Forsythe lists no fewer than 16 such pairs, plus three further "...instances in which one person held two consulships with two brothers or members of the same family." In addition, Forsythe notes the high frequency of repeat consulates in the twenty-five years after the reorganisation of 367 BCE. It is easy to pooh-pooh the *Consular Fasti*, the official list of consuls as recorded in the so-called *Fasti Capitolini*, as Millar does because they date only from the time of Augustus, but Forsyth based his observations on Livy's history as well, which was also written during the reign of Augustus.

On the basis of detailed prosopographical evidence, Ernst Badian found that "...the proportion of consuls who came from families that had already produced at least one consul never fell below 70 percent in the whole period between 179 and 49 BCE." (Badian 1990, pp. 371–413.)

Patronage or Clientela

Millar took issue with Matthias Gelzer's classic view, advanced in 1912, that the Roman Republic was dominated by "a homogeneous elite (or 'aristocracy' or 'nobility') controlling the mass of the people through a network of patronage relationships." (Millar, Ibid., p. 92.)

Gelzer may possibly have overestimated the importance of patronage in elections, but it is hard to believe that it played no role at all, considering its antiquity and the fact that it was clearly still alive and well in the Principate, not a time when it could suddenly have sprung into existence. In addition, there was a persistent aristocratic ethos throughout Roman history. A.H.M. ("Hugo") Jones described the people of Athens in the fifth century BCE as "...rather snobbish in their choice of leaders" (Jones 1957, p. 49) even though their regime was decidedly anti-aristocratic. The same can be said of the Roman *plebs* both during the aristocratic dominance of the middle Republic and in their support of *Populares* in the late republic.

Following Peter Brunt, Millar argued against Gelzer that "...such patronage relations cannot serve as the key to understanding the political process in Rome." I will take Millar's and Brunt's points one by one.

> *The citizen body of Rome was too large for such a system to have operated effectively* (Millar, as paraphrased by Guy Maclean Rogers as editor of Millar's *Rome, the Greek World, and the East*.) Referring to patronage or *clientela* as a "system" is a mistake. This mistake sets patronage up as an "Aunt Sally" or straw man, making it easy to knock down. In fact, *clientela* was not a "system" and cannot, therefore, be expected to have "operated effectively", whatever that is supposed to mean. Patronage *was* an *informal* social institution. And, of course, not *every* Roman would have been a patron or a client.

Patronage was "marginal" in the Republic but "...enjoyed a heyday under the principate" and "...flourished under the late empire" (Brunt 1988). There is little doubt about the importance of patronage in the later Roman Empire, more usually under the title *patrocinium*, which eventually morphed into the medieval seigniorial system. (See Arnheim 1972.) What about the Principate? The Epigrams of the Roman poet Martial, published between 86 and 103 CE, show that patronage was alive and well during the Principate but probably less political than social and financial. "With the commencement of the Principate," writes Yavetz, "the emperors became in a sense the *patroni* of the entire urban *plebs*." (Yavetz 1988, p. 152.) Garnsey, however, opines, "If everyone is a client, no one is." (Garnsey in McGill, Scott et al 2010, p. 44.)

This misses the point. According to Yavetz's cogent portrayal, the emperor was the patron "...of the entire urban plebs" but not of the whole population. There is a very big difference between the two. The *plebs* had long been opposed to the senatorial aristocracy and had their own champions, the *Populares*, culminating in Julius Caesar, a position which Augustus, as Caesar's heir, prized and cultivated. Hence, the use of the tribunician power by Augustus and all his successors. But Augustus was careful to balance his position as champion of the *plebs* with his claim to be the restorer of the Republic.

Brunt's idea that patronage relations during the Republic were "... fragile, peripheral, short-lived, and did not count for very much" may possibly be correct as far as the turbulent late Republic was concerned but less likely for the middle Republic. (Brunt 1988.) There is evidence of patronage going all the way back to the *Menaechmi* of Plautus (c. 254–184 BCE), which indicates that rich men liked to be the patrons of as many clients as possible.

I agree with Professor John North's characterization of the Brunt view as one of "sweeping negativity." Brunt's position was largely an argument from silence, based on the fact that "...clients are much less conspicuous in the sources" than we would expect if patronage was as important as was traditionally believed. North's comment is apt: "It is quite possible that the basic relationships of society, so familiar to contemporaries, should be assumed and rarely referred to in contemporary texts". (North 1989, p. 155.) But in fact, as Garnsey admits and as Brunt's own footnotes show, the sources are by no means silent on patronage.

Polybius Was Right

Up to now we have been concerned with the tendency on the part of certain modern writers to dismiss large amounts of ancient evidence out of hand, with the danger of throwing the baby out with the bathwater. We now come to the opposite tendency, namely to accept too uncritically certain other ancient evidence. Some writers even have managed to combine both these opposite tendencies in the same book. One particularly disquieting tendency is to accept too readily any suggestion that the Roman Republic was democratic and even that the Principate of Augustus had democratic elements.

The evidence is quite clear, however, that the Roman Republic was an oligarchy or an aristocracy controlled by a senatorial elite, which, however, was open to *novi homines*. This is a modified version of the traditional view that can be traced back to Matthias Gelzer's *Nobilität der römischen Republik* (1912). Until the 1980s there was a basic consensus, in the words of Professor Karl-Joachim Hölkeskamp, "that the social and political order of the *libera res publica* (free republic) had been aristocratic or even 'oligarchic', meaning that all institutions and positions of power were controlled by a particular kind of ruling class, which recruited not only magistrates, generals, priests, and senators from its ranks, but also the official representatives of the people, the *tribuni plebis*." (Hölkeskamp 2010, p. 86.) This picture emerged largely from prosopographical research. Since Gelzer's classic study, the existence of a "...complex system of patron-client relations" underpinning the political structure of the Republic had "...been generally accepted without further discussion." (Ibid.)

This consensus was broken by Fergus Millar, who, following Peter Brunt, not only poured scorn on the whole idea of the significance of patronage (*clientela*) but even "flatly denies the existence of the nobility or of any homogeneous patrician-plebeian political elite in general; for him, to put it in a nutshell, neither an aristocracy nor an oligarchy ever existed in Republican Rome." (Hölkeskamp, 2010, p. 108.) Instead, unduly impressed by the fact that elections and legislation were decided by popular assemblies, Millar even went so far as to refer to the "direct democracy" of the Republic:

> In the light of recent work, it is time to abandon the once established presuppositions of a hereditary 'nobility', of aristocratic factions, and of an all-embracing network of dependence and clientship. We might then be able to see the public life of the classical Republic in a rather different light: as an arena in which those who sought and held office competed before the crowd.... It was this crowd which, however imperfectly, symbolized and represented the sovereignty of the Roman people. (Millar 2002, p. 141 f.)

And again: "Using 'democracy' in a strictly neutral sense, it is undeniable that the constitution of the Roman Republic was that of a direct democracy" (p. 165). This appears to relate to the period around 150 BCE. That Millar was not referring only to the legal or constitutional position but also to political realities on the ground is clear from the longer passage quoted above, and in addition from the writings of Millar's staunch defender, T.P. Wiseman: "Fergus Millar forcefully insisted on the centrality of the People's role in the political life of the republic." (Wiseman, loc 76. referring to Millar 2002a, pp. 109–42.)

The first question to ask is what Polybius actually said. Then, whether he should be believed. And, if not, what was the true position? The response to these questions is as follows:

- *Polybius did not say that the Roman Republic was a democracy;*
- *His reference to democracy in this connection has been misconstrued;*
- *What Polybius actually said was that the Roman Republic had a "mixed" form of government, combining monarchy, aristocracy, and democracy;*
- *In reaching this conclusion, Polybius was unduly influenced by the tradition of constitutional classification by a long line of Greek writers culminating in Aristotle; and*

- *The true position is that the Roman Republic was an oligarchy, meaning rule by an elite minority or an aristocracy, namely a hereditary oligarchy, which, however, was not closed to* novi homines.

What Polybius Actually Said

Millar, claiming to be following the ancient historian Polybius (c. 200–c.118 BCE), maintained that a good deal of sovereignty was exercised by the Roman people. Here is what Polybius actually said: ὥστε πάλιν ἐκ τούτων εἰκότως ἄν τιν᾽ εἰπεῖν ὅτι μεγίστην ὁ δῆμος ἔχει μερίδα καὶ δημοκρατικόν ἐστι τὸ πολίτευμα. ("And so one might plausibly say that the people's share in the government is the greatest, and that the constitution is a democratic one.") (Polyb. 6.14.)

The key word here is εἰκότως (*eikotos*), meaning "in all likelihood, reasonably," which comes from the verb *eoike* (it seems). The point Polybius is making is *not* that the constitution was democratic but that, if one looked at the people's share in isolation, it might *seem* that their share was the greatest. Moreover, this passage is sandwiched between two other passages indicating that the Roman constitution was not a democracy but a mixed constitution.

It has to be remembered that Polybius was a Greek who had come to Rome as a hostage but stayed on and hobnobbed with some leading senators. His analysis of the Roman Republican constitution belongs to a well-known Greek genre going back to Plato and Aristotle and earlier writers. He classified the Roman constitution as mixed: a combination of monarchy, aristocracy, and democracy. The two consuls he identified as the monarchical element, which of course is arrant nonsense as the whole idea of the consulate was to prevent power from being concentrated in the hands of a single person. Polybius identified the Senate as the aristocratic element, which was fair enough, considering not only its elite composition but also the fact that it controlled all the finances, had jurisdiction over all serious crimes, and was in control of foreign affairs. "After this," writes Polybius, "we are naturally inclined to ask what part in the constitution is left for the people." As the people, through the popular assemblies, elected all office-holders, voted on laws, and decided questions of war and peace, he concludes with the sentence as quoted in Greek above. But he adds that, while the Senate must respect the people's wishes, "...the people must be submissive to the senate and respect its members both in public and in private." (Polybius 6.17.) So, it would be quite wrong to read Polybius as saying that Rome was a democracy. It is quite clear that he classified it as having a mixed constitution or government.

As a Greek writing in Greek for a Greek readership, Polybius's interest in Roman government is heavily influenced by the long Greek tradition of classifying constitutions in a formalistic or schematic way. That is why it is hardly coincidental that, as an adulator of Rome, Polybius should have chosen to classify its constitution as mixed, the form that Aristotle, among others, considered to be the best and stablest form of government. Polybius's interest in the actual operation of the Roman constitution in practice was minimal.

Millar, as paraphrased by Rogers, opines that, "At the center of the practice of Roman politics was not the Roman patron (*patronus*) imposing his will upon a client, but rather the orator, addressing the crowd in the Roman forum." See above for a discussion on patronage. But what about the idea that politics in the republic was all about orators persuading voters in debate?

Formal Rights vs. Practical Realization

"The orator addressing the crowd": Millar's idea that the popular assemblies were deliberative assemblies open to persuasion by rhetoric is illusory. Even the citizens of "democratic" Athens, who might have been expected to turn out enthusiastically in great numbers in anticipation of participating in their far more powerful assembly, were lackadaisical and had to be corralled by the police into attending. (See Chapter 6.)

Henrik Mouritsen provides a welcome dose of realism as a corrective to Millar's starry-eyed view: "The fact that political proceedings are public does not in itself make them 'democratic.'" (Mouritsen, loc 586.) And again:

> "The Roman 'democracy' is...founded on two—themselves indisputable—historical facts: the existence of a politically significant 'public' and the open access of all citizens to participate in this 'public'. These two facts do not, however, add up to a Roman 'democracy'. One crucial factor has been left out of the equation, which is the distinction between formal rights and their practical realisation." Mouritsen concludes that Millar's 'democratic' model "sits uneasily between, on the one hand, a very practical hands-on approach to politics and, on the other, an idealistic, almost naïve view of the relationship between constitutional principle and reality." (Mouritsen, 2008, loc 1841.)

Egon Flaig has pointed out that the popular assemblies almost always agreed with the bills presented to them, on the basis of which he denied that the assemblies were decision-making bodies, labelling them instead as "consensus-producing bodies". (Egon Flaig 1995, 77–91; 2003, 155–74; 184–93.)

What then about the *contiones* (informal non-voting public meetings), which Millar saw as the place where ambitious politicians employed persuasion to prepare the ground for later voting? (Millar 2002 6, 23, 136, 142, 158–61, 181–2.) As Hölkeskamp has stressed, these speeches do not necessarily imply a situation of open decision making. Rather, it was a situation where "...senators spoke and asserted what needed to be done, the People listened and followed their advice" (Hökeskamp 1995, 27–49; 2010 88 f).

Referring to the Senate, Millar remarked that, "The notion of that body as an 'aristocracy' in the modern sense has confused the study of the Republic for decades." (Millar 2002, p. 86.) It is not clear whether this remark refers only to the "early-middle- Republic" of about 390 to 218 BCE, or to later times as well. (Ibid., p. 85 f.). After consigning the Conflict of the Orders to the realm of myth and also rejecting the historicity of the Conflict of the Orders and of the "patricio-plebeian elite" that has generally been accepted as emerging after the resolution of that conflict, Millar provides us with a table purporting to show "Political Power in Mid-Republican Rome". (Ibid., p. 99.) However, the table, which covers the period 362 to 217 BCE, contains only ten items, most of which are examples of laws proposed by tribunes of the *plebs*. The purpose of this table is to illustrate "...that the constitutional structure of the state, the conditions of office-holding, and the duties of office are for determination by the People via the medium of *leges* [laws]." (Ibid., p. 98.) So what? Modern writers on ancient history tend to be dazzled by anything that smacks of democracy and especially of "direct democracy". (I note the same tendency in regard to Athens in Chapter 6.) It would, however, be a serious mistake to assume that we are dealing here with a genuinely deliberative assembly.

"Elective Dictatorship"

The present-day British constitution provides an apt parallel. The bedrock principle of the British constitution is the sovereignty of Parliament. Parliament, and more particularly the House of Commons, is where the debates take place, and no statute can be passed without a majority in both houses of Parliament, together with the royal assent. However, as Lord Chancellor Hailsham pointed out in his book titled *The Dilemma of Democracy*, the British system of government is really an "elective dictatorship," in which a government with even a narrow majority in the House of Commons can push through nearly any legislation it likes because of the iron grip that it has over its party members through the whip system, leaving not only the voters and Queen without any say but also even Parliament itself. So, though the sovereignty of Parliament has validity as a constitutional and legal concept, in practical terms, it is a sham. (Hailsham 1979.)

"Significance of Graduated Voting Absurdly Exaggerated"

Electoral system: As for elections, it is important to realise that voting in the *Comitia Centuriata*, the assembly which elected the top magistrates, namely the consuls, praetors and censors, was in wealth-order, and voting stopped once a majority was reached. This assembly was reorganised in 241 BCE to make it slightly more democratic. The *Comitia Tributa* (Tribal Assembly), which elected the lower magistrates, was more democratic, as the "tribes" voted in a random order selected by lot. But again, voting ceased once a majority was reached. The *Concilium Plebis* (Council of the *Plebs*) was essentially the same body as the *Comitia Tributa* but with the exclusion of patricians. It elected the Tribunes of the *Plebs* and Plebeian Aediles, according to tradition as a result of the so-called Conflict of the Orders. The *Lex Hortensia* of 287 BCE gave *plebiscita* (*Concilium Plebis* decisions), the status of *leges* (laws), after which most laws were in fact *plebiscita* but were called *leges*.

Millar, however, asserted: "The significance of the graduated voting, in descending sequence by groups belonging to different property levels, as found in the 'assembly of centuries' has been absurdly exaggerated." (Millar 2002, p. 178–9.) For more see Chapter 6 p. 208.

Millar did at least concede that "The consulate, for instance, was dominated by *nobiles*, the descendants of office-holders" for which he gave credit to Ernst Badian's sterling work (Ibid.). But Millar then goes on the attack again. I will quote Millar, with my own comments in italics.

"Does that of itself prove that in political terms the *res publica* was, or could be, run by an oligarchy for its own benefit? No: firstly, public office was, as indicated earlier, conceived of as a favour conferred by the people." M.A. *Maybe not "of itself", but, until the convulsions of the Republic's death-throes, the* res publica *actually was run by an oligarchy for its own benefit*.

Millar then provides us with "four fundamental points":

1. Millar: "(F)irstly, elections to the consulship tell us a lot, but not everything, about Roman political life." M.A. *Granted. But whoever said that consular elections told us* everything *about elections? Millar's point is a classic Aunt Sally or Straw Man.*

2. Millar: "Secondly, other offices, and above all the tribunate, were also reflections of popular support, and vehicles of popular politics. M.A. *Absolutely. The tribunate came into existence to protect the original plebeians in the Conflict of the Orders, the historicity of which Millar rejects. Later on, the tribunate became an important weapon used by* Populares, *demagogues with popular support like the Gracchi, against the* Optimates, *upholders of the dominant oligarchy, who finally lost out to Julius Caesar and then his heir, the future Augustus, who turned the oligarchic republic into a monarchy, all of which Millar rejected.*

3. Millar: "(T)hirdly, the use of words, oratory, before the people, was central to the political process in Rome. M.A. *Not at all. This is part of the illusion of the Roman Republic as essentially democratic. As Egon Flaig has shown (see above), the popular assemblies almost always agreed with the bills presented to them, on the basis of which Flaig denied that the assemblies were decision-making bodies, labelling them instead as "consensus-producing bodies."* (Egon Flaig 1995, 77–91; 2003, 155–74; 184–93.)

4. Millar: "(A)nd fourthly—the most important thing of all—the central focus of politics was *not* election to office but conflict about laws." (Millar 2002, p. 178.) M.A. *That there was a certain amount of conflict about laws is undeniable. Sometimes, this conflict turned violent, but this was all part and parcel of the conflict between* Optimates *and* Populares, *in which the latter (and, no doubt, the former as well) had lower class support. It is an illusion to see this conflict in terms of swaying voters by argument in debate. The violent conflict over the Gracchan reforms marked the beginning of the end of the oligarchic state that we know as the Roman Republic.*

"Rem Publicam...in Senatus Populique Romani Arbitrium Transtuli"

Augustus's vaunted restoration of the Republic: In his autobiography, Augustus claimed that, in 27 BCE, "I transferred the state from my own power to the control of the Roman Senate and People." (Aug. *R.G.* 34.) Fergus Millar appears to have taken this literally, meaning the "...restoration of the citizen body to its rightful place within the constitutional structure of the *res publica* and its politics," which "...provides the analytical framework for a very different understanding of what happened in 27 BC than we might gather from reading the *Annals* of Tacitus." (Guy MacLean Rogers, "Intro: Polybius Was Right" –Millar 2002, p. xiv.) Rogers emphasizes the phrase "and the Roman people" as if that is in some way significant. This is a misunderstanding of the passage in Augustus's autobiography, which is simply that he transferred the *res publica* (the state) from his own power to the *arbitrium* (discretion, or better, control or dominion) of the *Senatus Populusque Romanus*, (The Roman Senate and People) (SPQR), the traditional corporate designation of the Roman Republic. So, what Augustus is saying here is that he restored the Republic, which of course is false but which was a major theme in his propaganda. The mention of *populusque* (and the people), does not have any special significance.

Egypt: Rogers also makes much of the claim in Augustus's autobiography that he had added Egypt "...to the *imperium* of the Roman people." (Aug. *R.G.*, 27.) Why not again to the Roman Senate and People, SPQR? The omission of the "Senate" here is significant, but not for the reason that Rogers suggests. Augustus is *certainly not* claiming to have handed Egypt over to one of the popular assemblies. Egypt was newly conquered from Cleopatra (allied to Mark Antony), and Augustus ruled it as part of his own *patrimonium* (private estate) because he did not want the Senate or any senator to gain control of this rich province. So, the governor of Egypt was never a senator but always an equestrian with the title of "prefect", and no senator was allowed even to set foot in Egypt without express imperial consent. How was Augustus to publicize his acquisition of Egypt in his autobiography? He could not very well say, "I added Egypt to my own private estate." And he also did not want to say that he had given it to the Roman Senate and People, because then the Senate could have gotten its hands on it. So, he just said that he had added it to the *imperium*, of the Roman people. The term *imperium* in this context belongs to the category of what Lewis and Short call "publicists' language," with the multiple meanings of "supreme power, sovereignty, sway, dominion, and empire." (Lewis and Short, s.v. *imperium*.) This had nothing to do with the popular assemblies but was simply a vague propaganda claim that Egypt was now under Roman control and the "people" certainly never had any say over Egypt or over who was to govern it.

"Ironic victory": Rogers suggests that:

> [I]t is possible to argue" that the Augustan "monarchy itself was one of the (unintended) consequences of the struggle between some of the *nobiles* and the *populus Romanus* over the question of who was the sovereign power in the *res publica*. If we look at the breakdown of the Roman Republic from this perspective, we might see the emergence of a monarch from among the *nobiles* in 27 BC as an ironic victory for that democratic element in the Roman constitution, the Roman people. (Millar 2002, loc. 206.)

This is muddled. The fall of the Roman Republic was indeed the victory over the senatorial aristocracy by the people's champion, first Julius Caesar and then his heir, Augustus. But it makes little sense to suggest that this amounted to the victory of the "...democratic element in the Roman constitution, the Roman people." Moreover, if the Roman people had exercised as much power in the Republic as Millar and Rogers seem to believe, why would they have wanted to destroy the Republic? Yet Julius Caesar had made no bones about his contempt for the Republic by accepting an indefinite dictatorship and by describing the Republic as just "...a name without substance or form." Augustus's victory was not of democracy but of a form of monarchy that artfully concealed its true nature and managed to survive, with some modifications, for some 300 years.

Mommsen's "Dyarchy"

The famous German historian Theodor Mommsen (1817–1903) believed the Augustan regime was a "dyarchy" or "diarchy", in which power was shared between Augustus and the Senate. This view is not generally accepted. My own view, as mentioned above, is that what Augustus established was a monarchical regime based, as we have seen, on a combination of wide powers, with authority resting on broad support from the *plebs*, the *equites*, and the army, together with at least toleration by the surviving members of the Republican senatorial aristocracy and the support of the new men whom he had helped to qualify for entry into the Senate.

Syme: "A Monarchy Rules through an Oligarchy"

Against Millar's rejection of the characterisation of the Roman Republic as either an aristocracy or an oligarchy, we have this important statement by Sir Ronald Syme about the Roman Republic, based on detailed prosopographical evidence: "In any age of the history of Republican Rome about twenty or thirty men, drawn from a dozen dominant families, hold a monopoly of office and power." (Syme 1939, p. 124.) In his much acclaimed *The Roman Revolution*, a book about the rise to power of Augustus, written in 1939, Syme portrayed Augustus as an autocrat in all but name. But then Syme went off at a tangent and proclaimed in ringing tones, without any evidential basis that "In all ages, whatever the form and name of government or whatever may be the name and theory of the constitution, be it monarchy, republic, or democracy, an oligarchy lurks behind the façade." (1939, 7, 15.) Fifty years later, in 1989, his portrayal of Augustus's regime was still the same, describing it as "autocratic government" and adding; "The Princeps duly went on to exploit the 'res publica', encroaching on the functions of Senate, of magistrates, of laws." And:"'Potentia' now assumed the respectable name of 'auctoritas'." (Syme 1989, p. 1 f.)

I agree with Syme on the monopoly of office and power in the Roman Republic, but I certainly do not agree with the application of his one-size-fits-all oligarchic theory to the Augustan Principate. Accepting that Augustus initiated a monarchy, Syme tried to square the circle with the self-contradictory and erroneous oracular comment that "A monarchy rules through an oligarchy."

Monarchy and oligarchy are diametric opposites, representing the two poles of governmental power. (See Chapter 6 for a full discussion.) By "monarchy," I mean true, strong monarchy, a system in which power is concentrated in the hands of one person, usually with support from the lower classes, against the return of the oligarchy or aristocracy, which they have most likely overthrown. An oligarchy, on the other hand, is normally intent on perpetuating its shared group power and is, therefore, afraid of any one person becoming too powerful and having too much popular support. The vicissitudes of Roman history epitomize this type of conflict.

In the *Res Gestae*, as we have seen, Augustus makes a point of stating that he had no more *potestas* than any of his colleagues in office but surpassed everyone in *auctoritas*. (*R.G.* 34.5.) *Auctoritas* means "influence" and *potestas* refers to legally authorised, constitutional power. So, Augustus is trying to portray his position as conforming to the norms of the Republican constitution, which he claims to have restored. The fact that he had more *auctoritas* than anyone else was not unlawful. It was simply the expression of the esteem and prestige enjoyed by Augustus, similar to that which even great anti-monarchical Republican heroes of the past like Cincinnatus might have enjoyed. But what is *potentia*?

Syme does not mention *potestas* at all, but rather *potentia* and he does not suggest that this was ever given up, only that it masqueraded under the "respectable name of *auctoritas*." Unlike *potestas*, which is duly authorised, constitutional power, and *auctoritas*, which was not power at all, *potentia* was unbridled, naked power or might.

Syme's portrayal of Augustus is a gross exaggeration of Augustus's position, but it is correct insofar as the regime is shown to be monarchical. Yet, no sooner does Syme condemn Augustus as a lawless despot than we come across the bombshell quoted above: "In all ages, whatever the form and name of government, be it monarchy, republic, or democracy, an oligarchy lurks behind the façade." (Syme 1939, 7, 15.) Was

Augustus's rule not monarchical then? Syme certainly believed it was. So, how does he square this with his sweeping blanket theory of oligarchy? "A monarchy rules through an oligarchy," is Syme's baffling response. (Ibid., p. 8.) In 1989, Syme is still barking up the oligarchy tree: "Oligarchy is imposed as the guiding theme, the link from age to age whatever be the form and name of government." (Syme 1989, p. 13.)

This makes little sense. In a purely banal sense, it is of course true that no individual can single-handedly rule a state. The ruler will need the assistance and support of others in order to maintain power. But here we come to a crucial divide: between, on the one hand, those who serve a ruler in an inferior capacity and who are removable by the ruler at will, and, on the other hand, those who *share* his power. Where a ruler is surrounded by purely inferior minions who do his bidding, that is not an oligarchy because the minions have no independent power-base of their own. In that scenario, power is concentrated in the hands of the ruler, who exercises sole power. It is, therefore, a monarchy. By contrast, an "oligarchy" is a form of government where power is shared by the members of an elite group.

The essential difference between monarchy and oligarchy is the whereabouts of power. It is not always obvious whether the entourage surrounding a ruler is beholden to him, whether he is beholden to them, or possibly whether they are mutually dependent on each other.

The key question to ask is this: Who has the whip hand?

The existence of a ruling party, especially in a one-party state, may sometimes give a clue to the whereabouts of power but not always. So, for example, Adolf Hitler ruled Germany as "Führer" of the Nazi Party, but it would be a mistake to see power as vested in the Party, or any members of the Party, rather than in Hitler personally. The same applies to Communist Party leaders, such as Joseph Stalin in the Soviet Union, Cuba's Fidel Castro, and Mao Zedong (Mao Tse-tung) and Xi Jinping in China. As far as Rome is concerned, there was in fact no Augustan "party" although Syme seems to have thought there was; but even if there had been, that would not necessarily prove that the system was an oligarchy.

Augustus's *Consilium Principis*, drawn from his *amici*, which is discussed above, did not constitute a party in any sense. Nor was it a council or cabinet, whose advice he was obliged to take. Indeed, certain important issues on which we might expect him to have taken advice do not appear to have been referred to the *Consilium* at all (Sherwin-White). Membership of the *Consilium* was not fixed, its meetings were irregular, and the emperor was not obliged to accept its advice in any event. Informal chats *inter amicos* (among friends), likewise, do not constitute any kind of oligarchy.

Like strong monarchs throughout history who understood the realities of power, Augustus clearly recognized that the old Republican aristocracy, and especially the *nobiles*, "descendants of consular houses, whether patrician or plebeian in origin" (Syme 1989, p. 10), were foes or potential foes to his regime, just as they had been to Julius Caesar. But he recognized that Julius Caesar's blunt forthrightness was not the answer, so he developed much subtler tactics to neutralize potential enemies, which enabled him to establish one of the stablest and most durable regimes in history.

Syme recognized Augustus's defeat of the old nobility: "Not a mere faction of the nobility had been defeated, but a whole class." (Syme 1939, p. 490.) In addition, "Power receding, aristocrats looked to priesthoods for 'dignitas' and social eminence" (Syme 1989, p, 3 f), recognition of the fact that the defeated aristocrats understood the need to look outside government appointments to achieve or maintain a position in society.

> Hostility to the *nobiles* was engrained in the Principate from its military and revolutionary origins. In the first decade of his constitutional rule, Augustus employed not a single *nobilis* among the legates who commanded the armies in his *provincia*, and only three men of consular standing. When his position becomes stronger, and a coalition government based largely on family ties has been built up, *nobiles* like Ahenobarbus, Piso and Paullus Fabius Maximus govern the military provinces, it is true. But a rational distrust persists, confirmed under his successors by certain disquieting incidents, and leads to the complete exclusion of the *nobiles*, the delayed but logical end of Revolution and Empire. (Syme 1939, p. 502.)

Except for the suggestion of a "coalition government", of which there is no evidence whatsoever, Syme correctly highlights Augustus's reluctance to give military commands to *nobiles*. And Syme also looks ahead, beyond Augustus, to "...the complete exclusion of the *nobiles*." Yet Syme still failed to recognize that the regime established by Augustus was not an oligarchy at all but a different type or model of government altogether, a form of monarchy, in which power was concentrated in the hands of a single individual and that this form of government would continue long after Augustus.

Envoi: Augustus v. Alexander

ἀκούσας δὲ ὅτι Ἀλέξανδρος δύο καὶ τριάκοντα γεγονὼς ἔτη κατεστραμμένος τὰ πλεῖστα διηπόρει τί ποιήσει τὸν λοιπὸν χρόνον, ἐθαύμαζεν εἰ μὴ μεῖζον Ἀλέξανδρος ἔργον ἡγεῖτο τοῦ κτήσασθαι τὴν ἡγεμονίαν τὸ διατάξαι τὴν ὑπάρχουσαν. [p. 234]

> "Hearing that, after accomplishing most of his conquests by the age of thirty-two, Alexander was at a loss what to do for the rest of his life, Augustus expressed surprise that Alexander did not regard it as a greater achievement to stabilize the empire which he had won than to win it." (Plutarch, *Regum et imperatorum apothegmata*, Frank Cole Babbitt, 1931, p. 235, translated by M. Arnheim.)

The above passage comes from a collection of aphorisms or sayings of a variety of kings and emperors published by the prolific Greek biographer and essayist, Plutarch, probably in around 100, or about a century after the time of Augustus.

A neat contrast is drawn here between Alexander the Great (356–323 BCE), a military man obsessed with conquest, and Augustus, portrayed as a statesmanlike ruler, administrator and planner. Whether Augustus ever did comment on Alexander in this way is open to doubt. But, as they say in Italian, *Se non è vero, è ben trovato* (If it's not true, it's at least plausible). The contrast between the two men is certainly striking. By the age of 32, Alexander had conquered most of the known world, but he showed no interest in organizing his empire, and on his death soon after, it was split up among his generals. At 32, Augustus (63 BCE–14 CE) had just emerged as the victor of Actium and was about to embark on one of the most ambitious and enduring governmental or administrative feats ever achieved anywhere.

Nobody has ever accused Alexander of being a democrat (as far as I know, not yet, anyway!), and it is significant that, in Plutarch's probably fictitious little vignette, Augustus speaks as a ruler in complete control of his empire. There is none of the propagandistic double-talk that we find in his masterly autobiography discussed above. Yet, it is to his acumen and thoroughgoing, unblinking analytical understanding of the true countervailing forces at work in the power structure of his dominions that his success is attributable, making him perhaps the most effective ruler of all time, who was able not only to consolidate a stable regime for his own lifetime across the whole Mediterranean basin, but also to guarantee its survival for another 300 years.

The Roman Republic as "Direct Democracy"

Until Augustus's accession, the power structure of Roman history conformed to a general pattern shared by many other states, namely monarchy succeeded by oligarchy (minority rule) or aristocracy (hereditary minority rule), minority rule being the "default" form of government throughout history. Some modern writers on the Roman Republic, as we have seen, have managed to misunderstand this whole process, first, by dismissing much of the earlier evidence out of hand and then by going to the other extreme and uncritically accepting a passage of Polybius taken out of context as indicating that the Republic could possibly be regarded as a direct democracy, which is the exact opposite of the true situation.

Seeing the Roman Republic as at all democratic gives one a completely false impression of what it was like. But, as we have seen, modern writers who take this view of the Republic tend to compound their error by also adopting too uncritical a reading of Augustus's autobiography and misinterpreting that regime as democratic to some extent as well, a view which is wide of the mark, to say the least.

The Roman Revolution

As discussed above, Sir Ronald Syme, the author of the magisterial and aptly named *The Roman Revolution* on Augustus's rise to power, was well aware that the new regime was a monarchy, but his focus on the prosopography of the senatorial aristocracy led him into a blind alley: "A monarchy rules through an oligarchy." (Syme 1939, p. 8.) He continues: "In all ages, whatever the form and name of government or whatever may be the name and theory of the constitution, be it monarchy, republic, or democracy, an oligarchy lurks behind the façade." (Syme 1939, 7, 15.) Identifying monarchy with its diametric opposite, oligarchy, in this sweeping assertion is a serious logical category error.

"The First Emperor"

The section in Mary Beard's *SPQR* headed "The first emperor" is not about Augustus or even Julius Caesar, but Pompey. "Pompey," we read, "...has a good claim to be called the first Roman emperor." (Beard 2016, p. 273.) We are then treated to a catalogue of the honors and accolades showered upon Pompey. By the middle of the first century BCE, we are told, the stakes and "...the resources of cash and manpower available (were) so much larger that the rise of men such as Pompey was more or less unstoppable." (Ibid., p. 277.) Beard seems to assume that, had Julius Caesar not got the better of Pompey, he might have ended up in a monarchical role himself. There is very little evidence to back up this assumption. Unlike Caesar, Pompey certainly never identified with any particular political tendency. He was essentially a military man and a very good one too, it would seem. He was essentially an equal opportunity narcissist, happy to accept triumphs, honors, and kudos from any source. But did he really want to rule over Rome as a monarch, and would he even have known what to do had he been placed in that position? Elected consul in 70 BCE, Pompey promised to disband his army after his second triumph, and he kept his word though he could have seized power instead had he so wished. And, when as consul he had to preside over the Senate, such was his ignorance of the procedure that he had to ask a friend to jot down some pointers for his benefit. Much later, in 52 BCE, when he was made sole consul in the Optimate interest, Pompey asked the arch-conservative Cato the Younger to share power with him and advise him, which Cato agreed to do, but only in a private capacity (Plutarch, Pompey, 54; Cato the Younger, 47–49). And Pompey then brought his father-in-law in as his colleague for the last five months of his consulship.

In short, there is really no reason to believe that Pompey was aiming to become the first emperor. But it is not surprising that writers of largely narrative history, with inevitable concentration on individuals, should place undue emphasis on them at the expense of the bigger picture.

An even more egregious example of this tendency than in regard to Pompey is Mary Beard's similar assumption about the coins issued by the conspirator Marcus Brutus: "The portrayal of a living person on a Roman coin was taken as a sign of autocratic power." (Beard, p. 295.) In fact, however, as pointed out above, Brutus's coinage was so replete with traditional republican, aristocratic, and anti-monarchical symbolism as to make it inconceivable that he was aiming at "autocratic power" for himself.

2

Diocletian
Hammer of the Aristocracy

T he Emperor Septimius Severus (r. 193–211) is famously said to have advised his two sons, Caracalla and Geta, shortly before his death: "Be harmonious (between yourselves), enrich the soldiers, scorn all others." (Cassius Dio, 77.15). Caracalla soon got rid of his brother and behaved arrogantly toward most other people though, in 212, by the *Constitutio Antoniniana*, he extended Roman citizenship to all free male inhabitants of the empire. As his father had advised, his main concern was the army though his extension of citizenship actually had a detrimental effect on military recruitment. The army was made up of legions, recruited from Roman citizens, and *auxilia*, drawn from *peregrini*, non-citizen provincials, who became citizens automatically after twenty-five years' service. After 212, however, there was no longer any incentive for *peregrini* to enlist, and more "barbarians" were recruited than ever before.

Between Caracalla's assassination in 217 and the accession of Diocletian in 284, a succession of emperors met a similar fate. The period from 235 to 284 is known as the Crisis of the Third Century when the Roman Empire's very existence was threatened by a combination of threats, foreign, domestic, military, political, and economic.

Diocletian's solution stabilized the Empire, at least temporarily. As a military man, his focus was primarily on defense and security. By sharing his power with three other emperors in the so-called tetrarchy (rule of

Why Rome Fell: Decline and Fall, or Drift and Change?, First Edition. Michael Arnheim.
© 2022 John Wiley & Sons, Inc. Published 2022 by John Wiley & Sons, Inc.

four) and by greatly increasing the number of provinces, and separating military and civil commands, he secured the frontiers while tightening the administration of the Empire. The Christian writer Lactantius (c.250–c. 325) went so far as to claim that, under Diocletian, there were more men on the government's payroll than taxpayers! (Lactantius, *Mort. Pers.*, 7.3). This was an exaggeration, but modern estimates still suggest that Diocletian doubled the size of the civil service from about 15,000 to 30,000. (Treadgold 1997, p. 19.) On the basis of a population of between 50 and 65 million, this averages out at about one official per 2,000 inhabitants. (Jones 1964, p. 594. Cf. Bagnall 1987, p. 66.)

The corollary to this was the compilation of the Gregorian and Hermogenian Codes under Diocletian's direction, codification being a novelty at the time, which was to burgeon greatly in the future, right up to the present day. Diocletian took very seriously his responsibility as the fount of all law, and there are about 1,200 rescripts still surviving, probably only a fraction of those issued, chiefly from the period 293–294 alone. (See S. Connolly 2010.) Rescripts are legal responses, probably drafted by professional government lawyers in the *scrinium a libellis* (imperial secretariat), to petitions from people of varying degrees all around the Empire. (See Honoré 1979, pp. 51–64.)

Men of senatorial origin had a monopoly on provincial governorships under Augustus. This was one of the chief ways that this master politician was able to placate this important class, leading members of which had been responsible for that cataclysmic event on the Ides of March 44 BCE. As time went by, emperor after emperor continued to dilute the senatorial order with men of their own choosing from outside the order and, increasingly, from outside Italy. In the third century, emperors started appointing non-senators to governorships without even bothering to dunk them in the curia (senate-house) first. Diocletian completed this process, largely eliminating members of the senatorial order from positions of any importance.

Principate to Dominate

Diocletian's accession to power in 284 is an important watershed in the conventional chronology of the Roman Empire, marking the end of the Augustan Principate and the beginning of a new form of autocratic monarchy labeled by modern historians the Dominate, or simply as the beginning of the Later Roman Empire, or in French, as the transition from *Le Haut-Empire* to *Le Bas-Empire*. Adherents of the "World of Late Antiquity" school trace Late Antiquity as far back as to the period around the year 150. Oxford University in its wisdom also used to designate 284 as marking the beginning of its "Modern History Schools" syllabus!

My own view is that, though Diocletian's rule marks an important break with the past, it also represents the culmination of trends that can be traced back to the beginning of the Principate, including the sidelining of the senatorial aristocracy, which, however, was reversed in the West under Constantine, as is shown in Chapter 3.

Pomp and Ceremony

The pomp and ceremony associated with Diocletian's court are among the main reasons for the image of autocracy conjured up by his name. Here, for example, is a quotation from Sextus Aurelius Victor, writing in 361, stressing the outward trappings of Diocletian's rule that supposedly differentiated it from those of his predecessors: "He was the first to seek a robe made of gold and desired a large amount of silk, purple dye, and gems for his footwear. Although this finery was ostentatious and signs of a conceited and extravagant disposition, nevertheless these vices were insignificant compared to other things. For he was the first of all the emperors since Caligula and Domitian to allow people to openly call him *Dominus* (Lord) and to worship him, and address him as a god." (Aurelius Victor, *De Caesaribus*, 39.)

This is a gross exaggeration of Diocletian's responsibility for initiating these ceremonial features, most of which can be traced back to earlier emperors. Even the designation of the emperor as *dominus noster* (our lord), which is what made modern historians dub the period the Dominate, in fact first appeared in the reign of Septimius Severus (193–211) and became quite general during the third century, well before Diocletian's accession in 284.

Purple gradually became the imperial color. At the same time, the sceptre, long associated with Jupiter as chief god, became an adjunct to imperial costume from the time of the Severan emperors (combined reigns 193–235). The globe, symbol of rulership of the world, was to be seen on coins of Caracalla (r. 198–217) and Philip the Arab (r. 244–249.) To go with his elevated image, the emperor was even sometimes portrayed with a halo, or nimbus, a sign of divinity, as can be seen in representations of gods in wall-paintings from Pompeii (destroyed in the year 79) but only applied to living emperors from Constantine onward, notably on the *Missorium* (large ceremonial silver dish) of Theodosius I (r. 379–395.)

One innovation attributed to Diocletian by Ammianus Marcellinus, a much more reliable source than Aurelius Victor, is *adoratio* (doing obeisance) or *supplicatio*, before the emperor and kissing the hem of his purple robe. (Ammianus 15.5.18.) Some scholars have even found precedents for this among earlier emperors, notably Probus (r. 276–282), but the evidence for a Diocletianic origin is fairly strong. (See H. Stern 1954, pages 184–99.)

An oath by the emperor's *genius* (attendant spirit) was now considered more binding even than one by the gods. (*Dig.* XII.2.13.6; ILS 618.) And coin legends of Aurelian boldly describe the living emperor as a god: IMPERATORI DEO ET DOMINO AVRELIANO. (Mattingly-Sydenham V.1.264, 299, nos. 305 ff.) Descriptions of Diocletian's tetrarchy gave this formula a new twist. A marble milestone on the Via Egnatia on the way to Dyrrachium (later Durazzo, now Durres in Albania) in Illyricum is dedicated to: DIIS GENITIS ET/ DEORVM CREATORIBUS DD(OMINIS) NN(OSTRIS) DIOCLETIANO ET/ [MAXIMIANO INVIC]TIS AVGG(VSTIS) (To our Lords the invincible Diocletian and Maximian, offspring of gods and creator of gods) (CIL III.710 = ILS 629). The imperial pair are here described both as of divine descent and as the progenitors of gods, presumably the two Caesars who joined the tetrarchy in 293. From the early third century, everything connected with the emperor was described as *sacrum* or in Greek as *hieron* (sacred or holy).

However, certain other features associated with imperial claims to divinity are missing from the reign of Diocletian. One example is the radiate crown of the sun-god Apollo, first seen on coins portraying the deified Augustus and first worn on coins minted in his own lifetime by Nero (r. 54–68) (Mattingly-Sydenham, Vol. III, p. 178 f., and plate XI), followed, surprisingly enough, by coins minted in Antioch during the reign of Trajan (98–117). In the third century, this blatant symbol of the divinity of the living emperor was a regular feature on the imperial coinage, for example, under Aurelian (r. 270–275), but this fashion accessory was never adopted by Diocletian. (Rostovtzeff 1923, pp. 91–109.) A jewelled diadem, also associated with the sun-god, started appearing on coins of Gallienus (r. 253–268) but was also never affected by Diocletian though it became common later on.

The Imperial Cult

From the beginning of the Principate, there was always a tendency to revere the emperor in a religious sense. Though Augustus steadfastly refused divine honors for himself, he turned the deification of his adoptive father, Julius Caesar, to good account, styling himself *divi filius* (son of a god). Requests from the Greek-speaking provinces of Asia and

Bithynia as early as 30 BCE to worship the future Augustus as *sōter* (savior) were deflected by combining this worship with that of *Dea Roma* (the personification of Rome as a goddess). (Cassius Dio, 51.20.6–7.) The loyalty of Roman citizens living in the provinces was to be demonstrated by worship not of the living ruler but of Dea Roma and Divus Julius. (Suetonius, *Divus Augustus*, 52; Tacitus, *Annals*, 4.37.)

The title *Augustus*, meaning "the sublime one," initially used as a name, was redolent of divinity, associated as it was with Romulus, the eponymous mythical founder of Rome, who was worshiped as a god under the name of Quirinus. With a few exceptions, emperors were routinely deified upon death. Vespasian's deathbed joke, cited in the previous chapter, "Dear me, I think I'm becoming a god," represents a skeptical attitude towards imperial deification coupled with a recognition of it as a normal feature of Roman religion.

Sacrificial offerings were believed to propitiate the gods, and deified emperors were honored in the same way as the more established gods. The great majority of the population of the Roman Empire were not offended by the imperial cult. In the Eastern areas, particularly, there was a long tradition of worshiping even living rulers, going back well beyond their incorporation into the Roman Empire. So, the imperial cult formed a natural and integral part of the state religion.

In the West, and particularly in Italy, to avoid worshiping the living emperor, the emperor's *genius* was worshiped instead. Every Roman *paterfamilias* (head of the family) was believed to have his own *genius*, which was not the same thing as his soul, but rather was his attendant spirit. As all *genii* were divine, they were a proper object of worship, sidestepping the worship of a living person.

But the worship even of dead emperors was anathema to both Jews and Christians, who abhorred it as the worship of a graven image or idolatry, categorically prohibited in the Ten Commandments. It is sometimes suggested that the Jews were given special exemption from participation in the imperial cult. This does not appear to be correct, but Jews were certainly dispensed from the sacrificial duties associated with the cult, being allowed to substitute for it prayers for the emperor's well-being instead. (See Momigliano 1987.) The Jews could be recognized as a separate nation and so could normally enjoy the same toleration for their religion as was normally accorded by the Roman state religion to other communal religions. (See below.) But Christians did not form any distinct national, communal, or social element within the Empire. As far as the Roman authorities were concerned, Christians were simply members of Roman society, and their refusal to participate in the imperial cult, an integral part of the Roman state religion, could be regarded as seditious. So, the persecution of Christianity, a much rarer occurrence than is commonly believed (see below), was not motivated by any disagreement over doctrine, creed, or belief but was purely political.

The Great Persecution

Diocletian's persecution of the Christians, formalized by an edict issued in 303, was no exception to this rule. Eusebius, the Church historian, admitted that there was no persecution of Christianity in the early part of the reign. (Eus. *HE* 8.1.1-6.) And Diocletian's ire was first directed (in 302) only against the Manichees (Manicheans), a Christian sect with a good deal of support in the Eastern part of the Empire as well as in Egypt and North Africa. The Manichees were suspected of forming a pro-Persian fifth column, important at a time when a revived Persian Empire under the Sasanians posed a major threat to the Roman Empire.

But what was Diocletian's motive for then turning on the mainstream Christians? It had nothing to do with religious dogma or belief but was a response to Christian refusal to serve in the army or, once enlisted, to participate in the sacrificial ceremonials of the imperial cult.

The thorough research of Professor Candida Moss has revealed the falsity of the age-old Christian tradition that Christians had been mercilessly and systematically hunted down, persecuted, and executed by the Romans for 300 years until this was halted by Constantine. Candida Moss puts the Great Pesecution in context in a passage quoted in Chapter 10. (Moss 2013, p. 129.)

Why does this matter? It is important in relation to Constantine's later favoring of Christianity. (See Chapters 3 and 10.) In fact, the "pagan" religions of the Ancient world, including the old Roman state religion, were normally tolerant of one another. They were "communal religions", a term I coined in my books *Is Christianity True?* (1984), *The God Book* (2015) and *God Without Religion* (2018). This term meant that a person's religious identity was automatically bound up with their national, social or communal identity. Belief, dogma, or creed did not come into it. Unlike Christianity, which is a "creed religion" (another term I coined), communal religions mostly had no definite beliefs, only ceremonial and rituals. It was taken for granted that every nation had its own religion and its own gods, so one would respect foreign religions. Rome was exceptional in being (by ancient standards) a huge cosmopolis that attracted people from all over the Empire and beyond. These people brought their religions with them, so there were numerous foreign cults with their own gods, priests, and temples active in Rome. On the communal principle, these were generally tolerated even

though a number of them had long been separated from their communal roots and were simply what are sometimes described by modern
writers as "oriental mystery cults."

Foreign cults, such as those of Isis, Cybele (the *Magna Mater*, or
Great Mother), and Mithras (an all-male cult, very popular in the
Roman army) were all welcomed in Rome. Cf. Peter Garnsey's remark,
discussed in Chapter 10, that the Roman religion was "...disposed to
expand or absorb or at least neutralize" them. If that were so, why were
these religions allowed to flourish with their own temples and their
own priests at the heart of the Roman Empire? It was not under the
Roman pagan religion but under Christianity that they were closed
down and, especially after 391, banned, with the destruction of many
varied pagan temples, statues, and images and the murder of a number
of pagan priests. (See Chapter 10.)

Julian on Augustus and Diocletian

In Julian's satirical sketch, *De Caesaribus* ("The Caesars"), penned in
December 361, the Emperor Julian (r. 361–363), Constantine's nephew,
draws a marked contrast between Augustus and Diocletian. Here, first,
is his portrait of Augustus, whom he calls Octavian, presumably because
"Augustus" would have been confusing because it was a standard title
borne by emperors from the time of the original Augustus down to his
own day and by Julian himself:

> Octavian entered, changing color continually, like a chameleon, turn-
> ing now pale, now red; one moment his expression was gloomy, som-
> bre, and overcast, the next he unbent and showed all the charms of
> Aphrodite and the Graces. Moreover, in the glances of his eyes, he was
> fain to resemble mighty Helios, for he preferred that none who
> approached should be able to meet his gaze. "Good Heavens!"
> exclaimed Silenus, "what a changeable monster is this! What mischief
> will he do us?" "Cease trifling," said Apollo, "after I have handed him
> over to Zeno here, I shall transform him for you straightaway to gold
> without alloy. Come, Zeno," he cried, "take charge of my nursling."
> Zeno obeyed, and thereupon, by reciting over Octavian a few of his
> doctrines, in the fashion of those who mutter the incantations of
> Zamolxis, he made him wise and temperate. (Julian, *Caes.* 307, tr.
> Wright (1913) attalus.org/translate/caesars.html.))

After mocking Augustus for his apparently shifting identities as a young
man, Julian, a noted philosopher in his own right, concluded by praising him unstintingly as "wise and temperate" through his supposed

conversion to Stoicism (Zeno of Citium being the founder of the Stoic school of philosophy.)

Julian's portrait of Diocletian was rather different, coupling his pomp with the collegiate nature of the tetrarchy that he established:

> Next Diocletian advancing in pomp, bringing with him the two Maximians and my grandfather Constantius. These latter held one another by the hand and did not walk alongside of Diocletian, but formed a sort of chorus round him. And when they wished to run before him as a bodyguard, he prevented them since he did not think himself entitled to more privileges than they. But when he realised that he was growing weary, he gave over to them all the burdens that he carried on his shoulders and admired their unanimity and permitted them to sit far in front of many of their predecessors. (Julian, *Caes.* 315, Ibid.)

Imperial Power

Was the increased pomp and ceremony of Diocletian's court indicative of a genuine increase in imperial power, or was it just theater? Edward Gibbon, in his monumental *Decline and Fall of the Roman Empire*, first published in 1776, saw no real change in the power of the emperor in the transition from Principate to Dominate, just a change in style: "Like the modesty of Augustus, the state maintained by Diocletian was a theatrical representation.... It was the aim of the one to disguise, and the object of the other to display, the unbounded power which the emperors possessed over the Roman world." (Gibbon, vol I, p. 373.)

J.B. Bury, in his *History of the Later Roman Empire from the Death of Theodosius I to the Death of Justinian*, first published in 1923, referred to the emperor's "...gradual and steady usurpation of nearly all the functions of government which Augustus had attributed to the Senate. The republican disguise fell away completely before the end of the third century. Aurelian adopted external fashions which marked a king, not a citizen; and Diocletian and Constantine definitely transformed the state from a republic to an autocracy." (Bury, 1923, Vol I, p. 5.)

Bury follows Gibbon in referring to "disguise," but Bury also confusingly talks about a "gradual and steady usurpation." Disguise of course implies, as Gibbon made clear, that what lay behind the mask was the same throughout, whereas "usurpation" implies an actual escalation in imperial power.

More modern works tend to ignore the question whether Diocletian's accession marks an increase in imperial power. However, in Christopher Kelly's *Ruling the Later Roman Empire*, published in 2004, we come across these passages:

The extent of these changes [between Principate and Dominate] should not be exaggerated. The passage from the Principate to late antiquity was slow and intricate.... The difference between the government of the early and later Empire lies principally in a shift in the way power was organized and exercised, rather than in any great change in the social backgrounds of those involved in the business of government. (Kelly 2004, loc. 1396–8.) The transformation from the Principate to late antiquity was marked by a change in the way the Mediterranean world was ruled. For central government, the formation and promotion of an enlarged and sophisticated bureaucracy held out the attractive possibility of a more detailed and penetrating level of control. More formal structures permitted the development of an elaborate hierarchy of command, the more reliable allocation of tasks, and a greater degree of specialization. (Kelly 2004, loc 2384.)

These remarks, and Kelly's book as a whole, appear to rely a good deal on John Lydus's treatise (written in Greek), *De Magistratibus reipublicae Romanae* (The Magistracies of the Roman State), written in about 550, more than 260 years after Diocletian's accession in 284. It is primarily a source for the reign of Justinian (r. 527–565), under whom John Lydus, born in 490, served as praetorian prefect until 552. But this was the praetorian prefecture of the East, a century after the end of the Western Empire, which is traditionally dated to the year 476. The amount of light John Lydus's writings can shed on Diocletian's reign, or on the West at any time, is minimal.

Another modern writer with an Eastern focus is Peter Brown, who has observed that, "Despite the more drastic assertion of state power that characterized the fourth century, a system of government based upon collusion with the upper classes had continued to idle under a centuries-old momentum." (Brown 1992, p. 33.)

This model of "collusion with the upper classes" appears to refer to the curial class, who made up the decurions (town councillors) scattered throughout the towns and cities of the Empire. This class was a far cry from the senatorial aristocracy of the West, some members of which had genuine old noble pedigrees. The curial class was even a cut below the equestrian order, which *curiales* often aspired to join. So, even to call the decurions "upper class" is a stretch. As for "collusion" between Emperor and decurions, this too is misleading. The chapter on Decurions in the *Codex Theodosianus* (Theodosian Code), the longest chapter in that compilation, contains no fewer than 192 laws. Far from revealing an attempt by the emperor to curry favor with the decurions, these are mostly penal laws prohibiting decurions from seeking to evade their compulsory duties as members of local *curias* (town councils). Decurions' prime duty was as tax collectors, and any shortfall had to be made up out of their own pockets, failing which they could suffer forfeiture of their property or even execution.

What about the emperors' relationship with the actual upper classes, particularly the senatorial aristocracy? Diocletian had a visceral dislike of, or at least total disdain for, the traditional senatorial aristocracy of the West, and he completed the job begun by previous emperors of practically eliminating them from all offices of any importance, a policy that would be reversed by Constantine but only in the West. The distinction between Diocletian and Constantine is crucial. (See Chapter 3.)

Peter Brown's idea of "collusion with the upper classes" as some sort of ideal model of "autocracy" seems to have been inspired by William Beik in his *Absolutism and Society in Seventeenth Century France: State Power and Provincial Aristocracy in Languedoc* (1985) (cited by Brown, *op. cit.*, at p. 23.) Beik's book is a remarkable example of how myopic concentration on a narrow period and a narrow region can result in a complete misunderstanding of the main issues involved. Why was a supposedly anti-aristocratic reign (i.e. that of Louis XIV) "... sandwiched so tightly between the aristocratic Fronde and the aristocratic eighteenth century?" asks Beik. He sees Louis XIV's post-Fronde reign as a "success" amounting to a "class alliance" between King and aristocracy. (Beik, loc. 4506.) If Louis XIV's class alliance was such a success, why was his reign followed by a recurrence of the earlier problems? Beik does not even look at the later period. The Cardinal de Retz, a leading participant in the Fronde, an aristocratic rising against the French Crown, predicted in 1649 that "The parlements, which fanned the flames, will one day be consumed by them." (Cited by Cobban 1950, p. 64.) This prediction came to pass with a vengeance in 1789, 150 years later, showing that a contemporary had better insight into the forces at work than a historian viewing it with the benefit of hindsight three hundred years later. (See Chapter 6.)

Beik's error is compounded in his conclusion: "Absolutism was the political manifestation of a system of domination protecting the interests of a privileged class of officers and landed lords. Strong bonds linked the provincial nobility, the episcopacy, the various corps of royal officers, and the town oligarchies to the crown and to each other." (Beik, loc. 4449.) "What sort of absolutism is suggested by these findings?" asks Beik, regarding this as almost a rhetorical question. The correct answer, though, is "No kind of absolutism." For, far from being a picture of absolutism, this is actually a representation of some sort of shared government, a hybrid between monarchy and oligarchy, which is decidedly not a description of the reign of the "Sun King."

In analyzing power relations or power structures, one really should be a little more careful with terms like "absolutism," used by Beik throughout or "autocracy," Brown's preferred alternative to it. "Auto-crat" and "autocracy" are from the Greek, meaning "ruling on one's own," or "a monarch of uncontrolled authority; an absolute, irresponsible governor; one who rules with undisputed sway." (OED.) "Absolutism" has a very similar meaning. Coming from *ab+solutus*, from the Latin verb *absolvo*, it means literally (to free from, exempt, dispense from), as in Ulpian's famous description of imperial power, *Princeps legibus solutus est* (*Dig.* 1.3.31), which is discussed below. In short, therefore, both autocracy and absolutism refer to a form of monarchy with total power. Despite his famous (and arguably misinterpreted) remark, *L'état, c'est moi* (I am the state), Louis XIV's position was not one of total power, but it was also a far cry from a hybrid between monarchy and aristocracy. (See Chapter 6.)

Was Diocletian an Autocrat?

This brings us back to the fundamental question: Was monarchical power under Diocletian and the tetrarchy more autocratic than imperial power under the Principate? As mentioned above, unlike Augustus, Diocletian was not in the least bit bashful about revealing his power. Indeed, on the contrary, he revelled in displaying it. Gone was Augustus's demure, even modest demeanor, replaced by pomp and bombast although, as we have seen, a number of Augustus's successors had already blazed a trail toward the ostentation of the Dominate. We have the valuable insider view of the Emperor Julian, who was not taken in by the play-acting of either Augustus or Diocletian. And neither was Gibbon, from his very different vantage point. In sum, Diocletian's actual power was probably not much greater, if at all, than that of Augustus three centuries earlier.

The real difference between these two great rulers was in their perception of threats to their position. Augustus's elaborate charade was undoubtedly prompted by his concern not to meet the same fate as his adoptive father assassinated by a small band of aristocrats. Hence, he eschewed titles like "king" and "dictator" redolent of one-man rule while, at the same time, he fostered his inherited popularity with the masses, who shared none of the aristocracy's republican sensibilities but actually wanted a strong ruler to champion their cause.

Diocletian had nothing but scorn and disdain for the senatorial aristocracy, which he demonstrated by essentially removing them from practically all positions of power. They had already been largely sidelined by successive emperors, so Diocletian had nothing to fear from them. And, as for the *plebs urbana*, the common people of Rome, he did nothing to court them either. He hardly ever set foot in Rome, which he clearly regarded as the capital of the Empire in name only. He came to power through the army, and any threat to his position would come from that quarter. Enough of his predecessors over the past century had been overthrown by military force. Hence his close attention to the army, which not only protected his position as emperor but also shored up the integrity of the empire. So, although Diocletian's power may not have been any greater than that of Augustus, his power-base was very different.

Princeps Legibus Solutus Est

The reforms of Diocletian (r. 284–305) are generally lumped together with those of Constantine (r. 306–337). This is partly because of the scarcity of contemporary evidence of Diocletian's reign and partly because there undoubtedly was a certain common thread running through both reigns though there was also one very major difference starting in the latter part of Constantine's reign, as we shall see in Chapter 3. On the other hand, as we have already seen, some of the innovations attributed to Diocletian can be traced back to earlier emperors.

The great Roman jurist Ulpian (c. 170–228) summed up the emperor's law-making powers in the formula: *Quod principi placuit legis habet vigorem* (What pleases the emperor has the force of law). (*Dig.* I.4.1.) Any doubt about the scope of imperial power in this regard is dispelled by Ulpian's even more laconic and sweeping pronouncement: *Princeps legibus solutus est* (The emperor is not bound by the laws) (*Dig.* 1.3.31). Taken literally, this must mean that the emperor is above the law and, therefore, an absolute monarch. It has to be remembered that Ulpian's opinions had no official status until they were incorporated into the *Digest* as part of the *Corpus Juris Civilis* (Body of Civil Law) by the Emperor Justinian in the year 533. Yet Ulpian's *dicta* were written between 211 and 222 under the Severan dynasty, with reference to his own day, and they were not entirely theoretical. Ulpian himself served as Praetorian Prefect and chief adviser to the Emperor Severus Alexander (r. 222–235), which cost him his life at the hands of the praetorian guard, whose privileges he had reduced.

Ulpian's contemporary, Cassius Dio, (c. 155–c. 235), confirmed that the emperor was "absolved from the laws," and that this position could be traced back to the earliest days of the Principate. (Dio 53.18.1.) The *Lex de Imperio Vespasiani* (law concerning the constitutional powers of Vespasian"), dating from the year 69, confers upon the emperor a rather less comprehensive exemption from the operation of the laws, limiting it to the laws from which Augustus, Tiberius and Claudius had been exempted. However, this important document, only about half of which has survived on a bronze plaque, also contains a clause (number VI) conferring on Vespasian (r. 69–79) the right and power to do and execute "...whatever he shall consider to be in accordance with the public interest and the dignity of divine and human, public and private interests," just like Augustus, Tiberius, and Claudius. (*CIL* VI. 930 = *ILS* 244.) The less than pellucid language of this clause has aroused great controversy. What exactly is the scope of the power described here? Taken literally and in isolation, it would appear to confer on Vespasian an all-encompassing power. However, this is restricted by the clause about the emperor's dispensation from the laws, which exempts him only from those laws from which Augustus, Tiberius, and Claudius had been exempted. And even Clause VI makes it clear that Vespasian is not being granted any more power than had already been possessed by Augustus, Tiberius, and Claudius. There is a negative subtext here, as only the "good" emperors are cited as precedents, while the names of Gaius Caligula, Nero, Galba, Otho, and Vitellius are all studiously omitted. So, Vespasian is possibly being warned here not to assume any powers that the "bad" emperors may have arrogated to themselves. On the other hand, the broad powers conferred by Clause VI are far more extensive than the constitutional position depicted in Augustus's *Res Gestae*, discussed in Chapter 1. Although that document is a work of propaganda, the reason for the inclusion of Augustus's name in the *Lex de Imperio* may also have an ulterior motive, possibly to attribute to the revered founder of the regime novel powers being conferred on Vespasian.

Whatever the precise constitutional position of the emperor may have been in the Principate, in practice, Diocletian's position was not very different. What was of greater concern to him was to break the longstanding pattern of "absolutism tempered by assassination," a description originally applied to Tsarist Russia but equally applicable to the Roman Empire in the third century before Diocletian's accession.

The Tetrarchy

To solve this problem, Diocletian hit upon the novel expedient of the tetrarchy (not a term ever used by Diocletian), or four emperors sharing power, as illustrated in the famous more than life-size sculpture now in the Piazza San Marco in Venice, showing the four emperors in a group hug. The first step towards the tetrarchy was Diocletian's appointment of his comrade in arms Maximian as his junior partner in 285, with

Diocletian as "Augustus" and Maximian as "Caesar." To cement the power relationship, Maximian added Diocletian's family name, Valerius, to his own. The next step, in the following year, was to promote Maximian to share the title of Augustus with Diocletian, after which Diocletian took the name "Jovius" (associating him with the chief god, Jupiter) and Maximian became "Herculius," linking him with the semi-divine mythical hero, Hercules. In 293, the foursome was completed with the appointment of Constantius and Galerius as Caesars. Though each of the four emperors had his own base of operations, which kept changing as the need arose, the empire was not divided but remained a unitary state. The tetrarchy worked as a temporary expedient in the face of several security threats, but it broke down after Diocletian's abdication and peaceful retirement, itself a remarkable achievement, in 305.

Diocletian Chopped the Provinces into Pieces

Diocletian was also responsible for some major administrative reforms. Two are particularly noteworthy: rearranging the provinces and changing the provenance of office-holders. Besides his general hostility towards Diocletian for religious reasons, Lactantius (c. 250–c. 325) in his *De Mortibus Persecutorum* (Concerning the Deaths of the Persecutors) accused Diocletian of "chopping the provinces into pieces." (Lactantius, *de Mort. Pers.* 7. 4–5.) The provinces were nearly doubled in number, and Diocletian separated civil from military responsibilities (a policy completed by Constantine), civil authority being vested in a governor with the title of *praeses* (plural: *praesides*), while the armed forces were under the command of a *dux* (plural: *duces)*. The provinces were grouped into *dioceses*, of which there were twelve, under vicars (Latin: *vicarius*, plural *vicarii*) (deputies or lieutenants) because they were deputies to the praetorian prefects, their official title being *vices agens praefecti paetorio* (deputy to the praetorian prefect). Under Diocletian vicars and praetorian prefects combined civil and military authority, though this would change under Constantine. The praetorian prefects were essentially like chief ministers, or viziers, to the emperor. Initially, under Diocletian, there were two praetorian prefects, one attached to each Augustus. Under Constantine and his successors, there were always at least three, and more often four, praetorian prefects in office at the same time. After 312 the praetorian prefects' military authority was transferred to a new purely military official called *magister militum* (master of the soldiers) or, more specifically, *magister peditum* (master of the infantry) and *magister equitum* (master of the horse). The power of the praetorian prefects was reduced still further by the creation by Constantine of the post of *magister officiorum* (Master of the Offices), as Grand Chamberlain or head of the imperial civil service.

The provinces which suffered the greatest reductions were, predictably enough, the old proconsular provinces of Africa and Asia. The former was divided into three provinces: Africa, Byzacena, and Tripolitana; the latter was even more finely fragmented, into six provinces: Asia, Helespontus, Lydia, Caria, Phrygia I and Phrygia II. (Verona Codex). The truncated provinces of Africa and Asia were the only proconsular provinces under the tetrarchy and, as such, exempt from the authority of praetorian prefects and vicars. All the new African and Asian provinces, like all the other provinces everywhere else except for those of Italy and Achaea, were praesidial.

Titles of Honor

In this study, the terms "noble," "aristocrat," and "member of the (senatorial) aristocracy" are used interchangeably to refer to someone of senatorial birth or senatorial origin, by which is meant someone whose father at least was a *clarissimus* (literally highly distinguished). While this usage of the term "noble" is a departure from the strict Republican use of *nobilis* to refer to the holder of a consulate or one of his descendants, it accords with the meaning of the word as used in the fourth century by writers such as Symmachus (c. 345–402) and the historian Ammianus Marcellinus (c. 330–c. 400). (Symm. *Rel.* III.7; Amm. XVI.10.13.)

While all nobles were *clarissimi*, not all *clarissimi* were nobles. By the time of Diocletian, the title *vir clarissimus* had been in common use for well over a century to refer to a senator or a man of senatorial rank. The title was hereditary as we know from the examples that we have of the title *clarissimus puer* (highly distinguished boy), dating back at least to 197 (*ILS* 1143). The clarissimate was not confined to men and boys, for we also find the titles *clarissima puella* (highly distinguished girl) and *clarissima femina* (highly distinguished lady), the latter title coming to a woman from her father or her husband.

The clarissimate was the late Empire's equivalent to the *laticlavium* of the Principate, referring to the broad purple stripe on the tunic worn by senators. Just as, in that period, a *novus homo* (new man) could be awarded this honor by the emperor or be "adlected" (added), by the emperor to men of senatorial rank, a practice that appears to have been initiated by the Emperor Claudius (r. 41–54); so, in the late Empire individuals could be raised to the clarissimate by an imperial *codicillus clarissimatus* (diploma of clarissimate status), and the title could be extended to the holders of an ever-increasing number of hitherto equestrian state posts. (See *CTh* XII.74.5 (371); Cassiodorus *Variae 6.14.)*

Clarissimi became senators proper in the traditional way, namely by holding one or other of the republican magistracies, and it was still normal practice for young nobles to become senators unless too poor to be able to afford the expenditure which the tenure of a republican magistracy now entailed. Membership of the Senate was no longer of any practical significance because the Senate as an institution was powerless, and it is hardly surprising that its meetings were so unattractive to its members that the quorum had to be fixed at fifty. (Symm. *Or.* VI.)

Under the tetrarchy, the senatorial order formed a reasonably homogeneous group comprising men of senatorial birth, since, in the latter part of the third century, praetorian prefects were evidently the only *novi homines* to join its ranks. When, however, the senatorial *cursus honorum* ("career"), which Diocletian had turned into a cul-de-sac, became once again an important avenue of advancement under Constantine and his successors, this homogeneity came to an end. For now, in addition to men of senatorial birth, the order was flooded with office-holders whose positions had given them the clarissimate automatically and, as the fourth century passed, more and more offices came to carry senatorial rank with them.

This influx of new men into the clarissimate eventually reduced its significance, and as a result, office-holders in the upper echelons of power began to differentiate themselves from ordinary *clarissimi*, by adding to their titles *spectabilis* (notable) in the case of vicars and proconsuls and those equated with them in rank in the military and court hierarchies and *illustris* (illustrious) in the case of the praetorian and urban prefects, *magistri militum* (generals), and the major palatine officials. These new titles were not hereditary, and the son of an *illustris* would be a mere *clarissimus* until he earned a higher title through office. (See *CTh* 16.5.52 412.)

In the pre-Constantinian era, therefore, titles are much more precise indices of a man's social background than they are in the period from Constantine onward. The equestrian titles *egregius* and *perfectissimus* are, of course, always signs of non-senatorial birth, but the gradual increase during the fourth century in the number of posts carrying with them an automatic clarissimate made the equestrian titles obsolete and gave many men of non-senatorial origin the same title as that of the nobles. Thus, while under the tetrarchy, the clarissmate alone is sufficient evidence of nobility (except in the case of praetorian prefects) later, especially in the post-Constantinian period, it usually throws no light on a man's origins, and other criteria of nobility must be employed.

In the case of low-ranking governors such as *praesides*, however, the title *clarissimus* is a pointer to senatorial origin. Up to at least 379, the normal title for a *praeses* was *perfectissimus*, and any *praesides* who were *clarissimi* may be assumed to have been of senatorial origin, as it is inconceivable that the emperor would elevate a *novus homo* to senatorial rank just to appoint him a *praeses*, a position which he could and indeed should hold as an equestrian. In fact, the only datable cases known of *praesides* with the clarissimate under Diocletian were three *praesides* of Syria.

Emperor and Senatorial Aristocracy

In the three centuries before Constantine, the senatorial aristocracy had steadily been losing political power and influence. Conscious that imperial power and senatorial power were at opposite ends of a political seesaw, emperor after emperor encroached on the power of the Senate from the early Principate onward until it was left with only ceremonial functions. But though the Senate as an institution was no longer of any account, the men who comprised it continued to have a monopoly of most of the high state posts, notably provincial governorships.

In the Principate, the emperor controlled recruitment to the Senate, and the continued ascendancy of senators in government, particularly as provincial governors, and the hereditary nature of senatorial rank perpetuated the old Republican ethos. Once a man became a senator he was marked off by title, dress, and office alike from lesser mortals and from his own past life. Despite, therefore, the impotence of the Senate as a body, there was an imperial senatorial aristocracy with an *esprit de corps*. This aristocracy was very different, of course, from the self-perpetuating aristocracy of the Republic. Indeed, especially from the reign of Claudius (41–54), the huge bronze portals of the curia were continually welcoming new members from an ever- widening circle of provinces. New men rubbed shoulders with scions of ancient families and gradually became assimilated to the senatorial ethos. Yet at no time would the newcomers have outnumbered the more established elements, and not a few officeholders even in the third century could trace their senatorial rank back for a century or more. (Arnheim 1972, p. 32.) Among the surviving senatorial families in the third century were some ancient Republican lines, such as the Acilii Glabriones, Valerii Messallae, and even possibly the Cornelii Scipiones.

By the third century, the Senate as an institution had no power worth mentioning. Yet it was from this body, whose *esprit de corps* stemmed from a combination of heredity and assimilation, that the chief office-holders of the empire continued to be drawn.

At first, emperors worked through the Senate, subverting the position of the older families by introducing their own nominees into the Senate and then appointing them to governorships, thus keeping within the traditional constitutional framework.

In the course of the third century, however, this traditional framework was abandoned. Emperors, it is true, had always been able to appoint men of non-senatorial origin to high posts by introducing them into the Senate beforehand. But in the third century, there was a growing tendency to bypass the Senate by appointing non-senators directly to governorships without bothering to make them senators.

There already were precedents in the early Principate for the appointment of non-senators to high state posts. The positions of praetorian prefect and prefect of Egypt are cases in point, as are the governorships of Mauretania, Thrace, Judea, Raetia and Noricum, and smaller areas such as the Cottian and Maritime Alps and the Balearic Islands. All these provincial governorships, it is worth noting, were new posts, as emperors tended to be loath to break with tradition in any radical way.

However, in the latter half of the third century, emperors developed an appetite for appointing equestrians directly to governorships. By the end of the century, not only were most governorships open to equestrians, but they were also closed to senators.

A passage in Aurelius Victor has given rise to the belief that it was an edict issued by Gallienus (r. 253–268) that was instrumental in depriving senators of military commands. Because of the somewhat ambiguous phrasing of the passage in question, it has become the plaything of scholars. (Arnheim 1972, p. 34 ff.) There is, however, some evidence of senatorial governors exercising specifically military functions after the date of the supposed edict, for example, M. Aurelius Valentinianus in 283. (*CIL*.4102-03.) So, Aurelius Victor may well have been telescoping into a single "edict" a protracted development. For, there can be no doubt that there was a growing tendency in the period from Gallienus onward to appoint non-senatorial governors directly.

Among the proconsuls of Africa are to be found some of the noblest names of the age: T. Flavius Postumius Titianus, Amnius Anicius Iulianus, C. Annius Anullinus, Ceionius Rufius Volusianus. (See PLRE–Fasti.) The origins of these men contrast rather markedly with those of the governors, all *praesides*, of the new African and Asian provinces. The only *praeses* of Byzacena of known origin under the tetrarchy, (....) Junius Flavianus, was a *perfectissimus*. (*ILAlg*. I.3832.) In Tripolitana, two such *praesides* are known: C. Valerius Vivianus Obsequius and Aurelius Quintianus. Both of these were also non-senatorial. (AE 1929.4; VIII. 22763 = ILS 9352.) There are only three *praesides* of the various components of the old provinces of Africa and Asia under the tetrarchy whose origins are known: Fulvius Asticus and Aurelius Marcellus being governors of Caria and a Phrygian governor of whose name the only legible letters are Iu.... All of these were *perfectissimi*.

The pattern of equestrian appointments was repeated in praesidial appointments all over the Empire, with the single exception of Syria. For, though styled *praesides*, the three Syrian governors under the tetrarchy whose origins are known, namely L. Aelius Helvius Dionysius, Latinius Primosus, and Locrius Verinus, were men of senatorial origin.

The first of these had an ordinary senatorial career, two urban *curatelae* and the correctorship of Italy, before becoming *praeses* of Syria Coele, which post he evidently held together with appellate jurisdiction throughout the diocese of Oriens: *iudex sacrarum cognitionum totius Orien(tis)....* (VI. 1675 = ILS 1212.) This combination of a governorship together with diocesan appellate jurisdiction is also found in the pre-Diocletianic case of [*Vi*]irius Lupus, urban prefect from 278 to 280.

Of all Dionysius's offices, the only one which might be thought to be out of keeping with a senatorial career as it now was under Diocletian was his appointment as *praeses* of Syria Coele. The explanation for this anomaly may be that Dionysius was of equestrian origin and became a senator later. (Arnheim 1972, p. 42.) Even so, he was a senatorial *praeses*, a very rare animal indeed for the tetrarchy. But Syria also seems to have had at least one senatorial *praeses* under Constantine, and was one of the few Eastern provinces to change over to consulars under that emperor.

Locrius Verinus, who, like Dionysius, governed Syria under the tetrarchy, seems also to have had appellate jurisdiction at the same time over the diocese as a whole. (Symmachus *Ep.* 1.2.7; *CJ* 3.12.1.) In addition, Verinus was evidently a military governor of Syria, commanding an expedition against the Armenians. (Symmachus, Ibid.) He is probably to be identified with the Locrius Verinus who was vicar of Africa between 318 and 321 and urban prefect from 323 to 325.

These three cases leave Syria as the only province traditionally governed by senatorial governors styled "legates" (*legati Augusti pro praetore)* not to have been transferred to equestrian governors. This governorship was also to give birth, through the diocesan appellate jurisdiction attached to it, to the Constantinian post of *Comes Orientis*, as will be seen in the next chapter. (See Chapter 3.)

In addition to the governors of Syria, there are several other cases of *praesides* under the tetrarchy who have been claimed as noble, but none of these can be substantiated. (Arnheim 1972, page 43.) Of the 37 Western *praesides* datable to the tetrarchy, 27 are known to have been non-senatorial and the origins of the remaining 10 are unknown. So much for Diocletianic *praesides*.

In addition to the drastically pared proconsular provinces of Africa and Asia and that curious relic of a former age, Syria, the only offices left to the senatorial aristocracy under the tetrarchy were the Italian and Achaean governorships called correctorships, the urban prefecture, and the entirely ornamental ordinary consulate (i.e the position of one of the two first consuls of the year, who traditionally gave their name to the year.) Though long the popular term of reference for a legate of consular rank, the title *consularis* is not to be found in Italy until the reign of Constantine, who made it the official title of some Italian governorships.

In Achaea, the nobles suffered a temporary setback. L. Turranius Gratianus, a noble who was to become urban prefect in 290, was corrector of Achaea probably in the first years of the tetrarchy. (iii. 6103, cf. vi. 1128 and p. 845 = vi. 31241.)

Among the urban prefects under the tetrarchy were such men as Ceionius Varus, L. Caesonius Ovinius Manlius Rufinianus Bassus, L. Turranius Gratianus, Anicius Faustus, Nummius Tuscus, Aradius Rufinus, and T. Flavius Postumius Titianus. The last two were also ordinary consuls under the tetrarchy, and A. Annius Anullinus, an ordinary consul in 295, was to become urban prefect under Maxentius in 306–307. A member of the Anician house, Anicius Faustus, is known only as ordinary consul in 298, having already been a suffect consul, as is indicated by the number "II" after his name in the *fasti*. These noble consuls and urban prefects were representatives of families which, though now excluded from most positions of real importance, were within a generation to make their appearance in the *fasti* of a greatly enlarged and more significant range of posts.

The contrast between them and the Diocletianic vicars could hardly be greater, for, not surprisingly, Diocletian appointed to these new posts of his own creation men whom he could trust, men of humble origin who owed their rise to imperial goodwill. Though only six Diocletianic vicars can be traced, it is significant that four of these are known to have been of non-senatorial origin. (Lambrechts, 1937, pp. 110 ff.)

Similarly, of the five praetorian prefects whose names are known for the tetrarchy, three were of non-senatorial origin and the remaining two of unknown origin. Afranius Hannibalianus, whom Lambrechts claims as of senatorial birth, and his colleague Iulius Ascpepiodotus, pose an awkward problem. Basing himself largely on these two praetorian prefects, Lambrechts sees the period as one of "fusion" between the senatorial and equestrian orders. (*Ibid.*) However, though of senatorial rank from 292, neither Hannibalianus nor Asclepiodotus appears to have been of senatorial birth. Secondly, neither was appointed to an equestrian post while holding senatorial rank; the two men were already praetorian prefects when they became consuls in 292, and they appear to have continued as such through their consulships and beyond. Thirdly, and most significantly, these two are the only men of senatorial rank known to have held equestrian posts in the tetrarchy. At the same time, however, this period saw almost all the provincial governorships, hitherto the preserve of the nobles, concentrated in the hands of equestrians. What sort of fusion is this? While equestrians gain access to and, indeed, a monopoly of senatorial posts, senators are for the most part condemned to political impotence. There was no fusion between the two social groups, the nobles and equestrians, nor was there fusion between senatorial and equestrian titles, except in the cases of our two praetorian prefects. Though it was unusual to give a praetorian prefect an ordinary consulship while in office, the effect—namely the elevation of the prefect concerned to senatorial rank—was no different from that achieved by the lesser honor of the *ornamenta consularia*, which had long been conferred on praetorian prefects in office.

Under the tetrarchy, the two careers, the senatorial and equestrian, were quite separate, converging only at the ordinary consulate. A man of noble birth would begin his career with one or more of the traditional republican magistracies, after which the only positions open to him were the urban *curatelae*, the correctorships, the governorships of Syria, the proconsulates of Africa and Asia, the urban prefecture, and the ordinary consulate.

From the limited range of offices open to nobles it is clear that the senatorial *cursus honorum* (i.e. career) under the tetrarchy was a *cul-de-sac*. But, if so, why were praetorian prefects so ready to exchange their title *vir eminentissimus* for the clarissimate, as they did in assuming the ordinary consulate, which was still regarded as the crown of a man's career? The consulate was, as it had been for three centuries, merely a title of honor imbued with the aura of antiquity. Though the equestrian career was now the path to positions of importance in the imperial service, Roman traditionalism continued to rank the senatorial order above the equestrian, and to regard the ordinary consulship as a precious prize. A praetorian prefect would escape the disabilities of senatorial rank which affected the nobles, since he could rise no higher. The fact that a praetorian prefect could be a *clarissimus* while in office should mean that, theoretically speaking, the praetorian prefecture was open to nobles. But this was not actually the case. The anomaly was, of course, the result of a conflict between ceremonial tradition and practical policy. In theory a praetorian prefect with the rank of *eminentissimus* was of lower rank than any *clarissimus*, a title borne by all senators. In fact he was more important than anyone except the emperor. To reconcile theory and practice praetorian prefects were given senatorial rank, thus producing another anomaly, which has played havoc with historians.

In her very thoroughly researched study on *The Roman Empire from Severus to Constantine* (2015), Patricia Southern quotes my 1972 book as showing "...that senators still governed provinces as *praesides* and *consulares* well into the fourth century." (Southern, p. 245.) The words are not mine but Patricia Southern's, based on the *Fasti* (lists of office-holders), in an appendix to my book. Were there senatorial provincial governors "well into the fourth century"? Yes, but, as can be more clearly seen from Statistical Table I in my 1972 book, on "*The Social Origins of Western Praesides (284–337)*, there were no *praesides* of senatorial origin in the West under Diocletian and the tetrarchy, but nine under Constantine, with fifteen being of non-senatorial origin. As for *consulares*, this was a title specially created by Constantine for provincial governors of senatorial rank. Statistical Table II in my 1972 book shows forty-nine of senatorial origin as against four of non-senatorial origin. Similarly, there were no vicars of senatorial origin under Diocletian and the tetrarchy but six under Constantine (Statistical Table III). Likewise, none of Diocletian's praetorian prefects were of senatorial origin though one of Maxentius's was and six under Constantine as against three known to be of non-senatorial origin. (Arnheim 1972, p. 216 ff.)

In sum, therefore, Diocletian practically eliminated men of senatorial origin from all positions of importance, but Constantine reversed this policy. (See Chapter 3.)

Eunuchs

A much less well-known aspect of Diocletian's anti-aristocratic policy was his use of eunuchs, some of whom, according to Lactantius's attack on him, held powerful positions. (Lactantius, *De Mort. Pers.* 15.) From the time of Constantius II (r. 337–361) onward, the position of *praepositus sacri cubiculi* (provost of the sacred bedchamber), usually translated as "grand chamberlain," was regularly held by a eunuch. Though technically a servant in the imperial palace, the holder of this position in practice controlled access to the emperor, giving him tremendous power, and he headed up a bevy of junior *cubicularii*. It is possible that this important post was already held by a eunuch in the time of Diocletian, but there certainly were some eunuchs in his household, including some Christians, three of whom, namely Dorotheus and Petrus, *cubicularii*, and Gorgonius, an army officer, were executed during the Great Persecution.

Though sometimes attributed to deliberate aping of the Persian court on the part of Diocletian's junior colleague and successor, Galerius, the use of eunuchs as chamberlains made perfect sense as a counterweight to the established elites. Keith Hopkins's summary of the situation is probably only a slight exaggeration: "[T]he authority exercised by eunuchs not only by-passed the aristocracy but also served to supervise them." (K. Hopkins 1963, p. 74.)

Of servile and often foreign origin, eunuchs owed their position entirely to imperial favor; and their services and lives could be terminated at a moment's notice. However, with Diocletian, the long saga of the eunuch chamberlains was only just beginning. (See Chapters 4 and 5.)

Conclusion

Diocletian's accession in 284 marked both the culmination of several longstanding trends and also the introduction of some major new policies. His thoroughgoing reform of provincial administration secured the borders and tightened up the imperial bureaucracy. His concern with the army is also reflected in two very different policies. His persecution of Christianity was evidently a reaction to Christian reluctance to serve in the military. And his Edict of Maximum Prices of 301 was issued in response to soldiers' complaints about inflationary prices, though pegging the price of a live male lion or a pound of purple silk at 150,000 denarii probably did little to assist the average soldier.

Augustus had managed to hold the loyalty of the senatorial aristocracy by reserving provincial governorships to the membership of this order. This privilege was diluted by later emperors, who increasingly used senatorial status purely as a ploy, introducing outsiders into the Senate only to appoint them to governorships. Then, in the third century, emperors cut the Gordian knot (no pun intended) by bypassing the Senate and appointing non-senators to governorships directly. This trend was completed by Diocletian, who finally eliminated men of senatorial origin from practically all positions of importance.

3

Constantine the Reformer

I n *The Caesars*, the Emperor Julian's satirical sketch on his imperial predecessors, his remarks on his uncle Constantine are far from complimentary. Julian charges Constantine with being wholly given over to pleasure and the amassing of great wealth, and also alludes to Constantine's killing of his wife and son, worlds away from the image of "Constantine the Great." Julian, a staunch pagan, also mocks Constantine's Christianity, which, according to Julian, allowed Constantine to sin repeatedly with impunity. (Julian, *Caesares*, 336.) The diversity of opinion among writers ancient and modern on Constantine's character, motivation, success, and faith begs some big questions, including the following:

- **Constantine and the Dominate.** To what extent did Constantine continue the policies of the tetrarchy, and to what extent did he break with them? All too often, Constantine's rule is seen as essentially a continuation of the tetrarchy under the general heading of "the Dominate." That there was a good deal of continuity is undeniable. But Diocletian's failed "tetrarchy," under which senior emperors picked their own deputies and successors, was replaced with dynastic succession, which created its own problems. An area of continuity was the separation of the military from the civilian administration, which was largely finalized under Constantine. And Diocletian's systematic "chopping up" of the provinces and grouping them under vicars answerable to praetorian prefects was continued, with a few tweaks. However, regional praetorian prefectures only came well after Constantine's death.

Why Rome Fell: Decline and Fall, or Drift and Change?, First Edition. Michael Arnheim.
© 2022 John Wiley & Sons, Inc. Published 2022 by John Wiley & Sons, Inc.

- **What changes did Constantine introduce?** Constantine's reforms can be classified under four main headings:
  - The creation of new posts, military and civilian, notably *magister officiorum* and *quaestor* (*sacri palatii*).
  - Reopening appointment as provincial governors, vicars, and praetorian prefects to men of senatorial origin.
  - Adopting a pro-Christian policy and ultimately actually converting to Christianity himself.
  - Establishing a "New Rome" in Constantinople. The new capital was founded soon after Constantine's victory over Licinius in 324, and officially dedicated in 330. Constantine spent most of his time there in the latter part of his reign.
- **Why did Constantine make these changes?** Constantine played his cards close to his chest, and there is, in any event, no direct evidence of his motivation, which must inevitably remain speculative.
  - **Creation of new offices:** Constantine's creation of new offices follows on from his finalizing the separation of civilian and military posts, probably with the intention of allowing for greater specialization and centralization in the civilian administration and, on the military side, achieving the best possible frontier defense. It has been suggested that his creation of new high civilian offices, such as *magister officiorum* and *quaestor sacri palatii*, was intended to clip the wings of potentially overmighty praetorian prefects, but this seems unlikely. The holders of these new offices also sat on the (*sacrum*) *consistorium* which took the place of the *consilium principis* as a consultative and also judicial body.
  - **Concession to senatorial aristocracy:**
    - Pandering: Was Constantine pandering to the senatorial aristocracy?
    - If so, what was Constantine's motive?
    - Was it done in recognition of the strength of the aristocracy?
    - Or was it compensation for taxing them?
    - Or does it have a religious motive?
    - Or as it his intention to create a new composite aristocracy by fusion between the aristocracy of birth and the aristocracy of office?
  - **Christianity:**
    - The timing and degree of Constantine's commitment to Christianity remain controversial. These issues need to be clarified before his motivation can be tackled.
    - **Constantine's stealth:** There are four events particularly associated with Constantine's Christian leanings, interspersed among pagan elements:

- His pre-battle vision in 312
- The Edict of Milan of 313
- Constantine's convening of the Council of Nicaea of 325
- Constantine's deathbed baptism in 337

- **The strength of Christianity:** The idea that Constantine's support of Christianity was an act of political expediency dictated by that religion's strength is almost certainly wrong. Christianity probably accounted for only about 10 percent of the population of the Roman Empire at the time, concentrated chiefly in the East, which only came under Constantine's rule in 324.

- **Influence of Constantine's mother, Helena:** Was it the influence of his mother, Helena, evidently a committed Christian, that induced Constantine to embrace Christianity? There is no definite evidence, but see below.

- **Paganism of the senatorial aristocracy:** While the strength of Christianity was in the East, the senatorial aristocracy, which was still largely pagan, was concentrated in Rome itself and the West. So, could Constantine's concession to them have been counterintuitive to reassure them in view of his pro-Christian position? The problem with this theory is that Constantine's predilection for Christianity probably became well known only after 325, yet his appointment of members of the senatorial aristocracy started much earlier.

- **Constantinople:** Was the choice of Constantinople as the "New Rome" in the East motivated purely by strategic factors, or were there any religious and other considerations as well?

- **What effects did these changes have?**

  - **Creation of new offices:** The new civilian offices probably improved the efficiency of the administration, but the effectiveness of his military reforms remains controversial.

  - **Appointment of members of the senatorial aristocracy to high civilian offices:**
    - Fusion: This did ultimately result in a new composite aristocracy of office, but only in a nominal sense.
    - Inflation of honors: For, as titles of honor, notably the clarissimate, became devalued and largely meaningless, birth and origin continued to be valued in their own right, notably in the West.
    - Weakness of the central administration in the West.
    - The western empire gives way to "barbarian" kingdoms, with localized aristocratic power.

  - **Christianity:**
    - Constantine's conversion gave a huge boost to Christianity.

- Christianity becomes the official religion of the Roman Empire by the Edict of Thessalonica issued by Theodosius I in 380.
- The Catholic Church adopts and adapts the administrative arrangement of the Roman Empire.
- Paganism is stamped out.
- Religious toleration, a hallmark of communal religions, including the Roman pagan state religion, is replaced by the intolerance typical of a creed religion.

Let us examine these issues in more detail:

Constantine's Reforms

Constantine is still commonly lumped together with Diocletian and the tetrarchy in the "Dominate." That there was a good deal of continuity between Diocletian and Constantine is undeniable, but Constantine was also responsible for introducing some far-reaching innovations.

Imperial Musical Chairs

After clawing his way to the top of the pile, Constantine turned his back on the failed arrangement under which senior emperors picked their colleagues and successors at will and reverted to dynastic succession, though this too would have some problems of its own. (See Chapter 4.)

Diocletian's division of power among four emperors—the "tetrarchy" (a modern coinage, meaning, from the Greek,"rule of four")—backfired badly, partly at least because he ignored the basic Roman respect for heredity. The plan also does not appear to have been very carefully prepared. After assuming sole power in 284, Diocletian only raised a colleague to the purple in the following year, Diocletian being the senior emperor with the title of Augustus, while his colleague, Maximian, had the junior title of Caesar. In 286 Maximian became an Augustus as well, but the two emperors did not have equal status: Diocletian assumed the sobriquet *Jovius* (associating him with Jupiter or Jove), while Maximian only rated *Herculius* (from the demigod Hercules). In 293, the fully fledged tetrarchy took effect, with the appointment of Galerius and Constantius I (later known as Constantius Chlorus) as Caesars, or junior emperors, Galerius being Caesar to Diocletian, and Constantius to Maximian. On the simultaneous abdication of Diocletian and Maximian, Galerius and Constantius became joint Augusti, with Valerius Severus and Maximinus Daia, Galerius's nephew, as the two new Caesars. Maximian's son Maxentius and Constantius's son

Constantine were passed over in the succession. On Constantius's death (of natural causes) in July 306, Galerius promoted Severus from Caesar to Augustus to take Constantius's place, passing over Constantius's son Constantine, who, however, was proclaimed Augustus by his father's troops but was recognized only as a Caesar by Galerius. Meanwhile, the other ignored natural heir, Maximian's son Maxentius was declared Augustus in Rome itself in October 306, and then coaxed his father back from retirement by reinvesting him with the imperial purple. In 307, Maximian recognized Constantine as co-Augustus. Also in 307, Valerius Severus, unsuccessfully attempted to besiege Maxentius's Rome, and was either killed or executed, or was forced to commit suicide soon after. Galerius's choice as Severus's successor as Augustus in 308 was Licinius. After Galerius's death (of natural causes) in 311, he himself was succeeded by his nephew, Maximinus Daia (who had had the rank of Caesar since 305). Besides Constantine, the players left at this point were: Maxentius, Maximinus Daia, and Licinius, each of whom was eliminated in turn, leaving Constantine sole master of the Roman world:

- Maxentius was defeated and killed by Constantine at the famous Battle of Milvian Bridge, near Rome, in 312, trampled by his fleeing troops, and his body sliding into the Tiber.
- Maximinus Daia was defeated by Licinius in 313 for mastery of the East, after which he probably committed suicide.
- The final dénouement between Constantine and Licinius came in 324, after which Licinius was put to death by Constantine.

Provincial Administration

Constantine's reforms were not introduced all at once but in two main stages. First, after his victory over Maxentius at the Milvian Bridge in 312, which consolidated Constantine's grip over the western provinces. Then, even more so, after his defeat of Licinius in 324, which gave him control over the East, and united the whole empire under Constantine's sole rule. A key feature of Constantine's reforms was centralization of the imperial administration. The *Notitia Dignitatum*, a list of all government offices, both civil and military, dating from the 390s for the East and from the 420s for the West, is of only limited relevance in dating administrative changes. The Verona List (*Laterculus Veronensis*), dating as it does from around 314, has the opposite problem, of being too early to incorporate all of Constantine's reforms.

Constantine essentially retained Diocletian's arrangement of provinces, with a few minor changes. For example, he reunited some provinces that Diocletian had split, notably in Numidia and Egypt. Some of the governors of these reunited provinces were *consulares*, a new type of governor of senatorial rank. Jones plausibly suggests that "Constantine's motive may have been to enhance the dignity of the new senatorial governors rather than to improve administrative efficiency." (Jones, A.H.M., 1964, p. 107.) Constantine also retained Diocletian's grouping of the provinces into dioceses, each under a vicar (*vicarius*, short for *vices agens praefecti praetorio*, or "deputy of the praetorian prefect"), with one change, namely the splitting of Moesia into two dioceses, Dacia and Macedonia.

Praetorian Prefects

At the top of the civil hierarchy came the praetorian prefects, now minus any specifically military functions. The pagan historian Zosimus (460–520) wrongly attributed to Constantine the division of the whole Empire into regional prefectures, but this arrangement does not appear to have been formalized in Constantine's time. (Zosimus 2.33.1 f.) Under Diocletian there were only two praetorian prefects, one attached to himself and one to the other Augustus, Maximian. With the proliferation of Augusti in the free-for-all up to the defeat of Licinius in 324, the number of praetorian prefects also multiplied. There appear to have been five praetorian prefects in office toward the end of Constantine's reign, in 335, one attached to Constantine himself, one for each of his sons, all of whom had the status of Caesar, namely Constans, the future Constantine II, and the future Constantius II, plus Valerius Felix, described as prefect of Africa. But even this was not yet the final regional division with which Zosimus would have been familiar and which had not yet crystallized even by the death of Constantius II in 361. (See T.D. Barnes 1992, pp. 249–60.)

Separation of Military and Civilian Posts

Separation between civilian and military offices, already well advanced under the tetrarchy, was completed under Constantine, with two completely separate career structures.

Constantine created the posts of *magister equitum* ("master of the horse") and *magister peditum* ("master of the foot"), later amalgamated as *magister militum* ("master of the soldiers"), to take over the military functions previously exercised by a praetorian prefect. The pagan historian Zosimus blamed Constantine for the military collapse of the Western empire in his own day by reducing the number of troops stationed on the frontier. Jones disagrees with this judgment, which he describes as "obviously the fruit of religious prejudice." Adding: "It is true that Constantine somewhat reduced the number of the frontier army and lowered its quality and morale. But it is highly questionable whether the empire could have supported a frontier army strong enough to hold a barbarian attack at any point until reinforcements could be sent from the other frontiers; and a static army would probably in any case have gradually sunk in efficiency, even if it had not lost its best troops and been starved of good recruits." (Jones 1964, p. 100.)

Even the "top brass" of the army were career soldiers, often uneducated, and included "barbarians." By contrast, provincial governors, vicars and praetorian prefects, all now purely civil officials, were recruited chiefly from the educated classes, notably lawyers. To the argument that Constantine's motive was to weaken the praetorian prefecture, Jones responds with the alternative suggestion that Constantine probably realized "that the office had come to demand a combination of abilities and experience, military, judicial, financial, and administrative, difficult to find in one man." (*Ibid.*, p. 101.) While lacking any military functions, praetorian prefects under Constantine and his successors had great administrative power, second only to that of the emperor himself, including the power to make unappealable judicial decisions, a privilege shared only with the emperor himself. This is stipulated in an edict dating from 331: *A praefectis autem praetorio, qui soli vice sacra cognoscere vere dicendi sunt, provocari non sinimus, ne iam nostra contingi veneratio videatur.* ("We do not permit appeals from the praetorian prefects, who alone can truly be said to try cases as representatives of Our Sacred Majesty, lest veneration for us may seem to be affected.") (CTh 11.30.16. See Jones 1964, p. 374–5, 481–2.)

In many respects a praetorian prefect was the emperor's right-hand man. So, to attribute the praetorian prefects' loss of military functions as an attempt to clip their wings may well be wide of the mark.

And the same may apply to the suggestion that a similar objective lay behind the creation of the posts of *magister officiorum* (see below) and *quaestor* (later referred to as *quaestor sacri palatii*). (Zosimus 5.32.6) The title of *quaestor* goes back to the earliest days of the Roman Republic. It was the lowest rung on the senatorial career ladder, usually concerned with legal duties, and in the late Empire, quaestors were burdened with the duty of providing games at their own expense. In the early Principate one quaestor, known as the *quaestor Caesaris* or *quaestor Augusti*, had been responsible for reading out the emperor's speeches and messages to the Senate. The position of *quaestor* under Constantine had the similar, if less prominent, task of drafting imperial *constitutions*, or laws, with the aid of three *scrinia*, or secretariats.

Some New Administrative Posts and Honors

An important new civil post under Constantine was that of *magister officiorum*, or "master of the offices." We know the names of three of these officials in Constantine's reign, Heraclianus in 320, Proculeianus in 323, and Palladius in 332/4, and one, Martinianus, who served Licinius, and who, surprisingly, was elevated to the rank of Caesar, or junior emperor, in 324. The chief function of this post was to control the *officia*, or "offices," another word for the *scrinia*, or "secretariats," mentioned above. Heraclianus and Proculeianus are both described in laws as *tribunus et magister officiorum*—not a sign of very high rank. However, from at least 346 the rank of *magister officiorum* was raised from being a lowly *tribunus*—equivalent to the military rank of the same name, between centurion and legate—to being a *comes*. The newly created corps of *agentes in rebus*, or imperial couriers or special agents, reported to the *magister officiorum*.

Despite this fact and the fact that an early *magister officiorum*, Martinianus, was actually raised to the purple as nominal co-Augustus by Licinius in 324, it may be going too far to describe the creation of the post of *magister officiorum* together with that of *quaestor (sacrarum largitionum)* as "fragmentation of the praetorian prefects' vast area of responsibility" (Kelly 2004, loc. 4676), and as motivated by Constantine's desire to check the power of the praetorian prefect. The easiest way of doing that would surely have been to revert to the original pattern (when praetorian prefects were commanders of the imperial guard) of having two sharing office at any one time.

Also, besides their unassailable judicial authority and general responsibility for the army, it is worth remembering that the praetorian prefect remained in charge of taxation, with two high officials reporting to him, the *comes sacrarum largitionum* (responsible for collecting indirect taxes) and the *comes rei privatae* (in charge of the imperial estates). Instead of seeing the *magister officiorum, quaestor (sacri palatii)* and other officials as a check on the praetorian prefect, their relationship with the prefect should perhaps rather be seen as similar to that between civil servants and ministers in the British system of government, where the civil servants report to the minister, though they may in practice come to rule the roost in real terms. This may be the reason for the elevation of the *magister officiorum* from *tribunus* to *comes* (see below.)

Though long used as an unofficial term for members of the imperial entourage, the designation *comes* (plural, *comites*, literally "companion," which has given rise to English "count" via the French *comte)* was converted by Constantine into a title of honor bestowed by the emperor by codicil. The *comites* were divided into three grades, and, though the title was primarily just honorific, those who really were attached to the emperor and performed a service would be designated as *comites intra palatium, intra consistorium*, or *domestici* (see below on the *consistorium*.)

Another administrative innovation, probably predating Constantine, was the creation of the college of notaries, whose chief function it was to take the minutes of the imperial *consistorium*, or council. The head of the *notarii* had the grand title of *primicerius* (literally, "first name on a wax tablet"), who would become a really influential official in the fifth century, being responsible for compiling the *Notitia Dignitatum*, the formal list of administrative posts. The importance of this *scrinium* is evidenced by Chap. 6.16 of the Theodosian Code headed *De primicerio et notariis*.

The term *patricius* ("patrician") was originally applied to a member of the dominant aristocracy of the early Roman Republic which later fused with plebeian families to form a composite patricio-plebeian aristocracy. During the Principate emperors would elevate specially favoured supporters to the rank of *patricius*, but it was Constantine who converted the patriciate into a formal title of honor, which, according to Zosimus, even outranked the praetorian prefecture. (Zosimus 2.40.2.)

Standing Room Only

The *consilium principis*, an informal consultative body established by Augustus (see Chapter 1), which later became more formalized, was replaced under Constantine by the so-called *consistorium*, or *sacrum consistorium*, as anything to do with the emperor was deemed to be "sacred," or "holy." The name-change from *consilium* to *consistorium* indicates that, whereas the members had previously been seated, they now remained standing, in honor of the emperor, who presided. Besides high civil bureaucrats such as the *magister officiorum*, the *quaestor* (*sacri palatii*), and the *comes sacrarum largitionum* (a senior financial official probably created by Constantine, though first attested only after his death), who were *ex officio* members, there were specially appointed *comites intra consistorium*, or *comites domestici ordinis primi*, including, interestingly enough, members of the senatorial aristocracy, like the grand Marcus Nummius Albinus, who reached the pinnacle of honor of *consul ordinarius* not once but twice. (CIL. VI. 1748; PLRE- Albinus 13.) The degree of influence wielded by the *consistorium* presumably varied from one emperor to another. It seems to have dealt with policy as well as with much more mundane administrative matters, but the emperor was never bound by any of its recommendations. Valens, a weak emperor, for example, would act on disastrous military advice evidently proffered by the *consistorium*. (Amm. 31.4.4.) But the *consistorium* could also be used as a diversionary tactic. So, on the second embassy of Bishop Ambrose of Milan on behalf of Valentinian II to the usurper Magnus Maximus, who had control over a huge swathe of territory encompassing Britain, Gaul, Spain and Africa between 383 and 388, the bishop was refused a private audience with the usurper by his eunuch chamberlain, and was fobbed off instead with a meeting with Maximus's *consistorium*. (Amb. Ep.24.2-3.)

Fusion or Confusion?

Nowhere was there a sharper break between Diocletian and Constantine than in the recruitment of civil officials. As is shown in Chapter 2, Diocletian represents the intensification, and indeed the culmination, of an anti-aristocratic trend that can be traced back to the earliest days of the Principate. But Constantine reversed this trend by appointing nobles to high office once again.

Under the tetrarchy practically all provincial governors, known as *praesides*, were of non-senatorial status, with the equestrian title *vir perfectissimus*. Under Constantine we start finding *praesides* bearing the senatorial honorific, *vir clarissimus*, and, *pari passu*, an expansion of the equestrian order to ever lowlier office-holders. The equestrian titles, *vir egregius, perfectissimus* and *eminentissimus*, were not hereditary but were the automatic accoutrements of equestrian posts, which greatly increased in number, but as a result became debased in terms of prestige.

What we see is a form of inflation of honors. Under Diocletian the normal title of a provincial governor of praesidial rank was *vir perfectissimus*, but under Constantine an increasing number of *praesides* were *clarissimi*, whether or not they were of senatorial birth. Lowlier positions then came to carry the perfectissimate, so that by 362 it was accorded even to lowly *numerarii* ("accountants") of provincial governors with five years' unblemished service. With the inrush of so many *perfectissimi*, that title had to be split into three classes, and *vir egregius*, the entry-level equestrian title, completely disappears from view after 324.

During the Principate men of senatorial rank started giving themselves the title *vir clarissimus*. This became formalized in the third century, and Constantine awarded the title on a lavish scale. With more and more posts carrying an automatic clarissimate, the title *clarissimus*, which, unlike the equestrian titles, was hereditary, in itself tells us nothing about the origin of the office-holders concerned. We need to delve deeper, therefore, to determine which individuals were actually of aristocratic origin.

As we saw in Chapter 2, the only noble *praesides* known under the tetrarchy were governors of Syria, which did not undergo the change experienced by all other provinces under imperial legates from senatorial to equestrian governors. Under Constantine the majority of *praesides* remain equestrian, but a significant minority are men of senatorial birth. The provinces to which noble *praesides* were appointed were not chosen at random. First, all of them were Western provinces—and provinces in which large estates abounded: Byzacena and Numidia in Africa, and Gallaecia and Lusitania in the diocese of the Spains. In addition, we have examples of senatorial *praesides* of Lugdunensis Prima, Sardinia, and a possible one in Britain.

It is worth having a look at the statistics on pages 216–219 of my 1972 book. The names of 28 Western *praesides* are known under Constantine, of whom 9 were of senatorial origin, 15 of non-senatorial birth and 4 of unknown origin. In other words, three-eighths of all known Western Constantinian *praesides* of known origin were noble, and over a third of all whose names are known. This is particularly noteworthy by comparison with the figures for the tetrarchy, none of whose Western *praesides* are known to have been noble. It would be interesting and instructive to compare the proportion of noble *praesides* in the East and West, but the paucity of references to Eastern Constantinian *praesides* makes this impossible, though we should expect the nobles to be concentrated in the West, and all our cases of noble *praesides* under Constantine are indeed in that half of the Empire. One of Constantine's noble *praesides* was L. Aradius Valerius Proculus *signo* Populonius (*signo* indicating an additional *cognomen* or moniker, often printed in large letters above the regular name), whose career and family background are worth examining in more detail as an example of a new-style Constantinian provincial governor.

"Lineage Distinguished by its Nobility"

Proculus, as we shall call him, was a member of a prominent senatorial family. In a speech by the Emperor Constantine to the Senate in 337 proposing the erection of a statue to Proculus, his family is described as *insignem nobilitate prosapiam* ("lineage distinguished by its nobility"), and, less flatteringly, by Symmachus (c. 345–402), himself a proud aristocrat, as *clara quidem sed miserabilis domus* ("a distinguished but wretched house"). (Constantine's speech: CIL VI.40776 = AE 1934, 158 = AE 1982, 11; Symmachus Ep. 1.2.4.) Proculus's long public career, spanning the period 315 to 352, combined traditional senatorial posts with some novel Constantinian ones plus some pagan priesthoods and patronage of certain trade guilds and cities. (CIL VI. 1690–1694; Proculus 11–PLRE.) Notable milestones in his career include:

- **Praetor tutelaris**: The praetorship was the second highest (after the consulship) of the old Republican magistracies which made up the senatorial *cursus honorum* ("career".) The praetors had been the senior law officers of the Roman Republic. The position of *praetor tutelaris*, as held by our Proculus, was a specialized type of praetorship created by the Emperor Marcus Aurelius (r. 161–180) to appoint and oversee guardians for children and the mentally incompetent.

- **Legatus pro praetore Numidiae**: The position of *legatus pro praetore* is a title that harks back to the very earliest days of the Principate. Augustus divided all the provinces of the Empire into two categories: imperial and senatorial provinces. The senatorial provinces were governed by a proconsul chosen by lot from among senators who had served as either consuls or praetors, depending on the ranking of the province concerned. The provinces designated as imperial were in theory governed by the emperor himself, but in practice by someone appointed to stand in for him with the title *legatus pro praetor* (literally, "deputy, with praetorian rank"), the term *pro praetore* indicating that the appointee had reached the position of praetor on the senatorial *cursus honorum*. Numidia (now part of Algeria) had been a separate province with its own *legatus pro praetore* since 193, when the Emperor Septimius Severus detached it from the major senatorial province of Africa. As *legatus pro praetore* of Numidia, Proculus looks just like an old-style governor of a senatorial province—except that the title *legatus pro praetore* had ceased to exist by the accession of Diocletian in 284, being replaced by the title *praeses*. However, the proconsul of Africa was assisted by two junior governors with the rank of *legatus pro praetore*, one of whom was in charge of Numidia as part of the larger province of Africa. Though this arrangement formally came to an end in 193 when Numidia became a separate province, it appears to have continued in practice for well over a century. So, as legate of Numidia our Proculus was evidently not governor of Numidia as a separate province but as deputy to the proconsul of Africa. As it happens, in the year 319 the proconsul was someone named Proculus, probably an older relation of our Proculus. It certainly fits his career perfectly, as a legate of the proconsul of Africa was picked by the proconsul and would often be a member of his family. And holding the position of legate is yet further proof of our Proculus's noble birth. Note that, having held this junior governorship under the proconsul of Africa, Proculus became proconsul himself some years late. (See below).

- **Peraequator census Gallaeciae**: The post of *peraequator census* was created by Constantine to hear appeals against tax liability. Gallaecia was a Spanish province roughly equivalent to modern Galicia. Entrusting this new post to a member of the senatorial aristocracy is noteworthy. One might perhaps have expected this kind of position to have been occupied by someone less likely to be sympathetic to the aristocracy, the biggest taxpayers.

- **Praeses provinciae Byacenae**: This appointment as *praeses*, or governor, of the African province of Byzacena (roughly modern Tunisia) in 324 is symptomatic of the Constantinian reform of bringing aristocrats back into public service. For a *vir clarissimus*, or man of senatorial status, like Proculus to hold a praesidial post indicates that he already had this rank before his appointment, because the normal status of a *praeses* was that of an equestrian, with the title *vir perfectissimus*. There was no reason for a mere *praeses*, the lowest level of provincial governor, to be elevated to the senate—further evidence, if any was needed, of Proculus's senatorial status before his appointment as *praeses*.

- **Consularis Europae et Thraciae**: His next appointment, as "consular of Europa and Thrace," is a further rung up the gubernatorial hierarchy. Soon after Byzacena, he became *consularis provinciae Thraciae et Europae* ("consular of the province of Thrace and Europa.") As the provinces of Europa and Thrace were not contiguous, and, since *Thracia* was not only the name of a province but also of the diocese in which both that province and Europa were situated, Proculus was presumably in control of Europa and also of the other provinces of the diocese of Thrace, so effectively a *vicarius*. But, what exactly was a *consularis*? Its original meaning, going back to Republican times, was "ex-consul" and during the Principate came to be the informal popular term of reference for an imperial legate (*legatus Augusti pro praetor*) who happened to have held the consulship. But, it was only under Constantine that it first became the formal title for certain provincial governorships, evidently for Constantine's new brand of governors of senatorial origin for whom the title *praeses*, always associated with non-senatorial rank, was not considered a sufficient inducement. The provinces whose governorships were upgraded to *consularis* were the Italian provinces of Campania, Aemilia and Liguria, and Sicily, Numidia and probably Byzacena in Africa, and, in the East, Syria Coele, Phoenice, and temporarily Pontus and Bithynia, and Europa and Thrace. All

Constantinian *consulares* whose origins are known were of senatorial origin. (See Arnheim 1972, p. 57.)

- **Consularis Siciliae**: Another appointment as a *consularis* under Constantine.
- **Comes ordinis secundi**: The designation *comes ordinis secundi* ("companion [to the emperor] of the second rank") apparently denoted an appointment to the central imperial bureaucracy lower than that of *comes primi ordinis* ("companion [to the emperor] of the first rank"), a rank to which he was subsequently promoted.
- **Comes ordinis primi intra palatium**: As a title *comes* first appears under Constantine. The position of "companion [to the emperor] of the first rank" could be *comes primi ordinis intra consistorium*, or *intra palatium* or *domesticus*, which A.H.M. Jones plausibly suggests all "appear to be synonymous" terms. (Jones 1964, p. 333.) The *consistorium* was the imperial council of state, while *palatium* ("palace") or *sacrum palatium* ("sacred palace") denote the imperial court, as does *domesticus*. Proculus was twice appointed to this trusted position.
- **Proconsul Africa**: Proculus had held the junior position of legate to a relative also named Proculus serving as proconsul of Africa, and now, still under Constantine, he was appointed proconsul himself, and also acting praetorian prefect over all the other African provinces. (CIL VI. 1690–1694.)
- **Praefectus urbi**: He held this position twice, in 337–8 and again in 351–2. This high office, prefect of the City of Rome, or Urban Prefect, was one of the most ancient and honorable offices of the Roman state, first attested in the early days of the Roman Republic and possibly even dating from the monarchical period. It had always been reserved to members of the senatorial aristocracy. Its holders included (in 47 BCE) Lucius Julius Caesar, a cousin of the dictator; the famous pagan man of letters Q. Aurelius Symmachus (in 384 and 385 CE); and even Pope Gregory the Great (Pope from 590 to 604), a member of the noble Anician house, probably around the year 573. The authority of the Urban Prefect was largely concerned with law, and his powers were actually enhanced by the move away from Rome of the imperial court in the late imperial period. During this period the Urban Prefect's judgments and sentences were final, placing him on the same level as the Praetorian Prefects.
- **Consul ordinarius**: The position of consul was the highest office in the old Roman Republic, being shared by two men whose authority alternated month by month. In the Principate the consulship no longer conferred any power but became a purely honorific title. The "ordinary consuls" were the two who held office at the start of the

year and, according to Roman traditional dating, gave their names to the year. An ordinary consulship was considered a far higher honor than a "suffect consulship," as the consuls were called who filled in for the ordinary consuls later in the year. The honor of an ordinary consulship greatly outweighed that of a suffect consulship, but even as between the two ordinary consuls there was a slight difference, the one named first, or *consul prior*, being superior to his colleague, *consul posterior*. Proculus was *consul ordinarius posterior* in the year 340.

- *Augur*: Membership of an ancient pagan priestly college concerned to "take the auspices" by observing the flight of birds. In the Roman state religion, the will of the gods was believed to be revealed by this process, which was routinely practiced particularly before any major public decision was to be taken. The concept is still unconsciously embedded in present-day English, with such terms as *inaugurate, auspicious*, and, from a different root, *omen* and *ominous*.

- *Pontifex maior*: A *pontifex*, or "priest," (literally "bridge-builder") was a member of an ancient pagan religious college, headed up by the *pontifex maximus*, or "chief priest," a position which in imperial times was always held by the emperor until renounced by the Christian Emperor Gratian (r. 375–83) or even later, as suggested by Alan Cameron (Alan Cameron 2007, 341–84.) The next rank of *pontifex* below that of *pontifex maximus* was *pontifex maior*, or "major priest." The title of *pontifex maximus* was later assumed by the Popes, who still use it on official documents and coins. Cf. The English words *pontiff* and *pontificate*

- *Quindecimvir sacris faciundis*: This was membership of yet another ancient pagan priestly college made up of fifteen members charged, among other things, with guarding the sacred Sibylline Books, and also, significantly, with oversight of the worship of foreign religions introduced to Rome.

- *Pontifex Flavialis*: This was, curiously, a pagan priesthood established in Hispellum in honor of the Emperor Constantine in the year 333.

- *Benefactor of pagan temple*: The people of Carthage, in Africa, commemorate Proculus's restoration of both sides of the portico of a temple dedicated *Matri deum Magnae Idaeae et Atti* ("to the Great Idaean Mother of the gods, and Attis.") (CIL VIII. 24521.) This temple was devoted to Cybele, the Great Mother and her son and consort, Attis, a very popular cult, particularly in the western provinces of the Roman Empire.

- *Patron of pig farmers and butchers*: He was patron of the guild of pig farmers and butchers, who dedicated a statue to him. (CIL VI.1690. Other dedications: CIL VI. 1692, 1693, 1694; See CTh 14.41 (334).)

- **Patron of fishermen**: He was also patron of the guild of fishermen. (CIL VI. 1692.)
- **Patron of Puteoli**: He was also patron of the *ordo et populus Puteolanorum*, namely the town of Puteoli, who dedicated an inscription to him. (CIL VI. 1691.)

Our Lucius Proculus's brother Quintus Aradius Rufinus Valerius Proculus Populonius also served as *praeses* of Byzacena, in 321. (Proculus 12— PLRE.) An older Aradius Rufinus, probably the brothers' father or uncle, is recorded as urban prefect in 304–5, and another (or possibly the same) Aradius Rufinus was consul in 311 and urban prefect under Maxentius in 312 and then again under Constantine in 312–313. (Rufinus 10—PLRE). The Aradius Rufinus who was urban prefect in 376 may have been our Lucius Proculus's son. (Rufinus 11—PLRE.) According to a letter from Libanius to the urban prefect of 376, an ancestor of the Aradii also called Rufinus had been governor of Syria, probably the province known as Syria Phoenice under Gallienus. (Libanius Ep. 825, Teubner.)

The family goes back yet further, though probably not quite as far back as Symmachus would have us believe, who in a speech claimed descent for him from the Publicolae of the Republic. (Symmachus, Ep. 1.2.4.) . But in the third century CE there were several Aradii Rufini holding distinctly aristocratic positions, like that of the Q. Aradius Rufinus co-opted in 219 as a *sodalis Augustalis Claudialis*, a member of a pagan priestly fellowship instituted on the death of Augustus to attend to the cult of the deified emperor, to which that of the cult of the deified Claudius was later added. (CIL VIII. 14688 = ILS 3937; CIL VIII. 10602 = 14689 = ILS 3938 Thuburbo. PIR[1] A. 1017.) From the beginning it was open only to senators. Another family member was L. Aradius Roscius Rufinus Saturninus Tiberianus, who, among other typically senatorial appointments, held the position of *curio*, an ancient pagan priesthood restricted to men aged over fifty, who were not allowed to combine it with any other appointment... A Q. Aradius Rufinus was suffect consul probably in the early third century. Another namesake has left us a seal with his name together with that of his wife, Junia Aiacia Modesta, presumably daughter of Q. Aiacius Modestus, ordinary consul in 228. We know of two men called Aradius Roscius Rufinus Saturninus Tiberianus, one with the *praenomen* Lucius and the other Publius—unless they were the same person, as Groag believes. Both were *clarissimi*, Lucius being described as *triumvir stlitibus iudicandis, sevir equestrium turmarum, [quaestor] kandidatus, augur, curio*. He was also patron of Privernum. Publius appears in an inscription from Bulla Regia in Africa together with his daughter, [Aradia] Ros[cia]... Calpurnia Purgilla. (CIL. VIII. 14470) Other members of the family also had African connections. One Aradia Roscia and an early third century suffect consul Q. Aradius Rufinus Optatus Aelianus are recorded as patrons of Bulla Regia, and another or the same Q. Aradius Rufinus, also described as a suffect consul, set up dedications to the sun and moon at Thuburbo (in modern Tunisia).(CIL VIII. 14688 = ILS 3937.) In the fourth century the family's ties with Africa are no less manifest. Before becoming *praeses* of Byzacena, L. Aradius Proculus had been legate of the proconsul of Africa and would become proconsul himself later on together with the power of a vicar over all the other African provinces. In addition, the proconsuls of Africa in 319 and 340, each recorded simply as Proculus, were probably also Aradii. The family's longstanding African connections are a pointer to landed possessions there. Office therefore enabled the family to attend to their ancestral lands, and possibly also to add to them.

A bird's-eye view of Proculus's career reveals a combination of traditional senatorial posts with some new Constantinian appointments, and the whole suffused with pagan religious honors coupled with patronage of trade guilds and towns, signs of great wealth and influence.

Proculus the Pagan Priest

Despite Proculus's strong pagan ties, one modern writer dismisses descriptions of him as a "devout" or "zealous" pagan, a "païen engagé" a "grand seigneur païen," suggesting instead that "it is entirely possible that he simply acquired all these priesthoods before a late praetorship." (Cameron, 2013, p. 140.) This is complete speculation, and does not really help this author's attempt to play down the strength of paganism in this period in any case. The grouping of priesthoods together, as in Proculus's inscriptions, was a common convention and has no relevance in regard to date. Cameron resorts to more special pleading on Proculus's restoration of the portico of the temple of the Magna Mater, pointing out that "porticoes were public amenities" and that "it is unlikely that Proculus had a free hand. The probability is that he chose from a list of buildings needing renovation provided by local authorities. That he chose a temple rather than (say) baths may reflect his personal inclination, but it does not make him a zealot." Cameron's comment on Proculus's appointment as *pontifex Flavialis* is muddled:

> While the *pontificates Flavialis* was technically a 'pagan' cult, it was a cult sanctioned by and actually named after Constantine. Its award was a mark of imperial favor. Though an aristocrat of old Rome, Proculus enjoyed high favor with Constantine. His cursus lists three

conferments of the title of *comes*, the third time *intra palatium*, implying that he served at court in Constantinople. The base of his statue in
the Forum of Trajan preserves a flattering letter from Constantine
himself. A pagan who publicly reproduced such a letter from the first
Christian emperor can hardly be described as exercising 'independence...in the face of the Constantinian dynasty.' (quoted from Salzman
2004, p. 76.) Cameron concludes his special pleading on Proculus
with these words: "He may have been a pious pagan, who took his
priestly duties seriously. But it is a misunderstanding of the nature
and function of Roman state priesthoods to proclaim such men pagan
champions, let alone leaders of a pagan party. (Ibid., p. 141.).

Cameron is asking the wrong question. Instead of asking what
Proculus's attitude was to Constantine, we should turn that completely
around and ask why Proculus "enjoyed high favor with Constantine,"
as Cameron quite correctly puts it. The degree of favor enjoyed by
Proculus was remarkable but by no means unique among men of his
background. Indeed, it was part and parcel of Constantine's new
appointments policy of bringing aristocrats back into high government
office. And this begs the questions: Why did Constantine do this? What
was his motivation? And what effect did this change of policy have? I
will return to these important questions after examining some more
examples of Constantine's new policy. But, in the meantime, we should
be careful not to assume that Constantine's reformed appointments
policy must have been motivated chiefly, or at all, by religious considerations. And this policy change, deliberate though it undoubtedly was,
may well have had more than a single motivating factor.

Some New-style Vicars

Constantine's new policy went well beyond appointments to provincial
governorships. When it comes to vicars, the picture is similar. No vicars
of senatorial birth are known from the tetrarchy, but under Constantine,
we encounter five or possibly six of senatorial origin as against six of
non-senatorial birth, though there are twenty others of unknown origin. Five of the vicars of senatorial origin under Constantine were at the
head of Western dioceses, and in addition, there was one *comes Orientis*
(a new title created by Constantine for vicars of this large Middle
Eastern diocese), Q. Flavius Maesius Egnatius Lollianus *signo*
Mavortius, who held this post either late in Constantine's reign or soon
after. He began life with a standard senatorial career, as *quaestor candi-
datus*, urban praetor, next holding three of the urban *curatelae* traditionally reserved to senators and then consular of Campania. (Lollianus

5–PLRE. See Arnheim 1972, pp. 58, 80, 122.) He ended his career as a praetorian prefect under Constantius II between 355 and 356. The *signum* Mavortius, an old form of the name of the Roman god Mars, clearly identifies Lollianus as a pagan, as does the dedication to him of the astrology text *Matheseos libri octo* ("Eight books of astrology") by its author, Julius Firmicus Maternus, who was attacked by Augustine of Hippo for accepting that the planets were gods (and of course still bear the names of Roman divinities). (*Matheseos libri VIII*, ed. Kroll and Skutsch, Teubner: Stuttgart, 1968.) That the astrologer was himself a pagan cannot, therefore, be doubted. But he subsequently converted to Christianity, and in a book titled *De errore profanarum religionum* ("On the error of the profane religions"), written in about 346, dedicated to the Emperors Constantius II and Constans, attacked the pagan religions and entreated the emperors to stamp them out as a sacred duty. (*De errore profanarum religionum*, ed. Conrad Bursian, 1856.)

Aristocratic Praetorian Prefects

Constantine's new appointments policy did not stop at vicars, but went right up to the top of the administrative hierarchy. Of the eight praetorian prefects under Constantine whose origins are known (out of a total of fifteen), five were of senatorial origin.

The position of praetorian prefect was created by Augustus for commanders of the imperial guard. It always carried equestrian status, until Alexander Severus (r. 222–235), who acceded to power at the age of fourteen, appointed a senator to the post after a major breakdown of military discipline in the guard in 228. This praetorian prefect, Ulpian, the famous jurist—Gnaeus Domitius Annius Ulpianus, to give him his full name—was assassinated by his troops, after which the soldiers rioted for three days, setting fire to parts of Rome in the process. But Ulpian's appointment was atypical, and praetorian prefects continued to be of nonsenatorial stock until Constantine (and Maxentius, on whom see below).

Here are Constantine's five aristocratic praetorian prefects:

- **Petronius Annianus**: Consul ordinarius 314, Praetorian Prefect 315–317. (Petronius Annianus 2—PLRE) His consulship was shared with another noble, Ceionius Rufius Volusianus. And he was praetorian prefect together with Julius Julianus. Two inscriptions bear the names of both these prefects, both dating from 317. (CIL 13734 = ILS 8938; AE 1938, 85.) In both these inscriptions Annianus appears as *vir clarissimus*, the usual senatorial title, while Julianus is described by the equestrian title of *vir eminentissimus*. Julianus's non-senatorial origin is confirmed by his designation in 314 as prefect of Egypt, always an equestrian post. (P. Isid. 73.) But what about Annianus? The Petronii were a noble family connected by marriage in the fourth century with the Anicii and also, perhaps earlier on, with the Ceionii. The Anicii in turn were connected with the Annii. (See Arnheim 1972, p. 110.) Petronius Probus, Valentinian's famous praetorian prefect, was head of the Anician house in his day. (CIL VI. 1748, 1753; Ausonius Ep. 16.1.32.) That Petronius Annianus was related to Petronius Probus can hardly be doubted, both by reason of the *nomen* Petronius which they shared and the connection between the Petronii and the Anicii/Annii. Petronius Annianus was also therefore related to his contemporary, Petronius Probus's grandfather Petronius Probianus, the next praetorian prefect on our list.

- **Petronius Probianus**: consul prior 322, PUR 329–31 (Petronius Probianus 3—PLRE). He was proconsul Africa 315–6, Unknown office (praetorian prefect?) 321, consul prior 322 together with Anicius Julianus. His position in 321 was probably that of praetorian prefect. For, though not referred to as such, in 321 he received a law about the property of proscribed and condemned persons, that would normally go to a praetorian prefect but could conceivably also be addressed to a lesser official. Sent by Constantine from Serdica, the constitution is addressed simply: "Petronio suo salutem." ("Greetings to his own Petronius." The *suo* being a term of endearment. CTh IX.42.1.) The best reason for believing that Probianus was praetorian prefect in 321 is the fact that in the following year he was *consul ordinarius*—and indeed *consul prior*, or senior of the two ordinary consuls—together with Anicius Julianus, a member of the great Anician noble house, and then urban prefect from 329 to 331. The only office in order of precedence that could fall between proconsul of Africa (which he held in 315) and ordinary consul (322) was that of praetorian prefect or urban prefect. And, as he would become urban prefect in 329, that only leaves praetorian prefect for 321 (if correctly dated.) His seniority is further confirmed by the flattering tribute that he received from the elder Symmachus. (Symm. Ep. 1.2.6.)

- **(Acilius) Severus**: (Acilius Severus 16–PLRE.) The *consul ordinarius prior* in 323, the year after Petronius Probianus had had this honor, was Acilius Severus, his colleague as *consul ordinarius* being Vettius Rufinus. In 325–326 he was urban prefect. He was probably the Severus to whom two imperial constitutions were addressed, one in December 322 and the other in April 323. (CTh III.32.1; CJ III.12.3.) (Severus 3—PLRE). This is almost certainly the same person as the consul of 323, as no office besides that of praetorian prefect could be held simultaneously with an ordinary consulship and just before the urban prefecture. He would probably have been Praetorian Prefect or at least a vicar (in the West). Were these Acilii related to the Acilii Glabriones of the Republic? On the face of it, this seems unlikely. However, after more than a decade of research into this family, the French scholar Monique Dondin-Payre concluded that the family was involved in political life for over seven centuries, starting with Manius Acilius Glabrio, the conqueror of Antiochus III, for which he earned a triumph, consul in 191 BCE, and continuing into the fifth century CE. The distinctive *cognomen* Glabrio, literally meaning "bald-headed," we are told, was rationed, so to speak, limited to only one son in each generation. Between 191 BCE and 488 CE there were no fewer than thirteen Acilii Glabriones who were consuls, either ordinary or suffect. In addition, the cadet line of Acilii Balbi produced two consuls, both during the Republic; the Acilii Aviolae five, all during the Principate; and an assortment of other Acilii, including our consul of 323 CE, who account for another four consulships. The fourth century is a fallow period for the Acilii, with our consul of 323 as its only consul in that century. However, in 399 we encounter an Acilius Glabrio Sibidius signo Spedius as vicar of the seven provinces of Gaul. These worthies could simply have assumed names from Rome's glorious past without any genuine claim to them. However, certainly by the late fourth century CE the Acilii were recognized as noble by their relationship with the Anicii, one of the most distinguished noble families. The vicar of 399 was indeed married to an Anicia. The connection of the vicar with the old Republican Acilii is further corroborated by his *cognomen* Glabrio, which was also shared by an Acilius Glabrio recorded as a grammarian in Bordeaux in the first half of the fourth century. (Hagith Sivan 1991, pp. 435–439.) The connection with the Anicii is further evidenced in the name of the consul of 438, who served three times as urban prefect, and as praetorian prefect of Italy in 442: Anicius Acilius Glabrio Faustus, combining the signature *cognomen* Glabrio with both Anicius and Acilius, and was selected by the emperor Theodosius II (r. 402–450) to promulgate the Theodosian Code in the West. (Monique Dondin-Payre 1993, p. 180b.

- **Valerius Maximus:** Praetorian prefect 327–8, 332–3 and 337, consul 327. (Mennen 2011, p. 127, n. 26.) He is thought by Palanque to have been praetorian prefect in Gaul for ten years and by the PLRE to have been posted to different parts of the Empire for three short spells. (Palanque, 1933; Maximus 49—PLRE.) He was either the same person as, or a close relative of, the urban prefect of 319–23 recorded as Valerius Maximus Balbinus. a close relative. The urban prefect of 361/363, Valerius Maximus Basilius, was probably another member of his family and was certainly a noble, as we know that he was the son of a sister of Vulcacius Rufinus, *consul ordinarius prior* in 347 and praetorian prefect of Italy from 344 to 347. From the name of Melania the Elder's (c. 350-c.410) son, Valerius Publicola, one might conclude that Melania married into the Valerii Maximi, her husband probably being the Valerius Maximus who served as praetorian prefect in the early 360s. She herself was of the *gens* Antonia on her father's side, her grandfather being the Antonius Marcellinus who was consul in 341. Her son, Publicola, married Caeionia Albina (born c. 368), daughter of Caeionius Rufius Albinus, and their daughter was Melania the Younger. Both Melanias are Christian saints. (*Chron.* 354; Amm. 21.12.24. Publicola: Pall. Hist. Laus. 54, 58, 61.) Following Cardinal Rampolla's *Santa Melania Giuniore, senatrice romana* (Elena da Persico and Mariano Rampolla del Tindaro, 1909, pp. 111–117), Chastagnol sees our prefect, with whom he identifies the urban prefect of 319–23, as the father of the urban prefect of 361–2, whom he regards as the husband of Melania the Elder. (Chastagnol 1962, pp. 73, 155.) But this must be regarded as very tentative. (See Arnheim 1972, p. 70.) So, though related to no other Constantinian praetorian prefect, Maximus was evidently connected with that distinguished Constantinian noble acting praetorian prefect, L. Aradius Valerius Proculus Populonius, discussed above. Lucius Valerius Poplicola Balbinus Maximus was the seventh great-grandson of Valeria Messallia (Claudia Marcella Minor's daughter), making him a descendant of Octavia the Younger.

- **Annius Tiberianus:** (Tiberianus 4—PLRE.) *Comes Africae* 325/7, *comes* or *vicarius Hispaniarum* 332/5 *(CTh* XII.5.1—MSS. 326/ Seeck 325; CTh XII.1.15—327; *CJ* VI.1.6— *"ad Tiberianum comitem Hispaniarum"*—332; *CTh* III.5.6—*"ad Tiberianum vicarium Hispaniarum"*—335.) Under the year 336 Jerome includes a reference to him as praetorian prefect in Gaul and a man of culture. (Jer. Chron. s.a. 336.) Like many another noble of his day, Tiberianus had literary leanings, publishing a translation of some Plato into Latin. (Anth. Lat. 490, 719B, 809.) His *nomen*, Annius, is a pointer to noble birth. Tiberianus appears in a Tubernuc inscription of 337 together with three other praetorian prefects, Flavius Ablabius, Papius Pacatianus, and Nestorius Timonianus, all four being described as *viri clarissimi praefecti praetorio*. This is not the normal title for praetorian prefects, which was *vir eminentissimus*, the highest equestrian title but still below the standard senatorial honorific, *vir clarissimus*. In itself the title *clarissimus* tells us nothing about a person's origin. As it happens, both Ablabius and Pacatianus are known to have been of humble birth. Both men owed their clarissimates to their consulships, in 331 and 332 respectively. Annius Tiberianus's antecedents were very different. The Annii were related to two prominent noble houses, the Anicii and the Petronii. Tiberianus was therefore not the first member of his family to be a Constantinian praetorian prefect. That honor must go to Petronius Annianus, discussed above.

In all, a third of Constantine's praetorian prefects were nobles, a fifth non-nobles, and the origins of the rest unknown. This pattern contrasts completely with that under the tetrarchy and before. For example, Afranius Hannibalianus (Afranius Hannibalianus 3—PLRE), praetorian prefect under Maximian from 286 to 292, is described in the (often unreliable) *Historia Augusta* as an army commander under the Emperor Probus, a purely equestrian position (SHA V. Probi 22.3), and, later, as praetorian prefect, reliably, as *vir eminentissimus*, the distinctive equestrian honorific accorded to praetorian prefects. (Chastagnol, Fastes, p. 27ff.) He was apparently married to Eutropia, and their daughter Flavia Maximiana Theodora was to marry the future Emperor Constantius I (Chlorus), father of Constantine by his first wife Helena. But Theodora and Constantius were the parents of Julius Constantius, father of the Emperor Julian (r. 361–363). Eutropia evidently divorced Hannibalianus to marry the Emperor Maximian, to whom she bore two children, one being the future Emperor Flavius fius (r. 306–12). (Cf. Barnes 1982, p. 33 f.) It is worth noting not only that the imperial family was non-noble but also that they were content to take non-noble wives.

Another long-serving praetorian prefect, from 290 to 296, this time under Diocletian, was Julius Asclepiodotus (iulius Asclepiodotus 3—PLRE), who, like Hannibalianus, began as a *dux, or* military commander under Probus, and as praetorian prefects the two men are then described as *viri eminentissimi*.

The Maxentius Conundrum

It was a policy decision on the part of Constantine to throw high office open once again to members of the senatorial aristocracy. But this was anticipated on an individual basis by his arch-enemy, Maxentius, who appointed C. Caeionius Rufius Volusianus as praetorian prefect, probably in 309–310—with military as well as civilian responsibilities— and then as urban prefect from 310 to 311, after that worthy had held a suffect consulship in around 280 under Probus, the post of *corrector Italiae* from about 282 to 290, and that of proconsul of Africa from 305 to 306. (Volusianus 4—PLRE.) He was ordinary consul *prior* in 311, his colleague being Aradius Rufinus. Amazingly, even after Maxentius's defeat and death at the hands of Constantine in 312, Volusianus continued in high office under Maxentius's nemesis, Constantine. He was appointed one of the *comites* of the emperor, urban prefect again from 313 to 315, and is also described as *iudex sacrarum cognitionum*, evidently exercising high judicial function while urban prefect. In 324 he was again *consul ordinarius prior*, this time alongside Petronius Annianus. However, in late 315 he was dismissed from office and later exiled by decree of the Senate, evidently as a result of a whispering campaign against him by his enemies. A pagan, he held the priesthoods of *quindecimvir sacris faciundis* and probably *septemvir epulonum*. His family had estates at Volaterrae (in modern Tuscany) and in Africa. The PLRE plausibly suggests: "Volusianus was evidently a relative of Gaia Nummia Ceionia Umbria Rufia Albina *c(larissima) p(uella)*, *sacerdos publica* at Beneventum (perhaps his aunt or sister), and their ancestry in the female line appears to descend from the Nummii, Fulvii and Gavii of the late second and early third century, and through them from the Ceionii and from patrician and noble families of the late republic." (PLRE vol I, 1971, p. 978.) [*Caeionius* is a variant spelling of *Ceionius*, a sign of the shifting pronunciation of Late Latin.] Nummia Albina was active in the early third century, and is attested as *sacerdos publica* ("public priestess") of Venus and the Magna Mater in Beneventum. (AE 1968, 122.) She may have been related to M. Nummius Ceionius Annius Albinus, *consul ordinarius* in 206. For more on the Ceionii, see Chapter 4.

Maxentius was a very atypical emperor. He was the son of Maximian, Diocletian's hand-picked co-emperor, who abdicated together with and at the behest of, his senior colleague in 305, handing his position as "Augustus" to Constantius I (later known as "Chlorus"), who was next in line as Caesar according to Diocletian's carefully calculated plan. Left out in the cold, Maxentius had himself declared Augustus, which, needless to say, called down upon him the ire of the "official" Augusti, Galerius and his handpicked associate, Flavius Valerius Severus.

Unlike his father, Maximian, and the other emperors of the tetrarchy, Maxentius had no military skill or experience, and was based squarely in the City of Rome, venturing only occasionally to his estate on the Appian Way, less than two miles south of the city. While centered on Rome, Maxentius controlled most of Italy, Sardinia, Corsica, Sicily, and much of North Africa. Though no fighter, in 307 Maxentius managed to see off a challenge from two emperors in succession, Severus and then Galerius, just by sitting tight in Rome and bribing his troops with the promise of big handouts.

Maxentius and Constantine were now locked in a fight to the death, which Maxentius lost, together with his life, at the Battle of Milvian Bridge (in Northern Rome) in 312. As a result, Constantine, whose domain at that time comprised only Britain, Gaul and Spain, became ruler of the whole of the West.

Maxentius recognized the power of the senatorial aristocracy in Rome, pandered to them, with coins even claiming to be protector of the Roman Senate and People, the old Republican formula for the Roman state, while Galerius, when intending to overthrow Maxentius, advanced towards Rome, in which he had never previously set foot, according to Lactantius, resolved "to extinguish the senate and put the whole people to the sword." (Lactantius, *Mort. Pers.*, 26 f.)

Against this backdrop, it is not difficult to understand Maxentius's appointment of a high senatorial aristocrat as praetorian prefect, even investing him with military authority. And Constantine's continued favor to Caeionius Volusianus can be seen in the same light. His defeat of Maxentius brought him into contact for the first time with the senatorial aristocracy of Rome, and throughout his reign, which would last another 25 years, he visited Rome on only three occasions totalling five months in all.

For *iudex sacrarum cognitionum*, see CIL II. 2203, showing the career of Quintus Aeclanius Hermias (Hermias 3—PLRE), *vir perfectissimus*, so of equestrian rank, who is also described as *iudex sacrarum largitionum* while vicar of Spain under Constantine.

Short-term Appointments

Appointment to a governorship or higher position was generally for a comparatively short period, often of around two years, though there are some important exceptions, like Petronius Probus, who would serve repeatedly as praetorian prefect between 364 and 384, discussed in Chapter 4. But it is important to realize that, though his appointments would not have amounted to a service career, an office-holder would probably have been able to combine office with landholding in the same area, thus consolidating his wealth and power. And, from the provincials' point of view, they would have been under aristocratic control continuously.

The Senate as an Institution

Constantine's pandering to the aristocracy was not confined to appointments. Even the Senate itself as an institution gained a modicum of influence, in particular by regaining the right to elect quaestors, putting men on the first rung of the senatorial *cursus honorum*. This is commemorated in the inscription from about 337 honoring with a statue Ceionius Rufius Albinus, urban prefect 335–337, son of Maxentius's praetorian prefect C. Caeionius Rufius Volusianus. (CIL VI. 41318 = VI. 1708 = CIL VI. 31906 = D 1222: post Caesariana tempora id est post annos CCCLXXX et I primum sibi quaestorum omnium creandorum auctoritatem decreverit [statua honoravit]).

Constantine and Christianity

Though Constantine only formally converted to Christianity on his deathbed in 337, he is commonly represented as being favorably disposed toward it from a much earlier date. Constantine was, of course, the first Roman emperor to embrace Christianity, but he did so stealthily and with good reason. The old idea is quite wrong that Christianity must already have been strong in terms both of numbers and influence in order to attract as cold and calculating a ruler as Constantine. (Arnheim 1972, p. 73 n.) With all its splits, it appears to have accounted for only about 10 percent of the population concentrated in the East of the empire, which did not form part of Constantine's empire until 324. (See Chapter 4.)

Helena Augusta

So, how can we explain Constantine's apparent fascination with Christianity? One suggestion is that he was influenced in this regard by his mother, who appears to have been a devout Christian though it is not known from what date. She was invested by her son with the title Augusta, but only in 324 or 325, after he had united the whole empire under his rule. She was then sent on a special mission to locate Christian relics, probably in 326. Once launched, she proved an enthusiastic campaigner. Among other things, she ordered the destruction of the Temple of Venus (or Jupiter) built by the Emperor Hadrian two hundred years earlier on the supposed site of Jesus's tomb, where she found three crosses, one of which she claimed to be the "true cross." The pagan temple was then replaced by Constantine with the Church of the Holy Sepulchre. Helena would become venerated as a saint by both the Roman Catholic and Eastern Orthodox Churches. Despite Constantine's closeness to his mother, there is no way of knowing whether it was her example that attracted him to Christianity. (Cf. Drijvers 1997)

From Vision to Deathbed Baptism

Before the crucial battle against his erstwhile co-ruler Maxentius in 312 Constantine claimed to have had a vision of a *labarum* (military standard), bearing the Greek letters *Chi Rho*, a new abbreviation for *Christos*, with the message, *in hoc signo vinces* ("with this sign you will conquer"), or simply "by this, conquer," a more accurate translation of the Greek. This incident is related by Eusebius in his *Life of Constantine*, and a different version of it by Lactantius, but it is not mentioned in Eusebius's *Ecclesiastical History*. (Eusebius Vita Constantini 1.28 f., Lactantius, De Mort. Pers. 44.5-6.) The *labarum* does not appear on the coinage until 317, but it then plays a prominent part in Constantine's fight against Licinius, culminating in Licinius's defeat in 324, which made Constantine master of the whole Roman world.

In 313 Constantine and his colleague Licinius issued the Edict of Milan, which extended toleration to Christianity and to all other religions as well. Yet on his triumphal arch, the Arch of Constantine, erected in 315 to celebrate his victory over Maxentius, Christian symbolism is conspicuous by its absence, though there is no shortage of images of the pagan goddess Victoria and other pagan gods. As the arch was voted to the emperor by the Senate, this may reflect the staunch paganism of the senatorial aristocracy, or perhaps Constantine's reluctance to make his new faith known—assuming he had actually adopted Christianity by then, which he probably had not. He remained *Pontifex Maximus*, or Chief Priest of the Roman state religion, for the rest of his life, and his Christian successors continued to hold this position until it was finally renounced by the Emperor Gratian (r. 367– 75), or possibly only later (see above).

If any god was specially favoured by Constantine it was the pagan Sun god, *Sol Invictus* ("the Unconquered Sun"), whose image appears repeatedly on Constantine's coinage until 324, including magnificent gold single *solidus* and multiple *solidi* coins, showing jugate busts of Constantine and Sol in lockstep, minted in Ticinum as late as 316.

Constantine first came out openly as a Christian by summoning the ecumenical Council of Nicaea in 325, hard on the heels of Constantine's defeat of his co-ruler Licinius in 324, which, significantly, for the first time gave Constantine rule over the eastern provinces, the stronghold of Christianity.

We must resist the ambitious attempt by Jonathan Bardill to assimilate Constantine's pagan and Christian imagery to a single vision of himself "as elected by the supreme solar God to save his people and inaugurate a brilliant Golden Age....[T]he cultivation of this image made it possible for Constantine to reconcile the long-standing tradition of imperial divinity with his monotheistic faith by assimilating himself to Christ." (Jonathan Bardill 2012.) For example, to try to reconcile the radiate crown assumed by Constantine with Christianity is not persuasive. The radiate crown was associated with the sun god, and can be traced back as far as Nero (r. 54–68), and is much in evidence on the coinage of third-century emperors such as Gordian III, Aurelian, Probus, none of whom were Christian or even pro-Christian—and on the coins of Decius (r. 249–251), one of the fiercest persecutors of Christianity.

My own view is that Constantine hedged his bets on Christianity, but see more in Chapter 4. If the evidence about 312 has any validity—and there is something of a question-mark over it—Constantine was obviously not ready to "come out" openly in favor of Christianity at that point. The absence of Christian symbolism on his victory arch erected in 315 is telling. This may well be explained by the religious preferences of the Senate, but that must mean that the Senate either did not know about Constantine's Christian leanings or wanted to make clear its opposition to them.

Constantine's role in the Council of Nicaea is also not quite clear. That he convened the Council, presided over the opening session, and took part in the discussions is not in doubt, but, after acting in accordance with its rejection of Arianism, switched sides. For, though the assembled bishops resoundingly rejected Arianism (a non-trinitarian version of Christianity), Constantine, having banished its founder, Arius, eventually recalled him from exile and banished his nemesis, Athanasius of Alexandria, to Trier. And Constantine's confessor, by whom he was baptized, was in fact an Arian-leaning bishop who also happened to be a distant relative of his, Eusebius of Nicomedia, who also enjoyed the confidence of Constantius II (r. 337–361), an Arian, or at least a pro-Arian emperor (as would be the Emperor Valens, r. 364–378.)

Even as late as 333, as we have seen, Constantine instituted the position of *Pontifex Flavialis* in Hispellum (modern Spello, in Umbria), a pagan priesthood specifically named after himself and part, therefore, of the imperial cult, with the one proviso that there should be no sacrifices. This is a good example of Constantine's hedging of his bets. The ban on sacrifice no doubt salved Constantine's conscience, though it would not have gone far enough to satisfy Christians, who would not have been in favor of any kind of imperial cult.

The Religion of the Senatorial Aristocracy

Constantine's policy of appointing members of the senatorial aristocracy again to high office was a major concession to this class. But what was his motive for doing so? Among other possible reasons explored below, it could have been a counterintuitive response by a pro-Christian emperor to a staunchly pagan class, with a view to winning their support or at least their neutrality. But it is not certain how staunchly pagan the aristocracy was though they continued to hold traditional pagan priesthoods, and their stronghold in the West was much less Christian than the East in any case.

However, this counterintuitive explanation seems unlikely. For one thing, Constantine's aristocratic appointments started long before he came out unequivocally as a champion of Christianity, which occurred only after his defeat of Licinius in 324. Prior to that, the aristocracy would probably not even have known about his predilection for Christianity, his worship of *Sol Invictus*, as revealed in his coinage, continued until 325; so, he himself may have been in two minds about his religious stance. Nevertheless, the religious position of the senatorial aristocracy is worth exploring.

In 1971 Professor Werner Eck established, on the basis of a prosopographical study, that the senatorial aristocracy was solidly pagan in the early fourth century and that its conversion to Christianity was largely in the second half of the century, particularly in the reign of Theodosius I (379–95) and his successors (Eck 1971). This was confirmed by the massive prosopographical doctoral dissertation of Raban von Haehling, published in 1978. This position was attacked by T.D. Barnes in 1999, who sought to show that conversion of the senatorial aristocracy to Christianity started much earlier in the fourth century and also that Constantine's pagan appointees were fewer than had been previously believed (Barnes 1995). Yet, in his attempted "revision" of von Haehling's figures, Barnes places in the Christian column not only those who are attested as Christians but also those who are "probably to be regarded as Christian," while his pagan column is restricted to those "who are attested as pagan." However, even Barnes has to admit that there was a large majority of pagan appointees to high office under Constantine's youngest son, Constans (r. 337–350): no fewer than 12 out of 14. (Barnes 1995, p. 145.) Barnes tries to explain this away by suggesting that, "While that may reflect the strength of paganism among the senatorial aristocracy of Rome and Italy, it also reflects the weakness of Constans as a ruler and, in all probability, an implicit decision to allow the Senate more influence than it had enjoyed under Constantine." (Ibid., p. 144.)

The strength of the senatorial aristocracy does indeed correlate with weak imperial power in the West under Constantine's successors though that is more likely to be a result rather than a cause of increased aristocratic influence. Constans, who was an able general, was not a particularly weak ruler to begin with. If, as Barnes reluctantly admits, Constans' high pagan figures "...may reflect the strength of paganism among the senatorial aristocracy of Rome and Italy", it is inconceivable that the strength of paganism among them would have been less under Constantine. Christianity was on a positive trajectory, especially after Constantine's conversion. There was no likelihood of senators, or anyone else, reverting to paganism after converting to Christianity (except possibly later on during the brief pagan revival under the Emperor Julian between 361 and 363). And, even on Barnes's "revision" of von Haehling's figures, there are six "attested pagans" as against nine "attested or probable" Christians for Constantine between 324 and 337.

One of the problems with religious statistics in this period is that the religious affiliations of many appointees are unknown and that there are many other office-holders even whose names, let alone religious affiliations, are unknown. Of the total of 189 senatorial high office-holders for the period 324–61 in Barnes's "revision", the religious affiliations of 63, or one third, are unknown, and even the names of a further 64 are unknown. So, no conclusions can be reached on the religious affiliations of two-thirds of the senatorial office-holders of this period.

Constantinople: The "New Rome"

One of Constantine's best known achievements was his establishment of a new capital, later unofficially known as the "New Rome", in the old Greek city of Byzantium, which he renamed Constantinople. Rome itself was too far West, and too far from the frontier. It also happened to be the stronghold of the senatorial aristocracy, which Constantine favored in civil appointments, as was shown above, but which he probably never entirely trusted. Such was the strength of the senatorial aristocracy in Rome that as late as 392, when a grammarian and rhetorician called Eugenius (Eugenius 6—PLRE), who had served as *magister scrinii* (in one of the imperial secretariats), was raised to the purple by the Frankish-born *magister militum* ("general") Arbogast, the senatorial aristocracy persuaded the nominally Christian Eugenius to support the old pagan religion with public funding, notably by restoring the Altar of Victory (removed by the Emperor Gratian) and rededicating the Temple of Venus and Rome. Eugenius appointed senatorial aristocrats to high office, notably Virius Nicomachus Flavianus, father and son (Flavianus 15 and 14—PLRE) as praetorian prefect of Italy and urban prefect respectively.

Constantinople had no such associations. But Rome had not been the effective imperial capital from around 286, under Diocletian, and was not really in the running for Constantine's new capital. The choice was between Mediolanum (Milan), Sirmium, Nicomedia, and Augusta

Treverorum (Trier), which had served as the capitals of the itinerant imperial courts of the tetrarchy.

Constantine established a separate Senate in Constantinople, made up largely of new men, who were later held up to ridicule by Libanius for their lowly origins. (Lib. Or. 42.22-26; Cf. Chastagnol 1992, pp. 354–56; Jones 1964, pp. 538 and 546.) However, large landowners from the Eastern half of the Empire were also attracted into the new senate, not least in order to mitigate their tax burden. (Moser 2019.)

Conclusion: Constantine the Reformer

We are now ready to sum up our findings on Constantine as a reformer:

Constantine and the Dominate. To what extent did Constantine continue the policies of the tetrarchy, and to what extent did he break with them? All too often, Constantine's rule is seen as essentially a continuation of the tetrarchy under the general heading of "the Dominate." That there was a good deal of continuity is undeniable. But Diocletian's failed "tetrarchy," under which senior emperors picked their own deputies and successors, was replaced with dynastic succession, which created its own problems. An area of continuity was the separation of the military from the civilian administration, which was largely finalized. And Diocletian's systematic "chopping up" of the provinces and grouping them under vicars answerable to praetorian prefects was continued, with a few tweaks. However, regional praetorian prefectures, wrongly attributed to Constantine by Zosimus, only came well after his death.

- **What reforms did Constantine introduce?** Constantine's reforms can be classified under three main headings:
  - **Administrative:**
    - The creation of new posts, military and civilian, notably *magister officiorum* and *quaestor (sacri palatii.)* And the conversion of the *consilium* into the *consistorium*.
    - Reopening appointment as provincial governors, vicars and praetorian prefects to men of senatorial origin. Even the Senate as a body, which had become pretty insignificant, was accorded more influence by Constantine, in particular by being allowed to elect quaestors. This apparent pandering to the senatorial aristocracy was balanced by Constantine's introduction of the tax on senatorial real estate known as the *collatio glebalis* or *follis*, which may not have been quite as minor a burden on senators as suggested by A.H.M. Jones. (Barnish, 1989. Cf. Jones 1964, p. 431 and n. 51, pp. 465, 537, 555 f.) And it must never be

forgotten that the offices to which members of the senatorial aristocracy were now being appointed were purely civilian posts and mostly held only for comparatively short periods.

- Adopting a pro-Christian policy and ultimately converting to Christianity himself.
- Establishing a "New Rome" in Constantinople. Under the tetrarchy the imperial court was itinerant. The court was where the emperor happened to be. Under the tetrarchy each emperor had his own administrative captal. In 294 the four capitals were Mediolanum (Milan), Nicomedia, Sirmium and Trier, and other possible sites for Constantine's new capital included Ravenna, Serdica, and Thessalonica. Constantine's choice fell on the ancient Greek city of Byzantium, which he renamed Constantinople after himself, which had been renovated in the third century by Emperors Septimius Severus and Caracalla. The new capital was founded soon after Constantine's victory over Licinius in 324, and officially dedicated in 330. Constantine spent most of his time there in the latter part of his reign.

- **Why did Constantine make these changes?** Constantine must remain something of a sphinx, and some conclusions have to be couched in terms of probabilities rather than certainties.
  - **Creation of new offices:** Constantine's creation of new offices is not controversial, except that it is not always known when a particular post was first created, whether under Constantine or either before or after his time. However, in general his policy follows on from his finalizing the separation of civilian and military posts, probably with the intention of allowing for greater specialization and centralization in the civilian administration and, on the military side, achieving the best possible frontier defense. It has been suggested that his creation of new high civilian offices such as *magister officiorum* and *quaestor sacri palatii* was intended to clip the wings of potentially overmighty praetorian prefects, but this seems unlikely.
  - **Concession to senatorial aristocracy:**
    - Pandering: Was Constantine pandering to the senatorial aristocracy? In a practical sense, Constantine was evidently trying to win the support of the senatorial aristocracy, which may well have been because his purely western empire, as it was until 324, also happened to be the stronghold of the aristocracy.
    - Alternatively, were his concessions intended as a form of compensation for taxing the senatorial aristocracy? We simply do not know, but this may have been a factor.

- Could this policy have anything to do with religion? Probably not. See discussion above.
- Fusion: Was his intention to create a new composite aristocracy by fusion between the aristocracy of birth and the aristocracy of office? This may possibly have been a factor, which did in fact occur to some extent, but it did not materialize overnight.
- Antiquarianism: Constantine is known to have had antiquarian tastes—witness his creation of a new type of quaestorship, later known as *quaestor sacri palatii;* his innovative use of *patricius* ("patrician") as a formal title of honor; and his apparently genuine respect for long noble pedigrees, as in the case of the Aradii. But, as a calculating and ruthless ruler, Constantine would probably not have been too greatly influenced by his fascination with the past.
- **Christianity:**
  - The timing and degree of Constantine's commitment to Christianity remain controversial.
  - **The strength of Christianity:** The idea that Constantine's support of Christianity was an act of political expediency dictated by that religion's strength is almost certainly incorrect. (Cf. Burckhardt, Alfoldi, Rostovtzeff, and Schwartz.) Hans Pohlsander's more recent suggestion is no more persuasive, that Constantine's championing of Christianity "...served an entirely conservative end, the preservation and continuation of the Empire." Christianity probably accounted for only about 10 percent of the population of the Roman Empire at the time. (See Chapter 4.)
  - **Paganism of the senatorial aristocracy:** While the strength of Christianity was in the East, the senatorial aristocracy, which was probably still largely pagan, was concentrated in Rome itself and the West. So, it is possible that Constantine's concession to them was counterintuitive, to win their support, or at least their neutrality, in view of his pro-Christian position. The problem with this theory is that Constantine's predilection for Christianity probably became well known only after 325, yet his appointment of members of the senatorial aristocracy started much earlier.
  - **Influence of Constantine's mother, Helena:** Constantine's mother, Helena, was a committed Christian, who was given the title Augusta in 325, after which she was sent on a mission to the Holy Land to locate Christian relics. She was to be canonized as a saint.

- **Constantinople:** The choice of Constantinople as Constantine's new capital was probably largely dictated by strategic factors because Constantinople was within easy access of both the Danube and Euphrates frontiers of the Empire and was easily defensible. It also made an ideal choice for the Eastern, Greek-speaking half of the Empire. Although Constantine did not actually speak Greek and needed an interpreter whenever he spoke to a Greek-speaking audience, the fact that it was in the Greek East that Christianity was concentrated might have influenced his choice.
- **What effects did these changes have?**
  - **Creation of new offices:** The new civilian offices probably improved the efficiency of the administration, but the effectiveness of his military reforms remains controversial. See Chapter 4.
  - **Appointment of members of the senatorial aristocracy to high civilian offices:**
    - Fusion: This did ultimately result in a new composite aristocracy of office, but essentially only in the East. See Chapter 4.
    - Inflation of honors: However, as titles of honor, notably the clarissimate, became devalued and largely meaningless, birth and origin continued to be valued in their own right. See Chapter 4.
    - Weakness of the central administration in the West.
    - The Western Empire gives way to barbarian kingdoms with a strong aristocratic ethos. See Chapter 5.
  - **Christianity:**
    - Constantine's conversion gave a huge boost to Christianity. Even among the aristocracy, Christianity eventually became "fashionable," and in time a noble pedigree aids preferment even in the Church hierarchy. Pope Gregory I ("the Great," c. 540—604), for example, was of noble birth and had been urban prefect at the age of 30. And Gregory of Tours (c. 538—594) was a member of the new Gallo-Roman aristocracy.
    - Christianity becomes the official religion of the Roman Empire by the Edict of Thessalonica issued by Theodosius I in 380. This marks a complete break with the past. Though the old pagan Roman religion was a communal religion, it never excluded other religions, but actually welcomed them into a form of pagan syncretism.
    - The Catholic Church adopts and adapts the administrative arrangement of the Roman Empire, and the Pope would take the old pagan title of *Pontifex Maximus*, which until recently could be seen on coins of the Vatican

- Paganism is stamped out. Though Constantine began by encouraging the construction of pagan temples and tolerating traditional pagan sacrifices, by the end of his reign he was instrumental in ordering the destruction of pagan temples.
- Religious toleration, a hallmark of communal religions, is replaced by the intolerance typical of a creed religion. It is incorrect to suggest that the old pagan state religion was not really tolerant but attracted other religions and cults into Rome in order to stamp them out. (Cf. Garnsey.) See Chapter 2.
  - **Constantinople:** There had been a *de facto* division of the Empire from the time of the tetrarchy, with Diocletian ruling the East and Maximian the West. But the consecration of Constantinople in 330 marked the first step toward the formal division of the Empire into two distinct entities, which would come on the death of Theodosius I in 395. This division effectively spelled the end of the Western Empire, while allowing the East, now generally termed the Byzantine Empire, to survive, largely in attenuated form, for another thousand years. See Chapter 4.

4

The Christian Empire

As shown in Chapter 3, Constantine's impact on the long-term future of the Roman Empire and beyond was essentially threefold:

- **Christianity:** Though Constantine's true religious beliefs remain a subject of debate, the favors he showered on the Church and his death-bed baptism created a firm foundation for the declaration of Christianity as the official religion of the Empire in 380 and the banning of all pagan worship in 391. The creation of a Christian Empire, leading to a post-Roman Christian Europe, was Constantine's chief legacy.
- **Aristocratic appointments:** Constantine's reversal of Diocletian by bringing members of the senatorial aristocracy back into high office in the West proved long-lasting.
- **Constantinople**: The establishment of a new Eastern capital, leading eventually to a permanent split between East and West.

Constantine's Christian Legacy

At the accession of Diocletian in 284 the traditional polytheistic Roman civic religion had been in existence for about a thousand years. Since Caracalla's *Constitutio Antoniniana* of 212, all free male inhabitants of the Empire were Roman citizens. And all Romans were automatically members of this traditional Roman religion, which, however, did not

Why Rome Fell: Decline and Fall, or Drift and Change?, First Edition. Michael Arnheim.
© 2022 John Wiley & Sons, Inc. Published 2022 by John Wiley & Sons, Inc.

preclude their adherence to other cults or religions at the same time. Among the most popular of these were the cults of Mithras, Isis, and Cybele (or *Magna Mater*, "the Great Mother").

Communal and Creed Religions

Christianity is a creed religion, while the traditional Roman religion was a communal religion. The terms "creed religion" and "communal religion" were coined by myself in *Is Christianity True?* (1984) and amplified in *The God Book* (2015). Every separate Christian denomination or grouping is based squarely on a set of beliefs, acceptance of which is a prerequisite for adherence to that particular brand of Christianity. By contrast, the polytheistic "pagan" Roman religion had no creed at all. There was no concept of "religion" separate from society. Membership of the Roman state or civic religion was an automatic concomitant of membership of Roman society. It was part and parcel of a Roman's identity. And this traditional Roman civic religion coexisted quite peacefully with numerous "pagan" cults and religions.

A century after Diocletian's succession we find ourselves in a completely different religious ethos. The Roman Empire now had a single official religion, Christianity (or rather, a particular brand of Christianity), while all other worship was proscribed as "insanity," with the threat of condign punishment. This was a major sea-change indeed. For the first time in its thousand-year existence the Roman state had an exclusive official religion. The traditional old polytheistic pagan Roman religion had never been exclusive, and could be combined at will with any number of the foreign cults that had found their way into the Roman world. (See Chapter 10, "The Role of Religion.")

How had this sea-change come about?

- **Was it the result of the natural growth of Christianity in terms of birth-rate and conversions?** Most unlikely. Christianity does not appear to have made up more than about 10 percent of the population of the Roman Empire, and possibly quite a bit less. And numbers alone would not have been enough to give Christianity the dominant position that it achieved, becoming the sole official religion of the empire and banning and persecuting all the others.
- **Or was it the product of imperial favor?** This is almost certainly the answer. With an emperor who was not only openly Christian but also hostile to all other religions, many ordinary Romans would undoubtedly have wanted to follow the emperor's example, both

out of deference and fear. Once the emperor was Christian, the imperial government became an arm of the Church, and the Church became an arm of the state.

- **And, if the latter, was it the doing of Constantine or only of his successors?** The power of the Church grew steadily as time went by, checked only during the brief reign of Julian (361–363). But it was Constantine who gave it the kick-start that enabled it to attain the dominance that it was to achieve.

Christian Population Estimates

On the basis of a total population of 60 million for the Roman Empire in about the year 300, it is now commonly estimated that Christianity accounted for about six million or 10 percent of the whole. (Stark 2011, p. 157.) However, this is by no means certain, and Edward Gibbon's estimate was half of this. The figure of 60 million was influenced by Karl Julius Beloch's carefully calculated estimate, published in 1886, of 54 million for the Roman Empire on the death of Augustus in 14 CE though Josiah Cox Russell's 1958 article, "Late ancient and medieval population," based on factors such as life expectancy and fertility, posited a figure of only 39.3 million for the year 350. (Russell 1958.)

Rodney Stark, a modern writer on Christian demographics, identifies only two relevant population figures in the New Testament. According to Acts 1:15, the total number of adherents of the Jesus movement soon after the crucifixion was about 120, a figure which Stark accepts as "plausible": "That total is consistent with the early days of most new religious movements, since it seems that conversion is a person-by-person phenomenon that only slowly gains momentum through social networks. Sudden, mass conversions simply don't happen." (Stark, Ibid., p. 154.) Stark, therefore, rejects the claim in Acts 2:41 of "about three thousand souls" baptized on one day in response to a public sermon by Peter as "hyperbole." (*loc. cit.*) However, ignoring both these figures, Stark proceeds to estimate Christian membership in the year 40 at about a thousand. Then, using this arbitrary figure as a base, with growth at a speculative 3.4 percent per annum, Stark manages to reach the commonly shared estimate of six million, or approximately 10 percent of the population of the whole Empire, for the year 300. (*loc. cit.*)

However, even using Stark's speculative annual increments of 3.4 percent, a very different outcome is reached on the "plausible" basis of

120 Christians shortly after the crucifixion, which probably took place in about 33:

> Membership in 33: 120
> Rate of growth: 3.4 percent
> Time elapsed: 267 years
> Membership in 300: 903,993

Instead of six million Christians in 300, we now have fewer than one million. This shows just how difficult it is to reach a reliable estimate, and there is no reason in any case to assume an even rate of growth over three centuries.

A figure lower than the commonly accepted six million may also be supported by other factors, such as the dearth of churches, the earliest dateable church buildings in the city of Rome itself being from the mid-third century. (*loc. cit.*). "Instead," Stark comments, "Christians still met in one another's homes." (*loc. cit.*; Stark 1996, p. 1ff; Beloch 1886, p. 507; Russell 1958, 1–157; Cf Gibbon 1776.)

On the other hand, the 10 percent estimate may be supported by some calculations made on quite different bases, including Carlos Galvao-Sobrinho's study of Christian gravestones in the city of Rome and Roger Bagnall's calculations based on an analysis of the percentage of Christian names in Egyptian documents between 239 and 315. (Bagnall 1982 and 1987; Galvao-Sobrinho 1995.)

"Constantine was not Responsible for the Triumph of Christianity"

Having estimated the percentage of Christians in the Roman Empire at around 10 percent in 300, Stark then comes out with this rather surprising remark: "Constantine was not responsible for the triumph of Christianity. By the time he gained the throne, Christian growth already had become a tidal wave of exponential increase. If anything, Christianity played a leading role in the triumph of Constantine, providing him with substantial but well-organized urban support." (Stark 2011, p. 186.)

Even Stark's own estimates hardly qualify as "a tidal wave," especially when it is remembered that Christians were heavily concentrated in the East and that Constantine was a purely Western ruler until his defeat of Licinius in 324. So, it is hard to see how Christianity could possibly have "...played a leading role in the triumph of Constantine." There had always been many more Christians in the East than in the

West. Christianity radiated from Jerusalem. According to Acts 9:2–9, Paul's conversion to Christianity occurred while on the road to Damascus soon after the crucifixion, purportedly on orders from the Jewish High Priest to arrest Jesus followers and bring them back to Jerusalem for questioning. Twelve (or 71 percent) of the seventeen largest cities in the Empire within a thousand miles of Jerusalem had a church by the year 100 and all of them by 180, "...while of the fourteen cities more than a thousand miles from Jerusalem, only one (seven percent) had a church by 100 and eight (57 percent) by 180." (Stark 2011, p. 161.) The only exception in the West was Rome, which probably had one of the earliest Christian communities.

Stark's remark about "the triumph of Christianity" is strangely reminiscent of the previously fashionable view espoused by Jacob Burckhardt (1898), Schwartz (1913), Rostovtzeff (1926), and Alföldi (1948), who also believed that Constantine benefited from Christianity rather than the other way round. But their reason for believing this was quite different from Stark's. While Stark belongs to a group of modern writers who accept Constantine's pro-Christian leanings and subsequent conversion as genuine, the older scholars cited above were skeptical of his sincerity. Seeing him instead as a hard-headed, power-hungry political operator, they assumed that Constantine would not have favored Christianity had that religion not already enjoyed a certain dominance. The famous Swiss scholar Jacob Burckhardt (1818–97) summed up Constantine as "...a calculating politician who shrewdly employed all available physical resources and spiritual powers to the end of maintaining himself and his rule." (Burckhardt 1898, p. 292) And again: "In a genius driven without surcease by ambition and lust for power there can be no question of religiosity; such a man is essentially unreligious, even if he pictures himself standing in the midst of a churchly community....[A]ll his energies, spiritual as well as physical, are devoted to the great goal of domination." (Ibid., p. 281.) A more balanced position was taken by Baynes (1929) and A.H.M. Jones (1948 and 1964). Jones's sensible summing up of the situation after the defeat of Maxentius in 312 reads as follows:

> The motives and character of Constantine's conversion have been a subject of infinite debate. It has been assumed that he must have been swayed by prudential motives of a worldly character and that he wished to secure for himself the support of the Christian church. To this it must be answered that the church was not at this time worth courting. Christians were still a tiny minority, especially in the West, and they were on the whole people of no importance. The senate was and long remained a stronghold of paganism, and, what was more important, the army was pagan. Twelve years later, after intensive propaganda for the new faith, the veterans discharged after the defeat

of Licinius shouted: 'The gods preserve you, Constantine Augustus.' (Jones 1964, p. 81, quoting CTh 7.22.2 (326.))

Similar sentiments were expressed by veterans in 320: CTh 7.20.2. It is worth noting that Constantine was evidently happy to accept this outpouring of very pagan blessings from his troops as late as 326, well after his defeat of Licinius.

"Constantine Legislated not Christianity but Toleration."

In common with the school of "Late Antiquity," Stark is anxious to portray Constantine as genuinely committed to Christianity and tolerant of paganism at the same time, a difficult acrobatic posture to maintain. "Although Constantine played a central role in repressing all Christian dissent, he was remarkably tolerant of paganism throughout his reign. Constantine neither outlawed paganism nor did he condone persecution of non-Christians. In fact, although Constantine subsidized and gave official standing to the Christian church, he continued some funding of pagan temples." (Stark 2011, p. 177) Other defenders of Constantine adopt a similar position. A recent biography, by Randall Morris, is actually titled *Constantine: The Emperor of Tolerance*, and in Paul Stephenson's *Constantine: Unconquered Emperor, Christian Victor*, we read: "Constantine legislated not Christianity but toleration." Really? The Decree of Milan, issued jointly by Constantine and Licinius in 313, did extend toleration to all religions, though it appealed specifically to "the Supreme Deity," an understated but clear Christian reference. Moreover, all Christian property confiscated during the "Great Persecution" was to be returned without compensation, though those who had purchased such property could apply to be indemnified as a favor by the state. (Lactantius De Mort. Pers. 48.1-12; Eusebius Hist. Eccl. 10.5.)

To this extent Constantine did "legislate toleration." But what were Constantine's actual religious convictions? Was he really "tolerant of paganism throughout his reign"? This is not substantiated by the evidence taken all in all, patchy and apparently inconsistent though it appears to be.

Constantine's Ban on Animal Sacrifice

Constantine's attitude to animal sacrifice is relevant here. Animal sacrifice lay at the heart of the Roman pagan religion. Its purpose was either to seek divine favor, to placate a god or gods, to expiate a sacrilege, or as a thanksgiving offering. Constantine's attitude to animal sacrifice should, therefore, be a reliable gauge of his attitude to traditional Roman paganism in general. And, as it happens, we have some near-contempo-raneous evidence on this point. In Eusebius's biography of Constantine, written shortly after the Emperor's death in 337, we read that Constantine banned animal sacrifice shortly after his victory over Licinius in 324. In Eusebius's words, the law "restricted the pollutions of idolatry which had for a long time been practiced in every city and country district, so that no one should presume to set up cult-objects, or practice divination or other cult arts, or even to sacrifice at all." (Vita Constantini, 2.45) In an edict of 341 (CTh 16.10.2) Constantius II refers to a law of Constantine's banning sacrifice. This has raised a huge scholarly dispute characteristi-cally generating more heat than light. (See Averil Cameron's Commentary on Euseb, VC 2.44 at loc 3329). But why would Constantius's edict have referred to an earlier Constantinian ban on pagan sacrifice if none existed? This, coupled with the mention of a Constantinian edict by Eusebius, who was dead by 341, militates in favor of a Constantinian date for the original ban—confirming a visceral hostility toward pagan-ism on the part of Constantine, at least in the latter part of his reign. (Bradbury 1994, p. 139.) The fact that the ban had to be repeated in 341 indicates either that it had not been strenuously enforced or that it had not been obeyed—in either case pointing to a continuing attempt to stamp out pagan worship. (See Bradbury 1994, p. 139.)

According to Eusebius, Constantine was even responsible for the "destruction of idols, temples, and images everywhere" and "razing to their foundations" the chief pagan temples, while personally honor-ing leading Christian clerics. "He gathered them to his court from ev-ery province, received them into his palace, and even to his own private apartments and thought them worthy to share his home and table." (Eu-sebius, VC 3.52-56.) This may well be an exaggeration of Constantine's policy toward paganism though his partiality toward Christian bishops is not in doubt. Eusebius was intent on portraying Constantine as a com-mitted Christian. Religious toleration was not a virtue in his eyes.

Let us briefly trace here the chief vagaries of Constantine's religious experiences and policies, with those favorable to paganism *in italics*:

- *310—Constantine's "Pagan Vision":* *An anonymous panegyric delivered in 310 attributing to Constantine a pagan vision of Apollo, with the goddess Victory offering him three wreaths promising him a reign of thirty years, expressed as XXX. Possibly a variant of the Christian vision of 312 (below), though more likely separate, as it is referred to by Eusebius in his own Panegyric of Constantine of 336. (In Praise of Constantine 6.1; Panegyrici Latini 7 (6) 21.4–5.)*
- **312—Christian military standard:** According to Lactantius writ-ing within three years afterwards, on the eve of the crucial battle of

the Milvian Bridge in 312, Constantine was commanded by God in a dream to mark his troops' shields with a Christian symbol of some sort, possibly with the Greek letters *Chi Rho*, the initial letters of the word *Christos*. (Lact Mort Pers. 44.5-6.) Eusebius, writing shortly after Constantine's death in 337, describes an undated daytime vision of a cross of light above the sun, with the message "By this, conquer!" subsequently translated into Latin as *in hoc signo vinces* ("in this sign you will conquer.") (Eus V. Const 1.28.2.) Eusebius also describes being shown a *Chi Rho* standard by Constantine, which he specifically says was called by the Romans the *labarum*, though that term strictly applied only to the *vexillum*, or standard itself, to which the *Chi Rho* had been added. (Eus. V. Const. 1.31.1-2.) This standard first appears on a coin dating from around 317, and then not again until after the defeat of Licinius in 324.

- **313—Edict of Milan:** This extended toleration to Christians and pagans alike, though with special favors for Christianity. (See above.)
- *312–315—Arch of Constantine: This imposing triumphal arch in Rome, commissioned by the Senate to commemorate Constantine's victory over Maxentius in 312, incorporated several earlier arches, and contains no overtly Christian symbolism, though the inscription proclaims that Constantine had saved the res publica INSTINCTU DIVINITATIS MENTIS MAGNITUDINE "by divine inspiration and greatness of mind." The reference to "divine inspiration" is probably deliberately ambiguous, as it could apply equally to pagan as to Christian inspiration.*
- **318—Bishops' right to hear lawsuits:** A decree that any Christian who so wished could have his suit heard not by a regular civil judge but by an episcopal court. (CTh 16.2.1) Stephenson's comment smacks of special pleading: "One might observe in this ruling a desire to protect those who were vulnerable to the whims of the powerful." (Paul Stephenson 2011, p. 174.) And what about poor pagans, then, who made up the bulk of the population? A much more likely explanation of this law is as a privilege to Christians.
- *Until 324—Pagan symbolism on coinage: Until 324 Constantine's coinage was dominated by pagan symbolism, particularly celebrating* SOL INVICTUS *("the Unconquered Sun"). (See Chapter 3.)*
- **Ban on animal sacrifice:** There is strong evidence of a Constantinian ban on animal sacrifice predating that of 341, as discussed above.
- **325—Council of Nicaea:** Constantine summoned all 1,800 Christian bishops in the Roman Empire to a general Church Council, the first ever held, at the imperial palace at Nicaea. (Eus. V.C. 3.10.) Constantine was instrumental in convening the Council and provid-

ing the venue for it, and also paid for the travel and lodging of the participants out of public funds. (Theodoret 1.8.) He gave the opening address, calling for unanimity, and attended debates. (Sozomen 1.20.) When Arius's teachings were anathematized, and he and his followers were excommunicated when they refused to accept the agreed Creed, Constantine stepped in and banished them into exile. In 333 Constantine even went so far as to issue an edict ordering any writing by Arius to be burnt and sentencing to death anyone hiding any of his writings. (Athanasius, *Defense of the Nicene Definition 39.*) Constantine then switched sides, allowing Arius to return from exile on reformulating his ideas—and banishing his nemesis, Athanasius, who was to be banished four more times before his death in 373!

- **Hispellum:** As mentioned in Chapter 3, as late as 333 Constantine gave his consent to the construction of a pagan temple in Hispellum (modern Spello) in Umbria, for worship of the imperial cult, and in particular of Constantine's own family, the *gens Flavia*—on condition that no sacrifices were performed there, or, as Constantine phrased it, "on condition that the temple dedicated to our name shall not be polluted with the frauds of contagious superstition." (CL XI. 5265 = ILS 705) This is a good example of the way Constantine hedged his bets—consenting to the imperial cult in his own honor while attacking paganism in general at the same time.

- ***Pontifex Maximus***: Like all previous emperors, Constantine remained *Pontifex Maximus*, or head of the Roman state religion, all his life, and this example was followed by his successors until Gratian, or possibly even later, as discussed in Chapter 3.

- **Baptism:** While showing favor to Christianity from 312 onward, including convening the Council of Nicaea in 325 and, according to Eusebius, describing himself as "perhaps a bishop appointed by God over those outside the church" (Eus. VC 4.24.) He was technically only a catechumen until his deathbed baptism by Bishop Eusebius of Nicomedia. Constantine's son Constantius II followed his example in this respect.

Christian Intolerance

Is this really the record of a ruler intent on religious toleration as some of his recent defenders claim? Or is it rather the portrait of one who was ambivalent, hedging his bets, ducking and diving, or possibly flip-flopping from one position to another?

It hardly matters because intolerance is of the very essence of Christianity as a creed religion. With the best will in the world, there was no way that Constantine could have turned Christianity into a tolerant religion, not that there is any sign of his attempting or even wishing to do so. The Council of Nicaea, the first general council in the history of the Church, paved the way for centuries of Christian intolerance and persecution. Christianity demanded exclusivity. It was not possible to combine it with membership of any other cult or religion. Some people apparently did treat Jesus as just another god to be added to the pagan pantheon, but they cannot be counted as Christians. (Stark 2011, Ch 15.) And acceptance of the Christian creed (or, to be more precise, the creed of the particular branch of Christianity concerned) was strict, and any deviation was condemned as "heresy." As Christianity was not yet the official religion of the Empire, this persecution was initially directed primarily against other Christian groupings, notably Arians, Donatists, Pelagians, Marcionists, Montanists, Monophysites, Nestorians, and Manicheans, to name but a few "heresies". But, if Christians whose beliefs diverged in the slightest from the official line could be persecuted as "heretics," how much more deserving of punishment were non-Christians? The definition of "heretic" was very broad: "Those persons who may be discovered to deviate, even in a minor point of doctrine, from the tenets and the path of the Catholic religion are included under the designation of heretics and must be subject to the sanctions which have been issued against them." (CTh 16.5.28).

"What is Truth?"

There has been a multiplicity of Christian creeds over time, and variations from one denomination to another at the same time, every one of which has claimed to have a monopoly of "the truth." The difference in this regard between Christianity and the Roman state religion is glimpsed in the well-known passage in John's Gospel purporting to describe Jesus's interrogation by Pontius Pilate, governor of Judea. (John 18:37.) According to this account, Pilate taunts Jesus with the rhetorical question: "So, you are a king, then?" This is presumably intended to entrap Jesus into claiming that he is the Jewish Messiah, an essentially political figure expected by Jews to overthrow the Roman yoke. The Romans were not interested in Jewish infighting unless it threatened their control over Judea, which is precisely what a Messianic claim would do. But Jesus parries this blow by retorting: "*You* say that I am a king." Without quite denying the charge, Jesus neatly ducks it, adding: "To this end was I born, and for this cause came I into the world, that I should bear witness unto the truth. Every one that is of the truth heareth my voice." (Ibid. KJV).

Pilate's rejoinder has echoed down the ages: "What is truth?" (John 18:38.) Francis Bacon opened his essay *Of Truth* (1625) with this comment: "'What is truth?' said jesting Pilate, and would not stay for an answer." The reason that Pilate does not wait for Jesus to answer his question is that it is not really a question at all but rather a mocking dismissal of the whole idea of truth.

It is important to note that, while Jesus (twice) refers to "*the* truth," Pilate omits the definite article "the." He does not say "What is the truth?" but rather "What is truth?" Does this make any difference? I believe it is quite significant, though it is not a point that I have found raised in any commentary. Had Pilate's retort been "What is the truth?" that would have been a genuine question seeking to know to what "truth" Jesus claimed to be a witness. But, by omitting the definite article, what Pilate says is quite different. He not only shows a complete lack of interest in "the truth" of which Jesus claims to be a witness, but disdainfully dismisses the very idea of "truth," tantamount to denying that any such thing exists or is of any relevance.

The contrast between Jesus's fixation on "the truth" and Pilate's dismissal of the very existence of "truth" is a reflection of the difference between Christianity and the Roman state religion, or, more generally, between a creed religion and a communal religion. As a creed religion, Christianity stands or falls by a set of beliefs as constituting "the truth" (although there are as many creeds as there are Christian denominations.) By contrast, Roman paganism, as a communal religion, of which Pontius Pilate as a Roman citizen was automatically an adherent, had no creed or set of beliefs at all. There was a pantheon of multiple gods, about whom there were numerous myths, many of them far from flattering, but these were not taken too seriously, and Roman paganism had no concept of "heresy" or "blasphemy."

Did the exchange between Jesus and Pontius Pilate, as related in John's Gospel, actually take place? Almost certainly not. Majority scholarly opinion dates the final version of John to between 90 and 110 CE, or about seventy years after Jesus's death (Lincoln 2005, p. 18.) And there is no reference to either "truth" or "the truth" in the Synoptic Gospels' versions of Jesus's interrogation by Pilate, the earliest of which, Mark, probably dates from between 66 and 70 CE. (Perkins 1998, p. 241.)

In any case, in what language would Jesus's interrogation have been conducted? As a Roman military man, Pontius Pilate's native tongue would have been Latin, which lacks either a definite or an indefinite article. And he would have been unlikely to know any Greek, the lingua franca of Judea at the time, and the language of the Gospels. And an interpreter would have been unlikely to determine from the Latin word for truth, *veritas*, whether what was meant was "the truth" or simply "truth."

So, Pilate probably never actually threw down the famous challenge, *Ti estin alētheia*; ("What is truth?".) Does this matter? Not at all. Because it does not affect the important distinction between the Christian claim to possession of "the truth" and the pagan disdain for the whole concept of "truth", a distinction at which the philosophical author of John may well have been subtly hinting in the imaginary exchange.

The phrase "the truth" also occurs no fewer than ten times in the account of Jesus's acrimonious altercation with the Pharisees (not paralleled in the Synoptic Gospels), which includes the much-parodied verse, "Then you will know the truth, and the truth will set you free." (John 8:32-58.) As a committed believer in "the truth" as propagated by the new Christian faith, the author of John may have been attempting to deride Roman paganism in the Pilate episode, just as he had disparaged Pharisaic Judaism. "Unlike the Pharisees, we have a lock on the truth," the author of John may have been suggesting, "while the pagans don't even know the meaning of 'truth'."

But this assertion of the superiority of Christianity over all other faiths is at the same time an admission of Christian religious intolerance, foreshadowing centuries of persecutions, schisms, religious wars, and burnings at the stake. Christianity (or rather, each individual Christian denomination, division or sect) believes it has a monopoly on "salvation," while all non-believers and "heretics" are consigned to eternal damnation. Relevant Biblical verses include: "He that believeth on the Son hath everlasting life: and he that believeth not the Son shall not see life; but the wrath of God abideth on him." (John 3:36.) And: "He that believeth and is baptized shall be saved; but he that believeth not shall be damned." (Mark 16:16.)

The Papal bull *Decet Romanum Pontificem* excommunicating Martin Luther and his followers in 1521 is still in force. The schism, dating from 1054, between the Roman Catholic and Eastern Orthodox churches, centering on the word *filioque* in the creed, has still not been healed.

Constantine's Kick-start

What has Constantine's conversion to do with all this? Just this, that without Constantine's initial kick-start of imperial favor and support, it is unlikely that Christianity would ever have achieved the dominant position that it enjoyed from the mid-fourth century onward and, particularly, recognition as the sole official religion of the Roman Empire, which it achieved in 380, followed by the permanent banning of all pagan religions in 391. Without that recognition, internecine conflict, an integral feature of Christianity as a creed religion from the start, would undoubtedly have continued unabated, but Christianity would not have had the authority to proscribe or persecute any other religion even if Christianity had been the majority religion of the Empire in terms of numbers.

But, it may be objected, if Christianity is so inherently intolerant, how come it is so tolerant today? In fact, the reason for religious toleration in the modern world (or at least in the West) is the prevalence of secularism rather than any fundamental change in Christianity. Every Christian denomination still regards itself as having an exclusive key to "salvation." Even recognition of baptism across the divisions is by no means universal. And, as already mentioned, schisms going back hundreds of years are still unhealed.

"The Blending of Civil and Ecclesiastical Authority"

What William Boyd termed "the blending of civil and ecclesiastical authority in the later Roman Empire" is well documented in the Theodosian Code, a compilation of laws promulgated between 312 and 438, and published under the auspices of Theodosius II and his western co-emperor, Valentinian III, in 438. (See Boyd 1905, loc.16.) (Translations of the Theodosian Code are by Clyde Pharr.) Here are some examples: 318—CTh 16.2.1: Bishops' right to hear lawsuits: A decree that any Christian who so wished could have his case heard not by a regular civil judge but by an episcopal court. (Discussed above.)

- 341—CTh 16.10.2: "Superstition shall cease; the madness of sacrifices shall be abolished." (Discussed above.)
- 346—CTh 16.10.3: "Although pagan religious practices are banned, pagan temples are to be preserved because they host plays and circuses."
- 346—CTh 16.10.4: "Pagan temples are to be closed, access to them is denied, and violators may face the death penalty."
- 353—CTh 16.10.5: All pagan temples to be closed, sacrifices banned on pain of death, and even threatening confiscation of the property of governors who failed to enforce this edict. (Western edict.)
- 356—CTh 16.10.6: Those guilty of the worship of images or pagan sacrifices may be subject to the death penalty. (Western edict.)
- 356—CTh 16.2.14: "Clergy and their families are exempt from paying taxes."
- 379—CTh 16.5.5: "All heresies are forbidden by both divine and imperial laws and shall forever cease."
- 380—CTh 16.1.2, "Edict of Thessalonica": Issued jointly by Gratian, Theodosius I and Valentinian II, making Christianity the official

religion of the Roman Empire: "[L]et us believe in the one deity of the Father, the Son and the Holy Spirit, in equal majesty and in a holy Trinity. We authorize the followers of this law to assume the title of Catholic Christians; but as for the others, since, in our judgment they are foolish madmen, we decree that they shall be branded with the ignominious name of heretics, and shall not presume to give to their conventicles the name of churches. They will suffer in the first place the chastisement of the divine condemnation and in the second the punishment of our authority which in accordance with the will of Heaven we shall decide to inflict."

- 388—CTh 16.4.2: Public preaching and debate about religion is prohibited.
- 391—CTh 16.10.10: "Idol worship and pagan sacrifice are forbidden."
- 391 —CTh 16.10.11: "No person shall enter the pagan temples or perform sacrifices."
- 391—CTh 16.5.20: Gathering or assembly of any kind is denied to non-Catholics.
- 392—CTh 16.10.12: "No person of any class may sacrifice to an image…. Veneration of images with incense is banned."
- 393—CTh 16.8.9: "The Jewish sect is forbidden by no law. Hence We are gravely disturbed that their assemblies have been forbidden in certain places."
- 397—CTh 16.8.12: Jews are not to be insulted.
- 398—CTh 16.5.28: "Anyone who disagrees with the Catholic Christian faith even on a minor point of doctrine is considered a heretic."
- 399—CTh 10.10.16: Pagan temples in rural areas are to be destroyed.
- 399—CTh 16.8.14: Revenue collected by Jewish patriarchs is to be paid instead to the imperial treasury.
- 399—CTh 16.8.16: Jews and Samaritans are not allowed to be employed in the imperial service.
- 405—CTh 16.11.2: "[T]here shall be Christian unity throughout the empire."
- 405—CTh 16.5.38: "Worship shall be uniform, and all shall recognize the Trinity. There shall be one understanding of salvation."
- 409—CTh 16.5.46: "Donatists, Jews, and Gentiles should not suppose that laws previously passed against them have weakened."
- 409—CTh 16.8.19: "Christians may not be insultingly called Jews."
- 412—CTh 16.8.21: "Jews may not be persecuted for their religion or have their property taken without cause. They are cautioned, however, that they still may not disrespect Christianity."
- 415—CTh 16.5.56: Pagans who assemble publicly may have their property confiscated or even be executed.

- 418—CTh 16.8.24: "Jews may not enter imperial service."
- 420—CTh 16.2.44: "Priests may not marry after they have been ordained. However, they need not leave their wives if they were married before becoming priests."
- 423—CTh 16.10.22: "The regulations of constitutions formerly promulgated shall suppress any pagans who survive, although we now believe that there are none."
- 423—CTh 16.8.25: "Jewish synagogues may not be burned indiscriminately. If such an incident does occur, they will be compensated. However, they may not build new synagogues, and existing ones may not be improved."
- 429—CTh 16.8.29: Annual tribute is to be collected from the heads of Jewish synagogues.
- 435—CTh 10.10.25: Pagan temples are to be torn down and replaced with the symbol of Christianity, the Cross. Anyone mocking this law may be executed.
- 452—NVal 35.1.3: "No *originarius, inquilinus,* slave or *colonus* may become a priest or monk to evade his obligations." See p. 155 below.

Office-Holders under Constantine's Sons

Some months after the death of Constantine in 337, his surviving sons, the Caesars Constantine, Constantius and Constans, each assumed the title Augustus and divided the Empire among themselves. The eldest, Constantine II, became the ruler of Britain, Gaul and Spain, the same regions which had first come under the sway of his father; Constans, the youngest brother, who had become a Caesar only four years before, received Italy, Illyricum and Africa; while Constantius II was given the East as his share. But within three years fratricidal conflict delivered the whole of the West into the hands of Constans, and eleven years later, when he in turn had lost his life at the hands of a usurper and his death had been avenged by Constantius, the Empire was once again united under a single Augustus, namely Constantius II. (Zos. 2.39ff.)

Though not baptized until adult life, Constantine's sons were the first rulers of the Roman world to be brought up as Christians. Constans was a pious and orthodox Christian who followed the creed of Nicaea, while Constantius favoured the Arians, embroidering his religion with superstitious beliefs and having a taste for theological disputation. (Amm. 21.16.18.)

We have already noted several anti-pagan edicts issued by Constantius II. It was he also who was responsible for the removal of the altar of the winged goddess Victory from the curia, the meeting place of the Roman Senate, where it had stood for three centuries celebrating the future Augustus's victory over Antony at Actium in 31 BCE and as a symbol of Rome's majesty and grandeur, to which an offering of incense and wine was made before every session of the Senate. (Amb. *Ep.* 18.32.) The strongly worded anti-pagan legislation of Constantius and Constans should not surprise anyone. Unlike their father, they did not have to fight for their position. Their firm Christian underpinnings are enough to explain their hostility to paganism. Yet we have a tribute to Constantius for his tolerant attitude to paganism from none other than Q. Aurelius Symmachus (c. 345–402), whose name is a byword for paganism in the late Empire. (Symm. Rel. 3.7.) Symmachus, of course, had an ulterior motive in portraying the pious Christian emperor as a tolerant ruler, for it comes from the orator's well-known appeal for the restoration of the Altar of Victory to its traditional place in the Senate-house. His pleas, however, fell on deaf ears.

Despite this, Constans and Constantius continued their father's policy of appointing nobles to high office. This applies particularly to Constans as ruler of the West. None of his praetorian prefects is known to have been non-noble, and we have no information about the background of Ulpius Limenius, Eustathus, or Hermogenes. But Limenius and Hermogenes are each recorded in the *Chronography* of 354 as simultaneously urban prefect and praetorian prefect (Limenius in 347–9 and Hermogenes in 349–50), which is probably a sign that these men were merely stop-gaps, as may also have been the case with Eustathius, despite his unqualified description as a praetorian prefect in the Theodosian Code. Illyricum, if not Constans's whole empire, was under noble prefects throughout the period 340–50.

Constans's predilection for aristocratic praetorian prefects overlaps with his favoring the appointment of pagans to high office. It is important not to confuse religion with status. Not all nobles were pagans, though the Western senatorial aristocracy were evidently slow to convert to Christianity, which had made much more headway in the East. T.D. Barnes admits that "the appointees of Constans between 337 and 350 show a marked preponderance of pagans." (Barnes 1995, p. 145.) Barnes tries to explain this away by suggesting that "While that may reflect the strength of paganism among the senatorial aristocracy of Rome and Italy, it also reflects the weakness of Constans as a ruler and, in all probability, an implicit decision to allow the Senate more influence than it had enjoyed under Constantine." (Ibid. 144.) The strength of the senatorial aristocracy does indeed correlate with weak imperial power, though the latter is more likely to be a result rather than a cause of the former. Constans, who was an able general, was not a particularly weak ruler, especially in the early part of his reign.

One of the problems with religious statistics in this period is that the religious affiliations of many appointees are unknown. There also are many office-holders whose names, let alone religious affiliations, are unknown. Of the total of 189 senatorial high office-holders for the period 324–61 in Barnes's "correction" of von Haehling's figures, the religious affiliations of 63, or one third, are unknown, and we do not even have the names of a further 64. So, no conclusions can be reached on the religious affiliations of two-thirds of the senatorial office-holders of this period. (von Haehling 1978.) See discussion in Chapter 3.

Western vs. Eastern Appointees

Only one of Constantius II's Eastern praetorian prefects was noble, and that was Septimius Acindynus, who was vicar or *comes* of the Spains at some time between 317 and 326. Five of Constantius's Eastern prefects were certainly non-senatorial, and a further one probably non-senatorial. There could be no greater contrast than that between, for example, Vulcacius Rufinus and Flavius Philippus, whose prefectures, in the West and East respectively, were contemporaneous. Rufinus could trace his ancestry back to the Republic; Philippus was the son of a sausage-maker.

Though Constantius appears to have been less inclined to appoint noble prefects than Constans, Constantius's appointment of nobles to Western prefectures when he was sole emperor is an indication that the explanation is to be sought in the political and social circumstances in which the brothers found themselves rather than in their personal preferences. For it was in the West that the strength of the senatorial aristocracy was concentrated and here, too, therefore, that we find the great majority of noble appointments.

Of the thirteen praetorian prefects in the West appointed by Constantine's sons, only one, Flavius Taurus, prefect of Italy and Africa for the last six years of Constantius's reign, is known to have been of non-senatorial origin. Seven of these prefects, however, are known to have been nobles, and both C. Ceionius Rufius Volusianus Lampadius and Vulcacius Rufinus had more than one spell as prefect, the latter's terms amounting to a total of ten years under the sons of Constantine and Magnentius—and, as we have already noted, he was destined to return to office as praetorian prefect of Italy, Africa and Illyricum, for another three years under Valentinian.

It is also worth noting that the noble praetorian prefects Fabius Titianus, M. Maecius Memmius Caecilianus Placidus, Vulcacius Rufinus, and Egnatius Lollianus were all *comites ordinis primi*, the two last-named being *comites ordinis primi intra Palatium*, members, that is, of the imperial "cabinet." Placidus and Vulcacius Rufinus, it might be added, were also *comites Orientis* under Constantine's sons, and are in fact the only noble vicars known to us in this period in the East. In the West, however, we are not short of noble vicars. Six of the eight Western vicars appointed between 337 and 361, whose origins are known, were nobles.

Noble Office-Holders from Julian to Theodosius

Julian's reign was too short to have left us many examples of his policy as regards appointments, but the evidence that we have does not indicate a more pro-noble attitude on his part than was the case with Constantius II, Constans or Constantine I himself. His paganism must have given him greater security in the West than any of these emperors.

The effect of Jovian's short reign on the personnel of the imperial administration cannot be gauged, and so we pass on to consider his successor, Valentinian, a rough-hewn Pannonian soldier who would preside over the destinies of the Empire for more than a decade. A man of humble origins and only a commander of a *schola* of targeteers when he was raised to the purple, Valentinian had no personal inclination to favor members of the aristocracy. Indeed, we are told by Ammianus that the Emperor hated "well dressed men...learned men, the rich, and nobles."(Amm. 30.8.10.) His institution of *defensores plebis* is just one example of the concern felt by him and his brother Valens for the *humiliores* and of their determination to protect them from the wiles of the *potentiores*. The new emperor also brought several of his compatriots into government. An example is Viventius, who came from Siscia and who was praetorian prefect of Gaul in 368, a position that he held for almost three years. Before this, Viventius was prefect of Rome, a position hitherto normally held by nobles. Nor was he the only non-noble to have this office under Valentinian; Bappo, Principius, and Eupraxius also appear to have been non-noble, though there is no conclusive proof. Ampelius, another of Valentinian's urban prefects, came from Antioch and began his career as *praeses* of Cappadocia—a pointer to non-noble origin.

Maximinus, "of most obscure birth," is probably the most famous, or notorious, of Valentinian's intimates. He was governor in turn of Corsica, Sardinia, and Tuscia and Umbria before becoming *praefectus annonae*, when he emerged as the moving force behind the spate of indictments of nobles on charges of adultery, magic, and poisoning. The obvious favor with which Valentinian viewed this fierce attack on the aristocracy is reflected in the prosecutor's promotion, first to the vicariate of Rome and later to the praetorian prefecture of Gaul. The Emperor's abrogation of the senatorial immunity from arrest (CTh. 9.2.2.) and his anti-pagan edicts are further signs of his hostility to the aristocracy. Another facet of the same policy is the inflation of honors that Valentinian introduced.

Valentinian's antipathy toward the aristocracy and his inroads upon traditional strongholds of theirs like the proconsulate of Africa and the urban prefecture may lead us to see in him a new Diocletian. It is true that in his reign, and particularly in the latter part of it, the number of nobles in high state posts plummets to the lowest point since the accession of Constantine. (Cf. Schuurmans, 565ff.) However, alongside the *defensores plebis* Valentinian confirmed Constantius's institution of *defensores senatus*. (CTh 1.28.1 [361] and CTh 1.28.2 [364].) Though Valentinian may have appointed non-nobles to positions traditionally reserved for nobles and he may have introduced an inflation of honors which devalued the traditional clarissimate, unlike Diocletian, he did not turn senatorial rank into a political *cul-de-sac*. Instead, Valentinian worked within the Constantinian mould, and nobles retained their eligibility for high office. Admittedly, this in itself would be meaningless, as an emperor could appoint whoever he liked to any particular post. But Valentinian's successors returned to the pattern of appointments initiated by Constantine and his sons—and, while favoring men of humble origins in his appointments, even Valentinian himself entrusted the position second only to the imperial throne itself to two of the noblest men in the Empire, Vulcacius Rufinus (see above), and the towering figure of Sextus Claudius Petronius, the head of the Anician house, considered below.

Though no noble praetorian prefects are known under Gratian, familiar names such as Faltonius Probus Alypius and Alfenius Ceionius Julianus appear among the vicars. Gratian was a committed Christian and possibly the first Emperor to decline to accept the title *Pontifex Maximus*, high priest of the pagan Roman state religion, though this is disputed. (See Alan Cameron 2007.) He certainly was instrumental in removing the Altar of Victory from the Senate house in 382–after it had been reinstalled there by Julian—igniting a fire-storm that raged for more than a decade after his death. The acrimony of this dispute illustrates not only Gratian's Christian devotion but also the attachment of a (presumably) large number of Senators to the old religion. So there was no love lost between Gratian and the aristocracy, though Faltonius Probus Alypius was evidently a member of the Anician family, and, after his vicariate of Africa under Gratian in 378, appears as urban prefect in 391, a position that his father, Clodius Celsinus Adelphius, had held forty years before. In 393 he was sent to the court of the pro-pagan "usurper" Eugenius to celebrate the forthcoming consulship of Symmachus's friend Virius Nicomachus Flavianus, who had served as praetorian prefect of Italy from 390 to 394, under Theodosius and then under Eugenius.

Gratian's other noble vicar of Africa, Alfenius Ceionius Julianus, *signo* Kamenius (343–385, CIL VI. 1675; Iulianus 25—PLRE), a member of the leading noble house of the Ceionii, was another prominent pagan, holding priesthoods not only in the Roman state religion—*septemvir epulonum, quindecimvir sacris faciundis,* and *pontifex maior*—but also in some of the other pagan cults, including that of Mithras, Hecate, and Liber (i.e. Bacchus or Dionysus), and he had undergone the *taurobolium ceremony* associated with the worship of Cybele (*Magna Mater*). Alan Cameron, commenting on the fact that, in common with other pagan nobles, Julianus enjoyed the high rank of *archibucolus* in the cult of Liber, remarks: "If this was a battle against Christianity, it was fought by an army in which everyone was a general"—implying that the pagan revival in the late fourth century lacked a genuine following and was the artificial creation of a small band of aristocrats. (Alan Cameron, The Last Pagans of Rome, p. 150.) However, the furor aroused over the Altar of Victory, the courage of these nobles to resist the imperial onslaught against paganism—which was banned in 391—and the pro-pagan stance of the "usurper" Eugenius (nominally a Christian), indicate that the threat to paganism was taken seriously among members of the high aristocracy, but that this did not prevent them from being appointed to high office.

Theodosius I was no more favorably inclined to the pagan appeal for the restoration of the Altar of Victory than either Gratian or the youthful Valentinian II, and he encouraged pagan senators to convert to Christianity, (Zos. 4.59), yet his reign marks a new stage in the role played by nobles in the imperial administration.

The *comes ordinis primi intra consistorium* was evidently one of the emperor's leading advisers, who was actually present at court and took part" in meetings of the *consistorium*, the imperial "cabinet," (which from the time of Constantine replaced the *consilium principis* of the Principate). Up to the time of Theodosius no nobles are known to have had any of the specific ministerial portfolios, and it is not difficult to see why a noble would scorn to hold a position whose origin is to be sought in the work done in the early principate by the emperor's freedmen and which even in the fourth century retained a trace of its humble domestic beginnings. But time had made the palatine portfolios respectable, and under Theodosius we find Virius Nicomachus Flavianus as *quaestor sacri palatii*, and (Rufius) Festus and Caecina Decius Albinus as *tribuni et notarii*, the latter destined to become *magister officiorum* and probably also *quaestor sacri palatii* at the turn of the century. (Flavianus: CIL VI.

1782 = ILS 2947–8; Festus: CIL VI.32035 = XV. 7163; Albinus: Symm. Ep. 7.38.)

A Spaniard by birth, Theodosius was brought into the imperial college to rule the East after the death of Valens in the disastrous defeat of Hadrianople in 378. Like Valentinian, Theodosius brought some of his fellow countrymen into government with him, yet his first praetorian prefect was Q. Clodius Hermogenianus Olybrius, a member of the noble Anician family, who had a combined prefecture of the East with Illyricum. The first three Western praetorian prefects under Theodosius were all nobles, namely Petronius Probus (discussed below), Nonius Atticus Maximus, and Vettius Agorius Praetextatus.

Though the West passed on the death of Theodosius in 395 into the grip of the Vandal general Stilicho acting for Theodosius's young son Honorius, the nobles did not suffer a reverse. Indeed, under Valentinian III (r. 423–55), as Sundwall has shown, the Italian praetorian prefecture was virtually the preserve of the aristocracy, its holders including such names as Anicius Auchenius Bassus, Rufius Antonius Agrypnius Volusianus, Caecina Decius Aginatius Albinus, Anicius Acilio Glabrio Faustus, Nicomachus Flavianus, and Petronius Maximus (discussed below.)

At the time of Theodosius's death nobles had had access to high office for over eighty years. For a time, under Valentinian, whose hostility to the aristocracy was reflected in some of his appointments, it looked as though the new dispensation introduced by Constantine was threatened, but, as we have seen, even Valentinian entrusted the important central prefecture to nobles, and in general kept within the Constantinian mould. The emperor's personal preference was certainly an important factor in the selection of office-holders, but it had to be tempered by consideration of the political and social conditions of the day. It is this that explains the meager number of noble appointees in the Eastern half of the Empire in a period when the number of Western offices held by them was impressive. For it was in the West that their land, wealth, and family connections were concentrated.

The two leading noble houses in this period were the Anicii, who converted to Christianity (see above), and the Ceionii, who remained true to the old religion. Members of both families, however, were appointed to high office.

A Bird's-Eye View of the High Nobility—the Anicii

Though neither an attractive character nor an exemplary administrator, Sextus Claudius Petronius Probus was in office as praetorian prefect for the eleven years of Valentinian's reign, with a few short breaks.

Probus was a Christian, though whether he was the "first" Christian convert among the Roman aristocracy, as claimed by Peter Brown, or whether that honor belongs to an earlier relation of his, together with several other aristocrats, as claimed by T.D. Barnes, remains a moot point. (Brown 1961; Barnes 1995.) But the favors showered on Probus by Valentinian probably have less to do with his religious affiliation than his headship of the Anicii, one of the two leading noble houses of the day, the other being that of the Ceionii. Though Petronius Probus did not have the *nomen* Anicius, he is described in an inscription as ANICIANAE DOMVS CVLMEN ("Pinnacle of the Anician house"). (CIL VI. 1753 = ILS 1267.) It would seem, therefore, that his mother was an Anicia. His father was Petronius Probinus, consul in 341 and urban prefect in 344. His grandfather was Petronius Probianus, proconsul of Africa, ordinary consul, urban prefect, and probably also praetorian prefect under Constantine. (CIL V. 344 = ILS 1266.) The family goes back a bit further and was evidently connected with the Ceionii as well as with the Anicii.

After his first short spell in Illyricum he was appointed to the prefecture of Gaul, and for the last seven years of Valentinian's reign he was in control of Italy, Africa and Illyricum. The Emperor evidently allowed Probus a free hand, though Illyricum was the Emperor's native territory, and it was only late in his reign that Valentinian learned of his prefect's oppressive regime. But even then he failed to act against him, and Probus survived Valentinian in office. In 371 he was ordinary consul together with the Emperor Gratian, and in 383–384 he held the threefold praetorian prefecture once again. He was still alive in 390, when, according to the *Vita Ambrosii* (Life of Ambrose) by Paulinus of Milan, two Persian noblemen who came to see the Emperor Theodosius in Milan, made a special trip to Rome to gawk at *nobilitatis culmen* ("the pinnacle of the nobility".)

Ammianus portrays Probus as an arrogant and grasping man, who "owned estates in every part of the Empire, though whether or not they were honestly acquired is not for me to say." (Amm. 27.11.) If Ammianus is to be believed, Probus entered public affairs only in the interests of his family, so his appointment to a position of immense power by Valentinian can probably be seen as an attempt on the part of the Emperor to conciliate at least the most significant of the noble families in the Empire—with the consolation that, unlike the Ceionii, the Anicii were Christians.

Probus's sons, Anicius Probinus and Anicius Hermogenianus Olybrius, celebrated joint consulships in 395. Probinus then went on to serve as proconsul of Africa in 396–397. (Symm. Ep. 9; CTh 12.5.3.) His son Petronius Maximus was urban prefect in 420–421 and again at some point before 439, in the meantime celebrating a consulship in 433. Between 439 and 441 he was praetorian prefect of Italy, and was consul again in 443. In 445 he was raised to the patriciate, and between 443 and 445 he built the *Forum Petronii Maximi* in Rome. As the result of a series of court intrigues, and with the support of the Roman Senate and bribery of some palace officials, Maximus emerged briefly in 455 as Western Emperor before being murdered. Rome was then captured and sacked by the Vandal leader Gaiseric (or Geiseric). It was from this that the Vandals got the bad reputation that still attaches to their name today.

Remarkably, the family produced yet another, albeit almost equally shortlived, emperor, in the person of Anicius Olybrius, one of the very last emperors of the West, who reigned for a few months in 472 as a puppet of Flavius Ricimer, a Romanized general of Germanic extraction, who controlled the last vestiges of the Western Empire from 461 until his death in 472.

The famous philosopher Boethius, author of *De Consolatione Philosophiae*, was also a member of the Anician house, his full name being Anicius Manlius Severinus Boethius (c. 477–524). He entered public service under the Ostrogothic King of Italy Theoderic (or Theodoric), being given a consulship in 510 and being appointed to the high civil service post of *magister officiorum* in 522, the same year as when, as he proudly recalled, his two sons celebrated joint consulships. However, he soon fell out of favor and was executed.

Boethius was adopted and raised by Quintus Aurelius Memmius Symmachus, grandson of Quintus Aurelius Symmachus (c. 345–402), the famous pagan orator who in 384 pleaded in vain with the Emperor Valentinian II for the Altar of Victory to be returned to the Senate chamber, from which it had been removed by Constantius in 357, restored by Julian, and then removed again by Gratian in 382. His letters and other writings are a rich source of information on the period. He was proconsul of Africa in 373 and was also a pagan priest. After a somewhat chequered career, he found favor with Theodosius I, by whom he was granted a consulship in 391.

The family was honored with consulships for some time to come, ending with Anicius Faustus Albinus Basilius, consul in 541, the last person other than the East Roman Emperor to hold this title. Germanus, a cousin and leading general under the Emperor Justinian (r. 527–565), is said in Jordanes's *Getica* to have been a descendant of the Anicii, though this is by no means certain. Someone who was almost certainly a member of the family was Pope Symmachus (in office 498–513), who was born a pagan, and another likely member is Pope Gregory I, who started life as Gregorius Anicius and who served as urban prefect around 573, before becoming Pope in 590. He is thought to have been the great-great-grandson of Pope Felix III (in office 483–492). According to Jeffrey Richards: "Of the seventeen Popes between 483 and 604, seven were certainly or likely members of Roman aristocratic families, and three more had provincial aristocratic origins"— a good illustration of the way the aristocracy acclimated themselves to the changed religious environment. (Richards 1979, p. 243,)

A Bird's-Eye View of the High Nobility—the Ceionii

The great noble house of the Ceionii (or Caeionii) certainly had an impressive pedigree. They owned land in Volaterrae in Etruria and in Africa, and, though we need not take too seriously their vaunted descent from Volusus, the ancient Etruscan chief of the Rutuli, the family can nevertheless be traced back through the Nummii to patricians of the late Republic.

The very first noble praetorian prefect known to history was C. Ceionius (or Caeionius) Rufius Volusianus, who held this high post under Maxentius from 309 to 310, and is discussed in Chapter 3. (CIL VI. 1708 = 31906 = ILS 1222.; Volusianus 4–PLRE.) He went on to become urban prefect in 310 and again from 313 to 315. serving, therefore, under Constantine after Maxentius's defeat. His active paganism as the holder of two priesthoods, was not taken amiss by his new imperial master. His son, C(a)eionius Rufius Albinus, was *consul ordinarius posterior* under Constantine in 335 and urban prefect from 335 to 337. C. Ceionius Rufius Volusianus *signo* Lampadius, possibly his son, was praetorian prefect, probably first of Illyricum in 354 and then of Gaul from 354–355, and then urban prefect in 365 (Volusianus 5—PLRE.), a position held from 389 to 391 by yet another family member, P. Ceionius Caecina Albinus (Albinus 15–PLRE), father of Rufius Antonius Agrypnius Volusianus (Rutilius Nam. 1. 168 ff;), who corresponded with Augustine, politely parrying Augustine's arguments and refusing to be baptized. He was proconsul of Africa, urban prefect from 417 to 418, and praetorian prefect of Italy. He finally converted to Christianity when, as envoy of Valentinian III to Theodosius II in Constantinople to seek the hand of Theodosius's daughter on behalf of the Western emperor, he fell fatally ill and was persuaded to convert by his niece Melania the Younger, who was to become a Christian saint. Volusianus's sister Albina was married to Valerius Publicola, the son of Melania the Elder (another future saint) and father of Melania the Younger. We have two praetorian prefects and an acting praetorian prefect from this family in the early fifth century: Valerius Maximus, Valerius Messalla, a friend of Symmachus's, and Aradius Valerius Proculus, respectively. (Cf. J. Matthews, 1975, p.502.) In the Flavian Amphitheatre, we find another member of the family, Rufius Valerius Messala, *vir clarissimus et inlustris*, sitting next to the consul of 472, Rufius Postumius Festus, evidently a relative. P. Ceionius Caecina Albinus was the maternal grandfather of Eustochius, Bishop of Tours (in post from 443 to 461), who was succeeded in that position by his close relative Saint Perpetuus (in post 460 to 490), and in his turn by yet another relative, Saint Volusianus—quite a leap for this formerly staunchly pagan family.

A New Kind of Alliance

Emperors and aristocrats needed each other more now than at any time since the early Principate. Another feature worth noting is the marriage ties between aristocrats and the imperial families, and the desire of emperors to give themselves aristocratic lineages. A good example of these ties is provided by the aristocratic pagan Vulcacius Rufinus, who served as praetorian prefect of Italy under Constans from 344 to 347 and of Illyricum, initially also under Constans, from 347 to 352. He retained his post under the usurper Magnentius, who ousted Constans in 350, and was the only envoy sent by Magnentius to Constantius who was not arrested. (Petr. Patr. 16.) Constantius was not afraid to scorn the *de facto* ruler of the West but took care not to offend his aristocratic prefect. Indeed, after Constantius's defeat of Magnentius, Rufinus continued as praetorian prefect of Illyricum, and later also of Gaul, under Constantius himself, losing his position evidently because of his relationship to Constantius's cousin the Caesar Constantius Gallus, who, falling out of favor with Constantius, was assassinated at his instigation in 354. Rufinus returned to favor under Valentinian, serving as praetorian prefect of Italy and Africa from 365 to 368, and also of Gaul from 366 to 368. He died in office. His prominence can be gauged by the fact that he was *comes ordinis primi intra consistorium* the highest rank in the imperial *comitatus*) under either Constans or Constantius, or both, and his consulship in 347 was as *consul ordinarius prior*, the highest grade consulship, yet he also was not just a committed pagan but a *pontifex maior*. (CIL VI. 32051 = ILS 1237; Rufinus 25–PLRE .)

Vulcacius Rufinus was the brother, or (in view of the name difference) probably half-brother of Galla and Neratius Cerealis. (Amm. 14.11.27.) Galla was married to Julius Constantius, son of Constantius I (known posthumously as Chlorus) and half-brother of Constantine I. She predeceased her husband, who would father the future Emperor Julian by his second wife, Basilina, daughter of Julius Julianus, praetorian prefect under the Emperor Licinius from 315 to 324 and suffect consul after Licinius's defeat in 324.

The Constantinian family was probably of humble origin, though the notoriously unreliable fourth century *Historia Augusta* claimed a genealogical link for it with the Emperor Claudius Gothicus (.r. 268–270.) (*Historia Augusta, Claudius 12.1.*) Yet Galla clearly was of senatorial stock, as we know from the family background of her brother, Neratius (or Naeratius) Cerealis, urban prefect 352–353 and consul in 358, who erected a statue in honor of Constantius II in Rome, describing the Emperor as RESTITVTOR VRBIS ET ORBIS, EXTINCTOR PESTIFERAE TYRANNIDIS ("Restorer of the City and the world, exterminator of a pestilential tyrant"–CIL VI. 1158 = ILS 731–A reference to Constantius's defeat of Magnentius.) Galla and Julius Constantius had a son, the Caesar Constantius Gallus, a daughter who married Constantius II, and possibly another daughter, grandmother of the Galla who was daughter of Valentinian I and wife of Theodosius I. (Lenski 2006, p. 97.)

The Neratii were not only noble in their own right, but through the Betitii were linked to the Anicii, one of the two most prominent senatorial families of the period. In the public baths constructed by Neratius Cerealis, a loyal servant called Cursius Satrius put up two inscriptions, one to Cerealis and the other to Cerealis's (probable) son Neratius Scopius, the latter being described as consular of Campania. (CIL VI. 1745 and 1746 = ILS 1245 and 1246). Another inscription referring to Scopius gets the name of the emperor wrong, calling him Valerian instead of Valentinian. (CIL IX. 1566.) Satrius might well be proud to serve the Neratii, for, besides their connection to several emperors, the family could trace its ancestry back to the Principate, if not further back.

The Neratii came from Saepinum in Samnium, and we have a reference, dating probably from the late Republic, to a certain "C. Neratius Sexti filius IIvir iure dicundo." (*Not. Scav.* 1926, 245.) The first known consul in the family was the distinguished governor of Galatia and Cappadocia under Vespasian (r. 69–79), M. Hirtius Fronto Neratius Pansa, whose career has now been revealed to us in all its glory by Torelli's piecing together of eleven fragments of an inscription found in Saepinum, which includes the fact that Pansa had been adlected *inter patricios* meaning that he had been raised to the patriciate, an honor reserved for supporters of the emperor. (CIL XIII.1675 = ILS 4537. Torelli 1968, pp. 170–175.) Later members of the family include:

- L. Neratius Priscus, legate of Pannonia, a member of Trajan's *consilium*, and, according to the (unreliable) *Historia Augusta*, considered a potential successor to Trajan.
- L. Neratius Marcellus, brother of Priscus, and governor of Britain in 103 and ordinary consul in 129. Also *adlectus inter patricios*.
- Neratius Junius Flavianus, urban prefect 311–312.

Toward a Christian Byzantine Empire

The official foundation of Constantinople by Constantine in 330 replaced the tradition of an itinerant imperial court, with each emperor picking his favorite roosting spot: Nicomedia, Sirmium, Milan, Trier, Ravenna, Thessalonica. For more than a century before Constantine, most emperors were rough-hewn career soldiers who did not feel at home in Rome, the stronghold of the senatorial aristocracy. Some, like Diocletian, rarely visited Rome, which in any case was too remote from the frontier to afford protection against "barbarian" incursions. The choice of the ancient Greek city of Byzantium as the "new Rome," as it came unofficially to be known, was inspired. On the Bosphorus linking Europe and Asia, its position, geographically, strategically, and linguistically, proved most fortunate. Constantinople represented a unique departure from all other cities: it was the first city—and a capital to boot—to have a Christian character from the start, with all that went with it.

Its Christian character was of particular significance, enabling a symbiotic relationship between Church and state that set it apart from its Western counterpart, as is already noticeable from the time of Theodosius II (401–50), born in Constantinople, proclaimed co-Augustus with his father Arcadius when just nine months old, and sole emperor on his father's death in 408. Some parts of a recent compilation of articles on his reign smack remarkably of special pleading, especially Richard Flower's contribution on "heresiology." (Kelly 2013.)

Heresiology "A Recognized Intellectual Discipline"

The chapter on "heresiology" treats the wholesale condemnation of some twenty "heresies" in CTh 16.5.65 (issued in 428) as a branch of learning. No fewer than 37 "heresies" are listed in CJ 1.5.5, also dating from 428, including the Donatists, who had originally been regarded merely as "schismatics." Heresiology, we are told, was "a recognized intellectual discipline." (p. 175.) Like "the *Natural History* of Pliny the Elder or the medical treatises of Galen," heresiology "claimed to provide complete and secure information, guaranteed by the author's learning and experience" (p. 173.) Heresiologies are described as "carefully ordered catalogues of a new form of religious knowledge." If it were not made so earnestly, this comparison would be comical. "Heresiology" is simply an irrational and arbitrary torrent of bile spewed out against "heretics." How that can be compared to the rational, scientific researches of a Galen or a Pliny the Elder beggars belief. "Heresiology" has as much in common with any form of literature as crude graffiti on a bathroom wall have with the works of Shakespeare.

The title *De Haereticis* in the Theodosian Code contains 65 edicts, spanning a century, from 326 to 428. The edicts ranged in tone from a mild rebuke under Constantine in 326 (CTh 16.5.1) to a much shriller tone in 379, declaring, "All heresies are forbidden by both divine and imperial laws and shall forever cease" (CTh 16.5.5) to the hysterical CTh 16.5.65 of 428 so admired by the author of the chapter on "Heresiology." CTh 16.5.65 shrieks: "The madness of the heretics must be suppressed.... All the laws which were formerly issued and promulgated at various times against such persons and against all others who oppose our faith, shall remain in force forever." More than twenty "heresies" are listed. Though promulgated in the joint names of Theodosius II and his young Western co-emperor Valentinian III, the edict was issued in Constantinople and is redolent of the prevailing atmosphere of the eastern capital.

The parts of this same compilation written by the editor, Christopher Kelly, also contain some surprising remarks. When Theodosius II ordered synagogues seized by Christians to be returned to the Jews, we read, "the great Syrian holy man, Simeon Stylites," protested, and Theodosius immediately reversed his policy and sacked the praetorian prefect responsible. Does this prejudiced ascetic really deserve the title of a "great holy man"? And what does his influence over the emperor tell us about the ethos of the emerging Byzantine Empire? Kelly merely comments: "Such stories are not as one-sided as perhaps they might at first seem." (p. 47 f.) But the power of the church over the state was not confined to "holy men" perched on narrow pillars. Theodosius II is recorded as remarking, "I cannot give orders to a bishop," when requested to do so by the theologian Theodoret of Cyrrhus (c. 393–c. 458/466.)

This unhealthy relationship between church and state is just one feature that distinguishes East from West. Other features include the lack (at least in the early centuries) of a hereditary landed aristocracy and the growth of the power of an element that was far less prevalent in the West: eunuchs. These features are picked up in the concluding section of this chapter.

Constantine's Legacy

Constantine had a major effect on the future not only of the Roman Empire but indeed of European and world history, echoes of which are still felt today. It used to be fashionable for historians to judge events and characters in the past as either "good" or "bad." This tendency was parodied in that wonderful spoof history of England, *1066 And All That*, which, for example, characterized "WilliamanMary" as "a Good King." My own view is that passing judgment on the personalities or events of the past is not the job of a historian. Though complete objectivity may not be attainable, that is no excuse for overt subjective judgmentalism. In recent years, however, judgmental historical writing, including a certain amount of special pleading, is very much in evidence again—not least in regard to the period which is the subject of this book.

Constantine and Christianity

However, while eschewing the opportunity of classifying people or events as either "good" or "bad," I believe that there are certain values that can be accepted as objectively good, one of the most important of these being religious toleration. But what exactly is "religious toleration"? The word *toleration* comes from a Latin root meaning "to bear, to put up with, to endure," and even in modern English the term "religious toleration" still retains some negative connotations. A better term to use is "freedom of religion," as in Article 18 of the Universal Declaration of Human Rights adopted by the United Nations in 1948: "Everyone has the right to freedom of thought, conscience and religion; this right includes freedom...to manifest his religion or belief in teaching, practice, worship and observance." This is a fundamental human right linked to freedom of speech and expression. Both these rights are recognized in the US First Amendment as well as in Bills of Rights in other countries. There was no need for any such protection in the pagan Roman Empire, under which religious freedom was automatic—and the short periods of persecution of Judaism and Christianity were purely political. (Moss 2013, discussed in Chapters 2 and 10.) But the dominance of Christianity, a creed religion, put an end to religious freedom and introduced centuries of persecution of "heretics" and non-believers of all kinds.

And it is to Constantine that that dominance is ultimately attributable. Constantine's religious policy gyrations notwithstanding, the favors he showered on the Church and his deathbed baptism created a firm foundation for the declaration of Christianity as the official religion of the Empire in 380 and the banning of all pagan worship in 391. The creation of a Christian Empire, leading to a post-Roman Christian Europe, with all that that entailed, was a Constantinian legacy.

Constantine's Administrative Revolution

As a purely Western ruler until his defeat of Licinius in 324, Constantine recognized the value of aristocratic support and reversed Diocletian's policy of shutting members of this order out of high office. This policy, which was evidently motivated by political rather than religious considerations, was continued in the West by his sons and later successors, enhancing the power of the aristocracy at the heart of government while consolidating their wealth and power in the Western half of the Empire. Emperors and aristocracy were drawn to each other, leading to family alliances. And, as the power of Western Christianity increased, so did the mutual attraction of the church and the aristocracy, who began to occupy high posts in that institution.

As a result of Constantine's inflation of honors, the equestrian order gradually faded into insignificance, and the senatorial title of *vir clarissimus* was attached to more and more posts. The "entry level" equestrian title, *vir egregius*, is last recorded in 324 (CTh 6.22.1), and the highest equestrian grade of *eminentissimus*, usually reserved for praetorian prefects, is not found after the time of Constantine. Instead, prefects were accorded senatorial titles, while the clarissimate was held from birth by aristocratic prefects, who were more and more in evidence, in the West, from Constantine onward. The senatorial clarissimate, a hereditary rank, was cheapened too, and new titles were introduced for the holders of higher senatorial posts, namely *vir spectabilis* and *vir illustris* or *inlustris*. Initially, *clarissimus* and *inlustris* tended to be used together, as in the first use of the new title in 354 in reference to Vulcacius Rufinus as praetorian prefect, described as *vir clarissimus et inlustris*. (CTh 11.1.6) By the time of Justinian (r. 527–565), who briefly managed to reunite the Empire, even the title of *illustris* was subdivided, the holders of the top jobs being styled *gloriosus*—perhaps an inadvertent harking back to Plautus's *Miles Gloriosus* ("The Swaggering Soldier") of about 200 BCE!

'The new hierarchy," comments A.H.M. Jones, "effectively transformed the aristocracy from one of birth into one of office." (Jones 1964, p. 529.) This was true only on a superficial level, and chiefly in the East. In the West, however, the proud traditions of noble birth were kept alive, thus perpetuating the aristocratic ethos which had permeated Roman history since the early days of the Republic.

Constantine, First Byzantine Emperor

Constantine's establishment of Constantinople as a new Christian capital paved the way to a split Empire and then to a completely separate though gradually shrinking Byzantine Empire, while Western Europe fell under a mosaic of Germanic kingdoms and, much later, partly under the so-called "Holy Roman Empire," which Voltaire dismissed as neither holy, nor Roman, nor an empire. Yet even the European Union existing at the time of this writing is redolent of the Roman Empire, with a modern version of Roman Law prevalent in the majority of member states, Romance languages dominant in at least five, and an overarching European citizenship.

The word *byzantine* still carries with it a good deal of opprobrium coupled with a certain amount of amusement, implying a highly complex but ineffectual form of government operated in a devious and surreptitious manner. Just lately, however, it has become fashionable to attempt to rehabilitate the Byzantine Empire. One reason for its bad reputation, we are assured, was jealousy on the part of the crude Western Crusaders, gawking at the highly civilized, literate, silk-clad Byzantines, who ate their food with a fork (unknown in the West until much later.)

In the initial absence of a hereditary landed aristocracy like that of the West, the Dominate, or absolute monarchy, was perpetuated in the East—at least in theory. However, such was the power of the church and of court eunuchs, that the emperor was often merely a cipher. The tenth century saw the rise of a military aristocracy, who took over the imperial throne in the shape of the Komnenos (1081–1185) and Palaiologos (1259–1453) dynasties.

The important role played by eunuchs from the earliest days of the Byzantine Empire, and even more so from the eight century, differentiates it from the West, and also explains the low level of aristocratic power in Byzantium. Eunuchs were not a threat to the emperor. Initially employed as body-servants, they grew in power and influence as time went by, even serving on the imperial *consistorium*, or cabinet. Eunuchs were trusted not to try to usurp the throne, which was reserved for "bearded" men. However, the church hierarchy in the East was open to eunuchs, who are even found as patriarchs. By contrast, the church in the West has always been open only to "whole" men, and there is a persistent, though unverified, rumor that someone elected Pope has to undergo an inspection to verify that *habet duos testiculos et bene pendentes* ("he has two testicles and they hang well".)

5
Continuity and Change

Chapter 4 explored Constantine's legacy, the effects of his rule chiefly over the ensuing century. This chapter takes an analytical bird's-eye view of the two divergent worlds, East and West, in the longer term. The chief objective is to explain how and why the two halves of the Roman Empire developed so differently after the demise of the western empire. This analysis is undertaken with reference, *inter alia*, to the power relations that pervade this period—and, indeed, through every other period over the last three thousand years that I have studied—namely competition between two models of government: monarchy and aristocracy. (See Chapter 6, and Arnheim 2017a.)

The issues discussed in this chapter are the following:

- **Birth, Land, and Office**
  - The nexus between birth, land and office in the West in "late antiquity;"
  - The growth of self-contained and fortified estates;
  - The nature and significance of patronage in the East and West;
  - The use of *amicitia* by nobles in relation to "barbarian" generals;
  - The power-structure in the early Middle Ages in the West;
  - The unnecessary feud over "feudalism."
- **The Byzantine Paradox**
  - Much ado about nothing— whether Byzantium was an "empire" or not.
  - When is a schism not a schism? Special pleading to try to deny a thousand-year rift.

Why Rome Fell: Decline and Fall, or Drift and Change?, First Edition. Michael Arnheim.
© 2022 John Wiley & Sons, Inc. Published 2022 by John Wiley & Sons, Inc.

- An inconsequential pother: Whether the Byzantine Empire was a "Greek" Empire.
- Some unparadoxical paradoxes.
- Did Byzantium really last more than a thousand years? Yes, as a yo-yo empire, growing and shrinking (with more of the latter) by fits and starts.
- The Byzantine Empire's porous borders.
- The absence (until the late tenth century) of a hereditary aristocracy in the Byzantine Empire.
- The prominent role of eunuchs in government.
- The symbiotic relationship between church and state.
- The real significance of the Iconoclastic Controversy.

Birth, Land, and Office

Every society in history has had an elite of one kind or another, generally based on one or more of the following qualities: birth, wealth, power, status, and office. The Roman senatorial aristocracy from the time of Constantine combined birth, wealth, status, and office. (See Chapters 3 and 4.) Titles are not always very reliable indicia of anything other than status or office. In the late Roman Empire there was something of an inflation of titles and honors. While members of the senatorial aristocracy, who had birth, wealth and status on their side, also enjoyed the fruits of office and power under Constantine and his successors, particularly in the West, non-senatorial appointees, especially in the East, who shared the same titles, were not quite in the same bracket, especially as concerns wealth and local influence in the provinces. So, though there was a certain amount of fusion of honors, that did not equate to a merged aristocracy as long as the Roman Empire survived in the West, while in the East a hereditary aristocracy is not really in evidence until the eleventh century.

"Large Estates Have Ruined Italy, and Now Even the Provinces."

Senators had always drawn their livelihood from the land and were traditionally prohibited from engaging in trade. That senators were still essentially landowners in the fourth century is a commonplace and needs no proof. Perhaps the best indication of the fact that senators were primarily landowners is to be found in the fact that the tax levied on them from the time of Constantine, the *follis, collatio glebalis,* or *glebatio*, was a land-tax. (Zos. 2.38; CTh 6.2 and 3, passim; Jones 1964, pp. 462–469.) The Latin word *gleba* actually means a clod or lump of earth.

Nobles were not of course the only owners of estates. Decurions (town councillors), some soldiers, and even some Christian priests were evidently in this category, too. (CTh 5.2.3 and 6.) Though nobles, who often inherited landed property, probably had on average more extensive estates than non-senators; nevertheless, the general trends discernible in connection with landholding in the late Empire are relevant to estate-owners across the board.

"[L]atifundia perdidere Italiam, iam vero et provincias." (Large estates have ruined Italy, and now even the provinces.) (Plin. *N.H.* 18.7.35.) Thus wrote Pliny the Elder (c. 23–79) in his *Natural History* well over two centuries before Constantine. This dictum has been much discussed. Moses Finley (wrongly translating as present tense the perfect tense *perdidere*, an abbreviation for *perdiderunt*) dismissed the remark as "no more than moralizing archaism (....) a lamentation for the lost Roman yeomanry and the simpler good old days." (Finley 1973, p. 202 n. 51.) In fact, Pliny is not "moralizing" here at all. Instead, he is commending the practical (albeit traditional) advice "...that it was better to sow less land and plough it better." Pliny may have been exaggerating the degree to which large estates had "ruined" Italy, but he is unlikely simply to have invented their existence in a serious work of science as his *Natural History* certainly is.

Fast forward three centuries, and in the biography by Gerontius (written in about 452) of Melania the Younger (c. 383–439), a member of the noble *gens Ceionia*, granddaughter of Melania the Elder (c. 350–410/417), and, like her, venerated as a saint soon after her death, we read:

- "Of the nobles and wealthy patricians, it may be said briefly that their time was wholly devoted to pleasure, to the seeking for honors and magisterial dignities, the accumulation of riches, and the excessive increase of their estates, especially in those provinces of which they were appointed governors." This is a reference to the fourth century. (1.14.)
- "The orator Symmachus (c. 354–402), who, according to Olympiodorus, had relatively but a modest income, possessed three magnificent palaces in Rome, as well as fifteen villas to which he could betake himself whenever he needed change." (Gerontius, V. Melaniae 1.18.)
- "Unbridled love of pleasure, luxury, pomp and pride: such were the chief factors in the life of the Roman patrician." (Ibid., 1.18.)
- "During the first two years after she (viz. Melania the Younger) left Rome she restored to freedom no less than eight thousand slaves." (Ibid., 7. 83.)

- One of Melania's estates, which she donated to the church of Tagaste, was larger than the town. (V. Mel. 1.21.)

Agennius Urbicus, a writer on agriculture who probably lived in the late fourth century, had this to say about the size of privately owned estates, especially in Africa: "Many estates indeed are far larger than the districts: they have however in private estates a far from scanty (*exiguus*) plebeian population and villages around the villa in the manner of free towns." (Agennius Urbicus, *de Controversiis Agrorum, Corp Agrimensorum Rom.*, p. 45 (Teubner).) Both these examples point toward the tendency for private estates to become self-contained economic and social units. Palladius (full name: Rutilius Taurus Aemilianus Palladius), who wrote on agriculture in the late fourth or first half of the fifth century, assumes all along that his readers are owners of sizable estates and advises them to have craftsmen and artisans on their land so that their peasants will have no need to go to the cities. (Palladius, *de Re Rustica*, 1.6.)

The African mosaics corroborate this and show a multiplicity of activities going on within a single estate: the tending of sheep, goats, and cattle; horse-breeding; poultry-farming; the spinning of yarn; the production of wine and oil; hunting and fishing; and, of course, the farming of fruit and agricultural products. (Rostovtzeff 1926, Plates lxxvii, lxxix, lxxx.)

One of these mosaics, which depicts life on the estate of a certain Julius in Carthage, also shows the villa taking on the aspect of a fortress. (Merlin 1921, pp. 95–114.) This can also be seen in other mosaics, and there is in addition no lack of archaeological evidence even in Britain. (Paribeni 1940, pp. 131–48.) Inscriptions tell the same story. (CIL VIII.21531 = ILS 6021, Mauretania; CIL VIII. 19328 = ILS 6020 Numidia.)

An interesting example of a fortified villa is that of Zammac, brother of the rebel Moorish prince Firmus, which is described by Ammianus as constructed *in modum urbis* (in the manner of a city). The villa is also celebrated in an inscription with an acrostic down each end. (ILS 9351.)

The poet and bishop of Averna (Clermont) Sidonius Apollinaris (c. 430–c. 485) waxes lyrical in his poems on a number of rural estates belonging to members of the senatorial aristocracy in southern Gaul, including an Auvergne estate at Avitacum belonging to his wife (Ep. 2.2); estates named Vorocingus and Prusianum, north of Nimes owned by Tonantius Ferreolus (c. 390–475), a Roman senator and praetorian prefect of Gaul; and a villa called Octavianus Ager near Narbonne owned by one Consentius. Not least, in a poem addressed to his senatorial friend Pontius Leontius of the noble Anician house, Sidonius eulogizes his friend's estate, aptly named *Burgus* ("Castle, Fortress"), built by Leontius's father Pontius Paulinus, specifically stressing the impregnability of its walls with no less than thirty turrets:

"Those walls no engine, no battering-ram, no high-piled structure or near-built-mound, no catapult hurling hissing stones, no tortoise-roof, no mantlet, no wheel rushing onwards with ladder already in position shall ever have power to shake." W.B. Anderson comments: "Burgus is believed to survive in the modern Bourg-sur-Gironde." (Ibid., p. 259 n1.) These were heavy duty fortifications indeed, designed for protection against any attempted incursion. (See also: Goldberg 1995.)

Doubts have been expressed about the reliability of these descriptions. Sidonius's description of his Avitacum estate is couched as an invitation. Here is John Percival's comment: "The letter in which the description occurs is clearly a set piece, a literary exercise rather than a genuine attempt to provide information. Who, in real life, would invite someone to stay and include a detailed description of the property?" Percival's comment is apt:

> We are, of course, dealing for the most part with poetry, and some allowance must certainly be made for conventional literary motifs; but it is surely inconceivable that descriptions of this kind, some of which are in considerable detail, can have been wholly imaginary. The assumption must be that the villas in question existed, and the absence in the descriptions of any suggestion that they were exceptional must also be significant. (Percival 1976, p. 171 f.)

In an even more overtly literary description of another house, the Burgus of Pontius Leontius, other influences combine to produce an entirely different picture. (Sid. Carm 22.) Here the emphasis is on strength and security, both natural and artificial. Inside, it is true, are all the traditional comforts...but the feel of the place is different, and we seem to be in a different world."

Percival elsewhere proposes a plausible solution to this apparent incongruity: "So striking, indeed, is the contrast that one wonders, even from so few examples, whether an overall pattern can nevertheless be derived. It would be something as follows: Sidonius' Avitacum represents the survival of the traditional villa.... The Burgus, on the other hand, represents a new style.... In other words, if a villa survived into the fifth century, with its amenities intact or restorable, you might as well persevere with it and let it take its chance.... The idea of a change of this kind in the style and siting of villas is supported by a foreshadowing of it in a number of sites in the fourth century." (Percival 1992, p. 158.)

So important was this aspect of the *fundus* (villa or estate) that peasants tend to be referred to by formulae such as *coloni* of a particular fortified villa. Some landowners obtained imperial rescripts allowing them to collect the taxes from their estates themselves, a custom that came to be known as *autopractorium*, and was outlawed in a strongly worded edict of 409. (CTh 11.22.4.) Though addressed to Anthemius, praetorian prefect of the East, this practice no doubt existed in the West as well.

To this day, many towns and villages in Western Europe bear the names of owners of such self-contained *praedia* (estates, manor houses). (See Dauzat 1926, p. 112 ff.) Their size, fortifications, and social and economic self-sufficiency made the large estates resemble towns, and their owners tended to be placed on a par with municipal councils. People would confuse *civitates* ("cities") and *possessiones* ("estates"), and had to be reminded of the different titles for the administrative hierarchies in the two types of units: *ordines civitatum, sed procuratores possessionum.* (Victor Vitensis: Pers. Vand. 3.11.) Even the imperial government reluctantly recognized the power of the landowner within his estate. (CTh 16.2.31 (398) Milan.)

How much survival was there of such estates after the end of the Western Empire? Some interesting, if indecisive, evidence comes from France, where place-names ending in *–acum* or *–ville* are thought to point to prior Roman villas or estates around which settlements clustered and were later buried beneath them. This is based on the aerial surveys of the Somme basin published by Roger Agache, who suggested that some modern villages appear to overlie Roman villas. (Agache 1973; Percival 1992, p. 156ff.; Dauzat 1926.)

Peasants, Free and Unfree

Agricultural slaves were still abundant during the later Empire though it is not known how their numbers compared with those of *coloni* (free peasants). The gap between the relative status of the two groups was closing. As A.H.M. Jones put it: "While agricultural slaves rose to the status of serfs, free tenants gradually sank to a similar status." (Jones 1964, p. 795 f.) The idea, which is sometimes scouted, that the term *colonus* (plural, *coloni*) was an invention of Diocletian's, is completely wrong. *Colonus* is a classical Latin word, found in Cato the Elder's *De Re Rustica*, Varro, Cicero, and Vergil, among others in the sense of "cultivator of the soil, farmer," and especially "tenant farmer."

Agricultural workers could be either free tenant farmers or slaves, though it was only in Italy and Spain that slaves appear to have been particularly numerous. And even in Italy large estates were evidently worked chiefly by free *coloni*. As mentioned above, as the status of agricultural slaves rose, that of free *coloni* gradually declined. A law of Constantine dating from 332 tied *coloni* to the land. (CTh 5.17.1.) But

A.H.M. Jones believed that this occurred as a "by-product" of Diocletian's census and tax system. (Jones 1958, pp. 1–13; Jones 1964, p. 1327, n. 61.) This development foreshadowed what came to be called serfdom. This approximation of the status of free *coloni* to that of slaves is reflected in the terminology, the word *serf* itself being a Middle French version of Latin *servus* (slave).

Jones divides tenant farmers in the sixth century into three classes:

- *Adscripticii* (tenants registered in the census): A hereditary class of tenants chiefly descended from tied tenants registered in Diocletian's census. These were "...serfs, scarcely distinguishable from agricultural slaves." (Jones 1964, p. 801.) Two subdivisions of it were *originales* (or *originarii*), referring to tenants tied to the land of their birth: and *inquilini*, meaning cottagers domiciled on an estate who were not lessees.
- *Coloni*: Another hereditary class tied to the land for at least thirty years but of free status, meaning that they could even become the proprietors of their own land.
- Free men: Men who had short leases and so had the right of freedom of movement.

The Changing Economy

A master's power over his *coloni* was great, and a *colonus* who left the estate to which he was attached was guilty of a serious crime (CTh 5.17.1.1 332.) While binding *coloni* to the estates on which they had been born, this law, issued by Constantine in 332, nevertheless makes a clear distinction between *coloni* and slaves, and uses the threat to deprive *coloni* of their freedom as a deterrent against the abuse which it wishes to combat. Not surprisingly, the problem of *coloni fugitivi* was not solved by this constitution, which is only the first of a series of laws on the subject. (CTh 5. 17 & 18.) It is worth noting how the distinction between *coloni* and *servi*, which could be used as the basis of a threat in 332, had largely disappeared even by 365. Whether the distinction between *coloni* and *servi* meant anything in practical terms in 332 is not known, but by 365, even the law is well on its way to regarding *coloni* as slaves: "There is no doubt that *coloni* do not have the right to alienate the fields that they cultivate, to the extent that even if they have any belongings of their own, they may not transfer them to others without the advice and knowledge of their patrons" (CTh 5.19.1 365.) (On patrons, see below.)

A law addressed to Nebridius, proconsul of Asia in 396–397, actually uses the word *peculium*, a term traditionally associated with slaves, instead of the *propria* (possessions, belongings) of the law quoted above. (CJ 11.50.2.) The subordination of the *colonus* to his master, whose title, *dominus*, was also the traditional title of the slave-owner, was now complete.

The whole issue of landholding is complicated by the fact that for the majority of his estates the owner would be an absentee landlord. Does this mean that such estates were spared the development that I have been describing? Not at all.

On the favorite estate of a landowner, all life might well revolve around him, and he might spend very little time away from it, as was the case with Sidonius's Gallic friends in the fifth century. But this was obviously not the case on all *fundi*. For the most part, the estate proprietor was an absentee landlord, leaving the *coloni* to the tender mercies of a *procurator* ("agent") or *conductor* ("short-term lessee.") (On the management of estates, see Jones, A.H.M., 1964, pp. 788–92.)

As mentioned above, by no means all landowners were noble. Churches owned increasing amounts of land—and even individual bishops and lower clergy, as we know from a petition to Constantius II from clerical landowners for exemption from land tax. Their plea was curtly rejected by the Emperor, who specifically ordered the praetorian prefect to see to it that clerics were "compelled to pay taxes for the estates which they personally own." (CTh 16.2.15–360.)

Though the amount of land owned by absentee landowners was great and growing, peasant proprietors still continued to exist, albeit in declining numbers. Squeezed between what Jones terms "the inexorable demands of the tax collector," natural disasters and invasion, peasant freeholders would often resort to seeking the patronage of a powerful local personage. (Jones 1964, p. 775.) There is a good deal of legislation against patronage in the East. In the West we have the rantings of Salvian, which, though obviously grossly exaggerated, undoubtedly contain a kernel of truth, namely the oppression of peasants at the hands of rapacious patrons. In the fifth century, the central imperial government in the West was weak and indeed under the control of the very aristocratic class who themselves benefited from patronage, a topic to which I turn a little later on in this chapter.

We discern, then, an unmistakable tendency for estates to become self-contained social and economic entities, and also for their owners to spend more time on them than before. That this was so can be seen from mosaics, such as that of Julius at Carthage, mentioned above, depicting the *dominus* dispensing justice to his *coloni*. (A. Merlin 1921.)

The law of 356 fixing the quorum for meetings of the Senate at fifty was, like so many other laws, probably a reaction to events rather than a positive blueprint—reactive rather than proscriptive—and in this case the cause must surely have been the decline of the number of senators present in Rome. (CTh 6.4.9.) Similarly, the fifth-century law allowing senators to live wherever they pleased without leave (*sine commeatu*) must again be seen as a recognition rather than as an anticipation of the fact that many senators preferred not to live in Rome though legally obliged to do so. (CJ 12.1.15–undated. Dated by Seeck to between 426 and 442. *Regesten*, p. 137.*)* Indeed two laws of 354 and one of 395 had already implicitly recognized the new state of affairs in this regard, the earlier ones by their insistence that senators come to Rome to sponsor games for their traditional Republican magistracies, and the latter by the distinction between *senatores qui in sacratissima urbe consistent, licet habeant per longinquas provincias atque diversas possessiones* and those *qui in provinciis larem fovent.* (CTh 6.4.4–354; manuscripts 339); CTh 6.4.7—manuscripts 353, Seeck, pp. 42–354; CTh 6.2.16–395.) Though all those who had Roman residences also had estates elsewhere, there were evidently some who had no Roman abode at all.

This is what we have on the one hand, centrifugal forces at work; but that is not to say that those nobles who lived permanently in the provinces were out of touch with Rome, which, as we can see from Symmachus's letters, was still very much the social center of aristocratic life. And even later on, when travel became more difficult and large areas were lost to the Empire, contact was not altogether broken. Rutilius Namatianus, who wrote in the early fifth century, is himself a good example of such contact. His poem deals with his return from Rome to his ravaged estates in Gaul. Both he and his father held office in Italy. He himself had been *magister officiorum* and subsequently urban prefect, and his father Lachanius had been consular of Tuscia and Umbria, *comes sacrarum largitionum, quaestor sacri palatii*, and finally prefect, though of what sort is not known. (Rut. Nam. De Red. 1.561ff; 1.156ff.; 1.575ff.) Though Lachanius was probably not a noble, his son had close contacts with the high aristocracy of Italy, apparently through office. His friend Albinus, whom he visited at Volaterrae on his way home and who succeeded him as urban prefrct, was a member of the *gens Ceionia*, his full name being Caecina Decius Aginatius Albinus. Another member of that family with whom he was friendly was Rufius Antonius Agrypnius Volusianus, whom he congratulates on his urban prefecture in 417 and whose father Albinus, no doubt Ceionius Rufius Albinus, urban prefect 389–91, Namatianus also seems to have known. (Rut. Nam. 1.466ff.; 1.421ff.; 1.167ff.)In addition to the Ceionii, Namatianus had some contact with the Valerii, in particular Valerius Messalla, probably the praetorian prefect of the last years of the fourth century, *"primo de consule"*, literally "from the first consul," a (probably fictitious) claim of descent from the P. Valerius Publicola who was a founder of the Roman Republic and consul in 509 BCE. (Rut. Nam. 1.268ff.) If these were the contacts of a rank outsider, as Namatianus would have been, with the inner circle of Roman aristocrats, we can gain some impression of the degree of contact within it, at least throughout the West.

Even in the latter half of the fifth century, if the evidence of Sidonius Apollinaris is anything to go on, the senatorial aristocracy of Gaul had not yet lost touch with Italy. Sidonius himself was married to the daughter of Avitus, praetorian prefect of the Gauls and later emperor, who was on friendly terms with Theoderic, the Germanic king of Italy. Sidonius himself was made prefect of Rome by the Emperor Anthemius in 468. (Sid. Ap. Carm 2.)

So much, then, for nobles as owners of landed estates. We now turn to the relationship between office and landholding.

Land and Office

M. Ceionius Julianus *signo* Kamenius, urban prefect 333–334, was patron *a parentibus* of Bulla Regia in modern Tunisia, the designation *a parentibus* indicating that it was hereditary. (CIL VIII. 25525.) Similarly, Valerius Publicola, probably to be identified with the urban prefect of around 375 who was the son of Melania the Elder, husband of Ceionia Albina and father of Melania the Younger, is described in a dedicatory statue as *ab atavis* (by descent from his ancestors) patron of Beneventum (CIL IX. 1591). Similarly, Postumius Lampadius, urban prefect between 403 and 408 (CIL VI. 9920) and in 409 praetorian prefect of Italy under the usurper Priscus Attalus, is described in a dedicatory statue base in Capua as *patronus longe a maioribus originalis* (patron by descent through long ancestry) (CIL X. 3860 = ILS 1276; CIL X. 1704; PLRE2–Lampadius 7). Terms indicating hereditary patronage should not surprise us. It was standard practice to grant patronage to a man and his heirs in perpetuity.

What is noteworthy is that all three men were also governors of the provinces where their client communities were situated, and that none of these men was the only member of his family to govern the province concerned. Is it fanciful to infer from this fact that family interests existed in the localities concerned? What Ammianus tells us of Petronius Probus, namely that his main objective in entering government service was to further the interests of his family and dependents, (Amm. 27.11.1) may well also be true on a smaller scale of other nobles, and how better to further those interests than by holding government office in the same locality as one's family estates, or at least some of them?

Second only to Italy as a favorite area for combining land and office was Africa. The Aradii, for example, had a longstanding link with Bulla Regia and Thuburbo, going back to the early third century. In the fourth century, not only were both Quintus and Lucius Aradius Proculus (whom we met in Chapter 3) governors of Byzacena, in Africa, but Lucius, whose full name was L. Aradius Valerius Proculus *signo* Populonius went on to become proconsul and vicar of Africa (CIL VI. 1690 = ILS 1240). There were two other Proculi who were proconsuls of Africa, one in 319 and the other in 340, both no doubt members of the *gens Aradia*, which was related by marriage to the Ceionii. (See Stemma I in Arnheim 1972.) The Ceionii themselves had family ties with Numidia, another African province, four of whose 24 consulars known in the fourth century being members of that noble house. Similarly, thirteen, or more than a fifth of the proconsuls of Africa known in the fourth century, were Anicii, Ceionii, or collaterals, as were five of the ten noble vicars of Africa: C. Annius Tiberianus (325–7–CTh 12.5.1), Petronius (340–CTh 2.6.5), Virius Nicomachus Flavianus (377–CIL VI. 1782–3 = ILS 2947–8), Faltonius Probus Alypius (378–CIL VI.1185 = ILS 783), and Alfenius Ceionius Julianus *signo* Kamenius (381–ILS 1264).

It is hardly accidental that those provinces that tended to be governed by nobles in the fourth century were also the provinces noted for aristocratic landholding. The Italian, African, and Spanish provinces in particular fall into this category. Although Gaul, another favorite area for noble estates, was not often governed by nobles at provincial level and never at diocesan level so far as our records go, there were noble "praetorian prefects of the Gauls" in the fifth century.

It was also in Italy, Africa and Spain that the first governors called *consulares* were created by Constantine, a designation that may well have been introduced to pander to aristocratic pride, which turned its nose up at the all too equestrian title *praeses*. Appointment to a province such as Campania or Numidia would enable the office-holder to safeguard any family estates in that area and to add to them. Petronius Probus, according to Ammianus, was like a fish out of water when not in office as praetorian prefect, appointment to which he was actually compelled (*cogebatur*) to seek "...because of the constant lawlessness of certain families which on account of their boundless avarice were never free from guilt, and in order to carry out their many evil designs with impunity, plunged their patron into affairs of state." (Amm. 27.11.3) The reading here is in doubt, but the implication would appear to be that Petronius Probus was impelled to seek high office in order to defend his clients, which he evidently did regardless of the merits of their case. And the number of appointments, favors and recommendation of which a praetorian prefect could dispose must have been immense.

Ammianus describes Probus as "...carried on the swift wings...of a kind of congenital good fortune, which showed him to be now generous and ready to advance his friends, but sometimes a cruel schemer, working harm by his deadly jealousies. And although he had great power as long as he lived, because of the sums that he gave away and his constant resumption of offices, yet he was sometimes timid when boldly confronted, though arrogant against those who feared him; so that in his moments of confidence he seemed to thunder from tragic buskins, and when he was afraid, to be more humble than any wearer of the slipper." (Amm. 27.11.2. All translations of Ammianus are by John C. Rolfe, Loeb Classical Library, 1939.)

There was a general ban on purchases while in office, of land, houses, or slaves, and this was applicable to all office-holders irrespective of rank. This prohibition first appears under Constantine in 334 (CTh 8.15.1.), and the same rule is reiterated in laws of 364, 365, and 397, a sign that the imperial government was experiencing some difficulty in eliminating this offense. (CTh 8.15.3, 4 and 8.) In the year 451, Valentinian III, Emperor of the West, issued a law removing this ban, falsely claiming it was merely a reiteration of an earlier law issued by Honorius. (NVal. 32.1.) Valentinian's "novel" is phrased in such a way as to imply that it had never been illegal for office-holders to make purchases while in office, which is probably a tactical face-saving device. It is hardly irrelevant to note that the reign of Valentinian III (423–55) saw a succession of praetorian prefects of Italy whose names were representative of the noblest houses of the age: Flavius Anicius Auchenius Bassus, Rufius Antonius Agrypnius Volusianus, Caecina Decius Aginatius Albinus, Anicius Acilius Glabrio Faustus., Nicomachus Flavianus, Petronius Maximus. In these circumstances, it is difficult not to see the revocation of the ban on purchases as a result of noble pressure.

Another example of the influence stemming from office is furnished by a constitution of 380 dealing with betrothal gifts made by provincial governors. (CTh3.6.1.) The law contrives to protect families forced into an alliance with a high official against their will. Not only are they entitled to break off the betrothal with impunity, but they can also retain the official's betrothal gift.

A creditor wishing to hasten payment of a debt could resort to transferring the debt to a powerful man. The fact that the *potens* now appeared as the creditor was evidently sufficient to have the desired effect. This practice was outlawed by a law of 422, the penalty being the loss of the debt. (CTh2.13.1.) So successful was this sort of ploy that the name of a powerful man might be used in litigation even when he had not in fact given his consent. (CTh 2.14.1–400.)

Another sphere in which influence could prove efficacious was in evading taxation. The difficulty of collecting taxes from senators in general is well demonstrated by the imperial contortions in a vain effort to extract money from these errant subjects. Decurions were no doubt cowed or bribed by the great magnates, and the duty of collecting taxes from senators was transferred from them at an unknown date to members of governors' officials. But, in 397, the task reverted to the decurions. We do not have to read between the lines, easy enough though it would be to do so; we are told in a 397 law that in some provinces only half of the senatorial taxes had been paid. (CTh 6.3.4.)

In 399, the praetorian prefect of Gaul received a constitution abolishing all grants of *beneficia* (favors) to landowners. (CTh 11.1.26.) Though we are not told what form these *beneficia* took, we can only infer from the law that they were some form of tax exemption or reduction extended by the emperor to certain landowners, presumably those who had contacts at court. The law is probably a reference to *ad hominem* awards from the emperor, because seven years later we have a hint that *illustres* (the highest senatorial rank) were in a privileged position as regards taxes. A constitution of 406 addressed to the praetorian prefect of the East, Anthemius, decrees that the daughters of the Emperor (Arcadius) *tantum inlustribus privilegiis ac debitis potiantur* in the amount of tax that they should be required to pay on their land. (CTh 10.25.1.)

A powerful man could use his influence to ease not only his own tax burden but also that of others. Such a man would evidently sometimes take a tradesman under his wing and, no doubt for a share of his profits, help him to evade payment of the *collatio lustralis* (a tax imposed on all those engaged in trade). (CTh 13.1.1–2.) Though there is no evidence of how the protector set about shielding his protégé from the *fiscus*, we can assume that, as in other matters, personal influence was the decisive factor. It was of course the loss of imperial revenue that prompted Theodosius I to issue a law against this practice. (CTh 13.1.15–386.)

The influence of the powerful can also be seen in the earlier imperial decrees of Valentinian and Valens instituting *defensores civitatum* or *defensores plebis*. The new officials, who were to protect the lower classes *contra potentium iniurias* (against the wrongs of the powerful), were to be drawn from among former governors, barristers, *agentes in rebus*, and *principes* of the *officium* of prefects or vicars, while other officials and decurions were explicitly debarred. (CTh 1.29.1 364; CTh 1.29.3.) It is not difficult to account for the emperors' choice of *defensores*. All of these were either high-ranking officials, or, as in the case of the *palatine*, came to the locations concerned from the imperial court and were, therefore, much more influential than ordinary officials attached to governors' *officia*. The choice of *agentes in rebus* may have been prompted by their "secret service" activities. (Aur. Victor Caes.

39.44; CTh 6.29.4; See Jones 1964, 581 f.) And the exclusion of decurions is attributable to the fact that they themselves were among those needing protection. (See CTh 1.29.7.) In all, then, and not surprisingly, the choice of Valentinian for his new post fell on those office-holders who he thought would be most efficacious in protecting the *plebeii*.

But who were the *potentes* against whom the *defensores* were to extend their protection? The term was identified by Hoepffner with "the senatorial aristocracy." He admits that later emperors regarded the function of the *defensores* as protecting the humble against imperial officials, but he sees this as a change in the purpose of the institution. (Hoepffner, p. 226 ff. But cf. Harmand, p. 464 f.) Yet from a letter of 365 from Valentinian to a certain Seneca, evidently a *defensor*, it is clear that at least one of his functions was to act as a judge of first instance, deciding minor cases and referring more serious ones to the provincial governor. (CTh 9.2.2.) This does not conflict with later laws on the subject, and at least one of them shows how important it must have been for the poorer and humbler elements of society to have cheap or free access to the courts, since justice tended otherwise to be a very expensive luxury. (See CTh 1.16 on the venality of officials.) A law of 392 is instructive, in which Theodosius calls upon the *defensores* to remove *patrocinia quae favorem reis et auxilium scelerosis inpertiendo maturari scelera fecerunt* (those patronages which, by bestowing favors on the guilty and assistance to criminals have resulted in the growth of criminality). (CTh 1.29.8.) As so many patrons, in the West at least, were nobles, as we have seen, this law must be seen as aimed against them in that regard.

A very real advantage that noble office-holders had over their non-noble colleagues was an elaborate interlocking skein of relationships and family connections. (See *Stemmata* in Arnheim 1972, p. 247 ff.) All the major aristocratic families were connected with one another to greater or lesser extent. Marriages tended to be within the same aristocratic magic circle. This would tend to have knitted together the various noble houses into a more united social stratum, which it was not easy for an outsider to penetrate though Symmachus himself was only the second or third noble generation of his family. This interrelated network also served as a conduit of communication and influence.

The fact that nobles were prone, with or without justification, to claim descent from aristocratic figures of the Republic is itself an indication that this period, in common with most others, was one of aristocratic values. Lineage and birth were accorded exaggerated respect, another advantage that aristocratic officeholders had over their non-noble colleagues. The esteem for noble birth evinced even by Christian religious leaders like Jerome is no doubt a reflection of a common popular attitude that pervaded society. (See for example Epp. 54.2; 107.1; 108.1.)

There was even an aristocratic view of justice, as expressed, for example, by Symmachus, who as urban prefect in 384–5 would have had largely judicial functions. Symmachus acknowledged the need for fairness in judicial proceedings, "...but when it comes to nobles and respectable people there ought to be more moderation." (Symmachus Ep. 9.40.) It is instructive to find such blatant bias as a principle of justice on the part of a man who can be taken without much hesitation as a representative spokesman for his class though it is worth noting that his definition of justice privileges not only the aristocracy but also *probabiles personae*, an amorphous category of "respectable" people.

This aristocratic view of justice does not square with that held, for example, by Constantine, who, not surprisingly, regarded with no great favor the overmighty subject who attempted to pervert the ends of justice. A law of 328 instructs provincial governors to report to the praetorian prefect or to the emperor himself, any such person whom they were unable to punish or who disrupted the proceedings of a case. (CTh 1.16.4.) Whether such *insolentiores potiores* were nobles is not known, but, as their methods were evidently bribery and largess rather than armed force and violence, it is highly likely that they at least included some nobles. (See CTh 1.16.6.) The Emperor Julian, on the other hand, issued a law in 362 to protect the rights of senators and the authority of the senatorial order *in quo nos quoque ipsos esse numeramus* (in which we number ourselves). (CTh 9.2.1.) The law goes on to give senators immunity from arrest until convicted. Three years later, however, Valentinian decreed that judges should refer to the emperor "...either the merit of the case or the status of the person concerned," but that in the meantime, anyone suspected of a crime should be arrested "...whatever honor he may be said to hold." (CTh 9.2.2.) This is hardly surprising in an emperor who was a sincere and dedicated champion of the *laesi minores* (oppressed lower orders). (On Valentinian's hostility to nobles see Amm 30.8.10. For his predilection for Pannonians and policy on appointments, see Chapter 4. The term *laesi minores* occurs in a Constantinian law of 328: CTh 1.16.4.)

In an age in which bribery and corruption were as rife as the Theodosian Code reveals, wealth was obviously a factor of great importance in exerting influence. So venal do governors appear to have been in their capacity as judges that they were forbidden to receive visitors from their own provinces in the afternoon. (CTh 1.16.13 377.) It is hardly surprising that in so deferential and hierarchical a society the clarissimate should carry with it certain privileges. In addition to negative privileges, such as immunity from curial duties, senatorial rank accorded its holders positive influence and is specifically mentioned, for example, in a law of 400 dealing with the illicit use of *tituli potentium* in court cases. (CTh 2.14.1. See Jones 1964, p. 535 ff.)

Another example of such influence is to be found in a Novel of Theodosius II, which shows that the clarissimate still had sufficient aura to swing the result of a court action. (NovTheod. 15.1.2 439.) But, when added to official status, lineage and family connections greatly augmented the influence wielded by a man of senatorial rank.

By the latter half of the fifth century, rank, office, and lineage had also come to play a role in ecclesiastical appointments. For example, on being asked to recommend a bishop for the See of Bituriges (previously Avaricum, now Bourges), Sidonius Apollinaris admitted that two candidates were "rightly" thought superior to his own choice because they were *illustres*. (Sid. Ap. Ep. 7.9.18.)

Membership of the Senate still counted for something in this period. But to place beside evidence of the influence of the clarissimate we have examples of senators suffering at the hands of people below them in the social scale. However, it is worth noting that all the laws in the Theodosian Code dealing with *defensores senatus* are from the East, no doubt a reflection of the fact that senators of Constantinople, mostly new men, generally lacked the clout that their Western counterparts had owing to their much greater wealth and family connections. (CTh 6.3.2 396; CTh 1.28.1-4.) The number of nobles appointed to office in the East was very small by comparison with the West, and most of those appointed to Eastern positions were actually Westerners, men such as Q. Clodius Hermogenianus Olybrius (CIL VI. 1714 = ILS 1271), Postumianus (CTh 9.42.10), Vettius Agorius Praetextatus (CIL VI.1779 = ILS 1259), Maecius Memmius Caecilianus Placidus (CIL X. 1700 = ILS 1231), and Vulcacius Rufinus (CIL VI.32051 = ILS 1237), the first two of whom were praetorian prefects of the East, the third proconsul of Achaea, and the last two *comites Orientis*.

It was in the West that the large estates of the senatorial aristocracy were concentrated, and Eastern senators were more likely to have been poorer than their Western brethren. Also, the Eastern Senate seems to have been made up of self-made men with no elaborate family connections or long-established local position. (See Zos. 3.12; Jones 1964, 133 f., 551 ff.)

The advantages attaching to senatorial rank and the much greater benefits accruing to the holders of high office were, of course, far from the monopoly of the aristocracy. But nobles had the added advantage of wealth and intricate family networks, which served to conduct the influence of nobles in office to those living in retirement on their estates. For, of all the sources of influence, office was undoubtedly the most important, and the emperor's ear the most valuable commodity in the Empire, as can be seen, for example, in the successful appeals of Praetextatus to Valentinian. (Amm. 28.1.11; Zos. 4.3.) The addition of office to the previous amalgam of birth and wealth gave the senatorial aristocracy a more potent compound than was possessed by any other element of the civil population.

Patronage

Patronage, *patrocinium*, or *clientela*, was one of the oldest features of Roman society, going back to the Republic if not before. It was a relationship between two men, usually of unequal status. The patron (*patronus*) would offer his client (*cliens*) protection, including legal representation, and in return the client would be expected to support the patron politically and in other respects.

It is already encountered in the comedies of Plautus (c. 254–184 BCE), where we find patrons always eager to add to their stable of clients. How important a role *clientela* played in Republican elections is disputed, with Fergus Millar rejecting the widely held view that it was of central importance. Both extreme positions probably need to be modified.

During the Principate, the emperor was *pater patriae* (father of the fatherland) and liked to portray himself as protector of the lower orders, and especially of the *plebs urbana*, the masses of Rome. Members of the senatorial aristocracy had to tread carefully in attracting a personal following of clients, and the system became formalized, with a throng of clients lining up to pay their respects to their patron in the morning—*salutatio*—and, in return, receiving a small parcel of provisions or money, the *sportula* (small basket), as satirically portrayed in the writings of Juvenal and Martial.

Starting out as a relationship between two individuals, patronage could also extend to a relationship between a powerful man and a whole community. Both the individual and communal forms of patronage were very much in evidence during the late imperial period.

In this period, the landowner was the natural patron of his *coloni*, but where he was an absentee landlord or a man of no great influence, the *coloni* had to look elsewhere for protection against the imperial government, and particularly against tax-collectors. Our main evidence of this *patrocinium vicorum* comes to us from the Theodosian Code, Justinian's Code, and from Libanius (314–394), the Antiochene orator, who attacked the practice in a most impassioned address to the emperor. (CTh 11.24; CJ 11.54. Libanius, *Or.* 47.) There is no shortage of laws against patronage, all of them from the eastern part of the Empire, and Libanius is also concerned solely with that part of the world. But that is not to say that patronage of villages was confined to the East, and we do not entirely lack Western evidence of it, thanks to Salvian's mid-fourth-century *De Gubernatione Dei*. Though this emotive tract is far from being a systematic exposition of the workings of this form of patronage in the West, it does serve to characterize the Western brand as rather different in kind from the Eastern.

In the East, the patron was very often a military man. Perhaps the best example is Libanius's dispute with some of his own tenants, who enlisted the aid of their patron, a *stratēgos* (Greek for "general"), presumably the local *dux* (provincial military commander). After receiving a variety of gifts from his clients, the patron secured a favorable outcome for them. (Libanius, Or. 47.13-17.) We must not forget that what we have here is the testimony of the embittered loser. But even so, the influence of a patron of this kind is not difficult to believe, and the evidence of the learned rhetorician, written from the point of view of an indignant landlord who has been cheated of his natural right, is corroborated by imperial constitutions written from the point of view of a government defrauded of its rightful dues.

The imperial government's concern about loss of taxes appears explicitly in a law of 399: CTh 11.24.4. A law of 360 addressed by Constantius II to the praetorian prefect of the East and referring specifically to Egypt explains the cause for imperial concern over the patronage of *coloni*. We learn here that patrons were generally men of high rank, *duces* being singled out for special mention. (CTh 11.24.1.) A later constitution gives a more detailed array of the guilty, showing that, even in the East, holders of illicit patronage were not necessarily military men. (CTh 11.24.4 399.)

Military patrons were evidently less prevalent in the West. Though Salvian focuses his attention largely on the peasants who lose their property and become *coloni* in the service of the *maiores* (big-wigs), he is not altogether silent on the subject of the patrons. Most of what he has to say about them amounts to a torrent of abuse, but a very clear portrait emerges of them as grasping estate-owners greedy for more land. (Salvian, de Gub. Dei 5.8.34-50.) The province of Syria, where Libanius lived and wrote, was a particularly active one from the military point of view, and there is evidence of a close association between the people of the region and the troops. But it was in the West that *latifundia* were rife, while in the East there were relatively few large estates. It is not difficult to see the attractiveness as a patron of a territorial magnate with influence both locally and centrally. Such were the nobles whom we have already seen as the holders of high imperial appointments and as large landholders.

Those who came under the power of the patrons were not only *coloni adscripticii*, or tenants living on estates owned by others, but also freeholders, some of whom may have owned more than just a patch of land, as the terms *possessores* and *propria possidentes* may indicate. (CTh 11.24.4.)

What a *colonus* sought from his patron was, above all, legal assistance and protection against tax collectors, the most traditional sphere of a patron's activities on behalf of his clients, as we have seen. And there is certainly no lack of evidence of corruption in matters of taxation and judicial proceedings. The main object of the imperial constitutions against the *patrocinium vicorum* (patronage of villages) was to prevent tax evasion, and the law Codes are replete with imperial attacks on the corruption and venality of officials. Patrons took advantage of these traits, and in so doing fostered them.

So much for the peasants' aims in placing themselves under a patron. Whether they obtained what they wanted is a moot point, but those of them who were freeholders tended to lose their property as we learn from the classic statement or overstatement of their case by their champion Salvian. (Salvian 5.8.38ff.)

We are more concerned to view the whole process from the vantage point of the patrons. Their most obvious benefit was financial as can be seen from the second constitution against patronage of this kind. (CTh 11.24.2, dated to 370 in the manuscripts and by Seeck to 368). As a counter-inducement to peasants, the *fiscus* (imperial treasury) would demand only half of what they were accustomed to paying their patrons. (See de Zulueta, 1974, p. 20.) So usual had it become for patrons to receive payment that in later times in the East this due came to be known as *patrokinion*. (CJ 11.54.2.)

Patronage of villages could either benefit or harm the owner of an estate or even do both to the same man at the same time. An absentee landlord might well find his *coloni* in the clientship of a neighboring landowner, while he himself in turn might be the patron of another landowner's *coloni*. The tendency was for the patron to become the owner of property whose tenants were his clients, thus leading to the consolidation of neighboring estates under a single owner and the disappearance of absentee landlords. So common indeed was it for a patron to become the effective owner of an estate whose *coloni* were under his patronage that in 415 the imperial government recognized patrons who had been in this position for eighteen years as the legal owners of the estates concerned while forbidding the practice for the future. (CTh 11.24.6.)

Amicitia

Related to *clientela* were *amicitia* (friendship or political alliances), and the very ancient *hospitium* (reciprocal guest-friendship, both the English words host and guest are cognate with Latin hospes, meaning host or guest.)

Amicitia was usefully applied by skilful Roman nobles like Symmachus to smooth over relations with the "barbarians." This was no easy task. Symmachus's Christian nemesis over the Altar of Victory, Prudentius (348–c. 413), reflected the usual sneering attitude of upper-class Romans to the "barbarians" by likening them to four-footed animals. (Contra Symmachum, 2.816–817.) Sidonius Apollinaris, similarly, mocked the "barbarians" for dressing in animal skins, and being unwashed and illiterate. (Ep. 1.7.6; 2.1.2; 5.5.3.)

In an interesting analysis, Michele Salzman concludes:

> [T]he culture and language of late Roman *amicitia* was exceptionally useful for building social ties across the Roman/barbarian divide. Analysis of Symmachus's letters to the barbarian generals Stilicho (4.1–14), Richomeres (3.54–69), and Bauto (4.15–16) reveals how the language of *amicitia* smoothed over tensions and made it possible to ignore the 'barbarian' difference.... In the letters to Stilicho there is nothing to suggest the non-Roman origins or culture of this extremely powerful general. However, Symmachus's Letters to Bauto (Ep. 4.15-16) and two of his letters to Richomeres (Ep 3.59 and 61) are different. In both instances Symmachus calls attention to a failure of etiquette on the part of these two powerful generals. In establishing himself as the *arbiter amicitiae*, Symmachus demonstrates his cultured superiority to these men of non-Roman origins. At the same time, Symmachus defended his reputation and reasserted his influence.... Symmachus's letters to Bauto and Richomeres convey a carefully coded criticism of these two powerful non-Roman generals. (Salzman 2006b, pp. 352–67.)

Medieval Survival

Ernst Badian gives us this bird's eye view of the history of Roman patronage:

> The patronage of Roman individuals and families over cities, kings, and nations—inseparable from the Roman *Weltanschauung* and soon embodying kindred Greek and barbarian notions in its pattern—supplements and cements the empire of the expanding Roman city-state, even while (in the last age of the Republic) threatening to demolish it by rival systems of allegiance; in the *clientelae* of the Principate it combines with other methods of control into the very structure of the new state, while the *clientelae* of private citizens, politically neutralised, continue to perform an important social and economic task in the smooth running of the Empire; finally, surviving the decay of the Imperial organisation that restrained them, they emerge in undreamt-of triumph as one of the bases of the feudal system and thus of modern Europe. (Badian 1958, Review of Harmand 1957, pp. 774–7.)

Is Badian right to portray the *clientela* system as surviving the end of the Western Empire and emerging "...in undreamt-of triumph as one of the bases of the feudal system"? The importance of *clientela* or patronage in the late Roman Empire is not in doubt, as we have seen, and a combination of literary and archaeological evidence points to its survival, particularly in post-imperial Gaul and Africa as well. But is Badian's leap to "the feudal system" and "modern Europe" a bridge too far? "Feudal" has now become something of a taboo word, but Badian's point does not depend on that term. Were Badian writing today, he might say simply that patronage survived in one form or another into the Middle Ages, which ultimately gave rise to modern Europe. Put that way, his proposition has a claim to some validity.

The debate over "feudalism" has not abated, and it affects one's understanding of the whole nature of politics, society, and the economy of Western Europe, particularly between roughly 750 and 1200. A 1974 article by Elizabeth Brown, followed by a book by Susan Reynolds published twenty years later, succeeded in upsetting the apple cart of "feudalism," which had been a mainstay of historical writing for 200 years. (Elizabeth Brown 1974; Reynolds 1994) "I am not much concerned with the labelling exercises that occupy so much scholarly time and effort. My interest is rather in analyzing the substantive issues underlying the labels. But, in order to do so, it is necessary to clear away the terminological jungle that has grown up around not only *feudal* and *feudalism*, but also *vassal* and *fief*, and even *manorial* and *seigniorial*, or *seigneurial*."

Reynolds's denial of the existence of feudalism, until at least the twelfth century (if even then), is based chiefly on the absence of feudal terminology in contemporary documents. Reynolds sums up her position like this:

> Before the twelfth century the law of property, because it was customary law, probably reflected social values fairly well. Yet the standard form of property for nobles and other free men at that time was something more like the common modern idea of 'freehold property' than the modern idea of 'feudal property'. It certainly did not correspond to Weber's ideal type of the fief as a 'service tenement' that is granted in return for services. From the twelfth century on, property law did not reflect social values and social relations nearly so directly. Rulers and professional lawyers, as part of society, shared many of its values, but their interests and methods of work got in the way of reflection. Social values were therefore mediated through particular political and legal cultures. Yet it was in this period that the noble fief and the feudal pyramid or feudal hierarchy of tenure that came to be considered the keystones of feudalism became established in anything like the form they are supposed to have had. They were the creation of the stronger, more centralized,

more bureaucratic, and more effective government that developed after the twelfth century and of the professional law that went with it, not of the age of customary law before it. (Ibid., loc 1125–1133)

Though Reynolds's work is quite largely negative in tone, she does tentatively offer a classification of her own. She admits that "Social status was clearly an important determinant of everyone's life chances, including, naturally, the chances of the kind of people whom historians call vassals.... The layers of society were more like those of a trifle than a cake: its layers were blurred, and the sherry of accepted values soaked through." (loc. 610ff.) She suggests a three-fold classification of society (loc. 607–613):

- "The first or top category contained those whom historians generally call nobles—or, in England, nobles and gentry...."
- "The bottom category consisted of the plough-pushers, or rather, more broadly, of those who worked with their hands and bodies, owed rents and services to the top group, and could generally be described as more or less unfree peasants."
- "In between came another category that probably included a sizable proportion of the population. By and large these people did not actually push ploughs themselves, but they were more closely concerned with getting their own livings than the first group and supervised their own plough-pushers more directly." (loc. 607–613.)

This rather vague classification is intentionally purely economic, tying in with Reynolds's idea that, as quoted above, "...the standard form of property...was something more like the common modern idea of 'freehold property'...." I have to say that I am not persuaded of this, any more than of Reynolds's suggestion that feudalism, when it did eventually arrive, was the product of centralized, bureaucratic government coupled with "professional law." I give my reasons for disagreeing with her later in this chapter.

Surprisingly, perhaps, Chris Wickham, who has Marxist leanings, appears to agree with Susan Reynolds in certain respects, opining as he does that, "Historians who suppose that the break-up of the Roman world was to the benefit of aristocracies are wrong; in no case did they increase their prosperity. Indeed, in some places they lost wealth dramatically: most notably in the 'senatorial region' of southern Italy and the Rome-Carthage axis of the great families of late imperial Rome, which was destroyed by the regionalization of the Mediterranean." (Wickham 2006, p. 256.) Yet, his conclusion is that "...to an extent... the major shifts in the post-Roman aristocracies of Europe and the Mediterranean... mark continuities rather than change; in particular, at the level of cities and city-territories, the parameters of aristocratic power very largely remained as they were." (Ibid., p. 258.)

In a 1984 article, Wickham unabashedly asserted that "...feudalism already existed in 300 AD," and that this had become the dominant "mode of production" by the year 700. (Wickham 1984, pp. 3–36.) Mode of production is of course a typically Marxist buzzword. But was Chris Wickham here treating "feudalism" as a purely economic relationship, a restricted meaning that it did not usually have, even for Marxists? In *The Communist Manifesto*, written by Marx and Engels themselves, we read, "In the earlier epochs of history, we find almost everywhere a complicated arrangement of society into various orders, a manifold gradation of social rank... in the Middle Ages, feudal lords, vassals, guild-masters, journeymen, apprentices, serfs; in almost all of these classes, again, subordinate gradations." (Communist Manifesto, p. 14.) Central as the "mode of production" (or "means of production") is to Marxists, it is seen as the basis of political and social, as well as economic, power.

In a more recent incarnation, Wickham stresses this point:

> The dynamics of the lord-peasant relationship underlay not only all medieval economic history but all socio-political history too; it under-pinned the sharpness of the boundaries of social stratification and it made possible the whole politics of land...." (Wickham 2016, p. 66.) This strong assertion is based on the following: "Medieval political communities based their coherence and their success on the control of the land.... The reason is simple: all pre-industrial societies are based on agricultural wealth above all....But who was it that controlled land and its produce?" (p. 62ff.). "In some cases," he points out, "it was the peasants themselves," particularly in northern and eastern Europe between 500 and 1000 "But much of Europe was always owned by non-peasants: landowners who lived, and were prosperous, because they took rent from peasant tenant-cultivators. (Wage labour on the land was very rare before 1200.) Such landowners made up the aristo-cratic élites of Europe, the militarised lords whose loyalty (or not) to kings we have just discussed, and also the great churches—lands owned by churches could be as much as a third of the total land-area of kingdoms. Kings were themselves landowners, and their resources were, too, unless they taxed, overwhelmingly from the land they owned directly. (p. 62ff.)

Continuity or Change in the West?

Continuity or change? Here are a few points in response to Reynolds and Wickham:

- Reynolds's suggestion that property holding in the early Middle Ages was akin to modern freehold appears most unlikely.

- This ties in with her idea that economic relations were quite separate from socio-political ones, which is not very plausible, and there is some evidence against it. See below.
- Reynold's idea that feudalism, when it did finally appear, was the product of strong centralized, bureaucratic government is also not at all likely. Political power is a zero-sum game. The more powerful the king is, the less powerful the aristocracy and *vice versa*. This is the pattern in every society that I have studied (Arnheim 2016). To take an example almost at random, when the French monarchy was at its weakest, the aristocracy was most powerful as during the Fronde of the mid-seventeenth century; and, after Louis XIV strengthened the position of the monarchy, the aristocracy were reduced to social butterflies. (See Chapter 6.)
- Wickham's assertion in 2006 that the aristocracy did not benefit from "...the break-up of the Roman world" is based on their wealth. That may be true, but it does not necessarily mean that the aristocracy lost power, and the make-up of the aristocracy undoubtedly changed as "barbarians" entered its ranks.
- I prefer the Chris Wickham of 2016, who recognizes that economic relationships are not freestanding but underpin socio-political relationships.

An eminently sound evaluation of the whole period from 970 to 1215 was penned by Richard Southern in 1953, long before the whole "feudal" feud (pun intended) broke out; he was able to deal with the subject without using the terms "feudal" or "feudalism" while recognizing that the relationships between the different groups in society were not purely economic: "The slow emergence of a knightly aristocracy which set the social tone of Europe for hundreds of years contains no dramatic events or clearly decisive moments such as those which have marked the course of other great social revolutions." (Southern 1953, p. 15.)

But what about the period before 970? A very thorough study by Charles West comes to the rescue for Gaul in the ninth century:

[B]y 800, the lands between Marne and Moselle were already thoroughly caught up in networks of aristocracy control.... The archaeology, too, suggests village communities were thoroughly integrated into elite domination.... (West 2013, p. 64.) [O]wning large tracts of land could be less an abstract 'property' than a claim to exercise power. Indeed, occasionally, control over land was articulated precisely in the language of *potestas* (power), contrary to any assumption that this is a phenomenon only of the later period. (Ibid., p. 70.) Irrespective of practices of documentary representation, relations with the peasantry were only partly mediated through land ownership, and the direct exercise of power was never far away. (Ibid., p. 71.) [W]hat mattered during the ninth century was the central fact of lordship, and strategies for negotiating it. (Ibid., p. 77.) On the ninth century, West concludes: A social transformation, rooted in the ninth century, took place leading to a social formation that could conveniently (and for various reasons) be termed feudalism, it seems hard to set it aside.... (Ibid., p. 261.) And in the tenth century, West detects a 'retreat of royal power'. (Ibid., p. 132.)

Though this deals only with Gaul, and not the whole of it either, the features identified are of more general application, in particular, the fact that social relations were not purely a matter of economics.

Who were the Aristocrats in Early Medieval Europe?

But who were the aristocrats of early Medieval Europe? In the early years after Gaul and then Spain fell under Visigothic rule, beginning in 415, Roman aristocratic families continued both as estate-owners and as influential political players, not least by occupying most of the bishoprics in Gaul for a very long time to come. For example, King Euric (r. 466–484) protected aristocratic property in a decree providing, "The ancient boundaries are to stand, just as our father of blessed memory prescribed in another law." Similarly, Sidonius Apollinaris's friend Lampridius had his property rights restored by Euric. (Mathisen 2011a, loc 2952) In the Visigothic Code updated by Euric's son Alaric II in 506 (*Breviarium Alarici*), we read, "The assent of the venerable bishops and chosen provincials has strengthened (better understanding)", which alludes to the unity of interests of the aristocratic Gallo-Roman laity and episcopate. (Mathisen 2011, loc 2952.)

After the Franks gained control of most of Gaul after 486, the situation remained much the same as before, as we know particularly from the writings of Bishop Gregory of Tours (c. 538–594), who described the top echelon of society as *senatores*. Gregory's unclassical and not very accurate Latin coupled with his less than precise use of titles has created something of a dog-fight among scholars. But it seems that the term *senator* was used during this period to denote a member of a composite class of wealthy landowners partly of Gallo-Roman stock, partly drawn from the *curiales* or decurions (town councillors), together with an admixture of "parvenus", which eventually merged with the Frankish aristocracy. When the Mayor of the Palace Pippin (or Pepin) displaced the last Merovingian king in 751 and took the crown himself, this was done with the support of the aristocracy, and so under his

Carolingian dynasty, the title of *senator* came to denote a member of the king's council. (Gilliard 1979, p. 697.)

A strictly economic view of relationships in medieval society is plainly too narrow, and Reynolds's pooh-poohing of documents portraying socio-political relationships on the ground that they use the wrong language or language that is not precise enough is misconceived. Labels are affixed to cans only after the soup has been prepared and sealed in the cans. Similarly, relationships develop in real life, and it is only later that the lawyers are called in to name, categorize, and define their precise terms. And there are some documents that point to something like feudal relationships centuries before Reynolds is prepared to recognize any such phenomenon.

The Law of Fiefs 1037

Susan Reynolds does at least admit that the *Constitutio de feudis* (Law of Fiefs), decreed by the Emperor Conrad II in 1037, "...marked the foundation of the academic law of fiefs." (Reynolds 1994, p. 44.) But the wording of this law makes it clear that it had very practical, not just "academic," effects. The law stipulated that "...no knight (*miles*) who was the tenant of a bishop, abbot, marquess, count or anyone else was to be deprived of his fief unless he was convicted of a crime by the judgment of his peers....", with the right to appeal to the emperor. This gave knights an important right against their overlords, whom Conrad compensated by limiting his own right to collect a tax known as the *fodrum*.

Not only was this law practical, but Conrad states specifically that it was based on an earlier law, *constitutio antecessorum nostrorum* ("a law of our predecessors.") So, not only was this edict issued long before Reynolds claims any form of feudal system existed, but it itself was based on an earlier law.

Oath of Fealty 757

But, almost three centuries before this, under the year 757 in the *Annales Regni Francorum* (Annals of the Kingdom of the Franks), we read that Duke Tassilo III of Bavaria paid fealty to the Mayor of the Palace Pippin (Pepin) the Short, soon to be crowned King, Significantly, the words *vassus* and *vasaticus* are used to describe the relationship. This ceremony, which is referred to as *commendatio*, precisely the term used in full-blown feudalism, involved the relics of no fewer than five saints. The account relates that Tassilo *commendavit fidelitatemque iureiurando supra corpus sancti Dionysii promisit.* (Tassilo paid homage to Pippin and promised fealty to him by swearing an oath on the body of St. Dionysius.) *(Annales regni Francorum 741–829* Ed. Pertzius—Recognovit Frederck Kurze, Hannover: Hahn, 1895.)

It may be objected that this language is far too legalistic for the period, and probably represents a reworking of the original text by the Annalist. But it was plausibly suggested by the great German historian Leopold von Ranke that the Annalist was none other than Charlemagne's biographer Einhard. If this is right, the document as we have it (in two slightly different versions) must predate 840, when Einhard died.

Reynolds, needless to say, is quick to wave this case aside as "very special indeed" and to point out that "*commendare, commendatio* et cetera were words of many meanings." (Loc. 1383, 4877.) That may be so, but it is inconceivable that a whole new set of terms and elaborate ceremonial would have been invented just for this one very special case.

The Byzantine Paradox

During his five years at Eton, the popular historian John Julius Norwich recalled, "Byzantium seemed to be the victim of a conspiracy of silence. I cannot honestly remember its being mentioned, far less studied." (Norwich 1997, loc. 167.) Lord Norwich took it upon himself to rescue the Byzantine Empire from this conspiracy, which he proceeded to do with great verve in a delightful three-volume history, the first of which appeared in 1988. While favorably disposed to the Byzantines, Norwich took a balanced view: "[A]t bottom...the Byzantines were human like the rest of us, deserving of praise and of blame much as we are ourselves. What they do not deserve is the obscurity to which for centuries we have condemned them." (Ibid., loc. 7501.) For a writer like Norwich, for whom history was essentially a branch of the entertainment industry, to dole out praise and blame is perfectly understandable, but it is less forgivable in a professional academic historian. Yet there has recently been something of a wave of pro-Byzantine special pleading among a number of academic writers. Among academics, too, Byzantine History has lately exerted a certain fascination, which, however, has produced some disquieting results.

We have already had occasion to comment (in Chapter 4) on the special pleading, particularly in regard to "heresiology," found in two of the essays contained in the 2013 compilation, *Theodosius II: Rethinking the Roman Empire in Late Antiquity.* (Kelly 2013) But that is not the only book on Byzantium to show signs of special pleading.

Another such is a book titled *Byzantine Matters* (presumably a deliberate pun), which sets out its objective in these terms: "The field of Byzantine studies must be rescued from its continuing association with the competing claims of negativity and exoticism." (Cameron 2014, p. 115.) This is slightly misleading. It is not the "*field* of Byzantine *studies*" but the Byzantine Empire itself that has a longstanding negative reputation. And it is this that *Byzantine Matters* attempts to "rescue," entailing a certain amount of special pleading. But is such an approach really befitting an academic study? Objectivity is probably impossible to achieve in historical writing, but it surely behooves academics at least to attempt to get as close to it as possible. (See Chapter 7.)

An Exercise in Labeling

What label should be affixed to the Eastern Roman Empire? Was it a separate empire from the West? If so, when did the separation take effect? And was the East an "empire" in its own right, a "commonwealth," or just a "state" of some description? If an empire, was it a Greek empire or a Roman empire? Should it be labeled "Roman," "East Roman," or "Byzantine"? And from what date? These questions have greatly exercised historians in recent decades, most of whom have not stopped to ask what the relevance or significance is of any of these questions.

As part of her mission to "rescue" Byzantium's reputation, the author of *Byzantine Matters* is particularly anxious to claim the title of "empire" for what is generally termed the "Byzantine Empire." There is no indication of the significance, if any, of this bottling and labeling exercise.

First, we are presented with an elaborate definition of "empire":

> A basic definition of empire would probably include the ability to bring disparate and 'foreign' elements under central control, as well as the capacity to exploit population and territory by exacting some form of tribute ('tributary states.') Centralization of the means of exploitation is crucial ('state power'), and the key items of expenditure from the wealth that is extracted in this are likely to consist in the maintenance of an army and of the governing structures, including the court and the display that this entails. (Cameron 2014, p. 30.)

There are several serious problems with this:

- There is no recognition here that this definition of *empire* is a purely modern coinage (and not shared by modern European languages such as Dutch or German.)

- Latin *imperium*, from which the English word "empire" comes, is not generally used in Latin in a geographical or territorial sense, and *never* as the label for a historical period. Instead, it tended to be used by the Romans in the sense of *command, order, authority, power, government.*
- How then did the term "Roman Empire" come in English to mean the *period* when Rome was ruled over by an "emperor" (as distinct from being a Republic)?
- Blame it on Augustus, the first Roman "emperor," who styled himself *Imperator*—but used as a forename, *not* as a title—a precedent followed by most Roman "emperors" for three centuries.
- Why did Augustus do this? In a word, to avoid using the title *rex* ("king"), which was anathema to the senatorial aristocracy of the Roman Republic, which feared one-man rule—and Julius Caesar, Augustus's adoptive father, was assassinated precisely because of his monarchical ambitions.
- But wasn't Augustus a monarch himself? Certainly, but he concealed this fact for fear of meeting the same fate as Julius Caesar.
- Instead, he accepted the name Augustus ("the sublime one"), and adopted the inoffensive unofficial designation *princeps* ("first citizen")—which is why the first three centuries of the "Roman Empire" are now generally referred to in English as the "Principate" (followed by the "Dominate.")
- And took *Imperator* (commander) not as a title but as a *praenomen* (forename), a usage that continued with only a few exceptions until the time of Diocletian, and instances of which are still found much later, as for example in the formal *titulature* of Justinian's nephew and successor Justin II (r 565–574) in a law of 570: *Imperator Caesar Flavius Justinus...semper Augustus.* (Rösch 1978, p. 168.)
- Paradoxically, therefore, what we today refer to as the Roman "emperor" was meant to be *less*, not *more*, monarchical than a king.
- Similar thinking motivated Napoleon Bonaparte in 1804 to eschew the title of "king" in favor of "emperor"—which had more of a "republican" air.
- In most other societies in history there was not the same sensitivity attaching to the title of "king.," so there was usually no distinction between "king" and "emperor." So, for example, the Indian ruler Ashoka (r. 269–233 BCE), generally referred to in English as an "emperor," described himself (in the Kandahar Edict, for example) as "king"—in Greek *basileus*, and *melech* in Aramaic. (Sircar 1979, p. 113.)
- The same applies to the eastern half of the Roman Empire, most parts of which had experienced monarchical regimes prior to coming under Roman rule. So, even during the Principate, Roman

emperors were commonly referred to as *basileus*, the ordinary Greek word for "king." There is, for example, the oft-cited incident related by Cassius Dio, of the woman who approached the Emperor Hadrian (r. 117–138) while on tour in the eastern part of the Empire. When Hadrian waved her aside saying he had no time to attend to her request, she retorted, in Greek, *kai mē basileue* ("Then don't be king!"), the word *basileue* being a verb from the noun *basileus* ("king".) (Dio 69.6.3.)

- This informal usage survived into Byzantine times, and *basileus* was finally adopted by the Emperor Heraclius (r. 610–641) as the official imperial title in 629. We even find it transliterated into the Roman alphabet, as in coins of Leo VI (r. 886–912), while Leo's son Constantine VII (r. 913–959) is described in an ivory plaque as *autokrator kai basileus* (*imperator* and king) though *autokrator* was by no means reserved to emperors but was also applied to non-imperial military commanders, such as Justinian's general Belisarius and, much later, to military commanders such as David Arianites, appointed in 1018 by Emperor Basil II as *strategos autokrator* ("commander-in-chief") of Skopje (in modern North Macedonia.)

- The term "Byzantine Empire" is modern, less than two centuries old as a generally accepted label in the West. The Byzantines themselves referred to their state in Greek variously as *Basileia tōn Rhōmaiōn* (Kingdom of the Romans), *Politeia tōn Rhōmaiōn* (Republic/State/Commonwealth of the Romans), while Western contemporaries could refer to it in Latin as *Imperium Graecorum* (Empire of the Greeks) to distinguish it from the Holy Roman Empire, which also claimed to be the successor to the original Roman Empire.

- In brief, it really makes very little difference whether Byzantium is called an empire, a kingdom, a commonwealth (suggested by Obolensky 1974), or simply a "state" (Ostrogorsky 1986.) As it was the eastern successor to the Roman Empire it makes sense to continue to refer to it as an empire (though why "Byzantine" is another question: see below), but this issue hardly justifies all the energy expended on it.

- There is no sign of recognition of any of these points in *Byzantine Matters*.

- For all the above reasons, whether Byzantium matters or not, the question whether it should be called an "empire" or not certainly does *not* matter.

- Why, then, should *Byzantine Matters* be so concerned to justify this label for the supposedly beleaguered state? The only possible motive for claiming the label "empire" is the modern perception of it as more prestigious than "kingdom" or anything else. But why should that "matter" to a professional historian?

When is a Schism Not a Schism and Why Does it Matter?

In another attempted rescue operation in *Byzantine Matters*, we read that the "differences between the Roman Catholic and Orthodox churches" dating from 1054 are "no longer regarded by historians as a real 'schism' but certainly presaging future problems." (Cameron 2014, p. 16.) There are only three other references to "schism" throughout the whole of the 164-page book. The only mention of any length is a perfect example of special pleading, quietly sliding the definition of "schism" from "differences" to "contacts":

> Historians no longer believe that the so-called Great Schism of 1054 put an end to contacts between eastern and western churches. Yet for a period of five centuries thereafter Byzantium was engaged in a complex, emotional, and difficult tangle centering on the differences of doctrine and practice between east and west. (Ibid., p. 105.)

Nobody would suggest that there were no "contacts" between the two churches after 1054, but that is a completely different question from whether there was a rift between them, which, in fact, the "contacts" attempted and failed to heal. The passage carries on in the same vein for another 23 lines, including this "challenge":

> The real challenge for historians is to do justice to the vast effort and passion that went into these issues, including the outpouring of writing and debate that was dedicated to them. (loc. cit.)

The one-sidedness of this whole passage would be less disquieting if it even remotely resembled a logical argument. Perhaps one should simply dismiss it as a piece of crude special pleading and move on, but as it purports to be an academic treatment of an important subject, some basic points need to be made:

- The word *schism* comes from the Greek word *schisma*, meaning "a split, division." If the term *schism* is not a fitting label for the split between the Roman Catholic and Eastern Orthodox churches, then what is that rift to be called? In fact, the division has now lasted for nearly a thousand years, and despite some recent moves toward reconciliation, the breach has still not been healed. Just giving it a different label will not change that.
- I repeat that to define "schism" as an absence of "contacts" between the two churches, as *Byzantium Matters* tries to do, is simply wrong. Contact there certainly has been—but the split, which is what a schism is, remains unresolved nevertheless.

- "The real challenge for historians" suggested in *Byzantine Matters* amounts to no more than skating on the surface. The *actual* challenge for historians is to understand the *causes* and *significance* of the schism (often called "The Great Schism".)
- The schism is purportedly rooted in doctrinal differences, notably, but by no means solely, the *filioque* issue. The Eastern Orthodox churches believe that the Holy Spirit proceeds "from the Father," while the Catholic creed states that the Holy Spirit proceeds from the Father "*filioque*" (and from the Son.) There is no possible way of proving either of these completely arbitrary beliefs, so historians should rather ask:
  - How and why did this schism arise? In fact, it is rooted in a dispute over primacy between the Pope and the Patriarch of Constantinople.
  - Why is it so intractable? Because neither church is prepared to kowtow to the other. As recently as 2010, in an encyclical defending dialogue with the Catholic Church against those opposing it in "an unacceptably fanatical way," Patriarch Bartholomew I of Constantinople went out of his way to scotch "...false rumors that union between the Roman Catholic and Orthodox Churches is imminent." (*Catholic News Agency*, February 20, 2010.)
  - What is its significance? The Great Schism is the oldest currently existing split within Christianity but by no means the only one. Such stand-offs between different Christian denominations are an intrinsic feature of Christianity as a creed religion. (See Chapter 10.)
  - Why the reluctance in *Byzantine Matters* to admit the seriousness of the east-west schism? Presumably because such a longstanding rift does not show Christianity in a good light. But why should that bother a professional historian?

An Unparadoxical Paradox

Another book on Byzantium, which, if not guilty of special pleading as such, adopts an unduly pedantic attitude to the subject, is Fergus Millar's *A Greek Roman Empire*: *Power and Belief under Theodosius II (408–450)*. One of Millar's prime concerns is to answer this question: "[I]n what sense was this 'Roman' empire, now ruled by an Emperor established in Constaninople, really Greek?" (Millar 2006b, p. 4.)

In this connection, Millar identifies a "central paradox." It is not easy to tell what the supposed paradox is. A paradox is essentially a self-contradictory situation or statement, a statement that is a contradiction in terms, or a statement that is simply surprising. A basic example of a paradox would be the recognition that people in richer societies generally have fewer children than those in poorer societies though a richer population is able to support more children than a poorer population. A common type of paradoxical situation is a Catch-22, an example of which is the fact that to qualify for a bank loan you may have to prove to the bank that you don't need a loan.

On analysis, Fergus Millar's "central paradox" does not qualify as a paradox at all. Here is the relevant passage:

> It is time to confront the central paradox. On the one hand, as we have seen, Imperial legislation, all issued in Latin, embodied the principle of the collegiality of the Emperors, and of the unity of the "Roman" Empire. On the other hand, the entire administrative structure described by the *Notitia Dignitatum* is divided into two halves; and what it calls 'Oriens' (in the broadest sense) is a coherent and very extensive Greek-speaking world. So what justifies the claim made earlier, that in the first half of the fifth century the unity of the Empire, though very significant conceptually, was in practical terms an illusion? In reality, the claim made here is, there was a separate 'Greek Roman Empire', twinned with its western, Latin-speaking, counterpart—but separate all the same.
>
> The answer to the paradox comes in the form of two very simple propositions. Firstly, the imperial pronouncements which we normally (and contemporaries sometimes) refer to as 'laws' (*leges*) were in form, with only the rarest exceptions, letters, almost always addressed to officials, occasionally to the Senate.... [W]hat it means is that the entire body of "legal" material, on which in all essentials the Late Roman State has been based, consists of internal communications within the administration. All of them were issued in the name of the current Emperors, western and eastern, and virtually all of them were addressed to high officials, predominantly one or other Praetorian Prefect.
>
> Secondly, in spite of the principle of unity which informed both the authorship of *constitutiones* themselves and the compilation of the *Codex Theodosianus*, there are *(sic)* a set of perfectly clear and unambiguous criteria which allow an almost complete separation of western and eastern 'laws'. In summary, the criteria are: (1) the place of issue; (2) the post held by the official addressed; (3) the regions or cities referred to in the text; (4) the mode of reference to other Emperors, whether deceased or still alive. (Millar, Fergus, Ibid., p. 6ff.)

Let me take these points one by one.

- **A Greek Roman Empire?** "In what sense," asks Millar, "was this 'Roman' empire, now ruled by an Emperor established in

Constantinople, really Greek?" (Ibid., p. 4.) In fact, the Roman Empire had always been bilingual: Latin in the West, Greek in the East. While by no means always the first language of the inhabitants of the East, Greek had become the *lingua franca* of most of that area in the aftermath of the conquests of Alexander the Great (r. 336–323 BCE), though some parts of the Eastern Empire, like Dacia and Pannonia, were Latin-speaking. The first language of the Jews, for example, was Aramaic, but the Jewish authors of the New Testament naturally chose to write in Greek. And even the version of the Old Testament most familiar to Jews during Roman times was the so-called Septuagint translation into Greek compiled in Alexandria prior to 132 BCE. A.H.M. Jones put it in a nutshell: "The Roman government had from the beginning communicated with its Greek subjects in Greek." (Jones 1964, p. 988). This has nothing to do with the division of the Empire after the death of Theodosius I in 395, but goes right back to the beginning of the Principate. For example, Augustus's autobiography, the *Res Gestae Divi Augusti*, was exhibited in public places in the East in recognition of the practical situation—hence the title *Monumentum Ancyranum*, because the best surviving copy of the *Res Gestae* was the impressive bilingual version of it inscribed on marble in the forum in Ancyra (modern Ankara). However, until 397 formal written court judgments had to be in Latin (CJ 7.45.12), and it was only in 610, over a century after the demise of the Western Empire, that Greek became the official language of the Byzantine Empire, and coin legends were mostly in Latin until the eleventh century. Yet, Greek-language coins had already been in evidence during the Principate, issued by Greek cities like Ephesus, which even showed the image of a turret-crowned figure of the goddess ROMA (written in Greek letters) as early as the reign of Nero (r. (54–68). So, was the Byzantine Empire "Greek" or "Roman"? Beneath the official façade, Greek was the language of day-to-day administration as well as the *lingua franca* of communication generally—but not much more so than during the principate. Clearly, as time went by and the ties with Western Europe diminished (except during the period of Crusader control over a large part of the Byzantine Empire from 1204 to 1261), Byzantium took on more and more of a Greek character. But, why, in any case, does it matter how the Byzantine Empire is pigeon-holed or labeled? What is more important, surely, is to understand what made it tick.

- **One empire or two?** Fergus Millar makes much of the fact that the majority of the *constitutiones* in the Theodosian Code, while promulgated in the names of both or all the emperors reigning at the date of the particular law concerned, were issued in Constantinople. The basis for inclusion of laws in the Code is carefully explained in a preamble to the Code addressed jointly by Theodosius II and his western colleague Valentinian III to the Senate in Rome:

> [I]f in the future it should be Our pleasure to promulgate any law in one part of this very closely united Empire, it shall be valid in the other part on condition that it does not rest upon doubtful trustworthiness or upon a private assertion; but from that part of the Empire in which it will be established, it shall be transmitted with the sacred imperial letters, it shall be received in the bureaus of the other part of the Empire also, and it shall be published with the due formality of edicts. For a law that has been sent must be accepted and must undoubtedly be valid, and the power to emend and to revoke shall be reserved to Our Clemency. Moreover, the laws must be mutually announced, and they must not be admitted otherwise. (CTh 1.1.5–429, tr. Pharr.)

This makes it clear that a law originating in the East would have effect in the West as well, provided it was formally communicated to the West and officially promulgated there too. The phrase *coniunctissimum imperium* ("very closely united Empire") is undoubtedly an exaggeration, but to go along with Millar and discern here already two separate empires may be going too far in the opposite direction. There appears to have been at least a modicum of co-operation between East and West, though it has to be remembered that Theodosius II's half-cousin and western colleague Valentinian III (r. 425–455) had come to the throne in 425 at the age of six after a contested succession, and that during his long reign the West was under increasing pressure from civil war and invasion. and would formally cease to exist as a Roman state twenty-one years after his assassination. After the death of Theodosius II in 450 the East also entered a period of disputed successions until the reign of Anastasius I (r. 491–518), who is sometimes regarded as the first Byzantine emperor properly so called, marking the complete separation of East and West. But, so long as the situation on the ground is recognized for what it was, it really makes very little difference whether we slap a label on the period reading "one empire," "two empires," or "twin empires."

- **Notitia Dignitatum** ("List of Offices"): In the passage quoted above, Millar makes much of the fact that "the entire administrative structure described by the *Notitia Dignitatum* is divided into two halves." This is hardly surprising, as the Empire had two separate emperors when these official lists were compiled. The Eastern list dates from the 390s, while the Western one was evidently compiled only in the 420s. In fact, however, from the accession of Diocletian in 284 the Roman Empire had frequently been shared between two (or more) emperors, each of whom would generally have had his own administration. This occurred between 286 and 324; from 337 to 350; in 364 Valentinian I (r. 364–75) gave his bother Valens the eastern provinces (r. 364–78); then Gratian (r. 367–383) accepted Valentinian II as co-emperor in the West (r. 375–392) and appointed Theodosius I as Augustus ruling the East (r. 379–395.) Which brings us (skipping a couple of "usurpers") to the (probably unplanned) permanent division between the sons of Valentinian: Honorius in the West (r. 395–423), and Arcadius in the East (395–408.)

- **When is a law not a law?** Millar insists on denying the title of laws to the *constitutiones* collected in the Theodosian Code, because they were mostly letters addressed to officials, therefore amounting to "internal communications within the administration." This betrays a misunderstanding of the nature of legislation, which is what these *constitutiones* were. The motivation for the compilation of the Code was explained by Theodosius II in 438, just before the Code was due to go into effect. Deploring the confusion in the law resulting from the bulk of unsorted imperial *constitutiones*, Theodosius adds: "We have dispelled the darkness and given the light of brevity to the laws by means of a compendium." (Novellae Th 1.1) The way the Code was compiled is explained in CTh 1.1.5, which was published by the Senate as well. All *constitutiones* issued since 312 were to be collected together and classified under subject headings. Where a particular *constitutio* dealt with more than one subject, it was to be chopped up and each part filed under the relevant subject heading. So, the laws in the Code were no longer "letters" to officials. The reason for their arrangement under subject headings was precisely because they were now a legal reference book in which anyone could look up the relevant law on any topic. The fact that these laws originated in replies to officials is irrelevant. A great deal of legislation in modern times as well is prompted by particular topical concerns, hence, the so-called "mischief rule" of statutory interpretation, which assumes that any given piece of legislation is intended to cure a particular "mischief and defect."

- **"Central paradox"**: So much, then for Fergus Millar's "central paradox," which turns out upon examination not to be a paradox at all—and, as far as his denial of the title of "laws" to the *constitutiones* in the Theodosian Code is concerned, that is just simply factually incorrect.

Some Real Paradoxes

But that is not to say that there are no paradoxes associated with Byzantium. On the contrary, the Byzantine history is fairly bristling with paradoxes. Here are just a few of them.

- **Why "Byzantine"?** We have witnessed a great deal of gnashing of teeth over whether the Byzantine empire should be labeled an "empire" (see above), but none over why it should be labelled "Byzantine," which is a real paradox. Byzantium started life as a Greek trading post which had been in existence for nearly a thousand years by the time it was refounded by Constantine in 324, renamed Constantinople, and consecrated as a Christian Roman capital in 330. It retained that name even after it fell to the Ottoman Turks in 1453. Popular etymology derives its modern name, Istanbul, from the Greek phrase *eis tēn polin* ("to the city," presumably from phrases like, "I am going to the city.") But that only became its official name in the 1920s. Constantine would no doubt be turning in his grave if he heard the term "Byzantine Empire." Why not "Constantinopolitan Empire," or simply "Constantinople" (in the way "Byzantium" is frequently now used to refer to the whole empire)? In fact, the term Byzantine is quite a recent coinage, being first used by the German historian Hieronymus Wolff in 1557 and gaining currency in the West only in the nineteenth century.
- **Yo-yo Empire:** The Byzantine Empire is commonly said to have lasted for over a thousand years, until it fell to the Ottomans in 1453, but this is misleading. Starting out as the whole of the eastern half of the Roman Empire, the Byzantine Empire shrank and grew in fits and starts over the years like a yo-yo. Justinian (527–565) reconquered parts of the fallen western Empire, namely Italy, Africa and Spain, but Northern Italy is lost to the Lombards in 568, Egypt to the Persians in 619, and North Africa to the Arabs in 690. The whole Balkan peninsula, excluding Constantinople itself and the Peloponnese falls to the Bulgars as a result of the disastrous Battle of Achelous in 917. In 995 Basil II reconquers Syria from the Arabs and in the following year retrieves Greece from the Bulgars. At the death of Basil II in 1025 the Byzantine Empire was the most powerful state in the Mediterranean, encompassing the boot of Italy, Bulgaria, Thrace, Greece and Anatolia. However, southern Italy is lost to the Normans in 1055. The major defeat of Manzikert at the hands of the Seljuk Turks in 1071, at which the Emperor Romanos IV Diogenes was taken prisoner, ultimately results in the loss of most of Asia Minor, followed by Syria in 1075. In 1204 Constantinople falls to Crusaders from the West, who set up a "Latin Empire" that lasts till 1261. After Constantinople is recaptured, the Byzantine Empire limps on, rent by two civil wars between 1321 and 1347, and a pocket-handkerchief-sized remnant of the Empire finally falls to the Ottomans in 1453.
- **Porous borders:** The impregnability of Constantinople is yet another paradox. Defensive stone walls were first put in place by

Constantine and then greatly strengthened under Theodosius II (r. 408–450), hence often called the "Theodosian Walls." They have been described, with some exaggeration, as "...perhaps the most successful and influential city walls ever built—they allowed the city and its emperors to survive and thrive for more than a millennium, against all strategic logic, on the edge of [an] extremely unstable and dangerous world." (Ward-Perkins 1998, p. 391 f.) The walls really only protected Constantinople from the West, though the Byzantine Empire was also protected by certain natural features. With the exception of the soft, lowland underbelly of Asia Minor, both the Balkans in the West and the eastern frontier were protected by mountains. But the Seljuk Turks managed to establish themselves in Asia Minor and, as mentioned above, the defeat of Manzikert in 1071 ultimately deprived the Byzantines of their Anatolian heartland. "The Battle of Manzikert," wrote Sir Steven Runciman, "was the most decisive disaster in Byzantine history. The Byzantines themselves had no illusions about it. Again and again their historians refer to that dreadful day." (Runciman 1951, vol I., p. 64; Bazzaz, et al. 2012.)

- **Aristocracy without** *aristokratia*: Though the Byzantines avoided the term *aristocracy*, which is, after all, a Greek word, *aristokratia*, there was in fact an aristocracy of sorts throughout its history. (Sarris 2015, p. 60) It was essentially an aristocracy of service, yet neither office nor status was generally hereditary in Byzantine history. (Kouroumali 2013, p. 695 f.) Until the sixth century, there was an elite class made up of senatorial families of the Constantinopolitan senate, greatly inferior in lineage, honor, or status to those of Rome, and a hereditary landowning class also not in the league of the great landowners of the West. "By the ninth and tenth centuries the power-base had shifted to court-appointed officials in Constantinople, especially close personal attendants of the emperor, such as the eunuchs of the Imperial Bedchamber, and military landowning families in the Anatolian provinces and the North Balkans. This is indicated by the introduction and frequent appearance of patronymic names in the written sources from the ninth century whose families form the 'powerful' (*dynatoi*)." (Ibid.) They benefited from the so-called "theme" system (from the Greek *themata*), a reorganization of the Empire (particularly from the 780s to the 950s) into administrative divisions under military commanders, subordinating civil to military power.

The role of eunuchs is also relevant here. (See below.) The conflict between Leo VI (r. 886–912) and the aristocratic families of the Phokadai and Doukai is a case in point. The revolt of Andronikos Doukas in 906, caused by rivalry with the powerful eunuch and imperial favorite Samonas, led to Doukas's eventual defection to the Arabs in 906–7. His son Constantine escaped from Baghdad and returned to Byzantium, where he was pardoned by Leo and entrusted with senior military commands. He made a bid for the throne in 913, which cost him his life. Basil II's (r. 976–1025) struggle and eventual victory over the great military provincial Bardas and Phokas families drove them to seek closer ties with the imperial court. After Basil's death a power struggle ensued between the military aristocracy (which, unusually for Byzantium, was hereditary) and the court aristocracy, leading to the victory of the military aristocracy in the shape of Alexius I Comnenus (Alexios I Komnenos, r. 1081–1118), which gave greater prominence to family ties and lineage in the exercise of civil power as well as military power, alongside the existing provincial military aristocracy and the administrative service office-holders. So, it is really only from this period that we can speak of a hereditary Byzantine aristocracy. The last two centuries of the Byzantine Empire saw the rise to power of several aristocratic families, some of whom even provided occupants of the imperial throne—notably the Kantakouzenoi (Cantacuzene), and the Palaeologi (Palaiologoi). (Angold 1984; Cheynet 2018; Holmes 2005; Haldon 2008, pp. 212–32; Morris 1976, pp. 3–27.)

- **Eunuchs:** The term *eunuch* is from a compound Greek word meaning "guardian of the bedchamber." As castrated males, eunuchs were "safe" around women of the imperial court; and not being able to have families of their own (though some are known to have feathered the nests of relatives), they could be expected to be loyal subordinates to the emperor, which served another important purpose for a power-hungry ruler by making the eunuchs an additional counterweight to the aristocracy. This may explain the presence of eunuchs already in Diocletian's administration, as discussed in Chapter 2.
  - In 1929, Sir Steven Runciman, best known as a historian of the Crusades, remarked that the "...significance [of eunuchs in Byzantium] has never...been properly realized."(Runciman 1951, 29 f.) This gap has now been filled by a number of publications, notably Shaun Tougher's 2008 book on the subject. As early as 1963, Keith Hopkins set out to prove "that eunuchs did in fact exercise real power; that people who wanted important tasks immediately executed with the support of imperial authority regularly approached the court eunuchs rather than any other imperial officer or indeed the emperor himself. People believed that

eunuchs exercised power and acted upon that assumption."
(Hopkins 1963, p. 63.)

- What effect did this situation have on the emperor himself? Peter
  Brown, on the basis of no evidence or references whatsoever,
  opines that it did not cut the emperor off from his subjects. "The
  emperor's palace officials—above all the great eunuch-chamber-
  lains—were recruited from far beyond the traditional governing
  class. Thus, the backstairs government of the palace did not cut
  off the emperor from his subjects. Far from it, it was part of the
  secret of Byzantine rule that this all-important, shadowy fringe
  was often more closely in touch with the feelings of the provincials than was the polished mandarinate of the bureaucracy."
  (Brown 1971, p. 141.)
- This view flies in the face of the evidence. In his speech *De Regno*
  ("On Monarchy"), the neo-Platonist philosopher and bishop of
  Ptolemais in Cyrenaica, Synesius (c. 373-c. 413), advised the
  Eastern Emperor Arcadius (r. 395–408) not to allow himself to be
  shut away from the public, to lead his troops into battle in time-
  honored fashion, and to travel around the provinces in person to
  keep in touch with his subjects. (Synesius, *De regno*, PG 66.)
  Whether this oration was delivered in the presence of Arcadius or
  not, it was courageous of Synesius to alert the emperor to what he
  saw as weaknesses, and there can be no doubt that the problems
  that he identified were real. If Arcadius was out of touch with his
  subjects, his effete son and successor, Theodosius II (r. 408–450),
  cocooned with his eunuchs, was even more secluded and isolated
  from his subjects.
- Writing in the late fourth or early fifth century, the *Historia
  Augusta* fired a broadside against eunuchs in general: "These
  creatures alone cause the downfall of emperors, for they wish
  them to live in the manner of foreign nations or as the kings of the
  Persians, and keep them well removed from the people and from
  their friends, and they are go-betweens, often delivering messages
  other than the emperor's reply, hedging him about, and aiming,
  above all things, to keep knowledge from him." (SHA 18.66.3-4.
  Severus Alexander, tr. Magie 1924.) The *Historia Augusta* does
  not rate highly as a source, yet this passage rings true. Though
  occurring in the *Life of Severus Alexander* (r. 222–235), it seems to
  be an observation drawn from the author's own lifetime about
  150 years later, and it is corroborated by numerous incidents in
  Byzantine history.
- After demonstrating the power of eunuchs, Hopkins concludes,
  "Paradoxically, the political power of eunuchs in general, far from

being a sign of the emperor's weakness, was, in the Byzantine empire of the fourth and fifth centuries, a token of, and a factor in, the survival of the emperor as an effective ruler." (Ibid., p. 80.) He cites the example of strong emperors like Valentinian I and Theodosius I, whose strength was not impaired by their employment of eunuchs. The point is that these emperors were military men who were not secluded in their palaces and therefore not isolated. But that does not detract from the general points made by Synesius and the *Historia Augusta*, namely that seclusion cut the emperor off from his subjects and from reliable sources of information. As gatekeepers guarding access to their prize possession, namely the imperial presence, ambitious and cunning eunuch chamberlains were well placed to enhancing their own power at the expense not only of the populace at large but also that of the emperor himself.

- The first eunuch known to occupy a key position in the imperial administration as *praepositus sacri cubiculi* ("grand chamberlain") was Eusebius under Constantius II, After Eusebius, the next eunuch of note was Eutropius, who was even given a consulship while serving as close adviser to the Eastern Emperor Arcadius (r. 395–408.) No eunuch is known to have held office under Arcadius's brother and Western co-emperor Honorius (r. 395–423). Eunuchs are found in imperial service in the West as well as the East, even as late as under the Ostrogothic King Theoderic (r. 493–526), based in Ravenna. However, it was in Byzantium, where Diocletian's "Dominate" continued while the western Empire fragmented, where eunuchs really came into their own. "The absolute ruler," as Patterson puts it, "requires the ultimate slave; and the ultimate slave is best represented in the anomalous person of the eunuch." (Patterson 1982, p. 315; Hopkins 1978, pp. 179 and 190 f.) The use of eunuchs in high office enabled the Byzantine Empire to keep aristocrats on a short leash. Unlike in the West, aristocratic titles and appointments were not hereditary, so that, until the eleventh century, there was only a "service aristocracy". But, as is also indicated above, imperial dependence on eunuchs was more likely to enhance the power of the eunuchs than that of their imperial master. From at least the seventh century, eunuchs are in evidence in prominent positions in the church as well the state. Unlike in the West, where clergy had to be "whole," in Byzantium, we find eunuchs even as patriarchs from the eighth century. In imperial service, specific posts were designated for eunuchs as distinct from the "bearded ones," including, from the 960s, the high position of *proedros* (president), which carried with it presidency of the Senate in Constantinople, though this position was opened up to Bearded Ones in the eleventh century. (Tougher 2008.) The paradox here is that, though supposedly showing greater continuity than the West, Byzantium actually developed along its own idiosyncratic lines, not least owing to the prominence of eunuchs to a level never experienced in the Roman Empire.

- **Caesaropapism or Theocracy?:** There was a close, almost symbiotic, relationship between church and state, beginning with Constantine's convocation of the Council of Nicaea in 325. Was this a form of caesaropapism, as has sometimes been suggested, or a theocracy? The difference is that caesaropapism represents the subordination of the church to the state, and, more particularly, to a king or emperor; a theocracy is just the opposite, where the state is under the control of the church. In both cases, there is no separation between church and state. Emperors, as we have seen, certainly lent their support to the church by outlawing heretics and persecuting non-Christians but would also occasionally issue their own ecclesiastical edicts without the approval of a church council. Emperors would also convoke church councils, over whom they could exert a certain amount of influence, and exercised control over church appointments, including that of the Patriarch of Constantinople and, indeed, even of the Pope in Rome, though this latter power lasted only from 537 to 752. This close interrelationship between church and state, beginning with Constantine's convocation of the Council of Nicaea in 325, lasted throughout Byzantine history, with very few exceptions, and effectively resulted in mutual dependence of the two institutions, very different from the West where, for example, the so-called Investiture Controversy pitted church against state in a long-running conflict from 1076 to 1122, which resulted in the decline in monarchical power and an increase in the power of local lords throughout the Holy Roman Empire (chiefly Germany and part of Italy.)

- **Iconoclasm** (from Greek *eikonoklasmos* (breaking or smashing of images): In any Eastern Orthodox church today, there is a proliferation of icons, painted representations of Jesus, Mary, and myriad saints, which are the object of veneration by worshippers. Yet long before the Protestant Reformation in the West, which excoriated the representation of the human form in sculptures, paintings or any other medium, the Byzantines had their own iconoclastic controversy, the First Iconoclasm, as it is called, from 726 to 787, and the Second Iconoclasm from 814 to 842. In the first period, icons were banned by law by Emperor Leo III and, with greater vehemence, by his son Constantine V, and the Second Iconoclasm was initiated by Leo V ordering the removal of the icon of the Chalke Gate in Constantinople. It has been suggested that the iconoclasts adopted their position in the face of the Arab threat, fearing that Byzantium was being punished for breaking the prohibition in the Ten Commandments against making a "graven image." It is now fashionable, however, to reject any outside influence, whether Jewish or Muslim. At the time, iconophiles or iconodules (from Greek *eikon* + *douloi*, meaning "servants, slaves, worshipers of images") tended to reject the "graven image" argument on the ground that it had been superseded by the new Christian covenant. And, surprisingly perhaps, iconoclasts' attacks were concentrated on icons, and tended to be less bothered by statues and other forms of human representation. (Brown 1973; Doom 2016.)

The two most important features of the Iconoclastic Controversy tend to be ignored in the welter of academic articles on the subject. Firstly, unlike the Protestant Reformation in the West seven centuries later, the Byzantine iconoclasts were led by emperors, underlining the symbiotic relationship between church and state mentioned above. Secondly, despite all the arguments marshaled on either side, which modern commentators are too inclined to take at face value, the veneration of icons in Byzantium is essentially the same phenomenon as found in many other societies. Human nature finds it more appealing, more comforting, and much easier to worship tangible and visible objects like statues, images, and icons than a single invisible divinity. It is a problem that is confronted head-on in the story of the Golden Calf in Exodus 32.4. And the Second Commandment is a prohibition not only of idol *worship* but also even of *making* such an object because it was realized that the very existence of such a "graven image" would be likely to lead to veneration or worship. And the prohibition is not only of images of human beings but of any living creature. The strict insistence on this prohibition in Judaism—and also in (especially Sunni) Islam—lies at the very heart of the concept of monotheism. There is certainly a plausible argument that the veneration of statues, pictures and icons in certain Christian denominations makes it difficult for them to claim to be true monotheists. As a branch of Judaism, early Christianity would certainly have had no place for images of any kind. The veneration or worship of images must have been borrowed later on from the many religions and cults swirling around the Roman Empire.

Continuity and Change in East and West—Roundup

Birth, Land, and Office in the West

Stemmata quid faciunt? (What's the good of pedigrees?) asks the satirist Juvenal. "Virtue is the one and only true nobility." In mocking the bearers of ancient names, Juvenal actually puts them on a pedestal by holding them to a higher moral standard than mere mortals. (Juv. Sat. 8.) Writing in about the year 100, almost a century and a half after Cicero's death, he praises Cicero, a new man, for his patriotic service, together with others of low birth, and ends by pointing out that if you trace your ancestry back far enough you will come to a shepherd or worse. But, despite this, Juvenal is not advocating for any kind of meritocracy. He appears to accept that men of noble lineage should hold positions of power as provincial governors, provided they live up to the higher standards expected of them. (Malnati 1987, pp. 133–141.)

After being ousted from these positions of power by Diocletian and returning with a vengeance under Constantine and his successors, the old combination of birth, wealth and office is more in evidence than it had been under the Principate for two main reasons. Firstly, the posts now open to nobles were not just humble provincial governorships but even praetorian prefectures. Secondly, nobles were able to cement their power in imperial service with landholding and patronage in the areas where they held office, while the emperor himself was far away at the frontier fending off barbarian incursions, or in the new Eastern capital, Constantinople.

With the end of the Roman Empire in the West, estates become more self-contained, some even being fortified against attack, especially in Gaul, for which our sources are richest, where a new composite aristocracy of *senatores* is in evidence, made up of a substratum of Gallo-Roman nobles with an admixture of the descendants of former decurions (town councillors) and parvenus, ultimately merging with the Frankish aristocracy.

Society remained stratified throughout, with the king at the top, then the aristocracy, and finally the peasantry, often termed *villeins*, indicating their origin as attached to a villa, or *serfs*, indicating their position as little better than slaves, Latin *servi*. Relationships between these different strata were not purely economic, but also had an important socio-political element. Then, in the words of Charles West, "A social transformation rooted in the ninth century took place leading to a social formation that could conveniently (and for various reasons) be termed feudalism." (West, 2013, p. 261.) But whatever label is affixed, Richard Southern's description of the period from 950 to 1215 as one marked by "...the slow emergence of a knightly aristocracy which set the social tone of Europe for hundreds of years," still holds good. (Southern 1953, p. 15.)

The Byzantine Paradox

When we turn to the East, we find ourselves in a very different world. Hereditary aristocracy, the mainstay of Western European society throughout the period now labeled "late antiquity" and beyond, is largely absent in the Byzantine Empire. Instead, there is an aristocracy of service coupled with eunuchs in high places. There were even specific offices reserved for eunuchs as distinct from "the bearded ones." From the emperor's point of view, eunuchs were preferable to "the bearded ones" because they did not have families, and their loyalty could generally be counted on. Eunuchs were, however, permitted to hold high positions in the church, even including that of Patriarch, which was not the case in the West. The almost symbiotic relationship between state and church in Byzantium was also not replicated in Western Europe. Convening church councils, for example, which was an accepted imperial role in Byzantium, could simply not be imagined in the West. But the Byzantine emperor's closeness to the church could be a source of weakness to him as well, because he could be used by church leaders to lend legal support to particular doctrines by condemning different groups of "heretics," while refusing would probably have been more politic and more conducive to religious peace, which was rent apart on a regular basis. Emperors also tended to take advice from "holy men" with no official position as Theodosius II did from the "saintly" Simeon Stylites. (See Chapter 4.)

East vs. West

The biggest paradox of all is that there was less continuity in the East than in the West. Though the Byzantine Empire was supposedly a continuation of the Roman Empire, which is how it was known by contemporaries, it had less in common with the Roman Empire (properly so called) than the West did, in the following respects:

- Until near its end, Byzantium did not have a hereditary aristocracy, a mainstay of the Roman Empire, and a basic feature in the West long after the demise of the western Empire.
- One reason for this difference was the important role played by eunuchs in Byzantium—which was not replicated in the West after

the fifth century (except to the extent that *castrati* were later employed as singers in Italian opera, and in church choirs in the Vatican.)

- The symbiotic relationship between church and state in Byzantium resulted in continual persecution of "heretics." Though the Roman Catholic Church was not a lot more tolerant than its sister Orthodox church, on balance it can probably be said that it did not expend quite so much effort on persecution.
- Though much emphasis tends to be placed on the longevity of the Byzantine Empire, it was in fact a yo-yo state, enlarging and contracting (and more of the latter) by fits and starts. In the West, by contrast, the ideal of a renewed Roman Empire was kept alive by the Holy Roman Empire—though justifiably derided by Voltaire in the eighteenth century as neither Holy, nor Roman, nor an Empire—and survives today in the European Union.
- Though the Roman Empire was always bilingual in terms of speech, its official language was Latin, which was abandoned in the East in favor of Greek in 610. Latin continued to be the language of law and administration in the West for many years and also gave rise to a number of Romance vernaculars that are still alive and well today, while Greek ceased to be a lingua franca and shrank into a small local language.
- However, it was the fall of Constantinople in 1453 that gave rise to the greatest continuity of the Byzantine Empire with classical antiquity. The exodus of scholars to the West clutching precious manuscripts gave an impetus to the Renaissance. Many classical Greek texts owe their survival to this emigration—including some as unlikely as the brilliant but bawdy comedies of Aristophanes. This development coincided with Gutenberg's invention of printing. But western typographers and typesetters were baffled by the Byzantine manuscripts written in the highly abbreviated Greek minuscule script, so they just replicated it in print, and all Greek texts were printed in this form until the early nineteenth century, and all carried a Latin translation on the opposite page. The influx of classical Greek texts from Constantinople gave an impetus to the study of Greek, which entered the curriculum of Oxford and Cambridge in the 1540s. This gave rise to the incorporation of Greek words into English, or, more often, the construction of neologisms (itself from Greek *neos*, "new" plus *logos*, "word") coined by compounding Greek words, roots, prefixes or suffixes to produce new English words that never actually existed in Greek. Since the eighteenth century, there has been a flood of such Greek compounds, and Greek is the first port of call, particularly when it comes to finding a new medical, scientific or technical term. Hence, telephone, thermometer, isotope,

photography, dinosaur, helicopter, and zoology, to mention just a few. This line of continuity from Byzantium is perhaps the paramount paradox—or, the ultimate irony.

Power Structure and Ethos

As is shown in Chapter 6, monarchy and aristocracy are at opposite poles in terms of power structure. After nearly five centuries of aristocratic rule under the Roman Republic, monarchy became the order of the day. Augustus's Principate was a monarchy in all but name, and nobody (other than some modern writers, as discussed in Chapter 1) was fooled by the thin republican disguise. The troops were loyal to a commander-in-chief who gave them land and donatives; the urban plebs looked to a strong monarch as their champion; and even the senatorial aristocracy, who detested the very idea of monarchy, were grateful for still being allowed a role in the imperial administration.

In the "Dominate," the new dispensation introduced by Diocletian in 284, imperial power remains uppermost, dependent largely on the military, and using dispensable equestrian officials and eunuchs instead of aristocrats, who are now completely sidelined. The Dominate continued essentially in the Byzantine Empire, with imperial power now relying on the Church and on eunuch chamberlains, together with the military, in the absence of a hereditary aristocracy until the eleventh century. (See above.)

In the West, however, Constantine represents a marked change, bringing back members of the senatorial aristocracy into high office, which they were able to combine with land and wealth, often in the same regions which they governed, creating something of a centrifugal force—a situation that continued beyond the dissolution of the western empire and into the successor "barbarian" kingdoms.

What we have here, therefore, are three power structures, all of them monarchical, but with significant differences. Under the Principate and the Constantinian western model—but not under the Dominate or Byzantium—the aristocracy played a significant role, not enough to deprive the emperor, or ruler, of the whip hand, but sufficient to infuse these regimes with an aristocratic ethos, which has survived in the West down to the present day.

This ethos is based on an unstated belief in the inherent inequality of human beings, a stratified society, and social mobility. It finds expression at the time of this writing in the concept of "equality of opportunity," linked to that of a "meritocracy," or "rat-race." As is not sufficiently recognized, "equality of opportunity" is the diametric opposite of "equality" *tout court*. For, equality of opportunity means allowing individuals an equal chance to become *unequal*—or rather, for their inherent inequalities to be recognized. Similarly, the much-derided concept of "meritocracy" is based on the assumption that individuals should rise or fall in accordance with their inherent "merit."

What have these modern concepts to do with the aristocratic ethos, from which they ultimately developed? Just this, that both share a belief in the inherent—and unequal—worth of individuals. The word "aristocracy," after all, comes from the Greek *aristokratia*, meaning "the rule or power of the best." The aristocratic ethos bases this inequality on birth, lineage, and pedigree, while its modern successors base it on vague notions of "merit," comprising intelligence, ability, talent, achievement, or value. But both are worlds away from the concept of "equality" as such. See Chapter 6.

6

Two Models of Government

Aleitmotif of this book is power structure and, in particular, the relationship between monarchy and aristocracy. The significance of this feature is not often recognized, even by historians. I will go further and analyze the relationship between the power structure and the ethos of a society, a topic that is almost completely ignored.

Monarchy exerts a certain fascination on the human mind. It is hard to imagine what it was like to be a regular person in some past age. Evidence tends to be scarce and unreliable, and the subject matter may well turn out to be mind-numbing. The swashbuckling and flamboyant or scandalous and dissolute antics of rulers, on the other hand, and especially of those who "...bestride the narrow world like a Colossus" (Shakespeare's description of Julius Caesar as dictator for life) are the stuff not only of popular entertainment but also of the majority of historical writing, ancient and modern alike.

Monarchical titles are many, varied, and extremely misleading. For example, the title of king, emperor, president, or prime minister may or may not indicate the possession of genuine monarchical power because a minority may wield power under a titular head entrusted with purely ceremonial functions. Moreover, it is virtually impossible for one person to wield total, or absolute, power. Even the most apparently autocratic or absolute monarch is likely to have to share power to some extent with others. The test must be this: Who has the whip hand?

The formal division among modern western states into "monarchies" and "republics" has no real significance, as monarchy in the modern West is not real monarchy at all. The royal heads of state of

Why Rome Fell: Decline and Fall, or Drift and Change?, First Edition. Michael Arnheim.
© 2022 John Wiley & Sons, Inc. Published 2022 by John Wiley & Sons, Inc.

the United Kingdom, Denmark, Sweden, and Norway, have no more power—and those of Belgium, Spain, and the Netherlands have only marginally more power—than the presidents of republics such as Germany, Portugal, Greece or Switzerland.

Just as modern western monarchies are generally oligarchies in disguise, so the nominally republican governments of Vladimir Putin's Russia, Xi Jinping's China, Viktor Orbán's Hungary, or Turkey under Recep Tayyip Erdogan, can probably be labeled as essentially "populist" monarchical regimes.

In the modern West, royalty and nobility tend to merge, sharing common interests, such as horse-racing, polo, yachting, upmarket ski resorts, and exclusive private schools. No wonder the fundamental polarity between true monarchy and aristocracy (or oligarchy) is generally ignored or misunderstood. But this dichotomy is fundamental.

In every society, past and present, it is possible to identify an elite (or group of elites), whether labeled aristocracy, aristocrats, nobles, nobility, oligarchs, oligarchy, power elite, or simply elite (or élite), whether hereditary or not, and whether based on birth, wealth, status or office, or a combination of two or more of these factors. This elite (or combination of elites) is normally dominant socially and economically, and often politically as well, in the form of oligarchy or, if hereditary, aristocracy. Oligarchy (rule of the few) tends to develop into aristocracy (rule of the best), the term "aristocracy" being used to refer both to the hereditary ruling class itself and to the form of government which it controls. The ruling element in either, which can be described as a "power elite," intent on preserving and perpetuating its own group dominance, tends to have a deep-seated fear of one-man or monarchical rule.

At the same time, there is a natural antipathy inherent in the lower classes toward any oligarchy or aristocracy. This tends to impel the common people to give their support to a strong leader as their champion against the privileged classes, which may lead to the establishment of a form of popular, or "populist," monarchy or dictatorship.

There are only two pure forms of government: on the one hand, oligarchy, morphing into aristocracy, and, on the other, monarchy. True monarchy properly so called (from the Greek *monarchia*, "rule of one person"), is a form of government where power is concentrated in the hands of a single individual, whether a hereditary crowned head, a dictator, or an elected politician. Genuine monarchical power is essentially anti-aristocratic and, generally though not invariably, depends on lower class support, a form of what tends now to be labeled as populism.

Though monarchy and oligarchy/aristocracy are the only pure forms of government, hybrid forms are possible, combining populist monarchy with elitist, oligarchical or aristocratic features. Among these are the current or recent regimes of Narendra Modi in India, Boyko Borisov in Bulgaria, Andrej Babiš in the Czech Republic (Czechia), Evo Morales in Bolivia, Daniel Ortega in Nicaragua, Rodrigo Duterte in the Philippines, and Donald Trump's presidency of the United States.

What, then, about democracy? According to my analysis, Athenian "direct democracy" under Pericles and his successors was in reality a form of populist monarchy (see below), and modern "representative democracies" are in reality oligarchies. (Arnheim 2016.)

But why, you may well ask, does power structure matter in any event? The answer is that the whereabouts of power reveals who benefits from a particular regime. The power structure in a society goes to the very heart of that society, impacts directly on the degree of social mobility and equality in that society, and is related, directly or indirectly, to the ethos of the society concerned.

Preview

This chapter compares the power structure of a number of different societies with that of Rome as analyzed in the previous chapters, in terms of the following propositions:

- In every society, past and present., we find an elite group (or groups).
- This elite (or combination of elites) is dominant socially and economically, and often politically into the bargain.
- Elite political power manifests itself in the form of aristocratic (where hereditary) or oligarchic (where non-hereditary) government, or it is an oligarchy transforming into aristocracy.
- Elites are generally opposed to one-person rule, or monarchy properly so called.
- In every society, there is tension, competition, or antipathy between monarchy and aristocracy (or oligarchy). However, elites are rarely completely united, and competition between different factions or groupings within an elite, or among different elite groups, is common.
- From time to time, aristocracies (or oligarchies) are toppled by popular revolution and replaced by monarchical rule of some kind.
- Hybrids between monarchy and aristocracy are possible though appearances can be deceptive, and it is always necessary to look beneath the surface to see who really has the whip hand.
- Genuine monarchical power is essentially anti-aristocratic. Strong monarchy depends on subordinating elites to the monarch. Elites usually continue to exist but with diminished clout. If they can actually be eliminated altogether, so much the better for the monarch but this is virtually impossible.

- True absolute monarchy is practically unattainable.
- Isolation is not a good basis for strong monarchy.
- Strong monarchy generally, though not invariably, depends on lower class support, which is a form of "populism."
- This, paradoxically, links monarchy with democracy.
- However, the label of "democracy" is mostly misplaced. Most modern "representative democracies" are actually oligarchies.
- True democracy would need to be direct democracy, based on genuine equality, neither of which exists.
- Maximum social mobility occurs where there is maximum equality of opportunity.
- But equality of opportunity is an *equal* opportunity to become *unequal*.
- So, equality of opportunity is exactly the opposite of equality.
- And, as equal opportunity entails liberty, so liberty and equality are at loggerheads.
- Paradoxically, however, true equality of opportunity requires genuine equality, which does not exist.
- Even more paradoxically, the closest approach to equality is achieved by a monarchical ruler lopping off the heads of all poppies projecting above the rest and, thereby, creating a general leveling in society.

Case Study I: Rome

As shown in Chapters 1-5, Roman history provides us with a good example of the perennial conflict between monarchy and aristocracy. The government of the Roman Republic, which lasted from 509 to 49 BCE, was aristocratic, with a visceral hatred and fear of monarchy. (The idea that the Republic was some kind of "direct democracy" is a serious fallacy. See Chapter 1.) By accepting a "dictatorship for life," Julius Caesar effectively sealed his own death warrant—his assassination at the hands of leading members of the Roman senatorial aristocracy.

Caesar's heir, the Emperor Augustus, was not slow to learn this lesson. While retaining Caesar's popular support among the lower orders, he was careful not to offend the senatorial aristocracy, who were given a significant, albeit subordinate, role in government. This carefully balanced system, labeled by historians the "Principate," allowed considerable social mobility and achieved remarkable stability which would last, with certain modifications, and a few hiccups, for some three hundred years. (That the Principate was in any sense either a form of "direct democracy" or an "oligarchy" will not stand up to scrutiny. See Chapter 1.)

This system was abruptly terminated in 284 by the Emperor Diocletian, who replaced it with the "Dominate," a superficially more autocratic form of monarchy. Chapter 2 shows that Diocletian cut the senatorial aristocracy out of almost all government posts, appointing equestrians instead, and also relying to some extent on eunuchs.

In Chapter 3 we find that, in the West, Constantine brought members of the senatorial aristocracy back into civilian government appointments as provincial governors, and even as praetorian prefects. His motive is not clear. It does not appear to have been a counter-intuitive religious move, but rather a recognition of the social and economic status of the senatorial aristocracy in the Western half of the Empire, and also a consequence of the fact that after 324 his own focus shifted to the East, where he established a new custom-built Christian capital.

Chapter 4 shows that this policy of aristocratic appointments was continued by Constantine's successors in the West. What effect, if any, did this have on imperial power? It appears to have dented it somewhat because the great men who occupied positions of high trust in the imperial service had local interests in the shape of landholding and local influence in the provinces in which they served, which acted as a counterweight to central imperial power.

It would be wrong to think of this as amounting to a shift from monarchy to aristocracy but only as a move in that direction, which only materialized later after the grip of Rome over the Western provinces was replaced by "barbarian" kingdoms. The current taboo attaching to labels, such as *vassal*, *fief*, *feudal*, and *feudalism* should not blind us to the underlying realities. As Charles West puts it, "Historians who complain about the anachronism inherent in such terms might perhaps reflect on how far another label created by historians, that of the Middle Ages itself, shapes their research." (West 2013, p. 261.)

The very different power structure of the Eastern, or Byzantine, Empire, is dealt with in Chapters 4 and 5. Though conventionally described as "autocratic" or even "absolute," and despite the absence of a hereditary aristocracy until the tenth century, Byzantine imperial power was shared to greater or lesser extent with the Church and with court eunuchs.

Conclusion: Roman Social Mobility and Ethos

Social mobility fluctuated quite widely over the span of Roman history. As far as the Republic (509–49 BCE) is concerned, as explained in Chapter 1, I am prepared to go along with Syme: "In any age of the history of Republican Rome about twenty or thirty men, drawn from a dozen dominant families, hold a monopoly of office and power". (Syme 1939, p. 124.) This view is supported by Ernst Badian's conclusion that "the proportion of consuls who came from families that had already produced at least one consul never fell below 70 percent in the whole period between 179 and 49 BCE." (Badian 1990, p. 371–413.) This does not deny the existence of "new men," but it means that they were very much in the minority.

During the Principate (31 BCE–284 CE), the elites were more open. As shown in Chapter 1, detailed prosopographical research summarized by Mason Hammond shows that the proportion of provincial (i.e. non-Italian) senators of known origin increased steadily (with a couple of minor blips) from 16.8 percent under Vespasian (r. 69–79) to 56 percent in the third century. Under Vespasian, therefore, provincials made up only one-sixth of senators of known origin. There is a major jump to 32.4 percent under Trajan (r. 98–117), who was himself a provincial from Spain. Practically all subsequent emperors were also provincials, and from the end of the second century provincials made up more than half the senators of known origin. This ever-widening circle of senators, from whom most provincial governors were drawn, was an important reason for the stability and general tranquility of the Roman Empire over a long period. In keeping with this trend, in the year 212, the Emperor Caracalla extended Roman citizenship to all free male inhabitants of the Roman world by means of the so-called *Constitutio Antoniniana*.

Social mobility in the Later Roman Empire is more difficult to gauge. As was shown in Chapter 2, under Diocletian (284–305) senators were almost totally excluded from governorships, which became practically the exclusive preserve of equestrians. But, whereas senatorial rank, denoted by the title *vir clarissimus* (literally, "most distinguished man"), was hereditary, equestrian status was not hereditary but depended on the particular office held. By replacing senators with equestrians, and also relying to some extent on eunuchs, Diocletian clearly intended to enhance imperial power, which was demonstrated by his flamboyant dress and elaborate court ceremonial. Hence the modern label of "Dominate" attached to Diocletian's "tetrarchy."

Though the outward trappings of Diocletian's Dominate were perpetuated by his successors, the reality of power in the West underwent a major shift from the time of Constantine (r. 306–337), who brought members of the senatorial aristocracy back into high civil (but not military) government appointments, allowing them to combine office with local landholding. Constantine also began a long-continued process of inflation of titles of honor. For example, by the time of Valentinian I (r. 364–75) and Valens (r. 364–78) even the strictly equestrian post of *dux* (provincial military commander) carried the clarissimate. According to A.H.M. Jones: "The new hierarchy effectively transformed the aristocracy from one of birth into one of office." (Jones 1964, p. 529.) This was certainly true of the Eastern half of the Empire, which lacked a traditional senatorial aristocracy like that of the West, and where the *clarissimi* of the new Senate of Constantinople were parvenus. But in the West, once high office, including the position of praetorian prefect, was opened up to senators, appointees tended to be men not just of senatorial rank but also of senatorial *birth*. As a result, in the West there was no real fusion or merger between the old senatorial aristocracy and new men, and nobles were very proud, and conscious of belonging to the old senatorial aristocracy. Social mobility in the West was, therefore, far more limited than in the Byzantine East, where there was no real hereditary aristocracy until the tenth or eleventh century. Until then, as was seen in Chapters 4 and 5, imperial power, though theoretically unlimited, was shared with bureaucrats, generals, the Church, and, to a very significant extent, with eunuchs.

Caution: In a 1967 paper titled "The Caste System in the Later Roman Empire," A.H.M. Jones claimed that "...social mobility was greater in the later Roman Empire than it had been under the principate. We know of a surprisingly large number of persons of humble status, decurions (town councilors), *cohortales* (administrative assistants to provincial governors), and even urban workmen and peasants who rose through the law, the civil service or the army into the upper grades of the imperial aristocracy and even to the imperial throne itself." (Jones 1974, p. 418.) The article adopts a wide sweep down to the time of Justinian (r. 527–565), and these concluding remarks refer to the post-Constantinian East rather than the West.

This is the only place in Jones's article that the aristocracy is mentioned at all. What the article is actually about is the "hereditary classes" from much lower echelons of society. These, in Jones's words, fell into two main categories: "those whose personal service was required by the government, such as soldiers, agricultural labourers, and workers in the mints and the state factories and the public post, and those like the decurions [viz. municipal councillors] and also soldiers, agricultural labourers, the shippers, (*navicularii*), and the guilds of Rome, who, though they might have to perform certain personal services, were mainly required to make a financial contribution to various essential activities." (Ibid.) Focusing on these occupations, Jones declared his objective as endeavoring "...to prove that in practice status and occupation were to a large extent hereditary under the Principate, and that the later emperors did little more than give legal sanction to a system which was, through various social and economic causes, beginning to break down." (Jones 1974, p. 396.)

However, on the basis of the evidence assembled in the foregoing chapters of this book, comparing the Principate with the Later Roman Empire, what we find is this:

- Under the Principate, increasingly, senatorial status was conferred on those whom the emperor wished to appoint to high office.
- The same is largely true of the Eastern Roman Empire, from Constantine onward.
- But in the West, from Constantine onward, the situation was exactly the opposite: appointment to high office was largely vouchsafed to those who already had senatorial status by birth.

Case Study II: Classical Greek Tyranny

As mentioned above, true monarchy is essentially anti-aristocratic, and often populist. Ancient Greece provides us with a good example of this in the shape of the so-called *tyrants*, whose heyday was from 650 to 550 BCE, though tyrants pop up in later periods of Greek history as well. Tyrannies arose on the overthrow of aristocratic (or oligarchic) governments. Today the word "tyrant" has pejorative connotations, but these bad associations date only from the fifth century BCE. Before that the word had simply been a neutral synonym for "king," and there is strong evidence that in their own day the tyrants were genuinely popular leaders of anti-aristocratic movements.

Aristotle put the tyrants' typical power-base in a nutshell: "The majority of tyrants have generally developed out of demagogues who have gained the confidence of the people through their attacks upon the nobles." (Arist. *Pol.* 1310b 8ff = V.8.2-3.)

The tyrants' approach to the rich and noble is graphically illustrated by an anecdote related by Herodotus concerning Periander, tyrant of Corinth (r. c. 627–585 BCE), and his fellow tyrant, Thrasybulus of Miletus. Aristotle tells the same story, with roles reversed. (Arist. *Politics* 3.1284a and 5.1311a.) The story as told by Herodotus is that Periander sent a herald to Thrasybulus to ask his advice on the conduct of government. His advice was lost on the messenger, because it was mimed rather than spoken and amounted in fact to a graphic demonstration of the policy he was recommending:

> Thrasybulus led the man who had come from Periander outside the city and, entering a sown field, he walked through the corn questioning and interrogating the herald about his voyage from Corinth, and all the time he was lopping off any ears of corn that he saw projecting above the others, and he cast them aside as he cut them down until he

had destroyed the best and richest portion of the crop by this means. (Herodotus, 5.92, translated by A.D. Godley, Loeb Classical Library, 1989.)

Though this charade may have been wasted on the servant, it was certainly not lost on his master. This graphic demonstration epitomizes in itself the role of the tyrant as the enemy of the rich and noble and as a leveller.

Is this charming anecdote historical? Most probably. Not only does it ring true, but in view of the reversal of roles, Aristotle's version would appear to derive from a different source from Herodotus's. But it really makes no difference whether it is true or not. As they say in Italian: *se non è vero, è ben trovato*. ("If it's not true, it's plausible.") It neatly encapsulates the secret of monarchical power, sometimes labeled the "tall poppy syndrome", which is understood by many strong rulers throughout history, though, with a few notable exceptions, rarely by historians.

In a book specifically titled *The Greek Tyrants* by Anthony Andrewes, an Oxford professor, there is no mention at all of the famous anecdote. Even more disquieting, the book shows no sign of understanding the point made by Aristotle about the general anti-aristocratic basis of the tyrants' power. (Andrewes 1956.) The closest that Andrewes gets to any kind of general conclusion on the nature of Greek tyranny is in these vague remarks in the Epilogue (there is no "Conclusion"):

> The early tyrants '...were a product of the instability of their times, in their case of the breakdown of archaic aristocratic government.... The basic cause was a change in the conditions, above all the economic conditions, of Greek life, and the symptom of trouble was the incompetence or mere anarchy of the aristocrats. When the trouble came to a head, the immediate need of the city concerned was for strong government to repair the damage and pull the state together, and the tyrant's unfettered executive power answered this need.' (Andrewes 1956, p. 147)

There is no sign here of any awareness of the dominant thread of populism running through Greek tyranny. Instead, the rise of tyrants is confusingly associated with "...the incompetence or mere anarchy of the aristocrats." The term "mere anarchy" contradicts the very existence of aristocratic (or any other kind of) government, meaning as it does "no government." And the phrase "mere anarchy" makes about as much sense as "slight chaos" or "minor catastrophe." More important, if it means anything at all, the "mere anarchy of the aristocrats" should mean that aristocratic government had already broken down before the tyrant took power. Yet there is no evidence of that in any Greek state.

By contrast, Moses Finley, to his credit, drew a parallel between the tyrant Peisistratus and Pericles, the personification of Athenian democracy, recognizing the important truth that both were essentially "champions of the people" against the rich and noble:

> It is significant that of the few innovations by Pisistratus that have survived in the historical record, two were obviously designed to weaken the local power of the richer landowners by undermining major devices that fostered patron-client relations.... In that respect, Pericles was a direct heir of Peisistratus: he reestablished the apparently defunct board of deme judges and he instituted a long series of measures giving financial assistance to the poor from state funds.... (Finley 1983, p. 47.)

Tyranny and Democracy

In his *Rhetoric*, Aristotle names three demagogic tyrants, Theagenes of Megara (seventh century BCE), Peisistratus of Athens (died 527 BCE) and Dionysius I of Syracuse (c. 432–367 BCE), who are said to have won the confidence of the people by their "enmity towards the rich." The same three names recur in Aristotle's *Politics* as tyrants who were "the champions of the people" (*hoi prostatai tou dēmou*). (*Ibid.*, 1305a 18ff = V.4.5)—significantly, exactly the same phrase as used for Athenian democratic leaders.

The leveling regarded as most typical of tyranny was thought by Aristotle to have been invented by Periander, tyrant of Corinth. These measures included "The cutting down of the illustrious and the destruction of the proud, and also the prohibition of dining clubs, social clubs, education or anything of that sort." (Ibid., 1313a 38ff = V.9.2). All these measures were directed against the activities of the rich. The poor were not much given to joining dining clubs or cultural societies and would not have been able to afford that lifestyle in any case.

Athens: From Tyranny to Democracy

Referring to Athens, Plutarch remarks that: "From the beginning there had been a sort of hidden seam, as in iron, marking the difference between the popular and aristocratic parties."(Plutarch, *Pericles*, 11.3.) The Aristotelian *Athenian Constitution* (*Athenaiōn Politeia (AP)*, probably written by Aristotle himself or by one of his students) singles out two politicians in every generation, one billed as "the people's champion" (*prostatēs tou dēmou)* and the other as leader of the "notables" (*gnōrimoi*) or aristocracy. (Arist., AP 28.) The popular leaders are identified in chronological order as Solon, Peisistratus, Cleisthenes,

Themistocles, Ephialtes, Pericles, Cleon and Cleophon. Significantly, Peisistratus, a tyrant, is here lumped together with the popular leaders of the democracy, including Pericles.

Solon, the earliest of Aristotle's "people's champions", came to power in 594 BCE in the wake of an economic crisis, but, when called upon by the masses to become a tyrant, he demurred. The masses found a more reliable champion in Peisistratus, who first came to power in about 561 BCE and did not let them down. It is significant that the people were not seeking to take power into their own hands: they were looking for a champion to take power on their behalf.

Aristotle's *Athenian Constitution* rounds off its assessment of Peisistratus's long rule by describing him as popular (*dēmotikos*) and humane (*philanthrōpos*), ruling in accordance with the law and not favoring his own interests—even to the point of appearing in person to defend himself against a murder charge, although his accuser then took fright and left. Though deposed twice, we are told, he easily got back into power because most of the nobles (*gnōrimoi*) as well as the people were well disposed towards him, the former by his social interaction and the latter by his assistance to them in their personal affairs, and he "behaved impeccably (*kalōs*) to both." (*AP* 9.) Adding aristocratic support to his original populist power-base was an unusual—and far from easy—achievement for a tyrant, which presumably contributed to his resilience.

Peisistratus died in his bed in 527 BCE and was succeeded as tyrant by his son Hippias. The assassination of Hippias's brother Hipparchus in 514 BCE seems to have had more to do with a homosexual love triangle than with politics and his aristocratic murderers, Harmodius and his lover Aristogeiton, later fêted as "Tyrannicides" and even as "Liberators", were actually neither. Hippias's tyranny lasted another four years, until 510 BCE, when he was ousted by an aristocratic conspiracy and then only with the help of a Spartan army on its second attempt, under the personal command of King Cleomenes I. (*AP* 19.4.) The two aristocratic factions behind Hippias's ouster then fell out, and when Cleomenes took the Acropolis together with Isagoras and his aristocratic faction, "...the rest of the Athenians united and besieged them for two days", resulting in the surrender of the Spartan army. (Herodotus, 5.72; *AP* 20.3.) This remarkable achievement, the overpowering of the mighty Spartan army by a motley host of Athenians, is yet further testimony to the popularity of the tyranny.

Cleisthenes, a member of the noble Alcmaeonid family, now moved into the vacuum left by the tyrant, and, according to Herodotus, "...added the common people to his faction." (Herodotus 5.66) Aristotle, as we have seen, similarly lumped Cleisthenes together with Peisistratus as a champion of the people. (*AP* 28.) But, where Peisistratus's demagogy took the form of one-man rule, Cleisthenes' was translated into a major reform of the Athenian constitution, which established what later came to be labeled democracy but which Cleisthenes himself called *isonomia* (legal equality), the hallmark of which was sortition, i.e. selection by lot as distinct from election of most official positions.

"In Name a Democracy..."

There is no society in history that attracts more adulation among modern writers than Athenian "democracy." Athens is still fêted as the mother of modern democracy, but upon closer scrutiny the democratic credentials of Athenian democracy quickly unravel. The key feature of Athenian democracy is that it was a "direct democracy", in which all citizens were entitled to attend sessions of the *ecclēsia* (assembly). Yet, as we have seen, the ancient sources lump popular Athenian leaders together with tyrants as "champions of the people." This use by Aristotle of the same designation for tyrants and democratic leaders alike is extremely significant. What it appears to mean is that Aristotle recognized that the power-structure of Athenian democracy was essentially the same as that of tyranny. In the famous Funeral Oration in praise of Athens, Pericles (according to Thucydides 2.37) makes the interesting observation that the Athenian form of government "...is known as a democracy because it is administered not in the interests of the few but in the interests of the many" (*dia to mē es oligous all' es pleionas oikein dēmokratia keklētai.*) **Note**, this is **not** government **by** the many but only **in the interests of** the many! Did Pericles really say this? Though Thucydides does not claim that he was quoting the speech verbatim, A.B. Bosworth is probably justified in describing the Funeral Oration in Thucydides as a "...potent distillation of the speech Pericles actually delivered." (Bosworth 2000, p. 16.) To cap this important observation, we have Thucydides' own famous description of Periclean Athens: "In name a democracy, it became in fact rule by the first citizen." (Thucydides 2.65.)

Populist Generals

Selection by lot was the hallmark of Athenian democracy, election being considered a feature of oligarchical government because it played into the hands of aristocratic factions. Yet the most important office in the state remained elective. This was the position of *stratēgos* (general). There were ten *stratēgoi*, elected for a year at a time but with no restriction on the number of times they could be re-elected—unlike the huge number of officials chosen by lot, who could serve only one one-year term. Not surprisingly, the "champions of the people" tended to be elected as generals. Pericles is of course the best-known of these to be elected a general, but Themistocles, Ephialtes and Cleon were also elected to that position at one time or another.

In 461 BCE, Ephialtes, the father of "radical democracy," was assassinated after meeting with strong opposition from Cimon, the leader of the aristocratic party. Ephialtes was succeeded as "champion of the people" by Pericles (c. 495–429 BCE), a member of the noble Alcmaeonid family on his mother's side, who was elected as a general 15 times between 445 BCE and his death from the plague in 429 BCE. Pericles' pre-eminence in Athenian politics lasted from at least 461 until 429 BCE and was marked by the implementation of an ambitious program favorable to the masses.

Who Had the Whip Hand?

The central question is: Who had the whip hand in fifth century Athens—the masses in the Assembly or their demagogic leaders? Thucydides gave his assessment of Pericles in these words:

> [Pericles], deriving authority from his capacity and acknowledged worth, being also a man of transparent integrity, was able to control the multitude in a free spirit; he led them rather than was led by them; for, not seeking power by dishonest arts, he had no need to say pleasant things, but, on the strength of his own high character, could venture to oppose and even to anger them. When he saw them unseasonably elated and arrogant, his words humbled and awed them; and, when they were depressed by groundless fears, he sought to reanimate their confidence. (Thucydides 2.65.)

The historian, a younger contemporary of Pericles', clearly was a great admirer of his, and his description of Pericles as actually "ruling" a supposed democracy is not meant as criticism. The biographer Plutarch (45–120), writing in Roman times, cites some examples of attacks on Pericles as a "tyrant", but makes it clear that what underlay both these gibes and Thucydides' favourable judgment was a common truth, namely that Pericles really did rule the roost:

> He made the city, great as it was when he took it, the greatest and richest of all cities, and grew to be superior in power to kings and tyrants. Of his power there can be no doubt, since Thucydides gives so clear an exposition of it, and the comic poets unwittingly reveal it in their malicious gibes, calling him and his associates "new Peisistratidae" [that is

"sons of Peisistratus," i.e. tyrants] and urging him to take a solemn oath not to make himself a tyrant, on the plea that his pre-eminence was incommensurate with a democracy and too oppressive. Telecleides says that the Athenians had handed over to him lock, stock and barrel. And this was not the fruit of a golden moment, nor the culminating popularity of an administration that bloomed but for a season; no, rather he stood first for forty years among such men as Ephialtes, Leocrates, Myronides, Cimon, Tolmides and Thucydides. (Plutarch, *Pericles* 16.5.)

Pericles and the Aristocracy

A modern writer has mistakenly suggested that because Pericles was of aristocratic birth he must have engaged in politics as a member of an aristocratic elite: "The political machine of Pericles in fact drew from all elements of Athenian society, but predominantly from those very *chrēstoi* in whom we are supposed to see a party of the opposition." (Frost 1964.) This is incorrect for at least three reasons.

Firstly, to speak of organized "parties" in Ancient Athens is anachronistic and misleading. But, more important, it is plainly wrong to see Pericles as relying for his support on members of his own class, the *chrēstoi* ("the good", i.e. the aristocracy). On the contrary, he was an anti-aristocratic aristocrat and a "champion of the people", as we know from Thucydides, Plutarch and other ancient sources. Plutarch significantly tells us that Pericles refused all invitations to dinner and turned down all hospitality "...so that in the long time that he was engaged in politics he did not go to a single one of his friends for dinner, except that, when his cousin Euryptolemus got married, he stayed until the libations were poured and then immediately got up and left." (Ibid., 7.4.) In other words, Pericles deliberately eschewed the company of his own class. How convincing a champion of the poor would he have been if he was seen hobnobbing with the rich and noble, eating their food, and quaffing their wine? We can draw a parallel with his successor Cleon's dramatic renunciation of his friendships. The anti-aristocratic aristocrat or anti-wealthy millionaire is still with us today in the shape of the Roosevelts and the Kennedys, to mention but two.

Secondly, the fact that the champions of the people in the Athenian democracy included aristocrats like Pericles should not be dismissed with the remark that "...the Athenian people were rather snobbish in their choice of leaders." (Jones 1957, p. 49.) The question is: Why was this the case? The answer is that, though the regime was anti-aristocratic, the whole ethos of society remained aristocratic: the Athenian democracy, in common with ancient society in general, simply did not believe in equality. (Arnheim 1977, p. 158 ff.)

Thirdly, it is a fallacy to think of the dominant minority in any society as monolithic. Besides maverick members of the privileged minority who identify with the interests of "the many," there will always be factions and fissures within any dominant minority. In seventeenth century England, for example, the propertied classes, which alone were represented in Parliament, were divided into those supporting the Crown and those wishing to subject the monarch to Parliament. A bloody civil war, followed by the execution of one king and, fifty years later, by the deposition of another, decided the matter in favor of parliamentary power. (For more on this, see below.)

The history of the United States provides further examples of this. Populist presidents like Andrew Jackson (1829–37), Theodore Roosevelt (1901–09), Franklin D. Roosevelt (1933–45), Ronald Reagan (1981–89), and Donald Trump (2017–21) all combined support from (very varied) disaffected anti-elite elements of the population with the backing of portions of the elites themselves. (Osnos 2020.)

Beneath the Surface of the Athenian Democracy

The comfortable, gentlemanly idea of "government by discussion" applied to fifth century Athens by some of its adulators like A.W. Gomme and Moses Finley is totally misleading, especially in the period after the death of Pericles in 429 BCE. We must now explore what lies beneath the surface of that government. It will be found that the policies adopted by Athens in the latter half of the fifth century BCE had very little to do with the cut and thrust of debate in the Assembly but a lot to do with certain underlying factors, including populism, charismatic leadership and crowd psychology, aided by manipulation of the judicial system and bully-boy tactics.

Thucydides's respect and admiration for Pericles did not extend to Pericles's successors as "champions of the people" (*prostatai tou dēmou*). Cleon, who became the chief champion of the people after Pericles's death by plague in 429 BCE, was a charismatic leader with a booming voice, who knew how to whip up the passions of the Athenian masses. He increased the pay for service on the massive political juries favored by the Athenians, which, to prevent bribery, were made up of between 201 and 5,001 jurors selected by lot every day.

The ancient sources generally portray Cleon in a very negative light. It is easy to wave these aside as prejudiced because most Athenian intellectuals were conservatives hostile to the "democratic" regime, and Thucydides and Aristophanes also had personal grudges of their own against Cleon. Yet the picture of Cleon that emerges from the sources, including Thucydides' paraphrases of some of Cleon's speeches, has a ring of truth about it, which chimes in with the general pattern of popular dictatorship. Thucydides describes Cleon as "the most violent man in Athens" (Thuc. 3.36) and as "...a popular leader of the time and very powerful with the multitude." (Thuc. 4.21.) Aristophanes's portrayal of Cleon is much more vitriolic, especially in *The Knights* and *The Wasps*.

The comic dramatist Aristophanes (c. 446–c. 386 BCE) made no bones about his hostility to the Athenian democracy, and he had a personal run-in with Cleon (died 422 BCE). At one point in *The Knights*, the chorus addresses Demos (the people) with these words: "Demos, the rule that you possess is lovely, since everyone fears you like (*hōsper*) a tyrant. But you are easily led, enjoy being flattered and fooled, and you listen to the orators with mouth agape, and your mind is befuddled." (Aristophanes, *The Knights* 111–119.) Demos is said here to have "rule", but it would be a mistake to interpret this as meaning that Demos is a tyrant. What the Chorus is saying is that Demos is feared *as if* he were a tyrant. Does that mean that power in Athens was in the hands of the people? Clearly not, because Demos is told that he is under the thumb of the "orators", who are identified elsewhere in the same play as demagogues, notably Cleon. The question is who has the whip-hand: Demos or the demagogue? The answer is clear: it is the demagogue. To clarify this point further we might look at a passage from another of Aristophanes' plays, *The Wasps*, where the anti-Cleon son chides his pro-Cleon father for allowing someone like Cleon to rule (*archein*) over him. (*The Wasps* 666.) Here there can be no doubt: rule is in the hands of the demagogues and not of the people.

Whisper vs. Shout

The attacks in the ancient sources on Cleon and his demagogic successors touched off a belated rearguard action mounted from the mid-twentieth century onward to "rehabilitate" these demagogues. One of the more amusing non-arguments advanced in this cause is to be found in Moses Finley's article on demagogues, in which he dismisses the Aristotelian remark about Cleon being the first man to "shout and rail" as "...obviously a frivolous approach, nothing more than the expression of class prejudice and snobbishness." Finley poses a rhetorical question as his knock-out blow: "Are we to imagine that Thucydides the son of Melesias (and kinsman of the historian) and Nicias whispered when they addressed the Assembly in opposition to Pericles and Cleon, respectively?" (Finley 1962, p. 16.) Finley's point is completely illogical. He assumes that whispering is the only alternative to shouting, which is arrant nonsense. Not all politicians shout and rail, and those who do are more likely to be radical demagogues rather than conservative leaders. The most obvious example is the rantings of Adolf Hitler, whose strident tones were not matched, for example, by the rousing yet subdued fervor of Winston Churchill. So desperate is Finley to rehabilitate Cleon that he ultimately resorts to tarring all leaders with the same brush: "...the term [demagogue] is equally applicable to all leaders, regardless of class or point of view". (Ibid., p.19.) This completely obliterates the clear distinction drawn in the ancient sources between the conservative oligarchic leaders and the demagogic champions of the people.

"All Leaders Were Demagogues"

Finley's bad point about Cleon's rants is part of a more general, and equally fallacious, attempt on his part to tar all Athenian leaders with the brush of demagogy. This is based on Finley's mistaken belief that the system was one of rational discussion, debate, and deliberation:

> A man was a leader solely as a function of his personal, and in the literal sense, unofficial status within the Assembly itself. The test of whether or not he held that status was simply whether the Assembly did or did not vote as he wished, and therefore the test was repeated with each proposal. These were the conditions which faced all leaders in Athens, not merely those whom Thucydides and Plato dismissed as 'demagogues', not merely those whom some modern historians miscall 'radical democrats', but everyone, aristocrat or commoner, altruist or self-seeker, able or incompetent, who, in George Grote's phrase, 'stood forward prominently to advise' the Athenians. (Ibid., pp. 15–16.)

This picture of the Athenian Assembly as a sedate debating society is yet another example of Finley's getting hold of the wrong end of the stick. It is negated by (a) the whole new style of politics which came in with Pericles and was amplified by Cleon; (b) the use of bully-boy tactics by Cleon and others; (c) the citizens' lack of interest in participating in this supposed exercise of power on their part; (d) the existence of charismatic leadership on one side only; (e) the fact that there was very little real disagreement in the Assembly, with the majority simply endorsing their radical demagogic leaders' proposals; (f) crowd psychology; and (g) the highly irrational decisions taken by Athens under the leadership of the radical demagogues. (It is perhaps no surprise that Finley, pooh-poohing the ancient evidence, had to resort to George Grote (1794–1871), an activist radical British politician who never went to university and whose *History of Greece* was published between 1846 and 1856.)

"The New Politicians"

The radical demagogues undoubtedly *did* belong to a different leadership type from their conservative, oligarchic opponents like Cimon, Thucydides son of Melesias and Nicias. W. Robert Connor pointed out in *The New Politicians of Fifth-Century Athens* (1971) that these "new politicians" broke away from the traditional model of political support centered on a group of *philoi*, "friends", which were based on family connections and aristocratic clubs known as *hetaireiai*. The new model of politics was based instead on a direct personal relationship between the demagogues and the mass of lower-class citizens who attended the Assembly and served in the law courts as jurors on the enormous juries introduced to prevent bribery.

To symbolize this personal bond with the masses, Cleon, we are told by Plutarch, renounced his friends, declaring himself to be more deeply in love with the Assembly than with his friends. Thucydides and Aristophanes give further support to this picture. This model of politics rings true of charismatic populist demagogues in other societies and other periods as well, such as Benito Mussolini, Adolf Hitler, Fidel Castro and Mao Tse-tung (Mao Zedong). Despite the "...major doubts about Connor's presentation of the 'new style' in politics" expressed by a nitpicking reviewer (Davies 1975), Connor would actually have been justified by the evidence to take his theory of "the new politicians" even further. What there was in late fifth century Athens was not just a "new style" of politics but a new form of government, with power in the hands of a populist charismatic leader of the masses against the interests of the rich and noble.

Cleon and the Sycophants

Not surprisingly, in his discussion of the radical demagogues, Finley omits any mention of the devious means employed by Cleon, notably his use of "sycophants", meaning deceitful or calumnious informers against the rich and noble, enabling Cleon to bring lawsuits to strip them of their wealth and undermine them. The comic dramatist Aristophanes and other comic poets lost no opportunity to expose the nefarious practices of these informers and their links to Cleon and other populist demagogues. Some of the fragments of the Attic orators also throw some light on the sycophants. And we learn from Plutarch of the intimidation of the conservative leader Nicias by Cleon and Hyperbolus, another radical demagogue. The system was wide open to this kind of abuse because any Athenian could launch a prosecution against any other for alleged crimes against the state and collect a reward if his victim was convicted. As a result, the "profession" of sycophancy attracted a lot of dubious characters, whose unjustified threatened lawsuits against the rich amounted to blackmail, which could pay off twice over, once with a pay-out from their intended victim and possibly also a gratuity for their good work from the radical demagogue on whose behalf they had set the whole process in motion in the first place. It was possible, though, for two to play at the same game. In Xenophon's *Memorabilia of Socrates* (2.9.1–6), there is an amusing passage recording a conversation between Socrates and his friend Criton, who is at his wits' end being harassed by sycophants who believe that he would bow to their threats rather than go to court to face their untrue allegations. On Socrates' advice, Criton engages Archedemus as a sort of private investigator, who brings (justified) charges against the sycophant and only drops those charges in return for the sycophant's withdrawing his charges against Criton and rewarding Archedemus!

Charismatic Leadership

Charismatic leadership, first identified under that name by Max Weber (1864–1920), was an important aspect of this new style of politics which is not sufficiently stressed by Connor. There is now a welter of different definitions of charismatic leadership, but this definition by Professor Ronald E. Riggio is perhaps a useful starting point: "Charismatic leaders are essentially very skilled communicators—individuals who are both verbally eloquent, but also able to communicate to followers on a deep, emotional level. They are able to articulate a compelling or captivating vision, and are able to arouse strong emotions in followers." (Riggio 2012.) Arising out of this is charismatic authority, which has been usefully defined this way:

> [P]ower legitimized on the basis of a leader's exceptional personal qualities or the demonstration of extraordinary insight and accomplishment, which inspire loyalty and obedience from followers. (Kendall et al. 2000, pp. 438–439.)

Pericles, Cleon and Alcibiades, and others, including Hyperbolus and Cleophon, clearly were charismatic leaders with the broad support of the lower-class majority in the Assembly, with whom they had a reciprocal, almost symbiotic, relationship.

Max Weber classified the Greek *polis* in general, and Athenian democracy in particular, as belonging to the model of charismatic *Herrschaft*, which roughly translates as "institutionalized authority".

M.I. Finley predictably dismissed the whole idea of the applicability to Athens of charismatic leadership, rejecting the "mystical faith" that he charged Weber with, stressing and favoring instead an "instrumental view of politics" (whatever that is supposed to mean) locating the explanation for the workings of Athenian leadership "...in the area of programs and politics" and pouting,"To dismiss the Greek *polis* in general and Athens in particular as irrational does not advance our understanding." (Finley 1962, p. 93.) Josiah Ober, himself a strong admirer of Athenian democracy, makes the following sensible comment:

> Finley is certainly correct to attack as simplistic and misleading a purely charismatic view of Athenian leadership and to point out the overemphasis of the ancient critics on demagogic appeals to base emotions. But Finley himself seems to go too far in the other direction. His eagerness to debunk the critics of the democracy leads him to overrationalize the nature of the Athenian orator's appeal to his audience. (Ober 1989, p. 124.).

Government by Discussion?

In an attempt to boost its democratic credentials, Athenian democracy is often characterized by its adulators as "government by discussion", a phrase first used of (modern representative) democracy by John Stuart Mill, the liberal politician and theorist (1806–1873), and this phrase has since been bandied about by defenders of ancient direct democracy as well. Here is A.W. Gomme (1886–1959), a professor in the University of Glasgow, attempting to prove that Athenian government in the fifth century BCE was a true democracy. Referring to the *ecclēsia*, or Assembly, Gomme asks himself the question, "Did this assembly really rule or were its meetings only an empty show, and all decisions made elsewhere?"

Gomme's astonishingly naïve answer to the question is as follows:

> We can make a simple test: when government is by discussion, as it certainly was in Athens, where did the discussion take place, where were the great speeches made? In this country, in the eighteenth and early nineteenth centuries, they were made in parliament, in the Lords or the Commons, with a growing preponderance of the Commons; in the later nineteenth century in the Commons and on the hustings; now over the radio as well; the House of Commons, with some control by the people, rules. In Rome, in the great days of the Republic, the speeches were made in the senate; for the senate ruled. In Athens they were made only in the assembly... Government, then, was by the people. (Gomme 1962, p. 86.)

Besides being naïve, this is a circular argument if ever there was one. Starting from the premise that Athenian government was "government by discussion" it is hardly surprising that we arrive at the conclusion that Gomme wants us to. But was Athenian government really "government by discussion", and, for that matter, what does "government by discussion" mean?

Practically all Gomme's assertions are wrong. Let us examine them one by one:

- *In modern Britain, the House of Commons, "with some control by the people" rules—because it is in the House of Commons that discussion takes place.* This is naïve. First of all, there is very little actual discussion in the House of Commons. Members of Parliament are representatives rather than delegates, and so are theoretically free to vote any way they like in any debate, but voting against their party's line is a high-risk strategy. Important votes are designated as a "three-line whip", which means that members of each party are *obliged* to vote the party line, failing which they may be disciplined or even have "the whip withdrawn" from them, which means that they are cut loose and will not be nominated by the party at the next election. As a result, most parliamentary debates are highly predictable and are not intended to "persuade" the other side. Secondly, and even more importantly, it is simply not true to say that the House of Commons "rules" Britain. "The sovereignty of Parliament" is an important constitutional principle—in theory. But in practice the position is quite different. After a general election the political party (or coalition of parties) which has a majority of seats in the House of Commons automatically forms the government, which, precisely because it commands a majority of seats, can normally get its program passed into law without much difficulty; for, the overwhelming majority of laws passed by Parliament are proposed by the government. The government controls Parliament, not the other way round, and the notion that "the House of Commons rules" is arrant nonsense. Lord Hailsham (1907–2001), who served as Lord Chancellor under Edward Heath and Margaret Thatcher, coined the phrase "elective dictatorship" to describe the actual situation.
- *"In Rome, in the great days of the Republic, the speeches were made in the senate; for the senate ruled."* That the Senate ruled the roost in the heyday of the Republic is true enough, but that was not because the speeches were made there but for a very different reason, namely that the Senate was the chief bulwark of the ruling aristocracy. Moreover, even if that means that the Roman Republic was "government by discussion", it certainly does *not* mean that the Roman

Republic was a democracy. As is shown in Chapter 1, the Republic was ruled by a close-knit aristocracy or oligarchy.

- *"In Athens they [i.e. the speeches] were made only in the assembly... Government, then, was by the people."* The speeches were indeed largely made in the assembly. If it means anything at all, "government by discussion" must presumably mean that decisions are taken only after full and free debate, with the decision-makers being open to persuasion by speakers on either side. In reality, however, the outcome of the debates was almost always a foregone conclusion. We have only one example of a change of mind by a majority of voters on any of the "great issues" of Athenian politics in the whole period covered by Thucydides. To describe Athenian government as "government by discussion" is therefore misleading, and it is unrealistic to believe that the assembly "ruled". There was a succession of popular leaders with whom the masses had something of a reciprocal or symbiotic relationship. The most notable of these was Pericles, who held the position of *stratēgos* (general), one of the few elective positions in the state, for over thirty years, a period described by Thucydides, as we have seen, as "In name a democracy, but in fact rule by the first man" (2.65). And Pericles was succeeded by far more extreme demagogues like Cleon, Hyperbolus and Cleophon.

Greece: Conclusion

The Greek states of antiquity were mostly governed by oligarchies or aristocracies—in other words, by minorities, whether hereditary or not. Tyranny was an exception to this rule, representing as it did an anti-aristocratic populist form of government headed by an autocratic "tyrant," usually under the title of king. Another major exception to aristocratic government was democracy, as found particularly in Athens. The affinity between tyranny and democracy was not lost on ancient commentators including Aristotle, who, as we have seen, applied the label, "champions of the people" to both tyrants and democratic leaders. Athens' first tyrant, Peisistratus, essentially a populist leader, later managed to win over elements of the aristocracy. This was no mean feat, as the interests of the *chrestoi* (the aristocracy) and the *demos* (the masses) were essentially at loggerheads—as was graphically illustrated by the mimed advice referred to above, given by one tyrant to another: namely to lop off any ears of corn projecting above the others. Similarly, the radical Athenian democratic leaders after Pericles used the law courts with their huge juries to fleece the rich, as we know, among others, from Aristophanes, a contemporary of Cleon's.

Between 411 and 404 BCE, the Athenian government underwent some major changes. In 404 BCE, Athens suffered a crushing defeat by Sparta in the Peloponnesian War (431–404 BCE), but democracy was re-established in 403, which survived until 338 BCE, when Athens was defeated by Philip II of Macedon. But this was a far less radical form of democracy than before, with some oligarchic features.

A book by David A. Teegarden titled *Death to Tyrants!* turns out to have nothing whatsoever to do with the Greek tyrants as normally understood. (Teegarden 2013.) The book makes much of the Decree of Demophantos of 410 BCE, which obliged Athenians to take an oath to kill anyone who overthrew the Athenian democracy or attempted to become a "tyrant." This reference to "tyrants" does not refer to one-man rule at all but to its opposite, oligarchy. In 411 BCE, the Athenian democracy was overthrown in an aristocratic coup and replaced by an oligarchy of 400 men. Democracy was restored the following year; but, after Athens' defeat by Sparta in the Peloponnesian War in 404 BCE, the Athenian democracy was again overthrown, and this time replaced by a pro-Spartan oligarchy stigmatized by hostile contemporaries as the "Thirty Tyrants." This shows that by this time the Greek word *tyrannos* (tyrant), which had originally been a neutral term interchangeable with *basileus*, the ordinary Greek word for "king", had acquired the pejorative meaning that has clung to it ever since, referring to a cruel and repressive regime, whether headed by one man or a group of men. Teegarden confuses the issue still further by assuming that democracy and tyranny were opposites, when in fact, as we have seen, ancient Greek tyranny properly so called, in other words, anti-aristocratic monarchy, was actually closely aligned with democracy.

Muddled Perception

The failure or refusal of leading modern historians to recognize or understand the patterns of Greek power structure is worrying, because it reveals the shallowness of their understanding of Greek history as a whole, or, for that matter, of any history. Here is A. Andrewes's muddled perception of the relationship between tyranny and democracy in Athens. In reference to fifth century Athenian democracy we read: "The *demos* now becomes its own defender and the patron of its successive leaders. The corporate feeling which made this possible was in large part the creation of the Peisistratidae." (Andrewes, *op. cit.*, p. 115). The idea that the mass of the population became "its own defender" reveals a serious misreading of the ancient sources as well as an almost comical misunderstanding of the nature of politics. This is compounded by the next phrase, that the *demos* became "the patron" of its leaders. This is the exact opposite of the truth. As we have seen, it was the leaders who held the whip hand, so *they* were the patrons and the masses their followers. How in any case could a mass of 6,000 people be a "patron"? Though lost on Andrewes, the true affinity between tyranny and democracy was well understood by the ancients: tyrants and (especially radical) democratic leaders alike were "champions of the people," who won the support of the masses with populist policies and were rewarded in turn with varying degrees of obedience and respect.

Case Study III: France

At first sight, the history of France would appear to have little in common with that of classical Greece. While Greece was made up of a multiplicity of city states, France has been a unitary state for over a thousand years. The dominant character of Greek government in the classical period was oligarchy or aristocracy, with occasional interludes of tyranny or democracy. France, by contrast, was a monarchy continuously until 1792 and then intermittently until 1870, when it finally committed itself to a republican form of government.

Until the mid-nineteenth century, conflict between monarchy and aristocracy was a leitmotif of French history. A hard-fought victory over the *Parlements* was won by the monarchy under King Louis XV, only to be thrown away by Louis XVI on his accession in 1774. Monarchy did, however, stage a spectacular comeback under the Bonapartes in the nineteenth century. But at no time would I describe the French monarchy as "absolute," a term that is all too freely bandied about by protagonists on both sides. Absolute power means, literally, autocratic, arbitrary power untrammelled by limitations of any kind—which is virtually impossible.

"L'etat c'est moi" ("I am the state") is commonly attributed to King Louis XIV (r. 1643–1715), but it has been plausibly suggested that what Louis XIV meant was something rather less dramatic than it sounds, to the effect that his interests as king should be identified with the interests of the state. (Mettam 1988.) Louis XIV cultivated the image of himself as "The Sun King" (*Le Roi Soleil*). The portrayal of Louis XIV as an absolute monarch by historians goes back at least to Voltaire (1694–1778), who, though celebrated as a father of the French Revolution, was also a great admirer of Louis XIV—and not in spite of his putative absolutism but because of it. In recent years, however, this image of Louis XIV as an absolute monarch has been disputed. So, we have to ask, how powerful was Louis XIV actually in practice? And what about his predecessors and successors?

With the notable exception of Louis XI (r. 1461–83), until the accession of the first Bourbon king, Henry (Henri) IV (r. 1589–1610), the French monarchy was generally quite weak, and the country was dominated by the aristocracy. Henry IV and Louis XIII (r. 1610–43) were fortunate enough to have very able ministers who understood the fundamental truth that strong monarchy could only be established at the expense of the aristocracy. Early on in his long reign Louis XIV had to contend with a serious aristocratic rising, the Fronde, which was successfully rebuffed, after which the power of the monarchy was enhanced, a process culminating in the last few years of Louis XV's reign (1715–74) with the utter defeat of the *parlements*, the major thorn in the side of the Crown—only to have this great victory thrown away by Louis XVI (r. 1774–92) on his accession.

It is important to note that the *parlements* were not "parliaments" in the English sense but superior courts of law of appellate jurisdiction with a wide remit, especially in regard to taxation. The most important of these was the *Parlement de Paris*, but by 1789 there were twelve other provincial *parlements*, with a total of over a thousand members in the country at large, with twelve or more councilors sitting at any one time. One particularly important power exercised by the *parlements* was their control over legislation, whereby no royal decree had the force of law in any province until it was approved and published by the *parlement* of that area.

Henry IV: "A Chicken in Every Pot"

It is really only from the time of Henry (Henri) IV that a policy of establishing a strong monarchy at the expense of the aristocracy was pursued with any degree of consistency. Henry IV is also credited with the populist promise that there would be a chicken in every peasant's pot every Sunday. However, the introduction by Henry's otherwise very astute minister, Sully, of the Paulette tax in 1604, allowing office-holders to pass their offices on to their heirs or even sell them, antagonized the *noblesse d'épée* (aristocracy of the sword or the traditional hereditary aristocracy) while creating a formidable new aristocracy, the *noblesse de robe* (aristocracy of office-holders), which eventually joined the traditional aristocracy in opposition to the Crown. Henry's assassination in 1610 handed the throne to his not quite nine-year-old son, Louis XIII.

Louis XIII (r. 1610–1643)

The accession of a minor and the existence of a regency was a signal to the aristocracy to rise up in revolt. Some groups within the aristocracy even went so far as to raise private armies and conspire with foreign states against the French Crown. This opposition was successfully crushed during Louis's reign, especially after the appointment of Cardinal Richelieu (1585–1642) as chief minister in 1624, which turned out to be a great boon to the monarchy for, while Richelieu was intent on safeguarding his own position, he remained loyal to the king (contrary to the picture painted of him in the fictitious *Three Musketeers*, by Dumas) and to the task of aggrandizing the power of the monarchy and reducing that of the aristocracy. The means that he employed to this end included the demolition of all aristocratic fortified castles (unless needed for national defense); restricting the *Parlement de Paris* to judicial matters and prohibiting it from involvement in politics; and the setting up of an unofficial secret service, plus the imposition of press censorship. Richelieu was intent on creating in France a powerful nation state under a strong centralized monarchy. On Richelieu's death, he was succeeded by his hand-picked successor, Cardinal Mazarin, who was of Italian origin (under the name Mazzarino), and who served as chief minister of France from 1642 until his death in 1661.

Louis XIV (r. 1643–1715)

Louis XIV was only five years old when he ascended the throne. Once again, there was a regency, which once again was taken advantage of by the aristocracy to raise the banner of revolt in the Fronde, in which they were joined by the *parlements* and also enjoyed a certain amount of popular support, especially in Paris. The Fronde is usually divided into two stages: first, the *Fronde Parlementaire* (1648–49), sparked off by the Crown's shortage of money, leading to Mazarin's proposed suspension of judges' salaries for a few years, and his attempt to create new posts to subvert the position of the *Parlement de Paris*, which demanded the right to give consent to new taxes. Secondly, the *Fronde des Nobles* (1650–53), which ended with the bourgeoisie of Paris turning against the *frondeurs*. With remarkable foresight, Cardinal de Retz, himself a leading *frondeur*, predicted in 1649, "*Les parlements, qui soufflaient sur le feu, en seraient, un jour, consumés*" (The parlements, which fanned the flames, will one day be consumed by them). (Cobban 1950, p. 64.) This prediction was realized 150 years later!

The lesson of the Fronde was not lost on the young Louis XIV, who, following on from the policy of Richelieu, ordered the demolition of aristocratic castles, and required nobles to spend at least part of the year at Versailles, a huge palatial complex which was constructed for this purpose among others. Nobles here would be granted honors and favors in accordance with their closeness to the royal person. Only those deemed the most important personalities, numbering about a hundred, would be admitted every morning to the *Grande Levée* (following an even more intimate *Petit lever*, to which only a select few were admitted), during which the king was dressed and given breakfast (a bowl of broth), and a shorter version of the same ceremony took place when the king retired at night. (Saint-Simon, 2007.)

After Mazarin's death in 1661, Louis XIV effectively became his own chief minister. He deprived the *parlements* of their right to decide on the validity of laws, and he streamlined both criminal and civil procedure with the introduction in 1667 of the *Grande Ordonnance de Procédure Civile*, nicknamed the *Code Louis*—foreshadowing Napoleon in this respect. And law enforcement in Paris, and later in other cities, was placed under a lieutenant general of police. But French law in general still remained a patchwork quilt of different jurisdictions.

Louis XIV understood only too well the need to reduce the power of the aristocracy, and, besides the measures already mentioned, he deliberately chose as his ministers men of ability of non-noble backgrounds, like J.-B. Colbert, or from newly ennobled families, as in the cases of Michel Le Tellier, Hugues de Lionne and Nicolas Fouquet. Having no independent power-base of their own, these ministers depended on royal favor, in return for which the king could count on their loyalty and obedience. He would not tolerate malpractice on the part of a minister, so, when Fouquet, Superintendant of Finances from 1653 to 1661, was revealed to have made huge amounts of money out of his government position, he was arrested and imprisoned for life.

It would be hard to disagree with these remarks of Roger Mettam's:

> The conflicts which troubled the internal history of France in the seventeenth century almost all had one element in common—they were caused, or were at least prolonged and invigorated, by the unceasing struggle of the crown against the independent power of the varied groups who formed the privileged orders in French society. (Mettam 1977, p. ix.) Although most groups in French society—nobles of the sword and of the robe, clerics, municipal officials and the ordinary men of town and countryside—sometimes showed considerable hostility to each other, it was against the central government that their most vigorous protests were directed. (p. xiv) The result of this investigation may point to a degree of centralised control which, if it was on the increase, was far from absolute. (Mettam 1977, p. 16.)

However, while rightly rejecting the "absolutist" label, Mettam ends up tilting against windmills: "The historians who have exaggerated the effectiveness of centralised government under Louis XIV have tended particularly to inflate the importance of the intendants, whom they

have seen as the very basis of the absolutist regime they have described."
(Ibid., p. 16) Once it is recognized that, though not "absolute," Louis
XIV was a strong monarch, Mettam's objections about the intendants
fall away. These were royal officials with supervisory powers over
finance, justice and police in the provinces or *généralités*:

- Mettam remarks that, like government ministers (secretaries of
  state), the intendants came from "established bureaucratic families." This objection will not stand up to scrutiny. The position of
  intendant was a high-level administrative office, which could hardly
  be entrusted to just anyone off the street. (Cf. the "barefoot doctors"
  in Maoist China, discussed below.)
- However, Mettam admits that the post of intendant was not hereditary and was also "...not a position that could be bought, and was
  therefore one from which the holder could easily be dismissed." In
  addition, "unlike all other bureaucratic offices," the position of
  intendant of a *généralité* "...was always given to a man who was not
  a native of that generality and therefore had no personal vested
  interest in the life of the area." An intendant "...would use every
  legitimate means, and sometimes others, to demonstrate the efficiency of his administration and his suitability for higher office in
  his home district." (Ibid.)
- "During the ministry of (Jean-Baptiste) Colbert (1661–1683), the
  intendants were used more extensively than ever before, not just to
  spy on the bureaucracy but to send in highly detailed reports about
  every aspect of provincial France. Throughout the kingdom they
  acted as the eyes and ears of the Paris ministers.... Sometimes the
  intendants were sent on general tours of inspection in their area, on
  other occasions they were asked to investigate specific problems."
  (Ibid., p. 17.)

Not surprisingly, the very existence of intendants had been a major
grievance of the Frondeurs, who, as we have seen, plagued Louis XIV's
youth. Mettam grudgingly admits that under Colbert the intendants
"did indeed improve the efficiency of the administration, but slowly
and only to a partial degree. Throughout France they did root out the
worst examples of corrupt officialdom, though much sharp practice
remained." (Ibid.)

Louis XIV's France was divided into 34 *généralités*, most of which
were so-called *pays d'élections*, where the royal government was dominant through intendants. But there were a few *généralités*, designated
pays d'états, situated mostly around the perimeter of the country, where
elected provincial Estates still retained a certain amount of autonomy.
Here the intendants were less effective, and the King was forced to rely on

aristocratic provincial governors, who existed in all provinces but mostly with only nominal powers. But Louis XIV changed the system so that appointment to a governorship was initially for only three years and no longer depended on any hereditary or social right but on royal favor alone.

Another important area of royal power was religion. By the Concordat of Bologna of 1516, Pope Leo X granted King Francis (François) I (r. 1515–47) the right, known as the *droit de régale*, which had been claimed for several centuries before, to nominate bishops, archbishops, abbots and priors in certain parts of France. In 1673 Louis XIV issued a declaration extending the *régale* to the whole country. When Bishop François-Étienne Caulet of Montauban refused to recognize the *régale* in 1679, Colbert sent in the intendant Nicolas-Joseph Foucault, who annulled the bishop's administrative acts, "... and took control of the diocese's finances, leaving the bishop nearly starving." Caulet published a scathing attack on the *régale*, and then died. Foucault arrested the printers and clergy loyal to Caulet with *lettres de cachet* (an order signed by the king, generally ordering imprisonment without trial.) (Soll, J., 2009, p. 140.) Though this is just one case, it reveals Louis XIV's determination to rule the roost in as many different policy areas as possible. And in 1681 Louis XIV convoked a church Assembly in Paris presided over by the Archbishops of Paris and Reims, which had no trouble in siding with the King against papal authority on the question of the *régale*.

But Louis's best known religious move proved ultimately to be a costly mistake: the revocation of the Edict of Nantes in 1685, promulgated in 1598 by Louis's grandfather, Henry IV, which had extended religious toleration to Protestants, of whom Henry had been one before converting to Catholicism, reputedly with the famous words, *Paris vaut bien une messe* ("Paris is well worth a Mass.")

Though not "absolute," Louis XIV was undoubtedly a strong king who from his earliest youth understood the danger to the French crown posed by the aristocracy and the *parlements*—and greatly strengthened the monarchy in response. In Louis XIV's *Mémoires for the Instruction of the Dauphin*, a surprisingly frank guide for his son and heir (who would not live to put it into practice), the king makes clear his distrust of the nobility, and his reluctance to appoint members of their class to high office. Louis was particularly concerned about overmighty judges, notably the Parlements. "It was necessary for a thousand reasons, including the urgently needed reform of justice, to diminish the excessive authority of the principal courts." He prided himself on "humiliating" his judicial officials. What is even more noteworthy is Louis XIV's recognition of the other side of the coin, namely the suffering of the lower classes at the hands of the privileged elements: "All these elements, or rather their consequences and their effects, fell primarily upon the lower class, burdened, moreover, with taxes and pressed by extreme poverty in many areas, disturbed in others by their own idleness since the peace, and especially in need of relief and of employment." (Louis XIV, 1970, tr and ed. Paul Sonnino, New York: Free Press, p.21ff.)

This bond between the King and the ordinary people of France did not escape the notice of that perspicacious British diplomat and man of letters, Matthew Prior, who in 1698 observed of the French that: "The common people of this nation have a strange veneration for their king." (quoted in Mansel, P., 2019, p. 447.)

In rejecting the "absolutist" label traditionally attached to Louis XIV, Mettam argued that Louis XIV ruled traditionally and respected local privileges. (Mettam. R., 1988.) This is an over-reaction to the "absolutist" label, as is shown by the facts assembled above. In the *pays d'états*, as we have seen, Louis was constrained to rely on provincial governors, who, though drawn from the local aristocracy, were appointed not on the basis of birth and heredity but on merit, and only for three years at a time. As for the *pays d'élections*, which made up the majority of the *généralités*, here royal power was exercised through hand-picked intendants from outside their administrative areas, who were closely controlled by the Central Government. Colbert (whose long period in office, 1661–83, was only terminated by his untimely death from untreated kidney stones) was indefatigable in instructing intendants and other officials directly and in great detail. Torn between starting work early in the morning and retiring late after a full day's work, Colbert decided to do both. Totally loyal and trusted though he was, even Colbert was kept on a short leash, and was not in any sense "prime minister"—a position which Louis XIV himself advised the Dauphin should be "forever abolished in France."

Another modern writer, discussed in Chapter 2, who mistakenly classified Louis XIV's post-Fronde reign as a "success" amounting to a "class alliance" between King and aristocracy, compounded his error by labeling this as "absolutism," which he defined as "the political manifestation of a system of domination protecting the interests of a privileged class of officers and landed lords." (Beik, W., loc. 4506, 4449.) It is disquieting to find this kind of muddled thinking relied upon by historians of "late antiquity." (See Chapter 2.)

Roger Mettam at least recognized that seventeenth century French history was marked (as quoted above) by "the unceasing struggle of the crown against the independent power of the varied groups who formed the privileged orders in French society," and that, although royal power increased at the expense of these privileged groups, it did not reach the height entitling it to be labeled as "absolute," which would mean (contrary to Beik's idiosyncratic definition of the term) untrammeled autocratic royal power.

A welcome corrective to Beik and other "revisionists" is John Hurt's *Louis XIV and the Parlements*, published by Manchester University Press in 2002 (and unpersuasively attacked by Beik in, "The Absolutism of Louis XIV as Social Collaboration," *Past & Present* No. 188, (2005) 195–224.) Hurt argues with great force that Louis XIV's "political subjugation (not too strong a word) of the parlements should bulk larger in our assessments of the Sun King's reign. All the current general treatments, along with recent biographies, have underestimated the depth and significance of this achievement. It is time to give it due interpretative weight. Arguably, the victory won by Louis XIV was of such consequence that it influenced the government's relations with the tribunals into the middle of the eighteenth century." (Hurt, John, 2002, loc. 4840–4846.) The crucial importance of the relationship between the Crown and the Parlements right up to 1789 is discussed below.

Louis XV (r. 1715–74)

The death of Louis XIV, in 1715 after a reign of seventy-two years, plunged France into yet another minority, the third in succession, with the accession of his five-year-old great-grandson, Louis XV. Louis XIV's putative advice to the new king from the grave was sound and succinctly sums up Louis XIV's own philosophy of government: "Listen to the people, seek advice from your Council, but decide alone."

The Regent, the Duc d'Orléans, perpetuated Louis XIV's assertion of royal power, though it is as wrong to refer to his rule as to Louis's as "absolutist." But Orleans made it clear that he was determined to pass on to the young king royal authority in its entirety, as he had received it, and to stop the Parlements from meddling in affairs which were none of their business. (Mansel 2019, p. 448.)

In 1726, Louis XV appointed as chief minister his former tutor, Cardinal Fleury, who remained in office until his death in 1743. With the assistance of two successive controllers-general of finances, Fleury managed to balance the budget for a time and to stabilize the currency. He also instituted a major road-building program, including the construction of major highways, some of which are still in use today. The power of the *parlements* was curbed by dismissing 139 members of provincial *parlements* and precluding the *Parlement de Paris* from dealing with religious matters.

On Fleury's death in 1743, Louis XV effectively became his own chief minister, chairing meetings of the *Conseil d'en haut* (High

Council) consisting solely of the three most important ministers plus the *dauphin*, or heir to the throne; and he delegated most other decisions to ministerial committees.

Louis XV understood the need to stand up to the aristocracy but lacked the will to do so, so that the attempt, for example, to impose a new *vingtième* (twentieth) tax on nobles as well as commoners was abandoned in the face of vocal opposition from the *parlements*, the clergy, and from those aristocratically controlled provincial estates which still existed and retained rights over taxation. In 1753, the *Parlement de Paris* was sufficiently emboldened to proclaim itself the "...natural defender of the fundamental laws of the kingdom", which really meant the protector of feudal rights against the monarchy. The King's resolve was also sapped by the influence exerted over him by the aristocratic courtiers who surrounded him at Versailles.

The duc de Choiseul, Louis XV's influential foreign minister from 1758 to 1761 and again from 1766 to 1770, involved France in a number of mostly unsuccessful foreign wars, which did not assist the position of the Crown. Professor Alfred Cobban's comment is apt: "Under Choiseul it is almost true to say that capitulation to the *parlements* became official policy." (Cobban 1950, p. 75.)

Maupeou (1714–92)

However, everything changed with Choiseul's dismissal and the appointment of René de Maupeou as Chancellor of France in 1770. Having himself served briefly as President of the *Parlement de Paris*, Maupeou understood only too well the fundamental opposition between monarchy and aristocracy. Once ensconced in his new position, he devoted himself wholeheartedly to administering a knock-out blow against the *Parlement* on behalf of the Crown. In January 1771, Maupeou had the members of the *Parlement de Paris* exiled and their offices confiscated, replacing them with a royal court operating under the same name. Maupeou then took similar action against the provincial *parlements*. The practice of buying and selling offices was banned in the new *parlements*. These were intended as merely the first steps in a wholesale reform of the judicial system, but the whole enterprise was abruptly cut short by Louis XV's death and Maupeou's dismissal by the new king, Louis XV's grandson, Louis XVI. (Echeverria 1985.) The overhaul of the judicial system had to wait until Maupeou's secretary, Charles-François Lebrun, held office as Third Consul under Napoleon Bonaparte between 1799 and 1804.

Lebrun (1739–1824)

The drawn-out struggle between the Crown and the aristocracy centered on finance, with the aristocracy clinging to their privileges, including exemption from taxation, which it was in the interest of the Crown to abolish, an interest which the Crown shared with the ordinary people of France. It was Maupeou's secretary and right-hand man, Charles-François Lebrun, who first formulated the policy that came to be called the "Maupeou Revolution." "The Third Estate," he predicted, "would support the government against the views and interests of the nobility, the clergy and the parlements." (Echeverria 1985, p. 132.) This vision of a monarchy standing at the head of a popular "revolution" against the privileged elements was put in hand in 1770 and was operational until the death of Louis XV in 1774, when the policy was reversed by Louis XV's feckless grandson, Louis XVI. Maupeou threw up his hands in despair at the way the new king discarded this hard-fought victory. "*J'avais fait gagner au roi un procès qui dure depuis trois cents ans. Il veut le reperdre, il en est le maître*" (I had won for the king a case that has lasted three hundred years. He wishes to lose it again. He is the master of it).

Maupeou's interrupted overhaul of the judicial system, including the introduction of a uniform national code of laws, as proposed by Lebrun and Maupeou in 1771, and the reorganization of the national finances were eventually completed under Napoleon Bonaparte thirty years later, with the active participation of none other than Charles-François Lebrun, in his capacity as Third Consul (1799–1804) and then as arch-treasurer of the French Empire (1804). Remembering the struggle of the Bourbon monarchy against the aristocracy, Lebrun advised Napoleon against the restoration of titles of nobility though he himself was persuaded by the Emperor to accept the hereditary title *duc de Plaisance*. If only Louis XVI had had the sense to allow Maupeou to bring his victory to completion instead of reversing it, perhaps the French Revolution would never have happened!

"The Inevitable Liquidation of an Exhausted Expedient"

Durand Echeverria, author of a book on the *Maupeou Revolution* (1985), characterized Maupeou's dismissal by Louis XVI as "...the inevitable liquidation of an exhausted expedient." This is wrong on two counts. First, Maupeou's defeat of the *parlements* can hardly be called "an exhausted expedient" because no such complete victory over the *parle-

ments had ever previously been achieved. And secondly, why was its "liquidation" inevitable? Despite their pretenses, the *parlements* represented the interests of the privileged orders. So, what was inevitable was the liquidation of the *parlements*, not of an attempt to abolish them, and this is demonstrated by the speed and ease with which the *parlements* were in fact liquidated by the National Assembly in the early days of the French Revolution.

"Constitutional Consensus"

Munro Price, in his book on the Comte de Vergennes, likewise appears to misunderstand Maupeou's trouncing of the *parlements*, which he describes as follows: "This act, whose importance has recently been underlined by historians, dealt a major blow to the constitutional consensus on which the absolute monarchy rested". (Price 1995, p. 2.) This opinion should also be rejected on two counts. First, the inflated claims of the *parlements* can hardly be regarded as any kind of "constitutional consensus". On the contrary, the exaggerated claims made by the *parlements* in the 1750s had never been accepted by the Crown. And secondly, to suggest that the "absolute monarchy" rested on such anti-monarchical claims is a contradiction in terms. A succession of royal ministers over three centuries recognized that the relationship between the Crown and the *parlements* was a zero-sum game: the greater the power of the *parlements*, the less was that of the Crown, and vice versa. Absolute monarchy could only be achieved by completely subordinating, or even abolishing, the *parlements*. Which is why the label "absolute monarchy" is probably inapplicable to the *ancien régime* as a whole, because the knock-out blow administered by Maupeou to the *parlements* was so short-lived.

"Could Not Have Been Undone"

Professor Alfred Cobban's view of the subject is preferable. In his article, "The Parlements of France in the Eighteenth Century", he remarks that "Freed from the opposition of the parlements.... Terray [Controller General of Finances] was able to introduce important financial reforms. By 1774, he had reduced the debt to manageable proportions." (Cobban 1950, p. 76.) "In spite of widespread agitation the new courts were functioning...and the reform seemed to be definitive. There was no sign that Louis XV would desert the minister who had rid him of the turbulent parlements when the whole situation was changed by the king's death.

Whatever ill services Louis XV had done the French monarchy by his life, the greatest was in the moment of his death, when, if he had lived a few more years, time would have been gained for the new courts set up by Maupeou to consolidate themselves and his work could not have been undone." (Ibid.)

Run-Up to Revolution

Louis XVI, who succeeded his grandfather in 1774 at the age of nineteen, was indecisive and lacked Louis XV's perspicacity and cynicism. The reinstatement of the *parlements* was one of his earliest acts, undoing centuries of painstaking work (see above). When asked to explain his decision, he said: "It may be considered politically unwise, but it seems to me to be the general wish and I want to be loved." (Hardman 1993.) The trouble was that the *parlements* spared no effort or expense in portraying themselves as intermediaries between the Crown and the people. In the *Grandes Remonstrances* of 1753, for example, they had claimed that "...if subjects owe obedience to kings, kings for their part owe obedience to the laws", of which the *parlements* regarded themselves as the guardians. Alfred Cobban puts it like this: "As the last relic of the medieval constitution left at the centre of government, the parlement of Paris, though no more in fact than a small, selfish, proud and venal oligarchy, regarded itself, and was regarded by public opinion, as the guardian of the constitutional liberties of France." (Cobban 1965, vol. I, p. 67.) The *parlements* certainly knew how to manipulate public opinion, and a loose coalition of "Patriots" put out more than 500 books and pamphlets, or *maupeouana*, appealing to the "nation" against Maupeou's "despotism". But even these "Patriots" eventually saw through the pretensions of the *parlements*: "For it was the faithful remnants of the patriot party who, still under that banner, led the prerevolutionary charge in 1787–88 against the 'despotism' of the royal ministers Alexandre de Calonne and Lomenie de Brienne, who in turn followed Maupeou's example in subsidizing pamphlets that renewed the charge of 'aristocracy' against the parlements and their partisans." (Van Kley 1999, p. 252.) The clearest indication of the *lack* of popular support for the *parlements* is the fact that the *parlements* were suspended as early on in the Revolution as November 1789, with their formal abolition following in September 1790.

After several unsuccessful Controllers-General of Finance, Louis XVI appointed Lomenie de Brienne, who had just been named president of the Assembly of Notables. After an initial success by Brienne against the *Parlement de Paris*, that body finally consented to its own abolition, on condition that the Estates-General were summoned to tackle the national crisis. Brienne resigned his post in August 1788, and on January 24, 1789, the King reluctantly summoned the Estates General to meet on May 1, 1789.

Estates General to Guillotine

This august body, the equivalent of the English Parliament, had last met in 1614. It was made up of representatives of the three estates: the clergy, the nobility and the commons. Though some representatives arrived late in Paris (some only in 1791), the clergy initially had 303 representatives, the nobles 282, and the Third Estate, making up 95 percent of the population, was allowed a double representation of 578, drawn largely from the bourgeoisie together with a number of nobles, as there was no restriction on their standing for election by the Third Estate instead of by their own class. The franchise for the Third Estate was made up of property-owning males of at least twenty-five years of age. The double representation accorded the Third Estate by Louis XVI in response to a demand made in the press was an empty gesture because the King also went along with the requirement of the *Parlement de Paris* that the three estates sit and vote "by orders", i.e. separately, with each estate having an equal vote (as had been done in 1614), thus enabling the first two estates to outvote the Third Estate.

In practice, however, things worked out very differently. After a plenary session presided over by the King on May 5, 1789, the representatives got bogged down in a debate on "verification", including whether the three orders should vote together or separately as ordered by the King. On May 27, the nobles voted to confirm separate "voting by orders". On June 17, the Third Estate renamed themselves the National Assembly and invited the other two orders to join them. Under the influence of his Council, the King made another blunder by ordering the hall where the Third Estate had been meeting to be locked and guarded by troops. Undaunted, on June 20, the representatives simply moved to the royal *jeu de paume* (indoor tennis court), where they took the famous "Tennis Court Oath" swearing not to disband until there was a national constitution. After the majority of the clergy, followed by some nobles, had joined the Third Estate, the King, making a virtue of necessity, asked all three orders to meet together. On July 9, the National Assembly recreated itself once again, this time as the "National Constituent Assembly", thereby arrogating to itself not only the right to speak in the name of the French nation as a whole but even to frame a new constitution for it, something that was not even mooted in the *cahiers de doléances* (lists of grievances), which, on the contrary, had largely expressed loyalty to the king and the monarchy in its traditional form.

Just five days later, on July 14, 1789, came the storming of the Bastille, a medieval fortress and prison in the center of Paris, which was known to have held political prisoners incarcerated purely on the basis of *lettres de cachet*. One of its most high-profile inmates was the eccentric Marquis de Sade, who, however, had been transferred on July 2 to an insane asylum. On July 14, only seven old men were left in the Bastille, none of whom were of any political importance. Nevertheless, the significance of the event cannot be denied. The governor of the Bastille, the Marquis de Launay, was savagely murdered and his head paraded around the streets mounted on a pike, but what the fall of the Bastille really represented was an attack on royal authority. It was a warning by the reformist royalist Duc de la Rochefoucauld about the unrest in Paris on July 12, that prompted the King to enquire naïvely, "Is it a revolt?" To which the Duke famously replied, *"Non, sire, c'est une révolution"* (No, Sire, it's a revolution).

In the four months before the fall of the Bastille, it is estimated that there were more than 300 peasant riots in a number of provinces. (Herbert 2015, p. 93.) Interestingly enough, as testified to by a M. Conard of Dauphiné, "On the 29th [of July] the peasants everywhere believed that the pillage was ordered by the king;... that Louis XVI had taken the side of the peasants against their feudal oppressors." (Ibid., p. 99.) This shows that for the king to have adopted an anti-aristocratic stance, as indeed a number of his predecessors had done, was not beyond the bounds of belief, even in July 1789. Alas for Louis XVI, he lacked the imagination and political nous to follow this path. On the contrary, when the Assembly, impelled by the peasant riots, decided on that fateful night of August 4, 1789 to abolish "feudalism" root and branch (though mostly only in return for compensation to the feudal seigneurs and the church), Louis XVI demurred. "I will never consent," he naïvely wrote to the Archbishop of Arles, "to despoil my clergy and *noblesse*.... I will not give my sanction to decrees which would despoil them, for then the French people might some day accuse me of injustice or weakness". (Ibid., p. 108.) When the decree was presented to him for the royal assent, Louis procrastinated and finally signed it into law only on November 3, 1789 under pressure from unrest in Paris. After this, the Revolution continued to spiral out of control.

Mirabeau (1749–91): "L'indivisibilité Du Monarque Et Du People"

In 1791 Honoré Gabriel Riqueti, comte de Mirabeau, a reprobate aristocrat who was at once a leading revolutionary and a staunch royalist, advised Louis XVI in a secret *Mémoire* to move to Rouen or some other provincial capital, appeal to the people, summon a great convention, and effectively place himself at the head of the Revolution rather than impotently stand against it. Like some of Louis's more politically savvy predecessors and their ministers, Mirabeau recognized that there was a natural close reciprocal symbiotic or visceral bond between king and people which already existed beneath the surface but needed to be kick-started into action and power: "*L'indivisibilité du monarque et du people est dans le coeur de tous les Français; il faut qu'elle existe dans l'action et le pouvoir*" (The indivisibility of the monarch and the people is in the heart of all French people; it is necessary for it to exist in action and in power) (*Mémoire* to the Comte de la Marck and presented to the King by the Comte de Provence, the future Louis XVIII, quoted in Stephens 1911, location 124.) Mirabeau's sudden (but probably natural) death on April 2, 1791 robbed the King of what was probably his last chance to save himself and the monarchy, and the royal family were then confined as prisoners in the Tuileries Palace in Paris.

The King's attempt in June 1791 to flee to the royalist town of Montmedy (on the border of the Austrian Netherlands, modern Belgium) and seek the protection of Austria, which was ruled by Queen Marie Antoinette's brother, the Emperor Leopold II, was exactly the sort of thing that Mirabeau had counseled against. Ironically, the King was recognized from his embossed portrait on a revolutionary *assignat* banknote in the small town of Varennes-en-Argonne. The royal family were then ignominiously hauled back to Paris as traitors and prisoners. This episode dealt a fatal blow to the monarchy, leading to Louis XVI's deposition in 1792 and his beheading in January 1793, followed by that of Marie Antoinette in October of the same year.

Mirabeau's *cri de coeur* quoted above was actually an echo of what Maupeou and other astute ministers of the monarchy had been urging for generations, namely the common interest of the Crown and the people in abolishing or at least reducing the privileges of the aristocracy.

What Mirabeau was proposing was that, instead of cowering in the face of the Revolution, the King should place himself at the head of it. Could this possibly have worked? Possibly, but as Charles F. Warwick put it: "It is really not a question whether Mirabeau could have saved the monarchy, but rather a question whether Louis would have let him". (Warwick, 2018, location 4932.) The lessons of the *ancien régime* were finally learnt and put into effect by Napoleon, who established, albeit briefly, a popular monarchy with an efficient administration and a fair tax policy.

Alfred Cobban put the situation in a nutshell:

> If we compare the French monarchy in the eighteenth century with practically any other European monarchy of the same period, the striking fact that emerges is the comparative effectiveness of the limitations

on royal power in France, and this in spite of the fact that, in the absence of other checks, organised opposition to the crown was concentrated in a single institution. (Cobban 1950, p. 64).

Referring to the final abolition of the *parlements* by the Revolution in 1790, Cobban remarked: "The last stage in their history is the story of their unresisted elimination by the National Assembly, which thus achieved, almost without effort, what the monarchy had struggled so long to do in vain." (Ibid, p. 80.) "Thus was consummated the prophecy of the Cardinal de Retz in 1649 cited above: '*Les parlements, qui soufflaient sur le feu, en seraient, un jour, consumés*' ('The parlements, which fanned the flames, will one day be consumed by them')." (Ibid., p. 64.) As noted above, this remark, dates from the Fronde, of which Cardinal de Retz was a leader, 150 years before the Revolution.

Napoleon Bonaparte (1769–1821)

Napoleon Bonaparte (1769–1821) ruled France, initially as First Consul from 1799 to 1804 and then as Emperor from 1804 until 1814 and finally for a hundred days in 1815. In spite of the shortness of his rule and his final defeat at Waterloo, Napoleon made an indelible mark on history, not least by means of the Code Napoléon, which still forms the basis of codes of law in many countries around the world.

Napoleon is usually seen as heir to the French Revolution, both in terms of ideology and nationalism, which developed into imperialism. He was not only one of the most gifted generals in history but also an extremely adroit politician. Napoleon clearly understood the lessons of ministers of the *ancien régime* like Sully, Richelieu, Mazarin, Colbert, Fleury, Maupeou, Terray, and, not least, Lebrun, and their masters, Kings Henry IV, Louis XIII, Louis XIV, and Louis XV. So, Napoleon's rule also marks the fulfilment of the elusive goal of these astute monarchs and ministers, namely the establishment of a popular monarchy by means of a streamlined administration, the overhaul of the financial system, and the reorganization of the legal system.

Napoleon's defeat at Waterloo put an end to his career but not to his fame. Despite his defeat and ignominious last years as a prisoner of the British on the remote island of St. Helena, Napoleon continued to be revered by the French as a heroic figure. Before the adoption of the euro, the highest denomination French banknote proudly displayed a youthful Napoleon Bonaparte against a backdrop of victorious legionary standards. And, anyone unfamiliar with French history who has attended the *son et lumière* show at the Invalides in Paris, where Napoleon is buried, may be forgiven for being unaware of his inglorious end.

From Napoleon to Napoleon and Beyond

The Bourbon Restoration lasted only fifteen years, first under Louis XVI's brother, the conservative Louis XVIII, who died in 1824, and then under another brother, the reactionary Charles X (r. 1824–30), who was said to have "...learned nothing and forgotten nothing." He in fact completely failed to learn the crucial lesson that the aristocracy was no friend of strong monarchy, and he was overthrown in 1830 by a popular rising known as the July Revolution.

He was succeeded by his cousin Louis Philippe, who reigned as a constitutional monarch until he too was overthrown in 1848. He cultivated an unpretentious style, adopted the image of "Citizen King" and was nicknamed the "Bourgeois Monarch". To demonstrate his acceptance of popular sovereignty, he was styled "King of the French", in other words, King of the people, as against "King of France," the traditional title. However, this populist tone rang rather hollow. For example, only about two million of the nine million adult French males of voting age had the right to vote. To demands for universal suffrage, Louis Philippe's last Prime Minister, François Guizot, responded with a challenge: "Eclairez-vous, enrichissez-vous, améliorez la condition morale et matérielle de notre France: voilà les vraies innovations." (Have the sense to enrich yourselves, improving the moral and physical condition of our France: that is true progress.) (*Le Moniteur*, March 2, 1843. Quoted in "Guizot and Representative Government," Francois Guizot, The History of the Origins of Representative Govt in Eu, tr. Andrew Scoble, Indianapolis: Liberty Fund 2002.) The famous cartoon of 1831 showing Louis Philippe gradually turning into a pear was prophetic. By 1848, the pear was so rotten that a whiff of popular discontent was enough to dislodge it. Within three days, fearing for his life, the Citizen King fled to England unimaginatively disguised as "Mr. Smith."

The ensuing election, under universal manhood suffrage, swept to power Napoleon's nephew, Louis Napoleon Bonaparte, who, despite his unprepossessing appearance and monotonous speeches delivered with a slight German accent, won the presidency of the short-lived Second Republic with 74.2 percent of the votes cast. His program was unabashedly populist, but success was vouchsafed to him by one thing alone: the name Bonaparte. His endorsement by Victor Hugo's newspaper, *L'Evénement*, encapsulated his appeal: "We have confidence in him: he carries a great name." Debarred by the Constitution from re-election, the "Prince-President," as he styled himself, resorted to a coup d'etat to perpetuate his position. His action was approved in a plebiscite held in 1851 by 92 percent of the votes cast on a turnout of over 80 percent. The path was now cleared for him to follow in his late uncle's footsteps and declare himself emperor as Napoleon III, which occurred a year later on the strength of a 97 percent majority in another referendum.

France's defeat in the Franco-Prussian War of 1870 resulted in the Emperor's humiliating capitulation and brief captivity in Germany followed by exile in England. But the ignominious collapse of the Second Empire, as it was called, did not put an end to the French love affair with monarchy. After the establishment of the Third Republic in 1870, Henri, comte de Chambord (1820–83), grandson of Charles X (r. 1824–30), and a direct descendant of the first Bourbon King of France, Henry IV (r. 1589–1610), made a bid for the throne, which was seriously entertained by the royalist-dominated National Assembly. Had it not been for the comte de Chambord's insistence on the pre-revolutionary *fleur-de-lys drapeau blanc* (a white flag emblazoned with numerous fleur de lis) as the national flag instead of the red-white-and-blue tricolor, France may well have had yet another flirtation with monarchy.

Yet the fact that France has been a republic since 1870 has not prevented it from hankering after strong leadership, as personified particularly by President Charles de Gaulle, leader of the "Free French" resistance to Germany during World War II, who subsequently served as Prime Minister (1958–59) and then, from 1959 to 1969, as the first president of the Fifth French Republic, which was largely his creation. De Gaulle's leadership was summed up by the phrase used by his successor, Georges Pompidou, in announcing de Gaulle's death to the French nation: "Le général de Gaulle est mort; la France est veuve." ("General de Gaulle is dead; France is a widow.") At the time of this writing, France appears to be torn between two forms of populism, a more moderate variety represented by Emmanuel Macron, who won 66.1 percent of the vote in the second round run-off presidential election in 2017 and a right-wing nationalist form of populism represented by Marine Le Pen of the National Front (now renamed *Rassemblement National* or National Rally), who polled 33.9 percent of the vote in that same election. Neither type of populism is essentially anti-elite, but both combine support from different elements of society. Macron's presidency, though sometimes attacked as unduly autocratic, is in fact nothing of the sort, regardless of what his ambition may be.

Binary Power Structure

The key to a true understanding of the binary power structure of French history is the obscure figure of Charles-François Lebrun (1739–1824). We first meet him as Maupeou's perspicacious assistant in the victory over the aristocratic and anti-monarchical *parlements* in the reign of Louis XV. That victory was senselessly discarded by Louis XVI on his accession in 1774, with disastrous consequences for the monarchy and for France. But Lebrun never lost sight of the fact that there was a natural alliance between the people and a strong monarchical government against their common enemy, the aristocracy. And he was able to bring this alliance to fruition thirty years later under a new ruler with the same perceptive insight: Napoleon Bonaparte.

Case Study IV: England: 1066 And All That

The Norman kings of England were in a stronger position than their French counterparts. After the conquest of 1066, the king of England was able to wipe the slate clean and start from scratch, which the kings of France were never able to do. The early post-conquest kings did promise to honor the promises made to the aristocracy by their Anglo-Saxon predecessors, but they mostly ignored such undertakings. All land belonged to the king, who would distribute it to his followers as "barons" on feudal tenure, often in small scattered parcels to prevent the barons developing strong local power-centers rivalling that of the king. Initially, this gave the king great power. In time, however, the barons started ganging up on the king and forcing him to give them certain concessions. This is how Magna Carta (the Great Charter) came about. Contrary to all the ballyhoo surrounding it, the Magna Carta has nothing to do with democracy and everything to do with the ding-dong battle between the aristocracy and the Crown. And one of the reasons why the barons disliked King John (r. 1199–1216) was that he (quite rightly) distrusted them and in certain important respects favored the common people. It cannot be stressed enough that strong monarchy is not the enemy of the ordinary people. That role is repeatedly played by the aristocracy.

The rise of Parliament in the thirteenth century and its increasing control over grants of taxation weakened the English Crown further, while the French Crown gained the right to raise taxes without the consent of the Estates General, the equivalent of the English Parliament. Overall, the balance of power in the whole of English history from the Norman Conquest of 1066 until the advent of the Civil War of 1642 favored the aristocracy, and later Parliament, over the king.

Prelude to a Power-Struggle

William the Conqueror (r. 1066–87) and his successors gradually managed to impose on all free men (i.e. those with "freehold" tenures) who occupied a tenement (i.e. a feudal land-holding) a duty of "fealty" (i.e. feudal loyalty) directly to the Crown rather than to the immediate lords from whom they held their land. This was an early recognition by the Crown that aristocratic power was in competition with royal power, and that strong monarchy depended on keeping the barons in check. But as time went by land came to be concentrated in the hands of a small elite within the barons, which was bad news for the monarchy.

Needless to say, some kings were more successful than others in asserting their position. Henry I (r. 1100–35), an effective and ruthless ruler who had no compunction in keeping his eldest brother, Robert, prisoner for life, was also not afraid to punish barons for disloyalty. Many of his officials were of humble origins and he had a network of spies who reported back to him directly. (Green, 2009, p. 232 f.; Crouch, 2007, p. 17.) The legal reforms introduced by Henry I and Henry II (r. 1154–89) extended and centralized the scope of the royal courts—and there was certainly no hint yet of judicial activism!

Magna Carta

The Magna Carta was chiefly concerned with the relationship between the Crown and the barons, which continued to fester. People below the rank of baron got short shrift from this august document, with the exception of clause 39, which still survives today and reads as follows: "No free-man shall be seized or imprisoned, or dispossessed, or outlawed, or in any way destroyed. We will not condemn him, nor will we commit him to prison, except by the legal judgment of his peers, or by the laws of the land." The undertaking applied at the time only to "free-men", who are estimated to have accounted for only about one-seventh of the population. (Arlidge/Judge 2014, p. 47.) In 1354, in the wake of the Black Death of 1348–1350, the term "due process of law" was redefined to apply to everyone "...of whatever estate or condition he may be". (Holt 1992, p. 10.) But this clause did not prevent the Magna Carta from being essentially a capitulation by the King to his barons.

The Rise of Parliament

Before long, Parliament took over from the barons the role of chief obstacle to royal power, especially in regard to finance. Strong kings like Edward I (r. 1272–1307) were able to use Parliament for their own ends, as a way of uniting the country under the Crown and allowing Parliament to air their grievances in return for supply. A weak king like Edward II (r. 1307–27) could find himself actually forced to abdicate by Parliament, under the leadership of the barons.

The Hundred Years' War (1337–1453) was extremely costly, which gave Parliament the opportunity to insist that their consent was needed for the levying of taxes and also for the making of statute law, which became an established convention from this time forth. Towards the end of the reign of Edward III (1327–77) Parliament even impeached some of the King's ministers, a practice which was continued during the reign of Edward III's grandson, Richard II (r. 1377–99).

Richard II and the Peasants' Revolt

The Peasants' Revolt of 1381, sparked off by royal officials' attempts to collect unpaid poll taxes in Essex, gave Richard II an opportunity to assert himself against the aristocracy by siding with the rebels and acceding to their requests, including the abolition of serfdom. The rebels were not opposed to the King but to the aristocracy. John Ball, a rebel leader, posed the rhetorical question: *"When Adam delved and Eve span, who was then the gentleman?"* The word "gentleman" meant "nobleman", so this rhetorical question was an assertion that in primitive society everyone was equal, and that aristocratic privilege was a late and unnatural development, the result, as Ball put it, of "...the unjust oppression of naughty men." Recognizing that the King and themselves had a common enemy, namely the aristocracy, the rebels' slogan was "With King Richard and the true commons of England." (Sumption 2009, 423.) "True" here meaning that the rebellious peasants were rebelling against serfdom and privilege, not against the King, and that they expected the King to take their side, which he initially did. However, Richard II soon changed sides and ended up as a victim of the nobles himself and was effectively forced by them to "abdicate."

Henry VII (r. 1485–1509)

The Wars of the Roses, a conflict between rival claimants to the throne, which was fought on and off from 1455 to 1485 under a system of "bastard feudalism", in which rival nobles had private armies made up of mercenaries disguised as servants, weakened the Crown, and enhanced the power of Parliament, on which both sides depended for support. Once ensconced in power, the ultimate victor of the Wars of the Roses was the Tudor King Henry VII (r. 1485–1509), who passed laws to curb bastard feudalism. Henry used such devices as "bonds" and "recognisances" to ensure the loyalty of the aristocracy and thereby curbed their power. An important royal weapon against the aristocracy was the

Court of Star Chamber, made up of Privy Counsellors (senior advisers to the king) together with some common-law judges, one of whose main functions was to give ordinary people a channel for redress against the excesses of the aristocracy. The Star Chamber was also a court of equity, enabling it to impose punishments even for activities which, while strictly speaking legal, were considered by the court to be reprehensible. Although initially solely a court of appeal, it was also thrown open to plaintiffs at first instance by Cardinal Wolsey and Archbishop Thomas Cranmer, who presided over the court under Henry VIII (r. 1509–47).

Henry VIII (r. 1509–47)

Henry VIII's chief preoccupation was to obtain a male heir, which led to his reliance on Parliament in order to allow him to divorce his first wife, Catherine of Aragon. But in order to do so he had to break with the Roman Catholic Church and have himself declared "Supreme Governor" of the Church of England

Geoffrey Elton's *The Tudor Revolution in Government* (1953), which placed not the King himself but his minister Thomas Cromwell (1485–1540) in the driving seat of this development, together with a shift from "household government," centered on the person of the King, to a modern bureaucratic form of government, has now been consigned to the history of historiography.

But the very fact that Henry VIII only had to snap his fingers to destroy Cromwell shows just how much personal control the King exercised. Further examples are not hard to find, such as the King's dismissal of Cardinal Wolsey, who was on his way to certain execution when he died of natural causes in 1530, and the downfall of Wolsey's successor as Lord Chancellor, Sir Thomas More, in 1535, not to mention Henry's matrimonial antics, divorcing two wives and executing two more. Hans Holbein's iconic portrait of Henry VIII shows him as a masterful Renaissance ruler, especially when seen side by side with his father, Henry VII, who has something of the air of a conniving merchant.

Nevertheless, Henry VIII cannot be said to have exercised single-handed autocratic power. For his extremely ambitious program of religious reform he needed and, with Cromwell's help, he managed to obtain parliamentary support. In 1523, Parliament had already refused to agree fully to Henry's request for money. And the King's reliance on Parliament to implement his far-reaching legislative program only strengthened Parliament's hand for its future struggle against the Crown. In that respect, Henry VIII showed less than his usual perspicacity. "We be informed by our judges that we at no time stand so highly in our estate royal as in the time of Parliament." (Hist. of Parl.) Though couched in confident language, this remark, from a speech by Henry to a deputation from the House of Commons on March 31, 1543, is actually an admission of how much Henry had placed himself in Parliament's debt. And the fact that this bit of hypocritical flattery had evidently come from the judges is another ominous sign of the role that they would play in the seventeenth century in attacking royal power.

Elizabeth I (r. 1558–1603): "For it is Monstrous that the Feet Should Direct the Head."

Elizabeth I's Parliaments were not only comparatively few and far between but mostly also of very short duration, so that the days making up their sittings totaled less than three years of her 44-year reign. The Queen simply did not trust Parliament and wanted to curtail its discussion of sensitive topics such as the royal succession, her possible marriage, the problem posed by Mary Queen of Scots (1542–87) as heir apparent, and, not least, religion. So Elizabeth would try to get Parliament to vote supply as soon as possible and then send it packing. She was not averse to lecturing a Parliament in hectoring tones on the permitted limits of their deliberations: "For it is monstrous that the feet should direct the head." (www.elizabethfiles.com). And the Queen had no compunction about lodging Members of Parliament in the Tower of London for raising touchy issues in the House of Commons.

James I (r. 1603–25): "The Judges....may Easily Make of the Law Shipmen's Hose."

James I lacked Elizabeth's tact and finesse and made no secret of his belief in the divine right of kings, on which he had already written two treatises before his accession to the English throne. (He had been James VI, King of Scots, since 1567, when he was only one-year old.)

James's well-known sobriquet, "the wisest fool in Christendom", given to him by Henry IV of France, was intended as a compliment, not an insult. And James was under no illusion about the proper relationship between a king and the different categories of his subjects. Here are some of his views as expressed in his two treatises on monarchy:

> *On the nobility*: "...the nobility, although second in rank yet over-far first in greatness and power to do good or evil, as they are inclined." (James I, 1996, p. 124.) "The natural sickness that I have perceived this estate

subject to in my time hath been a feckless, arrogant conceit of their greatness and power...." From *Basilikon Doron* (Royal Gift) addressed to his eldest son, Prince Henry: "To remeid to these evils in their estate, teach your nobility to keep your laws as precisely as the meanest; fear not their orping or being discontented, as long as ye rule well."

On cultivating the lower orders: "...and weary not to hear the complaints of the oppressed, *aut ne rex sis* ['or you should not be a king']." (James VI/I 1996, p. 149.) Note also James's expansion and support of the Court of Requests under Sir Julius Caesar. The Court offered redress to the lower classes, whom it attracted away from the common law courts in great numbers thanks to its low charge for filing a complaint and its quick turnaround time—both resented by the common law judges, whose courts had neither of these advantages. With their characteristic lack of interest in justice, the common law judges went on a rampage against the Court of Requests.

On a king's superiority to the law: Kings existed "...before any estates or ranks of men, before any parliaments were holden, or laws made, and by them was the land distributed, which at first was wholly theirs. And so it follows of necessity that kings were the authors and makers of the laws, and not the laws of the kings."

James I was not content to assert these views in writing. He also acted upon them in practice. To his first Parliament in 1604, he remarked, "England has been conquered many times, Scotland never." Not surprisingly, James's relationship with his Parliaments was less than cordial. Nor was his relationship with the judiciary any more harmonious. When James asserted his right to try cases himself as king, he was rudely rebuffed by Sir Edward Coke (1552–1634), who claimed that this power belonged solely to legally trained judges. (*Prohibitions del Roy*, or *Case of Prohibitions* 77 ER 1342, 12 Co. Rep. 64 [1607] EWHC KB 123.)

But the King's rejoinder proved prophetic: "If the judges interpret the laws themselves and suffer none else to interpret, they may easily make, of the laws, shipmen's hose!", meaning that judge-made law would come to resemble the tattered and frayed stockings worn by sailors. (Hamburger 2008, p. 223; Bowen 1957, p. 304.)

Charles I (r. 1625–49): "I See the Birds Have Flown."

If James's problems with Parliament appear serious, they were of course dwarfed by the clash with Parliament under his son, which ultimately escalated into civil war, and resulted in the unprecedented execution of the King.

After four years of unproductive Parliaments, Charles ruled for eleven years without calling a Parliament. This period is variously portrayed by historians as the "eleven years' tyranny" or as a period of halcyon peace. Charles's loyal lieutenants, Thomas Wentworth, Earl of Strafford, and Archbishop William Laud, ably pursued their policy of "Thorough" to enhance the King's power by winning over the lower orders, offering them in the Court of Star Chamber genuine redress for their grievances against the privileged classes and checking the enclosure movement (the appropriation or privatization of commons, i.e. common agricultural land by wealthy landowners). The agrarian historian W.E. Tate called Charles I "...the one English monarch of outstanding importance as an agrarian reformer." (Tate 1967, pp. 124–7.) But Charles characteristically blotted his copybook by indulging in some enclosure of his own, in particular, by continuing his father's policy of draining the fenland commons to provide the Crown with additional revenue.

Finally forced in 1640 to call another Parliament by a need for money to finance a war against the Scottish Covenanters, Charles was rebuffed yet again and dissolved this "Short Parliament" after only three weeks. Reluctant to call another Parliament, Charles then took the exceptional and foolhardy step of calling a *Magnum Concilium*, or Great Council of Peers, an assembly of the nobility established in Norman times but which had not met since the reign of Henry VII (1485–1509). While offering the King a loan of £200,000 to pay the army, the Council advised him to call Parliament. In a remarkable parallel, Louis XVI of France—another king who did not understand the danger to monarchy posed by the aristocracy—was to make a similar mistake by calling an Assembly of Notables, which advised him to call the Estates General.

The "Long Parliament", summoned in 1640, was hostile to the King from the beginning. More than 350 of the 493 members of the House of Commons elected were opposed to the King. The Parliament lost no time in taking action against the King's most trusted and loyal advisers: Strafford, Archbishop Laud and John Finch, the former Speaker who was now Lord Keeper of the Great Seal. When Strafford's impeachment failed, the Commons passed a Bill of Attainder against him, which was approved by the Lords—and, after a good deal of prevarication, signed by the King. which amounted to Strafford's death warrant. Archbishop Laud, who was to suffer a similar fate in 1645, aptly commented that the King's abandonment of Strafford proved that he was "a mild and gracious prince, that knows not how to be, or to be made, great". (Trevor-Roper 2000, p. 409.) After this, Charles showed himself by turns weakly conciliatory and blusteringly bullying, a combination which ultimately undermined his position.

The most notable event was the King's unwise personal appearance in the Commons chamber on 3 January 1642, accompanied by an armed guard, in a vain attempt to arrest five members for high treason. "I see the birds have flown", remarked the King, and, seated in the Speaker's chair, asked Speaker Lenthall to reveal the whereabouts of the five men. On bended knees, the Speaker famously pleaded, "May it please your Majesty, I have neither eyes to see nor tongue to speak in this place but as the House is pleased to direct me, whose servant I am here." So strongly is this incident embedded in the national psyche that to this day the monarch's representative, known as (the Gentleman Usher of the) Black Rod, has the doors of the House of Commons ceremonially slammed in his face and has then to rap on the door three times before being admitted.

The incident regarding the five absent Members of Parliament marks the beginning of open hostilities between the King and Parliament, which erupted into full-scale war at the battle of Edgehill on 23 October 1642. After more than four years of a bloody civil war costing approximately 300,000 lives (amounting to 6% of the population of the country), Charles became a prisoner of Parliament in January 1647. At a show trial lasting a week on charges of high treason, 30 witnesses were called to testify against "Charles Stuart", as he was now referred to. Charles defended himself doughtily, claiming that the trial was illegal because the law was "that the King can do no wrong" and that "the arms I took up were only to defend the fundamental laws of this kingdom against those who have supposed my power hath totally changed the ancient government." (*Trial of Charles I*, 1963.)

The outcome of the King's "trial" was never in doubt, and neither was the sentence: death by beheading. Charles faced death with great composure, dignity and fortitude, which redounded to the royalist cause in the long run. The day of the execution, 30 January 1649, was a cold winter's day, and Charles made a point of wearing two shirts, so that his shivering would not be mistaken for fear. Most remarkably, humbly and perspicaciously, he attributed his fate to his failure to stand by Strafford in his hour of need: "An unjust sentence that I suffered to take effect, is punished now by an unjust sentence on me." And:

> For the people. And truly I desire their Liberty and Freedom as much as any Body whomsoever. But I must tell you, That their Liberty and Freedom, consists in having of Government; those Laws, by which their Life and their goods may be most their own. It is not for having share in government (Sir) that is nothing pertaining to them. A subject and a sovaraign are clean different things, and therefore until they do that, I mean, that you do put the people in that liberty as I say, certainly they will never enjoy themselves.... Sirs,...I tell you (and I pray God it be not laid to your charge) That I Am the Martyr of the People. (*Trial of Charles I* 1963.)

Had Charles come to a belated realization that Strafford and Laud were right and that true monarchy entailed a bond between king and people for the benefit of both against the interests of the privileged classes?

There is an indication also of the residual affection felt by ordinary people for their king. In the eye-witness account of Charles's execution by the young Philip Henry, a future nonconformist clergyman, we read: "At the instant when the blow was given, there was such a dismal universal groan among the thousands of people that were in sight of it, as it were with one consent." (Henry 1882, p. 12.)

Archbishop Laud's comment about Charles I quoted above was only too apt. Allowing Strafford and Laud to follow through on their policy of "Thorough" might have produced a popular monarchy, but Charles obviously did not understand the realities of politics. For example, he even allowed himself to be persuaded by Thomas Howard, Earl of Arundel, to cultivate the aristocracy as the main bulwark of royal authority, which led to his misguidedly relying on them in his war against the Scottish Covenanters in 1639, then after his defeat in his senseless summoning of a "Great Council of Peers" in 1640, and then finally in creating a royalist party of "Cavaliers" based on aristocratic support to counter Parliament in 1642, an image that did not do Charles any good in the English Civil War. (Cust 2007.)

Oliver Cromwell (1599–1658)

Oliver Cromwell, Member of Parliament for Cambridge, who became the commander of the victorious parliamentary army in the Civil War (1642–51), emerged from the war as "Lord Protector" of the "Commonwealth" (i.e. Republic), a position which he held from 1653 until his death in 1658

Cromwell rode roughshod over Parliament in a way that Charles I would never have dared. Even before his installation as Lord Protector, on April 20, 1653, Cromwell, accompanied by about 40 musketeers, marched into Parliament (the "Rump" of the Long Parliament, elected in 1640) and closed it down after hurling some choice insults at it. (Thomas Carlyle, The Letters & Speeches of Oliver Cromwell with Elucidations by Thomas Carlyle, edited in three volumes with Notes, Supplement and Enlarged Index by S.C. Lomas, with an Introduction by C.H. Firth, vol. II 1904, p. 263 ff.)

The dismissed Parliament was briefly replaced by a nominated assembly sometimes called Barebone's Parliament. Then, on December 16, 1653, under a written constitution, the only one in British history, known as the Instrument of Government, Cromwell was sworn in as Lord Protector of the Commonwealth for life. The form of government established by this very short document vested executive power in the Lord Protector and legislative power in the Protector in Parliament, not unlike the constitutional settlement that was to be introduced as part of the so-called "Glorious Revolution" of 1688–89. Cromwell was now addressed as "Your Highness" and he started signing his name "Oliver P" (P for "Protector"), copied from the royal style of signing "Charles R" (R for Rex). After reluctantly turning down the offer of the crown with expanded powers in 1657, he was re-installed as Lord Protector in a ceremony resembling a coronation, dressed in an ermine-trimmed purple robe seated on King Edward's Coronation Chair (dating back to 1296) and invested with all the trappings of monarchy except the crown itself and the orb. The coinage portrayed him in the guise of a Roman emperor, complete with laurel wreath and the legend OLIVAR DG RP ANG SCO ET HIB PRO (Oliver, by the Grace of God of the Republic of England, Scotland and Ireland, Protector).

Was Cromwell a Dictator?

Was Cromwell a dictator? Ironically, Oliver Cromwell probably came closer than any English king to exercising sole power. But his power was based on a standing army, which was disbanded only after the Restoration of the monarchy in 1660. The army's loyalty to the Protectorate was based on a combination of discipline and radical Protestant religious belief. Cromwell famously declared that he would "...rather have a plain, russet-coated Captain, that knows what he fights for, and loves what he knows, than what you call a Gentleman and nothing else". Does this mean that he ruled by "repression"? Not really. The army was indeed called upon to put down a number of opponents in what were essentially policing actions, but the only serious rising during the Protectorate was the Penruddock Uprising of 1655, which however was put down by a single troop of horse. The army could hardly be regarded as an oligarchy, because it did not share power with Cromwell but did his bidding.

Cromwell, being himself of gentry stock, attended a grammar school and Sidney Sussex College, Cambridge. He certainly was no social revolutionary. Here is what he said at the opening of Parliament in 1654:

> A nobleman, a gentleman, a yeoman; 'the distinction of these:' that is a good interest of the nation, and a great one! (www.olivercromwell. org/Letters_and_speeches/speeches/Speech_4.pdf.)

Cromwell clearly favored a hierarchical society, and he went on specifically to attack the egalitarian Levellers. On Oliver Cromwell's death in

September 1658, his son Richard Cromwell was appointed Lord Protector, but he proved ineffectual and was removed by the army seven months later. Oliver Cromwell's power-base was the "New Model Army." But once there was no longer a need for a standing army, the old elites were able to regain power. On March 16, 1660, the "Rump Parliament", which had been resuscitated, together with the addition of the members "purged" from it in 1648, finally dissolved itself after preparing the way for the Restoration of the monarchy under Charles I's son, Charles II (r. 1660–85).

Charles II: "The Merry Monarch"

After spending long years in exile abroad, Charles II, known as "the Merry Monarch," adopted the watchword, "I will not go on my travels again." Accordingly, he was prepared to toe the line and accept the reduced role offered to him by Parliament, which gave him more time to devote to his numerous mistresses.

"The Glorious Revolution"

His brother and successor, James II (r. 1685–89), had a very different attitude to royal power. His conversion to Catholicism during Charles's reign led to the "Exclusion Crisis" of 1679–81, in which the Whig party in Parliament launched an (ultimately unsuccessful) attempt to exclude James from the throne. However, though he ascended the throne on Charles II's untimely death in 1685, James was ousted in the so-called "Glorious Revolution" of 1688–1689, which was in fact neither glorious nor a revolution. It really was the recovery by Parliament of its preeminent position established by the Civil War and the execution of Charles I. Though James II is portrayed by his enemies and many modern historians as a power-hungry despot, probably the chief objection against him on the part of the parliamentary elite was his Declaration of Indulgence extending religious toleration to Catholics and Protestant Dissenters alike—including Quakers, a leading member of which, William Penn, founder of Pennsylvania, was a close friend of his. In his speaking tour to whip up support, James II struck a very modern note in a speech delivered in Chester: "Suppose... there should be a law made that all black men should be imprisoned, it would be unreasonable and we had as little reason to quarrel with other men for being of different [religious] opinions as for being of different complexions". (Sowerby 2013, p. 42.)

Was James genuine in wishing to extend toleration to all and sundry or, as his detractors maintain, was this was just a ruse to enable him to bring the country back into the fold of Rome? His Quaker friend William Penn certainly believed in his sincerity, but James's deposition deprived him of the opportunity of putting the policy into practice.

With some difficulty, Parliament then ensured a Protestant succession, passing over James's young Catholic son by his second marriage, who was heir presumptive to the throne. In a highly unusual move, Parliament gave the throne jointly to James's Protestant daughter Mary and her husband William of Orange, who reigned jointly as William III and Mary II. William was less than happy with the much reduced powers of the Crown as set out in the so-called Bill of Rights of 1689 (which still has the status of a statute). He complained in private that he had no more power than the doge of Venice, a personification of political impotence. (Claydon 2002, p. 72; Troost 2005, p. 212.)

Parliament's hopes of an Orange Protestant dynasty were dashed by the fact that William was gay, so the couple had no offspring. On William's death in 1702, the throne passed to James's second Protestant daughter, Anne (r. 1702–14), who had no shortage of offspring, all of whom, however, predeceased her. By means of some highly convoluted genealogical acrobatics, Parliament then traced the Protestant line back to James I and out again to the Elector George Louis of Hanover, who was offered the throne as King George I (r. 1714–27). Though he reputedly could speak no English (at least initially), this disadvantage was more than outweighed by his staunchly Protestant credentials, and the fertility of his line has ensured that the British throne has been occupied by a direct descendant of his to this day.

One important power initially left to the king was the right to select his own ministers. When Sir Robert Walpole, the first person to be referred to (originally in jest) as "Prime Minister," informed George I's son, George II (r. 1727–60), that his father was dead and he was now king, the new king snapped back: "That is one *big* lie!" (Thackeray, 2017.) That was on George II's assumption that nothing that Walpole said could be believed. However, as the King depended on Parliament for supplies and Walpole had a commanding majority in the House of Commons, Walpole was allowed to remain in office—which he only relinquished after losing a vote of no confidence in Parliament in 1742. It soon became apparent to successive kings that, instead of appointing a royal favorite as Prime Minister, who would have to scratch around to put together a parliamentary majority, it made more practical sense to appoint as Prime Minister a political leader who already commanded a parliamentary majority. In that way the king would be guaranteed supply—but at the cost of political power. By the time of Queen Victoria

(r. 1837–1901) this convenience had hardened into a constitutional convention, with the monarch being obliged to appoint as Prime Minister the leader of the majority party in the House of Commons. What little royal initiative was left was dealt a crushing blow by the crystallization of the party structure, especially since the Conservative Party started electing their leader in 1965.

The whole of British history has been dominated by a shifting power elite, originally by a hereditary aristocracy and later by more diversified elites. Though the make-up of the dominant elite has changed over the years, and, though the country or, until the Act of Union (1707), England and Scotland separately have nominally been a monarchy throughout almost the whole of its history, at no time has there been a populist anti-elite regime. The most obvious candidate for this title might have been expected to be Oliver Cromwell's short-lived Protectorate, but as we have seen, he owed his position to the army and was not actually opposed to a stratified or hierarchical society. Richard II (r. 1377–99) flirted briefly with the concept of popular monarchy, but, contrary to the usual historical view, the English monarch who came closest to forging a bond with the ordinary people against the elite was Charles I during his so-called "eleven years' tyranny" (1629–40), though it was his loyal lieutenants Strafford and Archbishop Laud rather than the King himself who carried a genuinely populist program into effect—and Charles only belatedly realized that his reluctant sacrifice of Strafford sealed his own fate.

That is not to say that there were not some strong British monarchs. Henry VII, Henry VIII and Elizabeth I immediately come to mind in this regard, but none of them attempted to forge an alliance with the ordinary people against the elite. Henry VII (r. 1485–1509) established strong monarchy by curbing the power of the aristocracy. His son and successor Henry VIII (r. 1509–1547) gave the impression of autocracy as portrayed by Hans Holbein; he had no qualms about sending two wives—and several erstwhile trusted ministers—to the block; and, in his pursuit of a male heir, he changed the religion of the country from Catholic to Protestant and had himself declared "Supreme Governor" of the Church of England. However, in so doing he had to pander to Parliament.

Elizabeth never made that mistake. But while being very wary of Parliament, it never occurred to her to appeal to the ordinary people over the heads of the elite. Her view of society was hierarchical. Her remark that "It is monstrous that the feet should direct the head," cited above, meant that she would take no instructions from Parliament, but her solution to their insolence as she saw it, was not to appeal against them to the wider population but simply to resort to calling Parliament as seldom as necessary, a power that the Crown lost after 1689.

Case Study V: Cuba

Traveling in a hypothetical time-machine, fast forward two and a half millennia, and we find the Cuban dictator Fidel Castro (in power 1959–2008) taking to heart the lesson of the "tall poppy syndrome," as it is sometimes called. (See above, under Greek Tyrants.) His "First Agrarian Reform," enacted just five months after his seizure of power in 1959, broke up large estates, confiscated the land and redistributed it to about 200,000 peasants. "[T]he first property he seized was his own family's farm. Castro's mother...never forgave her son." (Robinson 2005, p. Y07.) "[T]he revolution," Castro is quoted as proclaiming, "is the dictatorship of the exploited against the exploiters." (Mankiewicz 1976, p. 83.) Within a year, it is estimated, the Castro regime redistributed around 15 percent of the nation's wealth. Cubans who paid less than $100 a month had their rents halved. Judges and politicians' salaries were reduced, while low-level civil servants received a pay raise. Sugar production, the mainstay of the Cuban economy, was nationalized, together with the oil industry. In time, over 90 percent of the economy came under government control, and wages averaged less than $20 a month. (Sanchez 2010.) Education was greatly expanded, and a free healthcare system was established. The flip side of the coin was the abolition of elections, the arrest of hundreds of "counter-revolutionaries," and the suppression of freedom of speech and of the press. (Quirk 1993.)

Under the slogan *¡En cada barrio, Revolución!* (In every neighborhood, Revolution!), Castro set up what he called "a collective system of revolutionary vigilance, so that everybody knows who lives on every block, what they do, what relations they have had with the tyranny [viz. the previous regime, under Fulgencio Batista], in what activities they are involved, and with whom they meet." This system involved a "Big Brother" type network of thousands of *Comités de Defensa de la Revolución* (Committees for the Defense of the Revolution or CDR), charged with spying on everyone living in every apartment block in the country and reporting back to the police. In their defense, these committees also had a role in "...vaccination campaigns, blood banks, recycling, practicing evacuations for hurricanes...." (Sanchez 2010.)

The most prominent and enduring symbol of the Cuban revolution is the iconic image, not of Fidel Castro but of Ernesto "Che" Guevara, emblazoned on T-shirts still proudly worn by thousands of admirers around the world. An Argentinian by birth, second-in-command to Castro in the fight against the Batista regime, and then a key member of Castro's government for a few years, Guevara left Cuba in 1965 to foment revolution in Africa and later in Bolivia, where he was captured and summarily executed by firing squad at the age of 39 in 1967. What is not quite so well known is that Che's departure from Cuba and his doomed mission to Bolivia were encouraged by Castro, who evidently felt threatened by Che. And though "there was a guerrilla unit in Havana ready to deploy and rescue Guevara, Fidel never authorized the mission," abandoning Che to his fate. (Müller 2015.)

Castro's treatment of Che Guevara is of a piece with the tall poppy syndrome. Not only did Castro cut the former elite down to size, but he also could not brook sharing power even with his closest and most fervent supporters.

Case Study VI: Argentina

The only Latin-American figure to rival Che Guevara's iconic status was Eva "Evita" Perón (1919–1952), whose husband, General Juan Perón (1895–1974) owed his political success in no small measure to Evita's popularity, particularly with the industrial working class. In the 1946 presidential election, Juan Perón swept to victory with 299 electoral college votes out of 376, and 101 of the 158 seats in the Chamber of Deputies. Re-elected in 1951 by a margin of over 30 percent, Peron remained in power until removed by a military coup in 1955. Escaping first to Venezuela and then to Spain, where he was granted political asylum by Francisco Franco, he eventually returned to Argentina in 1973, greeted at Buenos Aires Airport by an estimated 3.5 million supporters. He swept back to power with 62 percent of the vote but died less than a year later, in July 1974. His funeral procession drew a crowd of over a million, chanting "¡Perón! ¡Perón! ¡Perón!"

When first elected in 1946, Perón embarked on a populist program inspired by Evita favoring workers and Labor Unions, nationalizing the Central Bank, the railroad, the merchant marine, public utilities, public transport, health care, the universities, the broadcasting system, and the labor unions. Perón attracted support and opposition from both left and right. Freedom of speech was stifled and dissidents imprisoned. That Perón was a dictator is not in doubt, but there is an ongoing debate on whether he was a fascist or more of a socialist. His admiration for Benito Mussolini and Adolf Hitler was not a secret, and he would later be given asylum in Franco's Spain. In the years immediately after World War II, Perón welcomed to Argentina a number of Nazis accused of war crimes, including Adolf Eichmann and Dr Josef Mengele. But in 1949, Perón's Argentina was the first country in Latin America to establish diplomatic relations with Israel while also allowing more Jewish immigrants than any other Latin American country.

Perón and Che Guevara, were on good terms, sharing a common enemy in the United States. Perón described Che as "...un utópico inmaduro—pero entre nosotros—me alegra que sea así porque a los 'yankees' les está dando flor de dolor de cabeza." (An immature utopian—but one of us—I am happy that it is so because he is giving the yankees a real headache). (O'Donnell 2011.)

What are we to make of all these paradoxes? Was Perón left-wing or right-wing? In fact, he was both or neither. He was a populist in the best "tall poppies" tradition, lopping off the poppies projecting above the rest with the active support of the generality of ordinary folk. Remarkably, three-quarters of a century since its inception, Peronism is still alive and well in Argentina and still drawing support from both left and right, though the two wings of the movement have drifted apart to some extent. But the essential "populist" nature of the movement comes out particularly in the second "principle" of Peronism: "Peronism is essentially of the common people. Any political elite is anti-people, and thus, not Peronist." (Modelo Argentino para el Proyecto Nacional 2015.) For 24 of the thirty-seven years since 1983, the presidency has been held by Peronists. The following presidents of Argentina are regarded as Peronists: Héctor Cámpora, Isabel Perón, Carlos Menem, Adolfo Rodriguez Saá, Eduardo Duhalde, Néstor Kirchner, Cristina Kirchner, and Alberto Fernández.

Case Study VII: Imperial China

On board our time-machine again, we find ourselves in China. It was an ancient Confucian principle that membership of the ruling class should be based on merit, through equal educational opportunity for all. This was put into practice by the T'ang dynasty in the seventh century by the introduction of a system of competitive written civil service examinations (upon which the modern Western examination system was modeled over a thousand years later.) This reform gradually achieved its objective of breaking the long monopoly of political power by the hereditary aristocracy. The Sung dynasty (960–1279) likewise deliberately utilized the examination system to counter the authority of regional military governors, enhance social mobility, and thereby increase imperial power.

According to Ho Ping-Ti's detailed study of Chinese social mobility, "The fact that there was more social circulation during the T'ang than during the previous three centuries cannot be much doubted, although it is difficult to say whether the truly humble and poor had much chance of social success.... [If] the hereditary aristocratic clans were no longer able to monopolize political power from the mid-seventh century onward, [they] remained the dominant political factor and enjoyed unrivalled social prestige down to the very end of the T'ang period." However, in the early Sung dynasty (960–1126), 46.1 percent of recorded officials came from *han-tsu*, (humble) clans or families, as against only 13.8 percent in the late T'ang period (756–906.) "The trend of increasing mobility continued after the founding of the Ming dynasty (1368), when the examination and academic degree system became more elaborate and the school system nationwide." However "... The early Manchu rulers (from 1644), unlike the Ming founder, who came from a poor peasant family, were mainly concerned with winning the support of the key social class in their conquered land, namely, the scholar-official class," resulting in a "...much curtailed opportunity structure for the humble and obscure." (Ho 1976, p. 262.) "It was perhaps more than coincidental that the Taiping Rebellion or Revolution (1850–64), the most massive civil war in world history, was precipitated by Hong Xiuquan (Hung Hsiu-ch'üan), a member of a small landowning peasant family who had repeatedly failed to obtain his first degree." (Ibid.)

In general, "[T]he most striking characteristic of the post T'ang society was that, on one hand, social success depended more on individual merit than on family status, and that, on the other hand, high-status families had little means of perpetuating their success if their descendants were inept.... For during the Ming-Ch'ing period (1368–1911), there were various institutionalized and noninstitutional channels which promoted the upward mobility of successful families but there were few institutionalized means to prevent the long-range downward mobility of successful families. In this sense, Ming-Ch'ing society was highly competitive in its peculiar ways." (Ibid., p. 257.)

Case Study VIII: Maoist China

At dinner at St. John's College, Cambridge, one evening in 1967, a young Chinese in a "Mao suit" came and sat next to me on the long student benches. He introduced himself as one of a small number of Chinese students who had just arrived in Cambridge. When I asked him why he was not wearing a student gown (then mandatory for dinner in "hall"), he explained that, as wearing a gown was a "class distinction," he and his colleagues had been given special dispensation from that obligation by the Senior Tutor. I pointed out that, if he looked around, he would find that *not* wearing a gown was a sign of class distinction. Within a few weeks my new-found friend was recalled to China to take part in the "Great Proletarian Cultural Revolution,", an attempt by Mao Zedong (Mao Tse-tung), or "Chairman Mao" (1893–1976), to replace with his own personal power the new elite that had supplanted the old ruling elite since the Communist takeover in 1949.

The "Cultural Revolution," enforced by youthful Maoist "Red Guards," resulted in the destruction of much of traditional Chinese culture, the imprisonment and death of thousands of "class enemies," and the upheaval of society. Teachers and educational authorities were among the prime targets. One of the best-known features of this was the "barefoot doctors" program, which brought peasants with just a few months' training from the countryside to work in city hospitals, replacing university-trained doctors, who were sent to work in the countryside. New political slogans were everywhere, on posters, banners, newspapers, and even on bus tickets and cigarette packets. "Long live the red terror!" was one popular slogan. Mao's personality cult was at the center of the whole movement, and even incidental remarks of his became sacred writ: "Sweet potato tastes good; I like it." Some slogans frankly revealed the true purpose behind Mao's fomenting this revolution: "Those who are against Chairman Mao will have their dog skulls smashed into pieces." (Huang, Shaorong, 2001.)

Mao's Cultural Revolution had two complementary sides. On the one hand, application of the tall poppy syndrome reduced everyone except Mao himself to the same level. But programs like that of the "barefoot doctors" opened an avenue of social advancement to some of the lowliest members of society while reducing the status of the newly emerging middle class. By contrast with Imperial China, which offered the prospect of advancement on the basis of merit as measured by competitive examinations, Mao's Cultural Revolution favored those with the least "merit" in any conventional sense. But that system proved short-lived. In due course, China allowed social mobility through an economy best characterized as state capitalism, which has resulted in huge inequalities in Chinese society, while the Constitution of the People's Republic of China entrusts supreme political authority to the Communist Party. Since 2012, political power has been concentrated in the hands of a single ruling figure, Xi Jinping, who combines the posts of General Secretary of the Communist Party and President with the unofficial designation of "paramount leader," without any term limit.

Conclusion

Equality, Equality of Opportunity, and the Aristocratic Ethos

In every society, past and present, we find inequality, with an elite group or groups at the top, and the bulk of the population below. In other words, to my knowledge, there has never been a society in which everyone was equal. Equality has sometimes been held up as an ideal or even as a description of a supposedly "natural" primitive state of society, but this has never been achieved in practice.

The slogan associated with the English Peasants' Revolt of 1381, is a good example: *"When Adam delved and Eve span, who was then the gentleman?"* This was a claim that originally everyone was equal, which is simply not true of any society in the past three thousand years. (See discussions above.)

Aristocratic Ethos

In practice, there has generally been what we may call an "aristocratic ethos" throughout history, meaning that there has been an (often unstated) acceptance of inequality as a natural state of affairs, and that society is stratified as a result even while protesting against that fact.

A.H.M. Jones's remark, in regard to Athenian democracy, that "... the Athenian people were rather snobbish in their choice of leaders." (Jones 1957, p. 49), begs the question: Why was this the case? The answer is that, though the regime was anti-aristocratic, the whole ethos of society remained aristocratic: the Athenian democracy, in common with ancient societies in general, simply did not believe in equality. (Arnheim 1977, p. 158 ff.)

And this does not apply only to ancient societies. The well-known hymn, "All Things Bright and Beautiful," first published in 1848, has a third stanza, now usually omitted, reading:

> *"The rich man in his castle,*
> *The poor man at his gate,*
> *God made them high and lowly,*
> *And ordered their estate."*
> (Cecil Alexander 1848, Hymns for Little Children.)
> The implication here is that social stratification is
> not only natural but God-given.

The *Déclaration des Droits de l'Homme et du Citoyen* (Declaration of the Rights of Man and of the Citizen), promulgated by the French Revolutionary National Assembly in 1789, was intended to do away with *privilege*, as enjoyed by the French nobility.

Accordingly, Article 1 of the Declaration proclaims: "Men are born and remain free and equal in rights. Social distinctions can be based only on the common good." Though ostensibly establishing equality, this Article recognizes the need for "social distinctions." Article 6 goes further: "All citizens, being equal in the eyes of the law, are equally eligible for all public dignities, positions and employments, according to their capacity, and without any distinction other than their virtues and talents." This is not a statement of equality at all, but of equality of opportunity, which is actually exactly the opposite. For, what is equality of opportunity if not equal opportunity to become unequal? The objective of equality of opportunity is meant to be meritocracy, which is commonly described as a rat-race.

Equality vs. Equality of Opportunity

But how can equality of opportunity be achieved? This is a problem with which modern Western societies have been grappling for some time. Standardized competitive tests, which have commonly been used to this end, are now often condemned as being intrinsically unfair, among other reasons because they tend to favor students with socio-economic advantages. The paradoxical logical solution would appear to be that there has to be actual equality first in order to achieve equality of opportunity. In other words, for the rat-race to be fair, all runners need to set off from the same starting line. But as we have already established, actual equality does not exist. So, to make up for the unfairness of the rat-race, the race has to be rigged, with losers being accorded special priority, based either on ethnicity, race, color, poverty, gender, or creed. Both equality and equality of opportunity are thereby jettisoned in favor of *privilege*, the very thing that the whole system was designed to do away with.

Justice Clarence Thomas of the U.S. Supreme Court, who was given a place at Yale Law School as part of an affirmative action program, recalled that the law firms to which he applied after graduating "...asked pointed questions, unsubtly suggesting that they doubted I was as smart as my grades indicated." As a result, he added, "I peeled a fifteen-cent sticker off a package of cigars and stuck it on the frame of my law degree to remind myself of the mistake I'd made by going to Yale. I never did change my mind about its value." (Thomas 2008 p. 143 f.) This system has an even more negative effect on those who feel cheated by it, like Allan Bakke, Barbara Grutter, and Abigail Fisher, who all brought high-profile lawsuits against universities for denying them a place in favor of minority students with lower grades than themselves: *Regents of the University of California v. Bakke* (1978), *Grutter v. Bollinger* (2003), and *Fisher v. University of Texas* (2013 and 2016).

Paradoxically, perhaps, the closest approach to equality is attained by means of the tall poppy syndrome, as practiced in populist monarchical systems like that of the Greek Tyrants, Castro's Cuba, or Maoist China (discussed above).

Monarchy vs. Aristocracy

As already mentioned, it is a serious fallacy to claim, with Syme, that "In all ages, whatever the form and name of government or whatever may be the name and theory of the constitution, be it monarchy, republic, or democracy, an oligarchy lurks behind the façade." (Syme 1939, pp. 7, 15.) And "A monarchy rules through an oligarchy." (1939, p. 8.)

Oligarchy (or aristocracy, where the ruling elite is hereditary), as shown in the foregoing Case Studies, is the polar opposite to monarchy. The Roman Republic is a prime example of an aristocracy with a visceral fear of one-man rule, but which ultimately succumbed to it. Though Augustus tried to conceal the true nature of the system of government that he established, its monarchical character is beyond doubt, and it is a serious mistake to believe that it was an oligarchy or even a dyarchy (power shared between the emperor and the aristocracy).

The history of France shows how a long and hard-won victory of monarchy over aristocracy was thrown away by Louis XVI, followed by two and a half centuries of oligarchy punctured by two brief interludes of monarchy. By contrast, English history presents us with a long and successful struggle of aristocracy or oligarchy against monarchical rule.

Monarchy: Real and Unreal

King Farouk of Egypt (r. 1936–52) reputedly predicted that, after his ouster, there would be only five kings left in the world: the king of England and the four kings on playing cards. However, as we have seen, despite the pomp and ceremony surrounding it, the British monarchy is not a monarchy in any real sense of the word, but what Walter Bagehot termed a "dignified" rather than an "efficient" part of the British constitution. (Bagehot 1867.) As already noted, though highly respected, and indeed adulated, the current British head of state, Queen Elizabeth II, has even less power than any of her predecessors. So, to refer to the current British form of government as a monarchy is misleading.

True monarchy is always anti-aristocratic, and its power is bolstered if it enjoys popular support—a "populist" form of government, to coin a phrase. Examples include the Greek tyrants, Athenian democracy, Peronist Argentina, Castro's Cuba, and Maoist China. The Roman Principate is more difficult to classify for, though undoubtedly monarchical and enjoying popular support, it also cultivated the elites around the Roman world without, however, sharing power with them.

The suggestion, sometimes made particularly in connection with Byzantium, that monarchical power is enhanced by "isolationism," is plainly wrong. It forces the monarch to depend on those around him, such as courtiers, or, in the Byzantine case, eunuchs, whose power was greatly enhanced without necessarily augmenting that of their master. (See Chapter 5.)

Monarchical power benefits not only from popular support but also from a sense instilled in the populace that the monarch is accessible. E.g. The well-known exchange (already discussed) between the Emperor Hadrian and a persistent supplicant, who, when rebuffed by the Emperor with the excuse that he had no time to hear her application, angrily retorted: "Then don't be king." (Cassius Dio 69.6.3.) It is significant that the woman expected a ruler to be accessible. And the use of the Greek word *basileue*, the verb from *basileus* (king), is also noteworthy. This incident is set in a Greek-speaking Eastern province, where rulers had long been worshipped and where the carefully contrived non-monarchical Latin terminology of the Principate had no place. To this woman, Hadrian was simply a king, and it was his duty to be accessible to his subjects. The story is probably apocryphal, and similar anecdotes are related in Plutarch and elsewhere about other rulers. But an ambitious and power-hungry emperor like Hadrian could not have been unaware of the benefits flowing to both ruler and subject from accessibility. Hadrian also happened to be a serious philhellene, so his concern for his Greek-speaking subjects was probably quite genuine. (See also Kritsotakis 2008.)

Writers unsympathetic to strong rulers are often unable or unwilling to understand or accept the possibility that such rulers may actually have a genuine affection for their subjects, which is reciprocated. An example of that is a recent book titled *Strongmen: How They Rise, Why They Succeed, How They Fall*, in which we read, "A strongman's fear and loathing of his people come through most clearly when his power is threatened." (Ben-Ghiat 2020, p. 256.)

Democracy

Athens in the fifth century BCE (and also later), modern Britain and France, are all commonly described as democracies, but this label tells us very little about the true power relations in those societies. For one thing, Athenian democracy was direct. Only adult male citizens could participate, which excluded not only women and slaves but also "metics," or foreigners. By contrast, modern democracy, as in Britain and France, is *representative* democracy, which means that voters choose someone to represent them. They are not *delegates* but *representatives*, so they do not have to vote in accordance with their constituents' wishes. (See Edmund Burke's "Speech to the Electors of Bristol," 1774, Burke's *Works*, Vol. I, pp. 446–448.)

An even more important point is that, as we have seen, fifth-century Athenian democracy was a form of anti-aristocratic populist government, with demagogic leaders in the driving seat. By contrast, with two brief Bonapartist interludes in France, modern representative democracy is essentially oligarchic. Jean-Jacques Rousseau (1712–78) summed up the essence of British government in his *Du Contrat Social* (The Social Contract) as follows:

> Le peuple Anglois pense être libre; il se trompe fort, il ne l'est que durant l'élection des membres du Parlement; si-tôt qu'ils sont élus, il est esclave, il n'est rien.(*Du Contrat Social*, ch. 15)

(The people of England regard themselves as free, but they are grossly mistaken. They are free only during the election of members of Parliament. As soon as they are elected, slavery overtakes the people, and they are nothing.)

This was written in 1762, well before the so-called Great Reform Act of 1832, when the electorate was restricted to only about 10 percent of the adult male population. Has the advent of universal suffrage invalidated Rousseau's harsh verdict? Actually, probably not. British voters today generally have to choose between three or four parties. As a result of the first-past-the-post or winner-take-all system, the winning party rarely polls over 50 percent of the total votes. The winning party forms the government, and, as long as it has a comfortable majority in the House of Commons, it can normally pass any legislation it likes, leaving the electorate, as Rousseau pointed out, on the sidelines. It is this situation that Lord Hailsham described as an "elective dictatorship."

In short, though a democracy in name, the British government of today is essentially an oligarchy. And, besides the elective dictatorship of the executive, there is also tremendous power vested in the senior judges, who are unelected, essentially irremovable, and not responsible to anyone.

In France, the President is very powerful though the electorate has slightly more say than in Britain because a candidate for the National Assembly needs at least 50 percent of the vote (in either one or two ballots) to win a seat. The winning candidate for the Presidency likewise needs 50 percent of the votes cast. But as in Britain, once the election is over, the people are essentially powerless, subject only to demonstrations or protests, like the protracted protests of the *gilets jaunes* (yellow vests) in France in 2018–19.

Part II

Conflicting Theories

Prologue to Part Two

*T*his *Prologue is essentially a bridge between Parts One and Two. A.H.M. Jones's masterly roundup of possible explanations for the demise of the Western empire is a useful sounding board. This is followed by a foretaste of my own conclusions on whether there was decline and fall or drift and change.*

In his magisterial *Later Roman Empire 284-602*, my esteemed and beloved doctoral supervisor, the late Professor A.H.M. ("Hugo") Jones of Cambridge, sums up in these words his explanation of what he unashamedly calls "the fall of the West": "[D]irectly or indirectly, it may be plausibly argued, barbarian attacks probably played a major part in the fall of the West." (Jones, 1964, p. 1027.) From the fact that, "[W]hile the Western parts were being parcelled out into a group of barbarian kingdoms, the East stood its ground," he concludes that "the empire did not, as some modern historians have suggested, totter into its grave from senile decay, impelled by a gentle push from the barbarians." (Ibid., 1026f.)

But Jones does not, nevertheless, completely discount evidence of internal "decline." In masterly fashion, he then weighs up one after the other of the possible explanations for the West's succumbing to barbarian attacks:

- **Division:** "Some critics have stressed the evil consequences of the division of the empire, particularly after 395, and have urged that if its whole resources had been pooled the Western fronts could have been held." (Ibid., p. 1031.) Jones's response to this is: "Much more might have been done if one emperor had ruled the whole empire, but it is doubtful if one man could have effectively controlled both the East and the West in the political and military conditions of the time..." (Ibid., p. 1032.) I agree with this, except that unity might have prevented certain problems from arising—notably the catastrophic defeat of Adrianople in 378 in which the Emperor Valens lost his life, which might have been averted had Valens had a unified army under him instead of needing reinforcements from the West, for which he unwisely decided not to wait. However, blame for this calamity may well belong to Valens's impetuosity rather than to the division of the empire.

- **Constitution:** "The succession of the empire has been criticised for its failure to provide a clear rule for the succession to the throne, and thus permitting, if not encouraging, usurpations." (Ibid., p. 1032.) Jones rejects this view: "[F]rom the time of Diocletian the college of emperors provided the continuity required." And: "From Constantine onwards the hereditary principle was *de facto* followed." (Ibid. p. 1032f.) But: "Unfortunately, dynasties were short-lived." (Ibid., p. 1033.) However, referring to the dynasties established by Constantine, Valentinian I, Theodosius I, and Justin I, he adds: "Nevertheless these families built up a certain tradition of loyalty." (Ibid.) I disagree slightly with Jones here. For one thing, I do not regard Diocletian's tetrarchy as a success, precisely because it ignored the hereditary principle by passing over Constantine, the son of Constantius, and Maxentius, son of Maximian—resulting in civil war, followed by a final war between Constantine and Licinius. And Constantine's attempt to implement orderly hereditary succession after his death also failed signally, with his three sons at each other's throats. However, these problems of succession affected the East as well as the West, so they cannot be regarded as a cause of the "decline" of the West.

- **Usurpations:** Jones comments that most usurpations took place in the West. "All these usurpations provoked civil wars, some minor, some of major importance." (Ibid.) p. 1033.) But: "In the East not only were legitimate emperors rarely challenged but when an emperor had not already designated his successor, an election was held in a constitutional manner, and its result accepted." (Ibid., p. 1033.) Jones plausibly attributes "the principal reason for the greater stability of the Eastern empire" to the fact that "monarchy was more deeply rooted there, and respect for royal authority had a longer tradition behind it. The Greek East had lived under kings from time immemorial, and had promptly hailed Augustus and his successors as kings." (Ibid., p. 1054.) As I mentioned in Chapter 5, during the

Principate the people of the Greek East did not bother to follow Augustus's careful sidestepping of monarchical language. To them, the Roman emperor was simply *basileus* ("king")—and, under the pagan empire, they also had no qualms about worshiping the living emperor as a god.

- **Regional or national sentiment:** "[S]ome modern historians," writes Jones, "have seen a growth of regional or national sentiment in the later empire, and a tendency of outlying provinces to break away from the empire." He is curtly dismissive of such views: "The evidence for such a view is very tenuous." (Ibid., p. 1034.) However: "That local loyalty played a large part in the devotion of many Africans to the Donatist cause and of most Egyptians to the Monophysite faith may be granted; the case of Syria is much more disputable. It is also true that the Donatists and Monophysites execrated those emperors who persecuted them, and violently resisted attempts to impose catholic or orthodox bishops upon them. This resistance certainly imposed an additional burden upon the imperial armies...But evidence is entirely lacking that either sect envisaged secession from the empire or gave welcome or support to the empire's enemies." (Ibid., p. 1034.) Like other divisive forces, then, "heresy" affected the East as well as the West, so it cannot be regarded as a cause of the "decline" of the West. It also challenges the idyllic picture of the Byzantine Empire painted by some adherents of the "Late Antiquity" school. (See Chapter 12.) But Jones's caution is here excessive. Religious schism could—and did—translate into political disloyaty. For example, a goodly proportion of the Monophysite population of Alexandria sided with the invading Muslims against their own Byzantine rulers during the Muslim siege of that city in 641. (See Chapter 14.)

- **Trade and industry:** Jones is dismissive of the view "that the fall of the empire in the West was due to the decay of trade and industry." (Ibid., p. 1038.) His reasoning was as follows: "There never had been a large-scale export trade beyond the frontiers." (Ibid., p. 1038.) And: "[I]t is very doubtful whether there ever had been any large-scale inter-provincial trade." (Ibid., p. 1039.) However, on the basis of laws about *agri deserti* ("deserted fields"), he does detect "some recession" in agriculture. This he attributes to "the heavy and increasing load of taxation." But Jones circles back to the "barbarians": "In so far as the high taxation was caused by the heavy military expenditure of the empire, the decline of agriculture was thus indirectly caused by barbarian pressure." (Ibid.) But he adds: "The extent of the decline must not be exaggerated." (Ibid., p. 1040.) However, more recently unearthed archaeological evidence has cast doubt on the very existence of agricultural decline. In the words of Cam Grey: "[I]n spite of the rhetoric of decline evident in legal and literary sources, the changes in settlement patterns evident from the archaeological evidence need not necessarily be interpreted as indications of widespread abandonment of the countryside brought on by an all-encompassing economic and demographic crisis." (Grey, 2007, p. 362) The current accepted view among scholars is that "legislation concerning *agri deserti* in the Late Empire is not necessarily an indication of a massive decline in agricultural productivity and the abandonment of land by a rural population in inexorable decline. Rather, the texts preserved in the Theodosian and Justinianic Codes were aimed primarily at ensuring that the taxes assessed on such land continued to be paid—that is, *agri deserti* were a fiscal rather than an agricultural problem." (Grey, 2007, p. 362) Grey contrasts the picture painted in the Codes with that gleaned from the *Opus Agriculturae*, written by Rutilius Taurus Aemilianus Palladius in the mid-fifth century: "One might expect, then, that the legislation emphasizes the exception rather than the rule, or responds to a particular, and particularly visible, phenomena..." (Ibid., p. 374.) "Archaeology also suggests that the fourth century, far from being the culmination of the [third century] crisis, saw in many provincial areas a growing rural landscape. *Agri deserti* in this context represent the marginal land, scarcely fertile, periodically unused and, depending on circumstances, undervalued by its owners or abandoned in order to concentrate on more fertile soils." (Soricelli, 2010, pp. 1–2.)

- **Depopulation:** Jones smartly bats this old chestnut away: "Depopulation has been regarded as a major factor in the decline of the empire. Unfortunately our information is so vague, and facts and figures are so sparse, that it is impossible to calculate what the population of the empire was at any date, or how much it declined, if, as is very probable, if not certain, it did decline." (Jones, p. 1040.) The evidence for this is largely tied to that for the decline of agriculture, which, as we have seen (above), may not have occurred, and Jones does not press the point: "Neither the poverty of the peasantry and the urban working class, nor the decline of the population, must be exaggerated." (Ibid., p. 1045.)
- **"Idle mouths":** "The basic economic weakness of the empire," opines Jones, "was that too few producers supported too many idle mouths." (Ibid., p. 1045.) There is no doubt some truth in this. Jones identifies the "idle mouths" as including: the poor of Rome, Constantinople, Alexandria, Antioch and possibly Carthage, who received free handouts of bread (and pork when available); the class of decurions, or town councillors; the army and civil service;

Christian clergy, monks and hermits; and, not least, the senatorial order.

- **Administrative abuses:** Jones identifies a number of administrative abuses, notably corruption. But he also blames excessive centralization for slowing up the processes of government without, however, achieving its object of checking corruption. (Ibid., p. 1056.)

- **Absence of public spirit:** A.H.M. Jones: "The most depressing feature of the later empire is the apparent absence of public spirit. The motive forces seem to be, on the one hand, compulsion, and on the other, personal ambition in its cruder forms, the desire to rise in the social scale and to get rich quick....Even more striking evidence of the lack of public spirit is the inertia of the civil population, high and low, in the face of the barbarian invasions. The upper classes were proud of being Roman, and valued Roman civilisation...The loyalty of the upper classes was, however, of a very passive character." (Ibid., p. 1058f.) This is discussed below.

- **Christianity:** Jones adopts a neutral position on this sensitive issue: "Christianity has been accused on the one hand of sapping the empire's morale by its otherworldly attitude, and on the other hand credited with giving the empire new spiritual energy and reforming it by its moral teaching. Neither allegation seems to have much substance. There is little to show that pagan worship promoted a patriotic spirit......But for the vast majority of ordinary men Christianity caused no fundamental change of attitude. To the ordinary man likewise the moral teaching and the otherworldly doctrine of Christianity seems to have made little practical difference. In some respects moral standards declined, and more people continued to devote their energies to the goods of this world. The average Christian does not seem to have worried greatly about the fate of his soul until he feared that death was near, and then he hoped to win access to heaven by the rituals of baptism or penance. In the meanwhile he pursued his worldly ends with no more, and sometimes less, regard for moral principles than his pagan forebears." (Ibid., p. 1062f.) But, as a minority withdrew into a monastic or ascetic life, "the service of the state tended to be left to ambitious careerists, and Christianity thus paradoxically increased the corruption of the government." (Ibid., p. 1063f.) For more on this, see below.

- **East vs. West:** Did the East suffer less from the weaknesses besetting the West? In some respects, more, says Jones, because "Christianity prevailed earlier in the Eastern parts and obtained a more thorough hold. Monks and clergy were more numerous and more richly endowed, and thus a heavier burden on the economy. Theological controversy was more widespread and more embittered, and the repression of heresy demanded a greater use of force and provoked more hostility." (Ibid., p. 1064.) Also: "The rules tying *coloni* to the soil and *curiales* to their cities were even more rigid in the East than in the West." (Ibid.) However, the East was evidently richer than the West, and wealth was probably more evenly distributed. "The East then probably possessed greater economic resources, and could thus support with less strain a larger number of idle mouths. A smaller part of its resources went, it would seem, to maintain its aristocracy, and more was thus available for the army and other essential services...The Western empire was poorer and less populous, and its social and economic structure more unhealthy. It was thus less able to withstand the tremendous strain imposed by its defensive effort, and the internal weaknesses which it developed undoubtedly contributed to its final collapse in the fifth century." (Ibid., p. 1067.)

- **Army:** Jones acquits the Roman imperial government on several major counts with which it is charged in regard to the army: its size and quality, and "for relying to excess on German troops and German officers." (Ibid., p. 1037.) "Under good leadership Roman armies could still defeat barbarian hordes which far out-numbered them, as the victories of Stilicho over Alaric and Radagaesus and of Belisarius over the Vandals and Ostrogoths amply demonstrate." (Ibid., p. 1037.) On the charge relating to Germanic troops, Jones is equally definite: "[N]o career officer of German origin—as opposed to tribal chieftains like Alaric and the two Theoderics who extorted high military commands from the government—is ever known to have betrayed the interests of the empire to his countrymen. The same applies to the rank and file." (Ibid., p. 1038.) But how then are we to explain the success of barbarians in taking over the Western empire? "The trouble," suggests Jones, "was caused when, from the time of Theodosius the Great, barbarian tribes which had forced their way into the empire were given the status of federates." (Ibid., p. 1038.)

- **Conclusion:** But this still begs the question of why the West fell while the East survived. Jones's convincing answer is in the last paragraph of his *magnum opus*: "[T]he internal weaknesses which it developed undoubtedly contributed to its final collapse in the fifth century..."But the major cause of its fall was that it was more exposed to barbarian onslaughts which in persistence and sheer weight of numbers far exceeded anything which the empire had previously had to face." (Ibid. p. 1068.) In his very last sentence he reiterates: "The internal weaknesses of the empire cannot have been a major factor in its decline."

Decline and Fall or Drift and Change?

"Hugo" Jones, therefore, had no qualms about referring to the "decline and fall" of the Western empire. He also had no hesitation in explaining this in terms of "barbarian onslaughts." In fact, he went even further, and detected what we might call a "double whammy" attributable to the barbarians. For, while identifying several subsidiary internal weaknesses, he held that "some of the more serious of these weaknesses were the result, direct or indirect, of barbarian pressure"—notably the need to maintain a vastly increased army, which necessitated heavy taxes, which in turn caused "a progressive decline in agriculture and indirectly a shrinkage of population.....The effort to collect this heavy taxation required a great expansion of the civil service, and this expansion in turn imposed an additional burden on the economy and made administrative corruption and extortion more difficult to control. The oppressive weight of the taxation contributed to the general apathy." (Ibid. p. 1067.)

This is an impressive logical edifice indeed! My own take differs from it chiefly in giving greater emphasis to certain internal factors—notably, the role of the senatorial aristocracy in the West as compared with the East, as established in Part I of this book. Emperors from Constantine onwards sapped the strength of the West by giving priority in its administration to members of the senatorial aristocracy, whose chief loyalty, with certain notable exceptions, was not to the imperial government but to themselves and their families, and who were able to cement their privileged position by combining great political power and influence in the provinces where they held office with extensive landed wealth in those same areas. This set the scene in the West for transition to the Middle Ages. In the "barbarian" successor kingdoms to the Western empire, however, the old Roman aristocracy was gradually supplanted by a new "Germanic" aristocracy.

These marked changes in the West, not unaccompanied by destruction and bloodshed, stand in stark contrast with the apparent unruffled continuity in the Greek East. The reality, however, was somewhat different. Though the Eastern, or Byzantine, Empire survived in name for nearly a thousand years beyond the conventional date of the end of the Western Empire, it was a pocket-handkerchief sized state that fell to the Ottomans in 1453. As for the vaunted impregnability of Constantinople, it was captured and sacked by members of the Fourth Crusade in 1204, who established the (Latin) Empire of Constantinople, which lasted until 1261. The Byzantine Empire's Northern and Eastern frontiers were in any case far less secure than Constantinople, and by

1204 the Empire had shrunk and grown by fits and starts, and lost territory to the Persians, Arabs, Seljuk Turks and Slavs. While technically an autocrat, in practice the Byzantine emperor shared power with the Church and with court eunuchs, who kept him isolated from the population at large.

It was, paradoxically, by its fall in 1453 that Byzantium made its greatest contribution to the continuity of the Roman Empire, when scholars and scribes escaped to the West taking precious classical manuscripts with them, contributing to the development in the West of the Renaissance, literally the "rebirth" of classical standards of art, architecture, literature, and philosophy. The influx of Greek scholars and texts also gave an impetus to the study of Classical Greek in the West, which for the first time entered the western university curriculum in the sixteenth century.

One major change from the Principate to post-Constantinian "late antiquity"—in East and West alike—was the prevalence of religious intolerance and persecution. Since the time of A.H.M. Jones, who died prematurely in 1970, and whose writings are just about as objective as it is possible to be, there has been a tendency among some writers on this period to play down or even deny this sea-change. For more on this see Chapter 10.

An important contrast between East and West was the survival of Latin—gradually morphing into the Romance languages—in the West, while the East, where Latin was never spoken, gradually lost its Greek lingua franca as large areas were engulfed, first by Arab conquests and later by Sejuk Turks, Slavs and others, before falling to the Ottomans. It is a tribute to the Romanization of the West that, despite being overrun by Goths, Vandals, Franks and other Germanic tribes, much of Western Europe—and, by expansion, most of South and Central America— remains to this day a latter-day Latin-speaking area, and that, even the Germanic tongue of the former province of Britannia, that remote outpost of the Roman Empire, came to be suffused with Latin derivatives.

Taking its cue from Caracalla's *Constitutio Antoniniana* of 212 giving Roman citizenship to all the free inhabitants of the Empire, the concept of a universal empire also survived better in the West than in the East. The Byzantines always referred to themselves as *Rhōmaioi* ("Romans"), but once their empire was swept away that identity perished (though Orthodox Christians living in modern Turkey were until recently referred to as *Rûm.*) In the West, by contrast, there has been a hankering after at least a European empire, which was partially realized, first by Charlemagne in the year 800, then by the Holy Roman Empire, dissolved in 1806, and today by the European Union of 27 nations.

The Roman Empire was always a monarchy, during the Principate down to 284, in Diocletian's Dominate to 305, in the Byzantine Empire until 1453—and even in the West, albeit somewhat weakened, after Constantine and his successors gave up some power to the senatorial aristocracy. But, from the fifth century onward aristocracy prevailed over monarchy in the West until the rise of nation states in the Early Modern period, and then again after parliamentary government eclipsed monarchy in the nineteenth and twentieth centuries. The French Revolutionary cry of *Liberté, Égalité, Fraternité* pointed to an unrealistic goal, as liberty and equality are inherently diametrically opposed to each other. Complete equality, though unattainable, is more closely approached in popular, or populist, monarchy—exemplified by such states as Maoist China or Fidel Castro's Cuba—than in an oligarchy. But it was by expansion of this latter form of constitution—into self-styled "representative democracy"— that the greatest degree of popular participation in government has been achieved.

7

Varieties of History

Over two thousand years ago, the great Greek historian Thucydides (c. 460–c. 400 BCE) identified what he considered the most fundamental criteria in the writing of history:

- The need for accuracy
- The analysis of causation
- The resemblance between past and future
- The utility of history as an aid to the interpretation of the future
- The long-term value of his history, composed "not as an essay for immediate commendation, but as κτῆμα ἐς αἰεί (a possession forever)." (Thucydides 1.22.4.)

Thucydides's ambition for his work to become a possession forever has been realized. But his criteria are still not universally accepted. This chapter discusses some of the many different approaches to the writing of history, with my own criteria summarized at the end. The issues dealt with are as follows:

- **"Proper historical writing"**: Moses Finley, who is credited with founding a new "school" for the writing of ancient history, defined "proper historical writing" as writing and teaching that is "morally and politically committed" and even "socially subversive."
- **The skeptical tendency:** A tendency of some historians exists to dismiss evidence accepted by most others, to the point of throwing the baby out with the bathwater.

Why Rome Fell: Decline and Fall, or Drift and Change?, First Edition. Michael Arnheim.
© 2022 John Wiley & Sons, Inc. Published 2022 by John Wiley & Sons, Inc.

- **Baby and bathwater:** Taken to an extreme, this tendency can result in a distorted or erroneous impression of whole periods.
- **"Drowning the Baby":** This is exactly the opposite fallacy, of credulously accepting weak or even non-existent evidence, perpetrated by some of the same writers engaged in throwing the baby out with the bathwater.
- **Ranke: "Wie es eigentlich gewesen ist."** The classic statement of the need for historians to stick to facts and eschew any "lessons" to be drawn from them.
- **History as "one damned fact after another":** A disparaging characterization of the Rankean approach which begs the question "What is a fact?"
- **"Cleopatra's nose":** The accidental theory of history, a rather superficial approach.
- **"An art of writing history":** Emphasis on elegant narrative, sacrificing analysis to style, does not necessarily prevent bias.
- **Torpedoing Torpor:** A case-study of how emphasis on narrative style may lead to erroneous interpretations.
- **The Oligarchy Trap:** This one-size-fits-all theory forces all forms of government into the same oligarchic straitjacket, blunting any ability to draw any distinctions between them.
- **"A monarchy rules through an oligarchy":** This is a curious example of "Oligarchy Club" thinking on the part of Sir Ronald Syme, resulting in a blurring of the dividing line between the Roman Republic and Augustus's Principate, and so obscuring a sea-change in Roman history.
- **Zero-sum game:** Lumping all governments together in a pot labeled "oligarchy" is a failure to recognize that monarchy and oligarchy are diametrically opposed to each other.
- **"Williamanmary was a good King":** This shows the dangers for a historian to rate people, events, developments or whole periods as "good" or "bad", a blatant rejection of any attempt at objectivity.
- **Causation:** In his *What Is History?* (1961), E.H. Carr opined, "The historian, like any other scientist, is an animal who incessantly asks the question, Why?" (Carr 1961, p. 113.) Not all historians would agree with this, though my own view is that, whether historians are regarded as "scientists" or not, Carr is correct.
- **Machiavellian History:** Machiavelli in *The Prince* is one of the very few writers ever to recognize the fundamental truth that in every society there is a mutual hostility between the aristocracy and the common people. A champion of the common people is likely to become a strong monarch, while a ruler dependent on the support of the aristocracy will be weak. Machiavelli draws his evidence

chiefly from the Italy of his own day and from classical antiquity. But the same analysis is applicable to societies in all ages around the world, as is shown in *Two Models of Government* (Arnheim, 2017a). (See Chapter 6.)

- **So What?** This is the ultimate test of the value and utility of the historian's researches.

Folk etymology derives "history" from "His story," meaning God's story, which cannot, of course, be taken seriously. The true origin of "history" is from the Greek *historia* (inquiry, investigation, research). The word entered Latin with the same meaning and, in Late Latin, was shortened to *storia* (story). So here we already have the two main classifications of history: history as literature, and history as science. The heroine of Jane Austen's *Northanger Abbey* (written in 1803) describes reading history as "...very tiresome: and yet I often think it odd that it should be so dull, for a great deal of it must be invention." This is a lighthearted caricature of the dilemma of historical writing, going to the heart of the question: "What is history?"

No one claiming to be a serious historian today would be likely to admit to being purely in the entertainment business, though by no means all professional historians would claim that history is a science either. There are a number of historical schools of thought, including the French *Annales* school as well as the so-called Frankfurt School, the Vienna School, the Toronto School, and a good many other more informal groupings, tendencies or traditions, each with its own answer to the question, "What is history?" Or, "What is the proper purpose of the study of history?" This chapter is devoted to a critical consideration of a number of different approaches to history.

"Proper Historical Writing"

Sir Moses Finley (1912–86), Cambridge Professor of Ancient History from 1970 to 1979, who had been highly critical of the state of ancient history writing, was asked in a 1985 interview by Keith Hopkins about his view of "proper historical writing." In the interview:

> (Finley) reflected on what he termed 'proper historical writing' and the part he had played in fostering it. He drew a contrast with the production of 'forty-page articles' on the detail of historical narrative: 'You offend nobody. You are acknowledged as a good scholar. It is easier.' He favoured instead the writing and teaching of history that was (as formulated by Hopkins) 'morally and politically committed' and even 'socially subversive.' He emphatically agreed that his own preferred way forward

was harder and made more enemies." (p. 57.) "'Do you think that you and your followers have in any way managed to change the normal way in which Ancient History is practised? You may not have been setting out to campaign against, but the impact was one of a campaign, wasn't it, setting up a new school?' To which Finley replied: 'Well, school, alright. (*sic.*) The difficulty is that there are too many ancient historians, any statement saying ancient historians now do this is easily falsified. But I don't have any doubt that...there is now an increasing number of ancient historians who do more of what I call proper historical writing. Now I am not suggesting that I did it, because of me, but I am prepared to accept that I have some responsibility for it. Whether they represent more than a minority in the field I doubt—because it's a bit the hard way to do things.' (Jew, Osborne, and Scott (eds.) 2016. p. 297.)

Several important points emerge from this exchange:

- Finley is critical of the traditional type of academic article on some "detail of historical narrative." (See the discussion below on Ranke.)
- Finley's own definition of proper historical writing is writing that is morally and politically committed and even socially subversive; in other words, it is tendentious writing supporting or even promoting a particular political, moral and social position. This is a far cry from the idea of the historian as a detached, neutral observer. (See the discussion below on Ranke.)
- Finley claims some personal responsibility for increasing the number of ancient historians doing "proper historical writing."

These points are begging the question in the following ways:

- Finley admits that what he calls proper historical writing is his own personal preference, but at the same time, he clearly takes pride in regarding it as superior to the conventional approach against which he had campaigned. There is no suggestion on Finley's part that there could be more than one type of proper historical writing.
- The writing of politically motivated history, i.e. Finley's proper historical writing, is nothing new. A good example is the Whig (or pro-parliamentary) interpretation of English history, which dominated the field for over two hundred years. But that would hardly have qualified as morally and politically committed, or socially subversive writing. Finley's left-leaning political sympathies are well-known, but it has to be said that, with some notable exceptions, there is little sign of an overtly left-wing bias in Finley's own writings.
- Finley's emphasis on how hard it was to write history in his preferred way may possibly explain his overly skeptical tendency to dismiss evidence that many other historians were prepared to accept.

The Skeptical Tendency

Here are just a few examples of Finley's skepticism:

Homer: In *The World of Odysseus* (first published in 1954), Finley categorically dismissed the idea that the Homeric epics threw any light on Troy or Mycenaean Greece: "...the narrative is a collection of fictions from beginning to end." (Finley 1954/2002, p. vii.) Finley essentially maintained this position for the rest of his life, for over thirty years — flying in the face of ever more impressive archaeological and linguistic evidence. The *Iliad* and the *Odyssey* make no claim to be historical records. They are epic poems reduced to writing probably between 800 and 700 BCE but evidently based on much older oral traditions relating to a war between Greeks and Trojans hundreds of years earlier. (West 2011, pp. 383–93.) The relevant evidence is threefold:

- First, Homer's Troy, or Ilium, has been reliably located on what is now called the mound of Hisarlik in present-day Turkey, a site occupied by a number of successive civilizations. The ones favoured by archaeology are Blegen's Troy VIIa or Manfred Korfmann's Troy Vii, dated to between 1260 and 1180 BCE. (Blegen 1995, p. 164; Korfmann 2013, p. 110.)
- This archaeological evidence is supplemented by archaeological evidence from Greece itself. Book II (lines 494–759) of the *Iliad* provides a "catalogue of ships" listing 164 Greek cities that contributed men to the campaign against Troy, most of which have been identified with archaeological remains dating from before 1150 BCE, when the whole Mycenaean world collapsed. In Homer, the Greek world is united in a loose confederacy under Agamemnon, King of Mycenae, which is reflected in the archaeological remains of Mycenae, Tiryns, Pylos, and other sites.
- The third source of evidence is Linear B, Mycenaean Greek as deciphered by Michael Ventris and John Chadwick. (Chadwick 1958.) This reveals a hierarchical society under a *wanax* (king), before the loss of the digamma, making it *anax* in Homer, which explains some anomalies in Homeric scansion as well as numerous other features, such as the appearance of a number of Homeric names like Hector and Achilles as the names of ordinary people in the Linear B tablets.
- Do the Homeric epics make some "mistakes" in representing Mycenaean society? Of course they do. The poems do not claim to be historical documents, and there was a long period of oral transmission before the traditions were eventually committed to writing. But the evidence of Mycenaean Greece reflected in the poems is so impressive as to make it counter-productive to simply discard it, as Finley did. (Finley 1954/2002; Cf. Arnheim 1977, p. 13 ff.; Wood 2015,)

Economies of scale: Finley dismissed the idea that the Romans had any idea of the commercial exploitation of land. He largely based this on a single letter from Pliny the Younger (61–c.113) to a friend asking for advice on whether he should buy an estate adjacent to one he already owned. "Apart from the bailiffs," opines Finley, "there is not a whisper of possible economies of scale that could or would follow the consolidation of two adjoining estates...." (Finley 1973, p. 113.) In fact, Pliny lists a number of potential economies of scale: "The same work could be carried on at both places, they could be visited at the same cost of travelling, they could be put under one steward and practically one set of managers.... Moreover, one must take into account the cost of furniture and head-servants, besides gardeners, smiths and even the gamekeepers, and it makes a great difference whether you have all these in one place or have them distributed in several." (Plin. *Ep.* 3.19.)

Latifundia: Finley pooh-poohed the famous stricture of Pliny the Elder (died 79 CE) on the rise of large estates: "*[L]atifundia perdidere Italiam vero et provincias*" (Large estates have destroyed Italy and even the provinces). (Plin. NH18.7.35.) Pliny's remark is unjustifiably dismissed by Finley, erroneously translating the perfect tense *perdidere*, short for *perdiderunt*, as present tense "(are destroying) as "...no more than moralizing archaism..., a lamentation for the lost Roman yeomanry and the simpler good old days." (Finley 1973, p. 202, n. 51.) Yet, Pliny had clearly put his finger on a development which was ultimately to transform the whole nature of the Roman economy and society. (See Chapter 5)

Cleon: One of Finley's more (unintentionally) amusing and palpably partisan enterprises was his spirited defence of Cleon, the Athenian demagogue who succeeded Pericles as the "champion of the people." Here, among other things, Finley omits any mention of the well-evidenced devious means employed by Cleon, notably his use of "sycophants," meaning deceitful or calumnious informers against the rich and noble, enabling Cleon to bring lawsuits to strip them of their wealth and undermine them. (See Chapter 6.)

Baby and Bathwater

The Roman historian Titus Livius (Livy), a contemporary of the Emperor Augustus, has been pilloried for being too uncritical of his sources. He admitted that the traditions of the early history of Rome were better suited to poetry than to history, but he decided nevertheless to repeat them, with the comment, "I have no intention of either confirming or rebutting them." (Liv. Pr. 6.) This left it up to later generations of historians to weigh up the pros and cons of accepting the early traditions.

However, there is no consensus among modern historians on this early period of Roman history. Tim Cornell, for example, has been criticized by Barry Forsythe and others for being "too trusting and overly optimistic." (Cornell 1995; Forsythe 2005, p. 4.) On the whole, I prefer Cornell's approach. (See Chapter 1.) At the opposite extreme from Cornell is Fergus Millar, who effectively throws the baby out with the bathwater: "So far as 'real' history goes, we should forget the earlier Republic, and begin where contemporary evidence begins, in the time of Hannibal." (Millar 2002, p. 85 f.) Hannibal lived from 247 to about 182 BCE and fought Rome in the Second Punic War, which lasted from 218 to 203 BCE. Millar continues: "The fourth century and the 'conflict of the orders' belong in the realm of myth. Yet so apparently purist a decision will not really do either....", and so he charitably stretches the period of "real" history two or three generations further back to allow for "collective memory."

An even clearer example of the baby-bathwater fallacy is Millar's rejection of Sir Ronald Syme's laconic conclusion, based on solid prosopographical evidence, that "In any age of the history of Republican Rome about twenty or thirty men, drawn from a dozen dominant families, hold a monopoly of office and power." (Syme 1939, p. 124.) This picture of the Roman Republic as dominated by a small elite was shared by Matthias Gelzer and his school, among others. (See Chapter 1.)

"Drowning the Baby"

However, as was shown in Chapter 1, Fergus Millar was also guilty of exactly the opposite fallacy from that of throwing the baby out with the bathwater to drowning the baby in an overflowing bathtub. This fallacy consists in the undue credulity of accepting weak or even non-existent evidence.

Though in a sense opposites, the two fallacies are actually correlative, or complementary, to each other. For, having thrown the baby out with the bathwater, Millar had to find a substitute for it. What he hit upon was a passage in Polybius that he misinterpreted as a description of the Roman Republic as a direct democracy: "Using 'democracy' in a strictly neutral sense, it is undeniable that the constitution of the Roman Republic was that of a direct democracy." (Millar 2002, p. 165.) From a purely legalistic, constitutional point of view, the "people" would indeed appear to have held center stage. But Millar was not referring only to the legal or constitutional position but also to political realities as is stressed by Millar's staunch defender T.P. Wiseman: "Fergus Millar forcefully insisted on the centrality of the People's role in the political life of the republic." (Wiseman, loc 76. referring to Millar 2002, pp. 109–42).

Ranke: "Wie Es Eigentlich Gewesen Ist"

It was in opposition to the idea of history as literature that Leopold von Ranke (1795–1886) famously characterized his approach to the writing of history as encapsulated in the phrase, *Wie es eigentlich gewesen ist* (How it actually happened or What actually happened). However, there is some doubt about what Ranke meant by this. A revisionist approach maintains:

> Ranke's oft-quoted dictum has generally been misunderstood in the English-speaking world as asking the historian to be satisfied with a purely factual recreation of the past. Ranke's writings make it clear that he did not mean this. In fact, the word *eigentlich*, which is the key to the phrase just quoted, has been poorly translated into English as "really" or "actually; 'essentially' would be a better rendition in this context. This gives the phrase an entirely different meaning, and one much more in keeping with Ranke's philosophical ideas. It is not factuality, but the emphasis on the essential that makes an account historical." "To history has been given the function of judging the past, of instructing men for the profit of future years. The present attempt does not aspire to such a lofty undertaking. It merely wants to show how it essentially was."—*blos zeigen, wie es eigentlich gewesen (ist)*. (Iggers and von Moltke (eds), 1973/2010, pp. xix–xx.)

Ranke is here drawing a contrast between history as a guide to the future and history simply as a straightforward factual account of the past, the latter being his approach. The revisionists may, therefore, be wrong to substitute "essentially" for "really" or "actually" in this context. But, either way, Ranke's emphasis is on the facts of history rather than on any "lessons" that may be drawn from them.

History as "One Damned Fact after Another"

So, is history just "one damned fact after another"? This disparaging characterization of the orthodox Rankean approach is sometimes attributed to Arnold Toynbee, whose 12-volume *A Study of History* (1934–61) adopted a whole different philosophy of history, identifying five stages through which Toynbee claimed 19 world civilizations had passed or were passing. (Toynbee)

This of course begs the questions: What is a historical fact? And is it possible for a historian to write purely factual history? In E.H. Carr's well-known book, *What is History?*, he remarks, "It used to be said that facts speak for themselves. This is, of course, untrue. The facts speak only when the historian calls on them: it is he who decides to which facts to give the floor, and in what order or context." (Carr 1961, p. 25.)

Ranke himself, perhaps inadvertently, provides us with examples of this. For instance, in his six-volume *History of England Principally in the Seventeenth Century*, we read in some detail of William Penn's visit to the Hague in the summer of 1686 in a failed effort to reconcile William of Orange with his father-in-law, King James II. (Ranke IV 389ff.) This visit is not even mentioned in Thomas Macaulay's five-volume *History of England from the Accession of James II*, covering the period 1685–1702. Why, then, did Ranke consider this abortive mission as a historical fact worth describing and indeed highlighting? William of Orange was, of course, a staunch Protestant, while James II was a devout Catholic, which was one of the factors eventually resulting in his ouster and replacement by William of Orange reigning jointly with James's daughter, Mary, as William III and Mary II. A striking fact about James II, and treated as such by both Ranke and Macaulay, was his close friendship with William Penn, the founder of Pennsylvania, a member of the Society of Friends (Quakers), the Christian denomination probably furthest removed from Catholicism. The King's "Declaration of Indulgence," seeking to institute a policy of religious toleration, is stigmatized as a fraud by Whig historians like Macaulay. But William Penn's evident acceptance of James's intentions as genuine must weigh in the balance, and this may possibly account for Ranke's decision to turn this otherwise insignificant and unsuccessful visit to the Hague into a historical fact.

Geoffrey Elton rejected Carr's distinctions between facts and historical facts, and Carr probably did make too much of this point. (Elton 1967.) Carr cites as a prime example the crossing of the Rubicon: "It is the historian who has decided for his own reasons that Caesar's crossing of that petty stream, the Rubicon, is a fact of history, whereas the crossing of the Rubicon by millions of other people before or since interests nobody at all." (Carr 1961, p. 27.) This is not quite correct. The Rubicon marked the boundary between Italy and Cisalpine Gaul, and it was strictly forbidden for a general to enter Italy with his army. Julius Caesar's crossing of the Rubicon was recognized as a significant fact at the time, as it amounted to a declaration of war against the Roman state. Hence Caesar's remark, as reported by Suetonius, *iacta alea est* (the die is cast) (Suet, Jul. 32.), or "let the die be cast," supposedly loudly declared in Greek, as Plutarch would have us believe. (Plut. Pomp. 60.2.9.) The crossing of the Rubicon was a bad choice on the part of Carr, as it does not actually support his distinction between *facts* and *historical facts*. But there certainly is no shortage of examples to support his distinction, William Penn's visit to the Hague in 1686 being one.

"Cleopatra's Nose"

"If Cleopatra's nose had been shorter," opined the great French mathematician and writer Blaise Pascal, "the whole face of the world would have changed." (Pensées 162.) This is what may be termed the accidental view of history.

Professor Sir Geoffrey Elton of Cambridge (1921–94), who championed traditional political history, went from one extreme to the other in this respect. He created a sensation in academic circles with his 1953 book *The Tudor Revolution in Government*, which sought to prove that a sea-change occurred in English history in the 1530s, when medieval household government, centered on the king, was replaced by a more impersonal bureaucratic form of government. To this double whammy, consisting of the *nature* and *date* of the revolution in government, Elton added one more: The architect and facilitator of this revolution was Henry VIII's chief minister, Thomas Cromwell and not the King himself, who played only a minor role in it. So major was this revolution, Elton believed, that it paved the way for England's future stability and greatness.

Before long, Elton found his theory assailed from all sides, and it is no longer an icon of historical orthodoxy. For one thing, it turned out that incipient bureaucratic government could be traced back at least half a century before the 1530s. Elton's demotion of Henry VIII to a walk-on part in his own show was also plainly wrong.

Robbed of his place in the vanguard of the historical revolution, Elton went almost to the other extreme of accidental history, playing down the role of Parliament in the sixteenth and even the seventeenth century:

> Prolonged involvement with Parliament has in the end convinced me that the customary concentration on it as the centre of public affairs, however traditional it may be, is entirely misleading. This is a message, it seems to me, that needs to be absorbed into the general history of England. We have been misled by the Victorians and their obedient successors who read the modern Parliament back into history; and I do not except the story of Parliament in the seventeenth century from these reservations. I now wonder whether the institution—one of the Crown's instruments of government—ever really mattered all that much in the politics of the nation, except perhaps as a stage sometimes used by the real contenders over government and policy. (Elton 1986, p. ix.)

But, if Parliament was not a "real contender", then who or what was? Elton rejects as "old hat" the theories that attributed the English Civil War either to a "rising" or "declining" gentry, two favorite explanations for the English Civil War, and he is equally dismissive of Puritanism as leading to an "irreconcilable conflict". He adds that "we are possibly ill-advised" to mistake (Sir Edward) Coke's personal battles with James I or Francis Bacon "for titanic conflicts of principle" over the common law. Professor Hugh Trevor-Roper's explanation in terms of the clash between "court" and "country" is equally curtly dismissed. Needless to say, Christopher Hill's Marxist interpretation gets short shrift, as does "a much subtler but essentially unchanged version of his earlier views concerning the bourgeois and urban revolutions against the economic and social structure of a gentry-run rural society."

Elton then rounds on the whole notion that the conflict was inevitable: "Most historians seem also convinced that there was something seriously wrong with the system of government inherited by the Stuarts: it is thought that when James I came to the throne nothing could have prevented conflicts with Parliament so serious as to call in doubt the whole survival of the structure. The Tudor constitution is considered ramshackle." "What these views have in common", opines Elton, referring to all the explanations that he has curtly rejected, "is a sense of inevitability, a feeling that so profound a disturbance as a civil war must have had roots so deep, causes so fundamental, that no analysis can be expected to discover them clearly enough... The mistake is one of logic: to suppose that because the civil war happened therefore it was bound to happen, and that because the civil war gave arms and voice to rival groupings therefore rival groupings made the war inevitable." And finally: "Under James I and Charles I, says Mr. Hill, the political nation 'was rent by political disagreements which led to civil war'. But is this strictly accurate? Assuredly, the nation was rent in those years, but in 1640 the one thing quite out of the question was a civil war. When the Long Parliament met, the gentry—the political nation—were remarkably united, and the king had no party to speak of". (Elton 2003, p. 164ff.)

With this feast of negativism, Elton appears to be close to the school of thought that sees history as "just one damned fact after another." Elton is undoubtedly right to reject the assumption that just because something happened, it was bound to happen. But he is wrong to go to the other extreme and concentrate exclusively on the immediate run-up to the events in question. Could the English Civil War have been averted? Quite possibly. But that does not alter the fact that there was a history of long-standing tension and intermittent clashes between Crown and Parliament from the fourteenth century. There had always been two alternative paths ahead, leading to two opposite destinations: monarchy or oligarchy. The situation in England was by no means unique. Most states in Western Europe reveal a similar clash between Crown and privileged classes. In most cases, as in France, Spain, and the German states, the Crown won at least initially. But in England the Crown lost. (See Chapter 6.)

The reasons for this defeat are more immediate, but to ignore the long-standing and deep-seated forces leading to the outbreak of the English Civil War in the first place, as Elton does, is to substitute the historian's role as explainer and interpreter with that of narrator and story-teller.

"An Art of Writing History"

Harvard's Professor Samuel Eliot Morison (1887–1976), the author of numerous chiefly narrative histories, made a special plea for historians to pay more attention to style: "American historians, in their eagerness to present facts and their laudable concern to tell the truth, have neglected the literary aspects of their craft. They have forgotten that there is an art of writing history." (Morison 1946.) But Morison's concern with literary style resulted in something of a superficial approach to historical developments and did not save him from espousing a partisan interpretation of history. In his presidential address to the American Historical Association in December 1950, he called for a history of the United States "...written from a sanely conservative point of view," in reaction against what he called "the Jefferson-Jackson-F.D. Roosevelt line" (American Historical Review, 56, 1951, pp. 272–3.)

Torpedoing Torpor

Emphasis on presenting a compelling narrative may also result in ill-considered interpretive conclusions. Here, for example, is a curious passage in Simon Schama's *A History of England* comparing Charles I (r. 1625–49) unfavorably with his father James I (r. 1603–25), and attributing James's greater success to "torpor":

> The problem with Charles Stuart was his good intentions, and the stubborn literalness with which he meant them to take effect. Conversely, in retrospect one can see quite clearly what enormous political assets his father's natural laziness and low threshold of distraction really were. (Uncannily, the same would be true of Louis XV and XVI. Benign torpor should perhaps have been on the list of recommended virtues for successful princes.) James I's tendency to leave government to others... was, since those others happened to be of the calibre of Robert Cecil and Francis Bacon and Lionel Cranfield, the

best thing he could have done for the country. Charles I, on the other hand, was positively driven by the itch to govern.... Just as it had for Augustus, for Constantine and, especially, for Alfred the Great, whose biography was commissioned by the king, Duty Called! (Schama, 1992, loc 1092 (Kindle).)

Is this intended to be some sort of joke? If so, it is not very funny. The point that Schama seems to be making is that "torpor" assists a monarch to become "successful", whereas conscientiousness and "the itch to govern" have the opposite effect. An amusing paradox? The only problem is that it simply has no basis. Louis XV is held up as a parallel example of "torpor" to James I, but it is not quite clear where Louis XVI fits in. Is he another example of "torpor", presumably because of his devotion to locksmithery and hunting? Or is he cited as an example of the opposite, because of his desire to be loved by his subjects? And what about Augustus, Constantine and Alfred the Great, who, driven by the call of "duty", are presumably cited as parallels to Charles I. Yet, were they not "successful"—except perhaps for Alfred's fabled burning of the cakes?

Here is the low-down on these monarchs:

James I enjoyed the races and liked to lavish time and money on his favorites. But torpor? Certainly not. Robert Cecil, Francis Bacon, and Lionel Cranfield undoubtedly were able ministers, but both Bacon and Cranfield were publicly disgraced. As for James himself, his fervent belief in the Divine Right of kings found expression not only in his writings but also in his dealings with Parliament, which were less than harmonious and presaged Charles I's ultimately fatal clash with that body. But was James I a "successful" king as Schama suggests? Only if escaping the fate of his mother, Mary Queen of Scots (beheaded), his son Charles I (beheaded), his grandson Charles II (in exile for ten years), and his grandson James II (deposed) constitutes success. (See Chapter 6.)

Louis XV certainly liked to keep himself amused and had no shortage of mistresses to this end, but he also understood that it was in the interests not only of the Crown but also of the ordinary people of France to keep the aristocracy in check. His reign culminated in the complete victory achieved by his astute minister Maupeou over the *parlements*, the protagonists of the aristocratic interest (See Chapter 6.)

Louis XVI on his accession senselessly gave up this hard-won victory and recalled the *parlements*, which led straight to the fateful summoning of the Estates General in 1789 and ultimately to the guillotine. (See Chapter 6.) Was Louis XVI an example of "torpor"? Quite possibly— but he can hardly be described as a success.

Augustus, the first Roman emperor, was without a doubt one of the most successful rulers of all time. As Schama admits, Augustus was driven by the call of duty, so it is hard to know why Schama even mentions him. (See Chapter 1.)

The same applies to **Constantine**, another largely successful Roman emperor who was anything but torpid. (See Chapter 3.)

As for **Alfred the Great**, he is the only English king to win the accolade of "the Great". Success but no torpor here.

The real point is that "successful" monarchy can be achieved only at the expense of the aristocracy, which simply cannot be done with torpor.

The Oligarchy Trap

There is no shortage of theories which lump all forms of government together as "oligarchies". The best-known of these are the theories associated with the names of Vilfredo Pareto, Gaetano Mosca, and Robert Michels. A recent recruit to this club is Jeffrey Winters, a political science professor at Northwestern University, with his 2011 book titled simply *Oligarchy*, who, however, is anxious to distinguish his theory from those of Pareto, Mosca, and Michels. "Oligarchy ranks among the most widely used yet poorly theorized concepts in the social sciences". (Winters 2011, p. 1.) This opening sentence of Jeffrey Winters' book, just titled *Oligarchy*, is surprising, to say the least. Winters is presumably familiar with the writings of Gaetano Mosca, Vilfredo Pareto and Robert Michels. Or is an oligarchy a different animal from an elite? Winters quotes the definition of oligarchy of the *International Encyclopedia of the Social Sciences* as ".a form of government in which political power is in the hands of a small minority". Elitist theorists like Mosca and Pareto would have no quarrel with this definition as applicable not only to oligarchies but also to what Pareto called a "governing elite", and Mosca labeled a "ruling class" or "political class". And Michels, a disciple of Mosca's, refers to *his* elitist theory as "the iron law of oligarchy."

Whether labelled oligarchy, aristocracy, ruling class, or elite, this is a one-size-fits-all theory that forces all forms of government into the same straitjacket, blunting any ability to draw any distinctions between different forms of government or different power structures.

"A Monarchy Rules through an Oligarchy"

A surprising member of the Oligarchy Club is Oxford's Sir Ronald Syme (1903–89), one of the most highly respected ancient historians of modern times. In Chapter 1 of this book, there is a discussion of a striking quotation from Syme's classic work, *The Roman Revolution*, which, at the risk of repetition, cannot be allowed to go unnoticed in the present context: "In all ages, whatever the form and name of government, be it monarchy, republic, or democracy, an oligarchy lurks behind the façade". (Syme 1939, pp. 7, 15.) Writing in 1939, Syme portrays Augustus essentially as a prototype of a fascist dictator. Was Augustus's rule not monarchical, then? Syme certainly seems to think it was. So how does he square this with his sweeping blanket theory of oligarchy? "A monarchy rules through an oligarchy," is Syme's baffling formula. (Ibid., p. 8.)

In a purely banal sense, it is, of course, true that no individual can single-handedly rule a state. The ruler will need the assistance and support of others in order to maintain power. But here we come to a crucial divide: between those who serve a ruler in an inferior capacity and who are removable by the ruler at will and those upon whose support the ruler *depends* to maintain his position and who *share* his power. Where a ruler is surrounded by purely inferior minions who do his bidding, that is not an oligarchy because the minions have no independent power-base of their own. In that scenario, power is concentrated in the hands of the ruler, who exercises sole power. It is, therefore, a monarchy. An oligarchy is a form of government where power is in the hands of a minority. (On Augustus, see Chapter 1.)

The essential difference between monarchy and oligarchy is the whereabouts of power. It is not always obvious whether the entourage surrounding a ruler is beholden to him, whether he is beholden to them, or possibly whether they are mutually dependent on each other. The key question to ask is whether they share power with him or whether they are completely subservient to him and removable by him at will.

The existence of a ruling party, especially in a one-party state, may sometimes give a clue to the whereabouts of power, but not always. So, for example, Adolf Hitler ruled Germany as "Führer" of the Nazi Party, but it would be a mistake to see power as vested in the Party, or any members of the Party, rather than in Hitler personally. The same applies to Communist Party leaders such as Joseph Stalin (1878–1953) in the Soviet Union and Cuba's Fidel Castro (in power 1959– 2008). As far as Syme's subject area is concerned, there was in fact no Augustan "party" in Rome, although Syme seems to have thought there was; but even if there had been, that would not necessarily prove that the system was an oligarchy. (See Chapter 1).

Zero-Sum Game

Syme's bald assertion that "A monarchy rules through an oligarchy", is a contradiction in terms. Monarchy and oligarchy are opposites although a hybrid combination between the two can sometimes exist. In other words, the relationship between monarchy and oligarchy is a zero-sum game in which the more power that is exercised by the one, the less is left to the other. But the existence of "shared pie" hybrid examples does not alter the fact that monarchy and oligarchy are diametric opposites (See Chapter 1.) Lumping all governments together in a pot labeled oligarchy amounts to a failure to recognize that there are in fact two polarized forms of government, monarchy, and oligarchy, which have opposite power-structures, resulting in major practical differences.

"Williamanmary Was a Good King"

1066 And All That, published in 1930, a delightfully amusing spoof of English History as taught at the time, claimed to include "103 Good Things, 5 Bad Kings, and 2 Genuine Dates." This is a parody of the highly subjective and moralizing tendency epitomized in the dominant Whig interpretation of English history, according to which King James II (r. 1685–89) was a "bad king" ousted in the "Glorious Revolution" and replaced by his daughter and son-in-law reigning jointly as William III and Mary II—converted in the parody into a composite "good king" called "Williamanmary."

On the other hand, there was a school of thought promoting objective history. A protagonist of this approach to history was Lord Acton (1834–1902), Regius Professor of Modern History at Cambridge. As prospective editor of the original *Cambridge Modern History*, Acton proclaimed that "...our Waterloo must be one that satisfies French and English, German and Dutch alike; that nobody can tell, without examining the list of authors, where the Bishop of Oxford laid down the pen, and where Fairbairn or Gasquet, Liebermann or Harrison took it up." (Acton 1906, p. 318.) While enunciating the goal of objective history, Acton neglected to ask how that was to be achieved or even whether it was feasible. As Acton himself wrote no history to speak of, except the text of a few lectures, he was unable to demonstrate how he would square his goal of objective history with the rather subjective aphorism for which he is best known: "Power tends to corrupt, and absolute power corrupts absolutely," to which he added the even more subjective: "Great men are almost always bad men, even when they exercise influence and not authority: still more when you superadd the tendency or the certainty of corruption by authority." (*Acton-Creighton Correspondence* (1887/2011) https://oll.libertyfund.org/titles/2254.)

Sir George Clark, editor of the *New Cambridge Modern History* (1957), was not quite as ambitious as Acton but refused to rule out objective history as an attainable goal, rejecting the view that "...since all historical judgments involve persons and points of view, one is as good as another, and there is no 'objective' historical truth." (Clark 1957, pp. xxiv–xxv.)

The main problem with objective history is simply that historians, like everyone else, inevitably have their own predilections, tendencies and biases, of which they may not even be aware. Many historians writing today are scrupulous in attempting to avoid overt bias of any kind, but the moment one allows oneself to characterize something or someone in history as "good" or "bad," one immediately falls prey to unconscious bias. "Democracy" is of course a particular buzzword at present. Any form of government labeled "democratic" is generally automatically considered "good," and, conversely, any government that is considered "good" is frequently labeled "democratic." Athenian "democracy" is a case in point, as is shown in Chapter 6, and, more surprisingly, the Roman Republic, discussed in Chapter 1.

Despite the mockery, not unmingled with scorn, heaped by *1066 And All That* on overtly judgmental historical writing, that type of writing has surfaced with a vengeance in recent years, particularly in the area of "late antiquity." Here are a few such assertions picked almost at random, which are more fully discussed in Chapter 12:

- **"The unnerving but mercifully brief reign of Julian"** (Brown,1997a, p. 638.) So, according to Brown, Julian presumably was "a bad emperor." The context makes it clear that this is simply because of Julian's paganism and ties in with Brown's special pleading for Christianity with which his writings are shot through and through. Is this sort of language and blatant prejudice really befitting a work of academic history?
- **"The sheer success of the post-Constantinian state"** (Brown 1997a.) The word "sheer" turns what might otherwise have appeared to be a genuine assessment of the achievements of the regime into cheerleader hype. There is in fact no attempt at analysis here at all.
- **"No lip service paid to the widespread notion of decay"** (Brown 1997b, p. 124 f.) Looking back at his *World of Late Amtiquity*, published in 1971, Brown opined that he had been able to write "...the entire history of the religious and cultural revolution associated with the end of the ancient world without invoking an intervening catastrophe and without pausing, for a moment, to pay lip service to the widespread notion of decay." (Ibid.) While limiting his claim to "religious and cultural" matters, Brown here manages to cast doubt on the very existence of any "catastrophe" or "decay."
- **"The barbarian invasions...brought no widespread destruction"** (Brown, loc. 826.) The detailed researches of Peter Heather,

and other historians labeled "counter-revisionists" by some adherents of Late Antiquity, provide us with a welcome corrective to Brown's rose-tinted view, revealing widespread "barbarian" destruction indeed in Italy, Gaul, Spain, and Africa: "Any attempt to reconstruct fifth-century events brings home just how violent the process was. In my view, it is impossible to escape the fact that the western Empire broke up because too many outside groups established themselves on its territories and expanded their holdings by warfare." (Heather, 2006, p. 434 ff.) (See Chapters 12 and 13.)

- **"Correct religion was the glory of the empire"** This is the ultimate good/bad judgment call. Is one religion, namely orthodox Nicene Christianity, not only "better" than all the others, but so much better that it alone is "correct," or, for "correct" read "true"? But Brown goes further: "Precisely because correct religion was the glory of the empire, it had to be imposed in a manner that reflected the overwhelming dignity of the imperial power." (Brown 1997a., p. 644.) This is doubly self-contradictory. First, if "correct religion" was the "glory of the empire," that could only have been because it suppressed all "incorrect" religions. What sort of "glory" is bigotry and persecution? This "correct religion" was so "glorious" that it "had to be imposed"! If one religion is really so much "better" than the rest, would it not attract adherents without having to be "imposed"? And, how is religion to be "imposed" on people in a way that reflects "the overwhelming dignity" of government power? There is a straight line from this to the burning of "heretics" at the stake by the Spanish Inquisition and Mary Tudor of England (r. 1553–1558.) But, is Brown here speaking in his own person, or simply relaying the views of people of the period? It would be hard to claim the latter, as there certainly was no agreed view on "correct religion" at the time. And the concept is just too redolent of other remarks of Brown's to be shrugged off.
- **"Awesome theologians"** This is a gushing, overtly subjective characterization, with no attempt to attribute it to anyone but Brown himself. (Brown 1971, p. 9.)

Causation

"The historian, like any other scientist, is an animal who incessantly asks the question, Why?" (Carr 1961, p. 113.) Of course, not all historians regard themselves as scientists. In fact, the majority probably do not. And there also are historians who do not keep asking why but who belong to the "Cleopatra's nose" school of narrative historians discussed above.

But I agree with Carr that a historian should keep asking the question Why? until it cannot be asked any more. I also agree with Neville Morley in his *Theories, Models and Concepts in Ancient History* on a "...basic assumption that the historian's task is to explain past events, rather than simply to record them, and to understand past society in terms of the underlying structures that shaped people's lives rather than simply describing the diversity of their experiences." (Morley 2004, p. 6.)

What exactly is the meaning of "causation" or "causality"? This is an important field of investigation not only in the study of history but also in science generally, medicine, philosophy, and law. Causes may be classified variously, for example as "necessary" and "sufficient" causes; or into the legal categories of proximate and remote cause, *causa causans*, and *causa sine qua non*. A useful classification for historians, though rarely actually discussed by them, is the division suggested by the French historian Marc Bloch, one of the founders of the *Annales* school, into "general causes" and "exceptional causes."

As an example of this classification one might take the English Reformation under Henry VIII (r. 1509–47). Henry was himself a staunch Catholic and the author of a theological treatise attacking Martin Luther, for which he was granted by the Pope the special title *Fidei Defensor* (Defender of the Faith). But because his wife was unable to bear him a male heir he asked the Pope to annul the marriage, a request that was denied. So, Henry cut the Gordian knot and broke with Rome, making the Church of England a Protestant Church with himself as its "Supreme Head." So, the "exceptional cause" of the English Reformation was Henry VIII's personal desire for a divorce. But that is hardly enough to explain it. One would also need to explain why the Pope refused Henry's request, which involves an analysis of international relations of the time. For Henry, to have himself declared Supreme Head of the Church of England required the consent of Parliament, which opens up a whole new avenue of investigation into the relations between Crown and Parliament. And, not least, one would need to factor in an explanation of the rise of the Reformation movement that was already in full swing on the Continent and had attracted English converts independently of the King's machinations. These factors would constitute the "general causes" of the English Reformation.

And what does a historian do once answers to all the Whys? have been exhausted? In other words, when your pursuit of causes, causes of causes, and causes of causes of causes finally either bears fruit or brings you up against a brick wall? The question to ask at that point is this: So what? (See below.)

But this does not detract from the fact that some of the most enjoyable, entertaining or informative works of history belong in the category of narrative history. Patricia Southern, for example, the author of a number of carefully researched and well-written books on Roman history, makes no greater claim than accuracy. Here is what she says in the introduction to *The Roman Empire from Severus to Constantine*: "This book attempts to document the changes in the Roman Empire between the end of the second century and the beginning of the fourth." (Southern 2015, p. xii.)

A more ambitious writer is Mary Beard, who describes her *SPQR: A History of Ancient Rome* as offering "...my contribution of why it (viz. Roman history) matters." (Beard 2016, p. 16.) Despite the word "why," the book is largely narrative, with very little that could be described as explanation. It certainly makes for a racy read containing some quirky observations and emphases, like the half-serious but completely baseless claim of Pompey to be regarded as "the first emperor" of Rome (Beard, 2016, p. 273 f.) and an equally groundless throw-away remark, based on a coin legend, implying that Caesar's assassin Marcus Brutus was aiming at "autocratic power." (Beard 2016, p. 295.) (See Chapter 1.)

It is also unhelpful to introduce Roman history to the general reader (to whom the book appears to be addressed) with a 32-page first chapter titled "Cicero's Finest Hour" focusing on the Catilinarian conspiracy of 63 BCE, by any account *not* a major event in Roman history except for Cicero, who was *not* a major player in Roman history but who owes his immortality to his loquaciousness in written form and to the longevity of his secretary, Tiro, who reputedly lived to the age of 99 and dedicated his life to editing and promoting his late master's works.

Machiavellian History

Machiavelli's The Prince *(1513) is one of the most perceptive works of history and political science ever written, recognizing the perennial hostility in every society between the common people and the aristocracy or privileged elite. A champion of the common people against the elite is likely to become a strong monarch.*

The name Machiavelli has long been almost a synonym for the devil, and in modern English the word *Machiavellian* still means cunning, scheming, or unscrupulous, especially in reference to politics. Niccolò Machiavelli (1469–1527) gained this reputation from his book of advice to rulers, titled *Il Principe* (*The Prince*). Though this little treatise ostensibly belongs to the well-known genre of "mirrors for princes," self-help books addressed to new or young rulers, its content and tone are very different from other books of the same genre. Instead of proffering conventional words of wisdom and diplomatic conduct, Machiavelli provides hard-edged amoral advice based on clear-eyed historical case studies.

Here is a key statement from Chapter 9 of *The Prince*, embodying an important insight into realpolitik: "In every state two distinct tendencies (humors) are found, namely that of the common people and that of the aristocracy. The common people do not wish to be ruled or oppressed by the aristocracy, while the aristocracy wish to rule and oppress the common people." (Machiavelli 1513, Chapter 9.) This theme of the mutual hostility between what Machiavelli calls *li grandi* (the aristocracy, nobility or privileged elite) and *il populo* ("the people," referring to the rank and file of the population, or the common people) runs right through *Il Principe*. The universality of the statement is noteworthy. This hostility between the aristocracy and the common people, says Machiavelli, is found *in ogni città* (in every city). The Italian word *città*, coming as it does from the Latin *civitas*, is used by Machiavelli to refer not only to the city-states into which the Italy of his day was divided but also to large states like France or Turkey, or to the Roman Empire of antiquity. Similarly, the word *principe* (prince), from Latin *princeps*, is used for the ruler of any state, regardless of title or status, including kings and emperors. This usage was paralleled in sixteenth and seventeenth century English, as for example in the phrase "Put not your trust in princes," found in the 1611 King James Version translation of Psalm 146, line 3.

Machiavelli continues:

"Monarchy is brought about either by the common people or by the aristocracy, according as one or the other of these parties has the opportunity. For, the aristocracy, seeing that they are unable to resist the common people, begin to escalate the reputation of one of their number and make him ruler, so that they can give vent to their ambitions under his protection. On the other hand, the people, finding themselves unable to resist the aristocracy, elevate the reputation of one man and make him ruler so as to be protected by his authority."

"One who comes to power with the assistance of the aristocracy maintains himself with more difficulty than one who becomes a ruler with the assistance of the common people, because the former finds himself surrounded by many around him who consider themselves his equals, and because of this he can neither rule nor manage them to his liking."

"But he who comes to power by popular favour, finds himself alone and has around him either none or very few who are not prepared to obey him...."

"A man who becomes ruler through popular favor, then, must keep the people well-disposed toward him. This will be easy, since they want only not to be oppressed. But a man who becomes ruler against the wishes of the people, and through the favour of the aristocracy, must above all else try to win over the people, which will be easy if he protects them.... I shall affirm only that it is necessary for a ruler to have the people well disposed toward him; otherwise, in difficult times he will find himself in desperate straits." (*The Prince*, Chapter 9.)

Machiavelli rejects what he calls

"...the trite proverb that he who builds on the people builds on mud.... A ruler who bases his power on the common people, who can command and is a man of courage undismayed in adversity and is not lacking in other preparations, and who keeps the whole citizen body inspired by his spirit and resolution, will never find himself deceived by them and it will be shown that he has laid his foundations well.... Therefore, a wise ruler ought to consider a course such that his citizens will always and in every kind of circumstance have need of the state and of him, and then they will always be loyal to him." (*The Prince*, Chapter 9)

"...[R]ulers should worry little about being plotted against if their subjects are well disposed toward them, but if their subjects are hostile and hate them, they should be afraid of everything and everyone. Well-ordered states and wise rulers have taken care with every diligence not to exasperate the aristocracy while satisfying the people and keeping them content, for this is one of the most important tasks for a ruler to undertake." (*The Prince*, Chapter 19.)

"I also conclude that a ruler ought to respect the aristocracy, but not so as to make himself hated by the people." (*The Prince*, Chapter 19)

And again:

"All recorded monarchies are found to be governed in two different ways: either by a single ruler with a body of servants who as ministers by his grace and favour assist him to govern the kingdom or by a single ruler and barons, who hold that rank not by the favour of the ruler but by the antiquity of their blood. Such barons have states and their own subjects, who recognize them as lords and hold them in natural affection. Those states that are governed by a ruler and his servants accord their ruler greater authority, because no one is recognized as superior to him in all his dominions; and if they obey any other they do so as to a minister or official and do not hold him in any particular affection." (*The Prince*, Chapter 4.)

Machiavelli's argument runs as follows:

- In every state, there is hostility between the aristocracy or privileged elite and the common people.
- Both sides select a leader.
- A leader dependent on aristocratic support will prove a weak ruler.
- Such a ruler will be dependent on "barons" with their own power bases.
- The people's loyalties will be to these barons rather than to the ruler.
- However, a ruler dependent on popular support will be a strong ruler.
- Such a ruler will govern through servants, who are totally beholden to him, so that popular loyalty is to him alone.
- But, while nurturing popular support, a wise ruler will take care not to exasperate the aristocracy.

One type of government that is absent from Machiavelli's schema is oligarchy or aristocracy. The closest we get to this is a weak monarchy dependent on the aristocracy but a monarchy nevertheless. The reason for this omission is not accidental. *The Prince* is a book of advice addressed to "princes" or monarchs. As Machiavelli makes clear right at the outset; therefore, it deals only with principalities, or monarchies. Republican forms of government are discussed in Machiavelli's *I Discorsi* (1517), a commentary on the first ten books of Livy.

Although Machiavelli's examples are drawn chiefly either from contemporary Italy or from classical antiquity, his theory applies to many societies throughout history, as is demonstrated in *Two Models of Government*. (Arnheim 2017a) The Greek tyrants are good examples of strong popular monarchy, while the position of the British Crown after the Glorious Revolution of 1689 is that of a weak monarchy subordinate to a privileged elite represented in Parliament. (See Chapter 6.) The Roman Republic, on the other hand, is an exemplar of oligarchy in which power was shared by a privileged elite eschewing any semblance of monarchy.

Machiavelli's writings, and particularly *The Prince*, have aroused great interest from his day to ours, yet his analysis of monarchy as set out in the bullet points above has been all but ignored. Discussion has largely focused instead on Machiavelli's own political views. Was Machiavelli really as cold, calculating, and amoral as would appear to be the case from *The Prince*? Or is that book a tongue-in-cheek satire? Alternatively, was Machiavelli a republican, or even a democrat, as the *I Discorsi* have sometimes been interpreted?

Sir Isaiah Berlin spent a whole essay debating these points, in his *Four Essays on Liberty*, without apparently realizing just how irrelevant they were. (Berlin 2002.) The more hidden Machiavelli's personal opinions are, the more likely it is that the advice which he proffers is objective and unbiased and the more valuable that advice then becomes.

As for Quentin Skinner, a vaunted authority on Machiavelli, I have encountered only one remotely relevant comment by him on the whole leitmotif of the hostility of people against aristocracy from his co-edited work *Machiavelli: The Prince*: "A ruler who wishes to hold on to power must ensure above all that the whole populace, nobles, and ordinary citizens alike, remain respectful and content with his government." This is no doubt a sound, if bland, principle of government It is supposedly a paraphrase of this remark of Machiavelli's, already quoted above, but taken out of context: "Well-ordered states and wise rulers have always been very careful not to exasperate the nobles and also to satisfy the people and keep them contented; this is one of the most important things for a ruler to do." (Machiavelli, Skinner/Price (eds), 2019.)

In fact, Machiavelli's actual point is very different from Skinner's insipid supposed paraphrase. What Machiavelli is talking about here is the danger of conspiracy, making the point that, while popular favor is essential for a wise ruler, he should not exasperate the aristocracy. And this harks back to the passages from Machiavelli's Chapter 9 quote about popular monarchy, (See above,) It would, of course, be ideal for a ruler to be able to count on the support, or at least the lack of discontent, among all his subjects. But this is not what Machiavelli is saying, because he knows just how difficult this is to achieve. That is why he couches the ruler's relationship with the two elements in quite different ways. He must "satisfy" the common people and "keep them content", very positive demands, while just not "exasperating" the aristocracy, a purely negative desideratum. What Machiavelli has in mind here is a monarch who depends primarily on popular support but recognizes that, in the interests of harmonious government, he should refrain from exasperating (the Italian is *desperare*) the aristocracy, meaning to avoid incensing the aristocracy so much as to spur them into resorting to desperate measures to overthrow the ruler's regime. Julius Caesar's disdainful treatment of the senatorial aristocracy is a case in point of how the aristocracy can be driven to desperation, leading to the Ides of March. Augustus represents the perfect statesmanlike antithesis to this, a ruler dependent on popular support who went out of his way to avoid offending the aristocracy whom he had just defeated.

So What?

I agree with Moses Finley's disparagement of pedantic academic writings that concentrate on minor details of historical narrative, like, for example, the debate about the precise date of birth of the Emperor

Diocletian. (Barnes, pp. 30, 46; Bowman, *Diocletian and the First Tetrarchy*, CAH, p. 68; Williams 1997, pp. 237–8; Rees 2004, *Diocletian and the Tetrarchy*, p. 86.) The question that needs to be asked is this: So what? What difference does it make whether he was born on December 22 (his official birthday) or any other date and whether it was in the year 244 or some other year? This could only have any significance if, for example, he led an army to victory at the age of six, or perhaps, if he had lived to the age of 120. But even that would be a curiosity rather than a matter of significance.

In this book, what I am concerned with, among other themes, is the relationship between causation, power structure, and ethos. But once these issues have been analysed and changes explained, it is important to stand back and throw down the challenge: So what? Why does it matter?

I believe it matters a great deal, which is one of the main reasons why I embarked on this quest in the first place. We are confronted here with a primary comparison between the two halves of the Roman Empire, one of which disintegrated and the other of which survived in some form for a thousand years. In trying to account for this major difference, we are forced to analyze the power-structure in the two halves, which, however, leads us into more and more comparative byways, both in our period and beyond—holding out as an ideal Thucydides' aspiration to write history "...judged useful by those inquirers who desire an exact knowledge of the past as an aid to the interpretation of the future, which in the course of human things must resemble if it does not reflect it." (Thuc. 1.22.4.)

Conclusion: "Proper Historical Writing"

There is certainly no shortage of approaches to the writing of history. But is there such a thing as proper historical writing? My own criteria are as follows. I hasten to add that I do not claim that these are the only possible criteria for proper historical writing:

- Pay close attention to factual accuracy, without allowing the tail to wag the dog or, in other words, without allowing trivial factual points to overshadow more important issues.
- Don't be in too much of a hurry to dismiss evidence out of hand. If in doubt, accept evidence on the basis of probability. Otherwise, you will be in danger of throwing the baby out with the bathwater, resulting in a misunderstanding or misinterpretation possibly even of a whole period.
- But also don't be too uncritical of dubious sources, which can also have a serious impact on your understanding of an issue or period. See above for examples.

- There is nothing wrong with fine writing, but don't sacrifice a proper understanding of a topic or period to stylistic elegance.
- Carefully think through the conceptual framework of your study. The oligarchy trap (see above) is a case in point. But don't abandon a search for a conceptual frameworks on that account.
- Then aim to be as objective as possible, trying to recognize and put your own preconceptions, prejudices and beliefs to one side.
- Don't judge historical figures, institutions, or societies as either good or bad, and stop well short of writing history committed to a particular political, social, or religious cause. Otherwise, what you produce will not be history but partisanship, special pleading, and propaganda, not to mention a distortion of the subject matter.
- Keep asking why until you can't ask it any more.
- Then ask "So what?" Look back at your period, problem, or issue, and test to see whether you can gain insight from other periods or subject areas.
- If, for example, you are exploring the causes of a particular war, cast a comparative eye over other wars. The same applies to the causes of a revolution, the rise or fall of an empire, or an economic upturn or crisis.
- I particularly commend to you the analysis of the power relations in all societies developed by Machiavelli. (See above.) My own studies of very different societies over a period of three thousand years confirm my own acceptance of this model, of just two diametrically opposed power structures: monarchy and oligarchy (or aristocracy). As I try to illustrate in this book, there is a relationship between the power structure of a society and its values and not least its social and political ethos.

8

Gibbon's *The Decline and Fall of the Roman Empire*

> **Please note:** Except where otherwise indicated, all the references in this chapter are to chapters of Gibbon's *Decline and Fall of the Roman Empire*.

"Another damned thick book!" was the less than complimentary acknowledgment by King George III's brother, William, Duke of Gloucester and Edinburgh, of a presentation copy of Gibbon's second volume. "Always scribble, scribble, scribble! Eh, Mr. Gibbon?" (Quoted by Leslie Stephen in the *Dictionary of National Biography*, 1921, Vol. 21, p. 1133.)

Fortunately for Edward Gibbon (1737–94), his reputation does not depend on this royal put-down. His six-volume *magnum opus*, the full title of which is *The History of the Decline and Fall of the Roman Empire*, published between 1776 and 1788, has remained in print uninterruptedly from that day to this, with several editions and abridgements available at any one time.

Decline and Fall?

Did the western Roman Empire fall at all? It is certainly undeniable that what had been a single political and administrative entity split up into a number of "barbarian" kingdoms. But was this change really sig-

Why Rome Fell: Decline and Fall, or Drift and Change?, First Edition. Michael Arnheim.
© 2022 John Wiley & Sons, Inc. Published 2022 by John Wiley & Sons, Inc.

nificant, or was it outweighed by continuity? Then, there are essentially two possible explanations for the changes in the West itself, one that may be labeled primarily *internal*, and the other primarily *external*. In short, was the western empire toppled when in a debilitated state, after suffering some form of "decline" or "decay" which sapped its strength and made it an easy prey. Or alternatively, was a largely healthy entity simply overwhelmed by unprecedented force?

Gibbon's position, as set out in his "General Observations on the Fall of the Roman Empire in the West," in Chapter 38 of his great work, can be encapsulated in the phrase that he immortalized: decline and fall. The "extinction" of the western empire, as he calls it, or "this awful revolution," Gibbon attributes largely to internal weakness. It is worth delving a little more deeply into his thinking:

- **"Immoderate greatness"**: "[T]he decline of Rome was the natural and inevitable effect of immoderate greatness. Prosperity ripened the principle of decay; the causes of destruction multiplied with the extent of conquest; and as soon as time or accident had removed the artificial supports, the stupendous fabric yielded to the pressure of its own weight." (Gibbon, Ch. 38.) This "natural and inevitable effect" is Gibbon's principal explanation for the demise of the western empire. But it is a complex cause, made up of several components, which need to be examined separately: the "overwhelming" of the Roman world by a "deluge of Barbarians"; resulting from the relaxation, and then the dissolution of "the vigor of the military government"; stemming in turn partly from a "base expedient" resorted to by a succession of weak emperors, and then "by the partial institutions of Constantine."

- **"Overwhelmed by a deluge of Barbarians"**: Gibbon characterized the "barbarian" takeover of the western empire as a "deluge" that "overwhelmed the Roman world," though it was of course only the western half of the empire that was lost. Gibbon's explanation for this "deluge" was that the "barbarians" were impelled by the Huns fleeing "before a victorious enemy." "The flying tribes who yielded to the Huns assumed in *their* turn the spirit of conquest; the endless column of Barbarians pressed on the Roman empire with accumulated weight." As a meticulous narrator, Gibbon does not shrink from describing the bloodshed and destruction involved in the takeover, though he exonerates both Christians and "Barbarians" from the worst excesses: "[T]he northern conquerors were neither sufficiently savage, nor sufficiently refined, to entertain such aspiring ideas of destruction and revenge....[A]nd, though incapable of emulating, they were more inclined to admire, than to abolish, the arts and studies of a brighter period." (Ch. 71.) Similarly, in regard to Christianity, Gibbon blames chiefly the Roman government, while going out of his way to exonerate both the mass of ordinary Christians and the popes: "The change of religion was accomplished, not by a popular tumult, but by the decrees of the emperors, of the senate, and of time. Of the Christian hierarchy, the bishops of Rome were commonly the most prudent and least fanatic; nor can any positive charge be opposed to the meritorious act of saving or converting the majestic structure of the Pantheon." (Chapter 71.)

- **"Military vigor"**: "Instead of inquiring *why* the Roman empire was destroyed, we should rather be surprised that it had subsisted so long." (Chapter 38.) But Gibbon still feels impelled to explain why Rome's long, though not entirely unbroken, record of success should have come to an end when it did. His answer is that Rome's military vigor was sapped from within, chiefly by deliberate imperial policy, including Constantine's "partial institutions" (presumably a reference to Christianity, on which more below.) There is still an ongoing debate on whether the Roman army of the fourth and fifth centuries was a less efficient fighting force than in the empire's glory days. On balance, I believe Gibbon was probably on the right track in identifying a lowering of military morale, though I do not agree with him that this is what brought the western empire down. For a discussion of this, see Chapter 10.

- **Split empire:** Gibbon then (also in his Chapter 38) considers the theory that ascribed "the decay of Rome...to the translation of the seat of empire. But he points out that "the powers of government were *divided*, rather than *removed*." "This dangerous novelty," as he calls it, of splitting the Empire in two, "impaired the strength, and fomented the vices, of a double reign; and a vain emulation of luxury, not of merit, was introduced and supported between the degenerate successors of Theodosius." But his conclusion is that, on balance: "The foundation of Constantinople more essentially contributed to the preservation of the East, than to the ruin of the West"—a fair verdict. For more on this, see the Prologue to Part II.

- **Bishops, Eunuchs, and Barbarians:** Besides the decline in military morale, Gibbon detects a passive spirit in the empire as a whole, exacerbated by the weak rule of the "incapable" or "degenerate" sons and grandsons of Theodosius I: "The empire of Rome was firmly established by the singular and perfect coalition of its members. The subject nations, resigning the hope, and even the wish, of independence, embraced the character of Roman citizens; and the provinces of the West were reluctantly torn from the bosom of their mother country. But this union was purchased by the loss of national freedom and military spirit; and the servile provinces, destitute of life and motion, expected their safety from the mercenary troops and governors, who were directed by the orders of a distant court. The happiness of a hundred millions depended on the personal merit of one or two men, perhaps children, whose minds were corrupted by education, luxury, and despotic power. The deepest wounds were inflicted on the empire during the minorities of the sons and grandsons of Theodosius; and, after those incapable princes seemed to attain the age of manhood, they abandoned the church to the bishops, the state to the eunuchs, and the provinces to the Barbarians." (Ch 38.) Though it contains more than a grain of truth, this last euphonious aphorism exaggerates the weakness of the imperial government, and the abandonment of the provinces to the Barbarians of course applies only to the West.

- **"Eclipse":** Another aspect of the "decline and fall" is attributed by Gibbon to the "feeble policy of Constantine and his successors," which allowed the Barbarians to subvert the western empire: "Cold, poverty, and a life of danger and fatigue, fortify the strength and courage of Barbarians....The warlike states of antiquity, Greece, Macedonia, and Rome, educated a race of soldiers; exercised their bodies, disciplined their courage, multiplied their forces by regular revolutions, and converted the iron, which they possessed, into strong and serviceable weapons. But this superiority insensibly declined with their laws and manners; and the feeble policy of Constantine and his successors armed and instructed, for the ruin of the empire, the rude valor of the Barbarian mercenaries....The splendid days of Augustus and Trajan were eclipsed by a cloud of ignorance; and the Barbarians subverted the laws and palaces of Rome." (Ch 38.) Gibbon was certainly no great admirer of Constantine, whose "feeble policy"—presumably including his partiality toward Christianity— he blames for causing the "eclipse" of "the splendid days of Augustus and Trajan." That the reign of Constantine marks a turning-point in government, administration and religion alike cannot be denied, but to blame him for the "the ruin of the empire" is going too far. See Chapter 3.

- **Christianity:** Gibbon has been mercilessly pilloried for his position on the role of Christianity in the demise of the western empire. He blames Christian otherworldly values for sapping the empire's morale, but concludes by praising Christianity for taming the "ferocious temper of the conquerors." Neither of these judgments will stand up to scrutiny. Here are Gibbon's exact words: "As the happiness of a *future* life is the great object of religion, we may hear without surprise or scandal that the introduction, or at least the abuse, of

Christianity had some influence on the decline and fall of the Roman empire. The clergy successfully preached the doctrines of patience and pusillanimity; the active virtues of society were discouraged; and the last remains of military spirit were buried in the cloister; a large portion of public and private wealth was consecrated to the specious demands of charity and devotion; and the soldiers' pay was lavished on the useless multitudes of both sexes, who could only plead the merits of abstinence and chastity. Faith, zeal, curiosity, and the more earthly passions of malice and ambition, kindled the flame of theological discord; the church, and even the state, were distracted by religious factions, whose conflicts were sometimes bloody, and always implacable; the attention of the emperors was diverted from camps to synods; the Roman world was oppressed by a new species of tyranny; and the persecuted sects became the secret enemies of their country. Yet party spirit, however pernicious or absurd, is a principle of union as well as of dissension. The bishops, from eighteen hundred pulpits, inculcated the duty of passive obedience to a lawful and orthodox sovereign......The sacred indolence of the monks was devoutly embraced by a servile and effeminate age; but if superstition had not afforded a decent retreat, the same vices would have tempted the unworthy Romans to desert, from baser motives, the standard of the republic. Religious precepts are easily obeyed, which indulge and sanctify the natural inclinations of their votaries; but the pure and genuine influence of Christianity may be traced in its beneficial, though imperfect, effects on the Barbarian proselytes of the North. If the decline of the Roman empire was hastened by the conversion of Constantine, his victorious religion broke the violence of the fall, and mollified the ferocious temper of the conquerors." (Ch 38.)

- Gibbon was prepared to accept that the Christian bishops "inculcated" patriotic loyalty though it was only "...passive obedience to a lawful and orthodox sovereign." In fact, however, Christians as well as pagans took pride in Rome's long and glorious past. For example, the sack of Rome by the Goths of Alaric I in 410 evoked a huge outpouring of grief among leading Christians from as far afield as Bethlehem, where Jerome (in the preface to his commentary on Ezekiel) lamented that "...the whole world perished in one city," and from Hippo in North Africa, where Augustine launched his *City of God against the Pagans*, aggressively fending off pagan allegations of Christian blame for the calamity, and claiming credit for Christianity for Rome's glorious past.
- However, Gibbon gives Christianity too much credit for mollifying "...the ferocious temper of the conquerors." While their warlike

spirit may have abated, the "barbarians'" eventual conversion to orthodox Christianity made them just as religiously intolerant as any Christian Roman or Byzantine emperor. There is a straight line from the Council of Nicaea of 325 to the Spanish Inquisition of more than a thousand years later.

- Gibbon's characterization of Christian persecution of "heretics" as "a new species of tyranny" is apt, and it is certainly true too that this turned at least the Donatists in Africa and the Monophysites in Egypt against the emperors who persecuted them.

Gibbon's Treatment of Religion

From the beginning, Gibbon's treatment of religion raised a firestorm around his work, which has not abated. Here is one of the best-known passages that earned Gibbon the reputation of being a paganist: "The various modes of worship, which prevailed in the Roman world, were all considered by the people, as equally true; by the philosopher, as equally false; and by the magistrate, as equally useful. And this toleration produced not only mutual indulgence, but even religious concord.... Such was the mild spirit of antiquity, that the nations were less attentive to the difference, than to the resemblance, of their religious worship." (Ch. 2.)

This is picked up in Gibbon's Chapter 15, which, together with his Chapter 16, attracted the most criticism, forcing him to publish a "Vindication" of those chapters in 1779: "We have already described the religious harmony of the ancient world, and the facility with which the most different and even hostile nations embraced, or at least respected, each other's superstitions."(Ch. 15.)

In fact, Gibbon shows a better understanding of ancient religion than many modern writers on the subject. Gibbon can be forgiven for not using the term "communal religion", coined by myself (Arnheim 1984) to refer to the normal type of religion in the ancient world. But it is precisely its communal nature that explains why religious toleration was the norm in the ancient world until the rise of Christianity.

As I explain elsewhere, a communal religion is one in which membership of the religion is an integral part of membership of the nation, society or community concerned (See Chapter 10.) For example, Egyptians would take it for granted that Babylonians had their own religion, and Babylonians would take it for granted that Egyptians had their own religion. As a result, before the advent of Christianity, the concept of proselytism, or conversion, was unknown. Because, for an Indian to convert to the Babylonian religion he or she would have to

become a Babylonian, and *vice versa*, which was not really possible—
except in the event of conquest (or in rare cases of migration, as in the
Book of Ruth. (See Chapter 10.) When one nation conquered another,
that was taken to mean that the gods of the conquerors had defeated the gods of the conquered, who would become absorbed into their
conquerors' nation and religion alike. Because of the close identity of
religion and society, most communal religions do not even have a distinctive name separate from their communities. The Roman state religion is a case in point. But, as a cosmopolitan center, Rome attracted
immigrants and, therefore, also religions from all over the world to
which not just toleration but indeed religious freedom was extended.
(The suggestion that Roman toleration of foreign cults had the ulterior
motive of absorbing and suppressing them is nonsense as can be seen
from the fact that the temples, shrines, and worship of these cults was
allowed to flourish alongside the Roman state religion until they were
all suppressed by the Christian emperors.) (See Chapter 10.)

As a conquered nation, the Jews should have expected to have to
give up their communal religion in favor of that of Rome, but Roman
indulgence treated them, both in their homeland and in the rest of the
Roman world, as if they were still independent. Gibbon puts it like this:
"According to the maxims of universal toleration, the Romans protected a superstition which they despised." But in 66, minor clashes
between pagans and Jews in Jerusalem escalated into a full-scale war
against Roman rule, which was succeeded by another serious Jewish
revolt between 135 and 138. Gibbon explains it like this: "But the moderation of the conquerors was insufficient to appease the jealous prejudices of their subjects, who were alarmed and scandalized at the ensigns
of paganism, which necessarily introduced themselves into a Roman
province. Their attachment to the law of Moses was equal to their de-
testation of foreign religions." (Ch. 15) But even after these revolts had
been brutally put down, until Christian dominance, the Jewish religion
continued to benefit from the normal respect accorded by one communal religion to another.

Why, then, was Christianity persecuted while the Jewish religion
was tolerated? Gibbon's answer is simple and direct: "The Jews were a
nation; the Christians were a *sect*: and if it was natural for every community to respect the sacred institutions of their neighbors, it was incumbent on them to persevere in those of their ancestors.... The laws
of Moses might be for the most part frivolous or absurd; yet, since they
had been received during many ages by a large society, his followers
were justified by the example of mankind; and it was universally acknowledged, that they had a right to practice what it would have been
criminal in them to neglect. But this principle, which protected the

Jewish synagogue, afforded not any favor or security to the primitive church.... The whole body of Christians unanimously refused to hold any communion with the gods of Rome, of the empire, and of mankind." (Ch. 16.)

Gibbon's explanation of the difference in Roman eyes between the Jewish and Christian religions shows remarkable insight into the mentality of a communal religion. Yet, as Gibbon also recognized, the frequency and severity of Roman persecution of Christianity has been greatly exaggerated, something that is now confirmed by the thorough research of Candida Moss. (Moss 2013.) Gibbon (ironically?) purports to treat the discrepancy as "a very natural mistake", i.e. "The ecclesiastical writers of the fourth or fifth centuries ascribed to the magistrates of Rome the same degree of implacable and unrelenting zeal which filled their own breasts against the heretics or the idolaters of their own times." (Ch. 16.)

Gibbon's understanding of religious motivation is lacking in only one important respect: a recognition that the root cause of Christian intolerance by contrast with pagan tolerance is simply that Christianity is a *creed* religion as against a *communal* religion. Every Christian denomination, sect or group believes that its particular creed or set of beliefs is *the truth*, holds the key to *eternal salvation*, and therefore entitles, or even obliges, them to convert "unbelievers" and "heretics" to the one and only "true faith"—and, failing that, to persecute them. Communal religions, by contrast, generally lack any creed at all, or are indifferent as to the beliefs embraced by their members, as is well illustrated by the myriad gods and beliefs in Hinduism, the biggest communal religion in the modern world.

"The Triumph of Barbarism and Religion"

How valuable is Gibbon's contribution to the debate on Roman "decline and fall"? Second in fame only to the phrase "decline and fall" is another of his aphorisms: "the triumph of barbarism and religion," which, in fact, appears only once, right at the end of his mammoth work:

"In the preceding volumes of this History, I have described the triumph of barbarism and religion." (Ch. 71.) It is commonly assumed that this oft-quoted phrase sums up Gibbon's explanation of the fall of the western Empire—which it does, encapsulating his view, set out in Chapter 38, that, once its proud military spirit was sapped by Christianity and general decline, the western empire was ready to fall to the "Barbarians."

But, for Gibbon, "the triumph of Barbarism and religion" also covers a much longer period. It is important to note that Gibbon's great work covers the whole period from the death of Marcus Aurelius in 180 to the fall of Constantinople in 1453, in East and West alike, and that Gibbon's principal interest, to which he returns repeatedly, is the City of Rome itself. "It was at Rome, on the fifteenth of October 1764,"Gibbon himself relates in his *Autobiography*, "as I sat musing amidst the ruins of the Capitol, while the barefooted fryars were singing Vespers in the temple of Jupiter, that the idea of writing the decline and fall of the City first started to my mind." His original concept, therefore, was a book not about the Roman Empire as a whole, but solely on the City of Rome.

And it is to the City of Rome that Gibbon is referring when he writes, "After a diligent inquiry, I can discern four principal causes of the ruin of Rome, which continued to operate in a period of more than a thousand years." (Ch. 71) "I have reserved for the last," he concludes this "inquiry" of his, "the most potent and forcible cause of destruction, the domestic hostilities of the Romans themselves." But there are here no longer strictures on "Constantine's feeble policy" or the "degenerate successors of Theodosius." Instead, Gibbon transports us well into the Middle Ages: "In a dark period of five hundred years, Rome was perpetually afflicted by the sanguinary quarrels of the nobles and people, the Guelphs and Ghibelines, the Colonna and Ursini." (Ch 71.) Much, therefore, as he regrets the passing of "the splendid days of Augustus and Trajan" to "a servile and effeminate age," Gibbon recognizes that the fall of the western empire did not mark the end of civilization, or even of Roman civilization. And it is perhaps his view of history, at once myopic and panoramic, that constitutes Gibbon's greatest contribution to the ages.

9

The Malaria Hypothesis

This book was composed during the Covid-19 pandemic that swept round the globe in 2020–2021, carrying death and destruction in its wake, creating havoc, and paralyzing the economy in a number of countries. No natural disaster had ever come close to this worldwide plague in scale, intensity or duration since the "Spanish Flu" of 1918–19 or the Black Death of 1348.

This totally unexpected catastrophe may have made at least some people conscious of the puniness of mankind in the face of nature and made them more open to the suggestion of the power of nature to disrupt, or even destroy, past societies. It is, therefore, necessary to take such claims seriously while guarding against jumping to conclusions.

There is no shortage of such hypotheses in regard to the ancient world, not least in respect of the "fall" of the Roman Empire in the West. One such view is offered in a recent book by Kyle Harper: "The fate of Rome was played out by emperors and barbarians, senators and generals, soldiers and slaves. But it was equally decided by bacteria and viruses, volcanoes and solar cycles.... In an unintended conspiracy with nature, the Romans created a disease ecology that unleashed the latent power of pathogen evolution. The Romans were soon engulfed by the overwhelming force of what we would today call emerging infectious diseases." (Harper 2017, p. 4 f.)

The latest culprit to be charged in this regard is malaria, giving rise to headlines in mainstream media, such as, "Did malaria bring Rome to its knees? A lethal outbreak could partly explain why antiquity's mightiest military machine was too enfeebled to repel the Visigoths, Huns and Vandals." (*The Guardian*, Feb 21, 2001.) This arises out of an archaeological "dig" in Lugnano, about 70 miles north of Rome. In excavating a cemetery in the ruins of an abandoned Roman villa between 1987 and 1991, the American archaeologist David Soren discovered 47 infant skeletons, most of them in pottery amphoras, dating from around 450. Most were too degraded to produce useful samples.

The much touted published results were in fact drawn from the skeleton of a single three-year-old girl, which was the only one that it was possible to analyze. Pitting in the skull just above the eye sockets raised the possibility that the child might have been suffering from malaria. This was confirmed by means of DNA tests, the first time that this technique had been used in archaeology. The strain of malaria identified in the child was *Plasmodium falciparum* (P. Falciparum), the most virulent of the four known species of malaria. (Soren/Noelle, 1999, p. 472; Sallares 2002; Soren 2003; Sallares, Bouwman, and Anderung, 2004.)

This extrapolation from one skeleton does seem to be a bit of a stretch. Even Robert Sallares himself, who was associated with Soren's research, admits that "...the most recent common ancestor (MRCA) of P(lasmodium) falciparum is approaching 100,000 years old although it has undergone a major population expansion within the last 10,000 years. Consequently, the view adopted here is that P. falciparum is indeed a very ancient human parasite." (Sallares 2002.) Malaria is also largely confined to marshy areas or areas with high temperatures, high humidity, and stagnant waters that provide a favorable breeding ground for anopheles mosquito larvae. As Sallares puts it: "Malaria did not occur everywhere.... Malaria did have considerable effects in Mediterranean Europe in antiquity...but usually only at a localized level." (Sallares et al. 2004.)

The Roman encyclopedist and medical authority Aulus Cornelius Celsus (c. 25 BCE–c. 50 CE) in his *De Medicina*, first explained the differential diagnosis between two types of malaria, semitertian fever and tertian fever, the latter being caused by P. Falciparum and both types being recognized by Celsus as very common and widespread in his own day. (Celsus 3.3.1 f.)

Most of the Roman armies that confronted the "barbarian" threat in the fifth century were so-called *limitanei*, stationed on the frontiers of the Empire and far from Lugnano, therefore unlikely to have suffered from malaria, which is not an infectious or contagious disease but can only be contracted from the bite of an infective anopheles mosquito.

Taken together, these facts make it most unlikely that Rome's military strength or morale could have been sapped by malaria. The opposite hypothesis is equally unlikely, namely that Rome was spared the attentions of Attila the Hun, who in 452, some two years after the burials at Lugnano, stopped his southern advance at the River Po in Northern Italy because of malaria or the fear of malaria. (Soren 1999). According to the chronicler Hydatius (c. 400–c. 469), Attila's troops were affected by "famine and some kind of disease." (Burgess 1993, Ed., p. 103.) If this is true, the disease in question was probably not malaria, to which an army on the march, as Attila's was, would not have been likely to be susceptible.

While malaria cannot be transmitted from person to person, other far more infectious diseases have taken a toll of human lives, yet none of them was able to sweep away, or even seriously debilitate, European civilization in whole or part:

- **"Antonine Plague" (165–180):** This pandemic, probably to be identified as smallpox, or possibly measles, evidently seriously depleted the Roman army on the frontier and may well account for the death of the junior emperor, Verus, in 169, and possibly even that of Marcus Aurelius himself, who died mysteriously in 180. The ancient sources include a contemporary account by the famous Roman physician Galen (*On the Natural Faculties*) and by Marcus Aurelius's tutor, Marcus Cornelius Fronto (Epp) and a much later reference in Eutropius (31.6.24.). Demographic estimates relating to the ancient world are notoriously unreliable, and some of the figures suggested for the death toll of the Antonine Plague appear grossly exaggerated. But the estimates, by R.J. and M.L. Littman, of an average mortality rate of probably 7–10 percent, and possibly 13–15 percent in cities and armies, seem plausible. (Littman/Littman 1973, p. 254 f.) Cassius Dio (c.155–c. 235) describes the recrudescence of the pandemic in 189 as the worst outbreak of which he was aware. (72.14.3 f.)
- **"Plague of Cyprian" (249–262):** Neither the identity nor the severity nor the geographical spread of this alleged pandemic is known. It is named after Cyprian, Bishop of Carthage, as its chief sources are Cyprian's *De Mortalitate*, and his biography by Pontius of Carthage. (Cyprian 8–14; Pontius Vita Cypr. 9.) Even the death of the Emperor Claudius Gothicus is sometimes ascribed to this plague, though it took place only in 270. (Harper 2017, p. 137.)
- **"Plague of Justinian" (541–549):** This is thought to have been the earliest known example of bubonic plague, which continued to recur until the mid-eighth century. There are three contemporary reports of this plague, by Procopius, John of Ephesus, and Evagrius Scholasticus. Procopius, Justinian's court historian, contracted the disease himself but recovered and, in *The Secret History of the Court*

of Justinian, he described the effects of the disease in lurid terms, claiming that it "...wiped out most farmers and left a trail of desolation in its wake." (Procopius, 23.20 f.) But the virulence and long-term effects of this pandemic have been doubted in some recent research. (Mordechai/Eisenberg, 2019, p. 246.)

- **"The Pandemic of 541–750"**: An ambitious compilation titled *Plague and the End of Antiquity: The Pandemic of 541–750*, with contributions by twelve academics, edited by Lester K. Little, and published by the Cambridge University Press in 2006, proclaims: "Plague helped carry out Antiquity and usher in the Middle Ages. Eight centuries before the Black Death did its part to carry out the Middle Ages and usher in the Renaissance, a similar pandemic of plague engulfed the lands surrounding the Mediterranean Sea and eventually extended as far east as Persia and as far north as the British Isles. Its sporadic appearances persisted from 541 to 750, the same period that witnessed the distinctive shaping of the Byzantine Empire, a new prominence of monasticism and of the Roman papacy, the gradual Christianizing of the Celtic and Germanic peoples, the beginnings of Islam, the rapid accumulation of the Arabic Empire, the ascent of the Carolingian dynasty in Frankish Gaul, and, not coincidentally, the beginnings of a positive work ethic in the Latin West." (Little (Ed.) 2006.) This is a tall order indeed! Even more so than other similar theories, this ambitious hypothesis, spanning two centuries of history across a vast geographical swathe, lacks the most crucial element needed, namely proof of causation, as discussed below. (Cf. A similar but less wide-ranging theory in William Rosen's *Justinian's Flea: Plague, Empire and the Birth of Europe*, 2008.)

- **Climate**: "In Europe, a shift towards wetter and colder weather began during the late fifth century and extended into the seventh. There was a less severe repeat of this phenomenon around the mid-ninth century....In southern Europe, studies of alluvial soils along the Arno and Po rivers indicate periods of intense flooding between 500 and 700, and again in the ninth century....More significant were the consequences for agriculture and settlement patterns. Over much of western Europe, the heavy clay soils and the river valleys that provide the richest soil for grain were abandoned. In the Paris basin and elsewhere in the north, the heavy soils would not be worked again in some areas before the eleventh or twelfth century." (Fredric L. Cheyette, (2008), pp. 127–165.) This "climatic anomaly" is too late to explain the "fall" of the West. And it is hard to see what political or other major events could possibly be attributable to it. It happens to coincide with the rise of the Frankish kingdom, exactly the opposite sort of development from what might have been expected from this "climatic anomaly."

- **The Black Death (1346–53):** This bubonic plague is the most serious pandemic recorded in human history, carrying off anything between 45 and 60 percent of the population of Europe. (Benedictow 2012.) By severely reducing the number of agricultural workers, it hastened the end of serfdom in Western Europe. But the key point is that it did not bring any country or society to its knees.
- **The Spanish Flu (1918–1920):** This influenza pandemic infected about 500 million people around the world, amounting to about one-third of the global population, killing anything between 20 million and 100 million. The spread of the pandemic was exacerbated by the debilitation caused by World War I, which had been raging for over three years when the disease was first reported.

Other Monocausal Explanations

Malaria, bubonic plague, smallpox, and measles are just a few of the many candidates in the monocausal stakes, factors identified as *the* cause or at least a contributory cause, of the "fall" of the Roman Empire in the West. Another favorite old chestnut is lead poisoning, based on the use of lead for plumbing [from plumbum (lead)] and drinking vessels. In 1983, Jerome Nriagu, a geochemist claimed that "lead poisoning contributed to the decline of the Roman empire." (Nriagu 1983.) Scarborough rebutted this contention by pointing out that lead poisoning was not endemic in the Roman Empire and did not cause its fall. (Scarborough 1984; Cf. Retief/Cilliers 2006.)

Already during the time of Augustus, the famous Roman architect Vitruvius warned against the use of lead and recommended clay instead. (Vitruvius, 8.6.10 f.) A similar observation is found in Columella's writings on agriculture (*De Agricultura* 1.5.2.) In addition, the water in Roman aqueducts generally contained dissolved calcium carbonate forming a limestone encrustation, which insulated against the introduction of lead into the water. A more serious contender for lead poisoning is the preparation of two varieties of grape syrup used to sweeten wine, namely *defrutum* and *sapa*, from *mustum*, (must or unfermented grape juice), for which lead cauldrons were often used. (Columella, 12.19.1; Pliny the Elder, Natural History, 14.136.) However, the Romans normally diluted their wine, *merum* (unmixed wine) being considered the drink of provincials, barbarians, and drunkards.

S.C. Gilfillan went so far as to claim that "...lead poisoning is to be reckoned the major influence in the ruin of the Roman culture, progressiveness, and genius," and contributing to the decline of the aristocracy. (Gilfillan 1965) But, as was pointed out by Needleman and Needleman, the decline of the aristocracy was more likely to be explained by their deliberate childlessness, which Augustus felt he had to counter by means of legislation promoting marriage and procreation. (Needleman/Needleman 1985.) "And yet," observed Tacitus, "marriage and child-rearing did not become more frequent, so powerful were the attractions of childlessness." (Ann. 3.25.) Walter Scheidel dismissed out of hand any impact of lead on fertility: "Nor is there any need to suspect that the incidence of marital sterility in the Roman ruling class might have been much higher than in other groups, times, and places." (Scheidel 1999.)

L. Cilliers and F.P. Retief, who have written extensively on the subject, from both a medical and historical viewpoint, make this instructive observation about lead poisoning during the Roman imperial period as a whole: "Although clinical lead poisoning probably occurred sporadically, archaeological evidence indicates that the mean skeletal lead content of the population was less than half that of the modern European in the same countries. The typical clinical picture of chronic lead poisoning was not described before the seventh century CE. It is thus unlikely that lead poisoning played a significant role in the decline and fall of the Roman Empire toward the fifth century CE." (Cilliers/ Retief (2018) in Wexler (Ed.) 2018, pp. 221–9.)

Conclusion

The endless fascination of the "fall" of the Western Roman Empire has elicited a vast number of causal "explanations," many of which, like the ones discussed in this chapter, will not stand up to scrutiny. The main reasons why they have so little validity include the following:

- If they brought down the West, why not the East as well?
- Malaria, and the other similar "usual suspects" were in existence long before—and, indeed, after— the "fall" of the Western Empire.
- The "fall" of the Western Empire was a complex event, which cannot be understood in terms of a monocausal explanation—or even a semi-monocausal explanation.
- Did the West really "fall," or was it more a case of continuity, drift and change?

- As for the widest and most ambitious theory of them all, namely that of *Plague and the End of Antiquity: The Pandemic of 541–750* (Little 2006), one event that is *not* attributed to the pandemic is the fall of the Roman Empire in the West because the theory only kicks in more than half a century after the conventional 476 date. But for two centuries after 541, whole clusters of very diverse and scattered events are held up as targets of the disease. There is no real proof of causation here. Instead, what we have is essentially the logical error, *post hoc, ergo propter hoc* (after this, therefore on account of this).

10

The Role of Religion

There are few subjects more controversial than religion, and few periods in which religion looms larger than in the historiography of "late antiquity." The period can fairly be characterized as a watershed in religious history across the whole Mediterranean basin and well beyond, seeing, as it did, the rise of Christianity to dominance throughout the Roman Empire; the rise of Islam; the development of rabbinic Judaism; the high incidence of religious intolerance and persecution; together with considerable continuity down to the present day. The main issues tackled in this chapter are the following:

- Communal vs. creed religions—why this is important
- Religious toleration, intolerance and persecution—Freedom of religion in pagan Rome
- "Christians to the Lions!"—A slogan that belongs more to Hollywood than to history
- The Roman treatment of Jews—Latitude shown to Judaism as a communal religion until the dominance of Christianity
- The origins, nature, and effects of rabbinic Judaism—Turning Judaism into a hybrid communal/creed religion
- How and why Christianity became the dominant religion of the Roman Empire—A critique of a number of varieties of pro-Christian special pleading
- The rise of Islam—Marking a watershed
- The impact of religion on politics
- Religious continuity and change down to the present day

Why Rome Fell: Decline and Fall, or Drift and Change?, First Edition. Michael Arnheim.
© 2022 John Wiley & Sons, Inc. Published 2022 by John Wiley & Sons, Inc.

Communal vs. Creed Religions

Religions can be classified in a variety of ways, most commonly as either monotheistic or polytheistic, as Abrahamic (chiefly Judaism, Christianity, and Islam) or non-Abrahamic, or as ethnic or universal. But for the purposes of the present study, the most important (but least recognized) classification is that of communal vs. creed religions, labels coined by myself in *Is Christianity True?* (1984) and further developed in *The God Book* (2015) and *God Without Religion* (2018).

Creed Religions

The two dominant religions in the world today, namely Christianity and Islam, are both creed religions. Each has a creed or set of beliefs that has to be accepted by adherents. To be more precise, every denomination, sect, or grouping within each of these religions has its own creed that has to be accepted by adherents. People failing to accept the creed in question are branded as "heretics" (if they belong to a deviant denomination within the same religion), or otherwise as "blasphemers," or "unbelievers." Differences between the several variants may appear trivial to outsiders, but are likely to be regarded as crucial by members of the individual groups themselves. A good example is the Latin word *filioque* (and from the son), the basis of an ongoing schism between Eastern and Western Christianity that has lasted since 1054. The issue is essentially whether the Holy Spirit proceeds only from the Father, or from the Father and the Son, i.e. filioque.

Communal Religions

By contrast, communal religions are based not on a creed or set of beliefs but on membership of a community, society, or nation. Membership of the religion is not separate from membership of the community but is an integral part of it. You are a member of a communal religion simply by virtue of your membership of the community, society, or nation concerned.

The largest communal religion in the world today is Hinduism. The English word *Hinduism* is a modern coinage, formed from *Hindu*, which is closely related to the words *India, Indus, Hindustan, Hindustani* and *Hindi* (the language.) Everyone born in India is automatically a Hindu, unless they (or their parents or ancestors) have converted to Islam, Christianity, or some other religion. Hinduism has no identifiable creed or set of beliefs, but a whole pantheon of gods and goddesses, and a plethora of rituals, festivals and practices. In 1966 the Indian Supreme Court defined Hinduism in these terms: "Unlike other religions in the world, the Hindu religion does not claim any one God; it does not subscribe to any one dogma; it does not believe in one philosophic concept; it does not follow any one set of religious rites." (Sen 2006, p. 15 f.)

The Roman "Pagan" State Religion

Most religions in the ancient world were communal religions, including the Roman "pagan" state religion. Like most communal religions, it did not have a distinctive name of its own for the simple reason mentioned above that membership of the religion was not separate or separable from membership of the society. All Romans were automatically deemed to be members of the Roman state religion. This religion had a pantheon of gods and goddesses but no creed or set of beliefs. Yet the fact that this was the Roman state religion did not make it exclusive and did not preclude Romans from being, *in addition*, adherents of any other cult or form of worship that they fancied. Judaism and Christianity, however, both posed (very different) problems in this regard as we shall see.

Religious Toleration, Intolerance, and Persecution

Why does it matter whether a particular religion is classified as either a communal or creed religion? In fact, it is of central importance. For, to put it at its simplest, communal religions tend to be tolerant, while creed religions tend to be intolerant, not only of other religions but also of different variants of their own religion. From a communal perspective, every nation is assumed to have its own religion and its own gods. In the ancient world, therefore, until the advent of Christianity, religious conversion was practically unknown. Conversion took place only as a by-product of conquest or in cases of migration or assimilation.

Ruth and Conversion to Judaism

The Biblical Book of Ruth gives us a rare glimpse into the communal attitude to conversion. The book tells of a Jewish family—Elimelech, his wife, Naomi, and their two sons—who moved from Bethlehem in the land of Judah to the nearby country of Moab, where the two sons married two Moabite women, Ruth and Orpah. After the death of all the male members of her family, Naomi returned to Bethlehem. Her two daughters-in-law accompanied her. Naomi entreated them to go back to their native Moab, and Orpah reluctantly did so. Ruth, however, decided to remain loyal to Naomi and immerse herself in Jewish life, expressing herself in these moving words: "Intreat me not to leave thee, or to return from following after thee: for whither thou goest I will go; and where thou lodgest, I will lodge: thy people shall be my people, and thy God my God: Where thou diest, will I die, and there will I be buried: the LORD do so to me, and more also, if ought but death part thee and me." (Ruth 1:16–17 KJV.) Ruth's pledge to become a member of the Jewish *people* is at the same time a pledge to convert to the Jewish *religion*. The two pledges merge. This is a perfect example of the communal identification of religion and society.

Greek Communal Religion

One of the few modern scholars who understood the prevalence of this communal attitude to religion in the ancient world was A.D. Nock. Here is an extract on religion in Classical Greece from his well-known book, *Conversion*:

> "The cults of Greek cities in the fifth and fourth centuries B.C. neither were nor could be missionary. Following tradition, a city honoured certain deities to whom it looked for the satisfaction of its needs. That was its own affair. A friendly city might be empowered, a colony or a subject city might be compelled, to take some part in this worship, but it was primarily a domestic matter.... What has been said of local cults in Greece is equally true of national cults. Just as an Athenian qua Athenian turned to Athena on the Acropolis, so an Ionian qua Ionian turned to Apollo on Delos and a Greek qua Greek to Zeus at Olympia or Apollo at Delphi. There was in all this a natural organic piety and no element of conversion or tenseness of religious emotion except in war or famine or plague, and again in the mystery dramas.... The gods of a people were one of its attributes." (Nock 1933, p. 17 ff.)

Resident aliens, however, might be allowed to worship their own gods:
> "The commercial importance of Athens brought with it a large influx of resident aliens. They were allowed to have their own associations to worship their deities: we possess the record of a permission granted in 333–32 B.C. to the merchants from Citium in Cyprus resident in Athens to acquire land to build a temple to Aphrodite (that is, their Semitic Aphrodite, often called Ourania), as the Egyptians have built the temple of Isis." (Ibid., p. 21.)

Roman Freedom of Religion

Imperial Rome was, of course, of even greater commercial importance than Athens had ever been and its population far more diverse. Not surprisingly, therefore, a proliferation of foreign cults sprang up, which, for the most part, were allowed to live and thrive alongside the Roman state religion. Was this religious toleration? Some modern writers deny this, claiming that what may appear to be toleration was actually subjugation, absorption, and suppression. (Garnsey 1984, p. 9.) If that is so, then why did these cults survive with their temples and shrines intact until suppressed by the Christian emperors, and beyond? In fact, the pagan Roman state extended more than toleration to other pagan cults. The term "toleration" has something of a negative connotation, meaning as it does permitting a practice with which one disagrees. The Roman state religion did not just tolerate other pagan cults: It extended freedom of religion to them. But, it may be objected, were some cults not banned? And what about persecution of Christians and Jews? Actually, there is no evidence of religious persecution as such under the pagan empire.

Bacchanalia

The most extreme example of what looks like religious persecution occurred during the Roman Republic: a *Senatus Consultum* (Decree of the Senate) of 186 BCE controlling the Bacchanalian cult. (CIL II. 581.) Writing during the Principate of Augustus, some 200 years later, Livy draws a lurid picture of the depravity of this Greek cult. He sums up the situation like this: "To consider nothing wrong was the highest form of their religious devotion." (Livy, 39.1; Gruen 1996, Ch. 2.; Walsh 1996, pp. 188–203; Takács 2000, pp. 301–10.) The outrage that the excesses of this cult evoked at the time was evidently motivated not only by morality but also by politics because leading forces in the cult were found to be plotting insurrection. Yet the cult was not actually banned, only placed under narrow constraints, which were later relaxed.

Druids

The only pagan cult to have been permanently banned by the Romans was that of the Druids. Julius Caesar, who encountered them during his conquest of Gaul, described them as leading members of Gaulish society with both religious and judicial functions, including presiding over rituals of human sacrifice. (Caesar BG 6.13-18.) Caesar's account has been much disputed, but the association of the Druids with human sacrifice was also made by Pliny the Elder (23–79), who claimed that the cult was banned by the Emperor Tiberius (r. 14–37) together with practitioners of magic. Pliny approved of the ban in the belief that it would end human sacrifice in Gaul. (Pliny *Natural History* 30.13.) Suetonius (c. 69–122) attributed the banning of the Druids by the Emperor Claudius (r. 41–54) to the *dira immanitas* (frightful inhumanity) of their religion, probably another reference to human sacrifice. (Suetonius, Claudius 25.5) The moral outrage may well have been combined with a political motive. In the words of R.G. Collingwood: "So long as Celtic religion wore an intolerant nationalistic shape, in the form of Druidism, Rome saw in it a danger to her own imperial policy." (Collingwwod/Myres 1936, p. 261.)

> Let us turn now to the treatment of pagan "mystery" cults in pagan Rome, among the most popular of which were the cults of Isis, Mithras, and Cybele (*Magna Mater* or Great Mother). Though these appear as "cults" rather than as full-blown religions, their origins were evidently as communal or national religions in their places of origin.

Cybele/*Magna Mater*

The goddess Cybele (*Magna Mater* or The Great Mother), was welcomed to Rome with great pomp during the Second Punic War (218–201 BCE). A favorable reception was also accorded at about the same time to the Greek gods Asclepius and Apollo, and the worship of the Greek goddess Demeter was assimilated to that of her Roman counterpart, Ceres. But the cult of Cybele was rather different. Originating as probably the national deity of Phrygia, she had very "un-Roman" associations, notably her castrated consort, Attis, and her *galli* (eunuch priests). Initiation into the cult of Cybele was either by *taurobolium* (a ceremony involving the sacrifice of a bull) or *criobolium* (the same with a ram). Despite these alien features, the cult was popular with the Roman upper classes, who alone would have been able to afford the outlay on the *taurobolium*.

Under Augustus, the *Magna Mater* came to be identified with the imperial order, and the Emperor Claudius promoted Attis to the Roman pantheon, and placed his cult under the supervision of the *quindecim-viri sacris faciundis*, one of the priestly colleges of the Roman state religion. But, this close association with the imperial regime did not rob the cult of its separate identity. The chief temple of the cult had an imposing position high up on the Palatine, reached by a long flight of stairs, at the top of which was a statue of the enthroned goddess wearing the mural crown, and with two lions at her feet. When the temple burned down during Augustus's reign, it was restored by him, and, when it burned down again, Augustus rebuilt it in more lavish style. But this was not Cybele's only temple. At least four others have been identified in Rome alone. The Emperor Julian was an initiate into the cult and wrote a hymn dedicated to the goddess. Even after Christianity had become the sole religion of the Empire, Augustine of Hippo reported seeing *galli* openly "parading through the squares and streets of Carthage, with oiled hair and powdered faces, languid limbs and feminine gait, demanding even from the tradespeople the means of continuing in disgrace," as he put it. (Augustine, Civ. Dei 7.26.)

Isis

Another mother goddess who developed a mass following in the Roman world was Isis, whose worship goes back to well before 2000 BCE in Egypt. Initiation and salvation are two major aspects of the cult, both of which later figure prominently in Christianity. Two characteristic Christian themes are particularly redolent of Isis, though direct borrowing cannot be proved, and Christians are often reluctant to admit that there was pagan influence on their religion. One such theme is Isis's frequent portrayal nursing her infant son, Horus, a possible foreshadowing of the ubiquitous Christian "Madonna and Child" motif, the other recurrent theme being the death and resurrection of Isis's husband, Osiris. Neither of these two themes had any counterpart in Judaism. In Apuleius's *Metamorphoses* (commonly known as *The Golden Ass*), dating from the mid-second century CE, the hero, Lucius, having been accidentally transformed into an ass, is saved and changed back into human form with the aid of the goddess. "This you must remember well," the goddess instructs Lucius, "and keep forever stored up in your inmost heart: the remaining course of your life right up until your last breath is now solemnly promised to me.... And you will live happily, you will live gloriously under my protection; and when you have completed your lifespan and descended to the shades, there also in that subterranean sphere I, whom you now behold, shall be there, shining amidst the darkness of Acheron and reigning in the secret depths of Styx, and you shall dwell in the Elysian Fields and constantly worship me and be favored by me. But, if by diligent service and pious service and steadfast chastity, you shall have deserved well of my godhead, know that I alone also have

power to prolong your life beyond the bounds fixed for you by your Fate."
(Apuleius, Bk 11, p. 172, tr. Kenny 1998) Finally, Lucius is initiated into
the cult of Isis, which is described, again with Christian overtones, as
"rebirth." (Ibid., p. 182.) As a new initiate, Lucius prostrates himself
before the statue of the goddess, and prays: "Hail, holy one, eternal savior
of the human race.... The gods above worship you, the gods below revere
you; you make the earth rotate, you give the sun its light, you rule the
universe, you trample hell under your feet." This single-minded devotion to one deity recognized as omnipotent comes close to monotheism
or what is sometimes termed henotheism. But initiation into the cult of
Isis did not preclude membership of other cults.

Like the *Magna Mater*, the cult of Isis reached Rome during the mid-
Republic, in this case some time in the second century BCE. Shrines and
altars to her are in evidence in pride of place on the Capitoline Hill from
the early first century BCE. These were private foundations, independent of the Roman authorities, who destroyed them on several occasions
between 59 and 48 BCE, without, however, banning the cult outright,
which they could have done had they wanted to. The reason for the destruction of the shrines was probably political. By this time Ptolemaic
Egypt was in turmoil and had become in effect a Roman protectorate.
Both Julius Caesar and, later on, Mark Antony, became embroiled in
Egyptian affairs (in more senses than one), and, after the future Augustus defeated Antony at Actium in 31 BCE, his victory was celebrated
two years later in separate triumphs, over Antony, and over Egypt in the
person of Cleopatra (both of whom had already committed suicide by
that time). After a further expulsion (together with that of the Jews), under Augustus's successor, Tiberius, in 19 CE, which was evidently trig-
gered by a sex scandal (Tac. Ann 2.85; Suet. Tib. 35–36; Josephus Ant.
18.3.4.), Isis, and her fellow Egyptian deity Serapis went from strength to
strength in the Roman world. They were venerated by the Emperor Vespasian (r. 69–79) and his successors, and Serapis then puts in occasional
appearances on the imperial coinage. His temple, the imposing Serapeum in Alexandria, built by Ptolemy III (r. 246-22 BCE), was closed under
Constantine in 325, and finally destroyed (together with Alexandria's
famous Library) by a Christian mob, or possibly soldiers, in or about 391.

Mithras

Another of the cults that competed with Christianity in the Roman
Empire was that of Mithras, probably originating in Persia. Evidently
an all-male cult, it appealed greatly to Roman soldiers between the first
and fourth centuries CE. The key imagery in this cult shows Mithras

slaughtering a bull (*tauroctony*). Another important scene shows Mithras and the sun-god *Sol Invictus* feasting on the slain bull. Initiation into the cult evidently involved a catechism (*not* a creed in any sense), and there were seven grades of initiates, culminating in that of *pater* (father.) Numerous temples of Mithras, or Mithraea, are found scattered throughout the Roman Empire, particularly in the Western provinces, including one in London. Like the other pagan cults, Mithraism was not exclusive. Almost all Mithraea contain statues of other gods, and dedications to Mithras are also found in the shrines of other cults, particularly those of Jupiter Dolichenus.

Roman Attitudes to Atheism

There was room in the Roman Pantheon for gods and cults of all kinds, shapes, and sizes, but complete denial of the existence of any gods at all was looked at askance. Because of their rejection of all pagan gods, Christians were sometimes placed in this category. The only philosophical group that could reasonably have been regarded as atheists were the Epicureans, who, while not denying the existence of the pagan gods, believed that they had no involvement or interest in human affairs and no power to reward or punish either in this world or in any afterlife, the existence of which they rejected in any case. Despite this, Epicurean philosophy was not "banned," and Lucretius's famous Epicurean didactic poem, *De Rerum Natura* (On the Nature of Things), which is referenced in the following well-known passage from the *Georgics* of Vergil (70–19 BCE), was evidently freely available in the late Republic and early Principate, and was also known to Cicero, Ovid, and Horace among others.

> *Felix, qui potuit rerum cognoscere causas,*
> *Atque metus omnis et inexorabile fatum*
> *Subiecit pedibus strepitumque Acherontis avari.*
> *Fortunatus et ille, deos qui novit agrestis,*
> *Panaque Silvanumque senem Nymphasque sorores:*
> *Illum non populi fasces, non purpura regum*
> *flexit*

Happy is he who has been able to understand the causes of natural events, and who has trodden underfoot all fear of inexorable fate, and the roar of hungry Hell. Lucky, too, is he who knows the rustic gods, Pan, old Silvanus, and the sister Nymphs. For him the symbols of public office hold no attraction, nor even the royal purple. (Vergil, *Georgics*, 2.490 ff., tr. M. Arnheim.)

Vergil presents us here with two parallel profiles. First, the Epicurean, with his scientific approach to life and scorn for divine retribution or the terrors of death followed by the humble, unambitious Roman husbandman, with his simple faith in the woodland gods. Vergil's sympathies clearly lie with the small-time farmer, with whom he identifies throughout the *Georgics*, but there are no recriminations against the worldly-wise Epicurean and no suggestion that his belief is in any way illegal, deserving of punishment, or even wrong. Remember, we are here in a communal religious world, where the very idea of true and false religions did not exist.

Ordinary people, too, evidently were skeptical about the gods. In Petronius's *Satyricon*, composed under Nero between 54 and 66, we are treated to some very down-to-earth remarks made by the guests at Trimalchio's lavish banquet. "Nobody now thinks," ventures one, "that heaven is heaven; nobody does any fasting; nobody cares a fig for Jupiter; but they all shut their eyes and count their own possessions." (Petronius, *Satyricon*, 44.) Petronius was known for his frankness, but this cannot have been the reason why he fell out of favor with Nero, whose confidante he had been, and was forced to commit suicide.

Homosexuality

Another prominent feature of Petronius's *Satyricon* is homosexuality. Indeed, the leitmotif of the whole work could be said to be a homosexual love triangle. Though sometimes mocked, homosexuality was not illegal during the Principate. There are a few references to a republican *Lex Scantinia*, possibly of 216 or 149 BCE, but it is not clear precisely with what aspects of homosexuality it dealt, and it appears to have been essentially a dead letter. (Cic. *Ad Fam.*8.12.3, 8.14.4; Suet, *Domitian* 8.3; Juv. *Satire* 2.) Under Philip the Arab (r. 248–249), male prostitution was criminalized, followed by laws against male sex with a minor, and male same-sex marriage. Under Jewish Law, homosexual intercourse was punishable by death (Lev. 18:22, 20:13.) The ban on homosexuality was picked up by Christianity. In 342 and 390, the death sentence was imposed on the passive partner in homosexual intercourse (CTh 9.7.3 = CJ 9.9.31-342; CTh.9.7.6-390), and under Justinian any kind of male homosexual activity was punishable by death (Justinian, Novellae 77 and 141.) The homosexual proclivities of the Emperor Constans (r. 337–350) were widely condemned, marking quite a contrast with Hadrian's love affair with the youthful Antinous two centuries earlier. After Antinous's accidental death in 130 at the age of 18, Hadrian had him deified, established a cult in his name, which became quite popular, and even founded a city in Egypt named Antinoöpolis in his honor, which became a center for the worship of Osiris-Antinous. A papyrus dating from 569, in the reign of Justin (565–574), still describes Antinoöpolis as "a very illustrious city." (P.Flor. 1.93.)

All these features—religious toleration, freedom of speech, and sexual liberalism—are characteristic of the laissez-faire attitude that typify the Principate, which no doubt contributed to what Gibbon called "... the indissoluble union and easy obedience that pervaded the government of Augustus and the Antonines." (V. Chapter 51.321–322.)

> Besides a few temporary bannings (except for the Druids, whose ban was permanent) for political reasons, pagan "mystery" cults were not only tolerated but accorded freedom of religion in pagan Rome. But what about the supposed persecution of Christians by pagan emperors?

"Christians to the Lions!"

"'Christians to the lions' was a powerful slogan." (Beard, North & Price 1998, p. 212.) Yes, in Hollywood. But the suggestion in a purportedly serious work of history that this was the long-term attitude of the Roman "élite" to Christianity will simply not stand up to scrutiny. This mistaken impression was first conveyed by the Christian apologist Tertullian, who lamented that Roman hostility to Christians was such that they would grasp at any natural disaster as an excuse to persecute them. "If the Tiber rises to the walls, if the Nile fails to rise and flood the fields, if the sky withholds its rain, if there is earthquake or famine or plague, straightaway the cry arises: 'The Christians to the lions'." (Tertullian Apology 20, cited Moss 2013, p. 127.)

In a thoroughly researched work of scholarship, Candida Moss brilliantly and wittily dispels the myth of persistent and widespread Roman persecution of Christianity. (Moss 2013.) She sums up her findings in a nutshell: "Between the death of Jesus around 30 CE and the ascension of Constantine in 313, Christians died as the result of active measures by the imperial government only (1) immediately following the Great Fire of Rome in 64, (2) around 250, during the reign of Decius, (3) briefly during the reign of Valerian in 257–58, and (4) during the 'Great Persecution' under the emperor Diocletian, which lasted from 303 to 305 and was renewed by Maximinus Daia between 311 and 313. These dates represent the largest time span before Constantine. As we shall see, not all of these episodes can reasonably be called persecution, and their implementation was often limited to specific regions and to months rather than years. Even putting these caveats aside, we are talking about fewer than ten years out of nearly three hundred during which Christians were executed as the result of imperial initiatives." (Ibid., p. 127 ff.) Moreover, these episodes were motivated by politics, not religious intolerance.

As a communal religion, the Roman pagan civic religion was part and parcel of being Roman. You were a member of the Roman religion by virtue of your membership of Roman society. The two were inextricably bound up together. As a Roman, you were expected to show loyalty to the Roman state and that meant to the emperor. And how better than by sacrificing to the *genius* ("divine spirit") of the emperor?

Nero and the Great Fire of 64

The conventional view is that state-driven Roman persecution of Christians got off to a sensational start when Nero blamed them for the Great Fire of Rome in 64 CE . This view is essentially based on a single passage in Tacitus (Ann 15.44), written between 110 and 120. Brent Shaw rejects the whole story, partly on the ground that the label "Christians" was not yet in use by this date. (Shaw 2015, pp. 73–100.) Shaw's forthright dismissal of the conventional view has stirred up a hornet's nest of criticism and angry opposition. Though Shaw is probably right to reject the conventional view, he places too much emphasis on the absence of the term "Christian" from Paul's letters, which are generally dated between 50 and 64. However, we should not expect this term to have been used by Paul, as it was evidently originally a pejorative label applied to Christians by outsiders. In Acts 11:26, we read : "And the disciples were first called Christians in Antioch." The "disciples" referred to here are Paul and Barnabas. The wording makes it clear that this was not a label applied to themselves by these two disciples, but by non-Christians. The incident is set around the year 43 CE, but the Book of Acts was probably written only between 70 and 90 CE. However, if this account is true and occurred more than twenty years before the "Great Fire," does that not allow quite enough time for Christians to be distinguished from Jews?

The problem is that, even if the Antioch incident in Acts is historical, there is no reason to believe that the "Christian" label would have percolated through to Rome by 64. The Romans had trouble distinguishing Christians from Jews much later than this. For example, in an oft-quoted passage, Suetonius (c. 69–c. 122) tells us that the Emperor Claudius, "Expelled from Rome the Jews who had been continually rioting at the instigation of Chrestus." (Suetonius, Claudius 25.4.) It is not clear from this whether it was only the rioters who were expelled or all Jews (as Act 18.2 would have us believe.) But a much more serious problem is whether Suetonius is referring to Jews or to Christians. If, as seems likely, "Chrestus" is a mistake for "Christus," then the reference must be to Christians rather than to Jews, yet Suetonius's statement specifically refers to Jews.

A century later, Cassius Dio (c. 155–c. 235), who, despite his Greek background, was a Roman senator and suffect consul in around the year 205, and who wrote a mammoth history of Rome in 80 books covering the period down to 229, had quite a lot to say about the Jews, yet does not once mention the word "Christian". He says that, without expelling them from Rome, Claudius prohibited the Jews, whose numbers had exploded, from holding meetings "...while continuing their traditional way of life." (Dio 60.6.6-7.) There are several marked differences between this and Suetonius's account if the two passages even refer to the same incident. Dio has no "Chrestus" and no expulsion, but the claim of a recent sharp increase in numbers points more to Christianity than to Judaism, which has never been a proselytizing religion.

Roman officialdom managed to distinguish Jews from Christians in 96, when the Emperor Nerva restricted the *fiscus judaicus* (Jewish tax) to people who actually identified themselves as Jewish. The tax, introduced after the destruction of the Temple in Jerusalem in 70, exempted Jews from having to sacrifice to the Roman gods (including the emperor's *genius*.)

It should also be mentioned that "Jewish Christians" or "Nazarenes", referred to in Acts 24:5, who accepted Jesus as the Jewish Messiah but otherwise remained Jewish and worshipped in regular Jewish synagogues, were not deemed "heretics" by Christianity until the Church Councils of the fourth century.

Decius and His *Libelli*

In the year 250 the Emperor Decius issued an edict ordering everyone in the Roman Empire formally to sacrifice to the Roman gods and the *genius* of the emperor—and to be given a *libellus*, or certificate signed by a Roman magistrate, to prove this fact. The edict is no longer extant, but a number of *libelli* have survived, which make no mention of Christianity. It seems that this edict did not actually target Christians at all, but was an attempt on the part of a very new and very insecure emperor to assure himself of the loyalty of his subjects. Most citizens would have had no problem sacrificing a little wine and incense on a patriotic altar. To Christians, though, this would have been anathema, and a number of them were executed. Besides Christians, the only people who would have objected were the Jews, who were exempt because of the *fiscus judaicus*. So much for the "Decian persecution of Christians."

Valerian: Targeting Upper Crust Christians

A stronger candidate for the title of "persecutor" was the Emperor Valerian (r. 253–260), who in 257 issued a letter addressed to the Senate calling for Christian clergy to perform sacrifices to the Roman gods on pain of banishment. This was followed up with a second letter requiring Christian senators and equestrians to sacrifice to the Roman gods or lose their titles and property, and, if they persisted, their lives as well. Unlike Nero's supposed scapegoating of the Christians for the fire of 64,—which probably never happened—and Decius's mandatory demonstration of certificated loyalty, which did not target Christians specifically, here we have a specific anti-Christian edict. But the fact that Valerian singled out, first Christian clergy, and then Christians in responsible positions in society, indicates that he was not attempting to root out the Christian religion but simply trying to get leading Christians to toe the line of loyalty to the Roman state, which was inseparable from the Roman religion. As Candida Moss puts it: "Christians had a reputation for being socially reclusive, refusing to join the military, and refusing to swear oaths. Once in the courtroom Christians said things that sounded like sedition. They were rude, subversive, and disrespectful. Most important, they were threatening." (Moss, C. 2013, p. 185.)

"The Great Persecution"

The Great Persecution of Christians by Diocletian, initiated in 303, looks much more like a religious persecution than anything that had gone before. In a series of four edicts, Diocletian gradually stripped away Christians' rights as Roman citizens, starting with the banning of Christian meetings and ordering the destruction of churches and Christian scriptures. Christians' legal rights to defend themselves in court were the next to go, coupled with loss of social status. The fourth and last edict demanded that everyone, not only Christians, assemble in a public place to offer sacrifice, on pain of death. After Diocletian's retirement in 305, the persecution in the East was briefly revived by Maximin Daia between 311 and 313.

Some Christians were indeed executed, including some in the East who were burned alive, as Diocletian's junior colleague, the Caesar Galerius, demanded. In general, the edicts were enforced much more severely in the East than in the West, where Constantine's father, Constantius (Chlorus), stopped the persecutions in 306, and even restored their confiscated property to affected Christians. The Christian accounts of the persecutions are greatly exaggerated, showing, in the words of Geoffrey de Ste Croix, "an increasing contempt for historicity." ("Aspects of the Great Persecution," p. 42, in de Ste Croix, Whitby & Streeter 2006.)

Candida Moss's conclusion is inescapable: "Christians were not the victims of sustained and continual persecution by the Romans on either an imperial or provincial level." (p. 160.)

Julian's Alleged Attack on Christianity

"You have defeated me, Galilean!" are the oft-quoted but almost certainly bogus dying words of the Emperor Julian (r. 361–363), first recorded by the highly partisan Christian writer and apologist, Theodoret (c. 393–c.458/466), in his *Church History*, compiled around 450. This spoof quotation was presumably intended to indicate Julian's admission of defeat by the "Galilean," namely Jesus, who was born in Galilee. More likely, it is simply Theodoret's gloating.

Was Julian a persecutor of Christianity? It is important to understand that, unlike the Christian emperors' policy toward paganism, Julian made no attempt to stamp out Christianity. He certainly restored pagan temples and worship and even planned at vast cost to rebuild the Jewish Temple in Jerusalem, which had been destroyed by Rome in 70, nearly 300 years before. (Amm. 23.1.1-3.) And he canceled the privileges enjoyed by Christian bishops, including their judicial powers, their right to be consulted on state appointments, and their receipt of state stipends. He also decreed that all public teachers be approved by himself, and, according to Ammianus, banned Christians from teaching rhetoric or grammar. (Amm.22.10.7 & 25.4.20.) However, it is more likely that he only banned Christians from using pagan classical texts in their teaching, presumably for fear that they would try to reinterpret such writings as conveying a Christian message. (Nazianzen, Oration 4. 100 ff) .)

In his zeal to promote paganism, Julian was himself initiated into at least three pagan cults, favored pagans in appointments, encouraged the troops to make an offering of incense to the gods on receiving their pay, appointed a pagan priest for each city and a high priest for each province, and, in imitation of Jewish and Christian charity, established hostels for the poor.

However, instead of trying to root out Christianity, Julian issued an edict guaranteeing freedom of religion and proclaiming the equality of all religions. (Bidez/Cumont 1922, Nos. 43–45.) He even went so far as to summon conflicting Christian bishops and lay leaders, and, according to Ammianus, "...politely advised them to lay aside their differences, and each fearlessly and without opposition to observe his own beliefs." (Amm. 22.5.4, tr Rolfe (1935), Heinemann.) Ammianus explains Julian's purpose as being to exacerbate internecine Christian strife: "On this he took a firm stand, to the end that, as this freedom increased their dissension, he might afterwards have no fear of a united populace, knowing as he did from experience that no wild beasts are such enemies to mankind as are most of the Christians in their deadly hatred of one another." (Ibid.) This interpretation of Julian's motivation may be unduly cynical. After all, was it not statesmanlike of Julian to try to get the warring Christian sects to settle their differences? And would it not have been more befitting the role of a ruler if the Christian emperors had done the same, instead of taking sides in the ongoing disputes as they did? Had the church leaders on all sides buried the hatchet, as Julian encouraged them to do, would that not have resulted in a more, rather than less, united Christian church? But perhaps, as Ammianus suggests, Julian understood only too well just how implacably at loggerheads the different Christian factions were with one another, an inherent feature of Christianity as a creed religion that he, as an "apostate" who had been brought up in that faith and rejected it, would have been ideally placed to appreciate.

Julian's short reign shows that, contrary to all the pro-Christian special pleading of a number of modern writers, the concept of religious toleration and, more than that, of genuine freedom of religion was not alien to the ancient world. On the contrary, what Julian was trying to do was essentially to turn the clock back to the heyday of the Roman Empire, when freedom of religion was so natural a concomitant of the communal ethos that it was scarcely ever mentioned or even consciously thought about. This spirit was not confined to Rome but was the normal rolled-up concept of religion as an integral part of society found in the ancient world generally.

Roman Persecution of the Jews?

In a state with a communal religion, you would be expected to show loyalty to that state or its ruler unless you were a resident alien, in which case you might be permitted to continue to worship your own communal religion. This was the anomalous position of the Jews under Roman rule. In 63 BCE, Judea fell under Roman control but was allowed its own king, who became a client king of Rome. In 6 CE, Judea came under direct Roman rule, which (except for a brief interlude between 41 and 44) remained the situation, with several name-changes and interludes of Persian (Sasanian) control until it was finally conquered by the Muslims in 636.

In keeping with the widespread pattern of the ancient world, Judaism was also a communal religion—with one important difference. While lacking a creed in the Christian sense, the Jews did have one central tenet, or article of faith, namely belief in a single invisible God, breach of which was punishable by death: "If there be found among you, within any of thy gates which the Lord thy God giveth thee, man or woman, that hath wrought wickedness in the sight of the Lord thy God, in transgressing his covenant, and hath gone and served other gods, and worshipped them, either the sun, or moon, or any of the host of heaven, which I have not commanded," then, after careful investigation, that person shall be stoned to death. (Deut. 17:2, KJV.) It is important to note that this harsh law, not found anywhere in the first four books of the Pentateuch but only in Deuteronomy, a sort of latter-day summary of the previous books, and commonly dated to the time of King Josiah (r. 641-609 BCE), applies only to apostates, namely to lapsed Jews, and not to members of any other religion. It also did not prevent Judaism from espousing a belief in freedom of religion. Here, for example, is a well-known extract from the Prophet Micah, purportedly composed before about 700 BCE, but more likely in the post-Exilic period, around 500 BCE:

> But in the last days it shall come to pass, that the mountain of the house of the LORD shall be established in the top of the mountains, and it shall be exalted above the hills; and people shall flow unto it.
>
> And many nations shall come, and say, Come, and let us go up to the mountain of the LORD, and to the house of the God of Jacob; and he will teach us of his ways, and we will walk in his paths; for the law shall go forth of Zion, and the word of the LORD from Jerusalem.
>
> And he shall judge among many people, and rebuke strong nations afar off; and they shall beat their swords into plowshares, and their spears into pruninghooks: nation shall not lift up a sword against nation, neither shall they learn war any more.
>
> But they shall sit every man under his vine and under his fig tree; and none shall make them afraid: for the mouth of the LORD of hosts hath spoken it.
>
> For all people will walk every one in the name of his god, and we will walk in the name of the LORD our God for ever and ever." (Micah 4:1-5, KJV.)

The overarching power of the one God of Israel is here envisioned as bringing about universal peace, but there is no suggestion that other nations should convert to Judaism or come over to the worship of this powerful God. On the contrary, the closing lines conjure up a world of communal religions, with everyone worshipping their own gods.

The relationship between Romans and Jews was something of a rollercoaster. As a separate nation the Jews were allowed a good deal of latitude by the Romans, even after two serious Jewish revolts against Roman rule: the Great Jewish Revolt, or Jewish War (66–73,) which resulted in the destruction of the Temple, and the Bar Kokhba revolt (132–135), which was brutally put down by Hadrian (r. 117–138) and resulted in Jews being banned (except for one day a year) from Jerusalem, now renamed Aelia Capitolina, and large numbers of Jews leaving Judea (now renamed Aelia Palaestina, the latter word being Latin for "Philistine," and presumably intended to sever all Jewish associations with the area).

Hadrian was not well disposed to Judaism, and his ban on circumcision (which as a staunch philhellene he regarded as a form of mutilation), may possibly have sparked off the Bar Kokhba Revolt in the first place. Yet, the ban was reversed (except in respect of Jewish-owned slaves and converts to Judaism) by Hadrian's successor, Antoninus Pius (r. 138–161); Jews were still given dispensation from pagan sacrifice in return for payment of the *fiscus judaicus;* and Jews were included in the extension of citizenship to all free male inhabitants of the Roman Empire by Caracalla's *Constitutio Antoniniana* of 212.

Under the Christian emperors, however, Jews gradually found themselves reduced to second class citizenship. A law of 418 excluded Jews from the imperial service and the army, though the profession of advocate was still open to them together with the decurionate, which was really a financial burden. (CTh 16.8.24.) The laws purporting to protect synagogues, but containing a sting in the tail, are discussed in Chapter 12.

Rabbinic Judaism

The destruction of the Temple in 70 shifted the focus of the Jewish religion from animal sacrifice under the control of a hereditary priesthood, the *kohanim*, in Jerusalem, to prayer services and *Torah* readings in synagogues scattered right across the Roman world. Though not all *kohanim* were Sadducees, there was a close association between the priests who officiated in the Temple service and this denomination, which believed solely in the written *Torah* (or Pentateuch), and rejected altogether the Pharisees' belief in an Oral Law. With the loss of the Temple, the Sadducees fade away, and the rabbis, the successors to the Pharisees, occupy center stage as far as the Jewish religion is concerned for about five centuries, during which period the *Talmud* is composed, made up of two components, namely the *Mishnah* (a rabbinic compilation of the Oral Law), and the *Gemara* (elucidation of the *Mishnah*.)

Probably the most important effect of rabbinic Judaism was to shift Judaism from a pure communal religion to a hybrid between a communal and a creed religion. The very belief in an Oral Law dictated by God to Moses on Mount Sinai, which became a principle of faith, is an example of this. Not only is there no evidence for this highly improbable belief, but the rabbinical authors of the Talmud themselves often disagreed with one another on the content of this Oral Law. By contrast, though no fewer than 613 commandments have been identified lurking within the *written* Torah, only one of those is a belief, namely monotheism. The remaining 612 commandments concern conduct, diet, and ritual. (Lieu, North, and Rajak, 1992, disappointingly, shows no sign of recognition of this important development in rabbinic Judaism.)

The result was to place Judaism at the crossroads (pun intended), with the worst of both worlds. As a communal religion, it recognized that every nation, society or community has its own religion, so there is no Jewish missionary zeal, or proselytism. But, insofar as it was now also a pseudo-creed religion, Judaism demanded literal acceptance not only of the existence of Oral Law but also of the (often extremely pedantic) details of the supposed content of that Oral Law. This has resulted in Judaism following the Christian route of splitting into a number of mutually intolerant branches, each with its own synagogues, clergy, liturgy, creed, and even its own separate *Beth Din* (rabbinical court).

Christian Dominance: How and Why?

There is a good deal of modern pro-Christian special pleading, but the writers concerned do not all sing from the same hymn-sheet. My comments are in italics.

- **Christian intolerance:** This is at least mostly admitted, but there is a reluctance to accept that religious toleration reigned while Rome remained under pagan control. Here is Peter Garnsey: "Roman-style polytheism was disposed to expand and absorb or at least neutralize other gods, not to tolerate them." (Garnsey 1984, 9.) *M.A. The fact that so many cults, including those of the Magna Mater, Isis, Serapis, and Mithras, survived intact—complete with their temples and shrines—until suppressed by Christianity, shows that, not only was there religious toleration under Roman paganism, but actual freedom of religion. It was Christianity, not Roman paganism, that used the "expand, absorb and neutralize" formula. Some of what*

became key features of Christianity were "borrowed" from other reli-
gions, which themselves were suppressed. These include Jesus's divin-
ity (contrary to Jewish tradition about the Messiah, who was never
envisioned as anything other than a purely human figure); the Trinity;
monasticism; Mariology; icons, and other types of images.

- **"Enduring myth":** Alan Cameron attempts to dispel the "enduring myth" of a major onslaught on paganism by the Christian
  Emperors Constantius II, Gratian, and Theodosius I. (Cameron,
  Alan 2013, pp. 3, 33 ff.) *M.A. Yet, how else is one to interpret the suc-*
  cession of punitive and vituperative edicts against paganism? Pagans
  were treated to a series of edicts repeatedly banning animal sacrifice,
  starting with the much-discussed CTh 16.10.2 of 341, which refers to
  an unknown earlier ban. The ban on animal sacrifice is repeated so
  often and over so long a period down to CTh 16.10.12 of 392 that it
  was clearly hard to stamp out or else officials were lax in enforcing it,
  which would indicate their lack of enthusiasm for the ban. The anti-
  pagan legislation also stripped pagan priests of their privileges (CTh
  16.10.14 396), banned pagans from public service (CTh 16.10.21
  415/416), and ordered the destruction of pagan temples (CTh
  16.10.16 399.)

- **Altar of Victory:** On Symmachus's pleas for the Altar of Victory to
  be restored to the Senate-house, Alan Cameron remarks, "As for the
  actual altar, Symmachus loyally represents it as the place where
  senators swore allegiance to the emperor, glossing over its far more
  obvious and significant role as a locus of pagan cult offerings, viv-
  idly evoked by Ambrose (two separate descriptions of Christian
  senators with eyes streaming from the smoke and choking on cin-
  ders)." (Cameron 2013, p. 42.) *M.A. Until removed by Constantius II*
  in 357, the Altar of Victory had stood in the senate-house since 29 BCE
  to celebrate the victory of the future Augustus over Mark Antony, one
  of the most significant turning points in Roman history. To talk as if it
  had two separate roles, one patriotic and the other religious, betrays a
  complete misunderstanding of Roman paganism (and of communal
  religions generally.) The two roles were rolled up (no pun intended)
  into one. The Roman pagan state religion was an integral part of being
  Roman. And the fact that the dispute over the Altar of Victory ran for
  nearly forty years (357–394) shows that there was strong feeling in the
  Senate recognizing its united twofold role. So much for Cameron's
  attempts to pooh-pooh it.

- **Red Herring:** H.A. Drake offers a red herring to explain away anti-
  pagan violence: "This article proposes an alternative way to think
  about the violence that swept the Roman Empire in the wake of
  Constantine's conversion to Christianity. Traditionally seen as the

inevitable result of Christian intolerance, recent experience suggests that this violence can be better understood by casting a broader net and including political as well as theological issues. The result shows this violence to be the by-product of a struggle between emperors and bishops to control access to the divine.... Bishops use martyrs to control emperors. But, as a famous confrontation between Ambrose of Milan and the emperor Theodosius shows, bishops also relied on their new role as patrons of a large and volatile constituency." (Drake 2011, pp. 193–235.) *M.A. Immediately after the orthodox Catholic creed has been laid down by the Council of Nicaea in 325 we find "heretics" lambasted in imperial edicts, starting with CTh 16.5.1 in 326 and culminating in CTh 16.5.65 of 428, containing a long list of "heresies". This internecine conflict, so aptly characterized by Ammianus (quoted above), was an inevitable concomitant of the fact that Christianity was a creed religion. Ambrose, often portrayed with a scourge or whip in hand, was an extreme bigot against pagans and Jews as much as against "heretics", but the Christian emperors could have remained aloof from religious disputes as the pagan emperors had mostly done.*

- **"Violence...was relatively infrequent"**: Michele R. Salzman similarly plays down the violence, taking issue with Ramsay MacMullen's view that coercion was necessary to convert the Roman Empire to Christianity. Salzman's counterblast to this reads as follows: "[V]iolence between pagans and Christians was relatively infrequent in the western empire.... There was religious conflict between pagans and Christians, but violence was far less typical and effective in Christianizing the Western Roman Empire than the steady dialogue that occurred between Christians and pagans." (Salzman 2006b, p. 267.) *M.A. Yet, even Eusebius admitted that Constantine's threats drove some pagans to convert to Christianity. (Cameron 2013, p. 182.) And it is hard to believe that the repeated hammer-blows of legislation (see above) had no effect, coupled with the desire of many to follow the faith of the reigning emperor. As for Salzman's "steady dialogue," there is very little sign of that. Christianity is not really open to dialogue. Every Christian denomination or sect has its fixed dogmas, none of which can be proved. Any apparent dialogue is merely coercion in disguise. Even Augustine, who approved of the suppression of paganism by the state, was not averse to coercion to bring "heretics" into line. "Why, therefore," he wrote in a late letter, "should not the church use force in compelling her lost sons to return, if the lost sons compelled others to their destruction?" (Epistula 185 to Boniface.) He particularly regarded it as a duty of the state to apply this force, and he also, rather disingenuously, asserted that coercion,* *or "rightful persecution," as he termed it, was a means of persuasion, "To compel them to come in"—an (inadvertent?) oxymoron.*

- **Aristocratic conversion:** T.D. Barnes and R.W. Westall, intent on proving that the growth of Christianity did not depend on coercion, date the start of conversion to Christianity by pagan aristocrats to before Constantine. (Barnes/Westall 1991, pp. 50–61.) In a separate article, T.D. Barnes opines, "The claim that a majority of the holders of high administrative offices under the Christian emperors continued to be pagan until the reign of Gratian is quite simply false." (Barnes 1995.) Yet Alan Cameron, who generally belongs to the same school of thought as Barnes, viewed this with a jaundiced eye: "As we shall see, this is probably true. But it is doubtful whether it can be proved by a handful of cases based on such uncertain evidence." (Cameron 2013, p. 178.) And he casts doubt on the religious identity of six office-holders under Constantine described by Barnes as "attested as Christians." (Cameron, Ibid.) *M.A. As was shown in Chapter 3, Constantine and his successors appointed aristocrats to high positions in the imperial service in the West. If a large number of them were pagans, as was evidently the case, this was only because there happened to be a preponderance of pagans among the aristocracy at the time.*

- **"Cramped existence":** A different tack is employed by Peter Brown, who, while admitting Christian coercion, plays down its intensity and success: "Having, in 423, been declared by the emperor Theodosius II not to exist, large bodies of polytheists, all over the Roman empire, simply slipped out of history. They continued to enjoy, for many generations, the relatively peaceable, if cramped, existence which, only two centuries after the reign of Theodosius II, would fall to the lot of Christians themselves in another great Near Eastern empire, raised up in the name of one God—that of Islam." (Brown 1997a, p. 641.) "The sheer success of the post-Constantinian state ensured that the edges of potential conflict were blurred in the golden glow of a God-given order." (Brown, Ibid., p. 652.) *M.A. If this opaque language means anything at all, it is presumably suggesting that the "sheer success" of the Christian empire reduced the intensity of the "potential conflict." In fact, however, religious conflict, or rather, Christian persecution of non-Christians and "heretics", was not "potential" but very real. And, far from reducing the severity of the onslaught, it was precisely the dominance of Christianity that caused it. As for pagans' "enjoyment" (an ironic term) of second-class citizenship "for many generations", it is hard to see how this is justified by the fact that Christians suffered a similar fate under Islam.*

- **John of Ephesus:** Brown is at least prepared to admit that paganism survived for "many generations" while Alan Cameron, intent on giving it an early quietus, outdoes himself in pooh-poohing a claim of pagan survival into the reign of Justinian (527–565): "John of Ephesus famously claimed to have converted 70,000 pagans and built 96 churches in mid-sixth century Asia Minor. But even here it depends what is meant by 'pagans.' There are bound to have been many places so remote that they had never heard of Christianity. Such people were certainly 'pagans,' but their practices are not likely to have had much in common with the civic cults of the Graeco-Roman world in their heyday. To cite them as proof of the 'tenacity' of paganism misleadingly implies a continuing entity that defiantly resisted the influence of Christianity—a Christian perspective." (Cameron 2013, p. 783.) *M.A. If these converts had simply never heard of Christianity, hardly likely, after 500 years of Christianity and in the most Christianized part of the empire, then a missionary outreach would have been all that was needed to bring them into the Christian fold. Yet they evidently needed to be bribed with money payments in order to achieve the desired effect—something that Cameron omits to mention. He also omits to mention that, in 546, some years after the initial campaign, Justinian, energetically assisted by John of Ephesus, embarked on a major persecution, by means of torture, of a large number of pagans, including many members of the aristocracy, in Constantinople itself, established in 330 as a specifically Christian capital.* (John of Ephesus, Joh. Eph., ed Nau (1897), p. 482; Whitby 1991, pp. 111–31.)
- **Religious liberty:** Next we have an (unintentionally) amusing extract from a book on Roman religion revealing a lamentable misunderstanding of the mindset of communal religion. (Beard, et al. 1998, p. 212.) My comments are in italics:
  - "No Roman propounded the view that Rome should respect the religious liberty of other peoples." *M.A. What about Themistius's appeals to the Emperors Jovian and Valentinian? Or Symmachus's oft-quoted remark in his 384 speech on the Altar of Victory: "It is not by one way alone that we can arrive at so sublime a mystery." Or the Emperor Julian's Edict of Toleration? But if Romans in earlier centuries never talked about freedom of religion, it was because it was taken for granted as part of their communal attitude to religion.*
  - "This does not mean that the Romans were therefore *intolerant* (indeed, the concept of 'toleration' is distinctively modern and does not apply at this period.)" *M.A. The concept of religious toleration is far from modern, and the pagan Romans knew all about it, or rather, about freedom of religion, which they embraced instinc-*

tively without even reflecting upon it, rather like Monsieur Jourdain in Molière's Bourgeois Gentilhomme, *who discovered belatedly that he had been speaking prose all his life without realizing it. So in ancient religion, where the very concept of intolerance on grounds of belief was alien.*

- "The issue is rather the degree of *exclusivity* of the Roman system, how it operated and how it changed—particularly as the empire prompted new ways of defining what was 'Roman', new ways of thinking about what was to count as 'Roman' and what was not." (Ibid., p. 212.) In setting boundaries between the legitimate and the illegitimate, between "us" and "them", the Roman élite identified a set of transgressive religious stereotypes (from horrendous witches to monstrous Christians) against whom they waged war, with the stylus and with the sword or with wild beasts in the arena: "'Christians to the lions' was a powerful slogan." *M.A. As we have already seen, the Roman pagan state religion was not at all exclusive. As for the "transgressive religious stereotypes," this is pure fantasy. Rome had no laws against witches (though magic was outlawed), and "Christians to the lions" belongs to Hollywood.* (Beard, et al. 1998, p. 212.)

- **"A firm religious policy"**: A bald assertion by Peter Brown is worth examining, revealing a misunderstanding of communal religion: "Emperors had always been expected to have a firm religious policy in order to be sure of the support of the gods."(Brown 2013, p. 73). *M.A. Note the word "always". In fact, emperors generally had no religious policy at all because the Roman communal religion was not seen as separate from Roman society. What then about the policy toward the Druids, Jews, and Christians? As we have seen, the suppression of the Druids was politically motivated as were the various restrictions on the Jews. As far as the alleged persecution of Christians was concerned, the whole Neronian episode probably never happened as Christians were not yet separable from Jews in the official Roman mind; Decius was not targeting Christians or any other religious group; and both Valerian and Diocletian, who did persecute Christianity, did so for political reasons.*

- **"Heresiology"**: The dominance of Christianity, of course, means the dominance of one brand of Christianity, while all others were condemned as "heresies". The gyrations of a modern apologist to avoid characterizing this exercise as what it was, i.e. simply a manifestation of extreme intolerance, are amusing and disquieting at the same time. The writer concerned characterizes "heresiologies" as "a recognized intellectual discipline," which, like "the *Natural History* of Pliny the Elder or the medical treatises of Galen, claimed to provide complete and secure information, guaranteed by the author's learning and experience." (Flower 2013, p.173.) Yet, any reading of the irrational and arbitrary torrent of abuse passing as "heresiology" should quickly conclude that it has as much in common with any form of literature or branch of learning as crude graffiti on a bathroom wall have with the works of Shakespeare. (See Chapter 4.)

The Rise of Islam

There are two reason for dealing with Islam. One is simply that the rise of Islam took place during "late antiquity." More important, though, is the fact that Islam was clearly influenced by Judaism and Christianity, and both the Jewish and Christian Bibles are sacred to it, after the Quran. The concept of monotheism probably came from Judaism, and the idea of being a creed religion was probably borrowed from Christianity.

Muhammad (c. 570–632), the founder of Islam, the second known creed religion in the world, is revered by Muslims but only as a prophet. He is not believed to be divine, and prayers cannot be addressed to him. Islamic monotheism is strict, obedient, for example, to the prohibition in the Ten Commandments on "graven images". That is why representations of human beings, and even animals, are largely absent from Islamic art. A striking example is the covering over in Constantinople's Hagia Sophia of all the Byzantine representations of Jesus and other figures when it was converted from a church to a mosque.

Under Muhammad's leadership, Islam spread very rapidly in the Arabian Peninsula between 622 and 632 and by 750 covered the Middle East, the whole of the North African coast, and most of Spain. Initially, conversion of the conquered peoples to Islam was actually discouraged by the introduction of additional requirements such as circumcision and recitation of passages from the Quran. The logic behind this may have been that, having obtained the key to eternal life, Muslims were reluctant to share it with outsiders. Another explanation puts it down to questions of taxation. However, before long, the more familiar pattern took over, promoting proselytism by means of tax incentives and a desire to retain social status. As "People of the Book," Jews and Christian were granted *dhimmi* (protected person) status, amounting to a form of second-class citizenship, in return for payment of the so-called *jizya* tax (per capita tax).

The basic Islamic creed is encapsulated in the *shahada* (profession of faith): "I bear witness that there is no god but Allah, and I bear witness that Muhammad is the prophet of Allah." However, accretions came to be added to this simple monotheistic credo, and before long,

Islam split into two main branches, Sunni Islam and Shia Islam, which are still the most important divisions today. The original dispute between them was political, over who was to be Muhammad's successor, but in time theological differences arose as well. Rancor between the two groups has not abated.

In fact, the reason Iran became the chief bastion of Shia Islam is purely political. Upon the conquest of Iran by Shah Ismail I (r. 1501–24), he proclaimed Shia Islam as the official religion of his newly formed state, which was consolidated by means of forced conversions. His chief motive appears to have been to differentiate Iran from its chief rival, the Turkish sultanate.

The Impact of Religion on Politics

Christianity was a a major divisive force in the Roman Empire, setting Christians against pagans, Jews, and, not least, other Christians. In the West, the hostility between Romans and "barbarians", more marked than ever before, could only have been exacerbated by the adherence of most "barbarians" to the Arian "heresy", which also seeped into relations between Roman themselves, with two emperors, Constantius II and Valens, showing partiality toward it.

As was seen in Chapter 4, one of the chief causes of the "fall" of the West to the "barbarians" was the fact that the strength of the West was sapped by the appointment of aristocrats to high posts in the administration and the tendency of these grandees to withdraw to their increasingly self-contained and fortified estates in the western provinces without bothering to assist the emperor to fend off the barbarians. As we have seen, they were not appointed to their imperial posts on the basis of religion, though paganism evidently remained strong among them right up to the end of the fourth century. This does not mean that they were necessarily anti-Christian, but their failure to resist the "barbarians"—by contrast with the attitude of their ancestors of earlier generations—says little for their loyalty to the imperial regime, which they failed to exert themselves to shore up.

That is not to say that the senatorial aristocracy would not have benefited from the survival of the Western Empire, which had enabled them to combine office with landholding and local wealth, and also to spread their landed interests over several provinces. Nevertheless, they displayed surprisingly little resistance to the "barbarian" takeover of the western provinces, which fell like ninepins one after the other in the fifth century. By that time the aristocracy had mostly converted to Christianity, and had come to realize, especially in Gaul, the advantages of gaining control of the church through bishoprics, which, by the same token, gave them leverage over their new "barbarian" masters.

Anxious to portray "late antiquity" as a "good thing," Peter Brown takes issue with Christian divisiveness in the East: "It has been said that the Council of Chalcedon [451 CE] divided the empire irreparably; that it rendered inevitable the loss of the eastern provinces to Islam in the seventh century....The exact opposite was the case. Despite the explosive nature of the issues involved, despite the fact that the ecclesiastical traditions of whole provinces were mobilized on both sides, the empire remained united. We can learn a lot about the resources of the east Roman state by seeing how this could be so. In the first place, the imperial administration had created a unified state; men paid their taxes and prayed for the success of the emperor whatever their shade of theological opinion." (Brown 1971, p. 145.)

No references are given to substantiate this wide-ranging bald statement, which, in fact, flies in the face of the evidence. Egypt, for example, was dominated by the Monophysites, who were the main target of Chalcedon, which would result in a Monophysite alliance with the Muslim invaders, ensuring them of a decisive victory over this jewel in the Byzantine crown. In general, there was very little resistance by the religiously divided local populations against the lightning-speed Muslim conquests which stripped the Byzantine Empire of the bulk of its territory (some of which was temporarily reconquered during the "Macedonian renaissance" of 867–1025).

Religious Continuity and Change down to the Present Day

The role of religion in this period is crucial. It marks a sea-change in the history of the Roman Empire, Europe, and the world. Christianity is still the dominant religion of Europe and its offshoots in other continents, and Islam is still the dominant religion of North Africa and the Middle East. These two creed religions, each inherently intolerant of other religions and of internal divisions, have marked world history indelibly with the bloodshed of religious wars and persecutions.

But, it may be objected, is that not a thing of the past, especially in the case of Christianity, which has become tolerant of dissent both internal and external, and, which has signed up to international charters and conventions guaranteeing freedom of belief and religion? It is certainly true that the principle of freedom of belief and religion is now loudly proclaimed from the rooftops, but how did that come about, and how genuine is it? It is really the product of the secularization of western society over the past two hundred years. Christian intolerance still lurks beneath. The "Great Schism" between the Roman Catholic and Eastern Orthodox churches, which has been a running sore since 1054, is still unhealed. And the Papal Bull issued against Martin Luther in 1520 is still in force.

But, is that pattern inevitable? In 1986, when Pope John Paul II was invited to address the European Parliament, the Reverend Ian Paisley, a member of that body elected from Northern Ireland, leader of the Democratic Unionist Party, and an extreme Protestant, greeted the Pope with a placard reading "You are the Anti-Christ," a message that he shouted out repeatedly in his stentorian voice. Under the so-called Good Friday Agreement of 1999, embodying a political settlement of the protracted Northern Ireland "troubles," Paisley became First Minister of Northern Ireland, with the Catholic Sinn Fein politician and former IRA commander, Martin McGuinness, as his Deputy. With the two men's diametrically opposed political and religious positions, they might have been expected to be totally incompatible. Yet, they not only forged a harmonious working partnership but also became close personal friends. From the number of times they were seen joking and laughing together, they were dubbed "The Chuckle Brothers." Had Ian Paisley changed his mind about Catholicism? Almost certainly not. But he had come to a practical realization that it was possible to put doctrinal religious differences to one side when the need arose. One did not have to be defined by one's religious views.

But in the meantime, the credal idea of "true religion" has been succeeded by the secular idea of "political correctness"—very different, but inspired by a similar sense of "holier than thou" rectitude—which, at the time of this writing, is killing free speech and free thought throughout western society.

Roundup

The religious changes of this period are a watershed that has had a continuous effect down to the present day. The fact that Christianity has been a creed religion, while the old pagan state religion of Rome was a communal religion, is of crucial importance. Communal religions tend to be tolerant, while creed religions are intolerant.

Where a communal religion is in place, there is no distinction between religion and society, church, and state. You are a member of the religion by virtue of your membership of the society. Communal religions expect every nation, society or community to have its own religion. Proselytism is simply out of the question because to change your communal religion, you would need to change your community or nationality.

Resident aliens are an exception and may be allowed to continue to worship their homeland gods in their new society alongside the gods of that society. This is what happened in Rome. As a result, a number of foreign cults were allowed to live and flourish in Rome alongside the pagan Roman state religion. There was no cunning plan, as has been suggested by some writers, to absorb and suppress these cults. With one or two exceptions for political reasons, these cults were welcomed at Rome with open arms, and their worship, priests and temples remained in place until suppressed by Christianity. In pagan Rome, there was not just religious toleration but in fact freedom of religion. But did pagan Rome not persecute Christianity? Only very briefly and then for political, not religious, reasons.

Christianity itself, however, was intolerant of paganism, Judaism, and Christian "heresies" and made a determined and successful effort to crush paganism and the "heresies" while reducing Jews to second-class citizens. There has been a huge amount of pro-Christian special pleading lately among academic historians, which has distorted much of the recent writing on the period.

Christianity contributed indirectly to the "fall" of the Western Empire and also to the shrinkage of Byzantium in the face of an Arab onslaught. The rise of Christianity to dominance was a watershed in world history, resulting in the rise of Islam as a creed religion, the morphing of Judaism into a pseudo-creed religion, and in centuries of bloodshed from religious wars and persecutions,

11

The Pirenne Thesis

*Note: Except where otherwise indicated, all references in this chapter are to page numbers in: Henri Pirenne (1954) *Mohammed and Charlemagne*, tr. Bernard Miall, London: Allen & Unwin.

> *"When our first parents were driven out of Paradise, Adam is believed to have remarked to Eve: 'My dear, we live in an age of transition'."*
> —Dean William Inge (1929), Assessments and Anticipations, p. 261

A solitary streetcar wends its way slowly on its accustomed route through a devastated city. The place is Hiroshima, Japan, and the date August 6, 1945.

The atomic bomb has just been dropped. This image, from a contemporary film clip, is burned into my memory. What it symbolizes to me is that, even in the midst of cataclysmic change and destruction, there is still some continuity. Business as usual? Certainly not but continuity nevertheless. (periscopefilms.com documentary footage: https://www.youtube.com/watch?v=4yTMkrMugH4.)

The applicability of this image to the Later Roman Empire and early Middle Ages is not far to seek. The period is replete with change, including violent, even cataclysmic change, coupled with long-term continuity. A prime task of the historian is to try to identify and distinguish the wellsprings of continuity and change as clearly and objectively as possible.

What, then, about the epigraph at the head of this chapter? Though jocular, does it not contradict our searing image of the Hiroshima streetcar

---

Why Rome Fell: Decline and Fall, or Drift and Change?, First Edition. Michael Arnheim.
© 2022 John Wiley & Sons, Inc. Published 2022 by John Wiley & Sons, Inc.

by implying that every age is an age of transition? I believe that there is no necessary contradiction here because change is endemic to all historical periods but so is continuity.

Periodization

Historians are prone to seize upon particular dates and events as supposedly representing "turning points" and ushering in discrete "periods", a process that is now dignified with the title of "periodization". One such event, conventionally identified as a watershed, was the deposition of Romulus Augustus—whose name fortuitously combines that of the mythical founder of Rome with that of the founder of Roman greatness—as the last Western Emperor in 476. The significance of this date is more formal than real, as the Western provinces had already by then been dismembered and converted into "barbarian" kingdoms, but that does not mean that it has no significance at all.

One of the biggest problems with periodization is the tendency to use it to dole out praise and blame. If the Western Roman Empire "fell" in 476, or at any other time, who was to blame? The usual suspects are the "barbarians" and Christianity, which had become the official religion of the Roman Empire in 380.

The Pirenne Thesis

Henri Pirenne (1862–1935), a leading Belgian historian, approached the subject not from Rome's classical past but from the other end, the Middle Ages, and not from a political but from an economic point of view. Pirenne focused on the unity of the Mediterranean, which he believed remained a "Roman lake" well beyond the "barbarian" invasions until it was disrupted by the Islamic conquests of the seventh and eighth centuries. Western Europe became more self-contained, and its center of gravity shifted to Northern Gaul and Germany. In the absence of gold (one of the imports from the East supposedly cut off by the Islamic invasions), the government was forced to pay its leading supporters in land, paving the way to the feudal system. So, hey presto, in Pirenne's unforgettable words: "It is therefore strictly correct to say that without Mohammed, Charlemagne would have been inconceivable." (p. 234.) Q.E.D.

The "Pirenne Thesis", as it was soon dubbed, has the virtue of simplicity coupled with a semblance of objectivity while resting, however, on some evidential stretches and fancy footwork. As a result, it raised a cloud of controversy from the start and is still hotly debated today. What follows is a brief summary of the thesis, with my comments interspersed in italics:

- **The Mediterranean as a Roman lake:** "Of all the features of that wonderful human structure, the Roman Empire, the most striking, and also the most essential, was its Mediterranean character." (Pirenne 1954, p. 17.) *M.A. This is the foundation of Pirenne's whole thesis. The centrality of the Mediterranean is almost self-evident though the term "Mediterranean character" is something of an exaggeration as the importance of* mare nostrum *(our sea), as the Romans called it, is largely confined to trade and transportation, or, as Pirenne himself put it:* "Thanks to the Mediterranean, then, the Empire constituted, in the most obvious fashion, an economic unity." (Ibid., p. 19.)

- **Romanized Barbarians:** "And there was no longer any question of closing the Empire to the Barbarians.... The Barbarians were needed, as soldiers, and as agricultural labourers. They asked nothing better than to enter the service of Rome. Thus the Empire, on its frontiers, became Germanized in respect of blood; but not otherwise, for all who entered the Empire became Romanized.... No sooner did they enter it than they adopted its language, and also its religion: that is to say Christianity, after the fourth century; and in becoming Christians, in losing their national gods, and frequenting the same churches, they gradually merged into the population of the Empire. Before long almost the entire army was composed of Barbarians; and many of them, like the Vandal, Stilicho, the Goth, Gainas, and the Suevian, Ricimer, achieved fame as soldiers of the Empire." (Ibid., p. 19 f.) *M.A. While insisting on Mediterranean unity until the Islamic conquests, Pirenne does not gloss over the changes brought about by the "barbarians" two centuries before. He is here gearing up to his bold contrast between the relationship that the Germans had with the Empire and that of the Arabs in the seventh century and beyond. [Pirenne is even prepared to concede as an exception to his thesis a law of Valentinian and Valens prohibiting marriages between* Provinciales *and* Gentiles, *under penalty of death* (CTh 3.14.1.), *an exception which, if Ralph Mathisen is right, there was no need for Pirenne to make:* "The general policy, according to a law of 428 C.E., was that Roman marriages were to be ...between persons equal in status, with no law impeding them." (CTh 3.7.3 428) (Mathisen 2009, p. 149.) Mathison concludes that "...it appears that the Roman-barbarian marital law was one more example of, and quite consistent with, Late Roman laws regulating marriages between persons of different legal status." (Ibid.)

- **The Barbarian Invasions:** *Pirenne is even prepared to speak of "barbarian invasions"*: "As we know, in the course of the fifth century the Roman Empire lost its Western territories to the Germanic Barbarians.... What was the cause of its final failure?... The Barbarians did not spontaneously hurl themselves upon the Empire. They were pushed forward by the flood of the Hunnish advance, which in this way caused the whole series of invasions." (Pirenne 1954, p. 20 ff.)

- **"Loss of the Mediterranean":** "For the Empire this was the decisive blow," says Pirenne referring to the Vandal conquest of North Africa in 427, and he quotes Salvian's lament that with this catastrophe "...the very soul of the Republic was destroyed." (Ibid., p. 27.) But Pirenne does not stop there: "When in 439 Genseric captured Carthage—that is the great naval base of the West—and then, shortly afterwards, took possession of Sardinia, Corsica and the Balearics, the position of the Empire in the West was completely shaken. It had lost the Mediterranean, which had hitherto been its greatest weapon of defence." (Ibid.)

- **Romulus Augustulus:** Pirenne continues in the same vein: "The fall of Romulus Augustulus delivered Provence into the hands of the Visigoths (476); and from this moment the whole of the Western Mediterranean was lost." (Ibid., p. 31.)

- **"'Romania' had lost very little":** *M.A. After Pirenne's rehearsal of the litany of losses and disasters befalling the Roman Empire—including what he termed the loss of the Western Mediterranean— we come upon this passage, which is actually much more in keeping with his general thesis*: "In reality, 'Romania' had lost very little: a strip of frontier in the north, and Great Britain, where the Anglo-Saxons had taken the place of the more or less Romanized Britons, many of whom migrated to Brittany.... But on the whole, Germanization en masse had occurred only where the German language was retained. 'Romania' had disappeared only in the latest conquests of Rome, along the outer rampart which protected the Mediterranean: the two Germanies, part of the Belgiums, Rhetia, Noricum and Pannonia. Apart from this, 'Romania' had remained intact." (Ibid., p. 34 f.)

- **"[T]he Germans wished neither to destroy nor to exploit the Empire. Far from despising it, they admired it."** (Ibid., p. 36) Pirenne contrasts this with "...the Normans in England, the Musulmans wherever they appeared, and even the Romans in the conquered provinces....," which he cites as cases where "...a minority can transform a people when it wishes to dominate it effectively, when it has only contempt for it, regarding it as fit only for exploitation." (Ibid., p. 36.)

- **"What the Germans destroyed was not the Empire, but the Imperial government *in partibus occidentis* ('in the parts of the West.')"** (Ibid., p. 139.) Then, in a footnote, Pirenne lists the Roman features that were retained after the "barbarian" takeover of the West: the language, the currency, writing (papyrus), weights and measures, the kinds of foodstuffs in common use, the social classes, the religion—the role of Arianism has been exaggerated—art, the law, the administration, the taxes, the economic organization. (Ibid., note 535 to p. 139.)

- **"Islam shattered the Mediterranean unity."** "The German became Romanized as soon as he entered 'Romania.' The Roman, on the contrary, became Arabized as soon as he was conquered by Islam.... There was a clean cut: a complete break with the past.... The Mediterranean unity was shattered." (Ibid., 151 f.) *On the Arab conquerors' mindset*: "What they proposed was not, as many have thought, their conversion, but their subjection." (Ibid., p. 150 f.) "After the conquest of Spain, and above all of Africa, the Western Mediterranean became a Muslim lake.... Islam had shattered the Mediterranean unity which the German invasions had left intact." (Ibid., pp. 161–4.)

- **Mohammed and Charlemagne.** *Pirenne is now poised to square the circle*: "With the Carolingians, Europe finally assumed a new orientation. Until their advent Europe had continued to live the life of antiquity. But all the traditional conditions were overthrown by Islam.... The *coup d'état* by which they replaced the Merovingian dynasty which had subsisted since the invasions, was itself very largely explained by the closing of the Mediterranean by the Saracens." (Ibid., p. 187.) "It is characteristic of the times that the great senatorial families which had furnished the ecclesiastical personnel of the dioceses and the great lay officers of the administration became increasingly rare in this profoundly changed environment." (Ibid., p. 196 f.) In a note, he adds the following: "The last mention of a person of senatorial rank in Gaul dates from the beginning of the eighth century." (Ibid., n. 684 to p. 197.) "It is evident that from the middle of the seventh century, society was becoming rapidly de-Romanized, and the process was complete, or nearly so, by the beginning of the eighth century. It was the same population, but it was no longer the same civilization." (Ibid., p. 197.)

- **The Church and continuity:** "The Church, on the fall of the Imperial government in the West, had loyally cherished its memories of and its reverence for that Roman Empire whose organization was reflected in its own, with its dioceses (*civitates*) and its provinces. It not only venerated but in a certain sense it continued the Empire, since the upper ranks of its personnel were composed entirely of descendants of old senatorial families who remembered the Empire with respect and regret. The whole Church was subject to Roman law. It regarded the events of 476 as having no real importance. It had acknowledged the Emperor of Ravenna; it now acknowledged the Emperor of Constantinople.... The Emperor himself, when things were normal, regarded and venerated the Pope as the first patriarch of the Empire, having primacy over the patriarchs of Constantinople, Jerusalem, Antioch, and Alexandria." (Ibid., p. 210.)

- **Charlemagne, Irene, and Pope Leo III:** *M.A. In 781, as king of the Franks and Lombards, Charlemagne (748–814) was asked by the Byzantine Empress Irene for the hand of his daughter Rotrude for Irene's son, the Emperor Constantine VI, aged 10. In 788, Irene broke off the engagement and supported the Lombard pretender Adalgis against Charlemagne and the Pope. In 797, Irene deposed her son and, in true Byzantine style, had him blinded, declaring herself sole ruler. As neither Salic law (i.e. that of the Franks) nor Roman law allowed female rulers, Irene's power-grab was used by Pope Leo III as a pretext for declaring the imperial throne vacant, thus enabling him to crown Charlemagne as emperor on Christmas day 800 but only after Charlemagne had been raised to the purple, in Byzantine fashion, by popular acclamation.*

- **Mohammed and Charlemagne:** "Without Islam, the Frankish Empire would probably never have existed, and Charlemagne, without Mohammed, would be inconceivable." (Pirenne 2014, p 27.) He added more fully that "The Empire of Charlemagne was the critical point of the rupture by Islam of the European equilibrium. That he was able to realize this Empire was due, on the one hand, to the fact that the separation of East from West had limited the authority of the Pope to Western Europe; and, on the other, to the fact that the conquest of Spain and Africa by Islam had made the king of the Franks the master of the Christian Occident. It is therefore strictly correct to say that, without Mohammed, Charlemagne would have been inconceivable." (Pirenne 1954, p. 233.) *Whew! Pirenne has finally squared the circle. Or has he?*

The End of Mediterranean Unity?

Pirenne's thesis depends on the disruption of trans-Mediterranean trade after the Arab invasions, particularly in luxury goods, such as silk and spices, and also papyrus, and, not least, gold. But the evidence is not nearly as self-evident as Pirenne seemed to think. Pirenne asserts that in the second half of the seventh century navigation with the Orient "...came to an end in the whole of the Western Mediterranean" and that by the beginning of the eighth century "...[t]here was no longer any traffic in the Mediterranean, except along the Byzantine coast." (Ibid., p. 165.) He quotes Ibn-Khaldoun as saying that (with the exception of Byzantium) "...the Christians could no longer float a plank upon the sea."(Ibid., p. 165.) "The great port of Marseilles," adds Pirenne, "which had formerly been the principal emporium of Western trade with the Levant, was empty. The old economic unity of the Mediterranean was shattered, and so it remained until the epoch of the Crusades. It had resisted the Germanic invasions; but it gave way before the irresistible advance of Islam." (Ibid., p. 166.)

Yet, David Abulafia, Professor Emeritus of Mediterranean History at Cambridge, tells a very different story: "By the sixth century, the unity of the Mediterranean had been shattered; it was no longer *mare nostrum*, either politically or commercially. There have been attempts to show that the fundamental unity of the Mediterranean as a trading space, at least, survived until the Islamic conquests of the seventh century (culminating in the invasion of Spain in 711), or even until the Frankish empire of the incestuous mass-murderer Charlemagne acquired control of Italy and Catalonia. There have also been attempts to show that recovery began much earlier than past generations of historians had assumed, and was well under way in the tenth or even the ninth century. It would be hard to dispute this in the case of the Byzantine East...or in the case of the Islamic lands that by then stretched from Syria and Egypt to Spain and Portugal, but the West is more of a puzzle. It is hardly an exaggeration to say that some historians observe decline at the same moments that others detect expansion. To this one can sensibly answer that there was enormous regional variation; but the question remains when and whether the Mediterranean lost, and then recovered, its unity." (Abulafia 2011, p. 297.)

The Real Question

But is that really the question? Even from an economic point of view, the West developed along its own lines. Innovations such as the horse-collar and the three-field system of crop rotation revolutionized agriculture regardless of the unity or disunity of the Mediterranean. And as for the disappearance of papyrus imports from Egypt on which Pirenne and his supporters place great emphasis, papyrus was evidently still in use in Gaul until the mid-eighth century and until 1057 in the papal curia in Rome. It was replaced by parchment, which was not only cheaper but also stronger and more durable and far better suited to the Northern climate.

The real question is to do with change and continuity generally, and here we encounter several major differences between East and West:

- **Language:** East and West diverged markedly:
  - **East:** The language of the former Byzantine and Roman areas conquered by the Muslims gradually became Arabic—which it has remained ever since, with the exception of the Iberian peninsula (which was brought back into the Christian fold by the *Reconquista*, culminating in 1492). Greek, which had been the *lingua franca* of the Byzantine Empire, eventually died out in the conquered territories, except Greece and Cyprus.
  - **West:** With the exception of Britain and the most recently acquired frontier provinces (listed above), the former western provinces of the Roman Empire have all continued to speak Romance languages, i.e. languages derived from Latin, including modern Italian, Spanish, Catalan, Portuguese, French and Romanian. Of these, French, deriving as it does from the *langue d'oïl* of Northern France, the least Romanized part of Roman Gaul, is the only one with any significant Germanic lexical component. Paradoxically, however, English, an essentially Germanic language, has accumulated—whether directly or via French—an overlay of Latin-based vocabulary accounting for about sixty percent of its lexicon.
- **Government:** Here, too, there was a marked divergence between East and West.
  - **East:** From the beginning, the ruler of the Islamic Empire was styled *khalifah* (caliph), meaning politico-religious successor to the prophet Muhammad with authority over the whole Islamic world, viewed as a single *ummah* (nation, community.) But despite this, Islam is not a communal but a creed religion. (See below.) There have been only four major caliphates: the Rashidun Caliphate (632–661), the Umayyad Caliphate (661–750), the Abbasid Caliphate (750–1517), and the Ottoman Caliphate (1517–1924), after which the caliphate was abolished. There have also been some regional Islamic states that have claimed to be caliphates, including, most recently (1999–2019), a terrorist organization, known as Daesh, claiming to be a caliphate under the title of the Islamic State of Iraq and the Levant.
  - **West:** Though Charlemagne never laid claim to the Byzantine throne, his coronation was resented in Constantinople because the assumption in both East and West was that there could be only one emperor of Christendom. Nevertheless, the Byzantine Emperor

Michael I (r. 811–813) recognized Charlemagne as both *imperator* and *basileus* (the ordinary Greek word for "king," which, however, had long been used as the Greek term for "emperor" as well). With the establishment of the Holy Roman Empire (a term first used in 1254 for an "empire" made up largely of autonomous German states) by the papal coronation of Otto I in 962, the problem of the two emperors reared its head once again. Otto's son and successor, Otto II, actually married Theophanu, the niece of Byzantine Emperor John I Tzimiskes. But later there was a stand-off, with neither emperor recognizing the other. In 1204, the Fourth Crusade sacked Constantinople and replaced the Byzantine Empire with their own so-called Latin Empire, which lasted until 1261, while recognizing the suzerainty of the Holy Roman Emperor. Strangely, perhaps, the Ottoman conquerors of the Byzantine Empire in 1453, regarding themselves as successors to that state, only came round to recognizing the Holy Roman Emperor after several defeats in 1606. The Holy Roman Empire, derided by Voltaire as "neither holy, nor Roman nor an Empire," was finally disbanded under pressure from Napoleon in 1806. The latest attempt to establish a Europe-wide authority is the European Union, now comprising 27 states, the majority of which have a form of Civil Law, i.e. Roman-based law ultimately deriving from the *Corpus Juris Civilis* of Justinian (r. 527–565), a compilation of centuries-old Roman law.

Religion: In the areas conquered by the Arabs, Islam soon became the established religion and this has remained the case down to the present day except for Spain and Portugal, which were gradually brought back into the Christian fold by the *Reconquista*, culminating in 1492. The West, by contrast, was officially Christian from the Edict of Thessalonica of 380 onward, and remains essentially Christian to this day. Neither the conventional end of the Western Roman Empire in 476 nor the "barbarian" incursions broke the continuity except that some of the Germanic successor-states initially adopted "heretical" Arian Christianity rather than the orthodox Nicene variety until Visigothic Spain converted to orthodoxy in 589 and Lombardy in 671. Those parts of Europe that formed part of the Roman Empire have largely remained Roman Catholic, with Protestantism being found chiefly in the Germanic-speaking countries of Northern Europe.

Conclusion

Pirenne was undoubtedly right to stress the importance of the Islamic conquests of the seventh and eighth centuries though he probably placed too much emphasis on their supposed disruption of Mediterranean unity. Their real significance is the perpetuation down to the present day of the split of the Roman Empire into two, with the East (except mainly for Greece and the Balkans) becoming Muslim, and the West (except for North Africa) remaining Christian.

This has resulted in tension, to say the least, between the world's two biggest religions, something that was completely unknown in the whole of ancient history before Constantine. Wars were endemic in the ancient world—wars of conquest, territorial wars, dynastic wars, and internecine conflict, but not religious wars. Every nation, society or community had its own gods and religion. Religion and society were one. Your membership of the religion was an integral part of your membership of the community—which is why I label this type of religion "communal." Above all, your membership of the religion did not depend on acceptance of any creed or set of beliefs. And there was no proselytism. The idea of, say, a Babylonian missionary outreach to Phoenicia would have seemed preposterous because conversion to the Babylonian religion would have required membership of Babylonian society. Conversion was, therefore, unknown, with two exceptions: first and foremost, conquest, where the vanquished would be assimilated into the community and, with it, the religion of the conqueror; and very secondarily, a rare case, like that of Ruth in the Book of that name, of voluntary migration to a foreign country, again entailing assimilation into both the society and religion of the new community. (See Chapter 10.)

Religious toleration and indeed, more than that, namely religious freedom, was, therefore, the order of the day in the pre-Constantinian ancient world. Christianity changed that, for the simple reason that it was (and is) a creed religion, a religion that requires a new member to accept a particular creed, set of beliefs, or articles of faith and claims to have a lock on "salvation". But, you may say, what changed after Constantine? Had Christianity not existed for three centuries before his time? It had, indeed, and its history had been marked by doctrinal disputes from the start, but until (thanks to Constantine and his successors) Christianity became the dominant religion of the Empire, these disputes were internal, without impacting on the wider community. But is Christianity not a tolerant religion today? It is certainly true that most Christian countries in the world today have signed up to charters guaranteeing freedom of religion, but the missionary zeal of the numerous Christian denominations, sects, and groups is unabated, each one activated by the belief that it is the only "true" faith and holds the key to eternal salvation. Some Protestant evangelical Christians not only anathematize Roman Catholicism but even denounce the Pope as the "Antichrist," while the Papal Bull excommunicating Martin Luther in 1520 has never been revoked, and the Great Schism that has existed since 1054 between the Roman Catholic and Eastern Orthodox churches still remains unresolved. (See Chapter 10.) As for Christian attitudes to non-Christians, even *Lumen*

Gentium (The Light of the Nations), the "Dogmatic Constitution of the Church," one of the most "liberal" statements of Catholic belief, promulgated by Pope Paul VI in 1964 after a near-unanimous vote of the Catholic bishops assembled at the Second Vatican Council, makes it clear that non-Christians need to convert to Roman Catholicism in order to "attain to salvation": "Whatever good or truth is found amongst them [viz. Jews and Muslims] is looked upon by the Church as a preparation for the Gospel." (*Lumen Gentium*, Chapter II, §16.) How, then, can we account for the prevalence throughout the modern western world of charters of religious freedom? These did not originate from the Christian churches but rather from the spread of secular and even anti-clerical sentiments in the wake of the Enlightenment of the eighteenth century, the French Revolution, and, among other factors, Darwinian evolutionary theory.

When Islam became the dominant religion in the Eastern half of the former Roman world and beyond, this pitted two equally intolerant religions against each other: a double novelty for world history because Islam is also a creed religion, and, like Christianity, has internal doctrinal schisms as well as intolerance of other religions, coupled with a very active missionary outreach. (For an unvarnished view of the treatment of Jews and Christians under Islamic rule. (See Ye'or 2013.)

It was no coincidence that the Roman Empire with its tolerant communal religion should have been taken over and ultimately split between two inherently intolerant creed religions. Though Islam is very different from Christianity in many respects, it was clearly heavily influenced by it as well as by Judaism, and the Quran is replete with echoes of the Bible. Jesus is mentioned repeatedly in the Quran, and Mary is referred to more frequently than in the Christian Bible.

There is no indication that Pirenne attached "blame" on the Muslims for their conquests though some of his latter-day supporters have been accused of harboring anti-Islamic sentiments. (See Scott 2012; Whitehouse/Hodges, 1983.)

The intolerance of Christianity is stubbornly resisted by a coterie of writers who seem as concerned as any Christian apologist of the fifth century to deny any "blame" on the part of Christianity for the end of the Western Empire. One such writer, Peter Brown, is so anxious to wave aside any talk of Christian violence against paganism that, in one of his writings, he resorts to an elementary logical fallacy to do so. Citing the highly tendentious sociologist, Rogers Brubaker (whose 2006 book, *Ethnicity without Groups*, targets what Brubaker labels "Groupism" and "Constructivism"), Brown remarks, "Observers of recent ethnic conflict have concluded that acts of violence are not necessarily driven in the first place by a sharp sense of ethnic difference. Rather, it is the other way round.... We should read accounts of what we call 'Christian intolerance' in action in the later empire with this insight in mind. The destruction of pagan temples was as much an exercise in boundary definitions as it was the expression of a pre-existing Christian rage against paganism." (Brown 2013, loc 1089.) Whatever this phraseology may mean, ethnic conflict, which is what the Brubaker quote is about, is strictly irrelevant to religious intolerance and persecution. Those engaged in ethnic conflict do not aim to "convert" anyone to their own ethnicity, while religious and specifically Christian intolerance, hostility, and violence do indeed have that very objective. Brown's assertion is a good example of argument by false analogy and, moreover, as is shown in Chapter 10, there is no shortage of evidence of Christian intolerance.

Pirenne's focus on the Islamic conquests helps us to gain perspective on the wellsprings of continuity and change in the Mediterranean world and beyond over more than a millennium and a half. The following features stand out:

- **Universal empire:** A continuing ideal and, to a lesser extent, reality, in East and West alike, of a universal empire, or at least of an empire predominant over a large geopolitical area.
- **Law:** The predominance in Europe and former European colonies in Asia, Africa, and South and Central America of Civil Law, i.e. Roman-based law ultimately deriving from the *Corpus Juris Civilis* of Justinian (r. 527–565), a compilation of centuries-old Roman law.
- **Language:** The survival of Latin, in the form of the Romance languages, with a current total of some 900 million native speakers, in most of the former Western provinces of the Roman Empire, plus the paradoxical prevalence of Latin-based loanwords in English, with currently about 400 million native speakers and a further 1.1 billion speakers of English as a second language worldwide.
- **Religion:** A permanent sea-change in the fourth century replacing the tolerant communal Roman "pagan" religion with an intolerant creed religion, initially Christianity across the whole Mediterranean world, and from the seventh century, Islam, in most of the Eastern Mediterranean and beyond, resulting in the predominance in the present-day world of two essentially intolerant creed religions. But that is quite a different, much larger, and strangely neglected issue, as against the narrow question of whether Christianity can be "blamed" for the "fall" of the Western Empire by weakening the resolve of the Romans in the face of the "barbarian" threat. My own view on this narrower question exculpates Christianity of the charge for lack of sufficient credible evidence though the jury is still out on the reasons

for the lack of Roman opposition to the "barbarian" incursions. If this could be ascribed to any extent at all to the fracturing of society as a result of religious persecution, then Christianity cannot escape blame for the takeover of the Western Empire by the "barbarians" though I do not believe that doling out praise and blame should form any part of the historian's métier. (For more on the military issues, see Chapter 13.)

12

"Late Antiquity"

L ate Antiquity is a period label that originated with Peter Brown 1971 in his book titled *The World of Late Antiquity*. Initially sub-titled *From Marcus Aurelius to Muhammad*, the period covered was subsequently extended in both directions to run from 150 to 750. There is no agreement on the precise extent of Late Antiquity. However, despite the association of the word "late" with death and decay, its protagonists have staked out a claim for Late Antiquity as an autonomous period as neither a debased version of the Roman Empire nor a "Dark Age" of any kind. Rejecting the twin notions of "decline and fall" and "dark ages", the proponents of "late antiquity" depict it in a positive light and in glowing colors, comprising new and improved forms of art, culture, philosophy, religion, society, economics, and politics. What emerges is not only a thoroughly upbeat, positive picture of growth and creativity, but also the subjective view that all these developments were "good," and anything countering them "bad."

Late Antiquity: Some of the Chief Claims

This chapter evaluates some of the main claims made on behalf of Late Antiquity by its chief protagonist, Peter Brown:

- **"The barbarian invasions...brought no widespread destruction"**: There is least an admission here that there was such a thing as the "barbarian" invasions, and also, tacitly, that they brought

Why Rome Fell: Decline and Fall, or Drift and Change?, First Edition. Michael Arnheim.
© 2022 John Wiley & Sons, Inc. Published 2022 by John Wiley & Sons, Inc.

some destruction. These pretty basic admissions are only worth noting because the writer concerned is generally so determined to view Late Antiquity through rose-tinted spectacles.

- **"Realization...that there was nothing wrong about not being Roman":** This claim simply does not gel with the general lamentation, by Christians as well as pagans, on the sacking of Rome and other disasters.
- **"The sheer success of the post-Constantinian state":** Another claim that will not stand up to scrutiny and amounting to special pleading.
- **"No determination to use the laws to convert unbelievers":** The one incident singled out to prove this assertion does no such thing.
- **"No evidence for a generalized, and inevitable, trend toward the victimization of Jews in the post-Constantinian empire":** Contradicted by the evidence.
- **"Correct religion was the glory of the empire":** Yet another example of special pleading.
- **"Religious toleration was, at best, a fragile notion":** An erroneous assertion.
- **"The unnerving but mercifully brief reign of Julian":** A bald subjective judgment without any supporting arguments or evidence.
- **Themistius: "not for real":** A subjective judgment arising out of a mistaken understanding of the concept of religious toleration.
- **"Large bodies of polytheists simply slipped out of history":** An unconvincing attempt to minimize the severity of Christian intolerance.
- **"Christian intolerance has been overblown":** A charming but irrelevant anecdote to try to minimize the degree of Christian intolerance.
- **"The most striking feature of the fourth century was the ability of the upper classes to muffle religious conflict":** True to some extent but puzzlingly attributed to the Christian emperors' subservience to the church.

"The Barbarian Invasions Brought No Widespread Destruction."

This position Brown adopts from Christopher Wickham's "magnificent book, *Framing the Early Middle Ages: Europe and the Mediterranean 400–800*." "In Wickham's view," writes Brown, "barbarian invasions...

brought no widespread destruction. But, in one way, the barbarian invasions and the civil wars of the early fifth century did prove decisive. They broke the spine of the empire as a tax-gathering machine." (Brown 2013, loc. 812-843.)

Brown likewise invokes Guy Halsall's *Barbarian Migrations and the Roman West 376–568*, as telling "...the story of the fall of Rome as a change.... He does not find evidence of widespread destruction in the wake of imagined barbarian hordes. Nor does he find a catastrophic drop in the standard of living of the Roman populations. Still less does he find evidence of monolithic immigration into Roman territory." (Brown 2013, loc. 781.)

And what, according to Brown, was the cause of this "silent change"? "After centuries in which Rome had been the central point of reference for ideas of civilization, of proper conduct, and of proper gender relations, [relatively well-to-do men and women—Romans and barbarians alike] had begun to see that, despite the fears of many of them, there was nothing wrong about not being Roman." (Ibid., loc. 781.)

So, are we to replace "decline and fall" with a vague psychological shift? In fact, despite Brown's *imprimatur*, Halsall does *not* shy away from the concepts of decline and fall, making the point that between 376 and 476, "...the western Empire lost control, one by one, of its provinces. Whether this resulted from a weakening ability to project its power and make its writ run in distant regions, or to defend its territories by force, or to prevent local societies from breaking away from its political control, or all three at once, matters little. In all cases it is reasonable to call this a decline in effective imperial rule: again, a decline which was felt in the ways in which people organised their identities and their relationships, in short their world. The power of the western Roman Empire declined and, as a political institution, it fell." (Halsall 2007, p. 21.)

So, here we have the taboo phrase "decline and fall" from one of Brown's own allies, placing the emphasis on the loss of the western provinces "one by one". Peter Heather sums up his carefully researched narrative like this: "Any attempt to reconstruct fifth century events brings home just how violent the process was." (Heather 2006, p. 434 ff.)

Even Wickham found that the barbarian invasions and civil wars "did prove decisive" in breaking the spine of the empire as a tax-gathering machine. This is perhaps rather too narrow a focus, but with cause and effect reversed, it ties in with Halsall's three factors, which in turn are not unconnected with my findings as summarized in Chapter 5: that the aristocrats' powerful positions in the imperial service, coupled with their great wealth and landholding in the very provinces where they held office, sapped the strength of the central government in the West, weakening its ability to fend off the barbarians.

"Realization that There Was Nothing Wrong about Not Being Roman"

A silent change without any "widespread destruction" translates, according to Brown, into a new realization among "reasonably well-to-do" Romans and "barbarians" alike that "...there was nothing wrong about not being Roman." (Brown 2013, loc. 781.)

How then are we to explain the lamentation even of leading contemporary Christians on the Goths' sack of Rome in 410? As Peter Heather puts it, "The sources, without being specific, speak clearly of rape and pillage. There was, of course, much loot to be had, and the Goths had a field day." (Heather 2006, p. 191.)

Even Jerome (c. 342/347–420), living though he was in Bethlehem, was badly shaken: "But when the bright light of all the world was put out, or, rather, when the Roman Empire was decapitated, and, to speak more correctly, the whole world perished in one city, 'I became dumb and humbled myself, and kept silence from good words, but my grief broke out afresh, my heart glowed within me, and while I meditated the fire was kindled,'" (Jerome, Preface to Commentary on Ezekiel.)

Pagans naturally used the sack of Rome as a stick with which to beat the Christians. It must have seemed pretty obvious to them that this unprecedented event must have been divine retribution for abandoning Rome's ancestral tutelary gods, which had occurred not long before. This point was still being pressed by pagans, like the historian Zosimus, nearly a century later.

Christians, equally unsurprisingly, were quick to counter any such charges. Armed with Livy's *Ab Urbe Condita*, Augustine of Hippo (354–430) retorted in his *City of God against the Pagans* that Rome had suffered a number of disasters even before the existence of Christianity. Where were the pagan gods then? Surprisingly, perhaps, Augustine claimed that Rome owed its successes to the Christian God. His argument then takes a sharp turn, developing the old concept, found in the Book of Revelation, of the two cities, the Earthly City and the City of God. For all its glory, claims Augustine, Rome is but one of many earthly cities that have existed throughout history, and Christians' loyalties must be focused not on the earthly City but on the City of God, which is attainable only after death. (Aug. *Civ. Dei*, 2.18.)

A very different message is conveyed by the *Carmen de Providentia Dei* (Poem on Divine Providence), composed by an anonymous Christian poet in Gaul in 417: "You, who weep over overgrown fields, deserted courtyards and the crumbling terraces of your burnt-out villa, should you not rather shed tears for your own losses, when you look at the desolate recesses of your heart, the beauty covered over with layers of grime, and the enemy rioting in the citadel of your imprisoned mind?" (As cited by Heather 2006, p. 235.) The distressing picture painted here, which is unlikely to have been made up, is blamed on the Christians' own lapses into sin. But then comes a call to arms: "If any mental energy remains, let us shake off the servile yoke of sin...."

When Rome was sacked again in 455, this time by the Vandals, Peter Heather wrote, "...the damage sustained was more serious than in 410. Geiseric's Vandals looted and ransacked, taking much treasure and many prisoners back with them to Carthage, including the widow of Valentinian III, her two daughters, and Gaudentius, the surviving son of Aetius." (Heather 2006, p. 379, from a reconstructed version of Sidonius Apollinaris, Poem 7.) The destruction lasted fourteen days as compared to the three-day Gothic (or Visigothic) attack in 410.

The mention of Carthage is significant because the Vandals had already captured this important provincial center in 439. Ancient sources, such as Victor of Vita, Quodvultdeus, and Fulgentius of Ruspe give the impression of widespread destruction on the part of the Vandals in their conquest of North Africa where they established a kingdom that lasted from 429 to 533. However, this has been disputed by some modern archaeologists, who point out that, though Carthage's Odeon was destroyed, the grid street pattern survived and that some public buildings were renovated. This evidence may not be as telling as Andrew Merrills and others claim. (Merrills 2017, p. 10.) A street pattern can survive even when the buildings themselves do not, and renovation is not called for except in cases of dilapidation or destruction. As for Merrills's argument from the large volume of African Red Slip pottery discovered across the Mediterranean, this seems to have tailed off in the fifth century, which is when the area was ruled by the Vandals. (Hayes 1972.)

A contemporary chronicler known as Prosper of Aquitaine reports that on June 2, 455, Pope Leo I implored the Vandal King Genseric (or Geiseric) to abstain from murder and arson, and to restrict his men to pillage alone. (Muhlberger, 1986, pp. 240–44.) If this papal plea is historical, which seems likely, it would appear that the Vandals' reputation for "vandalizing" captured cities was already established before their sack of Rome.

The two sacks of Rome of 410 and 455, and the barbarian takeover of Gaul and North Africa are not, of course, the only examples of barbarian incursions, and there are some examples of amicable arrangements between Roman and barbarians. But there is enough evidence to show that the experience of many in the fifth century, in particular, was marked by violence, destruction and, yes, catastrophe. And, though the response to these upheavals varied, there is no indication that any of the writers concerned, whether Christian or pagan, felt, as Brown puts it, "...that there was nothing wrong about not being Roman." On the contrary, the idea of being anything other than Roman does not appear to have occurred to them. Even Augustine was ready to take credit on behalf of Christianity for Roman successes. And though, as an "Earthly City", Rome was inferior in his view to the "City of God" to which Christians should aspire, he also originated the theory of "just war", according to which violence in defense of right and justice, and against evil, is justified.

"The Sheer Success of the post-Constantinian State"

"The sheer success of the post-Constantinian state ensured that the edges of potential conflict were blurred in the golden glow of a God-given order." (Brown 1997a, p. 652.) It is not easy to unpick this opaque and elliptical language. But in what respect can the Roman Empire between 337 and 425 be described in such glowing terms?

- **Imperial succession:** Constantine's death in 337 ushered in a family feud, starting with the massacre of several senior family members followed by a free-for-all among his three sons lasting until 350, representing the signal failure of Constantine's carefully laid plans of dynastic succession. The ultimate victor, Constantius II (r. 337–361), had his cousin, the Caesar Gallus, executed in 354. And Constantius ended his days in military conflict with Gallus's brother, Julian (r. 361–363), whom he finally recognized on his deathbed as his rightful successor.
- **Court intrigues:** Gallus's death was really caused not by Constantius but by his chief eunuch, Eusebius, *praepositus sacri cubiculi* ("grand chamberlain," literally "director of the imperial bedchamber"), a position listed in the *Notitia Dignitatum* ("Official List of Offices") as next in importance to praetorian prefect. So close was he to the emperor that on Constantine's death he was able to hide the emperor's will. He exerted a great deal of influence on Constantius II, whose pro-Arian leanings he shared. Eusebius was only the first of a long list of eunuchs who occupied the same influential position.
- **Military weakness:** In 376, Goths displaced by the Huns requested permission to settle in the Roman Empire. Valens (r. 364–378), ruling the Eastern half of the Empire, agreed. But, after being mistreated and starved by the Roman military commanders in Thrace, the Goths rose up in revolt, leading to the Gothic War. In 378, Valens rashly attacked the Goths without waiting for the reinforcements sent by his Western brother-emperor Gratian to arrive. It was one of

the worst defeats in Roman history, in which Valens himself was killed, abandoned by his guards. This emboldened the Goths, heralding the sack of Rome in 410 and the eventual establishment, by 475, of a so-called Visigothic Kingdom covering most of the Iberian peninsula and modern southwestern France; and a Ostrogothic kingdom in Italy from 493 to 553.

- **"[T]he edges of potential conflict were blurred":** What potential conflict? And how were its edges "blurred"? The conflict referred to here is evidently *religious* conflict, which is assumed to have been narrowly averted as a result of the "sheer success of the post-Constantinian state." In fact, however, as is shown in Chapter 10, religious conflict was endemic in the post-Constantinian age and beyond, as a result of one thing and one thing only, namely the dominance of Christianity, which, as a creed religion, was inevitably and constantly rent by internecine conflict. All this was the product of the post-Constantinian state. If this is the "sheer success" of the Roman Empire after 337, it was success in fomenting, not preventing, religious conflict. In the thousand years of Rome's existence up to the time of Diocletian, there had *never* been any religious conflict. Instead, there was not just toleration but actual freedom of religious belief and worship. And, as is also shown in Chapter 10, persecution of Christianity had taken place on only a few occasions and for political, not religious, reasons.
- **"[I]n the golden glow of a God-given order":** Is this eulogistic phrase Peter Brown's own view of the period, or is it meant to represent contemporary opinion? Either way, it is a highly partisan impression. By no means all contemporaries would have shared this view, least of all pagans, Jews, or "heretics."

"No Determination to Use the Laws to Convert Unbelievers"

While enthusiastic for the triumph of Christianity, Brown is reluctant to attribute it to state persecution of non-Christians and is anxious to minimize the degree and effect of Christian intolerance. He singles out one incident to prove that, despite the proliferation of laws against Jews and pagans, there was no "...determination to use the laws to convert unbelievers." (Brown 1997a, p. 641.) The incident in question was a bishop's confiscation of a Jewish synagogue, which was followed by an edict issued (evidently at the request of the praetorian prefect Asclepiodotus) at Constantinople in 423 ordering compensation to the local Jewish community. (CTh 16.8.25.) "The edict was not well received by the Christians of Syria," Brown admits, but omits to mention three important points. Firstly, that Theodosius II actually rescinded the edict under the influence of a "holy man"; secondly, that this apparently conciliatory edict had a sting in its tail; and thirdly, that the Emperor thenceforth adopted a hostile attitude towards the Jews. Let us consider these three points one by one:

- **Intervention of a "holy man"**: The edict of 423 evidently evoked a virulent attack on the Emperor by the "holy man" (always written without the quotation marks by Brown) Simeon Stylites, who spent thirty-seven years of his life sitting on top of a column in the Syrian desert. Accusing Theodosius of becoming a "...friend, associate and abettor of the unbelieving Jews," the "holy man" threatened the Emperor with divine punishment for his supposedly serious transgression. (Syriac *Life of Simeon*, *Acta Martyrum et Sanctorum*, Vol. IV, p. 648 f.; Evagrius, Eccl. Hist. 1.13.) According to the *Life of Simeon*, the Emperor responded by revoking the offending edict, dismissing from his post the praetorian prefect who had pleaded the cause of the Jews and sending a humble reply to the "holy man." (See Torey/Stylites 1899, pp. 253–76.)
- **Sting in its tail:** The apparently conciliatory edict of 423 had a sting in its tail. For, after decreeing that "...in future no synagogues of the Jews anywhere are to be demolished or burned down," and that compensation is to be paid for any synagogues confiscated in the future, the edict adds sternly, "Moreover, no further synagogues are to be constructed, and the old ones are to remain in their present state of repair." (CTh 16.8.25.)
- **New hostility to Jews:** Less than two months later, another edict was issued calling upon "...those persons who commit many rash acts under the pretext of venerable Christianity" to refrain from "injuring and persecuting" Jews. "No person," it added, "shall seize or burn their synagogues." Here again an apparently conciliatory edict has a sting in the tail: prohibiting Jews from circumcising any Christian or ordering a Christian to be circumcised, presumably in order to convert him to Judaism. And, while the punishment laid down for this crime by Jews is harsh, proscription of goods and exile for life, there is absolutely no punishment laid down for Christians guilty of persecuting Jews, or seizing or burning synagogues. (CTh 16.8.26.) The latter part of the edict is puzzling. As a communal religion, Judaism did not engage in proselytism at all and was less than welcoming to any prospective convert. So, in what circumstances would a Jew be in a position to circumcise a Christian? Only if the Christian were a slave owned by the Jew. This would then be covered

by Jewish law, namely the commandment in Genesis 17:12–13 requiring every Jew to circumcise all males in his household, specifically including slaves, whether home-grown "...or bought with money of any stranger", thus making the slaves part of their master's family and community. Jewish circumcision of a Christian slave had already been outlawed by Constantine in 335, though the penalty in that law was only that the slave be given his freedom, so that the Jewish master lost his investment. (CTh 16.9.1.) In 339, the penalty was increased to death for the Jewish slave-owner. (CTh 16.9.2.)

"No Evidence for a Generalized, and Inevitable, Trend toward the Victimization of Jews in the post-Constantinian Empire"

As far as the Jews were concerned, Brown claims that, in an unspecified number of provinces, "Judaism retained its ancient prestige, to the annoyance of Christian preachers such as John Chrysostom at Antioch." (p. 643.) And, while admitting five incidents of "the destruction or appropriation of synagogues" in one generation after 388, he adds that "...these incidents should be seen in proportion. They do not in themselves amount to evidence for a generalized, and inevitable, trend toward the victimization of Jews in the post-Constantinian empire."(Brown 1997a, p. 643; Seaver 1952, p. 84.)

In fact, however, a series of laws deprived Jews of more and more rights, culminating in Theodosius II's Third Novel of 438 banning all Jews and Samaritans from holding any public or administrative office; prohibiting the building of any new synagogues; and imposing the death penalty on any Jew daring to convert to Judaism any Christian, whether slave or freeborn. Justinian's Code contained no fewer than 33 anti-Jewish laws, one of which put an end to the legal privileges enjoyed by synagogues as places of worship; another ordering synagogues to be converted into churches; and the reissue of an earlier law prohibiting Jews from testifying in court against a Christian (except, after 537, where a Christian was being prosecuted by the state).

Byzantine Jews were subjected to forced conversion under the Emperor Heraclius (r. 610–641), and to official persecution at intervals thereafter up to the reign of John Tzimiskes (r. 969–976). Unsurprisingly, the Byzantine Jews revolted against Heraclius and assisted the Persian Sassanids in their successful invasion and capture of the whole of Roman Egypt and Syria. And many Byzantine Jews also sided with the Arabs in their conquering wave starting in 634.

Jews fared no better in the West, where the anti-Jewish laws of the Theodosian Code were incorporated into the "barbarian" codes and also in Canon Law. As in Byzantium, so in Spain, the brutal treatment meted out to the Jews at the hands of the Christians impelled the Jews to side with the Muslims during the long series of wars between Christians and Muslims between 1000 and 1492 when those Jews who had not converted to Christianity were forcibly expelled.

The lowly and ever-declining status of the Jews, in East and West alike, under the post-Constantinian empire and beyond, was a far cry from the status that they had enjoyed under the pagan empire, as discussed in Chapter 10.

"Correct Religion Was the Glory of the Empire"

The concept of religious toleration is clearly an embarrassment to writers like Brown, for whom the triumph of Christianity was evidently one of the greatest, if not *the* greatest, achievement of "late antiquity." "Precisely because correct religion was the glory of the empire," opines Brown, "it had to be imposed in a manner that reflected the overwhelming dignity of the imperial power." (Brown 1997a, p. 644.) Is this the view of Christians of the time, or is it Brown speaking in his own person, or possibly both? The label "correct religion," or "true religion," was (and still is) shared by Christians of every stripe but referring to something different for each of the many competing brands of Christianity.

In what sense could Christianity (presumably, of the dominant variety) be described as "the glory of the empire"? As a creed religion, Christianity was inherently intolerant, a really important point that I have mentioned before but is thoroughly explained in Chapter 10. If, as seems to be the case, the characterization of this extremely intolerant religion as "the glory of the empire" is Brown's own opinion, it robs the term "glory" of any meaning and must simply be dismissed as yet further evidence of special pleading.

As for the view that this "correct religion," had to be "imposed" in a dignified manner is something of an oxymoron. How do you "impose" something on someone, which indicates an element of coercion, in a dignified manner? But a more serious problem with this remark is that it is simply not true but yet another example of special pleading and, as discussed in Chapter 7, of an overtly subjective and judgmental approach, which is hard to square with any canons of academic historical writing.

"Religious Toleration Was, at Best, a Fragile Notion"

The assertion about "the correct religion" having to be "imposed" on non-believers begs the question, Why? Even if Christianity really was the one and only "correct" or "true" religion, as each of its variants claims to be; and even if there actually *was* such a thing as a single "correct" or "true" religion, why could other religions not simply be allowed to exist alongside the dominant one? The reason is that intolerance is an inherent feature of creed religions but not of communal religions. Had Constantine picked a different mystery religion other than Christianity, whether that of Isis, Cybele, or Mithras (to mention but three), this problem would never have arisen, because none of those cults claimed the exclusive loyalty of their adherents—and, above all, did not even have a creed. So the concept of "correct" or "true" religion would have had no relevance. The same applies to the old Roman state religion itself. However, with Christianity as a creed religion, demanding exclusivity and claiming a monopoly on correctness or truth, toleration was inevitably a problem.

It is against this background that we must understand this remark of Brown's: "Religious toleration was, at best, a fragile notion. It contributed little to the working-out of codes of coexistence between the adherents of different religions." (Ibid., p. 643.) It is only because Christianity was a creed religion that religious toleration was "fragile," or, in other words, difficult to achieve. And, contrary to Brown, it was not religious toleration that stood in the way of "the working-out of codes of coexistence"; it was Christianity itself that blocked peaceful coexistence. Recognizing the absence of toleration under the Christian emperors, Brown tries to sweep the whole idea of religious toleration under the rug: "The modern issue of toleration was swallowed up in a specifically late Roman insistence on civility." (Ibid., p. 644.) Toleration is here conveniently labelled a "modern issue," presumably meaning that it was irrelevant to the fourth and fifth centuries, without any reason being given for this. And then comes yet another of the fine-sounding vague phrases with which Brown's writings are peppered. After toleration is swept under the rug, an attempt is now made to bury it completely under the vague but false notion of "civility". The implication of this is that intolerance was justifiable because it was dished up in such a genteel manner. This not only makes little sense in itself but also happens to be untrue. Just as the imposition of Christianity was not performed with any "dignity," (see above), so religious intolerance and, we might add, persecution was not dished up with any civility, but instead with a torrent of abuse.

Far from being a fragile notion, religious toleration had been the hallmark of Roman religious life for a thousand years before Constantine. And not just toleration or tolerance, which implies grudging permission for people to worship religions other than the dominant one but, for the most part, *freedom of religion*. (See Chapter 10.)

"The Unnerving but Mercifully Brief Reign of Julian"

This bald and unbridled attack is not attributed to anyone, so we can only conclude that it represents Peter Brown's own personal opinion. And, as Julian is best known as an Apostate from Christianity and as an avid advocate for paganism, we can safely assume that Brown's hostility toward him is not unconnected this. The full quotation is as follows: "The fourth century was the Age of Authority *par excellence*. With the exception of the unnerving but mercifully brief reign of Julian, this authority supported the Christian church." (Ibid., p. 638.)

The terms of opprobrium used here are strong indeed. "Unnerving," means worrying or frightening? And "mercifully brief" implies divine disfavor for Julian. Julian's religious reforms and planned reforms certainly were highly controversial, and Christians may well have been apprehensive, but others, particularly members of the upper classes, welcomed a return to the old dispensation, which is what Julian set as his goal. However, by contrast with leading Christians like Augustine of Hippo, whose goal it was to eliminate paganism altogether, Julian never threatened the existence of Christianity, only its dominance and its persecution of non-Christians and "heretics." This is made clear by his edict guaranteeing freedom of religion to all, including "heretical" Christian sects. (Amm. 22.5.4.)

Julian's personal initiation into three separate pagan cults, including that of Mithras, as well as his planned rebuilding of the Jewish Temple in Jerusalem, indicate that he had no intention for the Roman state religion to absorb, smother or destroy rival forms of worship, but that, on the contrary, he looked forward to a return to the traditional freedom of religion, allowing all forms of worship to flourish without let or hindrance.

Brown's blatant subjective and judgmental characterization of Julian must take its place with *Williamanmary was a Good King* and other overtly judgmental characterizations held up to ridicule in that wonderful spoof history textbook, *1066 And All That* (1930). Complete objectivity may well be an unattainable goal, as E.H. Carr maintained (Carr 1961), but that does not exempt historians from at least making the attempt. Above all, purely subjective personal opinion, with its inevitable distortions, is a poor foundation upon which to construct any kind of reliable historical interpretation.

Academics, of course, have political and religious opinions, just like everybody else, but is it really fitting for these opinions to obtrude themselves upon their academic writings? With the best will in the world, academics may not be able entirely to prevent their prejudices from seeping in and influencing their writings. But what we have here is a blatant display of such views, without any attempt at justification. And this passage is far from isolated among the writings of the author in question, for whom the triumph of Christianity is clearly one of the greatest, if not *the* greatest, achievement of late antiquity.

"Slow Shift from One Form of Public Community to Another"

As Brown puts it in another of his writings: "During the late antique period there was a slow shift from one form of public community to another—from the ancient city to the Christian church." (Brown 1987, p. 1.) The use of "community" here is misleading. The old Roman pagan state religion, in common with most religions in the ancient world, was a communal religion, meaning that membership of the religion was not separate but an integral part of membership of the society or community concerned. Christianity, by contrast, is a creed religion, meaning that membership depends on acceptance of the specific creed or set of beliefs of the particular Christian denomination, sect or grouping concerned. Which is why Brown's characterization of "late antiquity" as a shift toward "the Christian church" as *the new* "public community" is so far from the mark. It glosses over the fact that many groups were excluded from the "community" of "the Christian church," such as Jews, surviving pagans, and (from the time of Muhammad) Muslims, not to mention the members of the large number of "heretical" Christian churches and sects. It also ignores the fact that many people, particularly in the West, defined their identity in terms of class or status group, nation, region or locality rather than as members of "the (Catholic) Church," and that there was a good deal of rivalry between secular rulers and the Papacy on the selection of bishops and abbots, which eventually in the eleventh century blew up into full-scale confrontation between Holy Roman Emperor and Pope in the so-called Investiture Contest (1076–1122).

Themistius: "Not for Real"

Brown's hostility to Julian is matched by his attack on the pagan orator, philosopher, and statesman Themistius (317-c. 390), who was in the good graces not only of Julian but also of a number of Christian emperors.

Characterizing Themistius as "not for real" and as "...a licensed maverick in an otherwise deadly serious class of persons", Brown remarked that Themistius "...usually made his appearance when the emperor was intending to back down from a course of action that had proved unfeasible or unpopular." (Brown 1995, p. 36 f.) Themistius's speeches on imperial policy "...were not resonant statements of principle. They were usually no more than making the best of a bad job." (Ibid., p. 37.) On the basis of a speech of Themistius's enabling the Emperor Valens to admit failure in negotiations with the Gothic king Athanaric, Brown rounds on two speeches by Themistius, one addressed to the Emperor Jovian in 363, and the other to Valens in 377, advocating religious toleration. "On both occasions," remarks Brown, "the context of Themistius' speech cancelled out its content." (Ibid., p. 37.) This is a *non sequitur* from the speech on the Gothic negotiations. In fact, the question of religious toleration was very topical in the immediate aftermath of Julian's reign, and, after initially re-enacting Constantius II's anti-pagan legislation, Jovian apparently issued his own edict of toleration, which has not survived, so we cannot be sure what it said. Themistius was, therefore, faced with a delicate task and used the ingenious argument, as if from a Christian standpoint, that the Christian God had made human beings free to adopt whatever form of worship they preferred and that Christianity and paganism were really just two aspects of the same universal monotheistic religion. (Themistius, Or. 5.)

As a pagan, Themistius saw religion as essentially communal, and the argument that he advanced is surprisingly similar to that of the Jewish Book of Jonah, which Themistius is unlikely to have encountered. Jonah, according to that book, is ordered by God to go to Nineveh, the capital of Assyria, the worst enemy of the Jewish people, and preach atonement for sins. As a Jew, Jonah is most reluctant to give the enemy an opportunity for divine forgiveness. So, he tries to run away, finds himself in the belly of a whale (or "big fish") and is then forced by God to go to Nineveh and preach. He reluctantly preaches to the people of Nineveh: "Repent, or you will be destroyed in forty days." To Jonah's utter dismay, the Ninevites repent and are forgiven by God. At no point is there any suggestion that the Ninevites should convert to Judaism. Jonah goes into a deep sulk, and God then points out to him that the Ninevites are just as much his creation as are the Jews. It is a parable with a universalist message. Each nation has its own religion and its own gods, but there is a single universal Creator.

Themistius was very courageous to adopt this kind of appeal to Christian emperors, but it was doomed to failure when confronted by the claim made by every Christian denomination to have a monopoly of truth and the sole key to salvation.

"[L]arge Bodies of Polytheists... simply Slipped Out of History"

While characterizing the triumph of Christianity as the glory of the empire, and dismissing religious toleration as a fragile notion, Brown is nevertheless anxious to minimize the severity of Christian intolerance:

> "Having, in 423, been declared by the emperor Theodosius II not to exist, large bodies of polytheists, all over the Roman empire, simply slipped out of history. They continued to enjoy, for many generations, the relatively peaceable, if cramped, existence which, only two centuries after the reign of Theodosius II, would fall to the lot of Christians themselves in another great Near Eastern empire, raised up in the name of one God—that of Islam. As a result, the religious landscape of the Mediterranean continued to be characterized by a patchwork of religious communities.... Rather than becoming uniformly 'Christianized', the Roman empire remained a land of religious contrasts.... Religious coercion on a large scale was mainly practised by Christians on other Christians.... [T]he imperial declaration of the triumph of the church posed the issue of coexistence with non-Christians in an acute form." (Brown 1997a, p. 641 ff.)

The train of thought in this passage would appear to run along the following lines, *with my comments in italics*:

- Though polytheism (i.e. paganism) was declared in 423 to have been eradicated, so mild or lax was the coercion brought to bear against it that polytheism continued to exist quietly "for many generations". *M.A.: This is a tacit admission of the failure of Christianity to persuade many pagans to convert, who then continued to practice their ancestral religion under the radar, which is what "slipped out of history" presumably means.*
- The existence of polytheists under Christianity was no worse than that of Christians under Islam. *M.A. The point here appears to be that Islam was no more tolerant of Christianity than Christianity was of polytheism though it is hard to see how this justifies the Christian treatment of polytheism. Christians (and Jews) were given* dhimmi *status (protected person) status in return for payment of a special tax known as the* jizya. *This status carried with it certain privileges (like the right to eat pork and drink alcohol), but it was generally inferior to the status enjoyed by Muslims.*
- As there was no uniform Christianization, the Roman Empire "... remained a land of religious contrasts." *M.A. This is an attempt to claim for the intolerant Roman and Byzantine states the same sort of*

religious diversity that had actually existed in Rome for many centu-
ries before Constantine. In reality, of course, the two situations were
like chalk and cheese. Traditional Roman diversity was a product of
religious toleration, or rather, of freedom of religion, whereas the
diversity under the Christian empire was diversity malgré lui *(diver-*
sity without toleration).

- There was more coercion against "heretics" than against polytheists. *M.A. This was probably true, but that is cold comfort to polytheists.*
- Once Christianity became the sole recognized religion of the empire,
  coexistence with non-Christians became a problem. *M.A. Coexistence*
  of multiple religions was not a problem before Constantine, so why
  now? Only because Christianity, as a creed religion, claimed a monop-
  oly of truth and, therefore, felt impelled to force everyone to toe the
  line, not just the Christian line but the line of the particular brand of
  Christianity that was dominant.

"Christian Intolerance Has Been Overblown"

So anxious is Peter Brown to minimize the seriousness of Christian
intolerance that he resorts to a lengthy, but less than persuasive, argument by analogy, based on a charming anecdote about his three-year-
old nephew's first visit to the zoo: "He had seen pictures of elephants,
giraffes, lions and walruses. But the only living animal that he had actually seen was his own pet cat, Teddy. Naturally, he assumed, therefore,
that all animals were the same size as that cat—and, consequently, that
they were smaller than himself: a flattering assumption. The fact that
the animals in the zoo were all of very different sizes—some, indeed,
immeasurably larger than himself—came as a great surprise to him."
(p. 29.) The object of this twenty-five-page exercise was to counteract
what Brown considered to be an exaggerated view of Christian intolerance: "Religious intolerance is a phenomenon that bulks large in any
history of late antiquity, to such an extent that it colours our perception
of the entire quality of the age." (Ibid.) Referring to the reign of
Theodosius I (379–395), Brown admits that "In this period, violence
against pagan sites was widespread. It was purposive and vindictive.
The hands and feet of pagan statues were broken; their faces and geni-
tals were mutilated; sacred precincts were 'purged' by fire. Yet, our
repelled fascination with such actions should not lead us to amplify
them unduly. Deliberate acts of desecration do not necessarily betray
the presence of uncontrollable multitudes. They may have been the
work of a determined few, briskly performed, possibly even so as to
avoid the mobilisation of a larger crowd" (Ibid., p. 49.) Brown does not

appear to realize that his desperate attempt to tone down the picture of Christian intolerance actually has the opposite effect. It is precisely the lead taken by highly respected Christian leaders in activating the extreme irrational, hatred-filled persecution of pagans, Jews, and heretics that makes this persecution so serious. Among the best-known examples of this are the rabid anti-Jewish rant of Bishop Ambrose of Milan against Theodosius over the burning down of the synagogue in Callinicum; the anti-pagan "depredations," as even Brown calls them, of another "saint," Shenoute of Atripe in the 420s; and the menacing letter by the "holy man" Simeon Stylites, yet another "saint" prevailing upon Theodosius II to revoke an order to Christians to restore to the Jews all the synagogues that had been taken from them. (See Chapters 4 and 5.) It is disquieting to find that, in waxing lyrical over Simeon Stylites (Brown 1995, p. 65 ff), Brown completely omits all mention of the major anti-Jewish policy role adopted by this "holy man" (never encased in quotes by Brown.) Zoo incident: Brown, 1995, pp. 29–54.

The fact that Peter Brown's little nephew *under*estimated the size of the zoo animals does not make it any more likely that the degree of Christian intolerance and persecution has been *over*estimated!

"[T]he Ability of the Upper Classes to Muffle Religious Conflict"

"The most striking feature of the fourth century was the ability of the upper classes to muffle religious conflict.... They tended, instinctively, to emphasize what they had in common—a common upper class culture and a common loyalty to the emperor." (Brown 1997a, p. 646.) There is a certain amount of truth in the common upper class culture, which bridged religious differences though it is necessary to distinguish between East and West, which Brown does not do here.

And it is important to stress that there was nevertheless a good deal of religious conflict as Brown admits by mentioning the "...destruction of temples throughout Syria in 386, the burning of the synagogue at Callinicum in 388, and the spectacular end of the Serapeum of Alexandria in around 391...." plus Theodosius I's policy of allowing "...the vehemence of local peer-groups, the Christian bishops and monks, to have a free hand, with occasional spectacular results that were remembered as decisive in later Christian sources." (loc. cit.)

But it is a *non sequitur* to attribute the common culture of the upper classes to the Christian emperors' subservience to the church. As Brown himself puts it: "One fact is indisputable. The late Roman revolution in government, which had placed the authority of the emperors at the service of the church, had, at the same time, created a governing class whose culture owed little or nothing to Christianity." (Ibid., p. 651.)

Aristocratic Ethos

The real reason for the shared upper class "culture", perhaps better termed "aristocratic ethos", in the West had nothing to do with the hand-in-glove relationship between the Christian emperors and the church. In the West there was an established old senatorial aristocracy. As was seen in Chapters 3 and 4, Constantine initiated a policy of appointing members of this class to high office, and this policy was continued by his successors. But it applied only to the West. The eastern empire, based in Constantinople, lacked anything resembling a hereditary aristocracy for several centuries. Holders of high government office there were mostly parvenus and eunuchs. The policy of appointing aristocrats in the West, a return to an older dispensation, does not appear to have had anything to do with religion, but was evidently motivated simply by the entrenched local power and influence, coupled with great wealth and landed estates, with which this class was endowed. With their ancestral ties to the Roman state religion in the form of priesthoods and other honorific positions both in Rome and in the Western provinces, members of the senatorial aristocracy were much less likely to have been Christians than their counterparts in the East, where the main strength of Christian numbers lay, and who in any event lacked ties to the old Roman traditions.

It would be hardly surprising if the "culture" of the senatorial aristocracy in the West "...owed little or nothing to Christianity", because this class was steeped in traditional Roman culture, including the ancestral Roman state religion. It is a complete *non sequitur* to attribute their non-Christian culture as Brown does to "the late Roman revolution in government, which had placed the authority of the emperors at the service of the church."

Aristocratic Conversion to Christianity

Of course, there came a time when the Western aristocracy converted to Christianity. This inevitably took place over an extended period, but the dating of this development is disputed. In 1971, Professor Werner Eck established on the basis of a prosopographical study that the senatorial aristocracy was solidly pagan in the early fourth century and that conversion to Christianity took place largely in the second half of the century, and particularly in the reign of Theodosius I (379–395) and his successors. (Eck 1971.) This was confirmed by the massive prosopographical doctoral dissertation of Raban von Haehling, published in 1978. (von Haehling 1978.) This position was attacked by T.D. Barnes in 1999, who sought to show that conversion of the senatorial aristocracy started much earlier in the fourth century, and also that Constantine's pagan appointees were fewer than had previously been believed. (Barnes 1995.) Yet, in his "revision" of von Haehling's figures, Barnes places in the Christian column not only those who are attested as Christians but also those who are "...probably to be regarded as Christian" while his pagan column is restricted to those "who are attested as pagan." However, even Barnes has to admit that there was a large majority of pagan appointees to high office under Constantine's youngest son, Constans (r. 337–350): no fewer than 12 out of 14. (Barnes 1995, p. 145.) Barnes tries to explain this away by suggesting that, "While that may reflect the strength of paganism among the senatorial aristocracy of Rome and Italy, it also reflects the weakness of Constans as a ruler and, in all probability, an implicit decision to allow the Senate more influence than it had enjoyed under Constantine". (Ibid., p. 144.) The strength of the senatorial aristocracy does indeed correlate with weak imperial power though the latter is more likely to be a result rather than a cause of the former. Constans, who was an able general, was not a particularly weak ruler to begin with. If, as Barnes reluctantly admits, Constans' high pagan figures "...may reflect the strength of paganism among the senatorial aristocracy of Rome and Italy", it is inconceivable that the strength of paganism among them would have been less under Constantine. Christianity was on a positive trajectory, especially after Constantine's conversion. There was no likelihood of senators, or anyone else, reverting to paganism after converting to Christianity except possibly later on during the brief pagan revival under the Emperor Julian between 361 and 363. And, even on Barnes's revision of von Haehling's figures, there are six "attested pagans" as against nine "attested or probable" Christians for Constantine between 324 and 337.

One of the problems with religious statistics in this period is that the religious affiliations of many appointees are unknown and that there are many other office-holders even whose names, let alone religious affiliations, are unknown. Of the total of 189 senatorial high office-holders for the period 324–361 in Barnes's revision, the religious affiliations of 63, or one third, are unknown, and even the names of a further 64 are unknown. So, no conclusions can be reached on the religious affiliations of two-thirds of the senatorial office-holders of this period.

Michele Salzman's figures show that under Constans and Constantius II, covering the period 337 to 361, 20.2 percent of (unspecified) high office-holders in the West were pagans, as against 13.7 percent who were Christian, and in the period 392 to 423, 22.1 percent were pagan, as against 54.7 percent who were Christian.

Pagan Survival among the Senatorial Aristocracy

Even at the very end of the reign of Theodosius I, we have unmistakable evidence that paganism was still alive and well among the senatorial aristocracy. According to both the Christian poet Prudentius and the pagan historian Zosimus, in 394, Theodosius visited Rome and called a meeting of the Senate at which he urged its members to "cast off their previous error," namely paganism, and convert to Christianity, "... which promises deliverance from all sin and impiety." According to Prudentius, the Senate then voted to approve this suggestion while Zosimus writes that "In an oration, he exhorted them to relinquish their former errors, as he termed them, and to embrace the Christian faith, which promises absolution from all sins and impieties. But not a single individual of them would be persuaded to this, nor recede from the ancient ceremonies, which had been handed down to them from the building of their city, and prefer to them an irrational assent; having, as they said, lived in the observance of them almost twelve hundred years, in the whole space of which their city had never been conquered, and, therefore, should they change them for others, they could not foresee what might ensue." (p. 86 Zosimus 4.59; Prudentius, Contra Symmachum 1.506-523; Salzman 2004, loc. 92.)

It is not certain whether there is any truth in either of these accounts, but though they appear diametrically opposed to each other, they have one very important feature in common. In both, Theodosius felt it necessary to try to persuade the senators to convert to Christianity, which would hardly have been necessary unless there had been a strong pagan contingent among them.

Shortly before this date, the historic Altar of Victory had been restored by the "usurper" Eugenius (r. 392–394) after it had been removed by Gratian in 382. Eugenius was at least nominally Christian, and had apparently been reluctant to restore the Altar. The fact that he did so just goes to show the strength of pagan opinion in the Senate at the time and, not surprisingly, earlier. The Altar of Victory had stood in the curia, or senate-house, since 29 BCE, to celebrate Augustus's victory over Antony at Actium. It was first removed by Constantius II in 357, restored by Julian, and removed again by Gratian in 382. In 384, after

Gratian's death, Quintus Aurelius Symmachus, a staunch pagan who was Urban Prefect of Rome at the time, appealed to Valentinian II to restore the Altar. (Symm. Rel. III.) His request was strongly opposed by Ambrose, Bishop of Milan, and Symmachus was rebuffed by the Emperor. Further unsuccessful petitions were addressed to Theodosius I, who instead banned all pagan worship by an edict issued in 391. In 403, the statue of the winged Victory (presumably without its altar) was still in the Curia, according to the pagan poet Claudius Claudianus. (Claud. VI Cons. Hon. 636.)

Round-up

"The most striking feature of the fourth century was the ability of the upper classes to muffle religious conflict.... They tended, instinctively, to emphasize what they had in common—a common upper class culture and a common loyalty to the emperor." (Brown 1997a, p. 646.) As discussed above, it is a fallacy to attribute to the Christian emperors' subservience to the church the existence of a common upper class culture in the West. And, it is also wrong to suggest that religious conflict was "muffled." On the contrary, it was actually encouraged and fomented by the intolerance or, indeed, persecution of "heretics," pagans, and Jews by Christian emperors themselves and their vituperative edicts—and "saintly" Christian "holy men" and bishops.

Though "late antiquity" is something of a movable feast, sometimes taken as starting as early as 200 or even 150, one of its most important features is the triumph and dominance of Christianity, which has continued in Europe down to the present day. Another important feature of the period was the rise of Islam in the seventh century, the product in many respects of both Judaism and Christianity. From Judaism it adopted the strict monotheism that has characterized it ever since, with Muhammad being greatly revered as a prophet but never regarded as supernatural while following the Christian model in becoming a creed religion, with inherent intolerance, both of "heretics" and of members of other religions.

Running through Brown's writings on "late antiquity" is a strong streak of special pleading, denying any image of "catastrophe," and rejecting the traditional picture of "decline and fall" of the Roman Empire in the West in favor of a thoroughly positive, upbeat portrayal of "late antiquity" as essentially a "Good Thing."

This raises two questions. First, how accurate is Brown's highly optimistic picture of the period? As indicated in this chapter, a number of his assertions will not stand up to scrutiny, including the following:

- The fundamental denial of "catastrophe"
- The assertion of "the sheer success of the post-Constantinian state"
- The claim that "...the edges of potential (religious) conflict were blurred" by this "sheer success" "in the golden glow of a God-given order." In fact, the dominance of Christianity only intensified religious conflict, which was fomented by Christian intolerance orchestrated by the Christian emperors themselves. As for the golden glow of a God-given order, this is a highly partisan view, expressed in the emotive language of eulogy.
- The attempts to minimize the severity of Christian intolerance
- The dismissal of religious toleration as "at best a fragile notion", when religious toleration, or indeed, freedom of religion, had been in force for a thousand years before Constantine, the few apparent exceptions to it being motivated by politics, not religious intolerance

The second question raised by Brown's approach to "late antiquity" is whether it is appropriate for an academic treatment of a subject to label a period, event, institution or a person as either "Good" or "Bad." The obvious danger of such an approach is that it justifies a partisan approach and special pleading, which is in evidence in abundance in Brown's writings on "late antiquity." The writings of my late mentor and doctoral supervisor, A.H.M. ("Hugo") Jones, can serve as an example here. Whatever his personal political or religious views may have been, it is quite impossible to detect them from his writings, which, I believe are all the more admirable for this. (See the Prologue to Part II of this book.)

13

Assassination or Accommodation?

The dissolution of the Roman Empire in the West remains one of the most highly controversial issues in history. Most empires have fallen either as the result of conquest by a rival power or under pressure from indigenous subject populations. Neither of these models fits the West Roman case. Rome did meet with a certain amount of resistance from local populations while it was building its empire. Britain and Gaul immediately spring to mind. And pockets of resistance occasionally flared up during the Roman occupation, notably in Judea. But, for the most part, Roman rule came to be not only well tolerated but also welcomed, and there was no prouder boast than *Civis Romanus sum* (I am a Roman citizen) as famously declared by Paul of Tarsus.

Did the Western Empire Come to an End?

Most writers on the period would agree that there came a time when the Roman Empire in the West ceased to exist and was replaced by a patchwork of "barbarian" kingdoms. There is considerable disagreement, however, on the significance and degree of disruption occasioned by this change and also, whether the disruption, if any, was a cause or effect of the dissolution of the Western Empire. Opinions range all the way from André

Why Rome Fell: Decline and Fall, or Drift and Change?, First Edition. Michael Arnheim.
© 2022 John Wiley & Sons, Inc. Published 2022 by John Wiley & Sons, Inc.

Piganiol's oft-quoted verdict of "assassination" to some modern writers' picture of the takeover of the Western Empire by "barbarians" as "accommodation," or even as settlements that took place "in a natural, organic, and generally eirenic manner." In between these two extremes comes the picture painted by the adherents of the school of Late Antiquity, replacing images of "decline", "crisis", or "catastrophe" with neutral or even positive terms like "change", "transition", or "transformation". (Ward-Perkins, Bryan, p. 4 ff.) Here are examples of some of these different takes:

- **Piganiol:** "La civilisation romaine n'est pas morte de sa belle mort, elle a été assassinée." (Roman civilization did not die a natural death: it was assassinated.) These are the final words of André Piganiol's *L'Empire Chrétien*. (Piganiol 1947, p. 732.) Without ignoring internal weaknesses, this sweeping conclusion appears to make the unwarranted equation of the end of the Western Empire with Roman civilization as a whole.

- **Jones:** "Hugo" Jones's monumental *Later Roman Empire* (1964) reached a similar conclusion, though specifically confined to the Western Empire, and couched in rather more prosaic language: "[D]irectly or indirectly, it may be plausibly argued, barbarian attacks probably played a major part in the fall of the West." (Jones 1964, p. 1027.) "[W]hile the Western parts were being parcelled out into a group of barbarian kingdoms, the East stood its ground," from which Jones concludes that "the empire did not, as some modern historians have suggested, totter into its grave from senile decay, impelled by a gentle push from the barbarians." (Ibid., 1026 f.) Jones's final sentence is: "The internal weaknesses of the empire cannot have been a major factor in its decline."(Ibid., p. 1068.)

- **Goffart:** Walter Goffart rejects the whole idea of "barbarian conquests", explaining the lack of Roman resistance by claiming that what the new "barbarian" masters obtained was not actual land but tax revenues: "At various dates in the fifth century, Visigoths and Ostrogoths, as well as Burgundians, settled in Roman Gaul and Italy. The settlements apparently took place peacefully, without visibly disturbing the resident landowners and cultivators. This was no conquest and forcible peopling; the initial steps were taken under the auspices of Roman generals." (Goffart 2009, p. 119.)

- **Eirenic settlements:** "Nearly all of the processes of change discussed in this volume, even the settlement of the barbarian peoples, took place in a natural, organic, and generally eirenic manner." (Mathisen/Shanzer (eds.) 2011b, p. 1.)

- **Late Antiquity:** "The so-called 'barbarian invasions' of the early fifth century.... were not perpetual, destructive raids; still less were they organized campaigns of conquest. Rather, they were a 'gold rush' of immigrants from the underdeveloped countries of the north into the rich lands of the Mediterranean." (Brown 1971, p. 122.) "It was not the barbarian invasions in themselves that changed the face of Europe. It was the synergy between barbarian groups, the long Roman practice of civil war, and the opportunism with which local Romans exploited both barbarians and civil war conditions for their own purposes. For this reason, it may be wise to abandon the term 'barbarian invasions' as a description of the period. It would be better to use the term 'convulsion': an involvement of all segments of the population in a shake-up from which a very different society would emerge." (Brown 2013, loc 906.)

Untangling the Threads

Which of these positions (if any) is right? The question that has attracted most attention is whether the fragmentation of the Western Empire was the result of war and conquest or of a more peaceful transition. This in turn raises a number of other thorny questions:

- **Did the Western Empire fall?** It would be hard to deny that there came a time when it ceased to exist and was replaced by a number of "barbarian" kingdoms.
- **External or internal?** The evidence identifies twin pressures: external and internal.
  - **External:** The external evidence in turn can be subdivided into "assassination" or "accommodation": in other words, "barbarian" conquest or peaceful takeover. The preponderance of the evidence points to the transition occurring mostly as a result of violence, war, and conquest. Where there is evidence of treaties and other "eirenic" arrangements, they mostly appear to have come about through extortion or threats of force.
  - **Internal pressures:** The empire's internal weaknesses made it vulnerable to takeover. My own view is that these internal pressures were uppermost.
- **So what?** Does it really matter what brought the Western Empire down? In my opinion, what is far more important is the degree of continuity and change since its demise.

Before tackling these issues in more detail, let us try to disentangle the skein of intertwined threads that make up the relationship between Romans and "barbarians" in the Later Roman Empire.

The Road to Adrianople

By the fourth century, the Roman Empire had long been engaged in periodic conflicts with the "barbarians" on its borders. In 365, the new Eastern Emperor Valens (r. 364–378) was faced by a mutiny supported by Gothic troops in Roman service. Valens's attempts to bring the Goths to heel proved ineffective, but he succeeded in getting their leader, Athanaric, to sign a treaty. Under pressure from the Huns, divisions arose among the Goths, many of whom sought refuge inside the Roman Empire in return for providing troops. At the prospect of gaining a large body of able-bodied recruits at no cost to the treasury and stabilizing the Danube frontier into the bargain, Valens agreed to allow these Goths (later referred to as Visigoths) to settle in the Balkans.

Tension between the two peoples resulted in frayed tempers, which broke out into open warfare, culminating in the disastrous Roman defeat of Adrianople (Hadrianopolis) in 378, in which Valens lost his life. Had Valens waited for the Western reserves under his nephew, Gratian, to reach him, the result of Adrianople might possibly have been different. But, as it was, the defeat, coupled with the death of an emperor, only emboldened the Goths, who immediately tried unsuccessfully to storm the fortified city of Adrianople, and then made their way to Constantinople, together with a detachment of Huns and Alans, but were repulsed by a troop of Saracen (i.e. Arab) mercenaries and by the city's stout walls.

However, according to Jordanes (Jordanes, *Getica.*, 26.138), "From this time, in consequence of their glorious victory, the Visigoths possessed Thrace and Dacia Ripensis as if it were their native land." This is probably an exaggeration because there was an ongoing Gothic War with Rome between 379 and 382. But there does appear to have been an agreement between Theodosius I and the Visigoths, probably in 382, allowing them to settle along the southern bank of the Danube in return for military service. (See below.)

Rome and the Barbarians under Theodosius I

To take the place of the slain Valens, Gratian (r. 367–383) appointed Theodosius I (r. 379–395), whose father had held high military office under Valentinian I (r. 364–375.) Theodosius was confronted with a crisis of army recruitment. The Theodosian Code shows that conscription was strictly enforced. The number of young men who evaded military service by entering a monastery was probably exaggerated by Gibbon and others. Chopping off a thumb to get out of the army is a desperate measure, but one evidently sufficiently common as to attract the attention of the law. Valentinian had ordered such men to be burned alive. Theodosius allowed them to serve, but landowners who offered such mutilated recruits to the army were penalized by having two such recruits count as one. (On conscription, see CTh 7.13.8-11, 380–82.)

The shortage of troops was strained still further by usurpations and civil war. Theodosius had begun his career in 367 in assisting his father, also named Theodosius, serving as *comes rei militaris* (a high military rank, just below that of *magister militum)* under Valentinian I, in putting down the "great conspiracy", a serious mutiny of the Roman garrison stationed at Hadrian's Wall in Britain. Described by Ammianus as *barbarica conspiratio* (a barbarian conspiracy), it was evidently an incursion by Picts, "Scoti," and Saxons, which managed to overwhelm a number of army outposts and sack and pillage several Roman cities. Evidently implicated in an internal Roman succession conspiracy, Theodosius senior was executed shortly after the death of Valentinian I in 375.

After being raised to the purple by Gratian (r. 367–383), Theodosius managed to reach a settlement with the Goths by offering them highly favorable terms. According to Jordanes (Getica 28.142), he went so far as to invite the Visgothic King Athanaric to Constantinople, where he showered him with gifts, and, on his death while still there, honored him with *digna sepultura* (worthy burial), with Theodosius himself as chief mourner.

The arrangement with the Visigoths is the subject of Themistius's panegyric of 383. But, as Jones points out, "Themistius veils the important point that the settlement was made by a treaty with the Visigothic people, who continued to be governed by their own chiefs and fought under their command as allies (*foederati*) of the empire." (Jones 1964, p. 157.) "The settlement was, in fact, a grave breach with precedent. Barbarians had served in large numbers in the Roman army, but under Roman officers and discipline.... The results proved disastrous..."(Jones 1964, p 157.)

Theodosius was himself engulfed in civil war twice. In 383, incensed by Gratian's perceived favoritism towards a regiment of Alan troops over Roman citizens, the army of Britain proclaimed the Roman general Magnus Maximus as Augustus. Maximus went on to invade Gaul, where Gratian, deserted by his troops, was killed. In 384, with the intervention of Bishop Ambrose of Milan, Maximus was formally recognized as Augustus by Theodosius and his young co-emperor, Valentinian II (r. 375–392.) Based in Trier (Trèves), Maximus ruled over most of the western provinces in Britain, Gaul, Spain and Africa, was evidently a popular emperor, and was the subject of a panegyric delivered by Symmachus. While championing orthodox Christianity, Maximus issued an edict censuring

Christians in Rome for burning down a Jewish synagogue, for which he was attacked by bishop Ambrose, remarking, "The Emperor has become a Jew." (Ambr. *Patrologia Latina*, 16–17 (1845) no 40.) Forcing Valentinian II out of Milan in 387, Maximus brought the ire of Theodosius down on himself, and, after being defeated in battle in 388, he was executed.

Now it was Theodosius's turn to fall foul of the intolerant Bishop of Milan. When in 388 the emperor ordered the bishop of Callinicum to restore the Jewish synagogue burned down at that bishop's instigation, Ambrose fired a broadside at the Emperor, persuading him to retract his order. He again attributed to the population at large the jibe that "The Emperor has become a Jew." He reminded Theodosius of the clemency he had shown to unruly mobs responsible for destroying many stately homes belonging to the rich, and also churches. (Ambr. Ep. 40.) However, in 393, Theodosius would again order the punishment of any Christians who attacked or destroyed synagogues. In 390, there was a major riot in Thessalonica against the garrison manned by Goths. Siding with the Goths, Theodosius ordered them to kill indiscriminately all the spectators at the circus, in the Massacre of Thessalonica. Ambrose rounded on the emperor again, this time justifiably, and banned him from the church until he had done penance.

In May 392, the 21-year-old Valentinian II, who had fallen out with his "barbarian" *magister militum* ("army chief") and puppet-master, Arbogast, was found hanged in his bedroom, almost certainly by order of Arbogast, who then proceeded to have a retired Roman professor of rhetoric serving as *magister scriniorum* (a fairly modest post in the imperial secretariat) with senatorial rank named Eugenius proclaimed as emperor. Though himself a nominal Christian, Eugenius made some concessions to the pagan Roman state religion, notably the restoration of the Altar of Victory to its place of honor in the Senate-house, from which it had been removed (for the second time) by Gratian. In 394, Theodosius took the field against Eugenius and Arbogast, defeating them in the Battle of the Frigidus.

In the civil war against Maximus and also in that against Eugenius, Theodosius relied heavily on "barbarian" federates. In fact, in both cases, the armies on either side contained large numbers of "barbarian" troops. In his fight against Maximus, Theodosius counted many Goths, Huns, and Alans. Against Eugenius, he deployed a large horde of Goths. In the words of Jordanes, "And since the Emperor knew that they (viz. the Visigoths) were faithful to him and his friends, he took from their number more than twenty thousand warriors to serve against the tyrant Eugenius, who had slain Gratian and seized Gaul. After winning the victory over this usurper, he wreaked his vengeance upon him." (Jordanes, *Getica*, 28.145 tr. Mierow.)

"Barbarians" were not only numerically significant in the Roman army, but they also played a leading role. Generals of barbarian origin serving the Roman Empire included Bauto, Arbogast, Richomer, Hellebich, Modares, Butheric, and, not least, the half-Vandal Stilicho, who essentially ruled the Western Empire from around 393 until his death in 408.

Alaric and the Romans

The leader of the Gothic forces who fought for Theodosius against Eugenius was a career soldier named Alaric. Despite losing a large number of his men whom Theodosius had deliberately placed in the front lines, Alaric received a rebuff from the emperor. Denied promotion to the rank of *magister militum* and command of a regular Roman regiment, Alaric mutinied and set out on a plundering raid from Thessaly down to Athens and the Peloponnese. (Jordanes, Ibid., 29.147)

Eventually, in 402, Alaric confronted Stilicho, who effectively controlled the Western Empire and with whom Alaric was subsequently reconciled and appointed *magister militum*. In 405 northern Italy was invaded by Radagaisus and a Gothic force, which ravaged the countryside until stopped by Stilicho near Florence. In 407, Alaric marched on Italy and extorted a payment of 4,000 pounds of gold from Stilicho to stop Alaric's advance on Rome and also to recruit him to fight the usurper Constantine III in Gaul. But before the ransom could be paid, Stilicho was executed on suspicion of plotting to place his own son on the throne of Constantinople on the death of the Emperor Arcadius in 408. This was not the first time that the puppet-master of the West had fallen foul of the Eastern Empire. In 399, he had put down a rebellion in Africa, part of the West, instigated by Constantinople. Stilicho's fall was a signal for Roman troops to slaughter barbarian *foederati* throughout Italy

In 408, taking advantage of Rome's weakened state after Stilicho's death, Alaric asked Honorius for gold and hostages but was refused. So, Alaric proceeded to march south sacking a number of cities on his way to Rome. The sixth-century pagan historian Zosimus likened Alaric's unopposed progress to a leisurely walk in the park: "Crossing the Po, being as it were at some festival, and having no enemy to obstruct him...he marched toward Rome, sacking all the fortresses and towns in his way." (Zos. 5.1162.) "Taking possession of the Tiber, Alaric cut off access for supplies, famine gave way to pestilence, and all places were filled with dead bodies." (Zos. 5.40 = 5.1164.) To Roman envoys sent to negotiate with him, Alaric arrogantly declared, "That he would not relinquish the siege on any condition but that of receiving all the gold and silver in the city, all the household goods, and the barbarian slaves. One of the ambassadors observing, 'If you take these, what will you leave for the citizens?' He replied, 'Their souls.'" (Ibid.)

Though Rome had not been an imperial capital since 286, it still had tremendous symbolic significance, and this was the first time it had been captured since the Gallic invasion of around 390 BCE, eight hundred years before. Christians and pagans blamed each other, and Pope Innocent I even agreed to the reinstatement of pagan sacrifices to win the old gods' support, provided these rituals were performed in private. However, with the pagan priests insisting that the sacrifices had to be performed in public, the whole plan was abandoned. But the incident is still good evidence of the vitality of paganism into the fifth century. But Christians were no less distraught. "The city that had taken the whole world," mourned Jerome, safely ensconced in Bethlehem, "was itself taken." (Jerome, *Ep.* 127, 12.) "If Rome can perish, what can be safe?" (Jerome, *Ep.* 123, 16.) "[W]hen the bright light of all the world was put out, or rather, when the Roman Empire was decapitated, and, to speak more correctly, the whole world perished in one city, 'I became dumb and humbled myself, and kept silence from good words, but my grief broke out afresh, my heart glowed within me, and while I meditated the fire was kindled.'"(Jerome, Pref. to Commentary on Ezekiel.) It was in response to the blame attached by pagans to Rome's abandonment of the old religion that Augustine of Hippo wrote his *De Civitate Dei contra Paganos* (On the City of God against the Pagans).

Alaric was finally bought off by payment of 5,000 pounds of gold, together with 30,000 pounds of silver and other valuables. Hearing that Honorius was trying to recruit 10,000 Huns to take the field against him, Alaric sent a delegation of bishops to Honorius, this time demanding land in the northern province of Noricum. Rebuffed yet again, Alaric renewed his siege of Rome. Addressing the Senate, he demanded the appointment of an alternative emperor to Honorius. Alaric's choice fell upon a leading pagan (but nominal Christian) senator, Priscus Attalus, who in return appointed Alaric as *magister utriusque militiae* (master of both infantry and cavalry).

Alaric and Attalus then marched to Ravenna to confront Honorius, who fearfully offered to share the West with Attalus. This offer was disdainfully rejected. Though Attalus was essentially Alaric's puppet, he refused to allow Alaric to send Gothic troops to Africa to secure it against Honorius. Alaric then deposed Attalus and renewed negotiations with Honorius, who, however, tricked him by setting a rival Goth, Sarus, against him at the head of a small Roman army.

This was the last straw as far as Alaric was concerned, and on August 24, 410, he entered Rome once again, which he proceeded to sack for three days. Taking Honorius's sister, Galla Placidia, as a hostage, together with some Christian clerics in tow, the Goths swept down into southern Italy, sacking and pillaging as they went., and, in Procopius's words, written over a century later, "...killed all the people, as many as came in their way, old and young alike, sparing nether women nor children. Wherefore, even up to the present time Italy is sparsely populated." (Procopius, *Wars*, 3.2.11-13.)

The Visigoths in Gaul and Spain

A few months later, in 411, Alaric died and was succeeded as Visigothic king by his brother-in-law Athaulf (r. 411–415), who would go on to marry Galla Placidia. Modern writers intent on drawing a picture of a peaceful "accommodation" tend to stress the treaty of 419 granting the Visigoths land in Aquitaine. However, the territory ceded to the Visigoths under this arrangement was a tiny sliver of land compared to the area that they subsequently brought under their control by force or extortion, eventually covering not only the whole of Gaul south of the Loire and west of the Rhône, but also most of the Iberian peninsula except for the Basque country and the northwestern Kingdom of the Suevi.

Even the area of Aquitaine ceded by the treaty of 419 had already suffered depredations between 407 and 409 when an alliance of Vandals, Suevi, and Alans crossed the Rhine and swept across Gaul and into Spain. The devastations of 407–409 were described by the Christian poet Orientius, no doubt with some poetic license, as engulfing the whole of Gaul: *uno fumavit Gallia tota rogo* (the whole of Gaul smoked on a single funeral pyre). (Orientius of Auch, *Commonitorium*, in *Poetae Christiani Minores*, ed. R. Ellis, *Corpus Scriptorum Ecclesiasticorum Latinorum*, XVI, Vienna 1888. Lines 179–84.)

The usurper Constantine III, who had been acclaimed emperor by the Roman troops in Britannia in 407, crossed to Gaul, where he battled against both "barbarians" and the regular Roman forces sent against him by Honorius, who, confronted in Italy by Alaric and his Visigoths (see above), backed down before Constantine III, whom he recognized as co-emperor in 409. However, in 411, encircled by enemies, notably the usurper Maximus in Spain, Jovinus in the Rhineland, and Saxon pirates in Britain, and with Honorius dishonoring his compact and sending troops against him under the future short-lived Constantius III, Constantine III surrendered but was beheaded, with his head mounted on a pole and presented to Honorius.

Britain was now permanently lost to Rome. Meanwhile, Athaulf led his Visigoths from northern Italy into Gaul, living off the land in time-honored fashion. In 413, after defeating two usurpers in Gaul, Athaulf patched up his differences with Honorius in an agreement cemented by his marriage to Honorius's sister Galla Placidia in 414. Relations with Ravenna soured again when the future Constantius III was authorized by Honorius to blockade the Mediterranean ports of Gaul. Athaulf retaliated by bringing Priscus Attalus out of retirement and proclaiming him emperor again. But, with the blockade succeeding, Athaulf led the Visigoths to a new home again, this time in Spain.

Gothia or Romania?

Though an Arian "heretic", Athaulf is recorded by the contemporary Christian historian Paulus Orosius as making a remarkably clear-throated pro-Roman Declaration, which may possibly be historical: "At first I wanted to erase the Roman name and convert all Roman territory into a Gothic empire. I longed for Romania to become Gothia, and Athaulf to become what Caesar Augustus had been. But long experience has taught me that the ungoverned wildness of the Goths will never submit to laws, and that without law a state is not a state. Therefore I have more prudently chosen the different glory of reviving the Roman name with Gothic vigor, and I hope to be acknowledged by posterity as the initiator of a Roman restoration, since it is impossible for me to alter the character of this empire." (Orosius, *Historiae Adversus Paganos Libri VII* 7.43.4-6. Tr. Williams 1997, p. 218.)

Whether Athaulf ever gave voice to any such sentiments, the Declaration proved prophetic. To this day, most of the area previously occupied by the Western Roman Empire now forms part of the European Union, is governed by Roman-based law, and speaks a form of modern Latin, chiefly Italian, Spanish, Catalan, Portuguese, Romanian, and French. In Britain alone did the language of the conqueror prevail. Yet, the Anglo-Saxon tongue, or Old English, would in due course become so heavily overlaid with French and Latin as to end up at the present day with a majority Latin-based vocabulary .

From Visigoths to Franks

Athaulf's successor but one as king of the Visigoths, Wallia (r. 415–418), quickly made peace with Honorius, and packed off the emperor's sister, Galla Placidia, back to Ravenna, where she proceeded to marry Athaulf's old nemesis, the future Constantius III. It was evidently as a reward for their success as Roman *foederati* that the Visigoths were granted land in Aquitaine (see above), which became the base of a Visigothic kingdom that would come to cover most of Gaul and Spain.

But the relationship between Romans and Visigoths had not yet stabilized. The death of Honorius in 423 ushered in a power struggle in Ravenna, which the Visigoth King Theoderic I (r. 418–451) used to his advantage by trying to capture Arelate (modern Arles) but was thwarted by the Roman general Aëtius with a force of Huns. Theoderic nevertheless managed to agree a treaty with Aëtius under which he was given Gallo-Roman hostages. Aëtius then turned his attention to the Salian Franks and the Bagaudae (or Bacaudae), i.e. marauding bands of impoverished peasants and other desperadoes resisting the Roman authorities, and lay and clerical landowners, whom he fought with the aid of Alans and other *foederati*. Aëtius, the de facto ruler of the shrinking Western Empire, at the head of an army made up of Romans, Franks and Visigoths, was responsible for seeing off the threat from Attila's Huns at the Battle of the Catalaunian Fields in 451.

Under Childeric I (r. 458–481) and Clovis I (r. 481–c. 511), the Salian Franks gained control over most of Roman Gaul. Victory over Syagrius in the Battle of Soissons in 486 handed the Franks the last vestige of the Roman Empire in Gaul. Clovis also conquered the Alemanni in eastern Gaul, and in 507 he saw off the Visigoths, pushing them into Spain.

The sixth and seventh centuries were a period of great turbulence in the area. Internecine conflict among the Visigoths broke out in 549, complicated by the intervention of the Byzantines under Justinian (r. 527–565). In 589, the Visigoths switched from Arianism to Nicene Christianity, giving the Church and the aristocracy great influence through the Councils of Toledo. The succeeding century was marked by conflict between the kings and the aristocracy. The Muslims, who invaded Spain in 711, faced little resistance and, after taking the capital Toledo where they executed several Visigothic nobles, they soon controlled practically the whole peninsula from which they were gradually expelled in the Christian *Reconquista* (Reconquest) culminating in 1492.

Romans, Vandals, and Huns

In 429, a Vandal army under Genseric, Geiseric, or Gaiseric (r. 428–477) landed in North Africa, carrying all before them on the coast of what is now Morocco, Algeria, and Tunisia. In 435, in what was probably a damage limitation exercise, the Western Roman Empire reluctantly concluded a treaty with the Vandals offering them considerable territory. In 439, the Vandals took Carthage, which became the capital of their kingdom. In 442, an alliance was forged between Valentinian III (r. 425–455) and the Arian "heretic" Genseric, King of the Vandals (r. 428–477), which was cemented by the betrothal of Genseric's son to Valentinian's daughter.

Between 433 and 450, the Western Empire, with its capital now (since 402) in Ravenna, was dominated by Flavius Aëtius, who developed good relations with the Huns, using Hun troops in his wars in Gaul and allowing some Huns to settle in Pannonia. With his eye on Gaul for himself, the Hun leader, Attila (r. 434–453), turned against Aëtius, who, with the help of Visigoths and Franks, defeated Attila in the Battle of the Catalaunian Plains in 451, in which the Visigothic king, Theoderic, lost his life. Not daunted, Attila invaded and ravaged Italy with a view to claiming the hand of Honoria, sister of Valentinian III, in marriage, demanding half the Western Empire as his dowry. After meeting with an embassy including prominent senators and Pope Leo I, Attila halted at the Po and retreated.

With the threat of a Hun invasion removed, Valentinian III, suspecting a plot by Aëtius to place his own son on the throne, suddenly drew his sword and killed him personally during a routine financial meeting in 454. Apollinaris Sidonius is credited with remarking to Valentinian that he had just cut off his right hand with his left. (Gibbon, Ch. 35.) Six months later Valentinian himself would be assassinated by a "barbarian" friend of Aëtius's.

The Western imperial throne was now briefly occupied by Petronius Maximus, a member of the great noble house of the Anicii, who was implicated in the assassination of both Aëtius and Valentinian III. His accession was obtained with the backing of the senate, by bribing key palace officials, and by forcing the late emperor's widow to marry him, and Valentinian's daughter to marry Maximus's son. But his scheme backfired when he canceled the betrothal of his new wife's daughter, Eudocia, to the Vandal king Genseric's son, Huneric. Incensed by this rebuff, Genseric set sail for Italy with an army. Meanwhile, less than three months after his accession, Petronius Maximus was stoned to death by an angry mob.

The Vandal Sack of Rome 455

By contrast with Alaric's three-day sack of Rome in 410, that by Genseric in 455 lasted fourteen days, during which huge amounts of treasure was looted, public buildings, including the Temple of Jupiter Optimus Maximus, were plundered, and a large number of prisoners were taken, including the Empress Licinia Eudoxia and her two daughters, Placidia and Eudocia, though the city was not burned down and there was no wholesale slaughter of the population. Eudocia, who had previously been betrothed to Genseric's son, Huneric, was subsequently married to him.

While recognized by the western Emperor based in Ravenna, the Vandal kingdom was attacked by the Byzantines, which launched several attempts to bring it back into the Roman fold. In 474, after promising toleration of Nicene Christianity, the Arian Genseric agreed to a peace treaty with Byzantium.

Genseric's grandson Hilderic, son Huneric and Eudocia, King of the Vandals from 523 to 530, struck up a close relationship with the future Emperor Justinian, who would accede to the Byzantine throne in 527. Hilderic, an Arian, was well-disposed toward the Catholic faith shared by his mother and his guest-friend Justinian. The spread of Catholicism among the Vandals alarmed the Vandal aristocracy, who, under the leadership of Hilderic's cousin Gelimer, deposed Hilderic. It was on the pretext of restoring Hilderic that Justinian, who by now had ascended the Byzantine throne, sent an army to Carthage, which reconquered Africa for the Roman Empire. In return for surrendering to Justinian's general, Belisarius, Gelimer was given extensive estates in Galatia, where he lived out the rest of his days, dying at the age of 73 in 553.

The Roman reconquest of North Africa was short-lived, as the whole area known in Arabic as the Maghreb would fall to the Muslims in three waves between 647 and 709. It is not clear for how long Christianity survived after this, but the longstanding conflict between Catholicism, Donatism, and Arianism can only have strengthened the position of Islam, which, together with the Arabic language, has remained dominant in the whole region to the present day.

The Significance of 476

What significance, if any, is there in the year 476, the conventional date for the end of the Roman Empire in the West, marked by the deposition of the sixteen-year-old Emperor Romulus Augustus, nicknamed Augustulus, "the little Augustus." The temptation was too great to pass up the opportunity of identifying the demise of the Western Empire with the removal of an emperor whose name combined that of Rome's mythical founder with that of its first emperor.

This event is now largely dismissed as irrelevant. The "little emperor" was a powerless puppet in the hands of his father, Orestes, a member of a Roman pagan aristocratic family from Pannonia who had served as a *notarius* (secretary) under Attila the Hun before being appointed *magister militum* and a patrician by the Western Roman Emperor Julius Nepos in 475. Orestes staged a coup, forcing Nepos to flee to his native Dalmatia. The little emperor was not recognized by either the Byzantine Emperor Zeno nor by the "heretical" (Miaphysite) usurper Basiliscus.

In August 476, Orestes himself faced a mutiny after refusing the demands for land of his "barbarian" *foederati*, Together with the Roman army of Italy, they transferred their loyalty to the Germanic (and "heretical" Arian) military leader Odoacer (Odovacer or Odovacar), who defeated and killed Orestes and gently deposed his son, the young emperor, who was exiled to Campania with a generous pension. Odoacer then sent a senatorial embassy to Constantinople, pledging his allegiance to the newly restored Zeno as sole Roman Emperor and investing him with the Western imperial regalia, merely requesting in return the rank of patrician. Scorning this flattery, Zeno urged the senators to allow Julius Nepos back from exile. (Malchus, fragment 14.) Odoacer then had himself proclaimed by his troops as king of Italy. (Anonymus Valesianus, 8.38; Jordanes, *Getica: Origin and Deeds of the Goths*, tr. C. Mierow.) A third of the land of Italy was then, we are told, distributed among Odoacer's troops though some modern writers claim that this is a reference to tax revenues rather than to actual land. The preponderance of evidence favors the view that the soldiery received allocations of land, but the proportion is not certain. (Cassiodorus, Variae 2.16, tr. Barnish. Liebeschuetz 1997 in Pohl (ed.), pp. 135–51; Ward Perkins, 2006, p. 64, arguing for land grants against Goffart.)

As Odoacer proceeded to consolidate his power in Italy, where he appears to have ruled with the approval of the Senate, Zeno engaged Theoderic (Theodoric), king of the Ostrogoths (r. 471–526), to destroy him, promising to give Theoderic free rein over the peninsula if he was successful. Between 489 and 493, a series of battles was fought between Odoacer and Theoderic, culminating in a three-year siege of Ravenna by Theoderic. At a banquet to celebrate a treaty between the two men, Theoderic suddenly killed Odoacer, hunted down his leading followers and family, and then proceeded to build a kingdom which came to include not only the whole of Italy, with its capital in Ravenna, but also southern Gaul, most of the Iberian peninsula in the West, and Dalmatia in the East, together with hegemony over Corsica, Sardinia, the Balearic Islands, the Vandal kingdom in North Africa, and the Burgundian kingdom.

The Byzantine emperor Anastasius (r. 491–518), with whom Theoderic had a harmonious relationship, was succeeded by Justin I (r. 518–527) and his nephew Justinian I (r. 527–565), who successfully reunited Italy, North Africa, southern Spain, and Dalmatia with the Eastern Roman Empire, most of which was lost in the Islamic Conquests in the period between 632 and 750, and Italy (with the chief exception of the so-called Exarchate of Ravenna) to the Lombards between 568 and 774.

Pulling the Threads Together

Having untangled the threads, it is now time to pull them together, to make some sense of them:

- **Adrianople:** Though the immediate cause of this catastrophic defeat was Valens's impatience in not waiting for Gratian's reinforcements, the underlying cause was the crisis of army recruitment, which can ultimately be at least partially blamed on Caracalla's extension of Roman citizenship in 212 to all free male inhabitants in the empire. After this, *peregrini*, or free provincials, no longer had an incentive to sign up for the army, which had earned them citizenship after twenty-five years' service. As a result, more "barbarians" started being recruited, and, from the time of Diocletian, conscription was introduced, which was always unpopular, and never worked very well.
- **Disastrous policy:** Theodosius's settlement with the Goths, which allowed them to fight as Roman *foederati*, or allies, under their own chiefs, proved disastrous. Their loyalties were not to Rome, but to their own leaders, who played fast and loose with all and sundry.
- **Usurpers:** The rise of usurpers was facilitated by the reliance on "barbarian" troops. Magnus Maximus, for example, was acclaimed as emperor by Roman troops who resented Gratian's favoring of his "barbarian" Alan contingent over themselves. Maximus came to rule over most of the West between 383 and 388, foreshadowing the loss of these provinces to "barbarian" kings. Yet in 390, Theodosius ordered the Gothic garrison of Thessalonica to kill all the spectators at the circus. Incidents like these did not help to knit together the fabric of society. In both the fight against Maximus and in that against Eugenius, the armies on both sides contained large numbers of "barbarian" troops. The defeat in 411 of Constantine III, a usurper in Britain and Gaul, marks the end of Roman control of Britain. And the defeat of two usurpers in Gaul by Athaulf gave the Visigoth huge leverage over the imperial government in Ravenna, followed by the conquest in 413 of Narbonne and Toulouse, and expanded by playing off competing Roman and "barbarian" commanders against one another.
- **"Barbarian" generals:** The dominance of "barbarians" is further underlined by the number of generals of "barbarian" origin serving Rome.
- **Ransom:** As a result of the heavy reliance on "barbarians", leaders like Alaric were in a position to hold the Roman state to ransom and to pick their own emperor.

- **"The whole of Gaul smoked on a single funeral pyre":** This description of the "barbarian" depredations of 407–409 is doubtless an exaggeration but not a total fabrication.
- **Attila the Hun:** Attila's defeat at the hands of a combined force of Romans and "barbarians" in 451 ended the Hunnic threat, but not before Attila had invaded and ravaged Italy to claim the hand of Valentinian III's sister in marriage, and claiming half the Western Empire as his dowry. But Attila's retreat did nothing to save the Western Empire from collapse. The Visigoths already controlled most of Gaul, and they shared Spain with the Suebi. The defeat by Clovis I of Syagrius, a Roman general and de facto ruler of northern Gaul in 486, gave the Franks control of most of Gaul, consolidating their position in 507. Despite Syagrius's defeat, his family did well under the Franks, one descendant being sent on an embassy to Constantinople in 585, another donating a large landholding to an abbey in 739, and another recorded as an abbot in 757.
- **Vandals:** Meanwhile, the Vandals went on a conquering spree in Africa between 429 and 439, when they conquered Carthage and then gave Rome a 14-day sacking in 455. Here a further ingredient was added to the mix, when Justinian reconquered Africa, but the whole Maghreb fell to the Muslims between 647 and 709, followed by most of Spain between 711 and 718.
- **The little emperor:** Besides its symbolic significance, the chief practical effect of the deposition of the last little western emperor in 476 was to turn Italy into a kingdom under the "barbarian" general Odoacer, who evidently ruled with the approval of the Senate. Byzantine intrigue set the Ostrogothic King Theoderic (r. 471–526) against Odoacer, leading to a series of battles between the two men, and Odoacer's murder at the hands of Theoderic, who proceeded to build a kingdom covering not only Italy but also southern Gaul, most of the Iberian peninsula, and Vandal North Africa, and the Burgundian kingdom. The Byzantine reconquest of much of this under Justinian would prove to be short-lived, mostly falling to the Muslims (between 632 and 750) and the Lombards (between 568 and 774.)

"Exceedingly Unpleasant" but "No Catastrophe"

Therefore, whether or not the period from about 375 to 750 constituted a "catastrophe", a label which is so emphatically rejected by the Late Antiquity school, it certainly was anything but a peaceful transition. Violence takes center stage, and the treaties, settlements, and marriage alliances that we encounter are merely bargaining chips used to lure, cajole, or threaten. Why, then, are so many modern writers on the period prepared to go to such lengths to fly in the face of the evidence and deny its fundamentally violent nature? In a word, these writers (or at least some of them) appear to be imbued with missionary zeal to depict Late Antiquity and, not least, Christianity, as a "Good Thing". Whether this is an appropriate approach to history by academics is another question.

- **"No catastrophe"** Did the Western Empire fall to "barbarian" invasions, was there an amicable "barbarian" takeover, or was the demise of the West chiefly the result of internal decay? Peter Brown, the founder of the Late Antiquity school, sometimes gives the impression of rejecting both conflict and decay. Here is one such remark of his: "Put bluntly: what brought down the western empire was the speed with which the barbarian armies were able to create local power blocs through collaboration with the local Romans.... The western empire was not so much destroyed as eroded and finally rendered unnecessary by a score of little Romes, rooted in more restricted areas of control. These little Romes were largely in the hands of the local nobilities, of energetic little men who had replaced and even helped to despoil the grandees of the imperial *ancien régime*." (Brown 2013, loc. 812.) Whatever the meaning is of this assertion, couched as it is in characteristically opaque elliptical language, it hardly accords with the picture that emerges from the evidence set out in the previous sections of the present chapter headed "Untangling the Threads" and "Pulling the Threads Together." Brown excoriates what he calls the "catastrophists" like Bryan Ward-Perkins, rejecting his "...vivid account of the violences *[sic]* that accompanied the barbarian invasions." (Brown 2013, loc. 970; Ward-Perkins 2006, p. 175.) Yet, Brown also dismisses Ward-Perkins's remark that "...it is now fashionable to play down the violence and unpleasantness of the invasions that brought down the empire in the West." (Brown 2013, loc. 812; Ward-Perkins 2006, p. 14.) Brown even goes so far as to express himself as "in entire agreement with" Wolfgang Liebeschuetz's assessment that "The fall of the Roman Empire was accompanied by changes which most people would view as a serious worsening of life if they were to happen to themselves." (Liebeschuetz 2004, p. 261.) Brown's objection to the catastrophsts is now concentrated more narrowly on his insistence that "...even the 'worsening of life' to which Liebeschuetz refers has a history, multiple causes which have to be understood." (Brown 2013, loc 969.) Brown provides no details of this process. Elsewhere, Brown is at pains to claim to have been able to write "...

the entire history of the religious and cultural revolution associated with the end of the ancient world without invoking an intervening catastrophe and without pausing, for a moment, to pay lip service to the widespread notion of decay." (Brown 1997b, p. 15; Gillett (2012) Review Article: "Rome's Fall and Europe's Rise," *The Medieval Review;* Ward-Perkins 2006, pp. 170 f. and 214 n.4.) This claim is limited to "the religious and cultural revolution" of the period. Before trying to define the contents of this "revolution", it would probably be a good idea to identify the span of the period involved. The original edition of Brown's *World of Late Antiquity* covered the period from Marcus Aurelius (r. 161–180) to Muhammad (d. 632), and the subsequent edition spanned an even wider period, from 150 to 750, a very long period for a "revolution." Elsewhere (2013, p. 83), Brown claims to identify a religious and social revolution in the reign of Constantine. However, regardless of the precise content or chronological bounds of these "revolutions," Brown and his followers seem to regard Late Antiquity as a Good Thing, often expressed in overtly subjective judgments, not least in the area of religion. (See Chapter 10.)

- **"Toxic discourse"**: While admitting that the "unravelling" of western society "could indeed be exceedingly unpleasant," Brown nevertheless views Late Antiquity through rose-tinted glasses and mercilessly attacks Ward-Perkins for being a catastrophist who "… steers dangerously close to those conventional images of the fall of Rome from which…extremist politicians and demagogues in contemporary Europe have conjured up a toxic discourse based on prejudice and fear." (Brown 2013, loc. 960.) This "toxic discourse" refers, inter alia, to a "notorious speech" in 2011 by the "extreme xenophobic" Dutch politician Geert Wilders drawing a parallel between uncontrolled migration into twenty-first-century Europe and the fall of the Western Roman Empire portrayed as an "unmitigated catastrophe." (Ibid., loc. 967.) Guy Halsall, a member of the "accommodation" school of thought, accuses Peter Heather, (who rejects that idea as smelling "more of wishful thinking than likely reality" (Heather 2018, pp. 80–100), of providing "succour to far-right extremists" opposed to immigration, including even the Norwegian mass murderer, Anders Breivik. (Halsall 2014, pp. 517–19; 2007, p. 58.) But it is equally unforgivable, especially in an academic, to distort the past just because one wants to combat what Brown refers to as "…toxic political movements in contemporary Europe." Before jumping to conclusions, the first step, which does not seem to have been taken, must surely be to see whether the individual migrants of the present day are even comparable to the incursions into the

Roman Empire of organized bands of "barbarians" under their own military leaders.

- **"Germans" or "barbarians"?** Another debate that is more about modern politics than ancient history concerns the identity of the "barbarians" who came knocking on the door of the Roman Empire. Reinhard Wenskus, of the "revisionist" Vienna School of History, maintained that the Germanic tribes of antiquity did not constitute distinct ethnicities but were rather diverse alliances led by a dominant elite continuing "core traditions" (*Traditionskerne.*) According to this school, members of the Germanic tribes were not actually related to one another; this was a figment of their own imagination. The Vienna School came up with the term *Stammensbildung* (ethnogenesis) to deconstruct the ethnicity of Germanic tribes. Pohl's hypothesis that the Germanic tribes had no traditions or values of their own has been criticized by Liebeschuetz as "extraordinarily one-sided" and a form of ideological "dogmatism" evincing "a closed mind". (Liebeschuetz 2015, p. xxi.) I agree with Liebeschuetz that one should not throw away the linguistic and literary evidence pointing to a common core of culture and identity among the Germanic tribes.
- **Did the Western Roman Empire come to an end?** In a political sense, the Western Roman Empire ceased to exist, either on the deposition of Romulus Augustus in 476 or possibly on the death of Julius Nepos in Dalmatia in 480. Theoretically, however, there was only one Roman Empire. So, as long as there was an emperor in Constantinople (or anywhere else), the Roman Empire could still be said to be subsisting. This was the argument used by Odoacer on packing the imperial insignia off to Zeno in Constantinople in 476. Charlemagne's coronation as emperor in 800 took place on the pretext that the imperial throne was vacant because it was occupied by a woman, Irene, but Charlemagne nevertheless carefully avoided the title "Roman emperor," contenting himself instead with the style *Imperator Romanorum* (Emperor of the Romans). The same title was borne by Otto I (r. 962–973), now regarded as the first emperor of the Holy Roman Empire, which, though it lasted until 1806, was essentially a nominal umbrella body covering a large number of independent (mostly German) states.
- **Did the dismemberment of the West take place by agreement?** Hardly. The Vandals' conquest of Africa was by no means the only example of a violent takeover. As discussed above, the much-touted agreement over Aquitaine in 419 accounted for only a small sliver of that area. The rest fell under Visigothic control as the result of a land-grab. Britain, Spain, and even Italy were subjected to

violent takeovers as well. The history of the relationship between Rome and the "barbarians" as related above justifies Bryan Ward-Perkins's verdict: "The Germanic invaders of the western empire seized or extorted through the threat of force the vast majority of the territories in which they settled, without any formal agreement on how to share resources with their new Roman subjects. The impression given by some recent historians that most Roman territory was formally ceded to them as part of treaty arrangements is quite simply wrong. Wherever the evidence is moderately full, as it is from the Mediterranean provinces, conquest or surrender to the threat of force was definitely the norm, not peaceful settlement." (Ward-Perkins 2006, p. 13.)

- **Land or tax revenues?** King Theoderic of the Ostrogoths (r. 475–526) tried to mollify the Roman Senate by stressing that their losses had actually enhanced the ties of friendship between the two peoples and that by losing land the Romans had acquired a defender (defensor adquisitus est) in the shape of his Ostrogoths. (Cassiodorus *Variae* 2.16, tr. Barnish, 29 f.) This is not the only clear evidence pointing to actual division of real estate after the "barbarian" takeover both in Italy and also elsewhere in the West. In Gaul, Sidonius Apollinaris's mock-playful but trenchant criticisms of a band of uncouth Burgundian "guests" at his villa underlines the pointed pun of hostility and the sham of *hospitalitas* (hospitals), including Paulinus of Pella's lamentation of the forced seizure of family property. (Sidonius Carm 12, Ep. 7.7; Paulinus of Pella *Eucharisticon, lines 422–25. Ausonius, Op. 295–351.*)

- **Tax revenues from cities?** Liebeschuetz, rejecting the idea that the "barbarians" received tax revenues rather than land, argues plausibly that, as tax revenues would have had to be paid by local cities, this would simply not have occurred because permission for this would have had to be obtained from the imperial government, which would not have been granted. (Liebeschuetz 1997, in Pohl (ed.), pp. 135–51)

- **"Hardly a ripple of protest"**: Goffart's argument appears to be based on faulty logic, resting on his observation that the "barbarian" takeover of the West "...raised hardly a ripple of protest from the Roman provincials." (Goffart 1987, p. 36.) "Such a result can hardly be explained unless the costs were chiefly absorbed by the state." (Ibid., p. 63.) "[T]he land given to barbarians was not ordinary property but a special mode of ownership made possible by late Roman tax law. The allotment that a barbarian initially received consisted of tax assessment and its proceeds, a superior ownership that did not extinguish or supersede the private proprietary rights of the

Romans owning assessed land and paying its taxes." (Ibid., p. 36 f.) However, as we have seen, this view is not supported by the evidence. What the "barbarians" received was actual real estate. And the reason for the low level of Roman resistance to the "barbarians" had nothing to do with this question of land vs. tax revenues. The reason for it was that loyalties were divided in a fractured society. (See below.)

- **The new masters:** What use, in any case, would a demobilized "barbarian" soldier have had for tax revenues even if paid in gold? He would, presumably, have wished to invest it in land. So, even if the "barbarians" initially received tax revenues rather than land, in time, this would been converted into real estate, and many of the major landowners of the post-Roman West are known to have been "barbarians". This is even recognized by Matthew Innes, generally a member of the Goffart school: "In the initial stages of settlement, particularly in the militarily denuded provinces of Gaul, violence and the threat of violence were central in allowing the systematic transfer of the fruits of landowning to barbarian incomers. In the second and third generations after the initial settlements, however, the legal and tenurial implications of these *de facto* transfers of rents and produce gave rise to litigation, as Roman landowners attempted to reclaim property, to assert their continuing title to lands which now housed barbarian settlers, even to claim rights over waste and woodland brought under the plough by newcomers." (Innes, 2006, p. 42.)

- **Thumb-chopping**: To resort to chopping off your thumb to avoid military service smacks of desperation, and it is probably unlikely to have been widespread. Yet it was sufficiently common as to attract the attention of the law (see above) and contrasts markedly with traditional Roman virtues. The problem seems to have been particularly acute in Italy. Ammianus Marcellinus contrasts Gaul and Italy in this respect: "No one of this nation (the Gauls) has ever mutilated his thumb from fear of the toils of war, as men have done in Italy, who in that region are called *murci* (cowards.)" (Amm. 12.3)

Self-mutilation of this kind was but one small problem relating to military recruitment in the later Roman Empire, which, together with the decline in tax revenues, explains why it was (reluctantly) prepared to allow "barbarians" to settle within the imperial frontiers, another marked contrast with earlier policy. For example, the attempt by the Marcomanni and others to cross the Rhine and Danube into Roman territory was repulsed by Marcus Aurelius (r. 161–180). And Caracalla's grant of Roman citizenship to all free inhabitants of the Empire in 212 did not extend to the Alemanni, whom he repulsed in 213 and who were subsequently beaten back from Gaul and Italy by Valerian and Gallienus (r. 253–268) and by Claudius Gothicus (r. 268–270), so named for his victory over the Goths.

- **Divided Loyalties:** If there was less overt opposition to the "barbarian" takeover of the West than might have been expected, the most likely reason was very different from Goffart's "tax revenues" explanation, but rather because the Roman Empire no longer enjoyed the same degree of loyalty and support as had traditionally been the case. Nevertheless, there certainly was *some* resistance, notably in Gaul. Sidonius Apollinaris (c. 430–c. 485), a member of one of the leading Gallo-Roman aristocratic families and bishop of Clermont between 470 and 485, has left us a valuable collection of writings, divided into two distinct periods: Book I dating from before 469, while the Visigoths were still loyal Roman *foederati* (allies), and a further eight books published after 476, by which time the Visigoths had conquered Gaul and there was no longer a Roman emperor in the West. His first book of letters adopts a conciliatory tone towards the Visigoths, including a highly flattering description of the Visigothic King Theoderic II, an Arian Christian. In 470 Sidonius converted to Nicene Christianity and became a bishop of Clermont. It was around this time that the Visigothic King Euric (r. 466–484) broke faith with the Romans and launched into a conquering spree around Gaul, which Sidonius actively opposed together with his brother-in-law, Ecdicius Avitus, son of the Roman Emperor Avitus (r. (r. 455–456). In 475, the Roman Emperor Julius Nepos ceded the rest of Gaul (including Clermont) to Euric in return for Provence. Because of his role in the resistance to Euric, Sidonius was himself exiled for two years, and his subsequent writings adopt a much more negative position toward the Visigoths and their Arian faith. In a letter to his brother-in-law, Ecdicius, dating from around 470, Sidonius makes an out-and-out attack on a high Roman official named Seronatus (evidently executed for treason in 471) for toadying to the Goths: "Every day he fills the woods with refugees, the villas with 'guests' (*hospitibus*), the churches with criminals, the prisons with clerics. He cries the Goths up and the Romans down.... He tramples underfoot the Code of Theodosius and replaces it with the laws of Theoderic (Theoderic II, King of the Visigoths, r. 453–466), raking up old charges to justify new imposts. Be quick, then, to unravel the tangle of affairs that makes you linger; cut short whatever causes your delay. Our people are at the last gasp; freedom is almost dead. Whether there is any hope, or whether all is to be despair, they want you in their midst to lead them. If the State is powerless to assist, if, as rumor has it, the Emperor Anthemius is without resource, our nobility is determined to follow your lead, and give up either their country (*patriam*), or the hair of their heads." (Sid Ap. Ep. 2.1.) Seronatus, who is also described as "... making a show of buying property but never thinking of paying" is the personification of the well-known type of self-serving, corrupt Roman official who existed even during much stabler periods, notably, for example, the head of the great aristocratic house of the Anicii, Sextus Claudius Petronius Probus, who served as Praetorian Prefect four times between 364 and 384 and who is described by Ammianus as constantly forced to seek high office in order to feed the criminal avarice of his family. (Amm. 27.11.3.) It is worth noting that, until Euric proved treacherous, Sidonius himself had initially been prepared to pander to the Visigoths.

- **Fractured society:** It has to be recognized that the resistance by Sidonius and Ecdicius to the Visigoths in Gaul was atypical. For the most part, as seen in the narrative part of this chapter, the "barbarians" encountered very little opposition. A key reason for this is that the Roman Empire of the fourth and fifth centuries was a fractured society. Under the Principate the elites had been open. Anyone in the Empire, no matter where they came from or what their background was, could aspire to Roman citizenship, equestrian status, senatorial rank, and even the imperial throne itself. Suetonius relates that Julius Caesar's enemies attacked him in ribald verse for allegedly allowing "long-haired" Gauls—whom he had just conquered—-to join the senate: "On the admission of foreigners to the Senate, a placard was posted: 'God bless the Republic! Let no one agree to direct a new senator to the Senate house.' The following verses too were sung everywhere: 'Caesar led the Gauls in triumph, led them to the senate-house; Then the Gauls discarded their trousers, and donned the purple-bordered toga .'" (Suet. Julius, 80) When the Senate really became accessible to Gauls a century later, at the behest of the Emperor Claudius (r. 41–54), there was still a certain amount of opposition to the idea, but the Senate acceded to Claudius's request without much ado. (Tac. Ann. 11.23 f. Lyons tablet) Access to the imperial throne itself was similarly liberalized. With the accession of Vespasian (r. 69–79), the top spot was occupied by someone of non-senatorial Italian stock; Trajan (r. 98–117), from Spain, was the first provincial emperor; Septimius Severus (r. 193–211) was of African origin; Diocletian (r. 284–305) came from Dalmatia; Constantine's family was Dacian; Valentinian was Pannonian; Theodosius came from Spain. Yet, in the late empire, none of the dominant "barbarian" figures felt able to assume the imperial title, even when they had marriage ties with the emperor of the day—neither Arbogast, nor Ricimer, nor Stilicho, nor Alaric, nor Athaulf, nor Odoacer, nor Theoderic the Ostrogoth, nor even Attila the Hun, though, as mentioned above, he demanded half the Western Empire as his dowry for marriage to Honoria, sister of Valentinian III. To what is this change to be attributed? Most of these men were highly Romanized. Stilicho (359–408), for example, had a Roman mother, though his father was a Vandal, and he married Theodosius I's niece and, on that emperor's death, became guardian to his young son and successor, Honorius; and Theoderic, king of the Ostrogoths (454–526), spent his formative years as a hostage in Constantinople. Attitudes had hardened: that was what had changed, no doubt partly for fear of a "barbarian" takeover, which of course was precisely what occurred, but also as part of a general tendency to pigeon-hole people—not least in terms of religion. (See below.)

- **Religion:** Until the time of Diocletian (r. 284–305) the inhabitants of the Roman world—with the exception of the Jews, who were treated as a separate nation—were all expected to owe loyalty both to the Roman state and, which was not distinguished from it, to the Roman state religion, including the imperial cult, though this did not preclude membership of other pagan cults, such as those of Isis, Mithras, and the Magna Mater. (See Chapter 10.) The whole situation changed in 381, when Christianity became the exclusive official religion of the Empire, and all those who were not adherents of that religion—and the dominant denomination of that religion—found themselves discriminated against and persecuted. No wonder the usurper Firmus was able to hold out against the imperial government in Africa between 372 and 375, with the support of the Donatists, a "heresy" that was particularly strong in that area. The ousting of the Eastern Emperor Zeno by Basiliscus in 475 was achieved with the support of another "heresy," Monophysitism, which was very strong in Egypt and Syria, and which later had the protection of the Empress Theodora, though her husband, Justinian (r. 527–565), was staunchly orthodox. Despite the strenuous efforts of some modern writers to convert the senatorial aristocracy to Christianity even in the early fourth century, it is clear from, among other things, the long saga of the Altar of Victory, that there were a good many pagans in the aristocracy up to and beyond the end of the century. It is significant that Eugenius, the puppet emperor chosen by Arbogast with the support of the Senate in 392, made a point of restoring the Altar of Victory to its place in the Senate house and appointed the influential pagan aristocrat Virius Nicomachus Flavianus as Praetorian prefect of Italy. It is also surely noteworthy that Priscus Attalus, selected by the Visigoths as emperor in 409 and again in 414, was a pagan. Alan Cameron, in his concern to kill off paganism as early as possible, went out of his way to disprove the existence of an active pagan resistance in the late fourth century. (Cameron, Alan, 2013) Yet, pagans did not need to be activists in order to feel less than loyal toward an intolerant, persecuting government. And, though supposedly extinguished by 423, paganism clearly continued to have considerable numbers of adherents for a long time. As late as the reign of Justinian (527–565), John of Ephesus boasted of converting 70,000 pagans in Asia Minor, one of the most Christianized parts of the Empire, and, in addition, a large number of pagans, including some highly placed men, in Constantinople itself, which had been established as a Christian capital in 330. (Ch. 10.)

Roundup

- **Fall of the West**: During the fifth century the Western Empire was dismembered piece by piece and converted into a changing patchwork of "barbarian" kingdoms. The year 476 (or 480) is of purely symbolic significance. The lack of an emperor in the West made no real difference to the realities of power, as Italy then also fell under direct "barbarian" control.
- **External or internal pressure?** The evidence identifies twin pressures: external and internal:
  - **External pressures:** The external pressures can in turn be subdivided into "assassination" or "accommodation" or, in other words, "barbarian" conquest or peaceful takeover. The preponderance of the evidence points to the transition occurring mostly as a result of violence, war, and conquest. Where there is evidence of treaties and other eirenic arrangements, they mostly appear to have come about through extortion or threats of force.
    - **Land or tax revenues?** Walter Goffart and others argue strenuously that the peaceful accommodation of the "barbarians" with the Roman state involved the handover not of actual land but only of tax revenues. (Goffart 1987, p. 36.) This argument seems to have been dictated, or at least influenced, by Goffart's claim that "...the settlements occasioned hardly a ripple of protest from the Roman provincials." (Ibid., p. 36.) "Such a result

can hardly be explained unless the costs were chiefly absorbed by the state." (Ibid., p. 63.) This is a back-to-front argument. The amount of resistance was indeed low (though not non-existent), but the explanation for that is the fact that the late empire had divided loyalties in a fractured society. (See below.)

- **"Barbarian" pressure:** It used to be believed that the main cause of the fall of the Western Empire was "barbarian invasions" or "barbarian migrations," under pressure, particularly, from the Huns sweeping across from Asia into Europe starting around 375. Guy Halsall and others see the migrations as the result of the collapse of the Western Empire rather than its cause. (Halsall 2007, Chapter 2.) This dispute begs the question: Why were the Romans unable to withstand the "barbarians" in the fourth and fifth centuries as they had always managed to do before? The answer to this lies in the internal weaknesses of the Empire. (See below.)

- **"Barbarian" land hunger:** If the "barbarian migrations" are seen as driven by land hunger, then this again begs the question: Why were the Romans not able to repulse them? The answer again lies in the internal weakness of the Empire and, not least, the Empire's shortage of troops, making it not only unable but also unwilling to repulse the "barbarians".

- **Attraction of Rome:** As early as 213, the highly Romanized Alemanni broke through the northern frontier of the Roman Empire with a view to settlement. The Emperor Caracalla, who had just extended Roman citizenship to all free inhabitants of the Empire, adopted a very different attitude to these would-be migrants, pushing the Alemanni back and strengthening the frontier against them. Why was the imperial government unable to hold back the "barbarians" who were similarly attracted to Roman civilization two hundred years later? The answer must again be sought in internal factors.

- **East and West:** It was quite largely Constantinople's strong strategic position that made the "barbarians" concentrate their efforts on the West. And this, indeed, had been one of Constantine's chief motivating forces in selecting Byzantium as the site for his new eastern capital. Between 324 and 330 the city's defenses were greatly strengthened, and the famous double Theodosian Walls, which made the city largely impregnable to naval attack, were constructed between 404 and 413, and repaired periodically thereafter. So, Constantinople was never captured until it fell to the Crusaders in 1204 (retaken in 1261), and finally to the Ottoman Turks in 1453, However, the Byzantine Empire's northern and eastern frontiers were much more vulnerable. As a result, it lost territory successively to the Arabs, Seljuk Turks, Slavs, Normans, and finally the Ottoman Turks.

- **Internal pressures:** The Empire's internal weaknesses made it vulnerable to takeover. My own view is that it was these internal pressures that were uppermost.
  - **Divided loyalties in a fractured society** led to the following:
    - **"The zest for civil war":** Under a sub-heading reading "From Civil War to Convulsion" (Brown 2013, loc 867), Peter Brown refers to the militarization of society in the late Roman Empire: "Of these military habits, the most upsetting to the civilian population was the zest for civil war. Again and again—indeed nine times in eighty-three years (from 312 to 395)—Roman soldiers had butchered their colleagues in murderous civil wars.... What happened in the fifth century was that civil war expanded to include 'proxy war' through the use of barbarian groups. Careful studies of the chronology and logistics of the civil wars of the early fifth century have shown that all the major breakthroughs by the barbarians either were part of maneuvers directly connected with civil wars, or at least were made possible by the distraction caused by civil wars.... It was not the barbarian invasions in themselves that changed the face of Europe. It was the synergy between barbarian groups, the long Roman practice of civil war, and the opportunism with which local Romans exploited both barbarians and civil war conditions for their own purposes. For this reason, it may be wise to abandon the term 'barbarian invasions' as a description of the period" and replace it with "'convulsion': an involvement of all segments of the population in a shake-up from which a very different society would emerge." (loc. 906.) Here Brown is prepared to admit that the "barbarian invasions" were actually violent, but he is anxious to push the blame for this on to internal factors labelled "convulsion". I agree that the prime causes of the dissolution of the West were internal but for a very different reason: the government's weakness in the face of the "barbarian" threat, resulting, as mentioned above, from divided loyalties in a fractured society, which in turn led to the following:
  - **Reduced tax revenues;** which, in its turn, resulted in:
  - **A shortage of troops,** leading to the need to hire "barbarian" troops, a most unsatisfactory arrangement as the imperial government was forced to hire the troops as *foederati* fighting under their own leaders, who could, and often did, change sides at will, and hold the government to ransom.
  - **Ethnic discrimination**, exacerbated by the separation between Roman units and "allied" troops under their own leaders, resulting

in massacres of one group by the other, and reflected in the fact that "barbarians" were not eligible for the imperial purple (something which changed later on in Byzantium.)

- **Religious persecution of "heretics" and pagans**, played down by Brown and his colleagues of the Late Antiquity school. (See Chapter 12.)
- **Aristocratic power.** One of the most important features of the Western Empire (though not in the East) from the time of Constantine was the renewed power of the senatorial aristocracy, who combined office, land, and local influence in the provinces, effectively acting as a centrifugal force sapping the power of the central imperial government and making it more vulnerable to "barbarian" takeovers.

So What?

This is the ultimate question that I believe a historian should always ask. In other words, in this particular case, what difference does it make whether the western Roman Empire fell, was pushed, or never came to an end at all? My own view is that the importance of this question has been grossly exaggerated. All the time and effort spent on the question of the fall of the Roman Empire could have been far better spent on the related, but quite separate, question of continuity and change, which has already been considered in Chapter 5.

The significance of this question becomes all the more apparent by comparing continuity and change in the West with those same features in the East. Though what is now generally called the Byzantine Empire lasted over a thousand years (albeit ending up in a very shrunken state), its heritage is rather restricted. The only territory that can be considered a linear descendant of Byzantium in the modern world is that now occupied by Greece and the Greek-speaking part of Cyprus. Only in these two states is Greek the official language spoken as their first language by the population at large. This is a major setback. Though the Byzantines always thought of themselves as "Romans" (and Orthodox Christians are still referred to in Turkish as *Rûm*), their empire was essentially a Greek empire. From the time of Alexander the Great (356-323 BCE), Greek became the lingua franca of the Eastern Mediterranean even though Roman rule made Latin the official language of the whole Roman Empire until it was replaced in the East by Greek in 610.

In terms of religion, Byzantium has left a more robust heritage. The Eastern Orthodox Church, made up of a number of autonomous (or autocephalous) national churches, is today the second largest Christian denomination in the world, with 220 million adherents, largely concentrated in Eastern Europe. However, most of the autonomous churches have quite a tenuous connection with Byzantium. The liturgical language in most such churches is either Church Slavonic or a vernacular language, and, though the Patriarch of Constantinople, known as the ecumenical patriarch, has priority over all other patriarchs, he is only *primus inter pares* (first among equals).

A third heritage of Byzantium which cannot be ignored is, ironically, the result of its demise, namely the rescue of thousands of Classical Greek texts, which were taken to the West after the fall of Constantinople in 1453, and are thought to have had some effect in developing the Italian Renaissance.

None of these features, however, really provides much continuity with the Byzantine Empire. The position in regard to the Western Roman Empire is very different. As Athaulf admitted, no "barbarian" kingdom of Gothia ever came into existence. The only "barbarians" who gave their name to a country were the Franks and the Angles though the language of France is a Romance language, like those of most of the rest of the Western Empire, and that of England (an integral part of Britain, from the area's Roman name) has become suffused with Latin loanwords. (See above.)

The Roman Catholic Church, with its subdivision into dioceses and provinces, terms taken over directly from the Roman Empire, still has its headquarters in Rome, under a bishop who is called in Latin by the same title as the Roman emperor as head of the old pagan state religion, Pontifex Maximus (chief priest). Politically, too, as discussed earlier in this chapter, the image of the western Roman Empire survives.

Three Revolutions

Three major revolutions can be traced back to Constantine. Firstly, Constantine initiated the dominance of Christianity in the Roman world though he was not actually baptized until on his deathbed in 337 and though Christianity did not become the sole official religion of the Empire until 380. The significance of this is that it replaced the tolerant communal Roman pagan state religion with an inherently intolerant creed religion, which has remained the dominant religion in Europe ever since. This represents both continuity and change, a major break with the past on the part of Constantine and his successors, and continuity from then on down to the present. That revolution also had two major continuing spin-offs, namely the rise of Islam, a creed religion that became intolerant on the Christian model, and rabbinic Judaism, which, under the influence of Christianity, changed from a tolerant communal religion into an intolerant quasi-creed religion. (See Chapter 10.)

By bringing members of the senatorial aristocracy back into high office, Constantine effected a second revolution, which endorsed, boosted, bolstered, and reactivated the aristocratic ethos that had been the hallmark of Roman society from the early Republic. This revolution, too, proved long-lasting, surviving until the French Revolution, and still not entirely extinct. (See Chapter 6.)

Thirdly, Constantine founded a new Christian capital in the East, which would ensure that there was a Roman emperor until 1453.

Structural or Individual?

One important question that has not received sufficient attention is how much of the continuity of the Western Empire was structural and how much was personal. We know, for example, that aristocracy and the aristocratic ethos survived the dissolution of the Western Empire. But who were the aristocrats who carried on this Roman tradition? Were they descendants of the old Roman senatorial aristocracy? Or were they "barbarian" aristocrats aping Roman manners and customs? The evidence is patchy, but the answer would appear to be that these later aristocrats were a mixture of the two. (See Chapter 5.)

Part III

Envoi

14

Conclusion

The full title of this book is: **Why Rome Fell: Decline and Fall, or Drift and Change?** The Wester Empire certainly ceased to exist at some point in the fifth century and was succeeded by a shifting mosaic of "barbarian" kingdoms. Though accompanied by some cataclysmic changes at the time, how significant was this transition in the long run? A bird's-eye view of the past two thousand years reveals two pre-eminent landmarks in Roman history: the reign of Augustus, and the reign of Constantine, with continuity after that—even after the transition to "barbarian" kingdoms in the west, and, in the East down to the fall of Constantinople to the Turks in 1453.

Constantine: Three Changes

There are three main changes attributable to Constantine: administrative, religious, and the founding of a new eastern capital. On the administrative front, the conventional view is that Constantine essentially perpetuated Diocletian's "Dominate," in itself a culmination of the trend toward autocracy. There is some truth in this, especially in the East. But in the West Constantine sharply reversed Diocletian's policy in an important respect. While Diocletian effectively excluded senators from provincial governorships, Constantine and his successors brought them back in, appointing them not only as governors but also as vicars and even as praetorian prefects in the West. The beneficiaries of this policy were not just *viri clarissimi*, men of senatorial *rank*, but included men of senatorial *birth*.

Power Structure

What, if anything, is the significance of this reform? As shown in Chapters 3, 4, and 5, this reversal of Diocletian's policy represents a meaningful shift in the power structure of the West. Power structure is a feature studied chiefly by sociologists, political scientists, and other "social scientists" while being largely ignored by those academics best placed to interpret the evidence required for such a study, namely historians. The power structure of a society identifies the whereabouts of power in that society, or, in short, who has the whip hand. It also relates to social mobility, which is ultimately a reflection of the degree of liberty in the society concerned. In addition, the power structure is related to the ethos of the society concerned.

Two Models of Government

My hypothesis, as set out in *Two Models of Government* (Arnheim 2016) and also in Chapter 6 of this book, is as follows. All forms of government for at least the past three thousand years have belonged essentially to one of two models: monarchy or oligarchy. By monarchy, I mean the rule of a single individual, whether hereditary, elective, or usurped, and whether that individual has the title of king or queen, emperor or empress, president, prime minister, dictator, chairman, first secretary, or no title at all. The opposite model, oligarchy (rule of the few), similarly includes the rule by elites of all kinds, whether hereditary, elective, or usurped, whether defined in terms of birth, wealth, ethnicity, or religion, and also whether access to the elite is open or closed. Where the ruling elite is made up of a hereditary oligarchy, even where access is not entirely closed, the form of government should rather be termed aristocracy, made up of members who may themselves be designated as aristocrats, aristocracy, nobles, or nobility.

Though the word "monarch" means the rule of one person (from the Greek *monarchia*), for one person to rule singlehandedly over a state of any size is practically impossible. The monarch, sovereign, or ruler will need support and assistance. This applies even to rulers considered to be autocrats or absolute monarchs. But the amount of power exercised by a monarch will vary greatly with the type of support and assistance relied upon.

Monarchy and oligarchy/aristocracy are polar opposites. So, where a monarch has aristocratic support, the monarch is either just delegating some of his power, or is merely a figurehead in what is essentially an aristocratic or oligarchic regime.

This latter case is the position in present-day European "constitutional monarchies", including those of Sweden, Denmark, Norway, the Netherlands, Belgium, Spain, and the United Kingdom. These countries are monarchies in name only. Despite all the elaborate trappings of power, pomp and ceremony, grandiose titulature, and all the bowing and scraping, the present-day "sovereign" of the United Kingdom, for example, is not sovereign at all. The king or queen is obliged to appoint as prime minister the leader of the majority party in the House of Commons and to assent to any legislation passed by both houses of Parliament.

Throughout world history, the monarchs who have wielded the greatest amount of power are those who enjoy broad popular support, generally from the lower classes. Such monarchs are often spearheaded to power by overthrowing an aristocratic regime. This enables them to rule as populists in the interests of the many and against the interests of the elite. Examples include most of the Greek "tyrants" of the period 650 to 550 BCE and dictators in the modern sense, such as Julius Caesar, Napoleon Bonaparte, Mao Zedong (Mao Tse-tung), and Fidel Castro.

This power structure was figuratively represented by lopping off all the ears of corn projecting above the others, as graphically illustrated in the well-known anecdote related by both Herodotus and Aristotle of one Greek tyrant advising another by means of a dumbshow transmitted through a herald. (Herodotus 5.92 f; Aristotle, *Politics* 1284a.) (See Chapter 6.) Aristotle describes Peisistratus of Athens and two other tyrants as "the champions of the people" (*hoi prostatai tou dēmou*). (*Ibid.*, 105a 18 ff = V.4.5). The populist nature of Greek "tyranny" is unfortunately missed by the modern author of one of the few books specifically on the subject. (Andrewes 1956.) (See Chapter 6.)

Aristotle put the tyrants' typical power-base in a nutshell: "The majority of tyrants have developed out of demagogues who have gained the confidence of the people through their attacks on the nobles." (Arist. Pol. 1310b.) In the Aristotelian *Athenian Constitution* (*Athenaiōn Politeia (AP)*), likewise, Peisistratus is lumped together with a number of democratic leaders, including Pericles, as "the people's champions", opposed to a list of leaders of the "notables" (*gnōrimoi*) or aristocracy. (Arist., *AP* 28.) Moses Finley, to his credit, following this evidence, characterized Pericles as "a direct heir of Pisistratus" in their common opposition to the rich and noble. (Finley 1983, p. 47.)

Every society of which we know has been stratified: in no society is everyone equal. From the earliest recorded history, we encounter dominant minorities or power elites of various kinds, which either rule as a group or select a leader as their head. If this person is installed as a monarch but remains dependent on or beholden to the elite group from which he emerged, he is either going to be a weak monarch or just a figurehead. In either case, the *ethos* of that society remains essentially oligarchic or aristocratic, a concept that is hardly recognized by historians.

Even demagogues tend to come from an elite background. "The Athenian people were rather snobbish in their choice of leaders," is A.H.M. Jones's explanation of the selection of Pericles, a high aristocrat, as champion of the people. (Jones 1957, p. 49.) This begs the question: Why was this the case? The answer is that, though the regime was anti-aristocratic, the whole ethos of society remained aristocratic: The Athenian democracy simply did not believe in equality. (Arnheim 1977, p. 158 ff.) Roman society was likewise thoroughly suffused with an aristocratic ethos even when the aristocracy was out of power.

Machiavelli

The only theory with which my "Two Models" hypothesis has anything in common is that set out in Niccolò Machiavelli's *Il Principe* (The Prince), written in 1513. (See Chapter 7.) Here is a key statement from Chapter 9 of that work, encapsulating the essence of his theory: "In every state two distinct tendencies (humors) are found, namely that of the common people and that of the aristocracy. The common people do not wish to be ruled or oppressed by the aristocracy, while the aristocracy wish to rule and oppress the common people." Though this hypothesis is a leitmotif running right through *Il Principe*, it has been all but ignored by modern commentators, including Quentin Skinner, a vaunted authority on Machiavelli. (See Chapter 7.)

Machiavelli's argument runs as follows:

- In every state, there is hostility between the aristocracy, or privileged elite, and the common people.
- Both sides select a leader.
- A leader dependent on aristocratic support will prove a weak "prince," and the regime will be essentially an oligarchy or aristocracy.
- Such a "prince" will be dependent on "barons" with their own power bases.
- The people's loyalties will be to these barons rather than to the "prince.".

- However, a prince dependent on popular support will be a strong ruler.
- Such a ruler will govern through servants who are totally beholden to him, so that popular loyalty is to him alone.
- But while nurturing popular support, a wise ruler will take care not to exasperate the aristocracy.

Roman Power Structure

Machiavelli's hypothesis in *Il Principe* is particularly well-suited to Roman history from Augustus's ascendancy onward, a period of unbroken monarchy, divisible into three types.

- **The Principate**: Initiated by Augustus, this type of monarchy would essentially last for three hundred years until the accession of Diocletian in 284 CE.
- **The Dominate:** A form of autocratic monarchy, introduced by Diocletian in 284, would essentially last in the Eastern Empire until its fall in 1453.
- **The Constantinian formula:** This form of monarchy with a certain amount of power delegated to the aristocracy, is found in western Europe from the time of Constantine until the rise of strong monarchy in the fifteenth century.

Power Structure: The Principate

Determined to avoid the fate of his adoptive father, Augustus restored the façade of the Republic while dismantling it from within. Under the thin disguise of *princeps* (first citizen), Augustus established a popular monarchy while conciliating the senatorial aristocracy by reserving to them all but a few provincial governorships, subject to his control.

Augustus's republican charade probably deceived very few of his contemporaries. The urban plebs regarded him as their protector (demanding, for example, when there was a food shortage in 22 BCE, that he accept the dictatorship), while the aristocracy were no doubt grateful for crumbs of imperial favor. Some modern historians have been more credulous. After discovering "direct democracy" in the Roman Republic on the basis of a misreading of Polybius, Fergus Millar then compounded this error by accepting at face-value Augustus's boast in his autobiography that he had restored the Republic. (See Chapter 1.)

A more disquieting fallacy, attached as it is to the name of Sir Ronald Syme, is the claim that the Augustan form of government was essentially an oligarchy. The author, of the magisterial and aptly named *The Roman Revolution*, was well aware that the new regime was a monarchy, but his myopic focus on the prosopography of the senatorial aristocracy led him into a blind alley: "A monarchy rules through an oligarchy." (Syme 1939, p.8.) "In all ages, whatever the form and name of government or whatever may be the name and theory of the constitution, be it monarchy, republic, or democracy, an oligarchy lurks behind the façade." (Syme 1939, pp. 7, 15.) Fifty years later, Syme is still barking up the oligarchy tree: "Oligarchy is imposed as the guiding theme, the link from age to age whatever be the form and name of government". (Syme 1989, p. 13.) Identifying monarchy with its diametric opposite, oligarchy, in these sweeping generalizations is a serious logical category error. (Chapter 1.)

According to Syme, Augustus harbored a particular "engrained hostility" towards the *nobiles*, the scions of consular families, and initially excluded them from any military appointments. However, "When his position becomes stronger, and a coalition government based largely on family ties has been built up, *nobiles* like Ahenobarbus, Piso and Paullus Fabius Maximus govern the military provinces, it is true. But a rational distrust persists, confirmed under his successors by certain disquieting incidents, and leads to the complete exclusion of the *nobiles*, the delayed but logical end of Revolution and Empire." (Syme 1939, p. 502.) Coalition government between emperor and aristocracy? How does this square with this remark, also by Syme that "Power receding, aristocrats looked to priesthoods for 'dignitas' and social eminence." (Syme 1989, p, 3 f.)

It is essential to an understanding of the Principate to realize that it was a monarchy, not an oligarchy of any kind, nor even a "coalition". Without appealing directly to the masses for their support against the aristocracy, the emperors nevertheless established themselves in the public mind as a bastion of strength and justice on whom ordinary people across the vast empire could depend, hence, for example, the huge number of letters petitioning the emperor and the bureaucracy set up to reply. People expected the emperor to be accessible as is reflected in the well-known anecdote about the petitioner who accosted the Emperor Hadrian (r. 117–138) on his travels in an eastern province. Trying to fob her off with the excuse that he was too busy, Hadrian received the angry retort: *kai mē basileue.* ("Then don't be king!") (Dio 69.6.3.) In the minds of ordinary people, it was an emperor's job to be accessible to his people. It is worth noting, too, that for this Greek-speaking woman— as, no doubt, in the eastern half of the empire generally—the emperor was simply *basileus*, (king).

The fact that the great majority of the emperor's lieutenants in the provinces, most of whom, indeed, bore the title *legatus Augusti pro praetore* (envoy of the emperor with praetorian rank), were senators did not mean that the senate or its members ruled the roost, as would have been the case in an oligarchic or aristocratic system. To change the metaphor, the question was who had the whip hand. And the answer was always the same: the emperor.

In the course of the third century, the old traditional framework was gradually abandoned until, by the end of the century, only very few posts of importance were open to senators. The tendency now was to bypass the Senate by appointing non-senators directly to governorships without bothering to make them senators first.

Power Structure: The Dominate

This process culminated in the reign of Diocletian (284–305), who excluded senators from all but a few provincial governorships, which effectively became the preserve of equestrians, while the senatorial career—the pinnacle of ambition for eight hundred years—-became a cul-de-sac. But, whereas senatorial rank, denoted by the title *vir clarissimus* (literally, "most distinguished man"), was hereditary, equestrian status depended on the particular office held. By replacing senators with equestrians, and also relying to some extent on eunuchs, Diocletian clearly intended to enhance imperial power, which was demonstrated by his flamboyant dress and elaborate court ceremonial. Hence the modern label of "Dominate" attached to Diocletian's "tetrarchy." (See Chapter 2.) This model of monarchy essentially continued in the eastern half of the empire, or the Byzantine Empire, until the fall of Constantinople to the Turks in 1453.

Power Structure: The Constantinian Formula

In the West, Diocletian's policy was reversed by Constantine. Under the tetrarchy, practically all provincial governors, known as *praesides*, were of non-senatorial status, with the equestrian title *vir perfectissimus*. But under Constantine an increasing number of *praesides* were *clarissimi*, whether or not they were of senatorial birth. And by the early fifth century the position of *praeses* carried with it an automatic clarissimate.

Constantine's policy of senatorial appointments to high office was perpetuated by his successors. By the time of Valentinian I (r. 364–375) and Valens (r. 364–378), for example, even the formerly strictly equestrian post of *dux* (provincial military commander) carried the clarissimate. Lower positions then came to carry the perfectissimate, so that by 362, it was accorded even to lowly *numerarii* (accountants) of provincial governors with five years' unblemished service. With the inrush of so many *perfectissimi*, that title had to be split into three classes, and *vir egregius* (entry-level equestrian title) completely disappeared from view after 324.

As more and more offices carried an automatic clarissimate, the once-proud senatorial title *vir clarissimus* itself became debased. Valentinian I introduced gradations within the clarissimate. (CTh 6.7.1; 6.9.1; 6.11.1; 6.14.1; 6.22.4-372.) The top grade, occupied, among others, by praetorian and urban prefects, was that of *viri illustres*, followed by *viri spectabiles*, borne, among others, by proconsuls and vicars, with plain *clarissimi*, including senators by birth bringing up the rear. By the reign of Justinian (527–565), active membership of the senate and even the designation as *senator* was confined to *illustres*, who by this time were further subdivided in the Byzantine Empire, with the top rank being *vir gloriosus*, or even *gloriosissimus*.

Inflation of Honors or Real Change?

Was this long process merely an inflation of honors, a form of "fusion" between the senatorial and equestrian orders? Or does it represent a genuine change of policy? The answer is emphatically the latter.

As is shown in Chapter 3, what we find, starting with Constantine, are *praesides*, vicars, and even praetorian prefects who not only bear the senatorial honorific, *vir clarissimus*, but are also of senatorial birth or origin. There are, however, two limitations. First, these aristocratic appointments are found in the West alone. And secondly, they are to purely civil posts.

What was Constantine's motive for making this major break with previous policy?

- **Pandering:** Was Constantine pandering to the senatorial aristocracy? In a practical sense, Constantine was evidently trying to win the support of the senatorial aristocracy, which may well have been because his purely Western Empire, as it was until 324, also happened to be the stronghold of the aristocracy.
- **Distrust:** The fact that these appointments were exclusively civilian may well be a sign of the reluctance with which this policy was embarked upon and the emperor's underlying distrust of the aristocracy.
- **Taxation:** Were Constantine's concessions intended as a form of compensation for taxing the senatorial aristocracy? We simply do not know, but this may have been a factor.

- **Religion:** Could this policy have anything to do with religion? It might appear a cunning, counterintuitive ploy for a Christian-leaning emperor deliberately to favor aristocrats, the majority of whom were still pagan (despite attempts by some modern writers to deny this). This was probably too devious even for the wily Constantine. See the discussion in Chapter 3.
- **Antiquarianism**: Constantine is known to have had antiquarian tastes: witness his creation of a new type of quaestorship, later known as *quaestor (sacri palatii)*; and his innovative use of *patricius* (patrician) as a formal title of honor. But he evidently had genuine respect for long noble pedigrees as in the case of the Aradii. And he even restored to the Senate as an institution its ancient right to elect to the quaestorship, the first rung on the ladder of the now again significant senatorial *cursus honorum.*

As mentioned above, this policy of appointing men of senatorial birth to high civil posts in the West was perpetuated by Constantine's successors. Of the thirteen praetorian prefects in the West appointed by Constantine's sons, only one, Flavius Taurus, prefect of Italy and Africa for the last six years of Constantius's reign, is known to have been of non-senatorial origin. Seven of these prefects, however, are known to have been nobles (i.e. of senatorial birth), and both C. Ceionius Rufius Volusianus Lampadius and Vulcacius Rufinus had more than one spell as prefect, the latter's terms amounting to a total of ten years under the sons of Constantine and Magnentius. He would return to office as praetorian prefect of Italy, Africa and Illyricum, for another three years under Valentinian, an emperor who was no lover of the aristocracy. Yet, the corrupt Petronius Probus, head of the great Anician clan, was praetorian prefect under Valentinian on three occasions, the last as praetorian prefect of the vast western region comprising Italy, Illyricum, and Africa for the whole period from 368 until Valentinian's death in 375, and again in 383–384.

Social Mobility and Ethos

This long-continued policy shift amounts to a significant change in the power structure of the Roman Empire, from one form of monarchy to another. Constantine's aristocratic appointments policy did not establish a "coalition" or hybrid form of government, but it modified the power structure enough to make a difference between East and West. While the Dominate ostensibly continued unabated in Byzantium, the West experienced monarchy tempered by an aristocratic ethos.

Besides identifying the whereabouts of power, power structure also relates to social mobility and equality of opportunity, which is ultimately a reflection of the degree of liberty in the society concerned.

Where power is held by a narrow hereditary aristocracy, as in the Roman Republic, social mobility is restricted. As Syme put it, based on solid prosopographical evidence, "In any age of the history of Republican Rome about twenty or thirty men, drawn from a dozen dominant families, hold a monopoly of office and power." (Syme 1939, p. 124.) This view is supported in regard to the Late Republic by Ernst Badian's conclusion that "...the proportion of consuls who came from families that had already produced at least one consul never fell below 70 percent in the whole period between 179 and 49 BCE." (Badian 1990, pp. 371–413.) This does not deny the existence of *novi homines* (new men), but it means that they were very much in the minority.

During the Principate, (to use a sociological expression) the elites were more open. As shown in Chapter 1, detailed prosopographical research summarized by Mason Hammond shows that the proportion of provincial (i.e. non-Italian) senators of known origin increased steadily (with a couple of minor blips) from 16.8 percent under Vespasian (r. 69–79) to 56 percent in the Third Century. Under Vespasian, therefore, provincials made up only one-sixth of senators of known origin. There is a major jump to 32.4 percent under Trajan (r. 98–117), who was himself a provincial from Spain. Practically all subsequent emperors were also provincials, and from the end of the second century, provincials made up more than half the senators of known origin. This ever-widening circle of senators, from whom most provincial governors were drawn, was an important reason for the stability and general tranquillity of the Roman Empire over a long period. In keeping with this trend, in the year 212, the Emperor Caracalla extended Roman citizenship to all free male inhabitants of the Roman world by means of the so-called *Constitutio Antoniniana*.

Social mobility in the Later Roman Empire is more difficult to gauge. Referring to Constantine's new dispensation, A.H.M. Jones remarked, "The new hierarchy effectively transformed the aristocracy from one of birth into one of office." (Jones 1964, p. 529.) This was certainly true of the Eastern half of the Empire, which lacked a traditional senatorial aristocracy like that of the West and where the *clarissimi* of the new Senate of Constantinople were parvenus. But in the West, once high office, including the position of praetorian prefect, was opened up to senators, appointees tended to be men not just of senatorial rank but also of senatorial birth. As a result, in the West, there was no real fusion or merger between the old senatorial aristocracy and new men, and nobles were very proud and conscious of belonging to the old senatorial aristocracy. Social mobility in the West was, therefore, far more limited than in the Byzantine East, where there was no real hereditary aristocracy before the eleventh or twelfth century. Until then, as was seen in Chapters 4 and 5, imperial power, though theoretically unlimited, was shared with bureaucrats, generals, the Church, and, to a very significant extent, with eunuchs.

Constantine and Christianity

Constantine's most important, best-known, and most long-lasting reform was his pro-Christian policy. Though not baptized until on his deathbed in 337, and though he continued to hedge his bets until at least 333, Constantine took several bold pro-Christian steps, notably his adoption of the *labarum* with the Chi-Rho christogram (either in 312, or possibly only after 317, and certainly after 324); his convening of the Council of Nicaea in 325; and the favors with which he showered Christian bishops. The idea that Constantine picked Christianity because of its dominant position numerically in the Roman world has been well and truly scotched. On the contrary, it was Constantine's favor that catapulted Christianity into dominance from being very much a minority religion. (See Chapter 3.) Nicene Christianity became the single official religion of the Roman Empire by the Edict of Thessalonica of 380, which condemned the adherents of all other variants of Christianity as "foolish madmen", branded them as "heretics", and threatened them with persecution (CTh 16.1.2.), a threat which was far from idle. Persecution of pagans and Jews was no less real.

Christianity Inherently Intolerant

What Constantine achieved by picking Christianity was to replace a thousand-year ethos of religious toleration or even religious freedom with one of religious intolerance and persecution. Constantine did not *make* Christianity intolerant: that feature was inherent in Christianity by virtue of its being a "creed religion". (See Chapter 10.)

In Paul's Epistle to the Galatians, written at some time between the late 40s and 60, we find a list of "works of the flesh" (vices) that amount to a denial of the Spirit. Not surprisingly, the catalog includes adultery, fornication, idolatry, and murder, but we then unexpectedly come across "heresies". (Gal. 5:19–21.) The reason for this is not difficult to fathom. The Epistle is chiefly concerned with that central question in early Christianity: whether non-Jewish converts to the new movement needed to regard themselves as proselytes to Judaism, involving circumcision, kosher food, and observance of other Jewish laws or, as Paul insisted, as converts to an entirely new religion quite separate from Judaism. From the start, therefore, Paul's position, which won out in the end against the "Judaizers" in the "Jerusalem Church", required a definition of the doctrines or beliefs of the fledgling movement, which turned it into something new, namely a creed religion, needing to define its beliefs, and inevitably making it intolerant not only of other religions but also of any deviation from the dominant sect's set of beliefs. Once Constantine selected Christianity for special favor, and, even more so, once Christianity became the sole official religion of the Empire, its intolerance became more marked, and it became able to enlist the support of the emperor in its persecutions.

The Severity of Christian Intolerance

So anxious are some modern writers, notably Peter Brown of the Late Antiquity school, to minimize the seriousness of Christian intolerance, that he resorts to a lengthy but less than persuasive argument by analogy, based on a charming anecdote about his three-year-old nephew's first visit to the zoo. As the only live animal he had ever seen was his pet cat, he is surprised by the large size of the zoo animals. (Brown 1995, p. 29 ff.) This is fully discussed in Chapter 12.

Peter Brown's unpersuasive argument is that, just as his little nephew *under*estimated the size of the zoo animals, so it is likely that the degree of Christian intolerance and persecution has been *over*estimated, an excellent example of a logical *non sequitur*.

Other Arguments Minimizing Christian Intolerance

To "correct" the supposedly magnified image of Christian intolerance, Brown repeats several well-worn arguments that have been given their quietus in previous chapters of this book:

- **"Paganism was not tolerant either"**: In trying to play down the severity and significance of Christian intolerance, Brown and his acolytes reach for the old adage that attack is the best defense and claim that paganism was no more tolerant than Christianity or even that religious toleration is a "fragile notion" and virtually unattainable. (See Chapter 12, and also Chapter 10, where it is shown that religious toleration, and, more than that, freedom of religion, had been the hallmark of Roman religious life for a thousand years before Constantine.)
- **"The punitive laws were not enforced"**: This is another old chestnut. Punitive and even savage as the laws against "heretics", pagans, and Jews may appear to be, runs this argument, the fact that they are

repeated so often with increasing shrillness shows that they were not enforced. (Ibid., p. 33.) In an empire as vast as that of Rome, the uniform enforcement of laws could not be expected. Also, some officials were more enthusiastic persecutors than others. Above all, though, the laws were not always obeyed. But the fact that "heresies" and paganism were gradually eliminated indicates either that the laws were working or that these banned forms of worship went underground or, of course, that their adherents converted to Nicene Christianity. In fact, all three developments probably took place. But even conversions to orthodoxy can hardly be regarded as entirely voluntary. There was a great deal of pressure, legal and extra-legal, to conform. And we know of major pockets of paganism surviving, even in Constantinople itself, into the reign of Justinian. (See Chapter 5.)

- "**The 'viscosity' of the mentality of the elites of the later empire**." (Ibid., p. 39.) This is what I would prefer to call an aristocratic ethos, as discussed above. Brown uses this concept as part of his attempt to minimize the severity of Christian intolerance, referring to the good relations on an individual basis between members of the elites who happened to belong to different religions. He explains further that "As far as the formation of the new governing class of the post-Constantinian empire was concerned, the fourth century was very definitely not a century overshadowed by 'The Conflict of Paganism and Christianity.' Nothing, indeed, would have been more distressing to a member of the late Roman upper classes than the suggestion that 'pagan' and 'Christian' were designations of overriding importance in their style of life and in their choice of friends and allies." (Ibid., p. 47.) This is probably true, but the idea must be dispelled of western aristocrats hobnobbing with parvenu eastern senators, with whom they would have had very little contact. It also does nothing to diminish the significance or severity of Christian intolerance, and the persecution of "heretics", pagans, and Jews, which went on unabated. However, this aristocratic ethos certainly survived the dissolution of the empire in the West, where, sensing, as always, which way the wind was blowing, the old noble families came to monopolize the top positions in the Church.

Christian Influence on Judaism and Islam

As the sole official religion of the Roman Empire, which remained dominant in both halves of the empire after the West was carved up into a number of "barbarian" kingdoms, Christianity naturally exerted great influence on Judaism and also on the new religion of the Arabs: Islam.

Rabbinic Judaism

Though the Jewish religion, in common with the other national religions of the ancient world, was a "communal" religion, the influence of Christianity impelled Judaism also to develop, at least partially, into a creed religion, leading to splits within it in later times.

In its original form as a communal religion, membership of the Jewish religion was part and parcel of being a member of the Jewish people. Judaism had no missionaries and was none too welcoming to would-be converts (as, indeed, would remain the case with orthodox Judaism down to the present day). The Hebrew Bible, or, more particularly, the Five Books of Moses (Pentateuch) contains 613 commandments, all but one of which are instructions on conduct, cleanliness, diet, and ritual, including Temple sacrifice. The sole exception is the fundamental belief in a single invisible God. And for disobedience to this law, the punishment is death. (Deut. 17:2–7.)

The Book of Deuteronomy is generally dated to the reign of King Josiah (640–609 BCE.) So, does this not mean that Judaism was in its essence just as intolerant as Christianity? No, because the passage in question is very careful to restrict this offense to Jews: "If there be found among you, within any of the gates which the Lord thy God giveth thee, man or woman that hath wrought wickedness in the sight of the Lord thy God, in transgressing his covenant, and hath gone and served other gods, and worshipped them, either the sun or moon, or any of the host of heaven, which I have not commanded; and it be told thee, and thou hast heard of it, and enquired diligently, and, behold, it be true, and the thing certain, that such abomination is wrought in Israel.....Then thou shalt bring forth that man or that woman, which have committed that wicked thing, unto thy gates, even that man or that woman, and shalt stone them with stones, till they die. So thou shalt put the evil away from among you." (KJB Deut. 17: 2-7.)

No non-Jew could fall foul of this law. It is also not aimed against any potential Jewish "heretics" who, whatever their beliefs, would still worship the one invisible God. In the time of Jesus, for example, all the different Jewish sects, including Jesus's own small band of followers, worshiped at the Temple in Jerusalem without let or hindrance.

After the destruction of the second Temple in 70, rabbinic Judaism, an offshoot of Pharisaism, developed a set of beliefs, probably as a way of competing with Christianity. (This important phenomenon seems to have been missed by the writers on rabbinic Judaism in the later Roman Empire.) These can be found in the Talmud, made up of the Mishnah, compiled in the early third century, and the Gemarah, comprising the Jerusalem Talmud, published between 350 and 400, and the Babylonian Talmud, dating from around 500. This whole development was based on the belief that, besides the Written Torah supposedly written by Moses at God's dictation on Mount Sinai, there was an even more voluminous Oral Torah (Oral Law), dictated by God to Moses at the same time, which was handed down orally and committed to writing by the rabbis. The most famous distillation of the supposed Oral Law is to be found in the Thirteen Principles of Faith, compiled by Moses Maimonides (1138–1204), which finally converted Judaism into a pseudo-creed religion, inevitably splitting it into a number of denominations, each with its own clergy, liturgy, and *Beth Din* (rabbinical court). The ambivalent attitude of the different groups to one another is well represented by this remark made by Orthodox Chief Rabbi Sacks of the United Kingdom from 1991 to 2013: "Reform Jews are Jews; Reform Judaism is not Judaism." (Sacks 1993, p. 34.)

Islam as a Creed Religion

As indicated in Chapter 13, Islam was heavily influenced by the Christian model of religion. Like Christianity, Islam is a creed religion, based on the Six Articles of Faith, five of which are already found in the Quran. (Quran 2:285.) The Third Article is belief in the divine authorship, not only of the Quran itself but also of the Torah, the Psalms, and the Christian Gospels. And Article Four is belief in Muhammad (570–632) as the final prophet, preceded by Jesus and several Jewish prophets. As a creed religion, Islam also had a natural tendency from the start to fragment, like Christianity. And this has certainly materialized though the split between the two main denominations, Sunni and Shia, was originally not doctrinal but concerned the question of the identity of Muhammad's rightful successor. Nevertheless, before long, divergences in belief, theology, and practice crept in as well as the development in Shia, but not in Sunni, of a formal clerical hierarchy.

After Muhammad's unification of Arabia into a single Muslim state, his successors made a series of lightning-speed conquests sweeping from Persia to Spain between 632 and 711. Largely, it seems for reasons of taxation, the conquered peoples were initially discouraged from converting to Islam, but conversions became very common from the eighth century, which exempted proselytes from the *jizya* tax imposed on *dhimmi* (protected person), namely Jews and Christians as People of the Book and later also the adherents of other religions as well. *Dhimmi* were essentially treated as second-class citizens though they also enjoyed certain privileges as in the later Ottoman "millet" system, under which *dhimmi* communities were allowed a good deal of autonomy. For example, the Ecumenical Patriarch of Constantinople was recognized as exercising both religious and political authority over all Eastern Orthodox subjects of the Ottoman sultan. (Cf. Sachedina, Abdulaziz Abdulhussein, 2001, p. 96 f.)

Constantine's New Rome

Constantine's third legacy, the establishment of a "Second Rome" in the ancient Greek trading port of Byzantium, renamed Constantinople, was probably not intended to split the Empire into two. Rome had effectively ceased to be the imperial capital after 286, early in the reign of Diocletian. Centers closer to the frontiers had taken its place, moving with the itinerant imperial courts during the tetrarchy. These new administrative centers included Nicomedia (in modern Turkey), Mediolanum (Milan), Sirmium (in modern Serbia), and Augusta Treverorum (modern Trier.) But Constantine had a longer vision, evidently seeking a grander, more permanent, defensible capital in the eastern half of the empire, which he only acquired after his defeat of Licinius in 324.

As was shown in Chapters 4 and 5, much of the modern special pleading for the Byzantine Empire (a modern coinage) is without foundation:

- Though much is made of its thousand-year survival after the dissolution of the West, by the time Byzantium fell to the Turks in 1453, it was a pocket-handkerchief size state and had been expanding and shrinking (mostly the latter) throughout its history.
- The vaunted impregnability of Constantinople is often given as the reason for the Eastern Empire's longevity. In fact, however, it fell to the Crusaders in 1204, 250 years before its final capture. And the Empire's porous eastern and northern borders led to its hemorrhaging large chunks of territory to the Persians, Muslims, Seljuk Turks, and Slavs.
- The idyllic picture painted by some modern writers of a joyful Byzantine Empire united in its devotion to an autocratic emperor and harmonious society simply does not gel. "Men paid their taxes and prayed for the success of the emperor whatever their shade of theological opinion." (Brown 1971, p.145.) This bald assertion, like so much else by the same author, is unsupported by evidence. What, then, about the major schism created by the Council of Chalcedon of 451, which anathematized Monophysites as "heretics"? This unleashed the merciless persecution and death of thousands of

Monophysites, especially in Egypt, a Monophysite stronghold (as, indeed, it would remain down to the present day). Brown's comment, another sweeping and unsupported generalization, is as follows:

"It has been said that the Council of Chalcedon divided the empire irreparably; that it rendered inevitable the loss of the eastern provinces to Islam in the seventh century....The exact opposite was the case. Despite the explosive nature of the issues involved, despite the fact that the ecclesiastical traditions of whole provinces were mobilized on both sides, the empire remained united." (Brown, 1971, p. 145.) This is pure bluster, as can be seen from a consideration of the facts of the Muslim conquest of Egypt between 639 and 641. Cyrus, Monophysite Patriarch of Alexandria and administrative head of Egypt, actually signed a treaty with the Muslims recognizing Muslim sovereignty over the whole of Egypt and agreed on behalf of the population of the diocese to pay the *jizya* tax. Forwarding the treaty to the Emperor Heraclius for ratification, Cyrus made it clear that he and his Monophysite Coptic flock would honor the treaty regardless of the emperor's response. When Heraclius repudiated the treaty and stripped Cyrus of his administrative position (though not of his Patriarchate), Cyrus specifically asked the Muslims not to make peace with the Byzantines even if they sued for peace but to enslave them as captives. During the siege of Alexandria in 641, the last obstacle to the Muslim takeover of Egypt, a good proportion of the population sided with the invaders. (Butler 1978, pp. 311–30.)

- As discussed above, the strongest type of monarch is one, like Augustus, who has popular support but who also does not antagonize the aristocracy. The form of the Dominate that survived under the Byzantine Empire was very different. Protected by elaborate court ritual and numerous layers of administrative officials, and cocooned with a small number of eunuchs, notably the *praepositus sacri cubiculi*, or "grand chamberlain," who doubled as body servant and confidential adviser, or even vizier, the Byzantine emperor was well and truly isolated from his subjects and, with certain notable exceptions, became a puppet in the hands of his own retainers. Brown's comment that the eunuchs' recruitment "...from far beyond the traditional governing class" proves that "...the backstairs government of the palace did not cut off the emperor from his subjects" is yet another unsupported, and unlikely, assertion. (Brown 1971, p. 141. Cf. Chapter 5 of this book.)

- The ultimate paradox (missed by the adulators of Byzantium in their anxious search for paradoxes) is that the Byzantine Empire's most lasting legacy was the result of its demise. The Byzantine swansong was the disgorging of scores of precious manuscripts of otherwise lost classical texts to the West in the hands of desperate refugees from Constantinople after its fall in 1453, jumpstarting, or at least giving a further fillip to, the Italian Renaissance.

Was Late Antiquity a "Good Thing"?

According to that wonderful parody of English history, *1066 and All That*, the Roman conquest of Britain was a "Good Thing". The book, written in 1930, mocks the tendency on the part of historians of that era to pass judgment on events and individuals alike. Academic historians, of course, have their own political opinions, views on issues ranging from nuclear weapons to euthanasia and, not least, their own religious beliefs or unbeliefs. With the best will in the world, it may not be possible for historians to set their views and beliefs completely to one side, but it is surely incumbent upon them as academics to at least make an attempt to do so, failing which their writings may well become contaminated, leading to a distorted vision of their subject. (See Chapter 7.)

Among historians of the later Roman Empire, the one most successful in attaining as "objective" an account as possible was probably my late supervisor and mentor, A.H.M. "Hugo" Jones (1904–70), from whose writings it would be hard to identify his political, social, or religious opinions. He and I used to have lively debates on the correct interpretation of the period, and though we did not always see eye to eye, at no time did he seek to impose his views on me. And in my doctoral dissertation, written under his supervision, I emphasized "internal" causes of the fall of the Western Empire, as against the "external" causes that he favored.

In recent years it has become fashionable among academic historians to be openly judgmental, at the risk of producing a distorted picture of the age in question. Members of the school of "Late Antiquity," in particular, tend to see the period as a "Good Thing," not unconnected with the fact of Christian dominance, which is also portrayed as a "Good Thing."

Here are a few examples:

- **"The unnerving but mercifully brief reign of Julian"**: Julian was obviously a "Bad Thing" in Brown's opinion. (p. 638). Is this really the language of scholarship? Here is the context of his 1066-ish remark: "The fourth century was the Age of Authority *par excellence*. With the exception of the unnerving but mercifully brief reign

of Julian, this authority supported the Christian church." (p. 638.)
The Age of Authority *par excellence*? What, if anything, does this
mean? And, for that matter, *which* Christian church did this "authority" support? Two fourth-century emperors, Constantius II and
Valens, favoured Arianism, and even Constantine himself teetered
on the brink of that "heresy". (For a fuller discussion of Brown's
view of Julian, see Chapter 12.)

- **"Awesome theologians"**: In the Preface to his initial *The World of
  Late Antiquity*, Brown looks forward to introducing the reader,
  among other things, to "...the awesome theologians of that time."
  (Brown 1970, p.9.) Is this supposed to mean that they inspire "awe",
  or is it being used in the modern teenage sense of "cool"? Either
  way, it is an unabashedly partisan description, not least because the
  "heretics" had their theologians too!

- **"Heresiology"**: When the anxious grandmother (in an old British
  TV ad) discovers that her shamefaced grandson did at least pass
  Sociology, "You have an-ology," she crows, "You're a scientist!" It is
  less amusing to witness the gyrations of academics purporting to
  create a "science" of "Heresiology" out of the noxious torrent of
  abuse spewed out against "heretics" in the Theodosian Code and
  elsewhere. "Heresiology" is described by one of these enthusiasts as
  "...a dynamic form of literary innovation and experimentation. As
  Averil Cameron has lamented, these texts are often too easily dismissed 'as sterile or boring, as mere scholastic exercises'." (Flower
  2013, p. 172.) Flower makes no secret of his admiration for these "...
  carefully ordered catalogues of a new form of religious knowledge."
  (Ibid., p. 172 f.) "The very appearance and structure of a heresiology, which mirrored other, less controversial branches of knowledge, reassured readers of its reliability and imbued the text with
  authority as a new late-antique form of technical literature." (Ibid.)
  Flower even goes so far as to compare "Heresiology" favorably with
  such genuine works of science as Pliny the Elder's *Natural History*
  and Galen's medical treatises, using the familiar arguments about
  how knowledge "...is never neutral, detached, objective." (Ibid.) But
  there is a world of difference between a Pliny or a Galen striving
  mightily to describe their observations as accurately as they can and
  the abusive discharge of arbitrary dogma activated by pure malice.
  All the talk about "Heresiology", while faintly amusing, is at the
  same time seriously disquieting because of its blatant bias and the
  failure to admit, or even recognize, that what we are dealing with
  here is the most unmitigated form of irrational religious intolerance
  and persecution. (See Chapter 4.)

Assassination or Senile Decay?

Beneath the bewildering welter of explanations for the dissolution of the Western Empire lies essentially a choice between two alternative causes: internal or external. The West either fell in the face of a largely violent takeover by "barbarians" or, in Jones's words, it tottered "...into its grave from senile decay, impelled by a gentle push from the barbarians." (Jones 1964, p. 1026 f) Nailing his colors firmly to the traditional mast of "barbarian" invasions, Jones concluded the following:

"Directly or indirectly....barbarian attacks probably played a major part in the fall of the West (Ibid.)....The internal weaknesses of the empire cannot have been a major factor in its decline." (Ibid., p. 1068) Was he right?

My own take emphasizes internal weaknesses without underestimating the violence of the "barbarian" takeover, the dismantling of the Western Empire, and the interplay between the internal and external forces, as demonstrated in Chapter 13. To aid the causal analysis, two major comparisons need to be made: one with the Principate, and the other with the Eastern Empire. Two questions can be teased out:

1. **Principate vs. Later Roman Empire:** Why was the later Roman Empire more susceptible to conquest by outside forces than had been the case under the Principate?

   - In a typical rotund phrase, and without undue exaggeration, Gibbon described the first two centuries of the empire as characterized by "...the indissoluble union and easy obedience that pervaded the government of Augustus and the Antonines." (Gibbon 1776-1789, Chapter 51, p. 321–22.) By contrast, as is shown in Chapter 13, the society of the later Roman Empire was fractured by profound divisions, of class, ethnicity, and religion, resulting in divided loyalties, weakening the empire's response to the "barbarians".

   - Ironically, Caracalla's *Constitutio Antoniniana* of 212, which extended Roman citizenship to all free male inhabitants of the empire, reduced recruitment to the army, more than half of which, constituting the *auxilia*, had been drawn from the *peregrini*, free non-citizen provincials, who were granted citizenship automatically on completing twenty-five years of service. Now that citizenship was universal, there was no such incentive, and the empire was forced to recruit "barbarians" in greater numbers than before, leading to the problems recounted in Chapter 13, and all the more so when, from the 370s, "barbarian" units were recruited serving under their own leaders, until, by 400, as indicated in the *Notitia Dignitatum*, a large number of regular units actually had "barbarian" names.

2. **East vs. West:** Constantinople's vaunted impregnability diverted the "barbarians'" attention from the East to easier pickings in the West. But, despite the strenuous efforts of the school of "Late Antiquity," the picture of an idyllic, united empire with everyone singing (literally) from the same hymn-sheet is no truer of the East than of the West. (See Chapters 4 and 5.) The weakening that this caused in the face of the Muslim invasion of Egypt in the seventh century has already been discussed. (See above.) And, with porous northern and eastern frontiers, the Byzantine Empire had gradually lost much of its territory long before succumbing to the Ottomans in 1453.

The Relevance of the "Fall" of the West

In Chapters 5 and 13, I set out my view that far too much emphasis has been placed on this question and that the more important issues of continuity and change could be considered independently of the presence of an emperor in the West. The following key aspects of continuity are discernible in the West:

- **Aristocratic ethos:** Though the "fall" of the Western Empire would be succeeded by monarchies of one kind or another for most of the next 1,400 years, the aristocratic ethos bolstered in the West by Constantine would survive, reinforcing the age-old values of inequality, elitism, and social stratification.
- **Political aspiration:** The dissolution of the Western Empire did not put an end to a hankering after European unity though the center of gravity moved with Charlemagne from the Mediterranean to Northern Europe, where it would remain for more than another thousand years.
- **Religion:** Constantine's conversion to Christianity made that the dominant religion in Europe and, in the world at large, to the present day. In so doing, however, it replaced religious toleration and, indeed, freedom of belief and worship, with intolerance and persecution, which has only very recently been eclipsed by a precarious recrudescent belief in religious freedom.
- **Language:** Unlike the early Arab conquests, the "barbarian" takeover of the West did not impose the language of the conqueror on their subjects. Instead, throughout most of the Western Empire, Latin survived, not only as the language of the Church and the law but also, in a variety of modified forms, as the vernacular from Portugal to Romania and in the New World and, not least, through an overlay of French and Latin on a Germanic language, in Britain and the English-speaking world.

- **Law:** Roman Law, as compiled, edited, and published in Justinian's *Corpus Juris Civilis*, remains to this day the basis of the law of most European countries, and of a large number of countries outside Europe as well.
- **Structural or Individual?** The aristocratic ethos of the Roman West survived the collapse of the Western Empire. But what about the aristocrats who carried on that tradition? Were they descendants of the old Roman senatorial aristocracy? Or were they "barbarian" aristocrats? Probably a mixture of the two. (See Chapter 5.)

Glossary

Monarchy   Rule by one person, or a state under such rule. From the Greek *monos* (alone) + *archein* (to rule). In this book, the term is not used of largely nominal monarchies, like those of contemporary western Europe and the United Kingdom, which are really oligarchies in disguise. See Chapter 6.

Aristocracy   Rule by a hereditary elite, a hereditary oligarchy; also, the members of such an elite. From the Greek *aristos* (best) + *kratos* (power or rule), so, literally "rule of the best." See Chapter 6.

Oligarchy   Rule by a non-hereditary elite; also, the members of such an elite. From the Greek *oligoi* (the few) + *archein* (to rule). See Chapter 6.

Noble, nobility   In this book, the terms **noble** and **nobility** (in Latin, *nobilis* and *nobilitas*, respectively) are used to refer to any member of the senatorial aristocracy by birth or origin, or, in other words, those born with the hereditary rank of *clarissimus* ---as against those who became *viri clarissimi* by virtue of holding a particular office. This usage contrasts with the stricter Republican convention under which the designation of **noble** was reserved to descendants of a consul.

Elite   A privileged minority, whether based on birth, wealth, race, or religion, and whether or not exercising dominant political power. A French term, *élite*, deriving from Latin *electus* (chosen or selected). See Chapter 6.

"Heresy"   In reference to Christianity, any deviant belief condemned and anathematized by a dominant Christian denomination. In particular, any deviant belief condemned and anathematized by a church council recognized by the Catholic Church, or, in the Byzantine Empire, any belief at variance with and condemned by the Orthodox Church. Examples of "heresies" include Arianism, Nestorianism, and Monophysitism. An adherent of a "heresy" is known as a "heretic". In this book, these terms, and also **"heresiology,"** are always encased in quotation marks to indicate that the author does not accept, endorse or condemn beliefs on either side of these religious disputes. See Chapter 10.

"Holy man"   In this book, this term is always encased in quotation marks to indicate that the characterization of individuals so described is tendentious. See Chapter 10.

Pagan, paganism   The adherent of any religion other than Judaism, Christianity, or Islam, first used as a pejorative term by Christians in the fourth century CE. Because of its negative connotations, it is sometimes now replaced by "polytheist" and "polytheism," referring, literally, to the worship of "many gods," as distinct from the monotheism of Judaism, Christianity, and Islam. However, "polytheism" is hardly less pejorative than "pagan," and not all pagans worshiped multiple gods in any case. So, in this book, "pagan" and "paganism" continue to be used, but without any negative connotations. See Chapter 10.

"Barbarians"   The English word **barbarian** comes from Greek *barbaros*, via Latin *barbarus*, a pejorative term used by the Romans to refer to anyone who was neither Greek nor Roman, and whose unintelligible speech sounded to the Romans like a babble of *bar-bar-bar-bar*. **"Barbarians,"** in quotation marks, is used in this book instead of "Germanic tribes," in deference to the ongoing debate among historians about whether peoples such as the Goths, the Vandals, and the Franks can be regarded as sharing an overarching "Germanic" identity. My own view is that there was a common bond, though there clearly were some non-Germanic "barbarians," notably the Huns and the Alans. Accordingly, the term "barbarians" is used in this book without any pejorative connotations. See Chapter 13.

Note: Except where otherwise indicated, all years referred to in this book are CE (Common Era) dates, equivalent to AD (Anno Domini), as distinct from BCE (Before the Common Era), or BC, dates.

Primary Sources and Abbreviations

> **Note:** This list contains only the most frequently cited primary sources

> Translations: Where primary sources are quoted in translation, the translations are by myself unless otherwise indicated by "tr." followed by the name of the translator.
>
> Bible: Unless otherwise indicated, biblical citations are from the King James Version, which is in the public domain in the United States.
>
> Inscriptions: Inscriptions referred to by just a number are from CIL.
>
> Papyri: Papyri are referred to in the text with an initial "P." E,g, P. Oxyrhynchus.

AE	*Année Épigraphique*
Amb. *Ep.*	Ambrose, *Epistulae*
Amm.	Ammianus Marcellinus, tr. John C. Rolfe (Loeb Classical Library), 1989
Anon. Val.	Anonymus Valesianus
Apuleius	Apuleius, *Metamorphoses* (The Golden Ass), tr. P.G. Walsh (Oxford World's Classics), 2008

Aug. *Civ. Dei*	Augustine, *De Civitate Dei* (The City of God), tr. R.W. Dyson (Cambridge Texts in the History of Political Thought), 1998
Aug. *R.G.*	Augustus, *Res Gestae Divi Augusti*
Aur. Victor	Aurelius Victor, *Liber de Caesaribus*
Ausonius	*Mosella, Ephemeris, Epigrammata, Caesares*
Boethius, *Consol.*	Boethius, *De Philosophiae Consolatione*
Cassiodorus	Cassiodorus, *Variae Epistolae*
Cassius Dio	Cassius Dio, *Historia Romana* (Roman History), tr. Earnest Cary (Loeb Classical Library), 1989
Cic. *Ad Fam.*	Cicero, *Epistulae ad Famiiares*
Cic. *Pro Sestio*	Cicero, *Pro Sestio*
Cic. *De Nat Deorum*	Cicero, *De Natura Deorum*
CIL	*Corpus Inscriptionum Latinarum*
CJ	*Codex Justinianus* (Justinian's Code)
Claudian	Claudius Claudianus, *De Consulatu Stilichonis*
CTh	*Codex Theodosianus* (Theodosian Code), Tr. Clyde Pharr, 1952
Dig.	Justinian, Digest (Pandects)
Epit. Caes.	*Epitome de Caesaribus*
Eus. *HE*	Eusebius, *Historia Ecclesiastica*
Eus. *V...Const.*	Eusebius, *De Vita Constantini*
Eutrop.	Eutropius, *Breviarium*
Evagrius	Evagrius Scholasticus, *Historia Ecclesiastica*
Gregory of Tours	Gregorius Turonensis, *Historia Francorum*
Hor. *Od.*	Horace, *Odes*
ILS	*Inscriptiones Latinae Selectae*, ed. H. Dessau
Jerome	Hieronymus, *Commentaria in Ezechielem*
Jerome, *Ep.*	Hieronymus, *Epistulae*
Joh. Eph.	John of Ephesus, *Historia Ecclesiastica*
Jordanes, *Get.*	Jordanes, *Getica*

Julian, *Caes.*	Julian, *De Caesaribus*
Julian, *Ep.*	Julian, *Epistulae*
Julian, *Mis.*	Julian, *Misopogon*
Juv.	Decimus Junius Juvenalis, *Satires*
Lactantius, *Mort. Pers.*	Lactantius, *De Mortibus Prsecutorum*
Libanius, *Ep.*	Libanius, *Epistulae*
Libanius, *Or.*	Libanius, *Orationes*
Livy	Titus Livius, *Ab Urbe Condita* (History of Rome), Tr. B.O. Foster, 1989 (Loeb Classical Library)
Lucr.	Titus Lucretius Carus, *De Rerum Natura*
Macrobius	Macrobius, *Saturnalia*
Mart.	M. Valerius Martialis, *Epigrams*
Not. Dig.	*Notitia Dignitatum Occidentalis/Orientalis*
Orosius	Orosius, *Historiarum adversus Paganos libri VII*
Petron.	C. Petronius Arbiter, *Satyricon*
Plautus	T. Maccius Plautus, *Miles Gloriosus, Stichus,*
Plin. *Ep.*	Pliny the Younger, *Epistulae*
Plin. *H.N.*	Pliny the Elder, *Historia Naturalis* (Natural History)
PLRE	*Prosopography of the Later Roman Empire*, 3 vols., Ed. A.H.M. Jones, J.R. Martindale and John Morris, Cambridge: Cambridge University Press, 1971-1992
Plut.	Plutarch, *Parallel Lives*
Plut. *Mor.*	Plutarch, *Moralia*
Plut. *Apoph.*	Plutarch, *Apophthegmata Laconica*
Procopius	Procopius, *Anecdota* (Secret History)
Rut. Nam.	Rutilius Namatianus, *De Reditu Suo*
Salvian	Salvianus, *De Gubernatione Dei*
SHA	*Scriptores Historiae Augustae* (Augustan History)
Sid. Ap. *Carm.*	Sidonius Apollinaris, *Carmina* (Poems), Tr. W.B. Anderson (Loeb Classical Library), 1936

Sid Ap. *Ep.*	Sidonius Apollinaris, *Epistulae* (Letters) Tr. W.B. Anderson (Loeb Classical Library) 1936
Socrates	Socrates, *Historia Ecclesiastica*
Soz.	Sozomen, *Historia Ecclesistica*
Suet.	C. Suetonius Tranquillus, *De Vita Caesarum*
Symmachus, *Ep.*	Q. Aurelius Symmachus, *Epistulae*
Symmachus, *Panegyrics*	Q. Aurelius Symmachus, *Panegyrici*
Synesius	Synesius, *De Regno*
Tac. *Agric.*	Tacitus, *Agricola (De Vita et moribus Julii Agricolae)*
Tac. *Ann.*	P. Cornelius Tacitus, *Annals*
Tac. *.Hist.*	P. Cornelius Tacitus, *Histories*
Themistius	Themistius, *Orationes*
Theodoret	Theodoret, *Historia Ecclesiastica*
Thuc.	Thucydides, *Peloponnesian War*
Verg. *Geo.*	P. Vergilius Maro, *Georgics*
Verg. *Aen.*	P. Vergilius Maro, *Aeneid*
V. Mel.	*Vita S. Melaniae Junioris*
Zosimus	Zosimus, *Historia Nova* (New History), tr. Ronald T. Ridley, 1982

Select Bibliography

This bibliography includes the secondary sources most frequently referenced in the text. See also PRIMARY SOURCES and GLOSSARY.

Abulafia, D. (2011). *The Great Sea: A Human History of the Mediterranean*. New York: Oxford University Press.

Acton, Lord (1906). *Lectures on Modern History*. Cambridge: Cambridge University Press.

Acton, Lord (1887/2011). *Acton-Creighton Correspondence*. https://oll.libertyfnd. org/titles/2254.

Agache, R. (1973). "La villa gallo-romaine dans les grandes plaines du nord de la France," *Archeologia* vol. 55, pp. 37–52.

Alföldi, A. (1948). *The Conversion of Constantine and Pagan Rome*. Oxford: Oxford University Press.

Andrewes, A. (1956). *The Greek Tyrants*. London: Hutchinson.

Angold, M. (1984). *The Byzantine Aristocracy: Ninth to Thirteenth Centuries*. British Archaeological Reports International Series.

Arlidge, Anthony and Judge, Igor (2014). *Magna Carta Uncovered*. London: Hart Publishing.

Arnheim, Michael (1972). *The Senatorial Aristocracy in the Later Roman Empire*. Oxford: Oxford University Press.

Arnheim, Michael (1977). *Aristocracy in Greek Society*. London: Thames & Hudson.

Arnheim, Michael (1984). *Is Christianity True?* London: Duckworth.

Arnheim, Michael (2015). *The God Book*. Exeter: Imprint Academic.

Arnheim, Michael (2016). *Two Models of Government*. Exeter: Imprint Academic.

Arnheim, Michael (2017a). *Two Models of Government*. revised ed. London: Black House Publishing.

Arnheim, Michael (2017b). *U.S. Constitution for Dummies*. New York: Wiley.

Arnheim, Michael (2018). *God Without Religion*. London: Black House Publishing.

Badian, Ernst (1958). Review of Louis Harmand (1957), *Latomus* pp. 774–777.

Badian, Ernst (1990). "The Consuls, 179–49 BC", *Chiron* 20, 37.

Bagehot, Walter (1867). *The English Constitution*. London.

Bagnall, Roger S. (1982). "Religious Conversion and Onomastic Change in Early Byzantine Egypt." *Bulletin of the American Society of Papyrologists*, vol. 19, 105–124.

Bagnall, Roger S. (1987). "Conversion and Onomastics: A Reply," *Zeitschrift für Papyrologie und Epigraphik, vol.* 69, 243–250.

Bardill, Jonathan (2012). *Constantine: Divine Emperor of the Christian Golden Age*. New York: Cambridge Universiy Press.

Barnes, T.D. (1982). *The New Empire of Diocletian and Constantine*. Cambridge, MA: Harvard University Press.

Barnes, T.D. & R.W. Westall (1991). "The conversion of the Roman aristocracy in Prudentius' *Contra Symmachum, Phoenix* Vol. 45, pp.50–61.

Barnes, T.D. (1992). "Praetorian prefects 337-361," *Zeitschrift für Papyrologie und Epigraphik*, Vol 94, pp. 249–60.

Barnes, T.D. (1995). "Statistics and the Conversion of the Roman Aristocracy," *Journal of Roman Studies*, Vol. 85, 135–147.

Barnish, S.J.B. (1988). "Transformation and survivalof the Western Senatorial Aristocracy, c.400-700." *Papers of the British School at Rome*, Vol. 56 (1988) 120–155.

Barnish, S.J.B. (1989). "A note on the *collation glebalis.*" *Historia* (1989) pp. 254–256.

Baynes, N.H. (1929). *Constantine the Great and the Christian Church*, Raleigh Lecture, *Proceedings of the British Academy*, vol. xv.

Bazzaz, Sahar et al. (2012). *Imperial Geographies in Byzantine and Ottoman Space*. Cambridge, MA: Harvard University Press.

Beard, Mary, John North & Simon Price (1998). *Religions of Rome*. Cambridge: Cambridge University Press.

Beard, Mary (2016). *SPQR: A History of Ancient Rome*. London: Profile Books.

Beik, William (1985). *Absolutism and Society in Seventeenth Century France: State Power and Provincial Aristocracy in Languedoc*. Cambridge: Cambridge University Press.

Beloch, Karl Julius (1886). *De Bevölkerung der griechisch-römischen Welt*.

Ben-Ghiat, Ruth (2020). *Strongmen: How They Rise, Why They Succed, How They Fall*. London: Profile Books.

Benedictow, Ole (2012). *The Black Death 1346–1353*. London: Boydell Press.

Berlin, Isaiah (2002). *Four Essays on Liberty*. Oxford: Oxford University Press.

Bidez, Joseph and Franz Cumont (eds.) (1922). *Julian, Epistulae, leges, poemata, fragmenta varia*. Paris: Les Belles Lettres.

Blegen, Carl (1995). *Troy and the Trojans*. Gazelle Book Services.

Bloch, Marc. (1992). *The Historian's Craft*. Manchester: Manchester University Press.

Bosworth, A.B. (2000). "The Historical Context of Thucydides' Funeral Oration." *Journal of Hellenic Studies*, Vol. 120 (2000) pp.1–16.

Bowen, Catherine Drinker (1957). *The Lion and the Throne*. Boson, Little Brown.

Bowman, Alan (2005). "Diocletian and the First Tetrarchy," *Cambridge Ancient History*. Cambridge: Cambridge University Press.

Boyd, William K. (1905). *The Ecclesiastical Edicts of the Theodosian Code*,New York: Columbia University Press.

Bradbury, Scott (1994). "Constantine and the problem of anti-pagan legislation in the fourth century," *Classical Philology* vol. 89, 120–139.

Brown, Elizabeth (1974). "The Tyranny of a Construct: Feudalism and the Historians of Medieval Europe," *American Historical Review*, pp. 1063–88.

Brown, Peter (1961). "Aspects of the Christianization of the Roman Aristocracy." *Journal of Roman Studies*, Vol. 51 (1961) pp. 1–11.

Brown, Peter (1971). *The World of Late Antiquity*. London: Thames & Hudson.

Brown, Peter (1973). "A Dark-Age Crisis: aspects of the Iconoclastic Controversy," *English Historical Review*, vol. 88, No. 346m pp. 1–34.

Brown, Peter (1987). *Late Antiquity*. Cambridge, MA: Harvard University Press.

Brown, Peter (1992). *Power and Persuasion in Late Antiquity*. Madison: University of Wisconsin Press.

Brown, Peter (1995). *Authority and the Sacred*. Cambridge: Cambridge University Press.

Brown, Peter (1997a). "Christianization and Religious Conflict," Chapter 21, *Cambridge Ancient History, Vol. XIII, 337–425*, pp. 632–664.

Brown, Peter (1997b). "The World of Late Antiquity Revisited," *Symbolae Osloenses*, vol. 72, 5-30.

Brown, Peter (2013). *The Rise of Western Christendom: Triumph and Diversity A.D. 200–1000*, third edition, London: Wiley-Blackwell.

Brubaker, Rogers (2006). *Ethnicity without Groups*. Cambridge MA: Harvard University Press.

Brunt, Peter and J.M. Moore (eds.) (1967). *Res Gestae Divi Augusti*. Oxford: Oxford University Press.

Brunt, Peter (1988). *The Fall of the Roman Republic and Related Essays*. Oxford: Oxford University Press.

Burckhardt, Jacob (1898). *Die Zeit Constantins des Grossen*, Leipzig.

Burgess, R.W. (ed.) (1993). *The Chronicle of Hydatius and the Consularia Constantinopolitana*: Oxford: Oxford University Press.

Bury, J.B. (1923). *History of the Later Roman Empire from the Death of Theodosius I to the Death of Justinian*. London: Macmillan.

Butler, Alfred J. (1978). *The Arab Conquest of Egypt*. Oxford: Oxford University Press.

Cambridge Ancient History, vol. 12 (2005). Alan Bowman et al. (eds.), Cambridge: Cambridge University Press.

Cambridge Ancient History, vol. 13 (1997). Averil Cameron et al. (eds.), Cambridge: Cambridge University Press.

Cambridge Ancient History, vol. 14 (2001). Averil Cameron et al. (eds.), Cambridge: Cambridge University Press.

Cameron, Alan (2007). "The Imperial Pontifex," *Harvard Studies in Classical Philology*, Vol. 103, 341-84.

Cameron, Alan (2013). *The Last Pagans of Rome*. New York: Oxford

Cameron, Averil and Garnsey, P. (1998). *Cambridge Ancient History*, Vol. XIII. Cambridge: Cambridge University Press.

Cameron, Averil (2014). *Byzantine Matters*. Princeton, NJ: Princeton University Press.

Carr, E.H. (1961). *What is History?* Harmondsworth: Penguin Books.

Chastagnol, A. (1962). *Les Fastes de la Préfecture de Rome au Bas-Empire*. Paris: Nouvelles Éditions Latines.

Chastagnol, A. (1992). *Le Sénat Romain à L'Époque Impériale*. Paris: Les Belles Lettres.

Cheynet, J-C (2018). *The Byzantine Aristocracy and its Military Function*. London: Routledge.

Cheyette, Fredric L. (2008). "Climate and the Early Medieval Environment." *Early Medieval Europe*, Vol. 16 (2008), pp. 127–165.

Cilliers, L. and F.P. Retief (2018). "Lead poisoning and the downfall of Rome: Reality or myth?" in Wexler, Philip (ed.) (2018). *Toxicology in Antiquity*, pp. 221–229. London: Academic Press.

Clark, G.N. (1957). *New Cambridge Modern History*, vol. 1. Cambridge: Cambridge University Press.

Claydon, Tony (2002). *William III*. London: Routledge.

Cobban, Alfred (1950). "The Parlements of France in the eighteenth century,' *History*, vol. 35, 65-80.

Cobban, Alfred (1965). *A History of Modern France*, 3 vols. Harmondsorth: Penguin.

Collingwood, R.G. & Myres, J.N.L. (1936). *Roman Britain and the English Settlements*. Oxford: Oxford University Press.

Connolly, Serena (2010). *Lives behind the Laws: The World of the Codex Hermogenianus*. Bloomington/Indianapolis: Indiana University Press.

Connor, W. Robert (1971). *The New Politicians of Fifth-Century Athens*. Princeton: Princeton University Press.

Cornell, Tim (1995). *The Beginnings of Rome*. London: Routledge.

Crook, John (1955). *Consilium Principis*. Cambridge: Cambridge University Press.

Crouch, David (2007). *The Normans: the history of a dynasty*. London: Continuum.

Cust, Richard. (2007). *Charles I: A Political Life*. London: Routledge.

Da Persico, Elena and Mariano Rampallo del Tindaro (1909). *Santa Melania Giuniore, Senatrice Romana*. Rome.

Dauzat, A. (1926). *Les noms de Lieux*. Paris: Librairie Delagrave.

Davies, J.K. (1975). Review of Connor (1971), *Gnomon* 47, 374–8.

Croix, Geoffrey De Ste., Michael Whitby & Joseph Streeter (2006). *Christian Pesecution, Martyrdom, and Orthodoxy*. Oxford: Oxford University Press.

De Zulueta, F. (1974). *Patronage in the Later Empire*. Oxford: Oxford University Press.

Dondin-Payre, Monique (1993). *Exercice du Pouvoir et Continuité Gentilice: Les Aciliii Glabriones*. Collection de l'École française de Rome.

Doom, Erin (2016). *Volcanoes and Heresies: Historiographical Perspectives on the Byzantine Iconoclastic Controversy*. http://core.ac.uk/download/pdf/276620084.pdf.

Drake, H.A. (ed.) (2006). *Violence in Late Antiquity: Perceptions & Practices*. Abingdon, Oxfordshire: Ashgate Publishing.

Drake, H.A. (2011). "Intolerance, Religious Violence, and Political Legitimacy in Late Antiquity," *Journal of the American Academy of Religion*, Vol. 79, No. 1, pp. 193–235.

Drijvers, J.W. (1997). *Helena Augusta: The mother of Constantine the Great and the legend of her finding the true Cross*. Leiden: Brill.

Drinkwater, J. and Elton, Hugh (eds.) (1992). *Fifth Century Gaul: A Crisis of Identity?* Cambridge: Cambridge University Press.

Echeverria, Durand (1985). *The Maupeou Revolution*. Baton Rouge: Louisiana State University Press.

Eck, Werner (1971). "Das Eindringen des Christentums in den Senatorenstand biz zu Konstantin," *Chiron* Vol; I, 381–406.

Elton, G.R. (1967). *The Practice of History*. London: Fontana Press

Elton, G.R. (1986). *The Parliament of England 1559–1581*. Cambridge: *Cambridge University Press*.

Elton, G.R. (2003). *Studies in Tudor and Stuart Politics and Government*, vol. II. Cambridge: Cambridge University Press.

Finley, M.I. (1954/2002). *The World of Odysseus*, New York: New York Review of Books.

Finley, M. I. (1962). "The Athenian Demagogues," *Past & Present*, vol. 21, 3–24.

Finley (1973). *Aspects of Antiquity.* Harmondsworth: Pengiuin Books.

Finley, M.I. (1983). *Politics in the Ancient World.* Cambridge: Cambridge University Press.

Flaig, Egon (1995). "Entscheidung und Konsensus," in *Jehne* (1995), 77–127.

Flaig, Egon (2003). *Ritualisierte Politik. Zeichen, Gesten under Herrschaft im Alten Rom.* Göttingen.

Flower, Harriet (2014). *The Cambridge Companion to the Roman Republic.* Cambridge: Cambridge University Press

Flower, Richard (2013). *The insanity of heretics must be restrained: heresiology in the Theodosian Code*, pp. 172–194, in Kelly, Christopher (ed.), 2013.

Forsythe, Barry (2005). *A Critical History of Early Rome.* Berkeley & Los Angeles: University of California Press.

Frost, F.J. (1964). "Pericles, Thucydides son of Melesias and Athenian politics before the war," *Historia* 13 (1964), 385–99.

Galvao-Sobrinho, Carlos R. (1995). "Funerary Epigraphy and the Spread of Christianity in the West," *Athenaeum vol* 83, 431–466.

Garnsey, Peter (1970). *Social Status and Legal Privilege in the Roman Empire.* Oxford: Oxford University Press.

Garnsey (1984). "Religious Toleration in Classical Antiquity," *Studies in Church History*, Vol. 21, pp. 1–27.

Garnsey, Peter (2010), "Roman Patronage," in Scott McGill, Cristiana Sogno, Edward Watts et al. (2010) *From the Tetrarchs to the Theodosians.* Cambridge: Cambridge University Press, 33–54.

Gelzer, Matthias (1975). *The Roman Nobility.* New York: Wiley-Blackwell.

Gibbon, E. (1776). *The Decline and Fall of the Roman Empire*, London.

Gillett, Andrew (2012). "Rome's Fall and Europe's Rise," *The Medieval Review.*

Gilfilla, S.C. (1965). "Lead Poisoning and the Fall of Rome," *Journal of Occupational Medicine*, Vol. 7, pp. 53–60.

Gilliard, Frank (1979). "The Senators of Sixth-Century Gaul," *Speculum* vol. 54, pp, 685–697.

Goffart, Walter (1987). *Barbarians and Romans.* Princeton: Princton University Press.

Goffart, Walter (2009). *Barbarian Tides.* Philadelphia: University of Pennsylvania Press.

Goldberg, Eric J. (1995). *The Fall of the Roman Empire Revisited: Sidonius Apollinaris and his Crisis of Identity*, Essays in History, Corcoran Dept. of History, University of Virginia.

Gomme, A.W. (1962). *More Essays in Geek History and Literature.* Oxford: Oxford University Press.

Grant, Michael (1971). *From Imperium to Auctoritas.* Cambridge: Cambridge University Press.

Grant, Michael (1986). *The History of Rome.* London: Faber & Faber.

Green, Judith A. (2009). *Henry I: King of England and Duke of Normandy.* Cambridge: Cambridge University Press.

Grey, C. (2007). "Revisiting the 'problem' of *agri deserti* in the late Roman Empire". *Journal of Roman Archaeology*, Vol. 20(1), p. 362–376.

Grote, George (1846-56). *History of Greece*. Cambridge: Cambridge University Press.

Gruen, Erich (1995). *The Last Generation of the Roman Republic*. Berkeley & Los Angeles: University of California Press.

Gruen, Erich (1996). *Studies in Greek Culture and Roman Policy*. Berkeley & Los Angeles: University of California Press.

Haehling, Raban von (1978), *Die Religionszugehörigkeit der hohen Amtsträger des Römischen Reiches seit Constantins Alleinherrschaft biz zum Ende der Theodosianischen Dynastie (324–450bzw. 455 n. Chr.)*. Bonn.

Hailsham, Lord (1979). *The Dilemma of Democracy*. London: Harper Collins.

Haldon, J.f. (2008). *Social History of Byzantium*. New York: Wiley-Blackwell.

Halsall, Guy (2007). *Barbarian Migrations and the Roman West, 376–568*. Cambridge: Cambridge University Press.

Halsall, Guy (2014). "Two Worlds Become One," *German History*, Vol. 32(4) 515–532.

Hamburger, Philip (2008). *Law and Judicial Duty*. Cambridge, MA: Harvard University Press.

Hammond, Mason (1957). "The Composition of the Senate, AD 68–235," *Journal of Roman Studies*, vol 47, 74–81.

Hardman, John (1993). *Louis XVI: The Silent King*. New Haven: Yale University Press.

Harmand, Louis (1957). *Le patronat sur les collectivités publiques des origins au bas-Empire*, Paris: Presses Universitaires de France.

Harper, Kyle (2017). *The Fate of Rome*. Princeton, NJ: Princeton University Press.

Hayes, John (1972). *Late Roman Pottery*. London: British School at Rome.

Heather, Peter (2006). *The Fall of the Roman Empire: A New History of Rome and the Barbarians*, New York: Oxford University Press.

Heather, Peter (2018). "Race, Migration, and National Origins," in Anna Maerker, Simon Sleight, and Adam Sutcliffe (eds.), *History, Memory and Public Life,"* pp. 80-100, London: Routledge.

Henry, Philip (1882). Lee, Matthew Henry (ed.) *Diaries and Letters of Philip Henry*. London: Kegan Paul, Trench & Co.

Herbert, Sydney (2015). *The Fall of Feudalism in France*. Miami: HardPress Publishing.

Ho, Ping-ti (1976). *The Ladder of Success in Imperial China: Aspects of Social Mobility 1368-1911*. New York: De Capo Press.

Hölkeskamp, Karl-Joachim (1995). *Senatus Populusque Romanus: Die Politische Kultur der Republik*. Wiesbaden: Franz Steiner Verlag.

Hölkeskamp, Karl-Joachim (2010). *Reconstructing the Roman Republic*. Princeton: Princeton University Press.

Holmes, C. (2005). *Basil II and the Governance of Empire (976–1025)*. Oxford: Oxford University Press.

Holt, J.C. (1992). *Magna Carta*. Cambridge: Cambridge University Press.

Honoré, Tony (1979). "'Imperial' rescripts 193–305: authorship and authenticity," *Journal of Roman Studies*, Vol. 69, pages 51–64.

Hopkins, Keith (1963). *Eunuchs in Politics in the Later Roma Empire*. Trübner.

Hopkins, Keith (1978). *Conquerors and Slaves*. New York: Cambridge University Press.

Huang, Shaorong (2001), "The Power of Words: Political Slogans as Leverage during China's Cultural Revolution." *Chinese Conflict Management and Resolution*, ed. G. Chen and R. Ma. Santa Barbara, California: Greenwood Publishing Group.

Hurt, John (2002). *Louis XIV and the Parlements*. Manchester: Manchester University Press.

Iggers, George G. and von Moltke, Konrad (eds.)(1973/2010). *Ranke: The Theory and Practice of History*. London: Routledge.

Inge, William, (1929). *Assessments and Anticipations*, London: Cassell.

Innes, Matthew (2006). "Land, freedom and the making of the medieval West," *Transactions of the Royal Historical Society*, Vol. 16, 39–74.

James I, Daniel Fischlin and Mark Fortier (eds). (1996). *The True Law of Free Monarchies*. Toronto: Victoria University Press.

James VI and I, King (2010). *Political Writings*. Cambridge: Cambridge University Press.

Jeffreys, E.M. (2006). *Byzantine Style, Religion and Civilization*. Cambridge: Cambridge University Press.

Jehne, M. (ed.) (1995). *Demokratie in Rom? Die Rolle des Volkes in der Politik der römischen Republik*. Stuttgart.

Jew, Osborne, and Scott (eds) (2016). *M.I. Finley: An Ancient Historian and his Impact*. Cambridge: Cambridge University Press.

Jones, A.H.M. (1948). *Constantine and the Conversion of Europe*. London: Hodder & Stoughton.

Jones, A.H.M. (1955). "Elections under Augustus," *Journal of Roman Studies*, Vol. 45, 1955.

Jones, A.H.M. (1957). *Athenian Democracy*. Oxford: Basil Blackwell.

Jones, A.H.M. (1958). "The Roman Colonate." *Past and Present* Vol. 13 (1958) pp. 1–13.

Jones, A.H.M. (1964). *The Later Roman Empire*. Oxford: Basil Blackwell.

Jones, A.H.M. (1974). *The Roman Economy*, Oxford: Basil Blackwell

Kelly, Christopher (2004). *Ruling the Later Roman Empire*. Cambridge, MA: Harvard University Press.

Kelly, Christopher (ed.) (2013). *Theodosius II: Rethinking the Roman Empire in Late Antiquity*, Cambridge: Cambridge University Press.

Kendall, Lothian, Murray and Linden (2000). *Sociology in Our Times*. Scarborough: Nelson.

Korfmann, Manfred (2013). *Troia-Wilusa Guidebook*. Troia Vakfi.

Kouroumali, Maria (2013). "Byzantine aristocracy," in Roger Bagnall, ed. (2013). *Encyclopedia of Ancient History*. Oxford: Blackwell.

Kritsotakis, Demetrios (2008). Hadrian and the Greek East. Ph.D. dissertation, Ohio State University.

Lambrechts, P. (1936). *La composition du sénat roman de l'Accession au Trône d'Hadrien à la Mort de Commode, 117–192*. Antwerp: *De Sikkel*.

Lambrechts, P. (1937). *La composition du sénat roman de Septime Sévère à Dioclétien (193-284)*. Budapest.

Lenski, Noel Emmanuel (2006). *The Cambridge Companion to the Age of Constantine*. Cambridge: Cambridge University Press.

Liebeschuetz, Wolfgang (1997). "*Cities, Taxes, and the Accommodation of the Barbarians*," in Pohl, W. (ed.) (1997) pp. 135–151.

Liebeschuetz, Wolfgang (2001). *The Decline and Fall of the Roman City*. Oxford: Oxford University Press.

Liebeschuetz, Wolfgang (2004). "The birth of late antiquity," *Antiquité Tardive* Vol. 12 (2004), 253–261.

Liebeschuetz, Wolfgang (2015). *East and West in Late Antiquity*. Leiden: Brill.

Lieu, Judith, John North, and Tessa Rajak. (1992). *The Jews Among Pagans and Christians in the Roman Empire*. Abingdon: Routledge.

Lincoln, Andrew (2005). *Gospel According to St John: Black's New Testament Commentaries*. London: Bloomsbury Publishing.

Lintott, Andrew (2003). *The Constitution of the Roman Republic*. Oxford: Oxford University Press.

Littman, R.J. and Littman, M.L. (1973). "Galen and the Antonine Plague," *American Journal of Philology*, Vol. 94, pp. 254–255.

Machiavelli, N. (2019). *The Prince*. Quentin Skinner & Russell Price (eds.). Cambridge: Cambridge University Press.

Malnati, T.P. (1987). "Juvenal and Martial on Social Mobility," *The Classical Journal*, vol. 83, pp. 133–141.

Mankiewicz, F.J. (1976). *With Fidel: A Portrait of Castro and Cuba*. New York: Ballantine Books.

Mansel, Philip (2019). *King of the World: The Life of Louis XIV*. London: Allen Lane.

Marx, Karl and Engels, Friedrich (1848). *The Communist Manifesto*.

Mathisen, Ralph W, (2009)." *Provinciales, Gentiles*, ands between Romans and Barbarians in the Late Roman Empire," *Journal of Roman Studies*, Vol. 99, pp. 140–155.

Mathisen, Ralph W. (2011a). *Roman Aristocrats in Barbarian Gaul*, Austin: University of Texas Press.

Mathisen, Ralph and D. Shanzer (eds.) (2011b). *Romans, Barbarians, and the Transformation of the Roman World*. London: Routledge.

Mathisen, Ralph and D. Shanzer (eds.) (2017). *Society and Culture in Late Antique Gaul*. London: Routledge.

Mattingly-Sydenham (1968). *Roman Imperial Coinage*, Vol. 3, Antoninus Pius to Commodus. London: Spink & Son.

Matthews, J.F. (1975). *Western Aristocracies and the Imperial Court 364–425*. Oxford: Oxford Univrsity Press.

Matthews, J.F. (1989). *The Roman Empire of Ammianus*. London: Duckworth.

Meier, Christian (2018). *Caesar*. London: Fontana.

Meier, Christian (2017). *Res Publica Amissa*. Wiesbaden: Franz Steiner Verlag.

Mennen, Inge (2011). *Power and Status in the Roman Empire, 193–284*. Leiden: Brill.

Merrills, Andrew (2017). *Vandals, Romans and Berbers*. London: Routledge.

Merlin, A. (1921). "La Mosaïque du seigneur Julius à Carthage," *BCTH*, 95–114.

Mettam, Roger (1977). *Government and Society in Louis XIV's France*. London: Macmillan.

Mettam, Roger (1988). *Power and Faction in Louis XIV's France*. Oxford: Basil Blackwell.

Millar, Fergus (1992). *The Emperor in the Roman World*. Bristol: Bristol Classical Press.

Millar, Fergus (2002). *Rome, the Greek World, and the East*. Chapel Hill: University of North Carolina Press.

Millar, Fergus (2006a). *The Roman Republic in Political Thought*. Boston: Brandeis University Press.

Millar, Fergus (2006b). *A Greek Roman Empire: Power and Belief under Theodosius II (408–450)*.

Momigliano, A. (1987). *On Pagans, Jews, and Christians*. Middletown, CT: Wesleyan University Press.

Mommsen, Theodor (1876). *Römisches Staatsrecht*. Leipzig.: S. Hirzel.

Mordechai, Lee and Merle Eisenberg (2019). "Rejecting Catastrophe: The Case of the Justinianic Plague," *Past and Present*, Vol. 244(1), pages 3–50.

Morison, S.E. (1946). *History as a Literary Art*.

Morison, S.E. (1951). Presidential Address, *American Historical Review*, vol. 56, pp. 272–3.

Morley, Neville (2004). *Theories, Models and Concepts in Ancient History*. London and New York: Routledge.

Morris, R. (1976). "The Powerful and the Poor in tenth century Byzantium," *Past and Present*, pp. 3–27.

Moser, M. (2019). *Emperor and Senators in the Reign of Constantius II*. Cambridge: Cambridge University Press.

Moss, Candida (2013). *The Myth of Persecution: How Early Christians Invented a Story of Martyrdom*. London: HarperCollins.

Mouritsen, Henrik (2008). *Plebs and Politics in the Late Roman Republic*, Cambridge: Cambridge University Press.

Mouritsen, Henrik (2011). *The Freedman in the Roman World*. Cambridge: Cambridge University Press.

Mouritsen, Henrik (2017). *Politics in the Roman Republic*. Cambridge: Cambridge University Press.

Mühlberger, Steven (1986). "Prosper's *Epitoma Chronicon*," *Classical Philology*, 1986, 240–244.

Müller, Alberto (2015). *Che Guevara. Valgo más vivo que muerte*, Kindle E-Books.

Needleman, Lionel and Diane (1985). "Lead poisoning and the Decline of the Roman Aristocracy." *Classical Views*, Vol. 4(1), pp. 63–94.

Nixey, Catherine (2018). *The Darkening Age: The Christian Destruction of the Classical World*. London: Pan.

Noble, Thomas (ed.) (2006). *From Roman Provinces to Medieval Kingdoms*. London: Routledge.

Nock, A.D. (1933). *Conversion*. Oxford: Oxford University Press.

North, John (1989), review of Brunt (1988), in *Journal of Roman Studies*, vol. 79, 151–6.

Norwich, John Julius (1997). *A Short History of Byzantium*, London.

Nriagu, Jerome O. (1983). "Did Lead Poisoning Contribute to the Fall of the Empire?" *New England Journal of Medicine*, Vol. 308, pp. 660–663.

Ober, Josiah (1989). *Mass and Elite in Democratic Athens*. Princeton: Princeton Univrsity Press.

Obolensky, D. (1974). *The Byzantine Commonwealth: Eastern Europe 500–1453*. London: Weidenfeld and Nicolson.

O'Donnell, Pacho (2011). "Opiniones de Perón sobre el Che," *El Pais*, October 8, 2011.

Osnos, Evan (2020). "How Greenwich Republicans Learned to Love Trump," *The New Yorker*, May 11, 2020.

Ostrogorsky, G. (1986). *History of the Byzantine State*. Rutgers University Press.

Paribeni, R. (1940) "Le Dimore dei Potentiores nel Basso Impero," *MDAI (R)* 55, 131–48.

Pascal, Blaise (1995). *Pensées*. Harmondsworth: Penguin Books.

Patterson, Orlando (1982). *Slavery and Social Death*. Cambridge MA and London: Harvard University Press.

Percival, John (1976). *The Roman Villa*. London: Batsford.

Percival, John (1992). "The fifth-century villa," in Drinkwater, J. and Elton, Hugh, *Fifth-Century Gaul: A Crisis of Identity? Pp.* 156–165, Cambridge: *Cambridge University Press.*

Perkins, Pheme (1998) pp. 241–258. In Barton, John, ed., *The Cambridge Companion to Biblical Interpretation.* Westminster: John Knox Press.

Piganiol, André (1947). *L'Empire Chrétien*: 325–395. Paris: Presses Universitaires de Franc

Pirenne, Henri (1954). *Mohammed and Charlemagne,* tr. Bernard Miall. London: Allen & Unwin.

Pirenne, Henri (2014). *Medieval Cities,* revised ed., tr. Frank H. Halsey. Princeton: Princeton University Press.

PLRE: The Prosopography of the Later Roman Empire. (1971–1992). A.H.M. Jones et al., (eds.), 3 vols. Cambridge: Cambridge University Press.

Pohl, W. (ed.) (1997). *Kingdoms of the Empire: The Integration of Barbarians in Late Antiquity.* Leiden: Brill.

Price, Munro (1995). *Preserving the Monarchy.* Cambridge: Cambridge University Press.

Quirk, Robert (1993). *Fidel Castro.* New York: W.W. Norton & Co.

Rampolla, Cardinal (1909). *Santa Melania Giuniore, Senatrice Romana*

Ranke, Leopold von (1875/2018) *A History of England Principally in the Seventeenth Century,* Oxford: Clarendon Press.

Rees, Roger (2004). *Diocletian and the Tetrarchy.* Edinburgh: Edinburgh University Press.

Retief, F.P. and L. Cilliers (2006). "Lead Poisoning in Ancient Rome," *Acta Theologica,* Vol. 26 (2),Supp. 7, pp. 147–164.

Reynolds, Susan (1994). *Fiefs and Vassals: The Medieval Evidence Reinterpreted,* New York: Oxford University Press.

Richards, Jeffrey (1979). *The Popes and the Papacy in the Early Middle Ages, 476–752.* London: Routledge Kegan Paul.

Riggio, Ronald (2012). "What is Charismatic Leadership? *Psychology Today,* 7 October, 2012.

Robinson, Eugene (2005). "The Controversial, Charismatic Castro," *Washington Post,* January 30, 2005.

Rosenstein, Nathan, ed. (2010). *A Companion to the Roman Republic.* London: Blackwell.

Rösch, Gerhard (1978). *Onoma Basileias.* Vienna: Österreichische Akademie der Wissenschaft.

Rostovtzeff, M.I. (1923). "Commodus-Hercules in Britain," *Journal of Roman Studies,* Vol. 13, pages 91–109.

Rostovtzeff, M.I. (1926). *The Social and Economic History of the Roman Empire,* 2nd ed., Oxford: Oxford University Press.

Rowe, Gregory (2013). "Reassessing the *Auctoritas* of Augustus", *Journal of Roman Studies,* 2013.

Royalty, Robert M. (2013). *The Origin of Heresy.* London: Routledge.

Runciman, S. (1951). *History of the Crusades,* vol. I. Cambridge: Cambridge University Press.

Russell, Josiah Cox (1958). "Late ancient and medieval population," *American Philosophical Society,* 1958.

Sachedina, Abdulaziz (2001). *The Islamic Roots of Democratic Pluralism.* Oxford: Oxford University Press.

Sacks, Jonathan (1993). *One People: Tradition, Modernity and Jewish Unity*. London: Littman Library of Jewish Civilization.

Saint-Simon, Duc de (2007). *Anthologie des Mémoires de Saint-Simon*. Paris: Livre de Poche.

Sallares, Robert (2002). *Malaria and Rome: A History of Malaria in Ancient Rome*. New York: Oxford University Press.

Sallares, Robert, Abigail Bouwman, and Cecilia Anderung (2004). "The Spread of Malaria to Southern Europe in Antiquity," *Medical History* Vol 48(3), pp. 311–328.

Salzman, Michele R. (2004). *The Making of a Christian Aristocracy: Social and Religious Change in the Western Roman Empire*. Cambridge, MA: Harvard University Press.

Salzman, M.R. (2006a). "Symmachus and the 'Barbarian' generals," *Historia* vol 55, pp. 352–367.

Salzman, M.R. (2006b). "Rethinking Pagan-Christian Violence," Chapter 22 in Drake, H.A. (2006).

Sanchez, Isabel (2010). "Fidel Castro marks 50 years of neighborhood watch group," CNN World, September 28, 2010. www.cnn.com.

Sarris, Peter (2015). *Byzantium: A Very Short Introduction*. Oxford: Oxford University Press.

Scarborough, John (1984). "The Myth of Lead Poisoning among the Romans." *Journal of the History of Medicine*, Vol. 39, pp. 469–475.

Schama, Simon (1992). *A History of Britain*, vol. 2. London: BBC.

Scheidel, Walter (1999). "Emperors, Aristocrats, and the Grim Reaper: Towards a Demographic Profile of the Roman Elite," *Classical Quarterly*, Vol. 49(1), pp. 254–281.

Schwartz, Eduard (1913). *Kaiser Constantin und Die Christliche Kirche*. Leipzig: Teubner.

Scott, Emmet (2012). *Mohammed and Charlemagnr Revisited*. Nashville: New English Review Press.

Seaver, James Everett (1952). *Persecution of the Jews in the Roman Empire (300–438)*. Lawrence: University of Kansas Publications.

Sellar, W.C. and Yeatman, R.J. (1930) *1066 And All That*. London: Methuen.

Sen, Ronojoy (2006). *Defining Religion: The Indian Supreme Court and Hinduism*. South Asia Institute, Dept. of Political science, University of Heidelberg.

Shaw, Brent D. (2015). "The Myth of the Neronian Persecution," *Journal of Roman Studies*, vol. 105, pp. 73–100.

Sherwin-White, A.N. (1957), review of John Crook (1955), *Journal of Roman Studies*, vol. 47, 252–4.

Sircar, D.C. (1979). *Asokan Studies*. Calcutta: Indian Museum.

Sivan, Hagith (1991). "A late Gallic branch of the Acilii Glabriones?" Notes on Ausonius' *Professores* 24 (Peiper)," *Mnemosyne* Vol 44, 435–439.

Soll, Jacob (2009). *The Information Minister: Jean-Baptiste Colbert's Secret State Intelligence System*. Ann Arbor: University of Michigan Press.

Soren, David and Noelle (1999). *A Roman Villa and a Late Roman Infant Cemetery*. L'Erma di Bretschneider.

Soren, David (2003). "Can Archaeologists Excavate Evidence of Malaria?" *World Archaeology*, Vol. 35(2), pp. 193–209.

Soricelli, G. (2010). "Agri deserti." *Encyclopedia of Ancient History*, pp. 1–2.

Southern, Patricia (2001). *The Roman Empire from Severus to Constantine*. London: Routledge.

Southern, Richard (1953). *The Making of the Middles Ages*, London: Hutchinson.

Sowerby, Scott (2013). *Making Toleration*. Cambridge, Cambridge, MA: Harvard University Press.

Stark, Rodney (1996). *The Rise of Christianity*, New Haven: Princeton University P

Stark, Rodney (2011). *The Triumph of Christianity*. London: Harper Collins.

Staveley, Stuart (2014). "The Nature and Aims of the Patriciate," *Historia*, vol. 32.1.

Stern, H. (1954). "Remarks on the 'Adoratio' under Diocletian," *Journal of the Warburg and Courtauld Institutes*, Vol. 17 (1954) 184–189.

Stephenson, Paul (2011). *Constantine: Unconquered Emperor, Christian Victor*. London: Quercus.

Sumption, Jonathan (2009). *Divided House: The Hundred Years War*, vol. III, London: Faber & Faber.

Syme, Ronald (1937). Review of Lambrechts (1936), *Journal of Roman Studies*, Vol. 27, p. 271f.

Syme, Ronald (1939). *The Roman Revolution*. Oxford: Oxford University Press.

Syme, Ronald (1989). *The Augustan Aristocracy*. Oxford: Oxford University Press.

Takács, Sarolta (2000). "Politics and Religion in the Bacchanalian Affair of 186 BCE." *Harvard Studies in Classical Philology*, Vol. 100 (2000) pp. 301–310.

Tate, W.E. (1967). *The English Village and the Enclosure Movement*. London: Gollancz.

Teegarden, David (2013). *Death to Tyrants!* Princeton: Princeton University Press.

Thackeray, William Makepeace (2017). *Four Georges*. London: A Word To The Wise.

Thomas, Clarence (2008). *My Grandfather's Son*. New York: Harper Perennial.

Torelli, M. (1968). "The cursus honorum of M. Hirrius Fronto Neratius Pansa," *Journal of Roman Studies*, vol. 58, 170–175.

Torey, Charles and Simeon Stylites (1899). "The Letters of Simeon the Stylite," *Journal of the American Oriental Society, Vol*. 20 *(1899) pp*. 253–276.

Tougher, Shaun (2008), *The Eunuch in Byzantine History and Society*. Abingdon: Routledge.

Toynbee, Arnold J. (1934–61). *A Study of History*, 12 vols. Oxford: Oxford University Press.

Treadgold, Warren (1997). *A History of the Byzantine State and Society*. Palo Alto: Stanford University Press.

Trevor-Roper, Hugh (2000). *Archbishop Laud*. London: Orion.

Troost, Wout (2005). *William III, the Stadholder-King*. London: Routledge.

Van Kley, Dale (1999). *The Religious Origins of the French Revolution*. New Haven: Yale University Press.

Ventris, Michael & Chadwick, John (1958). *The Decipherment of Linear B*. Cambridge: Cambridge University Press.

Walsh, P.G. (1996). "Making a drama out of a crisis: Livy on the Bacchanalia," *Greece & Rome, Vol* 43, *No*. 2 *(1996)* 188–203.

Ward-Perkins, Bryan. (1998). "The Cities," in *Cambridge Ancient History*, Vol. XIII, ed. Averil Cameron and Peter Garnsey. Cambridge: Cambridge University Press.

Ward-Perkins, Bryan. (2006). *The Fall of Rome: And the End of Civilization*. Oxford: Oxford University Press.

Warwick, Charles F. (2018). *Mirabeau and the French Revolution*. Miami: HardPress.

Werner, Karl-Ferdinand (1998). *Naissance de la noblesse*. Paris: Fayard.

West, Charles (2013). *Reframing the Feudal Revolution*. Cambridge: Cambridge University Press.

West, Martin L. (2011). "The Homeric Question Today," *Proceedings of the American Philosophical Society*, vol. 155, 383–393.

Wexler, Philip (ed.) (2018). *Toxicology in Antiquity*. London: Academic Press.

Whitby, Michael (1991). "John of Ephesus and the pagans," pp. 111–131, in Salamon, M, (ed.) (1991). *Paganism in the Later Roman Empire*. Krakow.

Whitehouse, David and Richard Hodges (1983). *Mohammed, Charlemagne and the Origins of Europe: The Pirenne Thesis in the Light of Archaeology*. London: Duckworth.

Wickham, Christopher (1984), "The other transition: From the Ancient World to Feudalism," *Past and Present*, no. 103, pp. 3–36.

Wickham, Christopher (2006). *Framing the Early Middle Ages*, Oxford: Oxford University Press.

Wickham, Christopher (2010). *The Inheritance of Rome*. Harmondsworth: Penguin.

Wickham, Christopher (2016). *Medieval Europe*. New Haven: Yale University Press.

Williams, Stephen (1997). *Diocletian and the Roman Recovery*. London: Routledge.

Winters, Jeffrey (2011). *Oligarchy*. Cambridge: Cambridge University Press.

Wiseman, T.P. (2009). *Remembering the Roman People*. Oxford: Oxford University Press.

Wood, Michael (2015). *In Search of the Trojan War*. London: Random House.

Yavetz, Zvi (1988). *Plebs and Princeps*. Oxford: Oxford University Press.

Yeatman, R.J. and Sellar, W.C. (1930). *1066 and All That*. London: Methuen.

Ye'or, Bat (2013). *Understanding Dhimmitude*. New York: RVP Press.

Index